Online Research Methods in Urban and Planning Studies:

Design and Outcomes

Carlos Nunes Silva
University of Lisbon, Portugal

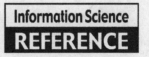

Information Science
REFERENCE

Managing Director:	Lindsay Johnston
Senior Editorial Director:	Heather Probst
Book Production Manager:	Sean Woznicki
Development Manager:	Joel Gamon
Development Editor:	Myla Harty
Acquisitions Editor:	Erika Gallagher
Typesetters:	Mackenzie Snader
Print Coordinator:	Jamie Snavely
Cover Design:	Nick Newcomer, Greg Snader

Published in the United States of America by
Information Science Reference (an imprint of IGI Global)
701 E. Chocolate Avenue
Hershey PA 17033
Tel: 717-533-8845
Fax: 717-533-8661
E-mail: cust@igi-global.com
Web site: http://www.igi-global.com

Library of Congress Cataloging-in-Publication Data

Online research methods in urban and planning studies: design and outcomes / Carlos Nunes Silva, editor.
    p. cm.
  Includes bibliographical references and index.
  ISBN 978-1-4666-0074-4 (hardcover) -- ISBN 978-1-4666-0075-1 (ebook) -- ISBN 978-1-4666-0076-8 (print & perpetual access) 1. City planning--Research. 2. Planning--Research. 3. Electronic information resource searching. I. Silva, Carlos Nunes.
  HT165.5.O55 2012
  307.1'2160285--dc23
                    2011042106

British Cataloguing in Publication Data
A Cataloguing in Publication record for this book is available from the British Library.

All work contributed to this book is new, previously-unpublished material. The views expressed in this book are those of the authors, but not necessarily of the publisher.

List of Reviewers

Alan Latham, *University College London, UK*
Amal K. Ali, *Salisbury University, USA*
Bengu Borkan, *Boğaziçi University, Turkey*
Bernhard Freyer, *University of Minnesota, USA*
Bernt Schnettler, *Bayreuth University, Germany*
Daniel Neyland, *University of Oxford, UK*
David Brown, *University of Wales Institute, UK*
David Roe, *RTI International, USA*
Elizabeth Buchanan, *University of Wisconsin-Stout, USA*
Elisabeth Gotschi, *Delegation of the European Union in Solomon Islands*
Gary Bowler, *Nova Southeastern University, USA*
Gillian Rose, *The Open University, UK*
Guangying Hua, *Bentley University, USA*
Hugh Busher, *University of Leicester, UK*
Johan van Rekom, *Erasmus University, The Netherlands*
John Grady, *Wheaton College, USA*
John Zacharias, *Concordia University, Canada*
Lynda Cheshire, *The University of Queensland, Australia*
Merrelyn Emery, *Concordia University, Canada*
Michelle M. Kazmer, *Florida State University, USA*
Peter Lindqvist, *Linnaeus University, Sweden*
Raymond Opdenakker, *Eindhoven University of Technology, The Netherlands*
Rene Ziegler, *Eberhard-Karls-Universität Tübingen, Germany*
Renaud Lambiotte, *Imperial College, UK*
Robert V. Kozinets, *York University, Canada*
Rob Perks, *British Library, UK*
Russell Belk, *York University, Canada*
Sabine Timpf, *University of Augsburg, Germany*
Sandra Edwards, *University of Utah, USA*
Stacey L. Connaughton, *Purdue University, USA*
Stephen Emmitt, *Loughborough University, UK*
Tomas A. Lipinski, *Indiana University, USA*

Table of Contents

Detailed Table of Contents

The chapter provides an overview of online research methods for urban and planning research. In examining different digital technologies and Web-based research methods, applied in different stages of the research process, in particular during data acquisition and data analysis, the chapter discusses critical differences and similarities between conventional paper-and-pencil research settings and online research environments. In this outline, the chapter addresses methodological procedures and ethical concerns in research conducted online with respondents or human participants, and ends looking to future directions for online research methods in the field of urban and planning studies.

Applied social science research has increasingly come to rely on surveys to generate detailed data, especially detailed data on firms, persons and households, needed to study social phenomena. The methods used to collect survey data have changed substantially in the past quarter century and appear on the cusp of changing yet again with the rise of Web-based technologies. These changes can be best implemented by adopting computational methods designed for relational databases. This is true not only for survey data, but also for administrative data that government agencies collect, store and use. The author explains how these changes are best accommodated and also explains how new telecommunications technologies, including Voice over Internet and smart phones, fit into this new paradigm. These techniques will likely dominate survey data collection for urban studies and other fields.

Web surveys have been widely adopted as a practical data collection tool notably due to their economic nature and a fast turn-around time. One of the popular types of Web surveys bases their sample on a group of Internet users who voluntarily join survey panels. Often labeled as a "volunteer panel Web survey," this approach is widely used in various social science studies including urban planning. Unfortunately, its practice appears to have highlighted its benefits and downplayed its limitations. This chapter provides an overview of the volunteer panel Web surveys, including their operational procedures and methodological advantages and disadvantages. Arguably, its main methodological disadvantage is lacking representativeness of the results arising from selection biases in the selected samples. A post-survey statistical adjustment based on propensity score analysis has been suggested as a potential solution. The author introduces detailed procedures of propensity score adjustment and discusses future research directions for improving the utility of the volunteer panel Web surveys.

Kathleen J. Hanrahan, Indiana University of Pennsylvania, USA
Mathew T. Smith, Indiana University of Pennsylvania, USA
Judith E. Sturges, Penn State Fayette, USA

Computer mediated communication is a part of everyday life for much of the population. People rely on email and instant messaging, post to chat rooms and blogs, and routinely use the Internet for a wide variety of functions. As a result, the options for qualitative study available to urban planners and researchers have expanded dramatically. This chapter examines the feasibility of online qualitative interviews. The chapter begins with an overview of the online options or venues (e.g., chat rooms, bulletin boards, social networking sites, email) currently available to the qualitative researcher. Next, issues of data quality in online interviews are discussed, and various online venues are compared with in person or face-to-face interview modes. Additionally, the authors discuss some of the central ethical and human subject protection issues involved in the online research landscape. The chapter concludes with an assessment of the potential for online qualitative interviews.

Peter Petocz, Macquarie University, Australia
Sue Gordon, The University of Sydney, Australia
Anna Reid, The University of Sydney, Australia

Researching people's ideas and experiences of Urban and Planning Studies can be carried out in a variety of ways, but maybe the most obvious is simply to ask them. This can be done qualitatively, using semi-structured or unstructured interviews, at an early stage of the research process, when it is important to explore participants' ideas prior to any quantitative investigation, or for investigations where in-depth and detailed information about individual thinking is important. Live, face-to-face interviews provide a 'gold standard' against which other qualitative methods of investigation can be compared. However, contemporary developments in technology provide a wider range of opportunities for qualitative researchers to collect rich data for analysis. Such technologies enable participation from any part of the world at any time, and allow the collection of video material that can capture many aspects of verbal and non-verbal interaction for further analysis. The use of e-mail interviews provides a relatively low-tech methodology for investigations and has some advantages over a live interview, on the one hand, and a high-tech video interview, on the other.

Instant Messaging (IM) programs are powerful and unique tools for conducting semi-structured or unstructured online interviews. However, there are many unanswered questions surrounding the use of IM interviewing. This is a design chapter that takes a storytelling approach to answer two specific research questions: (1) Do rich data collected via IM stand the test of time? (2) How can an IM program designed specifically for researchers be built? The chapter is consciously organized into three parts. Part one reviews recent, related research. Part two takes an unusual approach to answer the author's research question regarding the long-term power of IM data by re-visiting his experience from 2007 using IM to interview female participants about their feelings using online dating sites. Part three is a detailed description of the prototype IM program, Ethnochat. There are many IM clients in existence, but nothing has been made specifically for professional researchers for semi-structured or unstructured interviews. Having the best tool available helps urban planners conduct their research more efficiently and at a significantly reduced cost.

Chapter 7

In video-enhanced computer interviews, questions are presented by virtual interviewers by means of pre-recorded video sequences. To date, two strands of scientific interest in video-enhanced data collection are identifiable. On the one hand, video-enhanced data collection is employed for interviewing respondents with special needs (especially deaf respondents) and young respondents. On the other hand, research is focused on the impact on data quality. Following the previous results on enhanced data quality with audio-enhanced computer interviews, video-enhanced surveys are seen as a logical extension. In this chapter, previous research on both strands of applications of video-enhanced computer interviews is summarized to gain insight into preliminary evidence about the impact of these methods.

Chapter 8

Using visual material in a participatory interview process allows for broadening communication with users and developing a deeper understanding of residents' perspectives. Photographs taken by respondents as part of a research and future planning process provide the opportunity to see local spaces from users' perspectives, thus allowing them to contribute to urban planning in a meaningful way. This chapter introduces the method of participatory photo interview, its use in social science and its potential for urban and planning studies. It reviews literature on that topic, discusses opportunities for applying the method to spatial questions and reviews the method's strengths and weaknesses, illustrated by an example taken from urban studies. In conclusion, the author considers the feasibility of using the method online and highlights possible pitfalls and advantages.

Most research is conducted by teams rather than individuals, and due to a variety of technological advances, many research teams do not work face-to-face; they work virtually. The creativity literature that explores how working as a member of a virtual team differs from working as a member of a face-to-face team or as an individual is reviewed in this chapter, with a focus on the idea generation phase of the research process. The chapter offers practical techniques to help researchers effectively and efficiently brainstorm in virtual teams. Specific techniques to guide researchers are offered based on laboratory and field research in electronic, face-to-face, and virtual brainstorming.

The purpose of the chapter is to present an under-used technique for collecting ideas in scientific research teams, namely electronic brainstorming. This technique employs networked computer terminals and software designed to allow group members to communicate electronically during idea-generation tasks. A large number of studies have demonstrated that electronic brainstorming is a useful non-verbal technique for improving the efficacy of e-collaboration, but very few situations exist in which this technique has been used to collect ideas in scientific research teams. Nevertheless, writing articles, reports, white papers, and other scientific documents requires good ideas that can be generated through effective brainstorming. Brainstorming is also recognized as a problem-solving technique which can help researchers find solutions to complex problems by listing their potential causes. Although it is a simple technique that can gather ideas from a group of individuals rapidly by letting them express their ideas freely, it has not been widely used to collect ideas for complex research projects involving researchers working together or in geographically dispersed teams. After reviewing the literature in the field of (electronic) brainstorming, the challenges and opportunities for extending this technique to online research by scientific teams are discussed.

The Delphi research and investigation technique utilizes experts in any given field to generate information in greater abundance and specificity than what is currently known or available. The conventional and more widely used Delphi process strives for consensus so that target issues can be more fully investigated based on the feedback of the people who are most knowledgeable and involved. Policy Delphi differs in that it does not seek consensus but rather is meant to generate the strongest possible opposing viewpoints on an issue so that policy makers can consider divergent and opposing perspectives. Multiple iterations or rounds of data collection are the most unique aspect of both processes which allows the quality and relevance of the information concerning the target issue to become more precise and well defined. "Real-time" or "e-Dephi" uses the modern era of computers, electronic devices, and web-based communication to achieve the critical and unique group communication process utilized in a Delphi investigation.

Chapter 12

Thorsten Gruber, Manchester Business School, UK
Alexander E. Reppel, Royal Holloway, University of London, UK
Isabelle Szmigin, Birmingham Business School, UK
Rödiger Voss, HWZ University of Applied Sciences of Zurich, Switzerland

Laddering is a well-established research technique in the social sciences which provides rich data to help understand means-end considerations otherwise hidden from quantitative research. It does this through revealing relationships between the attributes of individuals, objects or services (i.e., means), the consequences these attributes represent for the respondent, and the values or beliefs that are strengthened or satisfied by the consequences (i.e., ends). The chapter describes how qualitative researchers can successfully apply laddering in an online environment. Through an explanation of the different stages of the online laddering process, the authors hope to interest fellow researchers in using this technique for their urban planning research projects. To illustrate the benefits of the technique, the authors describe a research study that successfully used the laddering technique in an online environment. The chapter concludes with the discussion of the limitations of using laddering online and suggests avenues for future research.

Chapter 13

Rosalind Hurworth, The University of Melbourne, Australia

This chapter examines the potential of the Search Conference (SC) and a later version, the Future Search Conference (FS), as useful participatory methods that can contribute to urban and other types of planning. An unusual feature of these approaches is that participants are expected to contribute to the implementation of any action recommended. The chapter begins with a definition and history of these conferences before outlining how traditional, face-to-face conferences are implemented. As an illustration, the Future Search Conference 'Bendigo +25' (carried out in a regional Australian city to determine ways forward for the next 25 years) is discussed. The same case study is then re-examined in the context of attempting to run the exercise in a Web-based environment. Both advantages and challenges of this mode of delivery are considered.

Chapter 14

Guido Lang, The City University of New York, USA
Stanislav Mamonov, The City University of New York, USA
Karl R. Lang, The City University of New York, USA

The advent of the Internet has facilitated many new forms of communication and thus has laid the foundation for new forms of interaction and social organization. The challenges of gaining insight into the social processes that occur in these newly emerging digital spaces require the development of new research approaches and methodologies. Netnography, or Internet ethnography, is one such example. It focuses on gaining cultural insights from virtual community environments and was originally developed for consumer research in the field of marketing, but has since been used in a number of other fields, including urban planning. This chapter examines the philosophical assumptions and specific methods of netnography as a newly emerging research approach. Findings from a qualitative analysis of ten cases of published netnography studies reveal interesting differences in both philosophical assumptions and uses as a research methodology, including the subject of research – community – and the role of the researcher. The chapter closes with some recommendations and a call for future research.

Chapter 15
Stefano Pace, Bocconi University, Italy

Videos on YouTube can be analyzed at two connected levels: (1) the content of the video, and (2) its context, which comprises viewers' comments and replies, tags, and related videos, and is both visual and textual. To fully comprehend the meanings of a video, researchers should focus on both levels and all contextual facets. This chapter provides suggestions on how to plan research pertaining to YouTube videos, with reference to videos that regard urban issues.

Chapter 16
Lesley Murray, University of Brighton, UK

The recent surge in interest in both mobile and visual methodologies reflects an increasing awareness of mobility and visualization in shaping social worlds. The 'mobilities turn' in social science draws attention to the significance of a range of mobilities, from everyday to global. In tandem, visualization of virtual and lived spatial and social contexts is increasingly central to daily life and wider social processes. Both mobile and visual methods have evolved to reflect the epistemological changes that accompany these realizations, leading to a mobility of method as approaches draw from a range of disciplines. Online resources present particular opportunities for the expansion of these methods. For example, video methods can be adapted for online use in collecting visual data; this data can then be disseminated in video form through the Internet. However, this interrelationship between online, mobile and visual methods has not been fully explored. This chapter explores the ways in which these methods can be combined to create knowledge in a unique way. It assesses the efficacy of these methodologies and methods by reviewing existing research and draws out key themes for analysis and further development.

Chapter 17
Susan Crichton, University of British Columbia, Canada

Digital tools can help simplify qualitative researchers' work. They can also add depth and richness by capturing data in a way that can be viewed and reviewed without preliminary transcription. This chapter explores an approach to working with digital data that honors participant voice and the lived experiences of those under study. The chapter also presents new tools and common software applications. Further, it suggests a workflow to guide researchers they begin to work to incorporate digital data into studies.

This chapter summarizes current empirical methods in virtual world research. Since 2001, virtual worlds have become an important form of social media as well as a new forum for general human interaction. Researchers have begun to study virtual worlds both for their inherent interest, as well as for insights about broader human behavior. The chapter addresses the quality of data that may be obtained, as well as early experience with surveys, experiments, ethnography, and direct observation in virtual worlds. The conclusions are that virtual worlds are a valid location for empirical research and many methods from the "real" world are suitable for deployment. At the same time, virtual worlds present some challenges in terms of technology and the nature of society, and researchers must not overlook these challenges.

Chapter 19

Mobility and orientation behavior research often requires the monitoring of pedestrian spatio-temporal behavior. A number of different empirical methods have been developed to investigate specific aspects of pedestrian behavior. However, each method has certain drawbacks, which aggravate the collection and analysis of relevant data. This chapter describes a new method which combines the advantages of simple observation and technological data collection. Pedestrian trajectories are collected by observing and annotating spatio-temporal tracks using a semi-automated shadowing tool. In this chapter, the authors first describe the background and related work in pedestrian spatio-temporal behavior research as well as most commonly applied methods and their respective advantages and drawbacks. Then, they present a shadowing approach with specific characteristics and implementation. Additionally, three case studies are described to illustrate potential fields of application. Finally, ongoing efforts to enhance the method through the use of additional sensors and features, as well as potential future developments, are described.

Chapter 20

The worldwide adoption of mobile phones is providing researchers with an unprecedented opportunity to utilize large-scale data to better understand human behavior. This chapter highlights the potential use of mobile phone data to better understand the dynamics driving slums in Kenya. Given slum dwellers informal and transient lifetimes, in terms of places of employment, living situations, and comprehensive longitude, behavioral data sets are rare. Working with communication and location data from Kenya's leading mobile phone operator, researchers have the ability to use mobile phone data as a window into the social, mobile, and economic dimensions of slum dwellers. This chapter discusses questions about the functionality of slums in urban areas in terms of economic, social, and migratory dynamics. In particular, the authors examine economic mobility in slums, the importance of one's social network, and the connectivity between slums and other urban areas. With four years until the 2015 deadline to meet the Millennium Development Goals, including the goal to improve the lives of slum dwellers worldwide, a great need exists for tools to make development and urban planning decisions more beneficial and precise.

Chapter 21

Almut Leh, FernUniversität in Hagen, Germany
Doris Tausendfreund, Freie Universität Berlin, Germany

This chapter explores developments in and prospects for online archival storage and retrieval of oral history interviews—with a focus on experiences and projects in Germany. The introductory section examines the contemporary history research method, oral history, which has led to extensive collections of interviews with witnesses of different historical periods, including survivors of Nazi persecution. To characterize the nature of oral history interviews, attention is given to their narrative form and biographical dimension. Emphasizing the specific value of this material, the authors discuss the particular demands involved in archiving such material framed by the expectations on both sides, witnesses as interview partners and researchers and other interested persons as archive users. A German example of state-of-the-art of online archiving strategies, called the "Forced Labor 1939-1945 - Memory and History" archive, is presented, outlining the technical challenges and research features as well as research functionality and further enhancements. Possible avenues for further development within the field are outlined: a meta-search engine covering multiple databases and an open online archive. A crucial ethical question is also presented in this chapter: How can a responsible online access policy ensure the protection of the contemporary witnesses' personal rights?

Chapter 22

Andrew Charlesworth, University of Bristol, UK

This chapter provides background to, and a broad understanding of, the legal (and ethical) risks that researchers face in their utilization of online mechanisms, in terms of the collection and analysis of research data, the communication of research results, and the retention and archiving of data generated by researchers and third parties. While researchers may understand the legal rules in the off-line research environment, research, dissemination and archiving on the Internet can pose more complex, and sometimes entirely novel, issues. The highly visible and accessible nature of the medium also means that existing legal risks may be significantly magnified in comparison to the off-line environment. Researchers should always seek advice specific to those jurisdictions they are targeting with their research, and particularly the jurisdiction in which they are located. Practical advice may be obtained from fellow researchers, institutional research support officers, or legal professionals. This chapter identifies activities that are likely to raise legal issues, or which are likely to require consideration of appropriate means of review, oversight and audit by researchers and ethical committees. Reference is primarily made to the law in the author's home jurisdiction, with some comparative references to other jurisdictions.

Online research methods are gaining popularity in several disciplines as they offer numerous opportunities that were not feasible before. However, online research methods also present many challenges and complexities that give rise to ethical dilemmas for online researchers and research participants. This chapter discusses key ethical considerations in the four stages of the research process: research design, online data collection methods, data analysis methods, and online communication of research outcomes. Issues of power, voice, identity, representation and anonymity in online research are discussed. The relationship between information and power and its implications for equity in online research is also examined. Rather than providing prescriptive recommendations, the authors use questioning as a strategic device to foster critical awareness and ethically informed decision-making among online researchers.

Preface

Research methods have experienced considerable changes in the past decades, in part as a consequence of the widespread use of computers and increasingly more sophisticated software applications, and appear to be changing yet again with the development of online versions of conventional research methods. In fact, in a multiplicity of disciplines, researchers have been converting conventional paper-and-pencil research methods into new digital and online versions, borrowing methods and tools from other disciplines, a pioneering work that provides valuable references for urban and planning researchers and practitioners. In the data acquisition phase of the research process there are now methods, based in digital technologies, similar to well-known paper-and-pencil research methods, as several chapters in this book show. Illustrations of this are the different forms of online observation, as well as the various types of online interviews and other modes of online data survey. In all these cases, it is not only the use of digital tools but their online application that is changing the way research is conducted in the field of urban and planning studies.

However, the extent of the impacts of this digital revolution in the professional practice of urban researchers and urban planners is still largely undetermined, notwithstanding the fact that data accessibility and the ever increasing size of databanks, made possible by the use of these new digital technologies, associated with continuous innovations in the supporting software, for both quantitative and qualitative analysis, contributed undoubtedly to the expansion of the methodological options available for urban research and urban planning. Data archiving and the publication of research outcomes have also experienced substantial changes, some of which created new or reinforced previous ethical and legal challenges that urban researchers need to address carefully.

Therefore, the goal of this book is to provide an overview of online research methods applied or likely to be applied in the field of urban and planning studies. In 23 chapters, written by 42 authors, from different academic and professional backgrounds, working in different parts of the world, the book explores and discusses the new digital technologies and Web-based research methods, as well as the legal and ethical challenges associated with the use of these methods. Its organization progresses from data collection and data analysis methods to archiving and publication of research outcomes and ends with ethical and legal considerations associated with research in digital and online environments.

The opening chapter of the book, "*Research Methods for Urban Planning in the Digital Age*," provides an outline of research methods for urban and planning research, examines different digital technologies and Web-based research methods, applied in the different stages of the research process, in particular during data acquisition and data analysis, and summarizes ethical issues in online research, some of which are examined in greater detail in the following chapters, namely in the last two. Randall J. Olsen in the second chapter, "*Infrastructure for Survey Data Processing in Urban and Planning Studies*," looks at the methods used to collect survey data, how they have changed in the last decades, and how they are likely to change again as a result of the rise of Web-based technologies, with a specific focus on how the new telecommunication technologies will probably dominate, in the future, survey data collection in urban studies. In the third chapter, *"Volunteer Panel Web Surveys in Urban Planning,"* Sunghee Lee provides an overview of the volunteer panel Web surveys, including their operational procedures and methodological advantages and weaknesses.

The next five chapters deal with different modes of digital and online interviews. In Chapter 4, *"Online Qualitative Interviews: Opportunities and Challenges for Urban and Planning Studies,"* Kathleen J. Hanrahan, Mathew T. Smith, and Judith E. Sturges examine the feasibility of online qualitative interviews, offer an overview and comparison of the online options available, and discuss research ethics issues related to human subject protection. This is followed by Chapter 5, *"Towards a Method for Research Interviews using e-Mail,"* where Peter Petocz, Sue Gordon, and Anna Reid explain how the use of e-mail interviews provides a relatively low-tech methodology for research in the field of urban and planning studies, and examines its advantages over live interviews and high-tech video interviews. Jason Zalinger in Chapter 6, *"The Story of Ethnochat: Designing an Instant Messaging Program to Conduct Semi-Structured or Unstructured Interviews,"* presents and discusses a tool for conducting semi-structured or unstructured online interviews, and offers a detailed description of his prototype Instant Messaging program, Ethnochat.

Joachim Gerich, in Chapter 7, *"Video-Enhanced Self-Administered Computer Interviews,"* reflects on the characteristics of this digital and online interview method, its strengths and shortcomings, especially when employed to interview respondents with special needs, in particular deaf or young respondents. In the last chapter of this section, *"Unveiling Space by using Participatory Photo Interview,"* Bettina Kolb reflects on how the use of visual material in a participatory interview process facilitates communication with human participants and a deeper understanding of their perspectives, offers an overview of the literature, outlines the strengths and weaknesses of this approach, and discusses prospects for the application of this method in the field of urban and planning studies.

The following chapters deal with methods that in different ways can be applied by researchers and urban planners to produce creative ideas or perspectives about the future of cities and regions. In Chapter 9, *"Brainstorming in Virtual Teams,"* Mary T. Dzindolet, Paul B. Paulus, and Courtney Glazer offer a review of the literature on virtual teams as well as on practical techniques that researchers can apply to effectively and efficiently brainstorm in virtual teams, with a particular focus on the idea generation phase of the research process. Nicolas Michinov in the following chapter, *"The use of Electronic Brainstorming for Collecting Ideas in Scientific Research Teams: A Challenge for Future Online Research,"* offers a review of the literature on brainstorming and reflects on electronic brainstorming as a method to create ideas within research teams, geographically dispersed, and as a problem-solving technique that can be used by researchers and urban planners to find solutions to multifaceted spatial problems. In Chapter 11, *"The Delphi Technique: Use, Considerations, and Applications in the Conventional, Policy, and On-Line Environments,"* Chia-Chien Hsu and Brian A. Sandford explain how the Delphi technique uses experts to produce information beyond what is currently known, and provide an overview of the different variants of this method, the conventional Delphi and the Policy Delphi, their main characteristics and differences, including, for both cases, the digital version, or e-Delphi, supported by Web-based forms of online communication.

Considerably different from brainstorming and from the Delphi method, the laddering technique is another example of a research method that should be used more extensively in urban and planning studies.

Thorsten Gruber, Alexander E. Reppel, Isabelle Szmigin, and Rödiger Voss, in Chapter 12, *"Designing Online Laddering Studies,"* offer a well informed account of this research method, its strengths and weaknesses, which, as they explain, can provide rich data to help understand means-end considerations, and describe how qualitative urban researchers can successfully apply laddering in an online environment, explaining the different stages of the online laddering process. This section ends with Chapter 13, *"Search Conferences and Future Search Conferences: Potential Tools for Urban Planning in an On-Line Environment,"* by Rosalind Hurworth. The author examines the potential of the Search Conference, and its more recent version, the Future Search Conference, as useful participatory methods in urban planning and discusses their strengths and shortcomings. As Rosalind Hurworth emphasizes, this is a method in which each participant is expected to contribute to the implementation of the proposals recommended during the participatory process.

The following section provides, in five chapters, an overview of methods and digital technologies for online observation of the new forms of interaction and social organization that takes place in the Internet, some of them developed outside the field of urban and planning studies. It is the case of Chapter 14, *"Netnography: An Assessment of a Novel Research Approach and its Underlying Philosophical Assumptions,"* by Guido Lang, Stanislav Mamonov, and Karl R. Lang, first developed for consumer research in the field of marketing and later applied in other fields. The authors elaborate on the philosophical assumptions and specific methods of netnography, present findings from several qualitative studies, and offer a number of recommendations that researchers and urban planners should consider. This is followed, in Chapter 15, *"Citizens on YouTube: Research-Method Issues,"* in which Stefano Pace provides methodological recommendations on how to research YouTube videos, in particular videos focused on urban issues.

Lesley Murray, in the chapter *"Online Opportunities for Mobile and Visual Research,"* explores the ways in which mobile and visual methods can be combined to create new knowledge and original insights, through the use of Web-based technologies, and assesses the effectiveness of these methods. In Chapter 17, *"Using Digital Tools in Qualitative Research: Supporting Integrity, Simplicity, Deep Insight and Social Change,"* Susan Crichton reflects on the ways new digital technologies can be used to respect participants' voices and experiences, and makes a number of suggestions and recommendations about new tools and software. In the last chapter in this section, *"Empirical Research Methods in Virtual Worlds,"* Travis L. Ross, Edward Castronova, and Gert G. Wagner provide an overview of empirical methods for research in virtual worlds, and address experiences in those virtual settings, concluding that virtual worlds are a valid venue to conduct empirical research.

The next three chapters deal with different issues: mobility in urban spaces; population characteristics in major informal urban areas, the slums, in the developing world; audio and video archives. In Chapter 19, *"Monitoring Pedestrian Spatio-Temporal Behavior using Semi-Automated Shadowing,"* Alexandra Millonig, Markus Ray, and Helmut Schrom-Feiertag address and discuss research methods for the study of mobility and orientation behavior, and describe a new approach, which combines simple observation with new data collection technologies for monitoring pedestrian spatio-temporal behavior. Amy Wesolowski and Nathan Eagle, in Chapter 20, *"Mobile Phones as a Lens into Slum Dynamics,"* explore and discuss the use of data produced by mobile phones as an opportunity to better understand human behavior, as well as the social, economic and mobility characteristics of the population living in slums. In the third chapter of this section, *"Archiving Audio and Video Interviews,"* Almut Leh and Doris Tausendfreund explore developments in online archival storage and retrieval of oral history interviews and reflect on its future prospects, focusing on experiences and projects in Germany, which should be seen as examples of technical and ethical issues likely to emerge in the field of urban and planning research.

The book ends with two chapters, "*Addressing Legal Issues in Online Research, Publication and Archiving: A UK Perspective*," by Andrew Charlesworth, and "*Ethical Considerations in Online Research Methods*," by Harsh Suri and Fay Patel. Andrew Charlesworth provides a broad and critical overview of the legal and ethical risks that researchers face when they use online research methods and Web-based technologies, for data collection and data analysis, for the communication of research outcomes, and in the archiving of data produced by the research team or by other researchers. Harsh Suri and Fay Patel outline and discuss critically a number of ethical dilemmas faced by researchers in each stage of the online research process.

In conclusion, these essays, written by distinguished colleagues, from different academic and professional backgrounds, give an updated and well informed overview of some of the ground-breaking online research methods, their strengths and shortcomings, examine and discuss important ethical and legal issues, and provide, when appropriate, practical guidance on how to conduct and apply each of these methods. For all these reasons, I trust the book will be useful for students, teachers, researchers and practitioners in the field of urban and planning studies, and in related disciplines. I hope the book will contribute to enhance the use of digital technologies and Web-based research methods and will stimulate the conversation, within urban and planning studies, about these digital technologies and online research methods.

Carlos Nunes Silva
University of Lisbon, Portugal

Acknowledgment

I wish to thank each of the contributors to this book for their participation in this project and for the excellent cooperation while preparing the book for publication. It has been an inspiring experience to work with this group of outstanding colleagues from different academic backgrounds.

I also wish to express my gratitude to the colleagues that accepted my invitation to assist me in the review process, which helped to improve the quality of this publication. Their names and institutional affiliations are listed at the front of the book.

Furthermore, for their continuous and excellent support during the entire editorial process, I am also grateful to the editorial staff members at IGI Global, in particular to Myla Harty, with whom I worked most directly throughout the development of the book.

Carlos Nunes Silva
University of Lisbon, Portugal

Chapter 1
Research Methods for Urban Planning in the Digital Age

Carlos Nunes Silva
University of Lisbon, Portugal

ABSTRACT

The chapter provides an overview of online research methods for urban and planning research. In examining different digital technologies and Web-based research methods, applied in different stages of the research process, in particular during data acquisition and data analysis, the chapter discusses critical differences and similarities between conventional paper-and-pencil research settings and online research environments. In this outline, the chapter addresses methodological procedures and ethical concerns in research conducted online with respondents or human participants, and ends looking to future directions for online research methods in the field of urban and planning studies.

INTRODUCTION

Conventional research methods have been complemented or replaced little by little by similar or comparable Web-based research methods, supported by increasingly sophisticated Internet technologies, at the same time as new methods, techniques and digital tools are being tested or are already well established in the social sciences, as the following chapters in this book illustrate.

This was in part the result of opportunities opened by the expansion of Internet, by innovations in the software for quantitative and qualitative research, and by the use of new visual sources and visual methods. These digital technologies, available for urban and planning research, in or via online environments, stimulated diversification of data collection and data processing methods and provided urban researchers with the capacity to work in larger research projects, for example with bigger samples and databanks, and offered new possibilities for data collection, as is the case

DOI: 10.4018/978-1-4666-0074-4.ch001

in cities and megacities in the developing world, punctuated by huge slum areas, as exemplified in Chapter 20 of this book.

If at the beginning of this process the software available for conducting Internet-mediated urban research was comparatively limited, the past two decades have witnessed an increasing sophistication in most of these digital technologies, a shift responsible for new opportunities for online research in urban and planning studies, a trend emphasized by consecutive methodological cross-fertilization within the social sciences and between these and information sciences. While most traditional research methods and tools have been transformed into digital versions, and when feasible also applied online, the digital revolution and the widespread use of the Internet were also responsible for the development of new methods and research tools, as is the case of Web-based geographic information systems, as a tool for data collection and data analysis in urban and planning studies.

This chapter offers an overview of online research methods and digital technologies applied, or with the potential to be applied, in urban and planning studies, and looks at ethical issues raised by the application of these online methods. However, in no way does the chapter intends to be an exhaustive account of these methods. In the first section, the chapter provides examples of how online research affects data collection and data analysis methods and compares these new methods with conventional paper-and-pencil offline research practice. In the following section, the chapter examines ethical concerns raised in digital and online research settings. Finally, the chapter presents a summary of main conclusions and points to some future directions in this field.

DIGITAL TECHNOLOGIES AND ONLINE RESEARCH METHODS

Research designs for Web-based environments are not essentially different from conventional research designs, although the way it is implemented and the ethical issues concerned can eventually be different. The classical experimental design or quasi-experimental designs, longitudinal or cross-sectional designs, described in numerous publications (e.g., Lavrakas, 2008; Silva, 2008a; Creswell, 2002; Newman, 2000; Frankfort-Nachmias et al., 2000), have the same types of structure and components, sampling designs, causal inferences, and control measures, independently of the research setting, conventional face-to-face or online research.

Qualitative and quantitative conventional research strategies, or even triangulation strategies that make use of mixed research designs and research techniques, also extensively described in the literature (e.g., Marshal et al., 2006; Creswell, 2002; Limb & Dwyer, 2001; Frankfort-Nachmias et al., 2000; Patton, 1999), do not differ in essence when applied to a Web-based research environment, even though some physical constraints and ethical issues may perhaps be online specific. The same happens with data collection methods, data processing, data analysis, research writing, publishing and diffusion of research results.

Online research is frequently easier and less expensive to implement than non digital and offline research and can allow a more flexible application of research designs, mixing interactively qualitative and quantitative methods and blending web-based questionnaires surveys with in-depth computer-assisted web interviews, as Lobe and Vehovar (2009) exemplify. Besides that, the use of the World Wide Web can improve sample recruitment and produce research outcomes that are more reliable and more convincing, if certain conditions are met (Dever et al., 2008; Ganassali, 2008; Porter & Whitcomb, 2005), as some of the following chapters also show. Nonetheless, they tend to require some form of adaptation, as is the case of online communication of geo-information (Jobst et al., 2010).

In both cases, paper-and-pencil and online, there are two broad categories of methods for data acquisition, each with different research techniques and tools, as is usually referred in the literature (e.g., Johnson et al., 2001): direct data collection or acquisition of primary data, where the researcher is the collector of the data, and indirect data collection. In this case, the reason for collecting the data is not necessarily the same that motivates the researcher, and those that did it usually do not know what use will be made of the data they collected.

Online Direct Data Collection

Methods and tools for online direct data acquisition, most of which adapted to a digital format from paper-and-pencil versions, and increasingly employed online, comprise, among others, Web-based questionnaire surveys, e-mail surveys, individual interviews, in-depth interviews, instant messaging interviews, online focus group, synchronous Web groups interviews in chat-rooms, e-Delphi or Web-based Delphi, Cyber-ethnography, photo-interviews in participatory research, participatory video, auto-photograph, video-diaries, audio-diaries, online participant observation, including action research, and non-participant observation, among other oral, textual and visual methods carried out in synchronous or in asynchronous formats, as described in the literature (e.g., Stewart & Williams, 2005; Buchwald et al., 2009; Chou, 2002; Madge & O'Connor, 2002; Murthy, 2008; Corbett & Mann, 2010), and in several of the following chapters.

Other examples of this potential use of ICT and the Web for data collection and data analysis in urban research and in planning processes include the analysis of municipal portals, local Internet forums, blogs, and discussion lists, especially those focused on the policies of the municipal

council (Staffans et al., 2010; Klessmann, 2010), or even in virtual worlds, as a new medium for human interaction, as Travis L. Ross, Edward Castronova and Gert G. Wagner explain in Chapter 18. Unknown facts or key details may appear in the course of these online conversations, pointing urban researchers and planners to new and often unexpected and more fruitful research directions.

These digital online sources have also the potential to increase the range of voices that are considered in the planning process, including therefore those usually left away in urban planning consultation processes (Bricout & Baker, 2010), through the employment of numerous new and innovative citizen e-participation procedures, some of which still experimental (Kubicek, 2010; Staffans et al., 2010; Horelli & Wallin, 2010), although the existing digital divide may prevent, or at least affect negatively the full participation of important groups within the urban population (Nordin & Berglund, 2010; Tregeagle, 2010; Elwood, 2006), due, for example, to the unequal access to the local council geographic information system or to the digital spatial data stored in the municipal internal information system.

This continuous development of new electronic devices opened indeed new possibilities to produce data for urban and planning research, as is the case of radio frequency identification (RFID), which can be employed in different urban research situations (Pang et al., 2010). RFID makes use of radio waves to exchange data between a reader controlled by the researcher and an electronic tag attached to an object, a car or a bicycle, for example, or directly to an object transported by the human participant, in order to identify and track human mobility in a variety of urban planning situations, such as urban transport planning or sustainable mobility studies, which raises new ethical challenges, as Glasser et al. (2007) show. Another example is the QR code, a two-dimensional barcode, containing encoded information which can be accessed easily, for example, by mobile phones (Rohs & Gfeller,

2004; Ohbuchi et al., 2004), to collect data or to share information, for example, about the built heritage within urban areas.

The use of internet-based geographic information systems, volunteered geographical information, online interactive maps, the use of multimedia representation of urban data, including 3D geo-visualization online applications (Bishop, 2012), virtual reality, and other geospatial technologies (Goodchild, 2007) are also responsible for the changes in the way urban researchers and planners can obtain and process urban data, how they build geospatial databases (Al-Kodmany, 2010), and how they can publicize and communicate research outcomes as well. Also Web 2.0 applications changed the way urban data is collected and processed and enhanced new forms of participatory urban planning, as Anttiroiko (2012) shows.

One of the methods often applied in urban research for direct data acquisition is observation, as Chapter 15 by Stefano Pace and Chapter 16 by Lesley Murray exemplify. As a data collection method, online observation can be direct or indirect, depending if the observation is focused on the events or on its consequences; structured or unstructured, depending if the researcher records systematically or not the behavior being studied; participant or nonparticipant, depending if the urban researcher participates regularly in the activities of the online group. Observation can also be uncovered or covered, raising ethical issues similar to those in conventional research.

Web-based participant observation has several advantages but also a number of shortcomings. Among its limitations is the fact that the researcher can influence or control the setting in which the research takes place, the small number of individuals researched, the lack of statistical representativeness, and the fact that it is time consuming and expensive. Despite these weaknesses, online fieldwork may require online participant observation, as is often the case in conventional research, and in that case, the researcher will participate in the online activities of the group,

for example involvement in a local forum focused on urban planning issues, which requires acceptance by the group and will act, up to a certain point, as a natural member of that online social network or Web-based discussion group. This can be complemented by information given by one or more informants belonging to the network.

Non-participant observation has been widely used by urban researchers and planners in conventional offline research settings, to collect data on human behavior, on the characteristics of neighborhoods, or on the use of urban space, for example, by pedestrians, disabled persons, old people or children, among other social groups. In this case, data is collected without any direct intervention or response by the person or group of persons observed. Non-participant observation can also be applied with digital devices, as Chapter 17, by Susan Crichton, and Chapter 16 by Lesley Murray, illustrate, or to be focused on the interactions within social networks. In this mode of observation, additional methodological and ethical concerns should be considered further than those established in conventional research, as emphasized by Guido Lang, Stanislav Mamonov and Karl R. Lang in Chapter 14.

Observation in a laboratory, including computer-supported face-to-face observation, can be replaced by online observation in a Cyber-Lab (Reips, 2001), with participants located in different places. This form of data collection provides control over the context or facts under observation, allows the use of a more rigorous experimental or quasi-experimental research design, compared to what is usually possible in a natural and uncontrolled urban research setting, but has the disadvantage that the observed will know in advance that he or she is being observed and for that reason may change behavior and attitudes.

Observation has also been employed in the study of the urban policy making process. Part of the planning decision-making procedures takes place in public meetings that are increasingly video-taped and published online in municipal planning portals. For that reason, there is now an enormous potential for urban researchers to apply online observation in the study of these processes, in a much larger number of locations than was imagined to be possible just few years ago, and for a much lower cost. Observation of municipal councils meetings, or public hearings, focused on urban planning issues, broadcasted live in the Internet, or available on a video archive, will probably provide a better understanding of what happened in that meeting or public hearing, and will provide a better interpretation of the decision-making process, compared to written statements, even when they are available online.

Nonetheless, not all situations faced by urban researchers and planners are accessible for direct online observations. Key local political or technical meetings dealing with sensitive urban planning issues are not open for direct observation and even less for online observation by an outsider urban researcher. Many of them are not even registered in written form and for that reason no evidence is left of key facts for a proper interpretation and understanding of urban planning decision-making processes. In a context such as this, the reconstruction of the planning decision-making processes may require a mixed methods approach, including the use of online computer-assisted interviews, questionnaires and email surveys, and the triangulation with conventional paper-and-pencil and face-to-face research.

Another frequent Web-based data collection method is the interview and the questionnaire. While conventional interviews are conducted face-to-face or over the phone, there are now new tools to conduct interviews, which comprises, for example, electronic mail interview and a variety of computer-assisted interview types, as some of the following chapters illustrate. Interviews conducted over the Internet can be highly structured, when a questionnaire is followed strictly, semi-structured or open-ended. Regardless of the type, paper-based or digital and online, the basics of this data collection method are comparable.

However, the physical detachment between the interviewee and the researcher raises additional technical and ethical issues.

The use of increasingly more powerful computational resources and web-based technologies, including Voice over Internet and smart phones, as Randal Olsen, in Chapter 2, shows, or numerous other online options, such as chat rooms, discussion forums, social networking sites, web surveys, or electronic mail, as Sunghee Lee, in Chapter 3, Kathleen J. Hanrahan, Mathew T. Smith and Judith E. Sturges, in Chapter 4, Peter Petocz, Sue Gordon and Anna Reid, in Chapter 5, and Jason Zalinger, in Chapter 6, elucidate, have been responsible for changes in the way interviews and questionnaires are executed, as well as in survey data processing, and the same can be said of more high-tech modes of interview, as the video-enhanced self-administered computer interviews, examined in Chapter 7, by Joachim Gerich, an interview mode especially recommended to interrogate respondents with special needs, such as deaf respondents, or children and young research participants. The use of visual material, in a participatory photo interview, as Bettina Kolb explores in Chapter 8, opens new opportunities for citizen participation in the urban planning process, allowing every citizen the possibility to offer his or her own perspective of the urban space through photographs taken by them.

Interactive online diaries, referred by Cohen et al. (2006), can be adapted and applied for monitoring and evaluation of spatial plans, as a new digital and online research tool. Among other advantages, it may allow real-time communication between members of the planning team and between them and other stakeholders, between those responsible for the implementation of the spatial plan and those in charge of its evaluation. Also solicited participant online digital diaries (Milligan et al., 2005; Kenten, 2010), guided by open-ended questions, can be excellent sources of data in urban and planning studies, when combined, for example, with computer-assisted online interviews.

Data mining and text mining online applications (Borzemski, 2010), namely Web usage mining techniques (Jansen et al., 2000), may also prove useful for urban and planning research, if employed to produce knowledge, from different types of digital footprints, valuable to support decision-making within the urban planning process. Online petition is another digital technology that urban researchers and planners can combine with other research tools to gain, at very low cost, useful insights on a variety of urban problems, as Briassoulis (2010) suggests. It can also be used to get support on urban or planning issues within the local community.

The use of artistic interventions in qualitative research is well established in a number of social sciences disciplines, and as Dwyer and Davies (2010) suggest can also be applied online. The online use, by urban researchers and planners, of different forms of artistic installations, exhibitions, films and other artistic forms, namely in participatory planning methodologies, in the framework of the collaborative planning paradigm (Healey, 1997), in particular with marginalized social groups within the city, in order to engage participants and respondents, is another example of Web-based methodological innovation that urban researcher and planners should consider more frequently than has been the case until now.

The use of wireless networks in urban and planning studies to collect data on the spatial distribution of physical and environmental characteristics, or the use of high-tech sensors and crowd sourcing, with human participants serving as sensors (Chun & Artigas, 2012), or volunteered citizen sensoring of urban issues (Goodchild, 2007), are examples of other types of technological innovations taking place in data collection methods in the field of urban planning. They can be used in emergency planning, in the study of spatial variations of certain air pollutants in the city or in the wider metropolitan area, as well as in the study of other physical or environmental characteristics that are relevant for urban planning. Also the use of a semi-automated tool to track and monitor spatial-temporal behavior of pedestrians in urban spaces, as explained by Alexandra Millonig, Markus Ray and Helmut Schrom-Feiertag, in Chapter 19, can change significantly the way data on urban mobility is collected and processed by urban researchers and urban planners.

Data acquisition about the future or on new ideas for urban development is a critical and perhaps the most difficult task in urban planning. Among other methods, Brainstorming, the Future Search Conference, the Delphi method or the Policy Delphi method, and to some extent also Laddering techniques, have been applied regularly in conventional planning processes. Similarly to what happened with other research methods, researchers developed electronic versions and when feasible also online applications, as Chia-Chien Hsu and Brian A. Sandford, in Chapter 11, explain for the Web-based Delphi method, or Mary T. Dzindolet, Paul B. Paulus and Courtney Glazer, in Chapter 9, and Nicolas Michinov, in Chapter 10, for the electronic online brainstorming method and its potential interest for urban and planning research, a move also supported by the evidence provided by Camarda (2010). Online laddering, addressed by Thorsten Gruber, Alexander E. Reppel, Isabelle Szmigin and Rödiger Voss, in Chapter 12, and future search conferences, by Rosalind Hurworth, in Chapter 13, are two additional examples of the recent migration of conventional research methods to online venues, and in the case of laddering, a good illustration of the methodological cross-fertilization between different disciplines.

Online Indirect Data Collection

In urban and planning studies, researchers depend over and over again on government and private organizations for textual or visual data to fulfill part of their information needs. For that reason, the Internet can be indeed a valuable research resource. Indirect online data collection from secondary digital sources, such as online official statistics, government reports, urban surveys data records, available in online digital archives or public repositories, are in most cases free or much less expensive than data collected directly by the researcher. However, the researcher doesn't control the data collection process and this data, easily available online, may not fulfill a number of needs the researcher has, concerning, for example, the time frame, geographical scale, variables or population covered.

Digital and online bibliographic databases, increasingly providing free access to full text, university repositories, online digital libraries, and other institutional digital archives, offering free access to text, images, maps, and statistical resources, covering an ever increasing time period, are just few examples of data sources available online which can have huge impacts in the practicalities of the urban research process, moving it from conventional paper-and-pencil to a fully developed digital and online research process. In addition to these strengths, online availability of digital data on urban structures and processes allows the use of sophisticated data and text mining software, for both quantitative and qualitative analysis, for content analysis of digital sources, in almost all sorts of urban and planning issues, making it easy to handle repetitive tasks in the data analysis stage of the research process.

The Choice of Online Methods

The choice of the appropriate online method for a particular research project depends on a number of factors. As a general guiding principle, urban researchers and planners should seek to apply the least obtrusive methodology. If data exists in official publications or in public archives, the option should be for indirect data collection, although the data, for the reasons mentioned before, may not match exactly the needs of the researcher. In that case, other options should be considered.

The choice depends also on the effect that the method may have on the case that is being studied. When someone knows he or she is being observed, or if the purpose of the observation is known in advance, the behavior can be affected, in one way or another, a characteristic particularly important in online research, when the observation takes place in chat rooms, in a local thematic forum, or in collective blogs developed around urban and planning issues related to the local community. A person may be averse to admit a certain social behavior or attitude regarding urban environmental issues during an online computer-assisted interview, but information on that fact, may perhaps be obtained by unobtrusive online methods, such as direct observation on a variety of digital environments, blogs, discussion forum, or chat rooms dealing with urban issues.

The selection of the digital technology and online method depends also on the population and issues to be addressed. If the problem is not feasible to deal with in an interview then other methods should be applied. That might perhaps be the case when a researcher, interested in the ethical behavior of urban planners or local politicians responsible for the planning department, decides to research unclear decisions, a situation that possibly will be unfeasible through online computer-assisted interviews with those that are suspected of such practices, and for that reason other data collection methods and other sources of information should be considered or should complement Web-based interviews.

Another critical factor is accessibility and data costs. As regards accessibility, online methods ease the access to respondents who are difficult to contact due to their geographical location or small numbers, and can allow, in certain circumstances, as explained by Amy Wesolowski and Nathan Eagle, in Chapter 20, the collection of data on excluded social groups within urban areas. Logistic aspects and repetitive tasks, in data collection and data processing, are also made easier and less time consuming by these digital technologies. In what concerns costs, digital technologies and online research methods are, broadly speaking, less expensive than their equivalent paper-and-pencil offline conventional methods.

Nonetheless, the type of questions that can be asked or the observations that can be done differ from method to method, are more limited in a few of them, and some are much easier to design and implement and less expensive than others. For example, while e-mail questionnaires or web-surveys, which are relatively low-tech methodologies, are among the easiest and cheapest online research methods, online public participation in urban planning processes, including 3-D visualization methods, are by far more complex and expensive to design and implement. Similarly, large scale online interviews are more expensive and time consuming than email surveys, and some direct observations in specialized forums on urban issues are more readily made than observations in similar digital tools with a more general focus.

ETHICAL CONSIDERATIONS IN URBAN AND PLANNING ONLINE RESEARCH

In social science research there is frequently a risk that human respondents or participants can be disturbed or distressed and for that reason ethical implications of urban and planning research projects must be made explicit from the start for all those involved, as is often suggested in the literature (Silva, 2007; Johnson et al., 2001; Newman, 2000; Patton, 1990). In other words, urban research, within or via online environments, must give proper consideration to ethical standards and legal regulations, including those related to human subject protection, professional integrity and intellectual property, as well as to information security risks, which need to be properly managed to ensure integrity, confidentiality and the privacy of every

citizen, as addressed and examined in some of the following chapters in this book, namely by Harsh Suri and Fay Patel in Chapter 23.

Where online research is intrusive of the privacy of informants and respondents or when there is any similar risk of harm for human participants there are certainly ethical issues that need to be addressed seriously, as is well documented in the literature on research ethics (e.g., Capurro & Pingel, 2002; Bassett & O'Riordan, 2002; Elgesem, 2002; Sheppard & Cizek, 2009; Creswell, 2002; Buchanan, 2004; Schultz, 2006; Madge, 2007). For that reason, urban researchers and planners must be prepared to consider and to act on a variety of ethical challenges (Silva, 2007, 2008b), throughout the online research process, even if the information collected and the method employed do not raise severe ethical dilemmas.

Since Web-based research creates specific ethical challenges and risks, within online communication and interaction processes with respondents, as is the case of research with children and young people (Nordin & Berglund, 2010; Battles, 2010) (for a broad view on ethical dilemmas in research with children and young people, see Morrow, 2008), which can even shape the research design and the type of data the researcher can collect, and how it can be done, additional care must be taken in each stage of the online research process.

Nonetheless, not all online research requires the same level of ethical consideration and review, and no one ethical approach fits all situations. Some may even be free from this review process, as is the case of research involving online data collection in public documents, when human participants cannot be identified, or when anonymous surveys are employed by email or similar digital tools, and other types of research may well require only minor ethical review controls.

Issues of physical harm or mental stress, psychological abuse, self-determination and paternalism, deception and informed consent, data privacy and privacy invasion, confidentiality, anonymity, the case of vulnerable populations, and the researcher' responsibilities after completion of the research, namely regarding anonymity and confidentiality, among other aspects, are not different, in essence, in research conducted entirely or partially in digital and online environments compared to conventional research settings, as is widely recognized in the literature (Buchanan, 2004; Silva, 2008b; Basset et al., 2002; Battles, 2010; Capurro & Pingel, 2002; Elgesem, 2002) and in several chapters in this book as well. Even so, urban researchers and planners, as mentioned in previous paragraphs, should be aware of potentially distinctive ethical challenges in fieldwork carried out in the World Wide Web. The characteristics of the digital environment emphasize the risk of harm, making the safeguard of privacy and confidentiality, after data has been collected, technically more complex.

The same can be said about ethical guidance regarding the archiving of research data and research outcomes, as well as the online publication of research findings and issues of intellectual property (Spinello, 2003; Blanke, 2004), since these may have a much greater negative impact than a traditional paper-and-pencil research report, if the privacy of participants or respondents is not properly protected, and if legal norms are not correctly considered, as Almut Leh and Doris Tausendfreund, in Chapter 21, and Andrew Charlesworth, in Chapter 22, explain. In fact, given that research findings have the possibility to influence future social behavior and social norms, increased accessibility offered by digital and online communication may well augment the impact research findings will have on social perception of particular urban problems and on urban planning ethics in general.

CONCLUSION

Notwithstanding the enormous potential digital technologies and Web-based research methods offer for research in the field of urban and plan-

ning studies, and the existence of a vast collection of actual experiences and practical applications, in a myriad of urban contexts worldwide, these online research methods and digital technologies are still not particularly widespread in urban and planning studies, and for that reason the field is still far from benefiting entirely from the strengths and opportunities offered by digital technologies and online research methods.

Even so, it is reasonable to expect that this increasing diffusion of Internet technologies will represent a major methodological innovation in the field of urban and planning studies, will expand the use of participatory research methodologies in urban planning and will stimulate the implementation of different forms of collaborative planning as well, although part of these changes requires new developments and improvements in digital technologies and in Web-based research methods. Changes are also required at the level of urban knowledge management and urban databanks management systems, within planning departments, and among them and other external urban data sources, which need to become more integrated, open and accessible to ordinary citizens and other urban stakeholders.

However, while these digital technologies reduce numerous research problems, namely logistic ones, they also tend to introduce new restrictions that require a revision of standards and practices that govern urban and planning research. For that reason, urban researchers and planners need to be reflexive and critical in the design stage and during the research process itself. For example, the persistent digital divide along a number of social dimensions, such as social class, income, age, gender, or ability, as Mossberger et al. (2008) and Bricout and Baker (2010) demonstrate, and other conditions as well, as Littleton (2007) and Cantrell and Lupinacci (2007), among others, suggest, may prevent, in some circumstances, at least for some time, a generalized adoption of online research methods in urban and planning studies.

Considering all these aspects, a balanced combination of Web-based research methods and conventional research approaches, will offer urban researchers and planners more research tools, will reach a larger number of respondents and participants, will be more socially and geographically inclusive, enhancing the participation of citizens in the research process and in the planning process as well.

In sum, although digital technologies and Web-based research methods have several advantages over conventional research methods, they also have shortcomings that urban researchers need to balance in each specific context. The use of sophisticated online methods can improve the overall quality of urban and planning research designs but will not change per se the essence of the urban research endeavor. Ultimately, it is the nature of the study, the research question, the philosophical perspective and, in some circumstances, also its potential contribution for community empowerment that will determine the choice of the research method, conventional or online, or the exact combination of the mixed-method approach.

REFERENCES

Al-Kodmany, K. (2010). Political power, governance and e-Planning. In Silva, C. N. (Ed.), *Handbook of Research on E-Planning: ICTs for Urban Development and Monitoring* (pp. 143–166). Hershey, PA: Information Science Reference. doi:10.4018/978-1-61520-929-3.ch008

Anttiroiko, A.-V. (2012). Urban Planning 2.0. *International Journal of E-Planning Research, 1*(1), 16-30. doi: 10.4018/ijepr.2012010103

Bassett, E. H., & O'Riordan, K. (2002). Ethics of Internet research: Contesting the human subjects research model. *Ethics and Information Technology, 4*, 233–247. doi:10.1023/A:1021319125207

Battles, H. T. (2010). Exploring Ethical and Methodological Issues in Internet-Based Research with Adolescents. *International Journal of Qualitative Methods, 9*(1), 27–39.

Bishop, I. (2012). On-line approaches to data delivery and visualisation in landscape planning and management. *International Journal of E-Planning Research, 1*(1), 31-41. doi: 10.4018/ijepr.2012010104

Blanke, J. M. (2004). Copyright law in the digital age. In Brennan, L. L., & Johnson, V. E. (Eds.), *Social, Ethical and Policy Implications of Information Technology* (pp. 223–233). Hershey, PA: Information Science Publishing. doi:10.4018/978-1-59140-168-1.ch013

Borzemski, L. (2010). The Experimental Design for Data Mining to Discover Web Performance Issues in a Wide Area Network. *Cybernetics and Systems: An International Journal, 41*, 31–45. doi:10.1080/01969720903408763

Briassoulis, H. (2010). Online petitions: new tools of secondary analysis? *Qualitative Research, 10*(6), 715–727. doi:10.1177/1468794110380530

Bricout, J., & Baker, P. (2010). Deploying information and communication technologies to enhance participation in local governance for citizens with disabilities. *International Journal of Information Communication Technologies and Human Development, 2*(2), 34–51. doi:10.4018/jicthd.2010040103

Buchanan, E. (Ed.). (2004). *Readings in Virtual Research Ethics: Issues and controversies*. Hershey, PA: Information Science Publishing.

Buchwald, D., Schantz-Laursen, B., & Delmar, C. (2009). Video Diary Data Collection in Research with Children: An Alternative Method. *International Journal of Qualitative Methods, 8*(1), 12–20.

Camarada, D. (2010). Beyond citizen participation in planning: multi-agent systems for complex decision-making. In Silva, C. N. (Ed.), *Handbook of Research on E-Planning: ICTs for Urban Development and Monitoring* (pp. 404–419). Hershey, PA: Information Science Reference. doi:10.4018/978-1-61520-929-3.ch010

Cantrell, M. A., & Lupinacci, P. (2007). Methodological issues in online data collection. *Journal of Advanced Nursing*, 60(5), 544–549. doi:10.1111/j.1365-2648.2007.04448.x

Capurro, R., & Pingel, C. (2002). Ethical issues of online communication research. *Ethics and Information Technology*, 4, 189–194. doi:10.1023/A:1021372527024

Chou, C. (2002). Developing the e-Delphi system: a web-based forecasting tool for educational research. *British Journal of Educational Technology*, 33(2), 233–237. doi:10.1111/1467-8535.00257

Chun, S. A., & Artigas, F. (2012). Sensors and Crowdsourcing for Environmental Awareness and Emergency Planning. *International Journal of E-Planning Research*, 1(1), 56-74. doi: 10.4018/ijepr.2012010106

Cohen, D. J., Leviton, L. C., Isaacson, N., Tallia, A. F., & Crabtree, B. F. (2006). Online Diaries for Qualitative Evaluation. *The American Journal of Evaluation*, 27(2), 163–184. doi:10.1177/1098214006288448

Corbett, J., & Mann, R. (2010). Tlowitsis Re-Imagined: The Use of Digital Media to Build Nation and Overcome Disconnection in a Displaced Aboriginal. *International Journal of Information Communication Technologies and Human Development*, 2(3), 33–54. doi:10.4018/jicthd.2010070103

Creswell, J. W. (2002). *Research design. Qualitative, quantitative, and mixed methods approaches* (2nd ed.). London, UK: Sage.

Dever, J., Rafferty, A., & Valliant, R. (2008). Internet survey: can statistical adjustments eliminate coverage bias? *Survey Research Methods*, 2(2), 47–60.

Dwyer, C., & Davies, G. (2010). Qualitative methods III: animating archives, artful interventions and online environments. *Progress in Human Geography*, 34(1), 88–97. doi:10.1177/0309132508105005

Elgesem, D. (2002). What is special about the ethical issues in online research? *Ethics and Information Technology*, 4, 195–203. doi:10.1023/A:1021320510186

Elwood, S. (2006). Critical issues in participatory GIS: Deconstructions, reconstructions, and new research directions. *Transactions in GIS*, 10(5), 693–708. doi:10.1111/j.1467-9671.2006.01023.x

Frankfort-Nachmias, C., & Nachmias, D. (2000). *Research Methods in the Social Sciences* (6th ed.). New York, NY: Worth.

Ganassali, S. (2008). The influence of the design of web survey questionnaires on the quality of responses. *Survey Research Methods*, 2(1), 21–32.

Glasser, D. J., Goodman, K. W., & Einspruch, N. G. (2007). Chips, tags and scanners: Ethical challenges for radio frequency identification. *Ethics and Information Technology*, 9, 101–109. doi:10.1007/s10676-006-9124-0

Goodchild, M. F. (2007). Citizens as sensors: the world of volunteered geography. *GeoJournal*, 69, 211–221. doi:10.1007/s10708-007-9111-y

Healy, P. (1997). *Collaborative planning: Shaping places in fragmented societies*. Basingstoke, UK: Palgrave-Macmillan.

Horelli, L., & Wallin, S. (2010). The future-making assessment approach as a tool for e-planning and community development – the case of Ubiquitous Helsinki. In Silva, C. N. (Ed.), *Handbook of Research on E-Planning: ICTs for Urban Development and Monitoring* (pp. 58–79). Hershey, PA: Information Science Reference. doi:10.4018/978-1-61520-929-3.ch004

Jansen, B. J., Spink, A., & Saracevic, T. (2000). Real life, real users, and real needs: a study and analysis of user queries on the web. *Information Processing & Management*, *36*, 207–227. doi:10.1016/S0306-4573(99)00056-4

Jobst, M., Dollner, J., & Lubanski, O. (2010). Communicating Geoinformation effectively with virtual 3D city models. In Silva, C. N. (Ed.), *Handbook of Research on E-Planning: ICTs for Urban Development and Monitoring* (pp. 120–142). Hershey, PA: Information Science Reference. doi:10.4018/978-1-61520-929-3.ch007

Johnson, J. B., Reynolds, H., & Josylin, R. (2001). *Political Science Research Methods* (4th ed.). Washington, DC: CQ Press.

Kenten, C. (2010). Narrating Oneself: Reflections on the Use of Solicited Diaries with Diary Interviews. *Forum Qualitative Sozialforschung / Forum: Qualitative. Social Research*, *11*(2). Retrieved from http://nbn-resolving.de/urn:nbn:de:0114-fqs1002160

Klessmann, J. (2010). Portals as a tool for public participation in urban planning. In Silva, C. N. (Ed.), *Handbook of Research on E-Planning: ICTs for Urban Development and Monitoring* (pp. 252–267). Hershey, PA: Information Science Reference. doi:10.4018/978-1-61520-929-3.ch013

Kubicek, H. (2010). The potential of e-Participation in urban planning: a European perspective. In Silva, C. N. (Ed.), *Handbook of Research on E-Planning: ICTs for Urban Development and Monitoring* (pp. 168–194). Hershey, PA: Information Science Reference. doi:10.4018/978-1-61520-929-3.ch009

Lavrakas, P. J. (Ed.). (2008). *Encyclopedia of Survey Research Methods*. Newbury Park, CA: Sage.

Limb, M., & Dwyer, C. (Eds.). (2001). *Qualitative Methodologies for Geographers. Issues and debates*. London, UK: Arnold.

Littleton, D. (2007). Navigating Pitfalls of Web-Based Survey Development and Administration. *Medical Reference Services Quarterly*, *26*(4), 75–83. doi:10.1300/J115v26n04_06

Lobe, B., & Vehovar, V. (2009). Towards a flexible online mixed method design with a feedback loop. *Quality & Quantity*, *43*(4), 585–597. doi:10.1007/s11135-007-9146-7

Madge, C. (2007). Developing a geographers' agenda for online research ethics. *Progress in Human Geography*, *31*(5), 654–674. doi:10.1177/0309132507081496

Madge, C., & O'Connor, H. (2002). On-line with e-mums: exploring the Internet as a medium for research. *Area*, *34*(1), 92–102. doi:10.1111/1475-4762.00060

Marshall, C., & Rossman, G. B. (2006). *Designing qualitative research*. London, UK: Sage.

Milligan, C., Bingley, A., & Gatrell, A. (2005). Digging deep: Using diary techniques to explore the place of health and well-being amongst older people. *Social Science & Medicine*, *61*, 1882–1892. doi:10.1016/j.socscimed.2005.04.002

Morrow, V. (2008). Ethical dilemmas in research with children and young people about their social environments. *Children's Geographies*, *6*(1), 49–61. doi:10.1080/14733280701791918

Mossberger, K., Tolbert, C., & McNeal, R. (Eds.). (2008). *Digital citizenship. The Internet, Society, and Participation*. Cambridge, MA: MIT Press.

Murthy, D. (2008). Digital EthnograpShy: An Examination of the Use of New Technologies for Social Research. *Sociology, 42*(5), 837–855. doi:10.1177/0038038508094565

Newman, W. L. (2000). *Social research Methods. Qualitative and quantitative approaches* (4th ed.). London, UK: Allyn and Bacon.

Nordin, K., & Berglund, U. (2010). Children's Maps in GIS: A Tool for Communicating Outdoor Experiences in Urban Planning. *International Journal of Information Communication Technologies and Human Development, 2*(2), 1–16. doi:10.4018/jicthd.2010040101

Ohbuchi, E., Hanaizumi, H., & Hock, L. A. (2004). Barcode Readers using the Camera Device in Mobile Phones. In *Proceedings of the 2004 IEEE International Conference on Cyberworlds (CW'04)* (pp. 260-265).

Pang, L., Morgan-Morris, V., & Howell, A. (2010). RFID in Urban Planning. In Silva, C. N. (Ed.), *Handbook of Research on E-Planning: ICTs for Urban Development and Monitoring* (pp. 388–403). Hershey, PA: Information Science Reference. doi:10.4018/978-1-61520-929-3.ch020

Patton, M. Q. (1990). *Qualitative evaluation and research methods* (2nd ed.). London, UK: Sage.

Porter, S., & Whitcomb, M. (2005). E-mail subject lines and their effect on web survey viewing and response. *Social Science Computer Review, 23*(3), 380–387. doi:10.1177/0894439305275912

Reips, U.-D. (2001). The Web Experimental Psychology Lab: Five years of data collection on the Internet. *Behavior Research Methods, Instruments, & Computers, 33*(2), 201–211. doi:10.3758/BF03195366

Rohs, M., & Gfeller, B. (2004). Using Camera-Equipped Mobile Phones for Interacting with Real-World Objects. In *Advances in Pervasive Computing* (pp. 265–271). Zurich, Switzerland: Institute for Pervasive Computing, Department of Computer Science, ETH Zurich.

Schultz, R. A. (Ed.). (2006). *Contemporary issues in ethics and information technology*. London, UK: IRM Press.

Sheppard, S. R. J., & Cizek, P. (2009). The ethics of Google Earth: Crossing thresholds from spatial data to landscape visualisation. *Journal of Environmental Management, 90*, 2102–2117. doi:10.1016/j.jenvman.2007.09.012

Silva, C. N. (2007). Urban Planning and Ethics. In Rabin, J., & Berman, E. M. (Eds.), *Encyclopedia of Public Administration and Public Policy* (2nd ed.). New York, NY: CRC Press/Taylor & Francis Group. doi:10.1201/NOE1420052756.ch410

Silva, C. N. (2008a). Experimental Design. In Lavrakas, P. (Ed.), *Encyclopedia of survey research methods*. Thousand Oaks, CA: Sage.

Silva, C. N. (2008b). Research ethics in e-public administration. In Garson, G. D., & Khosrow-Pour, M. (Eds.), *Handbook of Research on Public Information Technology* (*Vol. 1*, pp. 314–322). Hershey, PA: Information Science Reference. doi:10.4018/978-1-59904-857-4.ch030

Spinello, R. (2003). The future of intellectual property. *Ethics and Information Technology, 5*, 1–16. doi:10.1023/A:1024976203396

Staffans, A., Rantanen, H., & Nummi, P. (2010). Local Internet Forums. Interactive land use planning and urban development neighborhoods. In Silva, C. N. (Ed.), *Handbook of Research on E-Planning: ICTs for Urban Development and Monitoring* (pp. 80–102). Hershey, PA: Information Science Reference. doi:10.4018/978-1-61520-929-3.ch005

Stewart, K., & Williams, M. (2005). Researching online populations: the use of online focus groups for social research. *Qualitative Research, 5*(4), 395–416. doi:10.1177/1468794105056916

Tregeagle, S. (2010). Participation in child welfare services through information and communication technologies. *International Journal of Information Communication Technologies and Human Development, 2*(2), 17–33. doi:10.4018/jicthd.2010040102

ADDITIONAL READING

AAS. (1999). *Ethical and legal aspects of human subjects research on the Internet.* Washington: American Association for the Advancement of Science.

ACM. (1992). *Code of Ethics and Professional conduct.* New York: Association for Computing Machinery.

ACM. (1997). *Software Engineering Code of Ethics and Professional Practice.* New York: Association for Computing Machinery.

Aikins, S. K. (2010). E-Planning: information security risks and management implications. In Silva, C. N. (Ed.), *Handbook of Research on E-Planning: ICTs for Urban Development and Monitoring* (pp. 404–419). Hershey, PA: Information Science Reference. doi:10.4018/978-1-61520-929-3.ch021

Anderson, R., Johnson, D., Gotterbarn, D., & Perrole, J. (1993). Using the new ACM code of ethics in decision making. *Communications of the ACM, 36*(2), 98–106. doi:10.1145/151220.151231

Anttiroiko, A.-V., & Malkia, M. (Eds.). (2006). *Encyclopedia of Digital Government.* Hershey, New York: Information Science Reference. doi:10.4018/978-1-59140-789-8

AoIR (2002). *Ethical decision-making and Internet Research. Recommendations from the AoIR Ethics Working Committee.* AoIR - Association of Internet Researchers.

Blaikie, N. (2000). *Designing social research: The logic of anticipation.* London: Polity.

Bonometti, R. J., & Jun, T. (2006). A dynamic technique for conducting online survey-based research. *Competitiveness Review, 16*(2), 97–105.

Bowker, N., & Tuffin, K. (2004). Using the Online Medium for Discursive Research About People With Disabilities. *Social Science Computer Review, 22*(2), 228–241. doi:10.1177/0894439303262561

Brennan, L. L., & Johnson, V. E. (2004). *Social, Ethical and Policy Implications of Information Technology.* London: Information Science Publishing.

Brewer, J., & Hunter, A. (1989). *Multimethod research. A synthesis of styles.* London: Sage.

Cappelle, C. (2010). Intelligent Geolocalization in Urban Areas Using Global Positioning Systems, Three-Dimensional Geographic Information Systems, and Vision. *Journal of Intelligent Transportation Systems, 14*(1), 3–12. doi:10.1080/15472450903385999

Capurro, R. (2005). Privacy: An intercultural perspective. *Ethics and Information Technology, 7*, 37–47. doi:10.1007/s10676-005-4407-4

Castells, M. (2010). *The Information Age: Economy, Society and Culture, Vol I-III.* Oxford: Wiley-Blackwell.

Christensen, L. B. (1994). *Experimental methodology.* Boston: Allyn and Bacon.

Cliford, N., & Valentine, G. (Eds.). (2005). *Key Methods in Geography.* London: Sage.

Cole, S. T. (2005). Comparing Mail and Web-Based Survey Distribution Methods: Results of Surveys to Leisure Travel Retailers. *Journal of Travel Research, 43*(4), 422–430. doi:10.1177/0047287505274655

Danielson, P. (2007). Digital morality and Ethics. In Ari-Veikko, A., & Malkia, M. (Eds.), *Encyclopedia of Digital Government* (pp. 377–381). Hershey, New York: Idea Group Publishing.

DiCicco-Bloom, B., & Crabtree, B. F. (2006). The qualitative research interview. *Medical Education, 40*(4), 314–321. doi:10.1111/j.1365-2929.2006.02418.x

Fine, G. A. (1988). *Knowing children. Participant observation with minors*. London: Sage.

Flowerdew, R., & Martin, D. (2005). *Methods in Human Geography. A guide for students doing a research project*. Harlow: Longman.

Garson, G. D., & Khosrow-Pour, M. (Eds.). (2008). *Handbook of research on Public Information Technology*. Hershey, New York: Information Science Reference. doi:10.4018/978-1-59904-857-4

Gilbert, N. (1995). *Researching Social life*. London: Sage.

Gray, A. (2004). *Research practice for cultural studies. Ethnographic methods and lived cultures*. London: Sage.

Hakim, C. (1987). *Research design: strategies and choices in the design of social research*. London: Routledge.

Hambridge, S. (1995). *Netiquette guidelines*. IETF - The Internet Engineering Task Force.

Hodges, M. (2000). Seeing Data In-depth. *Computer Graphics World, 23*(5), 43–49.

Holloway, I. (1997). *Basic concepts for qualitative research*. Oxford: Blackwell.

Holmes, S. (2009). Methodological and ethical considerations in designing an Internet study of quality of life: A discussion paper. *International Journal of Nursing Studies, 46*(3), 394–405. doi:10.1016/j.ijnurstu.2008.08.004

Hudson-Smith, A., Evans, S., & Batty, M. (2005). Building the Virtual City: Public Participation through e-Democracy. *Knowledge, Technology & Policy, 18*(1), 62–85. doi:10.1007/s12130-005-1016-9

IEEE. (1999). *Software engineer's code of ethics and professional practice*. Washington: Institute for Electrical and Electronic Engineers.

Jansen, B. J. (2008). Searching for digital images on the web. *The Journal of Documentation, 64*(1), 81–100. doi:10.1108/00220410810844169

Jiyeong, L. (2007). A Three-Dimensional Navigable Data Model to Support Emergency Response in Microspatial Built-Environments. *Annals of the Association of American Geographers. Association of American Geographers, 97*(3), 512–529. doi:10.1111/j.1467-8306.2007.00561.x

Kenny, A. J. (2005). Interaction in cyberspace: an online focus group. *Journal of Advanced Nursing, 49*(4), 414–422. doi:10.1111/j.1365-2648.2004.03305.x

Köninger, A., & Bartel, S. (1998). 3D-GIS for Urban Purposes. *GeoInformatica, 2*(1), 79–103. doi:10.1023/A:1009797106866

Lefever, S., Dal, M., & Matthíasdóttir, Á. (2007). Online data collection in academic research: Advantages and limitations. *British Journal of Educational Technology, 38*(4), 574–582. doi:10.1111/j.1467-8535.2006.00638.x

Melville, R. (2007). Ethical dilemmas in online research. In Ari-Veikko, A., & Malkia, M. (Eds.), *Encyclopedia of Digital Government* (pp. 734–739). Heshey, PA: Idea Group Publishing.

Nicholas, D. B. (2010). Contrasting Internet and Face-to-Face Focus Groups for Children with Chronic Health Conditions: Outcomes and Participant Experiences. *International Journal of Qualitative Methods, 9*(1), 105–121.

Noveck, B. S. (2009). *Wiki Government. How technology can make government better, democracy stronger, and citizens more powerful.* Washington: Brookings Institution Press.

Parr, H. (2002). New body-geographies: the embodied spaces of health and medical information on the Internet. *Environment and Planning. D, Society & Space, 20,* 73–95. doi:10.1068/d41j

Parsell, M. (2008). Pernicious virtual communities: Identity, polarisation and the Web 2.0. *Ethics and Information Technology, 10,* 41–56. doi:10.1007/s10676-008-9153-y

Perkins, G. H. (2004). Will Libraries' Web-based Survey Methods Replace Existing Non-Electronic Survey Methods? *Information Technology & Libraries, 23*(3), 123–126.

Potter, S. (Ed.). (2002). *Doing Postgraduate Research.* London: Sage.

Ryan, G. W. (2004). Using a Word Processor to tag and Retrieve Blocks of Text. *Field Methods, 16*(1), 109–130. doi:10.1177/1525822X03261269

Sade-Beck, L. (2004). Internet Ethnography: Online and Offline. *International Journal of Qualitative Methods, 3*(2), 1–14.

Schultz, R. A. (Ed.). (2006). *Contemporary issues in ethics and information technology.* London: IRM Press.

Silva, C. N. (Ed.). (2010). *Handbook of Research on E-Planning: ICTs for Urban Development and Monitoring.* Hershey, PA: Information Science Reference: IGI Global.

Silva, C. N. (Ed.). (2010). Special issue "Local Governance in the Digital Age: e-Participation of Children and Citizens with Disabilities". *International Journal of Information and Communication Technologies, 2*(2).

Silva, C. N. (Ed.). (2010). Special issue "Local Governance in the Digital Age: Citizen E-Participation in Rural Areas and in Displaced Aboriginal Communities". *International Journal of Information and Communication Technologies, 2*(3).

Silverman, D. (2000). *Doing qualitative research: A practical handbook.* London: Sage.

Verbree, E. (1999). Interaction in virtual world views-linking 3D GIS with VR. *International Journal of Geographical Information Science, 13*(4), 385–396. doi:10.1080/136588199241265

Vuorinen, J. (2006). Ethical codes in the digital world: comparisons of the proprietary, the open/free and the cracker system. *Ethics and Information Technology, 9,* 27–38. doi:10.1007/s10676-006-9130-2

Walters, G. T. (2002). *Human Rights in an information age: A philosophical analysis.* Toronto: University of Toronto Press.

Weinstein, M. (2006). TAMS Analyzer: Anthropology as cultural critique in a Digital Age. *Social Science Computer Review, 24*(1), 68–77. doi:10.1177/0894439305281496

Wyld, D. C. (2008). Blogging. In Garson, G. David e Khosrow-Pour, Mehdi (Eds.). *Handbook of Research on Public Information Technology.* New York: Information Science Reference, pp. 81-93.

Yigitcanlar, T., Baum, S., & Stimson, R. (2003). Analyzing the Patterns of ICT Utilization for Online Public Participatory Planning in Queensland, Australia. *Assessment Journal, 10*(2), 5–21.

Chapter 2
Infrastructure for Survey Data Processing in Urban and Planning Studies

Randall J. Olsen
Ohio State University, USA

ABSTRACT

Applied social science research has increasingly come to rely on surveys to generate detailed data, especially on firms, persons, and households, needed to study social phenomena. The methods used to collect survey data have changed substantially in the past quarter century and appear on the cusp of changing again with the rise of Web-based technologies. These changes can be best implemented by adopting computational methods designed for relational databases. This is true not only for survey data, but also administrative data that government agencies collect, store, and use. In this chapter, the author explains how these changes are best accommodated and how new telecommunications technologies, including Voice over Internet and smart phones, fit into this new paradigm. These techniques dominate survey data collection for urban studies and other fields.

INTRODUCTION

A quarter century ago, survey research had two key tools—pencil and paper. The situation in the late 1980s was ripe for fundamental changes in how surveys handled the flow of data. There were two

DOI: 10.4018/978-1-4666-0074-4.ch002

general responses to that problem—computerize the process a step at a time with solutions targeted on particular stages of the process, or target the process as a whole, reconstructing how surveys handle their data. In this chapter, we describe the second approach. In our judgment, survey organizations will find themselves there sooner or later; the only issue is how painful the trip will be.

Today, when interviewers set out to do interviewing, paper and pencil is largely relegated to generating sticky notes and jotting down reminders. For the serious business of data collection, we discourage interviewers from writing things down lest they (a) constitute a breach of security; or (b) make it difficult and costly to store and process all the data that a project needs to collect, store and keep organized in order to achieve the scientific goals of the study. For surveys, our invitation to the prospective respondent is increasingly, our keyboard or yours? That is, aside from relatively rare mail-out interviews that send booklets for the respondent to fill out, we either call the respondent on the telephone, with the interviewer entering the data on a PC at his or her workstation, or the interviewer visits the respondent's home or place of business, again using a computer, this time a stand-alone laptop, to enter answers and other data secured during the interview. Even in the event we ask the respondent to enter the data him or herself, the preferred approach is a Web site rather than a booklet that needs to be mailed out, mailed back in, received and tracked, data entered, edited and cleaned to deal with the inevitable respondent or data entry errors that result from failing to read the instructions, skipping items or writing down answers that are blatantly inconsistent with previous responses.

The process of handling what was, often, literally tons of paper was labor intensive to say the least. Even before the first interviewer did the first case, forms needed to be printed, bound and mailed to interviewers. That was the easy part. For face-to-face interviewing, the completed forms needed to be mailed back to the central office, receipted, tracked against the case load, and packaged together with all the other relevant paper materials, such as any consent forms, receipts for incentive payments, specialized questionnaire modules for self-administered components, and paper forms that may have been filled out as part of the interview process, such household rosters, calendars that were marked up for event histories, answer forms for tests and other items. These materials needed to be assembled into a folder, identifiers checked and, if necessary, added to the loose forms. Each expected item was systematically recorded as either present or missing, and this information was passed along to the interviewer's supervisor so she could track the interviewer's performance and productivity.

After receipt, the interview booklets passed to an editor who reviewed the form for completeness, unclear markings, missing answers and other irregularities. Depending on the study and the protocol, this initial review might lead to the case being set aside for a call to the interviewer asking her to clarify those items that were garbled, missing or in error, and if the interviewer could not do this and the items in question were crucial, either the interviewer or a member of the central office staff might place a call to the respondent to retrieve the necessary information.

Assuming the editor found the interview to be in order, the next step was data entry, often double entry to catch errors. Then came cleaning, often based upon cleaning specifications that had to be designed, agreed upon, programmed, tested and then run. Usually the process was iterative with multiple passes through the cleaning program until all errors were either resolved or accepted as irreconcilable. Once the data were cleaned, they were assembled into one or more files and frequencies run, usually with a program such as SAS or SPSS. From that point, staff created additional variables and the data were usually distributed on magnetic tape with a printed codebook that ran for hundreds of pages.

One can appreciate that such a complex process used a lot of time and a lot of money. The labor-intensive process started with, and was driven by, a printed questionnaire. Besides making the survey process labor intensive, paper questionnaires made it expensive to add questions as each additional question not only absorbed interviewer time, it also required, editing, data entry, cleaning and documentation.

Urban and planning studies is a data driven discipline. The modalities for data collection are changing and on line data collection is becoming a significant factor. In the past fifteen years, survey data collection has changed significantly and we anticipate on line methods will change data collection once again. In this chapter, we step the reader through the entire process of data collection, describe how technology changed that process and point out how on line methods are instigating yet more change.

SURVEY DATA PROCESSING

Steps in the Process

Design

The survey process begins with design. The effect of survey computerization on the design process is fairly modest in most cases. The goals of a survey are usually set without regard to whether the instrument is printed or computerized. There are three ways, however, that computerization has affected the design process. First, the layout of the question the interviewer sees and reads has changed substantially. The ability of a computer to handle text fills—to use the correct tense, pronoun, case and number, and even to reference names from a roster—substantially simplifies the interviewer's task but puts more of a load on the designer to build in those text fills. The first time we trained interviewers to work on a CAPI survey, we said, only half in jest that the instruction manual consisted of three words: Read. The. Screen.

The second change that designers must bear in mind is that questions appear in an entirely different context. When we mounted a study of mode effects from our 1989 randomized experiment of CAPI vs. paper and pencil, we searched for questions that generated different response patterns in the two modes. The differences in the response patterns achieved the 5% level of significance in

only about 5% of the questions, an encouraging result. However, there were two response patterns that suggested a mode effect—the effect of scrolling and the effect of what else the interviewer sees on the page. When a question had such a long pick list that some choices required the interviewer to scroll down to read them, they were less likely to be selected. In another interesting case we had two questions on a printed page, the first of which asked the respondent for the easiest way to report their earnings on a job, whether by the hour, day, week, month, or year. The second question asked those respondents not reporting an hourly wage whether they were, in fact, paid by the hour and if so, how much they earned. More respondents answered the first question with an hourly wage in paper interviews than in computer interviews, suggesting that interviewers using paper forms realized the design team wanted to learn the hourly rate of pay if that was how the respondent was paid. Paper questionnaires are more intuitive and clear, and that has an effect on the interview process.

The third way computerization affects the design process is via complexity. When paper and pencil was the norm, the interview had to be simple enough for the interviewer to negotiate her way through the booklet. Routing instructions had to be fairly simple. Complex "check" items that referenced several of the respondent's previous answers, either in the current or previous interviews, were not feasible and hence the design process could not be too complicated. With the computer performing the checks, the design process has become unconstrained by issues of complexity. This ability to deal with complexity provides great latitude to the designer—for example, it is easier to recover data that may have been missed by a few respondents in previous waves due to item or wave non-response—and can be exploited to make an interview much more efficient, avoiding questions whose responses could be easily inferred from earlier answers.

Complex questions that can infer subtle respondent attitudes by means of posing a sequence of hypothetical questions by building on previous responses—such as attitudes concerning risky lotteries—or questions driven by visual stimuli presented on the screen that are themselves conditional on how the respondent reacted to earlier stimuli, are suddenly possible instead of impossible. Survey designers have been quick to exploit the complex possibilities offered by computerization.

The downside of this complexity is that the overall flow of the interview has become opaque. Users of the data may be uncertain in which circumstances a particular question is posed to the respondent. The number of data items produced by an interview increases, the number of check items the user must negotiate is much larger, and taken as a whole, the datasets constructed from an interview are more difficult to understand. This creates new problems for the process of documenting and disseminating the data – topics we take up below. An important upside of computer assisted interviewing is that it greatly reduces the cost of processing the data from an additional minute of interviewing. This leads to longer interviews at only a modestly higher cost and can make the survey data substantially more powerful by increasing the scope of the data collected.

Instrument Preparation

Unlike the process of instrument design, which for the most part involves subject matter specialists or members of a scientific team, the process of preparing the instrument for fielding is mostly a task for survey professionals. Starting at this point, computerization has a stronger impact on the survey process and the precise implementation of computerized interviewing has a large effect. Because the first computerized surveys were done on mainframes or super-minicomputers, the programming language used had to be native to that equipment. For the most part, this was roughly co-incident with when PCs became popular. The languages available for PCs, and even the

address space MS-DOS supported, were very limited. Consequently, the languages in which the first programming efforts were mounted were off-the-shelf commercial software, not a system designed for the purpose at hand. This meant the design work done for a survey was given to a programmer whose understanding of how the survey was to work might be somewhat limited. Complicating the situation was the fact that surveys, unlike batch data cleaning programs, are inherently interactive. When an interviewer or respondent makes a mistake, that error needs to be undone. This may require going back several questions, or even several sections, to correct the error and then returning to where the error was discovered, with the caveat that a changed answer early on can change the flow of control for an interview, requiring new questions to be asked and abandoning other questions if they become "off path".

The computerized instrument must handle break-offs, so the interview can resume in the future without the loss of data that might require many questions to be re-asked. In addition, programming must account for jumps or checks that need to be executed in the event a respondent gives either a "don't know" or "refuse" answer to an item. Add in the handling of text fill items, control over loops, rosters and the answer file, and it is clear that programming an instrument can be a difficult task. These up-front costs were quite costly if handled in a manner that consumed large amounts of time from skilled programmers, and this technically demanding task imposed serious schedule risks on the project team. Further, certain technical constraints of early computers had serious operational consequences. For example, a limited address space could mean that a large, complex interview done on an early PC had to be programmed as several independent programs. Early computerized surveys did not allow the interviewer to back up over these program segment boundaries imposed by a limited address space. If an error were made in an earlier section, the problem could only be rectified in the central office by hand-editing the data.

A major divide in the industry is how to represent an instrument. The first efforts at computerization were to represent the instrument as a program, but a very few organizations choose to represent the instrument at a series of data records. This has some very considerable strategic advantages, so we outline this alternative strategy next—a strategy that has considerable appeal for a great many social science research projects that deal with large amounts of data.

The core technology for a great many data management applications is an integrated database facility built around modern relational databases. Now, if one is dealing with a small, simple questionnaire almost any method for data collection and data management will work. As the scale, scope and complexity of a survey project grows, one needs to plan carefully for the questionnaire, how the survey collects the data, the management of the data it produces, and making the resultant data readily available for analysis.

For these steps to run smoothly and flow smoothly from one to the other they need to be integrated. There are compelling reasons why relational database management systems (RDBMS) are the most effective tools for achieving this integration[1]. It is essential that the data file preserve the relationships among the various questions and among the questionnaire, respondent answers, the sampling structure and respondent relationships. In more complex survey applications, such as birth cohort or household panel studies, there are often complex relationships among persons from the same family structure or household. In longitudinal surveys there are also complex relationships among the answers in various rounds that result from prefills (data carried forward) from previous surveys and bounded interviewing techniques that create event histories by integrating lines of inquiry over multiple rounds of interviewing. Using an RDBMS strategy for a longitudinal survey will reduce administrative costs and for large, complex

cross-sectional surveys the RDBMS strategy also offers advantages.

In the RDBMS system, each question or check item in the survey is represented as a record in the database. Instead of programming an entire questionnaire using a computer programming language, the survey staff enters the database records for each question and then creates a program that processes each question record in turn and links the results together. Preparing the instrument consists of "filling in the blanks" in a form that captures all the necessary attributes of the tables that make up the transaction formed by a question. Questionnaire preparation becomes not a programming task but, for most of the instrument, a clerical operation. While there are some complex "records" used to guide Boolean comparisons or roster operations, these are fairly standard. The "heavy lifting" in code generation is handled by the utilities that process the question records, and those are shared, and unchanged, across surveys.

Paper and pencil surveys only required secretarial staff to prepare the printed booklets. With computerized surveys instrument preparation is more costly. In effect the editing and cleaning tasks become front-loaded in the sense they precede rather than follow the field work. Given one is going to computerize a survey, as virtually all surveys are, the major issue is whether to use an RDBMS strategy or a programming approach. That decision also dictates how the rest of the survey process must be handled and the resources and time needed to carry them out. We will expand upon this throughout this chapter.

Testing and Diagnostics

Once the computerized survey has been designed and implemented, the next major task is testing. As mentioned above, complexity has become a distinguishing feature of these surveys, and this complexity makes the testing phase difficult. There are two parts to testing—what computers and software can do and what people must do. On the machine side of testing, the first line of defense against error is the diagnostics one's system can run. The first set of diagnostics in any approach is a syntax checker. Whether one deals with a compiler, parser or record processor, the first step is to check whether the commands satisfy the system's requirements. When one represents the instrument as data, the process of devising and running diagnostics becomes simpler.

The advantage of a system designed for computer assisted surveys over systems built around a general purpose compiler is that for the former, the syntax checker will be designed around the survey application as opposed to a compiler that is not focused on any particular application. When the instrument is data, one can write customized diagnostics – all that is necessary is the ability to write a structured query language (SQL) statement. Some systems designers have written diagnostics in SAS utilizing the ability of SAS to access relational databases from a variety of vendors using standard SQL statements. When one is dealing with a general purpose compiler, the ability to integrate customized diagnostics into the compiler will be between very limited and non-existent. For complex surveys, flexibility in generating diagnostics has great advantages.

Just as compilers have "debuggers" that are used to ferret out errors in a program, one can construct a debugger that can be used to catch errors and track the functioning of a computer assisted interview. Because the database approach breaks an interview down into a series of question records, the debugger can be simple to implement and powerful to use as it allows the designer to step through the interview and examine how rosters, output files, symbol lists, or other working arrays are being handled, modified, read and written. The debugger can also allow the survey designer to drill down on certain types of errors common to surveys.

Another approach to testing, which is relatively easy to execute when the instrument is represented as a series of data records, is to simulate cases.

This involves processing the question records one at a time and randomly selecting items from the pick list, or values from the range of allowed responses for questions collecting amounts, dates or times, and then moving to the next question. This can be done on several machines simultaneously. Whenever the program encounters a fault, a message is written to a file, and the system starts simulating another case. In this manner, one can simulate hundreds or, using several computers working independently, thousands of cases overnight. While this is a mindless exercise, it will find errors in unexpected and unusual parts of the instrument. Often human testers focus on standard scenarios or response patterns they feel are likely to occur in practice. While these biases are likely correct, it is the unexpected response pattern that can create the most havoc in a computerized survey. The strength of simulation is that it can uncover a great many errors in a short amount of time using very little labor, catching problems that diagnostics don't uncover. Simulation is very poor at uncovering logic errors, but to uncover logic errors efficiently, one needs to have an instrument that is mostly clean of programming errors. By having a testing regime that is layered, starting with diagnostics and then simulation, one can get to the last stage of testing more quickly and efficiently.

At the other end of the spectrum from the random simulation process is the logic checking undertaken by humans, preferably people who know how the instrument should function. Typically, the human testing phase starts with a set of scenarios the tester should work through, looking for errors. These scenarios focus on parts of the instrument with complex skips, specialized functions, difficult text fills and the like. Simple, "linear" parts of the instrument require less testing, but still require what might be better described as proofreading. This phase can require many hours, depending on the complexity of the instrument, and requires a mix of people who understand how the instrument should work and hence can detect subtle skip pattern errors, and people who are less connected to this particular instrument but know, in general, how questionnaires should work. Some detachment from a survey is very helpful—with repeated testing, testers can become "jaded" and no longer notice errors that are evident to fresh eyes, especially after repeated cycles of testing and revising.

Testing has always been difficult. We suggest the right way to look at the problem of testing is to consider the error detection and correction process as a whole, utilizing multiple approaches to testing, especially when one method is strong for one type of error and weak on others. Errors often creep in when one does something new or makes a change in one part of the instrument that has an effect (often unexpectedly) in another part. Unfortunately, projects need to plan under the presumption that they will not find all the errors in an instrument and that their computer-assisted interview will need modification at some time during the field period. This leads to the next topic—how should a project plan to manage the computers used for data collection?

Managing Machines in the Field or (Virtual) Central Office

In this section, we will speak to managing field machines that we use outside the central office or call center. Centrally located and managed machines for interviewing will likely be handled as any other personal computer, the data collection software simply being yet another application. For decentralized call center work (see below) or machines used for in-person interviewing, the situation is different. The most important point to make about managing remote computers is that this is not a problem unique to surveys. Many organizations must deal with exactly the same problem; there is nothing special about data collection that calls for a customized solution. The system we have used with great success is Kaseya, which allows us to centrally manage remote machines and inspect them when we encounter problems. Being able to inspect a remote machine is a must-have capability. When something goes wrong, most frequently one cannot diagnose the problem without close examination of the data files and other internal logs that track how the software was functioning around the time the problem arose. When a problem occurs, prompt action is essential so that one can fix the problem quickly before more cases are affected. As a general proposition, it is easier to replace data files than program files on a machine, so once again, representing the instrument as data has an advantage in that it simplifies the correction process. However, this advantage is less significant than it once was simply because remote synchronization of PC images has improved so dramatically.

If this section were being written ten years earlier, it would have needed to reflect the constraints imposed by the limited bandwidth of dial-in connections. Today, high-speed Internet connections are ubiquitous, and this has had a salutory effect on the process of centrally managing remote machines. The ability to run diagnostics, scan the machine, replace files and perform other managerial tasks has improved not only because bandwidth has improved, but also because more organizations rely on this capability and the market for software that manages this process has become so competitive. Given these developments, a survey organization that writes its own software to achieve these goals should articulate some compelling reasons for why it has adopted software autarky instead of relying on the excellent products on the market.

Data Flow to Repository

To be usable, survey data need to be where they can be readily accessed and understood. While virtually any data collection program can generate a file containing responses, the more difficult part is to make the data readily available in a form project staff and others can understand and use.

There is, of course, a natural connection between the data file and the questionnaire—the former is generated by the respondent interacting with the latter. When one represents the questionnaire as a series of data records that describe the attributes of the question, the process of managing the data flow to the central repository becomes straightforward. Virtually everything one needs to document a data item is present in the questionnaire data records. The table structure of the questionnaire (that is, the set of fields that describe what the question is, how it branches, question text, range restrictions, data type, indexing, and so forth) provides the information needed to understand and document the data that flows from the interview into the data repository. Setting up the structure of the data repository for incoming data is a fairly direct task inasmuch as the tables that define the structure of the incoming survey data are derived from the tables that describe the structure of the questionnaire. With this direct correspondence, utilities that load the incoming data into the master relational database are easily constructed and designed to run automatically. Current practice is to have the incoming data represented as an XML file.

Once interviewers connect to the Internet and download their completed cases to the repository, the data are available for examination and analysis either using a conventional statistical program in SAS, SPSS or Stata, or by issuing SQL commands that direct the master database to dump certain variables or cases for examination. While most attributes of the incoming data are derived from the questionnaire data base, certain attributes are generated independently from the data collection program. These attributes are characteristics that describe the data collection process. For example, the program that executes each question record in turn will produce a file of "transaction" outcomes from each question record. This file will contain information that is very useful for monitoring the field activity. Each question transaction typically contains the date and time when the question record was encountered, the date and time

when the transaction finished, which language the interviewer used, whether the interviewer referenced a "help" record, whether an audio or video playback feature was turned on, the linkage to a sound file in the event that question record turned on the microphone to record the interaction between the respondent and interviewer, and so on. Such data is typically not a part of the analysis file, but can be a very useful adjunct to quality control monitoring. Using such data, one can track what was going on at each moment of the interview, reducing the need for validation interviews and, when one does use a validation interview, gaining access to much more detailed information on the putative interview to query the supposed respondent. Often just being able to time how long the interviewer spent in each question and at what time of the day is enough to reveal inappropriate behavior.

The survey process does not end at data collection. Frequently the project needs to code verbatim items from the interview, such as industry and occupation codes, disease codes and the like. Very frequently the coder needs a variety of information from the interview to do an accurate job of coding a response. For example, in order to accurately code an occupation, one frequently needs to know the respondent's level of education or the industry in which he or she works. With the sort of highly structured data file that is produced using the database approach to generating an interview, one can prepare a prepackaged SQL query to the data base that extracts all the variables the coder is likely to need and places them into a form or spreadsheet the coder can work with. Carrying all these "tags" along with the coding file keeps the work organized and enhances supervisor review of how well a particular coder is handling verbatim items.

While the data are being processed, the archivists create many variables and edit others. Using a RDBMS to manage the data makes this process more efficient as it allows the data processing staff to edit data points one at a time without having to rewrite the entire dataset, as is the case when the data are stored in a sequential data set—examples of which are conventional SAS, Stata or SPSS datasets. While these systems are excellent for statistical processing, as systems to manage large and complex datasets they are not the preferred alternative compared to the RDBMS approach.

ORGANIZING THE DATA RESOURCES TO SUPPORT DATA COLLECTION

Above, we point out several reasons why representing a questionnaire as data has important advantages. The key tool enabling such an approach is an RDBMS that serves as the organizing hub of virtually every aspect of the survey process from design through data dissemination. Relational database software is a major, mature software industry segment. Some of the suggested standards for codebooks and for documenting survey data, such as the data documentation initiative (DDI), are similar to relational database designs, but arrived on the scene decades after RDBMS methods. Superimposing a DDI structure for documentation fails to make an organic connection between the management of the instrument, management of the data and the dissemination of the data. Rather than specifying the questionnaire specification in an RDBMS at the outset, the DDI approach requires the documentation file to be retrofitted into DDI form with additional labor time and its attendant costs; this approach fails to exploit the economies of scope RDBMS methods provide. On the other hand, once the instrument has been represented as data in an RDBMS table structure, it is a simple process to create a DDI structure from it—it is primarily a matter of cross-walking fields. DDI does more than just document the questionnaire—it also encompasses documentation of various sampling and surveying procedures, but for the purposes here, those ancillary features can be added onto the core documentation features for

the instrument regardless of how the survey data flow is organized.

The key to a successful RDBMS system is organizing the correct table structures to support the tasks of programming the instrument, fielding the survey, and documenting the data collected.

Organizing the Table Structure

Instrument

One can think of each question in a survey as a row within a table with a variety of attributes that are linked in a flexible manner with other tables. The attributes (or "columns") within a question table would contain, at a minimum, the following:

- The question text
- What information or other features the screen should, or should not, display
- Whether the question should be displayed with other questions in sequence on the same screen
- Whether the answer should be concealed from viewing after data entry (this is often used for in-person interviews when a sensitive question is presented and the respondent is asked to directly enter an answer. Once the respondent hits "enter" his or her answer cannot be seen by the interviewer even after backing up to the question again)
- A set of questions or check items that leads into the question (in practice this information is contained in the skip patterns of predecessor questions)
- A set of allowable responses to the question and data specifications for these allowable responses (whether the answer is a date, time, integer, currency value, textual response, or a numerical value assigned to a categorical response, such as 1 = yes, 0 = no). This sets up a "mask" to guide data entry, so the designer can specify whether a currency answer will be in dollars and

cents, just dollars (or use another currency), whether commas are used, etc. An appropriate mask simplifies entering items such as telephone numbers that have a particular format.

- Whether, for pick-list questions, the respondent can choose just one answer or all answers that apply
- Real-time edit specifications imposed upon dates, currency amounts and other numerical (i.e., non-pick list) data, such as numerical values that require interviewer confirmation (soft range checks) or limits on permissible values (hard range checks)
- Routing instructions to the next question, including branching conditions driven by the response to the current question, or complex check items that are contingent on the response to the current question as well as previous responses
- For internal checks, whether the (or which) condition holds and the interpretations of the outcome codes from the check item
- Pre-loaded, or "default" values for the answer
- Whether an answer to an item is automatically loaded into an "information sheet" file that contains data to be used if and when the respondent is interviewed again. This feature is especially useful in longitudinal surveys.
- Text fill specifications
- Instructions to assist the interviewer and respondent in completing the question
- Any other information needed for the question, such as audio files used for audio computer assisted self-interviews or graphic images that are used as a visual stimulus, for example "which of these pictures most closely corresponds to the meaning of this sentence?" or "Which of these bones most closely resembles the femur in the skeleton you are looking at?"[2]

For multi-lingual surveys, there would be separate tables for question text and pick lists for each language. This greatly simplifies the preparation and management of different survey versions for different languages that share the same core structure.

In addition to these, each question record should have a table used to store information about how to document a question. For example:

- Archival comments about the accuracy or interpretation of the item or its source or "see also notes" referring the user to associated variables that are available to users in the data set
- Notes to the support staff about complexities associated with the question to document the internal operation of the survey
- Options that describe the security handling of the answer record – which tiers of users should, or should not, be able to view the data
- Links to supporting documentation produced by the survey organization or, in the case of standard scales or psychometric items, a URL to more comprehensive documentation on the item
- The "pedigree" of the question, that is, which survey first asked it and when; changes or modifications made and why
- Words or phrases used to index the question
- A unique name for the question by which it can be identified
- When the instrument is especially complex and the skip pattern difficult to decipher, it can be very helpful to include a field that describes the universe for a question in fairly simple terms.
- Particular cases for which the values for the variable were edited or imputed
- A short descriptive title, or titles, for the question that can be used in statistical programs

- In longitudinal or repeated cross-sectional surveys, instances when the question or a similar question have been asked.

This is a large number of attributes for question records, to be sure. The important thing to bear in mind is that this information gets carried with the response to that question throughout the process and at each stage of survey operation, staff will be able to link this information to the data. In addition, these question records can be copied from survey to survey, making the survey process more efficient because so much information will be carried along with the question text.

Respondent Contact Information

While data capture is the central objective of surveys, this objective requires respondent co-operation. The second most important data organization system for surveys is the one that tracks respondents and contacts with respondents. While respondent information has little direct relevance for the survey data, an RDBMS strategy is likely the best approach for managing these data as well. Like the primary survey data, respondent information has a lot of structure to it. Address and telephone number data obey standard formats and, when tracking down respondents, it is useful to be able to maintain several records for this contact information as the respondent moves about. This is a functionality that RDBMS systems do very well with – maintaining multiple record types with the multiplicity for a particular record type varying from respondent to respondent.

Managing the data collection process also means tracking what kind, when and how many contacts the interviewing staff made with the respondent. Again, the description of the contacts made with a respondent tend to follow a fairly common format with information on the date, time, type of contact, who made the contact and what the respondent's (or their family member's) reaction was. This information needs to be stored in a central repository so it is not lost if a particular interviewer leaves the project or the case is transferred to a different interviewer. Especially when automated telephone systems are used to manage calls to the respondent, capturing a record detailing the call just made and storing it in a repository allows one to strategically choose the next time to call a respondent, or even whether to call at all. The scientific management of a telephone effort requires good data recording the fate of all calls to a respondent. This is probably best achieved from within a RDBMS.

When one wants to investigate the survey process in detail, being able to combine call data with respondent data is a useful capability. Again, the advantage goes to an RDBMS architecture—both the survey data and the call record data will be indexed by the respondent ID number; "joining" record types in an RDBMS using a shared ID number is a standard operation and will readily generate the required data which combines the desired elements of both.

The Special Case of Longitudinal Surveys

Longitudinal surveys are the most difficult surveys to manage for several reasons. First, in a long-running longitudinal survey the number of variables can be large. We manage longitudinal survey databases with well over 100,000 variables. Second, longitudinal surveys frequently make extensive and repeated use of data collected in previous rounds of interviewing to manage and guide the conduct of the current interview. For one survey we are conducting, the information sheets, or 'preloads' to the interview contain about 2,000 items. There are large surveys that don't collect this many variables, let alone carry them forward to the next interview. Managing this flow of data between rounds requires an organized system for handling the data. Just the act of putting together (and correcting!) such a large amount of data to feed into an interview is a daunting task. Keeping such a large effort organized is much easier working within an RDBMS system. In fact, because rosters and other items repeatedly flow from one interview to another, one can, as mentioned above, carry an indicator that a response is to be loaded into both the answer file and the preliminary information sheet or preload file to be made available to the next interview. Because the data type of each element will be known by virtue of its definition in the question record file, the management of these different files is simplified.

Third, longitudinal surveys make repeated use of the same questions and one needs a way to keep these items straight across rounds but also make it evident when items are repeated several times during the study. Researchers must be able to locate and link the same questions over time. Using common question records to generate each instance insures that protocol for entering the answer is the same, or nearly the same, over time, the documentation elements are similar, and the questions are indexed in the same way so that when one finds one item it is nearly certain one will be able to find the same question in other years.

DOCUMENTING THE SURVEY

The penultimate step in the survey process is generating documentation. A lot of the documentation produced involves an explication of procedures, sampling, how the field work was conducted and the generation of summary or created variables. There are two major elements of documentation we will discuss here—the codebook and the flowchart. Different projects put different amounts of information in the codebook, but as a general proposition more is better. Besides the question text, answer categories (and frequencies), users should expect to see explanatory notes, branching instructions from the question, branching into the question, means, maximums, minimums and counts for various categories of missing values

and, where applicable, the location of the variable in a file and the data format.

Statistical programs such as SAS, SPSS and Stata will generate minimal codebook pages with variable titles and, if the data include value labels, also will document the pick list item codes and their labels. However, statistical programs will not document the universe or how the skip pattern affects when the question is asked or to where it branches. The programming approach to instrument design can be used to generate value labels and point to the next question asked, but skip and branching information would be a different matter. When the instrument is represented as data, these documentation elements become much easier to assemble into the codebook page, including any other notes, comments, or even hyperlinks to supporting articles or reports that back up the question item. With so many survey resources being put on the Web, having URLs a part of the codebook page is an important part of supplying good documentation. Finally, with the questionnaire represented as data, we can produce customized documentation products with SQL commands to the questionnaire and a unified database.

As surveys have become more complex, understanding the skip pattern and the universes for the variables has become more important. The RDBMS approach to representing the instrument allows the survey team to simplify the skip pattern. This is done by "compressing" the skip pattern to remove machine checks and other internal "housekeeping" records that do not affect which questions a respondent is asked and hence are not necessary to understand the universe of respondents who are asked a question. This can substantially reduce the amount of data the user must deal with and simplify the structure of the file. By breaking the instrument up into discrete steps, this compression operation can be executed fairly readily. Once the instrument is simplified, putting the instrument into a series of discrete steps allows for software to generate a flowchart for users to reference. Constructing a flowchart manually is labor intensive.

DATA DISSEMINATION

The final step in the process is data dissemination. When a survey is too large to put all the variables in a single file, the most common approach is to break the data into several files, and require the user to pull down each file he or she needs and select the variables they need from each file. For longitudinal surveys that contain many tens of thousands (or hundreds of thousands) of variables, this approach is inconvenient and possibly infeasible. An alternative strategy again exploits the RDBMS framework. That strategy is to create an online system that includes all variables in the survey and indexes them by subject matter, year, question name and title. If one enables the user to peruse the codebook page online for each variable in the collection, the system can allow users to "tag" the variables they want to use, and then allow the system to query the underlying RDBMS, select the desired variables, and write out the data file with control cards that match the user's desired statistical program. When the data file is large, having indexed variables in the underlying RDBMS allows Web-based software to query the RDBMS using a combination of characteristics (word in title, year, subject matter area, etc.) taking either the union or intersection as desired. Done in this way, survey organizations can lift a substantial burden from the user.

MODERN DATA CAPTURE

The Problem of Multiple Modes—and its Solution

With the exception of self-administered interviews done over the Web, survey data collection is a fairly labor-intensive process. Labor intensive processes tend to be expensive processes. The cheapest mode of data collection is a self-report, with self-reports over the Web cheaper than self-reports using mail-out booklets. Interviews done by telephone are more costly, and in-person interviewing is the most expensive method, but also the method most likely to secure the cooperation of reluctant respondents. A very cost-effective way of securing respondent cooperation is to start with a self-administered option over the Web and then move to a telephone effort for those not cooperating over the Web, with the last step being an in-person effort for those whose cooperation could not be secured over the Web or telephone. This approach is referred to as a multi-modal survey. If it is to be efficient, the cost of switching among the various modes must be minimal. Currently, the best strategy for multi-modal surveys is to build data capture around a Web browser as the user interface. One builds a Web site that serves up each question record in turn and that site can be used either by respondents who log into the site after receiving an invitation, or by telephone interviewers who bring up the Web site at their workstation, whether that workstation is in a traditional bricks-and-mortar call center or located in their home, connected to the Internet. (Below, we discuss the evolution of call center work in more detail.) For in-person interviewing, the set-up of the laptop is somewhat more complex, because the survey must function without Web access. The survey program therefore includes both a "server" application that produces the "Web" pages, and a browser client that displays those pages for the interviewer to read and enter the data. The data collected is then merged with the rest of the survey data in the central office when the interviewer returns home and logs onto the central system.

Note that with all four modes, one has a server and a client – the difference is where the server is located and who is logged into the client – the respondent, the call center agent, the interviewer in the home working with a laptop connected to the Web, or doing in-person interviewing not connected to the Web. The servers and clients are, with minor exceptions, identical. The same survey infrastructure handles all four modes of data collection. Perhaps the greatest difference is in how the server is supported. For Web and call center interviewing, the server is usually in the central office or central computing facility. For in-person efforts the server is on the laptop. This is more difficult configuration to manage, but as mentioned above, by utilizing commercial PC management software, the management of hundreds of laptops with server applications running on them is not terribly difficult. We have collected well over a hundred thousand cases using this multimodal client-server approach with minimal problems.

What Ever Happened to the Call Center?

The rapid evolution of telephony is evident for all to see – from Skype and Vonage to cable TV based telephone systems. Since the late 1980s, we have seen a great many changes reflecting the rapid evolution of PC operating systems, processor speed, memory, storage and input/output speed. Oddly the rapid changes in modern telephony have not been tracked and exploited in the survey industry as aggressively as one might think. The reasons for this are unclear, but the result is that there are unexploited opportunities for improving data collection operations. However, these opportunities will likely be disruptive in that large parts of the survey process may need to be abandoned and completely redesigned.

As above, we start by describing call center approaches ten or more years ago and then point out how things have changed. In terms of infrastructure, call centers were built around large buildings housing hundreds of seats. These facilities had large circuit-switched private branch exchanges (PBXs) connected to the public switched telephone network (PSTN). The "floor" allowed supervisors to roam, offering support, encouragement, training and monitoring. In less advanced facilities,

the agents would dial the number either on a telephone or from their PC keyboard. Telecommunications providers had near-monopolies on connections to the PSTN; even if long-distance calling was more competitively priced, the cost of "trunk lines" connecting the call center to the PSTN was not. The switching equipment used was highly specialized and expensive. Features such as remote monitoring and call recording were highly specific to the type of switching equipment used. Predictive dialers were specialized pieces of equipment.

In the past ten years, the market for telephony has become completely disrupted with incumbents losing market share and the technology changing. The impetus for this is Voice over Internet Protocol (VoIP). This technology uses the Internet not just to transmit data, but also to transmit voice, broken down into small chunks called "packets". Instead of dedicating a circuit to a conversation (at least locally) the sound file the conversation creates is broken into packets, and the packets are routed around the Internet in real time as if they were so many Web pages being served up to users. This is referred to as "packet switching" as opposed to circuit switching. Thus, the infrastructure used to provide Internet service is being turned into telephone infrastructure as well, with virtually no additional investment except for on-going improvements in speed and capacity. The capacity needed to display pictures and You Tube videos is appreciably greater than what it takes to carry a telephone conversation. The quality of VoIP is significantly better than what one gets from a good cell phone conversation and in recent years is the equal of a landline connection, only because landline infrastructure imposes sound quality restrictions on VoIP.[3]

Perhaps more importantly for survey operations, VoIP has generated multiple generations of PBX switches that are based on high-speed servers without any special circuit boards or chips. The PBX has become a software application, not a hardware product. The descent of Nortel into bankruptcy is emblematic of the changes in this market segment. Vendors such as Cisco and Avaya, who had a preferred position in the VoIP market, are coming under competitive pressure—both on price and features. In our experience, the best buys on VoIP "soft switches" are not these major vendors, but smaller, more nimble companies. The half-life of soft switches is fairly short, so little is lost by looking to upstart companies. In fact, there are "freeware" software PBX applications available (Asterisk), although they require a greater reserve of telephony skill on the part of survey technical staff. Similarly, cheaper software options (or even in-house development) are available for recording interviews and utilizing predictive dialers, putting these technologies within the reach of smaller operations. Whereas these capabilities previously required substantial scale to be economically implementable, the barriers to obtaining these technologies have been lowered, making it possible for smaller survey call centers to compete on something more like a level playing field.

The second force for disruption in this market, which benefits more flexible survey organizations, is the rise of Session Initiation Protocol (SIP). This is a protocol for handling voice packets, call set up, termination and other switching operations. This standard protocol has lead to SIP "trunking" providers to emerge in the market. Instead of having to lease a PRI, T1 or T3 connection from the phone company, one simply contracts for capacity with a SIP trunking provider that connects via one's existing Internet provider. These contracts offer substantially greater flexibility in terms of costs, simultaneous conversations and features. SIP trunks match up very well with software PBXs, which increasingly are built around the SIP protocols. In addition, instead of expensive desk phones, one can equip agents with a high quality headset that plugs into the USB port on a PC. The software equivalent of the dialing mechanism becomes an inexpensive piece of software that costs under $30 and can be integrated with

the PBX and used as the desktop appliance for sophisticated dialers and call schedulers.

Because all the technical infrastructure of a call center is now based on the Internet, we have seen the rise of the "virtual call center". We have mounted large national survey efforts that use VoIP, SIP and software PBXs to stitch together hundreds of interviewers across the U.S. and in overseas call centers to mount a complex survey effort, all with very modest start-up costs. Those efforts retain all the ability of a traditional call center to monitor calls, track interviewer performance, record calls and manage widely separated interviewers as if they were all co-located in a traditional call center. We can "build" a virtual call center that is based in kitchens all across the U.S. with great speed.

Traditional call centers still have advantages in providing quick access to training new staff and provide a better framework for supervision for less experienced and more transitory staff. However, for survey organizations looking to keep a national staff of interviewers in place and ready to work large in-person survey efforts, the virtual call center can keep them on staff and employed with telephone surveys between those large in-person field efforts. While it is unlikely the virtual call center technology will completely replace the bricks-and-mortar call center, it will almost surely eat into a significant part of its market share—the economics and flexibility are just too compelling.

WHY THE EVOLUTION TO THE RDBMS APPROACH HAS BEEN SLOW

Survey organizations that did not start out with a strategy of using RDBMS as the organizing approach to data management and instead adopted the strategy of programming their instrument in Basic, Pascal or some other language perhaps unknowingly started down a trajectory that would not lead toward an integrated RDBMS strategy. The legacy of installed systems places a substantial impediment in the way of making a change, primarily because of the heavy investment in staff skills that are oriented toward the programming approach. Moving those systems and human skill sets toward the RDBMS strategy will take time and the press of business makes change very difficult. The other major obstacle is in generating the sub-systems, utilities and other infrastructure necessary to implement the RDBMS strategy. Change will come slowly, but we predict that the change will come. The operational advantages are simply too great.

The other vector of change that may emerge is in how work gets divided between the ultimate customer and the project sponsor. The RDBMS strategy makes it possible for project sponsors that have a significant portfolio of work to move many of the data processing tasks in-house, contracting out for the pure data collection tasks. Project sponsors are typically also data users and questionnaire designers. This should make an integrated strategy attractive. In addition, because the interface to almost any system can be handled over the Web, the sponsor can maintain control of the survey process without a large investment in infrastructure. Another advantage of this strategy is that it makes procurements of survey services more generic as one is contracting for data collection rather than co-mingling data collection and data processing in a single statement of work. Competing data collection vendors can be evaluated on a more nearly uniform basis, allowing more straightforward evaluations of bids. A corollary to all this is that smaller survey start-ups, who have less of a problem with legacy systems, should seriously consider starting out with the RDBMS strategy and using its efficiencies as a method of competing against incumbent firms with less latitude to change.

FUTURE RESEARCH DIRECTIONS

Perhaps the most significant trend for on line research in the area of urban and planning studies is the rise of mobile technologies that exploit smart phone resources. This reflects two important factors—market penetration and the ability to retrieve location. While smart phones allow people to access the Web as conveniently as if they were at a home computer, the situation is far more radical. First of all, the diffusion of smart phones in the mobile phone market has been rapid, especially among the young. The screen size on mobile phones is limited and the keyboards awkward, but anyone who spends a few moments watching people realizes many are nearly continuously fiddling with their phones. Not only are people connected to the Web, many are nearly continuously connected. Marrying data collection methods to smart phones offers a dominating technology—if the subject can be induced to use it. Just over the horizon we see smart phones used for purchasing goods and services. This opens the way for a creative approach to paying respondent incentives for replying to a survey on their mobile phone. This is a development that bears watching.

The second factor is that smart phones generate a stream of location data for the bearer, either using global positioning satellite (GPS) technology or by triangulating among cell phone towers using the strength of signal. The former approach reputedly will soon have a precision less than ten feet, the latter being significantly less precise. For studying how people interact with an urban environment, the ability to track people in nearly real time offers a unique flow of data that, when combined with traditional survey information, will generate data sets with unique power for understanding how people interact with their environments. While there are clear privacy and confidentiality problems with this technology, there are many other, more sensitive domains, where people are willing to sacrifice some privacy and confidentiality for study that has face validity and secures the trust of the respondent.

Marrying survey and locational technologies together calls for considerable technical and conceptual research and development as well as imagination in terms of the sorts of questions that were heretofore infeasible to ask that will soon be well within our grasp. The flow of locational data from such a data collection effort will fit in with the framework described above.

CONCLUSION

Modern data collection is undergoing radical changes, driven by technological change which allows some modes of data collection to be more cost-effective than other forms and substantially more cost effective than the methodology used twenty-five years ago. As computer-based technologies have arisen, the entire framework to support data collection has changed, reflecting the need for the data collection system to be compatible with the rapid and accurate dissemination and documentation of the survey's results. This has lead to the marrying of relational data base management techniques with computer assisted survey methods. This marriage dominates survey data collection in the social sciences in general and Urban and Planning Studies in particular. The ascendency of smart phones and disruptive changes in telephone technology are leading the way to yet another generation of data collection techniques that will require even more sophisticated data systems to support the collection of data. This chapter has described how data collection has evolved and how new techniques have altered how surveys are designed, managed, archived and the results disseminated.

ACKNOWLEDGMENT

This chapter is primarily based upon an ongoing effort at Ohio State University to reformulate the approach to collecting, managing, documenting and disseminating survey and other social science data. This effort started in 1988 and reflects the cumulative efforts of our past and current employees as well other approaches implemented by other organizations. These developments unfolded as best practices in the field rather than on the pages of publications. While the paternity of many of these approaches is ambiguous, my objective is to make their utility clear.

ADDITIONAL READING

Botman, S. L., & Thornberry, O. T. (1992). *Survey Design Features Correlates of Nonresponse*, pp. 309-314 in Proceedings of the Section on Survey Research Methods. Alexandria, VA: American Statistical Association.

Cheung, G.-Q. (2007). *Mixed-Mode Sample Management System: An Early Glance*. Presented at International Blaise Users' Conference, Annapolis, MD.

Costigan, P., & Thomson, K. (1992). 'Issues in the Design of CAPI Questionnaires for Complex Surveys' in Westlake et al (eds). *Survey and Statistical Compu*ting, pp.147-156, London: North Holland.

Couper, M. P. (1998). *Measuring Survey Quality in a CASIC Environment*. Presented at the Survey Research Methods Section of the American Statistical Association.

Couper, M. P., Baker, R. P., Bethlehem, J., Clark, C. Z. F., Martin, J., Nichols, W. L., & O'Reilly, J. M. (Eds.). (1998). *Computer Assisted Survey Information Collection*. New York: John Wiley.

de Leeuw, E., & de Heer, W. (2002). Trends in Household Survey Nonresponse: A Longitudinal and International Comparison. In Groves, R. M., Dillman, D. A., Eltinge, J. L., & Little, R. J. A. (Eds.), *Survey Nonresponse* (pp. 41–54). New York: Wiley.

Elmasri, R. A., & Navathe, S. B. (2001). *Fundamentals of Database Systems*. New York: Addison-Wesley.

Forster, E., & McCleery, A. (1999). Computer Assisted Personal Interviewing: A Method of Capturing Sensitive Information. *IASSIST Quarterly*, *23*(2), 26–28.

Gray, J., & Reuter, A. (1992). *Transaction Processing: Concepts and Techniques*. San Francisco: Morgan Kaufmann.

Groves, R.M. (1987). Research on Survey Data Quality. *Public Opinion Quarterly* 51(2: 50th Anniversary Supplement): S156-S172.

Groves, R. M. (1989). *Survey Errors and Survey Costs*. New York: Wiley.

Kroenke, D. M. (2001). *Database Processing: Fundamentals, Design and Implementation*. Upper Saddle River, New Jersey: Prentice Hall.

Kroenke, D. M. (2001). *Database processing: Fundamentals, design and implementation*. Upper Saddle River, New Jersey: Prentice Hall.

Olsen, R. (2008). Computer Assisted Personal Interviewing. *Encyclopedia of Survey Research Methods*, Paul J. Lavarakas, (ed.), Sage, p. 118 – 120.

Olsen, R. (2008). Computer Assisted Self-Interviewing. *Encyclopedia of Survey Research Methods*, Paul J, Lavarakas, (ed.), Sage,p. 121 – 122.

Olsen, R., & Sheets, C. (2008). Data Management. *Encyclopedia of Survey Research Methods*, Paul J. Lavarakas, (ed.), Sage, p. 177 – 180.

Olsen, R., & Sheets, C. (2008). VoIP and the Virtual Computer Assisted Telephone Interview (CATI) Facility. *Encyclopedia of Survey Research Methods*, Paul J. Lavarakas, (ed.), Sage, p. 950 – 952.

Saris, W. E. (1991). *Computer-Assisted Interviewing*. Newbury Park: Sage.

Stern, J., Stackowiack, R., & Greenwald, R. (2001). *Oracle Essentials: Oracle9i, Oracle8i and Oracle 8*. Sebastopol, CA: O'Reilly.

Windle, R. (2010). *The Big Picture: What the Decline of Fixed Line Telephones will Mean to Mobile Research*, Presentation at the 2010 Mobile Research Conference. London.

KEY TERMS AND DEFINITIONS

Call Center: This is an office containing from five to as many as a thousand work stations each of which has a telephone (or telephone-like device reflecting the technical change in telephony) and a computer for the entry of data. Call centers are typically multi-purpose facilities, being used for conducting surveys, providing customer assistance, doing out-bound sales or fund raising campaigns, or providing a port of entry into an organization for the purpose of directing calls to agents who can provide the desired service. Call centers have sophisticated systems for placing, receiving and routing calls. Agents who work the telephones are overseen by floor supervisors who are responsible for enforcing protocols and standards of service as well as serving as resources when problems arise. The first line agents then refer problem cases to their supervisor who either resolves the problem or refers it up the line for more detailed service. Call centers have substantial operational flexibility and maintain substantial indigenous training capabilities to allow them to re-task the staff to new projects in response to client demands.

CAPI: An acronym standing for Computer Assisted Personal Interviewing, although common usage has led many to use the term to refer to the use of any computer assisted method for collecting survey data, whether in person, over the phone or over the Web – any medium which relies on a computing device as the portal by which data are entered into the system. The heart of any CAPI system is structure used to manage the flow of data into and out of the system as well as to document both how the survey is supposed to operate and what the data elements produced by the survey are, how they are measured, and what the various values mean in the context of the questions asked of the respondent.

Multi-Modal Survey: This refers to the growing practice of designing survey operations to allow respondents to provide data by whichever method the respondent finds most attractive. This means a survey may be designed to be collected either on a paper form that is mailed or handed out, over the telephone by an interviewer working in a call center, in person by an interviewer making a personal call on the respondent's home or business, or over the Web using a browser connected to the survey organizations computing facility.

Relational Database: A term to refer to a collection of data, often both extensive in terms of numbers of variables and substantial in terms of numbers of distinct units whose information is being stored, within an organized structure that greatly facilitates data storage, retrieval, editing archival and maintenance.

Schema: This is the design of a relational database that summarize the tables containing the data, the fields that correspond to particular elements in the table, and the relationships among those elements, including the indices used to link the various tables and elements.

SIP: This acronym stands for Session Initiation Protocol, which is a relatively recent Internet technology for setting up a telephone conversation between two devices (traditionally known as telephones, although technology changes appear to be making the term "telephone" obsolete) by signaling between the devices that they are to send and receive a set of voice (and possibly video) packets over the Internet between one another so as to support a conversation and exchange information on the algorithm by which sound is to be converted to data in the voice packets.

Smart Phone: A term used to refer to a device that can not only support a voice conversation between two or more parties, but can also access the Internet and bring to bear substantial computing power, data storage, Web browser and e-mail capabilities in the same device to support a variety of computational and data access tasks.

VoIP: This acronym stands for Voice over Internet Protocol, which is a system for transmitting "packets" of data that encode sound over the Internet between two or more parties to support a conversation. The flows of packets are directed from the speaker to the listeners, one packet at a time. This process is often referred to as "packet switching", which directs the conversation a packet at a time, as opposed to "circuit switching" which connects two or more telephone devices over a dedicated circuit to facilitate the rapid routing of sound from one party to another. In the traditional telephone technology, the device used for switching at the customer's premises was referred to as a PBX, which stands for private branch exchange. PBX equipment is currently considered obsolete, with the function of the PBX being taken on by a general purpose server provisioned with software to handle local switching tasks and which can communicate with the public switched telephone network, using a protocol known as "SIP".

ENDNOTES

[1] A major theme of this chapter is that relational database management systems (RDBMS) have significant advantages as the backbone of the survey data management process. RDBMS are hierarchical in the sense that

each of many different "tables" contains a set of related variables that are linked to other tables by a set of linking or "key" variables. A "primary key" is a variable whose value is unique among all tables to which it might be connected, whereas a "key" is a variable that is used to link various tables but whose values may not be unique. For example, in survey applications, a respondent ID would be a primary key as the same value must not be shared by other respondents; each question in survey will also have an identified that is a primary key with unique values so one can keep the different questions straight. On the other hand, one might use ordinary key values to link pick lists or skip instructions to questions. While these ordinary keys must be unique in their own domain (pick lists or skip instructions), it is possible to reuse an identifier used for skips to identify pick lists. RDBMS are workhorses of enterprise-level computing, being used for accounting, inventory and personnel systems, among others. These are sophisticated, complex and well-developed software applications with a wide variety of applications and users. Relational database methods center on Structured Query Language (SQL), which is a standard syntax for operating on, loading data into and extracting data from an RDBMS.

2 Survey programs can be used as a tool for data entry that doesn't involve questioning a live respondent. For example, we have used a CAPI system to guide the entry of data about ancient skeletons in a project to understand the health and well-being of primitive societies.

3 VoIP calls not routed through the PSTN can have remarkable sound quality.

Chapter 3
Volunteer Panel Web Surveys in Urban Planning

Sunghee Lee
University of Michigan, USA

ABSTRACT

Web surveys have been adopted as a practical data collection tool notably due to their economic nature and a fast turn-around time. One popular type of Web survey bases the sample on a group of Internet users who voluntarily join survey panels. Often labeled as a "volunteer panel Web survey," this approach is widely used in various social science studies, including urban planning. Unfortunately, its practice appears to have highlighted its benefits and downplayed its limitations. This chapter provides an overview of volunteer panel Web surveys, including their operational procedures and methodological advantages and disadvantages. Arguably, its main methodological disadvantage is lacking representativeness of the results arising from selection biases in the selected samples. A post-survey statistical adjustment based on propensity score analysis has been suggested as a potential solution. The author introduces detailed procedures of propensity score adjustment and discusses future research directions for improving the utility of the volunteer panel Web surveys.

INTRODUCTION

Technological developments have made Internet an everyday communication medium in many places around the world. According to World Bank (http://data.worldbank.org/indicator/

IT.NET.USER.P2), over twenty countries show an Internet penetration rate over 70%. It is now a standard practice to use email address as main contact information, and Internet has become a solid communication channel in the society. Especially with the emergence of smart phones, Internet is more accessible than ever before.

DOI: 10.4018/978-1-4666-0074-4.ch003

Most research data for social sciences including urban planning as opposed to natural science are collected through communication with people. Of course, there are social science studies using data from administrative or patient records or researchers' pure observations, hence, not involving any communication. However, because human society is the ultimate research object in social sciences, communication is indispensable in data collection. Any changes in how people communicate directly influence data collection methods (Dillman, 2000; Tourangeau, 2004). Naturally, researchers and non-researchers alike speculate the utility of Internet as an emerging data collection and research tool. The field of survey methods has examined the possibility of using Internet as a data collection medium (Couper & Miller, 2008). Internet provides unique benefits and challenges and has its own place in research. Data are collected to generate new knowledge. This knowledge is at times aimed to be exploratory and other times generalizable. For population-based research which relies on sample survey data, Internet is still regarded as having numerous inferential issues to overcome as theoretical underpinnings are lacking to support inferential representativeness (Couper, 2007).

It is important to note that there is a fine difference between Internet as a research tool and a data collection tool. Data collection is one part of research activities. Other research activities, such as facilitation of research topics (e.g., behavior interventions, educational curricula) or dissemination of research information, can be carried out successfully via the Internet. While seemingly convenient, lumping different Internet research activities may blur assessing the value of Internet as a research tool (e.g., Farrell & Petersen, 2010). Therefore, this chapter will focus on the Internet as a data collection tool.

More specifically, this chapter will attempt to provide practical understandings about inferential properties of volunteer panel Web surveys. In the following section, different types of web surveys will be reviewed, and volunteer panel Web surveys will be compared to other types of Web surveys with respect to sampling and operation processes. The main focus of the chapter will be on the problematic inferential statistical properties of volunteer panel Web surveys. Propensity score adjustment, a remedy proposed for such problems, will be introduced in detail along with its caveats. Potential future research topics will be suggested as a way of improving the effectiveness of propensity score adjustment. A discussion on the trade-off between cost savings and expected errors of volunteer panel Web surveys will conclude the chapter.

BACKGROUND

The most frequently noted data quality issue of Internet-based surveys is their lacking coverage for the general population. Unlike the telephony communication system where only a small proportion of the general population may be missed in the developed parts of the world, Internet is not used by a sizable amount of the general population. Moreover, Internet nonusers are known to be different from users: they are likely to be older, less educated and less affluent. This is termed as, "digital divide," which in turn is related to numerous characteristics that research addresses.

One of essential element of any survey data collection is the frame from which samples are drawn. Often, frames are a list of individual units in the well-defined population of interest. They contain contact information of the units which allows researchers to contact sampled units and conduct interviews to collect data. An issue more troubling than the coverage for the Internet to become a practical single-mode data collection tool is the fact that there are no reliable frames. When considering an Internet survey targeting the general population, a list of email addresses of all population units where one individual unit in the population is matched to one email address would be ideal but is not known to exist. Even when the Internet covers the entire population, this issue is not likely to disappear. The absence of frame means that samples cannot be drawn in a probabilistic manner. Probability samples are essential for scientific research attempting to make generalizations at the population level. This is possible because probability samples are theoretically proven to produce results that are unbiased of the population quantities. In sum, for single-mode Internet surveys, the most pressing challenge stems from the absence of usable frames. Of course, this frame issue does not cause a serious concern when making generalizations to a broader population is not of interest. This may include case-control studies, psychological experiments, and qualitative research (e.g., focus groups, instrument pre-testing).

There are special subpopulations whose members have a Web access universally and have verifiable one-on-one contact information over the Web. Examples may include employees at municipality planning departments in a country or students at a university. In these cases, one may prepare frames that contain Web contact information of individual employees or students without too much difficulty and use the frames to draw samples. Web surveys targeting these special populations are not likely to experience the same type of frame problems.

Clearly, not all Web surveys are the same. There are many different ways to use the Web for survey data collection, and each approach has its own distinctive methodological implications for both survey operations and statistical inferences. For this reason, while it may seem convenient, discussing all Web surveys as one category blurs evaluations on the data quality and may reach a misleading conclusion (e.g., Evans & Mathur, 2005; Farrell & Petersen, 2010). Therefore, it is important to classify Web surveys based on their methodological distinctiveness and to evaluate the data quality accordingly (e.g., Couper, 2000).

There are other types of popular Web surveys that borrow frames from other data collection modes (e.g., telephone, mail, face-to-face). First, the Web can be mixed with other modes. One may give respondents a chance to select their preferred mode of interview. Survey of Earned Doctorates (SED) by U.S. National Science Foundation is an example. SED uses paper questionnaires at the first contact. However, according to the respondents' preference, a URL link to SED is provided with PIN and password to the respondents. SED reports an increase the Web completion rates (http://www.nsf.gov/statistics/srvydoctorates/). Alternatively, one may consider a strategy of sequentially changing contact mode depending on the response status (de Leeuw, 2005). For instance, a face-to-face survey may send a postcard to nonrespondents and invite them to complete a shortened questionnaire on the Web.

Second, a probability sample survey may be conducted to recruit people into a Web panel. If a contacted person is not a Web user, he or she will be provided with Web access device. The panel may serve as a frame for subsequent surveys. Knowledge Networks in U.S. (Dennis, 2010) and MESS Panel by CentERdata at Tilburg University in the Netherlands are some of the first applications of the Web panel approach based on random digit dial telephone probability samples. These surveys do not experience problems arising from the absence of the frame and inadequate coverage of the population. Because they borrow frames prepared for other survey modes, they may not be considered as a true single-mode Web survey.

VOLUNTEER PANEL WEB SURVEY APPROACH

This chapter focuses on the volunteer panel Web survey approach as it is the only true single-mode Web survey attempting to make the population-level generalizations. This approach has its own statistical properties for inferences, as indicated above. Before examining the inference issues, we will first provide an overview of this Web survey approach with its actual operational procedures, its advantages and disadvantages over other types of surveys, and applications in the field.

The first step of operating volunteer panel Web surveys involves establishing a pool of panel members. There are numerous ways to recruit panel members. Some may consider using banners or pop-up windows on popular Web sites and advertising opportunities to join Web survey panels. Others may consider using commercially available email lists and sending out emails with an invitation to join the panel. Once those who are exposed to these invitations accept them, the panel recruitment surveys begin. Each panel member is asked to provide his or her Web contact information, mainly email addresses, and basic background information. The background information can range anywhere from socio-demographic characteristics to chronic health conditions and to recent consumer goods purchase history. The background information plays a crucial role in adding advantages to this type of Web surveys as examined shortly. It should be noted that the panel members must not only have their own Web access but also agree to join a panel and participate in subsequent surveys. Unlike traditional surveys where researchers have control over who are included in the sample, panel members control this part in volunteer panel Web surveys. Therefore, researchers using volunteer panel Web surveys do not have much room to control and monitor who does and does not respond to the recruitment and come into the sample.

Through the recruitment process, a list of panel members individually linked with contact and background information is prepared. This list is used as a substitute for frames to draw samples. However, these samples are considered as a non-probability convenient sample because the list drastically differs from the traditional sampling frames. One advantageous feature of these lists is the richness of the available background informa-

tion. With such a list, people with rare traits (e.g., Native Americans with asthma living in rural areas) can be easily identified and selected for surveys. Otherwise, an extensive screening effort will be required to locate these persons which may be prohibitively expensive. Therefore, volunteer panel Web surveys provide a cost-effective opportunity to collect data for rare populations. The magnitude of cost savings depends on the characteristics of the study population—the rarer the target population, the higher the savings. However, if the number of panel members is not large enough, this will yield only small sample sizes, not providing the adequate statistical power.

Volunteer panel Web surveys provide a number of other benefits over traditional surveys. By eliminating a screening procedure and contacting samples and conducting surveys on a real-time basis, researchers may expect a much faster turnaround time. There are situations where the data must be collected for an urgent manner. A study of a new infectious virus outbreak in a certain city can be an example. Traditional surveys are likely to be limited in providing timely data, whereas volunteer panel Web surveys may be conducted timely because panel members' residential geography is likely to be available in the list. Due to this, data can be collected in a short time period.

Just like any other Web-based surveys, volunteer panel Web surveys offer an opportunity for researchers to easily incorporate multimedia components in the survey instruments. Sound bites, animated images and video footages can be easily displayed on the instruments. Of course, most computerized instruments allow such features, but multimedia files must be preloaded in the instruments. Web-based instruments do not require preloading files as the multimedia components can be accessed through hyperlinks. This adds flexibility in operations as different files may be prepared and tested at different time points during data collection. For instance, if a city planning department is testing the preference of bicycle routes with its residents, Web surveys provide numerous options for displaying the routes.

Survey research literature has shown that interviewer administered surveys are more likely to be influenced by social desirability than self-administered surveys especially on sensitive topics, such as racial discrimination issues. This is because the presence of an interviewer triggers a respondent to feel necessary to report something more presentable and pleasing to the interviewers rather than what is true. This well-known social desirability bias can be minimized in Web surveys, as they do not involve interviewers.

Given these benefits and strengths, volunteer panel Web survey may appear as a promising and attractive approach. It is not surprising to find volunteer panel Web surveys considered as a viable data collection tool in market research and opinion polls (e.g., Sparrow, 2006; Sparrow & Curtice, 2004). Additionally, they have been used in traditional academic research, such as social science and public health. In particular, studies focusing on men with and without erectile dysfunction (Cameron, Rosen, & Swindle, 2005), examining pain at the vulvar vestibule (Reed et al., 2004), and exploring the effect of social desirability on discrimination related topics (Kuran & McCaffery, 2004, 2008) have used volunteer panel Web surveys.

In order to evaluate data collection methods thoroughly, one must consider trade-offs between costs and errors (Groves, 1989). An economical method may not be useful if it is plagued with a large amount of errors. In the same way, an error-free method may not be practical if it requires a large amount of resources. A careful examination between the required costs of the expected errors will be a practical guide for determining whether to use volunteer panel Web surveys.

Proponents of volunteer panel Web surveys often reason lower costs as their strength (e.g., Cobanoglu, Warde, & Moreo, 2001; Farrell & Petersen, 2010; Faulx et al., 2005; Wright, 2005). However, it should to be noted that a certain amount of fixed costs are required for all survey operational tasks regardless of the specificity of methods or the sample sizes. Costs for questionnaire developments are an example. In fact, Web surveys may require higher fixed costs than other survey modes (e.g., Cobanoglu, Warde, & Moreo, 2001). It is the marginal costs that are lower in Web surveys than in other surveys. The substantial savings from lower marginal costs may be expected when the data collection size is large, and the overall savings may not be as large as one may expect (Converse et al., 2008).

Discussions around the errors of volunteer panel Web surveys are focused on the representativeness of survey results. Empirically speaking, while some researcher report evidence favoring this approach (e.g., Bethell et al., 2004; Taylor, 2000; Taylor et al, 2001), others find the opposite (Chang & Krosnick, 2009; Yeager et al., 2009). Theoretically speaking, volunteer panel Web surveys are not in the position to produce consistent and representative results. The debate over the blogoshpere between the proponents and opponents provides respective viewpoints further. Rubinson argues strongly for the non-probabilistic approach with volunteer panel Web surveys (http://blog.joelrubinson.net/2009/09/how-do-online-and-rdd-phone-research-compare-latest-findings/). Krosnick and his colleagues (http://blogs.abcnews.com/thenumbers/2009/09/guest-blog-more-on-the-problems-with-optin-internet-surveys.html/) demonstrate the superiority of probability samples. Baker adds a layer of evidence against volunteer panel web surveys (http://regbaker.typepad.com/regs_blog/2009/07/finally-the-real-issue.html). Given these, the cost benefit of volunteer panel Web surveys may not be justified especially when the representativeness of study results cannot be compromised. The limitation on generalizability is thoroughly examined and documented in *Report on Online Panels* by the American Association for Public Opinion Research (AAPOR, 2010).

Issues

The volunteer panel Web survey method was introduced to the survey research field as a potentially viable tool mainly by Harris Interactive at the turn of the 21st century (Terhanian, 2000; Terhanian & Bremer, 2000). This introduction has started a meaningful discussion about the benefits and limitations of this new data collection method within the survey methodology community. Unfortunately, these discussions do not appear to have transferred to other disciplines. In spite of the benefits, researchers or users of volunteer-based Web survey data should be aware that this approach does not stand on a firm statistical ground. This is especially true when the data are used for population-based research.

Central to the generalizability controversy is the nonprobabilistic nature of the volunteer panel Web sample. What is the difference between probability and nonprobability samples? First, it is implicitly assumed that probability samples are drawn from reliable and usable frames that have a reasonable coverage of the population of interest. Because of this, the probability of one unit in the frame selected into the sample can be calculated prior to data collection. With nonprobability samples, including those for volunteer panel Web surveys, selection probabilities cannot be calculated. One may wonder whether the list of panel members can serve the role of a frame. Unfortunately, the volunteer panel members do not cover the general population and are likely to be different from the population as a whole, unless the panel members themselves are the population of interest. This list is not equivalent to frames used in probability sampling and is ineffective in substituting frames.

Second, probability theories support the representativeness of the results from probability sample surveys. This is because the actual sample selection mechanism follows a randomized fashion. This guarantees the selection not contaminated or influenced by any particular characteristics of

individual units. Nonprobability samples, on the other hand, do not have such theoretical support. Therefore, the results from volunteer panel Web surveys are viewed not safeguarded from potential sample selection biases.

Two arguments often used to support volunteer panel Web surveys are that probability sample surveys are experiencing declining response rates and that the frames for traditional landline telephone surveys, a very popular survey mode in North America, is losing its coverage due to an increasing proportion of cellular phone only users in the general population. These have presented as indicators of diminishing representativeness of the probability sample surveys and as a reason to use volunteer panel Web surveys. These arguments are not invalid because probability sampling theory itself assumes a complete response and an ability to cover the target population. These trends are a threat to these assumptions. However, literature has not provided clear evidence supporting volunteer panel Web surveys over probability sample surveys. In fact, the opposite evidence has been shown (e.g., Keeter et al., 2000; Merkle & Edelman, 2002; Montaquila et al., 2007; Lee et al., 2009). It is because of the well-known facts that response rates and coverage rates are not a direct measure of respective biases (Groves, 1989; Groves & Couper, 1998) and that the relationship between these rates and the biases does not take a clear positive form (Groves & Peytcheva, 2008). Moreover, if these rates are to be used to gauge biases, volunteer panel Web surveys suffer even greater challenges with representativeness because their coverage is less desirable as discussed previously and their response rates are known to be much lower than traditional probability sample surveys (Couper et al., 2007; Couper & Miller, 2008).

It is natural for survey practitioners to explore volunteer panel Web surveys as an option because they are often constrained by tight budgets and timelines. In contrast, academics have yet to give meaningful methodological considerations to this type of surveys. The apparent gap between survey practice and methodological research appears to have resulted in the absence of scholarly guidance on volunteer panel Web surveys for the practitioners. This chapter attempts to reduce this gap by illustrating a statistical remedy proposed for potential biases in volunteer panel Web surveys. In the remainder of the chapter, we will discuss how this statistical remedy is relevant for volunteer panel Web surveys and describe the actual procedures. We will then examine the effectiveness and limitations of this approach shown in the literature. As volunteer panel Web surveys are a new data collection tool, so is the statistical remedy in the discussion. Hence, this chapter will conclude with future research questions.

Solutions and Recommendations

The representativeness issue of volunteer Web panel surveys can be understood with the framework of sample selection bias, as their samples are a group of Web users who self-select to join a survey panel. It is reasonable to assume that these individuals as a group are different from the general population. Clearly, when collecting data only from these people, the results are likely to deviate from what would be expected with the general population or its probability samples. Conceptually, selection bias is the same as this deviation. Of course, the level of selection bias differs across variables, as biases are a property of a variable not of a survey or a sample. Some variables may be highly related to the Web survey volunteering pattern than others variables, resulting in larger selection biases.

The selection bias is not a new topic in many disciplines. In fact, there is an on-going debate on this in the causal inference literature (see the 1996 special issue of the *Journal of the American Statistical Association* [vol. 91] for this discussion). In causal inference, the desired statistics is the effect of an experimental treatment (e.g., a new transportation route, a new fibromyalgia medicine, a new job training program). Ideally,

there will be two groups of people, where one receives the treatment (i.e., treatment group) and the other does not (i.e., control group). These two groups will differ only by the treatment status. When outcomes are compared between the two groups, the difference is viewed as caused by the treatment alone and, therefore, is an unbiased estimate of the treatment effect. When human subjects are involved in research, it is not always feasible to randomize the sample selection and treatment assignment. In some cases, it may be unethical. Consider a study on the effect of a new job training program. Not offering an opportunity to be trained with the new program to those who may benefit from it will jeopardize the fair treatment of study subjects.

Under these circumstances, data are collected through sample observations rather than randomizations. Nonrandomized sample selection means that the treatment and control groups may differ not only by the treatment status but also by some other characteristics. For instance, those who are enrolled in a new job training program may have lower educational backgrounds than those who are not. Treatment effects calculated by comparing these groups become confounded by the difference in educational attainment. Therefore, it becomes necessary to consider decreasing or eliminating the effect of potential confounders in inference.

Propensity score adjustment first introduced by Rosenbaum and Rubin (1984, 1983) attempts to make the treatment and control groups as comparable as possible by taking into account potential confounders in the treatment effect estimation (Guo & Fraser, 2010). D'Agostino (1998) provides a readable account of this method. A statistical model is adopted to estimate propensity of a sample unit being in the treatment group over the control group using a set of potential confounder variables as follows:

$$e\left(\mathbf{x}_i\right) = \Pr\left(i \in s^T \mid \mathbf{x}_i, i = 1, ..., n\right),$$

where $e(x_i)$ is the propensity of ith unit of the total sample (s) of a size n being in the treatment group (s^T) over the control group (s^C) The total sample is comprised of both the treatment group and the control group (i.e., $s = s^T + s^C$). The propensity score is estimated by using a set of covariates (x_i) identified as potential confounders often in logistic regression models as the dependent variable (i.e., treatment status) is binary. If all relevant covariates are observed in the data, then $x_i = x_{obs,i}$ Using a specified model, estimated propensity scores are assigned to each individual unit. The propensity scores represent all observed confounders and summarize their effects into a scalar format. The idea is that treatment and control units given a particular propensity score differ only by the treatment status. In other words, the treatment effect is adjusted by propensity scores. Therefore, comparisons between treatment and control cases conditioned on propensity scores provide an estimate of the confounder-free treatment effect.

There are a number of critical assumptions in propensity score adjustment. Two particular assumptions relevant to survey statistics are shown below. First, given a set of covariate values, a unit must have a nonzero probability of being in the treatment or control group, and that probability must be estimable from the total sample, s. If some units in the sample have absolutely no chance of being in the new job training program, for example, then this assumption will be violated. Second, the set of observed covariates (x_{obs}) is assumed to represent unobserved confounders. If x_{obs} excludes any important confounders, then the estimated propensity scores, $\hat{e}(\mathbf{x}_{obs})$, will be biased of $e(\mathbf{x})$ and the assumption unmet.

This statistical procedure for the selection bias in causal inferences is considered for the sample selection bias in volunteer Web panel surveys. Here, a Web survey using a volunteer panel Web sample is considered as a treatment group and another survey using a probability sample, called a reference survey, as a control group. (Reference surveys will be discussed in detail later.) Generally speaking, the required assumptions indicate that this type of propensity score adjustment will fail if the probability of volunteering for the Web panel survey cannot be described with a common model for the reference sample and the Web panel sample.

The application of propensity score adjustment for volunteer panel Web surveys was first suggested by Harris Interactive. This technique calls for a reference survey as mentioned above. Ideally, the reference survey should be of high quality with a probability sample from a frame with good coverage properties for the target population. Additionally, it should include a set of variables that are also collected in the volunteer Web survey. The content of the reference survey does not need to be much larger than a list of potential confounder variables. Therefore, one reference survey is often used for multiple Web surveys. These variables are to be used as covariates to predict the propensity of being in a volunteer panel Web sample (s^W) over a reference sample (s^R) The distributions of propensity scores are likely to differ between s^W and s^R due to selection biases.

Propensity score adjustment is attempted at this stage to make the distribution of Web sample's propensity scores similar to that of the reference sample.

While the propensity score estimation resembles the one described for the causal inference, the actual application of propensity score is not the same. This is because the desired estimates of Web surveys are population-level characteristics not treatment effects. Based on the estimated propensity score, $\hat{e}(\mathbf{x}_{obs})$, its distribution of the Web sample is rearranged so that s^W resembles s^R in terms of $\hat{e}(\mathbf{x}_{obs})$. Mechanically, this is done first by sorting the combined sample (s) by $\hat{e}(\mathbf{x}_{obs})$ and then partitioning s into C subclasses, where each subclass is about the same size. Following

Cochran (1968), the conventional choice is to use five subclasses based on quintile points. Ideally, all units in a given subclass will have about the same propensity score or, at least, the range of scores in each class is relatively narrow. Naturally, use of more than five classes is likely to help in creating more homogeneous classes. Then, an adjustment factor is calculated by simply taking a ratio of two proportions: the proportion of the reference sample in the cth subclass and that of the Web sample. When applying this factor to the Web sample, the propensity score distributions become similar between the Web and reference samples. This factor can be used as itself or can be added in the weighting process.

While the body of literature is still growing and will certainly benefit from more empirical research, propensity score adjustment has shown to be effective in decreasing bias in volunteer panel Web surveys (e.g., Harris Interactive, 2008; Lee, 2006; Schillewaert & Meulemeester, 2005; Schonlau et al., 2009; Taylor et al., 2001). However, the reduction in bias does not hold a universal pattern across all variables. In some cases, the bias may become larger after the adjustment. This is not surprising given that propensity score adjustment is a mere post-hoc remedy intended to help alleviating selection biases, unlike probability sampling theoretically guaranteed to be free from such biases by design. Although less frequently discussed, the major drawback of this adjustment is a decrease in statistical precision due to increased variability in point estimates (Lee & Valliant, 2009). Increased variance means wider confidence intervals, hence, lowered power to detect differences. In a sense, the reduced bias in estimates by propensity score adjustment comes at the cost of increased variance of the estimates. From the total survey error perspectives that consider both bias and variance, the gain from propensity score adjustment may not be as large as when only the bias is considered.

Propensity score adjustment is not new to survey sampling statistics and has been examined for post-survey adjustments (for a review, see Lee & Valliant, 2007).

Nonresponse and noncoverage biases in probability sample surveys are viewed analogous to selection biases in observational studies, as they may violate complete randomization assumptions in probability sampling theory. For this reason, propensity score adjustment has been applied to correct for the nonresponse (e.g., Göksel et al., 1991; Iannacchione, 2003; Lepkowski et al., 1989; Smith et al., 2001), late response (e.g., Czajka et al., 1992) as well as noncoverage biases (e.g., Brick, Waksberg, & Keeter, 1996; Duncan & Stasny, 2001; Garren & Chang, 2002; Hoaglin & Battaglia, 1996). For example, propensity of responding versus not responding is modeled based on age, gender, and urbanicity, characteristics well known to be associated with response patterns. Using the estimated model, nonresponse propensity score is predicted for each sample unit. Estimating such a model requires both respondents and nonrespondents, but the adjustment itself is applied only to respondents. With predicted propensity scores, weights are adjusted in a way that those with higher nonresponse propensity scores receive higher weights. These are respondents resembling nonrespondents with respect to the characteristics included in the model. The logic itself does not differ from traditional post-survey adjustments, such as post-stratification. What differs is that propensity score adjustment is free from challenges of including multiple variables in adjustment as it summarizes all variables as main effects or in interactions with other variable into one scalar score. This is not possible with the traditional approaches.

FUTURE RESEARCH DIRECTIONS

The application of propensity score adjustment to volunteer panel Web surveys is at an infant stage, and much is remained to be examined. There are four areas where future research can delve into: (1)

quality of reference surveys; (2) an investigation of covariates; (3) propensity score modeling; and (4) properties of estimated propensity scores. The first two issues are unique to Web surveys, whereas the latter two are applicable for all surveys.

Propensity score adjustment for volunteer panel Web surveys requires high quality reference survey with respect to coverage, nonresponse and sampling properties. It is interesting to find the research by the proponents of volunteer panel Web surveys have used a telephone sample to conduct reference surveys while they have asserted that the representativeness of telephone sample surveys is declining rapidly. Alternatively, one may consider conducting a reference survey through face-to-face interviews using an area-probability sample drawn from a well-constructed frame. Design features, such as financial incentives or a shorter interview length, may further enhance the quality. It should be noted the reference survey data are also collected from a sample, meaning that there are sampling errors associated with the estimates. While this issue is clear, the literature has not shown how sampling errors of the reference survey can be incorporated in the propensity score estimation process.

It is well known in the statistics literature that the quality of post-hoc adjustment is influenced by covariates in the model at a larger extent than by types of the models

(Groves, 2006; Little, 1993; Little & Vartivarian, 2005). Also, one of the critical assumptions for propensity score adjustment is how well observed covariates represent unobserved ones. Unlike nonresponse issues in probability sample surveys which benefit from a large volume of literature consistently showing a set of variables related to nonresponse, such as age, gender and urbanicity, volunteer panel Web surveys literature does not provide such information. Therefore, it is difficult to identify critical covariates influencing one's propensity to voluntarily participate in Web surveys and to assess the consistency of covariates between different Web surveys and between

different volunteer Web panels. For these reasons, identifying these covariates throughout various Web panels maintained by different companies will increase our understanding about the adjustment.

It is imperative for removing of selection bias to specify correct models and select relevant covariates in estimating propensity scores. However, because it often calls for subjective judgments, researchers faced with such tasks may naturally seek to support their subjective judgments with objective yet practical rules. Propensity score literature has seen an active development in model building and refinement strategies recently. For example, generalized boost regression suggested by McCaffrey, Ridgeway and Morral (2004) may be a potential solution when the specification of predictors' functional form is an issue. An application of new modeling techniques and an evaluation of their relevance would benefit the post-hoc survey adjustments. Additionally, guidelines for testing the sensitivity of violating critical assumptions in propensity score models would promote the correct application of propensity score adjustment.

Predicted propensity scores are the essential tool in propensity score adjustments. However, the predicted scores do have standard errors as propensity models have assumed errors. The less predictive the propensity model, the larger the standard errors of the predicted scores. Just as in any social science fields where statistical models are shown to be limited in explaining human behaviors, propensity score models for volunteer panel Web surveys may not show large predictive power. The literature has so far focused on the application of predicted scores and has not considered the effect of using models with low predictability. Therefore, discussions around the consequences of inadequate model fit and the incorporation of model errors will benefit propensity score adjustment literature.

CONCLUSION

An effort to improve the quality and inferential adequacy of volunteer panel Web survey data is indispensable as this type of data collection is practiced popularly. However, it should be recognized that the results of volunteer panel Web surveys are not free from being contaminated by selection biases and unlikely to represent the population, especially when targeting the general population. Applying propensity score adjustments for such surveys may reduce the selection bias, but its effectiveness is not guaranteed as it is dependent upon many aspects not fully examined.

It is true that the costs and the timeliness of volunteer panel Web surveys are appealing to survey practitioners. Current literature suggests that this appeal should be understood with a caution. This is well noted in a comment by Kim Dedeker, then Vice President for Global Consumer and Market Knowledge at P&G at a market research conference in 2006: "Two surveys a week apart by the same online supplier yielded different recommendations. I never thought I was trading data quality for cost savings."

REFERENCES

American Association for Public Opinion Research (AAPOR). (2010). AAPOR report on online panels. *Public Opinion Quarterly*, *74*(4), 711–781. doi:10.1093/poq/nfq048

Bethell, C., Fiorillo, J., Lansky, D., Hendryx, M., & Knickman, J. (2004). Online consumer surveys as a methodology for assessing the quality of the United States health care system. *Journal of Medical Internet Research*, *6*(1), e2. doi:10.2196/jmir.6.1.e2

Brick, J. M., Waksberg, J., & Keeter, S. (1996). Using data on interruptions in telephone service as coverage adjustments. *Survey Methodology*, *22*(2), 185–197.

Cameron, A., Rosen, R. C., & Swindle, R. W. (2005). Sexual and relationship characteristics among an Internet-based sample of U.S. men with and without erectile dysfunction. *Journal of Sex & Marital Therapy*, *31*, 229–242. doi:10.1080/00926230590513447

Chang, L., & Krosnick, J. A. (2009). National surveys via RDD telephone interviewing versus the Internet. Comparing sample representativeness and response quality. *Public Opinion Quarterly*, *73*(4), 641–678. doi:10.1093/poq/nfp075

Cobanoglu, C., Warde, B., & Moreo, P. J. (2001). A comparison of mail, fax, and Web-based survey methods. *International Journal of Market Research*, *43*, 441–452.

Cochran, W. G. (1968). The effectiveness of adjustment by subclassification in removing bias in observational studies. *Biometrics*, *24*, 295–313. doi:10.2307/2528036

Converse, P. D., Wolfe, E. W., Huang, X., & Oswald, F. L. (2008). Response rates for mixed-mode surveys using mail and e-mail/Web. *The American Journal of Evaluation*, *29*(1), 99–107. doi:10.1177/1098214007313228

Couper, M. P. (2000). Web surveys: A review of issues and approaches. *Public Opinion Quarterly*, *64*, 464–494. doi:10.1086/318641

Couper, M. P. (2007). Issues of representation in eHealth research (with a focus on Web surveys). *American Journal of Preventive Medicine*, *32*(5S), S83–S89. doi:10.1016/j.amepre.2007.01.017

Couper, M. P., Kapteyn, A., Schonlau, M., & Winter, J. (2007). Noncoverage and nonresponse in an Internet survey. *Social Science Research*, *36*, 131–148. doi:10.1016/j.ssresearch.2005.10.002

Couper, M. P., & Miller, P. V. (2008). Web survey methods: Introduction. *Public Opinion Quarterly*, *72*(5), 831–835. doi:10.1093/poq/nfn066

Czajka, J. L., Hirabayashi, S. M., Little, R. J. A., & Rubin, D. B. (1992). Projecting from advance data using propensity modeling: An application to income and tax statistics. *Journal of Business & Economic Statistics*, *10*(2), 117–132. doi:10.2307/1391671

D'Agostino, R. B. Jr. (1998). Propensity score methods for bias reduction for the comparison of a treatment to a non-randomized control group. *Statistics in Medicine*, *17*, 2265–2281. doi:10.1002/(SICI)1097-0258(19981015)17:19<2265::AID-SIM918>3.0.CO;2-B

de Leeuw, E. (2005). To mix or not to mix data collection modes in surveys. *Journal of Official Statistics*, *21*(2), 233–255.

Dennis, M. (2010). *KnowledgePanel®: Processes & procedures contributing to sample representativeness & tests for self-selection bias*. Retrieved from http://www.knowledgenetworks.com/ganp/docs/KnowledgePanelR-Statistical-Methods-Note.pdf

Duncan, K. B., & Stasny, E. A. (2001). Using propensity scores to control coverage bias in telephone surveys. *Survey Methodology*, *27*(2), 121–130.

Evans, J. R., & Mathur, A. (2005). The value of online surveys. *Internet Research*, *15*(2), 195–219. doi:10.1108/10662240510590360

Farrell, D., & Petersen, J. C. (2010). The growth of Internet research methods and the reluctant sociologist. *Sociological Inquiry*, *80*(1), 114–125. doi:10.1111/j.1475-682X.2009.00318.x

Faulx, A. L., Vela, S., Das, A., Cooper, G., Sivak, M., Isenberg, G., & Chak, A. (2005). The changing landscape of practice patterns regarding unsedated endoscopy and propofol use: A national Web survey. *Gastrointestinal Endoscopy*, *62*(1), 9–15. doi:10.1016/S0016-5107(05)00518-3

Garren, S. T., & Chang, T. C. (2002). Improved ratio estimation in telephone surveys adjusting for noncoverage. *Survey Methodology*, *28*(1), 63–76.

Göksel, H., Judkins, D. R., & Mosher, W. D. (1991). Nonresponse adjustments for a telephone follow-up to a national in-person survey. In *Proceedings of the Survey Research Methods Section, American Statistical Association* (pp. 581-586).

Groves, R. M. (1989). *Survey errors and survey costs*. New York, NY: John Wiley.

Groves, R. M. (2006). Nonresponse rates and nonresponse bias in household surveys. *Public Opinion Quarterly*, *70*(5), 646–675. doi:10.1093/poq/nfl033

Groves, R. M., & Couper, M. P. (1998). *Nonresponse in household interview surveys*. New York, NY: John Wiley.

Groves, R. M., & Peytcheva, E. (2008). The impact of nonresponse rates on nonresponse bias. *Public Opinion Quarterly*, *72*(2), 167–189. doi:10.1093/poq/nfn011

Guo, S., & Fraser, M. W. (2010). *Propensity score analysis: Statistical methods and applications*. Thousand Oaks, CA: Sage.

Harris Interactive. (2008). *Election results further validate efficacy of Harris Interactive's online methodology*. New York, NY: Author.

Hoaglin, D. C., & Battaglia, M. P. (1996). A comparison of two methods of adjusting for noncoverage of nontelephone households in a telephone survey. In *Proceedings of the Survey Research Methods Section, American Statistical Association*.

Iannacchione, V. G. (2003). Sequential weight adjustments for the location and cooperation propensity for the 1995 National Survey of Family Growth. *Journal of Official Statistics*, *19*(1), 31–43.

Keeter, S., Miller, C., Kohut, A., Groves, R. M., & Presser, S. (2000). Consequences of reducing nonresponse in a large national telephone survey. *Public Opinion Quarterly, 64*, 125–148. doi:10.1086/317759

Kuran, T., & McCaffery, E. J. (2004). Expanding discrimination research: Beyond ethnicity and to the Web. *Social Science Quarterly, 85*, 713–730. doi:10.1111/j.0038-4941.2004.00241.x

Kuran, T., & McCaffery, E. J. (2008). Sex differences in the acceptability of discrimination. *Political Research Quarterly, 61*(2), 228–238. doi:10.1177/1065912907304500

Lee, S. (2006). Propensity score adjustment as a weighting scheme for volunteer panel Web surveys. *Journal of Official Statistics, 22*(2), 329–349.

Lee, S., Brown, E. R., Grant, D., Belin, T. R., & Brick, J. M. (2009). Exploring nonresponse bias in a health survey using neighborhood characteristics. *American Journal of Public Health, 99*, 1811–1817. doi:10.2105/AJPH.2008.154161

Lee, S., & Valliant, R. (2007). Weighting telephone samples using propensity scores. In Lepkowski, J. M., Tucker, C., & Brick, J. M. (Eds.), *Advances in telephone survey methodology* (pp. 170–186). New York, NY: Wiley. doi:10.1002/9780470173404. ch8

Lee, S., & Valliant, R. (2009). Estimation for volunteer panel Web surveys using propensity score adjustment and calibration adjustment. *Sociological Methods & Research, 37*, 319–343. doi:10.1177/0049124108329643

Lepkowski, J., Kalton, G., & Kasprzyk, D. (1989). Weighting adjustments for partial nonresponse in the 1984 SIPP panel. In *Proceedings of the Survey Research Methods Section, American Statistical Association* (pp. 296-301).

Little, R. J. A. (1993). Post-stratification: A modeler's perspective. *Journal of the American Statistical Association, 88*, 1001–1012. doi:10.2307/2290792

Little, R. J. A., & Vartivarian, S. (2005). Does weighting for nonresponse increase the variance of survey means? *Survey Methodology, 31*, 161–168.

McCaffrey, D. F., Ridgeway, G., & Morral, A. R. (2004). Propensity score estimation with boosted regression for evaluating causal effects in observational studies. *Psychological Methods, 9*(4), 572–606. doi:10.1037/1082-989X.9.4.403

Merkle, D., & Edelman, M. (2002). Nonresponse in exit polls: A comprehensive analysis. In Groves, R. M., Dillman, D. A., Eltinge, J. L., & Little, R. J. A. (Eds.), *Survey nonresponse* (pp. 243–258). New York, NY: Wiley.

Montaquila, J., Brick, J. M., Hagedorn, M. C., Kennedy, C., & Keeter, S. (2007). Aspects of nonresponse bias in RDD telephone surveys. In Lepkowski, J. M., Tucker, C., & Brick, J. M. (Eds.), *Advances in telephone survey methodology* (pp. 561–586). New York, NY: Wiley. doi:10.1002/9780470173404.ch25

Reed, B. D., Crawford, S., Couper, M. P., Cave, C., & Haefner, H. K. (2004). Pain at the vulvar vestibule—A Web survey. *Journal of Lower Genital Tract Disease, 8*, 48–57. doi:10.1097/00128360-200401000-00011

Rosenbaum, P. R., & Rubin, D. B. (1983). The central role of the propensity score in observational studies for causal effects. *Biometrika, 70*(1), 41–55. doi:10.1093/biomet/70.1.41

Rosenbaum, P. R., & Rubin, D. B. (1984). Reducing bias in observational studies using subclassification on the propensity score. *Journal of the American Statistical Association, 79*(387), 516–524. doi:10.2307/2288398

Schillewaert, N., & Meulemeester, P. (2005). Comparing response distributions of offline and online data collection methods. *International Journal of Market Research, 47,* 163–178.

Schonlau, M., van Soest, A., Kapteyn, A., & Couper, M. (2009). Selection bias in Web surveys and the use of propensity scores. *Sociological Methods & Research, 37*(3), 291–318. doi:10.1177/0049124108327128

Smith, P. J., Rao, J. N. K., Battaglia, M. P., Daniels, D., & Ezzati-Rice, T. (2001). Compensating for provider nonresponse using propensities to form adjustment cells: The National Immunization Survey. *Vital and Health Statistics, 2*(133), 1–17.

Sparrow, N. (2006). Developing reliable online polls. *International Journal of Market Research, 48,* 659–680.

Sparrow, N., & Curtice, J. (2004). Measuring the attitudes of the general public via Internet polls: An evaluation. *International Journal of Market Research, 46,* 23–44.

Taylor, H. (2000). Does Internet research work? Comparing online survey results with telephone survey. *International Journal of Market Research, 42,* 58–63.

Taylor, H., Bremer, J., Overmeyer, C., Siegel, J. W., & Terhanian, G. (2001). The record of Internet-based opinion polls in predicting the results of 72 races in the November 2000 US elections. *International Journal of Market Research, 43*(2), 127–135.

Terhanian, G. (2000). *How to produce credible, trustworthy information through Internet-based survey research.* Paper presented at the Annual Meeting of the American Association for Public Opinion Research, Portland, OR.

Terhanian, G., & Bremer, J. (2000). *Confronting the selection-bias and learning effects of problems associated with Internet research.* New York, NY: Harris Interactive.

Wright, K. B. (2005). Researching Internet-based populations: Advantages and disadvantages of online survey research, online questionnaire authoring software packages, and Web survey services. *Journal of Computer-Mediated Communication, 10*(3).

Yeager, D. A., Krosnick, J. A., Chang, L., Javitz, H. S., Levendusky, M. S., Simpser, A., & Wang, R. (2009). *Comparing the accuracy of RDD telephone surveys and Internet surveys conducted with probability and non-probability samples.* Retrieved May 24, 2011, from http://comm.stanford.edu/faculty/krosnick/Mode%2004%20online%20supplement.pdf

ADDITIONAL READING

Bethlehem, J. (2010). Selection bias in Web surveys. *International Statistical Review, 78*(2), 161–188. doi:10.1111/j.1751-5823.2010.00112.x

Bethlehem, J. (2011). Can Web surveys provide an adequate alternative to phone and face to face surveys? *The Survey Statistician, 63,* 10–14.

Couper, M. P. (2008). *Designing effective Web surveys.* New York, NY: Cambridge University Press.

Couper, M. P. (2011). Emerging methodology of Web surveys. *The Survey Statistician, 63,* 22–24.

Das, M., Ester, P., & Kaczmirek, L. (Eds.). (2010). *Social and behavioral research and the internet: Advances in applied methods and research strategies.* London, UK: Routledge.

Das, M., Toepoel, V., & Van Soest, A. (2007). *Can I use a panel? Panel conditioning and attrition bias in panel surveys*. CentER Discussion Paper Series. Retrieved May 24, 2011 from http://ssrn.com/abstract=1012252

DiMaggio, P., Hargittai, E., Neuman, W. R., & Robinson, J. P. (2001). Social implications of the Internet. *Annual Review of Sociology*, *27*, 307–336. doi:10.1146/annurev.soc.27.1.307

Fielding, N., Lee, R. M., & Black, G. (Eds.). (2008). *The SAGE handbook of online research methods*. London, UK: Sage.

Howell, R. T., Rodzon, K. S., Kurai, M., & Sanchez, A. H. (2010). A validation of well-being and happiness surveys for administration via the Internet. *Behavior Research Methods*, *42*(3), 775–784. doi:10.3758/BRM.42.3.775

Kolodinsky, J., Harvey-Berino, J. R., Berlin, L., Johnson, R. K., & Reynolds, T. W. (2007). Knowledge of current dietary guidelines and food choice by college students: Better eaters have higher knowledge of dietary guidance. *Journal of the American Dietetic Association*, *107*(8), 1409–1413. doi:10.1016/j.jada.2007.05.016

Lee, S. (2006). An evaluation of nonresponse and coverage errors in a Web panel survey. *Social Science Computer Review*, *24*(4), 460–475. doi:10.1177/0894439306288085

Moloney, M., Dietrich, A., Strickland, O., & Myerburg, S. (2003). Using Internet discussion boards as virtual focus groups. *ANS. Advances in Nursing Science*, *26*(4), 274–286.

Ploderl, M., Faistauer, G., & Fartacek, R. (2010). The contribution of school to the feeling of acceptance and the risk of suicide attempts among Austrian gay and bisexual males. *Journal of Homosexuality*, *57*(7), 819–841. doi:10.1080/00918369.2010.493401

Rookey, B. D., Hanway, S., & Dillman, D. A. (2008). Does a probability-based household panel benefit from assignment to postal response as an alternative to Internet-only? *Public Opinion Quarterly*, *72*(5), 962–984. doi:10.1093/poq/nfn061

Ross, M. W., Rosser, B. R. S., Stanton, J., & Konstan, J. (2004). Characteristics of Latino men who have sex with men on the Internet who complete and drop out of an Internet-based sexual behavior survey. *AIDS Education and Prevention*, *16*, 526–537. doi:10.1521/aeap.16.6.526.53793

Schonlau, M., van Soest, A., & Kapteyn, A. (2007). Are Webographic or attitudinal questions useful for adjusting estimates from Web surveys using propensity scoring? *Survey Research Methods*, *1*, 155–163.

Sills, S., & Song, C. (2002). Innovations in survey research: An application of Web-based surveys. *Social Science Computer Review*, *20*(1), 22–30. doi:10.1177/089443930202000103

Strabac, Z., & Aalberg, T. (2011). Measuring political knowledge in telephone and Web surveys: A cross-national comparison. *Social Science Computer Review*, *29*(2), 175–192. doi:10.1177/0894439310371340

Traugott, M. (2001). The polls: Performance in the 2000 campaign. *Public Opinion Quarterly*, *65*, 389–419. doi:10.1086/322850

Valliant, R. L., & Dever, J. A. (2011). Estimating propensity adjustments for volunteer Web surveys. *Sociological Methods & Research*, *40*(1), 105–137. doi:10.1177/0049124110392533

Vehovar, V., Lozar Manfreda, L., Zaletel, M., & Batagelj, Z. (2002). Nonresponse in Web surveys. In Groves, R. M., Dillman, D. A., Eltinge, J. L., & Little, R. J. A. (Eds.), *Survey nonresponse* (pp. 229–242). New York, NY: Wiley.

KEY TERMS AND DEFINITIONS

Coverage (or Noncoverage) Error: Coverage error arises due to the fact the sampling frame does not cover the target population adequately and there is a systematic difference between those who are covered by the frame and those who are not.

Nonprobability Sample: Any samples that do not meet the criteria of probability samples are classified as nonprobability samples.

Probability Sample: When samples are drawn from the population in a randomized fashion and the selection probabilities are known prior to sampling, the sample is considered a probability sample.

Random Digit Dialing (RDD) Telephone Sample: RDD sampling method is based on the frame of all telephone numbers. It exploits the structure of telephone numbers, for instance, a combination of an area code, a three-digit exchange code and a four-digit suffix in US. The frame is often created by appending suffixes to the prefixes that combine area codes and exchange codes. The main idea is to draw a sample from this type of frames at random, but the actual sampling operation can take different forms by using a telephone list assisted approach or a dual frame approach.

Sampling Error: Sampling error arises in sample surveys due to the fact that only a fraction of the population is studied. This is the common error in all data collection using samples.

Selection Bias: When samples are selected disproportionately over- or under-sampling certain groups by design but by some other uncontrolled factors, inferential results using data from such samples are confounded by such factors, resulting in selection bias. Nonprobability samples are subject to selection bias be definition unless the all confounders are controlled in the inference procedures. Probability samples themselves are free from selection bias, but this may be violated by nonresponse and frame coverage.

Weighting: Weighting is a statistical procedure typically placed after completing data collection. There are two reasons for weighting. First, by design, sampling may target subgroups at different rates, resulting in differential sampling rates. Second, surveys often experience glitches in operations due to nonresponse and noncoverage issues and these can differ systematically by subgroups. These mean that the distribution of a sample in hands may depart from that of the population. Weighting corrects for this departure using known characteristics for both the sample and population by projecting the sample distribution to the population level.

Chapter 4
Online Qualitative Interviews:
Opportunities and Challenges for Urban and Planning Studies

Kathleen J. Hanrahan
Indiana University of Pennsylvania, USA

Mathew T. Smith
Indiana University of Pennsylvania, USA

Judith E. Sturges
Penn State Fayette, USA

ABSTRACT

Computer mediated communication is a part of everyday life for much of the population. People rely on email and instant messaging, post to chat rooms and blogs, and routinely use the Internet for a wide variety of functions. As a result, the options for qualitative study available to urban planners and researchers have expanded dramatically. This chapter examines the feasibility of online qualitative interviews. The chapter begins with an overview of the online options or venues (e.g., chat rooms, bulletin boards, social networking sites, email) currently available to the qualitative researcher. Next, issues of data quality in online interviews are discussed, and various online venues are compared to in person or face-to-face interview modes. Additionally, the authors discuss some of the central ethical and human subject protection issues involved in the online research landscape. The chapter concludes with an assessment of the potential for online qualitative interviews.

INTRODUCTION

Qualitative research allows us to enter the subjective experience of our respondents – to see their world through their eyes. At the heart of this research tradition is the interview. Whether interviewing is the main or only method used to learn about respondents' worlds, or supplements a broader ethnographic project, we learn about people by talking with them.

Qualitative research encompasses a remarkably rich variety of epistemological traditions, methods, and techniques, and has a place in both

DOI: 10.4018/978-1-4666-0074-4.ch004

academic and applied research settings. Many academic researchers are more comfortable with the structure and shared assumptions of the quantitative paradigm. However, qualitative research has its academic proponents, and applied research often relies on qualitative methods, particularly on qualitative interviews.

Qualitative interviews are often described as a "conversation with a purpose." What is most critical about the interview is the transaction between the researcher and the respondent. Indeed, reactivity – the influence that the data collection method has on the information gathered – is particularly an issue in the design and analysis of qualitative research. Thus the data gathered via interviews reflect not only the information offered by the respondent, but also matters like the influence of the researcher's characteristics, the setting, question wording and sequence, and duration of the interview. The data also reflect, to some extent, the selection of interview mode, or the method of interviewing. Traditionally, interview mode has referred to matters such as whether the interview is conducted face-to-face, or over the telephone, and whether it is a personal interview with one researcher and one respondent, or a group interview with one researcher or facilitator and several respondents.

Online interviews represent yet another mode, and one that is expanding rapidly. As noted by Markham (2008), the opportunity for Internet-based qualitative research is "beguiling: A researcher's reach is potentially global, data collection is economical, and transcribing is no more difficult than cutting and pasting" (p. 255). Yet, much needs to be learned about this evolving option for qualitative research.

As a practical matter, online interviewing is not a unitary mode in the sense that telephone interviews constitute a single mode of data collection. Perhaps when the Internet was new, and online options limited and more or less entirely text-based, it made sense to think of "online interviews" as a unitary mode. However, as the options have increased, and the virtual-physical world interface has become more permeable, a "single mode" view simply is not correct. And increasingly, the difference between online and traditional communication is diminishing; broadband technology has made "today's media landscape one of increasing convergence" (Gies, 2008, p. 312) (see also Sade-Beck, 2004; Bowker & Tuffin, 2004).

Of perhaps more interest are the implications of these new modes of interviewing. As Markham (2008) notes, "Simply put, our methods are still more suitable for research in physically proximal contexts... our epistemological frameworks have not yet shifted to match this [online] reality" (p. 278). Certainly, what we know about traditional qualitative interviews does not transfer directly to online options. Instead, as Markham (2008) and others have suggested, we need to explore the extent to which online interviews are similar and dissimilar to traditional face-to-face interviews, and to consider carefully the implications for our findings.

Ten years ago, Seymour wrote "while online research is exciting, it is no longer new" (2001, p. 164), and experience and reflection about online interviewing have grown over the past decade. At the same time, the nature of "online" options has continued to expand, and the pace of change has quickened. What we attempt in this chapter, therefore, is a modest summary of what we know about using online technologies to conduct qualitative interviews.

These methods are relevant to urban planning studies, the focus of this text. Recent trends in urban planning include sustainability and inclusion of the full range of stakeholders in the planning process. While not without controversy (Astrom & Granberg, 2007), the move to incorporate citizen perspectives through increased participation via survey and discussion is widespread. The potential for such participation is vastly increased when citizens, planners, and policy makers can rely on electronic or computer mediated communication

Table 1.

Chart 1 – Online Research Venues
Venue
Search Engine Queries
Chat Rooms and IRC [Internet Relay Chat]
Email
Instant Messaging and ICQ [I Seek You]
Listservs
Internet Forums (e.g. message boards, bulletin boards)
Blogs
Homepages
Social Networking Sites (e.g. Facebook, MySpace)
Video and Audio Chats
Massively Multiuser Online Games and Communities (e.g. Second Life)
Wikis (e.g. Wikipedia and other user-modified sources)

(Astrom & Granberg, 2007; Komito, 2007; Stern & Dillman, 2006), and makes online interviews increasingly appealing.

ONLINE RESEARCH VENUES

The key to successful research is clarity about the question to be answered, and the fit between that question and the data collection and analysis techniques. The online data collection methods afforded by the Internet and new technologies are always subject to change. At this point in time, the online venues most commonly used for qualitative research are shown in Table 1.

Not surprisingly, online qualitative research is becoming as varied as research conducted in the physical world (and of course both real and virtual world research settings can be included in a single project). Here, we want to recognize three broad and overlapping foci of online study that may use one or more of the venues listed above.

First, there is a fascinating body of research that seeks to understand how people use the Internet, particularly the creation and participation in online communities in which participants adopt online personas (Second Life, for example), or participation in games that permit or require adoption of such personas (World of Warcraft, for example). These online or virtual worlds can be quite elaborate creations involving multiple users, graphical representations of the virtual world, website stability, and they can be recorded. Researchers typically use an ethnographic approach to study these virtual communities; this may include participation to some degree, interviews with participants or their personas, recording of website content, collection of virtual artifacts, and related approaches (Hine, 2008; McKee & Porter, 2009).

A second broad area of online inquiry seeks to learn from the byproducts of Internet usage: blogs, social networking sites, and forum postings of formal and informal online groups (Hookway, 2008). Here, the strategy may involve participation in online groups, and perhaps interviews, or it may simply involve content analysis of "harvested" real time or archived postings. This method has the advantage of being natural talk, but perhaps not on the topic of interest. More importantly, and as discussed below, participants in even public forums often have an expectation of privacy, and gleaning information this way raises ethical concerns. There are numerous references in the literature to online participants taking a very negative view of "lurking" – reading the online discussion without participating – even on public forums.

The third area of research, and the one most commonly meant by "online research", is the use of the Internet to locate and recruit respondents to interview in order to understand the respondents' views on matters related to their offline, physical selves (Bowker & Tuffin, 2004). For example, researchers have conducted online interviews with gay men about sexual practices (Ayling & Mewse, 2009), with handicapped persons about their disability (Bowker & Tuffin, 2004), with young adults about HIV/AIDS (Graffigna & Bosio, 2006), with adolescents about the HPV vaccine (Battles, 2010), and many other populations and topics. Holt (2010) provides a very useful overview of criminological studies of this type. This third area of research is the main focus of this chapter.

MODES OF ONLINE INTERVIEWS

Once the online qualitative interview is selected as the data collection technique best suited to the research question, the next consideration is selection of venues (email or chat, for instance), and a decision about the temporal aspect of data collection. That is, will the interviews be conducted in real time, or not (Graffigna & Bosio, 2006; Steward & Williams, 2005)? Synchronous interviews, those conducted in real time, can use one of the chat or instant messaging options, for example, for a near conversational forum. Data from asynchronous interviews, conducted by email for instance, can be collected over extended periods of time during which the respondent has time to consider, craft and perhaps revise responses. Bowkin and Tuffin (2004), for example, report that their online interviews were conducted over a period of "weeks and months" (p. 234).

Another design decision, related to choice of online venue, is the extent to which the interview data will be text-based. Increased bandwidths, and the ready availability of programs like Skype, have made visual online interviews a relatively straightforward matter. More sophisticated options exist; researchers can create virtual environments, ask respondents to participate in the virtual world, and discuss it with them. For example, Kaliski (2006), suggests this option using utilities such as those provided by CommunityViz (www.communityviz.com), and Howard and Gaborit (2007) report on the results of developing a virtual planning environment.

At the time of this writing, researchers generally have made use of email, online bulletin boards, and Internet forums for asynchronous data collection. Real time interviews can be conducted by Internet chat, instant messenger, by phone with or without visual contact, or via webcam-assisted chat. Researchers can use existing Internet forums or can create one dedicated to the research project. In the latter case, invited participants can be asked to provide demographic or screening information and to execute a formal consent agreement, and the researcher has more control over information security. For example, for their study of gay men's use of the Internet to make sexual contacts, Ayling and Mewse (2009) established this type of private website and after collecting demographic data and participant consent, asked respondents "to download [encrypted] secure Internet chat software" (p. 567). Use of existing forums and message boards, on the other hand, makes sampling or recruiting respondents easier by offering some assurance that the respondents will be knowledgeable about the topic under study. Table 2 summarizes some of the choices.

Finally, the researcher must make a decision familiar to traditional qualitative studies: should the interviews be one-to-one, or should group interviews be used? The majority of the online interviewing discussed in the literature involves online group interviews (e.g., Franklin & Lowry,

Table 2.

Chart 2 – Online Research Venues				
	Asynchronous	Synchronous	Software*	Hardware**
Venue	○	○	○	○
Search Engine Queries	○	•	○	○
Chats/IRC	○	•	•	○
Email	•	○	○	○
Instant Messaging/ICQ	○	•	•	○
Listservs	•	○	○	○
Internet Forums	•	○	○	○
Blogs	•	○	•	○
Homepages	•	○	•	○
Social Networking Sites***	•	•	○	○
Video and Audio Chat	○	•	•	•
Massively Multiplayer Games and Communities	○	•	•	○
Wikis	•	○	○	○

*Requires additional software
**Requires additional hardware
***Incorporates both synchronous and asynchronous aspects

2001; Graffigna & Bosio, 2006) and even within this category of data collection, there is variety. Asynchronous group interviews have been conducted via chat rooms, bulletin boards, email, and even educational course management software. Alternately, a "virtual focus group" can be conducted in real time. Respondents can be recruited and asked to log on to a chat room at a particular time; webcams can show respondents as they speak if face-to-face interaction is desired. In still another approach, Franklin and Lowry (2001) brought respondents onsite, but used networked computers and group support software to conduct onsite, computer mediated focus groups.

In short, the Internet offers a growing variety of venues for qualitative interviews. The researcher must take into account the venue's technological demands on both the potential respondent and the researcher. Options that use other than widely available technology pose additional challenges. As Graiser (2008) points out,

It is one thing to commit your time to participate in an interesting discussion; it is yet another to have to spend time configuring your computer... The other dilemma of needing to instruct participants to configure an application is that the [researcher], by default, becomes the technical support staff (p. 301).

Some of this difficulty can be addressed by relying on simpler technologies like Gmail, which is a browser based program and does not require the installation of additional software or hardware. Figure 1 summarizes the technical demands of the commonly used venues.

Figure 1.

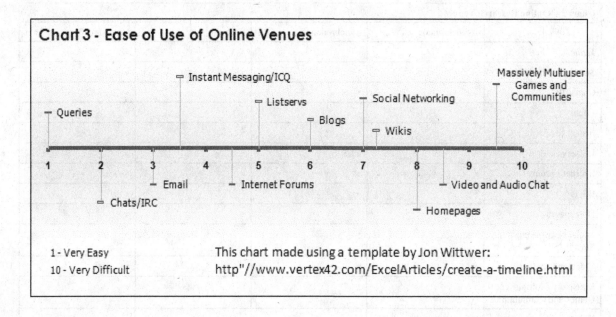

Access and Sampling

One of the selling points for online research is the extraordinary reach or connectivity of the Internet. As Markham (2008) notes, the potential for recruiting or sampling on the Internet is "potentially global" (p. 257) and it seems particularly well suited to contacting some otherwise hard to access respondent groups. For example, online interviews have been conducted with those with disabilities (Bowker & Tuffin, 2004), or suffering from chronic illness (Nicholas et al., 2010), and with respondents who are widely dispersed geographically. However, actual access to this vast range of participants is only potential. There are real obstacles to online recruitment of respondents.

First and foremost, there is a "digital divide" when it comes to computer access and fluency, and this has obvious and central significance in the design of online research. Even among educated professionals who use the Internet in daily work, access is a continuum. In our experience, county level agencies, human service agencies, and not-for-profits are the least likely to have access to technology and generally lag everyone else in adoption of new technologies. This has obvious implications for studies that might rely on workers in these and related occupations.

The situation with regard to the general public is more varied. As Komito (2007) points out, the digital divide is diminishing, and efforts to increase free or affordable access by, say, local libraries have helped. However, increasing access to the Internet addresses only physical access. Computer literacy, keyboarding skills, and/or and ease with written expression (for purely text-based modalities) comprise the other side of access. If the goal of the research project is inclusion, some groups will be vastly underrepresented in research that is conducted online: the poor, the uneducated, the non-native speaker, the incarcerated, the homeless, and the elderly. Other groups are more likely to be included, particularly the young (Borkan, 2010) and the well-educated. As noted by Markham (2008), the populations most commonly available at this point in time for study via the Internet tend to be both privileged and relatively small.

Considered against this backdrop, the global reach of the Internet is more limited than we hoped, but it is still vast. It has been estimated that Americans, for example, currently spend an average of 18 hours a week online (up from 2.7 hours in 2000), that about 350 billion emails are sent each day, and that over 140 million blogs are active (Rodriguez, 2010). But this bounty of potential respondents has a downside: determining which groups to sample, or the parameters of the sampling frame, is challenging. There are numerous websites, message boards, etc. but neither they nor their members are permanent. As a result, specifying the population of interest is another design feature that emerges during the research, rather than being specified in advance (Markham, 2008).

To date, the practice of "taking advantage of existing social groups online is by far the most common and successful method of recruiting participants" (Stewart & Williams, 2005, p. 398). As described more fully below, access via these groups can raise ethical issues, and will require, at a minimum, the standard recruitment process: approval from a gatekeeper, followed by contact with individual group members. And of course, using an existing online group requires that such a group exists. Existing groups are commonly tapped in research related to medical issues, and some education issues; professional associations and similar groups are a likely source of respondents. As use of the Internet grows, one can easily imagine that groups of every possible stripe will be available. At the moment, however, some groups, particularly those at the margins, are not readily accessible.

Thus, the researcher who plans to conduct interviews online must consider, as does every other researcher, the extent to which respondents are representative enough of the population of interest to yield useful data. While qualitative researchers do not seek generalizability in the statistical sense, we certainly seek information that is credible and trustworthy. Access to appropriate respondents is one half of the equation; the quality of their responses is the other.

Online Interview Data Quality

Assessing the validity and reliability of qualitative interview data is challenging, particularly when viewed from the vantage point offered by the dominant quantitative paradigm. Unlike the positivist tradition, qualitative research assumes a subjective reality, co-created in the interview process. Thus, assessment of data quality in qualitative research tends to be more subjective as well. A variety of suggestions have been advanced for defining and assessing reliability and validity in qualitative research (Lewis, 2009). As is always the case, good research depends on matching the method with the research question and population of interest. Thus, choice of interview mode can enhance or impede research success.

A few issues with respect to the quality of online interviews are raised with some regularity: the truthfulness of respondents, lack of visual cues to help the researcher judge response quality, and the nature of the data compared to face-to-face interview data.

A concern commonly expressed about online interviews is that the lack of face-to-face interaction makes deception easy, and perhaps more attractive. We all have heard of chat room participants who present themselves as teenage girls but later turn out to be middle-aged men trolling for sex. Couldn't online research participants pretend to be very different from their actual selves? If so, what good are the data?

This is an empirical question: are online respondents less truthful than face-to-face respondents? Answering this question is far from simple, but researchers with experience conducting online interviews do not give this notion much purchase. Gies (2008) has suggested that the very characteristics that permit deception may also lead to greater honesty: "the appeal of the Internet is not invariably that it allows us to be someone else but also that it allows us to be ourselves" (pp. 317-318). Others agree (e.g., Bowker & Tuffin, 2004; Sade-Beck, 2004; Shields, 2003; Ayling & Mewse, 2009).

The respondent groups of interest, and the nature of the research question, play a role here. Surely, sensitive research questions seem better suited to methods that permit some sense of anonymity for the respondent. Researchers make the same observation about telephone vs. face-to-face interviews (Holt, 2010; Sturges & Hanrahan, 2004). Online data collection affords some privacy to the respondent; it can offer a sense of pseudo-anonymity. Speaking of telephone interviews, Holt (2010) observes that certain groups at the social margins are frequently subjected to the "surveillant other" – to the "professional gaze" of social workers, school officials, etc. – and might welcome less intrusion.

The lack of face-to-face interaction in most contemporary online venues raises another concern; namely the lack of visual interpersonal cues. Does the lack of this information – facial expression, voice, body language, demographic information – mean impoverished communication between the researcher and participants? Again, there is little systematic information to address this question. Many researchers point out that regular users of the Internet and those fluent in computer mediated communication have developed a variety of substitute cues (e.g., Gies, 2008; Markham, 2008; Seymour, 2001; James & Busher, 2006) that can compensate for the lack of visual feedback. The most obvious are the use of emoticons and changes in font to indicate emotional content or emphasis (e.g., YELLING IN CAPITAL LETTERS). More subtle cues also exist; frequent users of message boards and similar media can recognize each other's style of presentation or "signature style" (Geis, 2008). Ayling and Mewse (2009) comment that the researcher needs to be experienced in the media being used in order to "receive and work with the subtle nuances that are present in dialogue of this form" (p. 571) and to increase engagement

in the interview. Moreover, the increasing availability of visual options, like Skype, mitigates this concern in cases where visual data is important.

Perhaps the central concern for data quality is how well the respondents can express themselves in writing, if the project is entirely or largely text-based. According to Markham (2008): "If one is simply using the Internet as a tool to expand one's reach to participants and interviewing them online is merely a convenience, one should consider the extent to which people can and do express themselves well, truly, or fully in text" (p. 268). In turn, the ability to express ideas depends not only on the respondent but on the venue selected as well.

Taking the face-to-face interview as the benchmark for qualitative interviews, it is useful to consider how well the online methods can produce text of the nature required by the research question. That is, how does the data from online interviews compare with that from a face-to-face interview? Does the transcript contain rich qualitative data? Here, the experience to date is mixed and dependent on the venue (email or chat, for instance) and mode (personal or group interview) selected.

The early literature about online research is replete with discussion and speculation about the potential for online data collection. As experience with online interviewing has grown, researchers have offered thoughtful reflection about the data themselves (e.g., Shields, 2003). Researchers have commented on the condensed nature of online interview data and the resultant dense coding of the transcript (e.g., Ayling & Mewse, 2009; Nickolas et al., 2010). Franklin and Lowry (2001), for example, comment on the text of transcripts, alternately referring to the focus group data as "a concise discussion of the topic" (p. 179) and noting that the data lacked depth, with the transcript looking more like "a list of ideas than well-developed thoughts or in-depth exploration of attitudes and opinions" (p. 180).

Direct comparisons between online data collection and traditional face-to-face interviews, and comparison of interview data collected using different online venues, are available. And it appears that there is a difference in the data gathered. Bowker and Tuffin (2004) interviewed people with disabilities using three online options (mostly email, but also using IRC and ICQ) and face-to-face interviews. Their generally favorable reflection on the data collection process includes discussions of many of the obstacles to and challenges of using the online approach (for both researcher and respondent) and its impact on the nature of the data collected.

Graffigna and Bosio (2006) compared face-to-face focus group interviews about HIV/AIDS with online group interviews conducted using different venues. Specifically, they compared two face-to-face focus groups with two chat room discussions (synchronous), two online forums (asynchronous), and two mixed approach (online forum plus chat). They note differences between online and face-to-face interviews, and also differences among types of online group interviews. All methods produced "rich and articulate discourse" and "some key themes" were produced regardless of how the data were generated. The authors note some interesting and useful differences. For instance, they characterize chat room discussions as more similar to brainstorming, while forum participants produced more fully developed and nuanced discussions.

Nickolas et al. (2010) conducted face-to-face focus groups with children suffering from chronic health problems and compared the method and results with online asynchronous group discussion using a chat room. They report that "parallel patterns of topics were observed in both modalities" (p. 114) but that there were obvious differences in expression. On one hand, online participants reported greater feelings of privacy and security which resulted in "increased disclosure and transparency" (p. 116). Yet face-to-face discussions contained more relational and non-topic conversations, while online groups produced "less descriptive, elaborative and social use of

language" (p. 115) leading to "more direct and cryptic" data (p. 115).

Other researchers have reported similar findings. Steward and Williams (2005) note that in transcripts of synchronous interviews, those conducted in real time, the text tends to be spontaneous, quick and less fully developed and more like normal conversations. It can also be hard to follow (O'Connor, Madge, Shaw, & Wellens, 2008). Asynchronous interviews, conducted by email for example, tend to result in lengthier, more carefully constructed postings. At the same time, the postings are less spontaneous and may reflect greater concern with social desirability (O'Connor et al., 2008). Stewart and Williams (2005) characterize asynchronous data collection as "literate" and synchronous data as "oral" (p. 405).

The forgoing suggests that online interviewing is neither the same nor predictably different from face-to-face interviews. The venue, mode, epistemological stance, research question, type of analysis, and population of interest must be complementary in order to conduct successful online interviews.

HUMAN SUBJECT PROTECTIONS

Given the conclusion that online interviewing is neither the same nor predictably different from face-to-face interviews, it is not surprising that the ethical issues it presents are also neither quite the same nor predictably different from conventional interview studies. Seymour (2001) suggests that ethical conduct within online research projects may be more important than in offline situations, and that there is a good chance that the implications of online research procedures will be fully understood only in retrospect because of the rapid development of the online medium. Institutional Review Boards for the Protection of Human Subjects (IRBs), or similar bodies charged with oversight of human subject protections, may be challenged by these modes of data collection as well. McKee and Porter (2009) note the current lack of guidance in these matters. Thus, the researcher proposing online methods, particularly online qualitative methods, should expect to assume more of the burden of anticipating the human subject protection issues and sharing that information with the IRB or other oversight body.

Another area of potential ethical challenges more common to online research is due to the global reach of the Internet. Global connectivity permits respondent pools to cross national and cultural boundaries. Thus the researchers must consider differing legal, social, and cultural aspects of human subject protection. As noted by the Association of Internet Researchers (Ess, 2002):

Different nations and cultures enjoy diverse legal protections and traditions of ethical decision-making. Especially as Internet research may entail a literally global scope, efforts to respond to ethical concerns and resolve ethical conflicts must take into account diverse national and cultural frameworks (p. 3).

Freed-Taylor (1994) compiled an overview of European ethical codes. In her summary of principles, she states that researchers who study diverse nations, cultures or ethnic groups "have a special responsibility" (Principle 3) to heed differences in national law and its implementation and to comply with any appropriate regulations governing data collection, storage, or dissemination. Her recommendations are referenced on the UNESCO website (www.unesco.org/most/ethissj.htm) and are reflected in those promulgated by the Council of European Social Science Data Archives (CESSDA, 2010).

We take as a starting point that online researchers are required to abide by all the human subject protections evident in face-to-face data collection. However, as noted, the form of these protections and even their meaning may be somewhat changed in the online environment. Here, we focus on the following set of interrelated issues: the possible intrusiveness of online interviews, documenting voluntary consent to participate, confidentiality and privacy given the thin line between public and private discourse, and protection of research data.

The Internet and the communities within it can provide a robust source of information on a variety of topics, but there exist the possibility that the presence of the researcher will be unwelcome, or that efforts to recruit will be viewed as spam (O'Connor et al., 2008). Battles (2010) argues this may be especially so when the researcher "lurks" (watches members of a community interact without actively interacting) within online communities - particularly those that that are organized around personal issues such as grief or medical matters. Holt (2010) notes that open forums (those that do not require users to register) are less likely to raise ethical issues than are closed forums.

Informed, voluntary consent to participate in a research study is the most central of all the human subject protections. Yet the very breadth of the pool of potential respondents in an online setting makes consent more complicated than in face-to-face interviews. Some researchers have questioned whether consent is even necessary in some online settings. Battles (2010), for example, argues that gleaning information from a MySpace page or other public source may not require consent of the author, and McKee and Porter (2009) make the same argument about aggregate data from public sources that have been stripped of identifiers. Under some circumstances, however, even public sources of this type are viewed by their authors and others as at least "quasi-private" and negative reactions to perceived intrusion are to be expected.

While face-to-face interviews and focus groups typically involve consent forms signed before beginning the data collection, consent in the online world may not always function in a similar manner. Lack of face-to-face contact and the ability of Internet users to adopt online personas, mentioned above, makes it difficult to be sure about the personal characteristics of the respondent. Of particular concern here is whether or not the respondent is of legal age to consent to a research interview. Most researchers indicate the desired demographics, including age range, in their recruitment posting or email and must simply accept the respondent claims as accurate. Both Seymour (2001) and Ayling and Mewse (2009) suggest that informed consent be sent to the participant's email address so that a record of said consent can be maintained by the researcher.

Perhaps the best way to approach consent online is to recognize that the distinction between public and private postings on the Internet is truly a moving target (McKee & Porter, 2009), and to attend to the three levels of consent outlined by Battle (2010) and others: consent from the participant or guardian, consent from the community being studied, and consent from the company that owns the website or community. Stewart and Williams (2005, p. 411) suggest paying attention to the "acceptable use policies" (AUP) of the service provider and becoming informed about any legal issues related to the website.

Protecting the privacy of respondents is a challenge with online research. If confidentiality or anonymity is promised, it must be provided. However, assuring such privacy is problematic in the case of online communication. One concern is the possibility that respondents could be personally identified by their participation in online research. Battles (2010) notes that even if participants rely on anonymous usernames during the research project, individuals may inadvertently provide enough information to allow for identification of their true identity. This is particularly an issue in small online communities. In such settings, as noted earlier, participants may be able to recognize each other's style of presentation or "signature style" (Geis, 2008). Thus, it is important to consider how privacy can be maintained, to assess the "risk of deductive disclosure" (Stewart & Williams, 2005, p. 411), and to specify in the consent document the nature of both the guarantee and risk.

A related possibility is that use of a search engine and a direct quote could lead to respondent identification. Because of the nature of qualitative data analysis, use of direct quotes is desirable for providing insight into the respondent's viewpoint. While search engines do "crawl" the Internet and store data (including direct quotes), website administrators can opt-out of such functions. Additionally, communities which require a username and password to access content tend to not be crawled. Using such websites and communities may negate this concern.

A final ethical issue raised by online data collection is the protection of research data throughout the life of the research project (Nicholas, 2010; Battles, 2010; Ayling & Mewse, 2009; Seymour, 2001). While many of the authors cited throughout this section mention the importance of protecting data after it is gathered, Ayling and Mewse (2010) specifically mention the practical issue of data interception during the online dyad. The authors mention the possibility of the discourse between the researcher and the respondent being gathered by an unauthorized third party. Ayling and Mewse suggest the usage of novel e-mail addresses not personally connected to the subject. A portion of the informed consent should include information about data interception and what measures have been taken to prevent it. Additionally, novel e-mail addresses could be used to send informed consent and register for communities and communication services unique to the research[1]. While this may offer protection during data transmission, several authors also cite the importance for maintaining data security after it is collected. This protection will likely be well known to seasoned researchers. Ayling and Mewse (2010), however, suggest keeping chat and message board transcripts in a locked file on a locked computer. Hardcopies and CD records of said transcripts should be kept in secure filing cabinets.

Each of the measures discussed here is intended to protect the respondent from harm. Sensitivity to perceptions of researcher intrusiveness, informed consent, protection of privacy, and data security are all facets of the same goal. There are other methods mentioned in the literature to safeguard respondents. Ayling and Mewse (2009), for example, conducted online interviews with gay men about online sex-seeking and sexual preferences. Clearly, this is a sensitive topic. In addition to fairly elaborate procedures to safeguard respondent privacy, the authors also offered "an online debrief" to their respondents to allow them "the opportunity to process their feelings about the interview" (p. 568) and suggested that future researchers might consider making transcripts available to participants for their review and reflection. The latter approach was used successfully by Bowker and Tuffin (2004) in their study of the online experiences of people with physical and sensory disabilities.

As Stewart & Williams (2005) observe: "old ethical guidelines and procedures must be revisited and reframed in this new style [of data collection], and anticipated carefully in the design stage of the research" (p. 410). We would add that the researcher also has the responsibility to make transparent to respondents, IRBs, and other researchers the ways in which the conventional guidelines and procedures have been reframed or adapted to the online setting.

CONCLUSION

There is much to recommend online interviews. Numerous advantages, or at least potential advantages, have been noted: the global reach of the Internet, the opportunity to connect with hard to access populations, the benefits of pseudo-anonymity for discussion of sensitive topics, the expanding set of online venues, the design flexibility afforded by additional interview modes, and cost savings over face-to-face interviews. In addition, asynchronous interviews allow the respondent to answer at their own pace, time, and location, and to consider, revise, and rewrite their responses. The latter can potentially result in what James and Busher (2006) refer to as an "enriched interview" (p. 406).

There is also a frequently mentioned "technical" advantage to online interviewing: text-based online interviews eliminate the need for transcription. In the words of Markham (2008), transcription becomes "no more difficult than cutting and pasting" (p. 255). Qualitative researchers who rely on audio recording of face-to-face interviews can attest to the drudgery and cost of transcription, and to its less obvious demands, such as deciding how to punctuate to preserve the speaker's meaning, how to deal with dialect, how to ensure systematic, standardized transcription decisions, and similar matters (e.g., McLellan, MacQueen, & Neidig, 2003; Warren & Karner, 2005). While the absence of "transcriber bias" is indeed valuable (Franklin & Lowry, 2001; Bowker & Tuffin, 2004), it is not without cost.

One of the strengths of qualitative research is researcher immersion in the study. Here we refer not only to immersion in the field, but also to immersion in the data. Painstakingly transcribing interviews is a time-honored way to become intimately knowledgeable about what the respondents have said. For some projects, researcher transcription of the data is worthwhile. And, of course, the researcher needs interview content to analyze. To the extent the data collection process generates a transcript that is superficial or truncated due to the method (by, say, using a chat room when more reflective narration is needed), nothing is gained. Several researchers have noted the difference in depth of interview information generated by the various online venues, as noted above, and researchers must take care in the selection of venue.

Online interviews present additional challenges. Asynchronous data collection can drag on for "weeks and months"; the same flexibility that allows respondents to reply when it is convenient for them can slow down the entire research project (James & Busher, 2006). More importantly, the digital divide is real, and members of existing online groups may deny or impede researcher access. Norms for online interaction are evolving and mediated by venue, and procedures for insuring protection of human subjects are still under development. In particular, the boundaries of public and private communication are blurred in online environments. Finally, the implications of these challenges and others for data quality are not fully understood.

Many of these issues are matters that arise because of the newness of the Internet – to both researchers and potential respondents. In our view, online research will soon be simply one of the options open to qualitative researchers and for some disciplines, it will become the norm for interview studies. Use of online interviews to learn from citizens and other stakeholders and to connect communities of interested parties seems particularly useful for urban studies. As access expands, so too will reliance on online methods for urban planning.

Caution in adopting online methods is still in order, however. It would be a serious mistake to think that mode and venue are simply technical decisions; both have implications for the nature and the quality of data or information generated. We agree with Ayling and Mewse (2009) that the challenges on online research "can be addressed with creative adjustments to and fuller preparation of existing methods" (p. 575). Overcoming these constraints will require that researchers consider the implications of using the Internet to recruit respondents and to collect data, and the fit between their own epistemological leanings and the options available to them. Finally, researchers need to make these considerations and their conclusions known to respondents, IRBs, and other researchers.

REFERENCES

Astrom, J., & Granberg, M. (2007). Urban planners, wired for change? Understanding elite support for e-participation. *Journal of Information Technology & Politics*, *4*(2), 63–77. doi:10.1080/19331680802076116

Ayling, R., & Mewse, A. J. (2009). Evaluating internet interviews with gay men. *Qualitative Health Research*, *19*(4), 566–576. doi:10.1177/1049732309332121

Battles, H. (2010). Exploring ethical and methodological issues in Internet-based research with adolescents. *International Journal of Qualitative Methods*, *9*(1), 27–39.

Borkan, B. (2010). The mode effect in mixed-mode surveys: Mail and Web surveys. *Social Science Computer Review*, *28*(3), 371–380. doi:10.1177/0894439309350698

Bowker, N., & Tuffin, K. (2004). Using the online medium for discursive research about people with disabilities. *Social Science Computer Review*, *22*(2), 228–241. doi:10.1177/0894439303262561

Council of European Social Science Data Archives (CESSDA). (2010). *Research Ethics*. Retrieved March 27, 2011, from http://www.cessda.org/sharing/rights/4/index.html

Denzin, N. K., & Lincoln, Y. S. (Eds.). (2008). *Collecting and Interpreting Qualitative Material*. Thousand Oaks, CA: Sage.

Ess, C.Association of Internet Researchers Ethics Working Committee. (2002). *Ethical decision-making and Internet research: Recommendations from the AoIR Ethics Working Committee*. Chicago, IL: Association of Internet Researchers.

Fielding, N., Lee, R. M., & Blank, G. (Eds.). (2008). *The Sage Handbook of Online Research Methods*. Los Angeles, CA: Sage.

Franklin, K. K., & Lowry, C. (2001). Computer-mediated focus groups sessions: Naturalistic inquiry in a networked environment. *Qualitative Research, 1*, 169–184. doi:10.1177/146879410100100204

Freed-Taylor, M. (1994). Ethical considerations in European cross-national research. *International Social Science Journal, 46*(4), 523–532.

Gies, L. (2008). How material are cyberbodies? Broadband Internet and embodied subjectivity. *Crime, Media, Culture, 4*, 311–330. doi:10.1177/1741659008096369

Graffigna, G., & Bosio, A. C. (2006). The influence of setting on findings produced in qualitative health research: A comparison between face-to-face and online discussion groups about HIV/AIDS. *International Journal of Qualitative Methods, 5*(3), 55–76.

Graiser, T. J. (2008). Online focus groups. In Fielding, N., Lee, R. M., & Blank, G. (Eds.), *The Sage Handbook of Online Research Methods* (pp. 290–306). Los Angeles, CA: Sage.

Hine, C. (2008). Virtual ethnography: Modes, varieties, affordances. In Fielding, N., Lee, R. M., & Blank, G. (Eds.), *The Sage Handbook of Online Research Methods* (pp. 257–268). Los Angeles, CA: Sage.

Holt, A. (2010). Using the telephone for narrative interviewing: A research note. *Qualitative Research, 10*(1), 113–121. doi:10.1177/1468794109348686

Holt, T. (2010). Exploring strategies for qualitative criminological and criminal justice inquiry using on-line data. *Journal of Criminal Justice Education, 21*(4), 466–487. doi:10.1080/10511253.2010.516565

Hookway, N. (2008). Entering the blogosphere: Some strategies for using blogs in social research. *Qualitative Research, 8*(1), 91–113. doi:10.1177/1468794107085298

Howard, T. L. J., & Gaborit, N. (2007). Using virtual environmental technology to improve public participation in urban planning process. *Journal of Urban Planning and Development, 133*(4), 233–241. doi:10.1061/(ASCE)0733-9488(2007)133:4(233)

James, N., & Busher, H. (2006). Credibility, authenticity and voice: Dilemmas in interviewing. *Qualitative Research, 6*(3), 403–420. doi:10.1177/1468794106065010

Kaliski, J. (2006). Democracy takes command: The new community planning and the challenge of urban design. In Saunders, W. (Ed.), *Urban Planning Today. A Harvard Design Magazine Reader* (pp. 24–37). Minneapolis, MN: University of Minnesota Press.

Komito, L. (2007). Community and inclusion: The impact of new communications technologies. *Irish Journal of Sociology, 16*(2), 77–96.

Lewis, J. (2009). Redefining Qualitative Methods: Believability in the Fifth Moment. *International Journal of Qualitative Methods, 8*(2). Retrieved September 4, 2010, from http://ejournals.library.ualberta.ca/index.php/IJQM/article/view/4408/5403

Markham, A. N. (2008). The methods, politics, and ethics of representation in online ethnography. In Denzin, N. K., & Lincoln, Y. S. (Eds.), *Collecting and Interpreting Qualitative Data* (pp. 247–284). Thousand Oaks, CA: Sage.

McKee, H. A., & Porter, J. E. (2009). *The ethics of Internet research: A rhetorical, case-based process*. New York, NY: Peter Lang.

McLellan, E., MacQueen, K. M., & Neidig, J. L. (2003). Beyond the Qualitative Interview: Data preparation and transcription. *Field Methods, 15*, 63–84. doi:10.1177/1525822X02239573

Nicholas, D. B., Lach, L., King, G., Scott, M., Boydell, K., & Sawatxky, B. (2010). Contrasting Internet and face-to-face focus groups for children with chronic health conditions: Outcomes and participant experiences. *International Journal of Qualitative Methods*, 9(1), 106–121.

O'Connor, H., Madge, C., Shaw, R., & Wellens, J. (2008). Internet-based Interviewing. In Fielding, N., Lee, R. M., & Blank, G. (Eds.), *The Sage Handbook of Online Research Methods* (pp. 271–289). Los Angeles, CA: Sage.

Rodriguez, N. (2010, July 26). Exactly how much are the times a changing? *Newsweek, 56*(17).

Sade-Beck, L. (2004). Internet ethnography: Online and offline. *International Journal of Qualitative Methods*, 3(2), 45–51.

Saunders, W. (Ed.). (2006). *Urban Planning Today: A Harvard Design Magazine Reader*. Minneapolis, MN: University of Minnesota Press.

Schroeder, R., & Bailenson, J. (2008). Research uses of multi-user virtual environments. In Fielding, N., Lee, R. M., & Blank, G. (Eds.), *The Sage Handbook of Online Research Methods* (pp. 327–342). Los Angeles, CA: Sage.

Seymour, W. S. (2001). In the flesh or online? Exploring qualitative research methodologies. *Qualitative Research*, 1(2), 147–168. doi:10.1177/146879410100100203

Shields, C. M. (2003). "Giving voice" to students: Using the Internet for data collection. *Qualitative Research*, 3(3), 397–414. doi:10.1177/1468794103033007

Stern, M. J., & Dillman, D. A. (2006). Community Participaton, Social Ties, and Use of the Internet. *City & Community*, 5(4), 409–422. doi:10.1111/j.1540-6040.2006.00191.x

Stewart, K., & Williams, M. (2005). Researching online populations: The use of online focus groups for social research. *Qualitative Research*, 5(4), 395–416. doi:10.1177/1468794105056916

Sturges, J. E., & Hanrahan, K. J. (2004). Comparing telephone and face-to-face qualitative interviewing: a research note. *Qualitative Research*, 4(1), 107–118. doi:10.1177/1468794104041110

Warren, C., & Karner, T. (2005). The interview as social interaction and speech event. In Warren, C., & Karner, T. (Eds.), *Discovering qualitative methods: Field research, interviews, and analysis* (pp. 137–155). Los Angeles, CA: Roxbury Publishing.

ADDITIONAL READING

Borkan, B. (2010). The mode effect in mixed-mode surveys: Mail and Web surveys. *Social Science Computer Review*, 28(3), 371–380. doi:10.1177/0894439309350698

Bowker, N., & Tuffin, K. (2004). Using the online medium for discursive research about people with disabilities. *Social Science Computer Review*, 22(2), 228–241. doi:10.1177/0894439303262561

Denzin, N. K., & Lincoln, Y. S. (Eds.). (2008). *Collecting and Interpreting Qualitative Material*. Thousand Oaks, CA: Sage.

Ess, C. & the Association of Internet Researchers Ethics Working Committee (2002). *Ethical decision-making and Internet research: Recommendations from the AoIR Ethics Working Committee*.

Fielding, N., Lee, R. M., & Blank, G. (Eds.). (2008). *The Sage Handbook of Online Research Methods*. Los Angeles: Sage.

Franklin, K. K., & Lowry, C. (2001). Computer-mediated focus groups sessions: Naturalistic inquiry in a networked environment. *Qualitative Research*, 1, 169–184. doi:10.1177/146879410100100204

Gies, L. (2008). How material are cyberbodies? Broadband Internet and embodied subjectivity. *Crime, Media, Culture, 4*, 311–330. doi:10.1177/1741659008096369

Graffigna, G., & Bosio, A. C. (2006). The influence of setting on findings produced in qualitative health research: A comparison between face-to-face and online discussion groups about HIV/AIDS. *International Journal of Qualitative Methods, 5*(3), 55–76.

Hine, C. (2008). Virtual ethnography: Modes, varieties, affordances. In Fielding, N., Lee, R. M., & Blank, G. (Eds.), *The Sage Handbook of Online Research Methods*. Los Angeles: Sage.

Hookway, N. (2008). Entering the blogosphere: Some strategies for using blogs in social research. *Qualitative Research, 8*(1), 91–113. doi:10.1177/1468794107085298

Howard, T. L. J., & Gaborit, N. (2007). Using virtual environmental technology to improve public participation in urban planning process. *Journal of Urban Planning and Development, 133*(4), 233–241. doi:10.1061/(ASCE)0733-9488(2007)133:4(233)

James, N., & Busher, H. (2006). Credibility, authenticity and voice: Dilemmas in interviewing. *Qualitative Research, 6*(3), 403–420. doi:10.1177/1468794106065010

Komito, L. (2007). Community and inclusion: The impact of new communications technologies. *Irish Journal of Sociology, 16*(2), 77–96.

Lewis, J. (2009). Redefining Qualitative Methods: Believability in the Fifth Moment. International Journal of Qualitative Methods, 8(2). Retrieved September 4, 2010, from http://ejournals.library.ualberta.ca/index.php/IJQM/article/view/4408/5403

Markham, A. N. (2008). The methods, politics, and ethics of representation in online ethnography. In N. K. Denzin and Y. S. Lincoln, Eds. *Collecting and Interpreting Qualitative Data* (247-284). Thousand Oaks, CA, Sage.

McKee, H. A., & Porter, J. E. (2009). *The ethics of Internet research: A rhetorical, case-based process*. New York: Peter Lang.

Nicholas, D. B., Lach, L., King, G., Scott, M., Boydell, K., & Sawatxky, B. (2010). Contrasting Internet and face-to-face focus groups for children with chronic health conditions: Outcomes and participant experiences. *International Journal of Qualitative Methods, 9*(1), 106–121.

O'Connor, H., Madge, C., Shaw, R., & Wellens, J. (2008). Internet-based Interviewing. In N. Fielding, R. M. Lee, and G. Blank. *The Sage Handbook of Online Research* (271-289). Los Angeles, Sage.

Sade-Beck, L. (2004). Internet ethnography: Online and offline. *International Journal of Qualitative Methods, 3(2)*, 45-51.

Seymour, W. S. (2001). In the flesh or online? Exploring qualitative research methodologies. *Qualitative Research, 1*(2), 147–168. doi:10.1177/146879410100100203

Warren, C., & Karner, T. (2005). The interview as social interaction and speech event. In C. Warren and T. Karner, Eds. *Discovering qualitative methods: Field research, interviews, and analysis (*137-155). Los Angeles, Roxbury Publishing.

KEY TERMS AND DEFINITIONS

Asynchronous Interviews: Interviews conducted over a period of time; interviewer and interviewee respond not at the same time, but sequentially, as time permits; the interview may be conducted over an extended time period.

Digital Divide: A term used to describe the uneven distribution of access to digital technology and the skills needed to use it effectively. Some people have ready access to both equipment and knowledge; others have little or no access.

Interview Mode: The manner in which the interview is designed, including both whether the interview relies on face to face contact, or contact mediated by electronic means (telephone, computer), and whether the interview is conducted one to one or in a group setting.

Online Interviews: Interviews conducted through electronic means rather than in person.

Online Venue: One of several available means of contacting others via the Internet; including but not limited to: forums, blogs, chat rooms, listservs, social networking sites, and many others.

Reactivity: The influence that the data collection method has on the information gathered; related to method and mode.

Synchronous Interviews: Interviews conducted in real time; such that both interviewer and interviewee are responding to each other immediately and in the same time period.

ENDNOTE

[1] Such a service might include X-IM (http://x-im.net), suggested by Ayling and Mewse (2010). X-IM is an anonymous chat client that provides a high degree of information security between communication partners (256 bit protection).

Chapter 5
Towards a Method for Research Interviews using E-Mail

Peter Petocz
Macquarie University, Australia

Sue Gordon
The University of Sydney, Australia

Anna Reid
The University of Sydney, Australia

ABSTRACT

Researching people's ideas and experiences of Urban and Planning Studies can be carried out in a variety of ways, but the most obvious is to ask them. This can be done qualitatively, using semi-structured or unstructured interviews, at an early stage of the research process, when it is important to explore participants' ideas prior to any quantitative investigation, or for investigations where in-depth and detailed information about individual thinking is important. Face-to-face interviews are a 'gold standard' against which other qualitative methods of investigation can be compared. However, contemporary developments in technology provide a wider range of opportunities for qualitative researchers to collect rich data for analysis. Such technologies enable participation from any part of the world at any time, and allow the collection of video material that can capture many aspects of verbal and non-verbal interaction for further analysis. The use of e-mail interviews provides a relatively low-tech methodology for investigations and has advantages over a live interview, on the one hand, and a high-tech video interview, on the other.

INTRODUCTION

In this chapter, we present an approach to using e-mail for carrying out semi-structured interviews. We have developed this approach during the course of conducting several research projects in the area of pedagogy, using students and lecturers as participants. We will trace our approach from initial, serendipitous e-mail interviews to the development of a mature e-mail interview protocol. We illustrate the various stages with several excerpts from our interviews. In addition, we have asked some of our lecturer respondents what they think about e-mail interviews and how

DOI: 10.4018/978-1-4666-0074-4.ch005

they view the relationship between interviews and online pedagogies. We include an analysis of their reactions and insights. We review advantages and disadvantages compared to both live interviews and high(er)-tech approaches involving online video interviewing using tools such as Skype.

Face-to-face interviews are synchronous in time and space lending themselves to spontaneous and responsive interactions between interviewer and interviewees. Other interview methods that are synchronous in time but not space are interviews that take place by telephone, or use computer mediated communication, such as MSN messenger, a chat room or Skype. Each of these methods has relative advantages and disadvantages to the researcher, such as whether interviews can be standardised, how important social cues are for interpretation of communication and what disruptions or distractions the interviewee is likely to experience during the interview. For instance, in a telephone interview, the interviewer has no view of the respondent's environment, while a video interview may enable a remote researcher to see more of the respondent's situation.

Web-based technologies for communication and content creation are widespread among the 'Net Generation' (Gray, Chang, & Kennedy, 2010). Online activities in higher education and daily life include blogging, using wikis, media authoring and publishing, socialising and other formal or informal virtual interaction. In universities, course management systems such as Blackboard are common resources that support learning of distance students as well as learning on-campus. Web-based technologies are also integral to many current research projects in education, particularly when participants are geographically or temporally remote, or diverse in some way, such as mobility or hearing impaired. The internet as a data-gathering tool is perhaps most commonly used for surveys and questionnaires, as current software enables both collection and statistical analysis to be carried out with relative ease. Online, open-ended questions may be less successful in eliciting full

responses from participants, depending on the particular format used (Denham, 2004).

BACKGROUND

Research approaches in the field of Urban and Planning Studies closely mirror those in the broad field of social research. They often incorporate statistical analyses – particularly for market research projects – but also utilise qualitative approaches, such as interview studies or observations or a combination of different methods, to illuminate different aspects of the problem under investigation. For instance, Popkin, Leventhal, and Weismann (2010) explored the difficulties faced by female adolescents growing up in high-poverty neighbourhoods. They approached their sensitive research topic by the random allocation of families to three different treatment groups. Following the seven-year experimental phase, 1000 families participated in an evaluation process, which incorporated semi-structured interviews with family members and an ethnographic study involving a subset of the families. The research team considered their approach to be 'family focused' (p. 724) as it utilised a variety of different methods to build a broad picture of the researched situation. The role of interviews in this study was to add richness to the complex problems involved in urban poverty. Martin (2004) also described a mixed-methods approach to researching neighbourhood activism. In her study, the mix utilised (quantitative) archival analysis of documents and (qualitative) interviews. Her analysis of the documents uncovered two different philosophies surrounding land use, which then led to an appreciation of alternate views obtained by speaking with people. She claims that 'much of urban politics involves the interactions of these spaces' (p. 593) acknowledging the complex diversity of views.

For qualitative researchers a major focus is on the collection of diverse views and subjecting these views to some form of analysis. Although live interviews with individuals or groups are the simplest and most common ways of gathering qualitative research data, the qualitative research interview is a "very artificial" situation, comment Myers and Newman (2007, p. 3). The researcher is usually talking to a stranger and asking questions that require immediate answers. The researcher may be intruding or potentially interfering with people's behaviour or changing it – possibly merely by conducting the interview. The interviewees may not be representative of the broader group in a given situation and the language used may be ambiguous. Further, as Myers and Newman maintain, the face-to-face interview is largely unexamined and the interview process is treated as unproblematic. To help solve some of these problems and sensitise the interviewer to the complexity of the interview process, these researchers suggest the metaphor of the research interview as drama, with actors, stage, props, a script and a performance.

Developments in technology have suggested some refinements to the collection of interview data. For instance, the advent of the telephone offered the possibility of a form of randomness to interviews (and hence a form of scientific validity loaned from quantitative methods). Telephone interviews also have the practical benefit of allowing an investigator to collect data from respondents in distant or dangerous places (Opdenakker, 2006). However, we must question the *form* of the interview undertaken; in many cases, telephone interviews are simply short responses to a read questionnaire, while others are more conversational, and probe particular points. More recently, the computer has supported different forms of synchronous and asynchronous interactions. Hamilton and Bowers (2006) claim that it is easy to adapt interviewing techniques to e-mail format (p. 822), developing one more skill in the "craftsmanship of interviewing" (p. 827). We would contest the concept of 'ease' by suggesting instead that e-mail interviews need to

be carefully planned and executed to allow rich data to be collected.

E-mail, as a qualitative research tool, was critiqued more than a decade ago by Selwyn and Robson (1998), who pointed out positive features such as convenience and ease of use, a potentially less biased or coercive setting than in face-to-face communication, and logistic advantages such as eliminating transcription with an associated reduction in researcher time and errors. They noted that at that time the method was constrained by the limited demographic of computer users. Kivits (2005) described a project in which she used e-mail to interview volunteer 'online health information seekers'. She highlighted the importance of building and maintaining an online rapport with respondents in order to collect rich interview data, continually balancing personal and research information. Her interviews were open-ended, some lasting up to a year, with as many as 40 e-mail interchanges, a few finishing abruptly after a few exchanges, sometimes for unspecified reasons. More recently, Ison (2009) has reported that interviewing people with impaired verbal communication by e-mail can increase opportunities for participant involvement and enhance the authenticity and inclusiveness of research data. This is particularly important for sociological researchers, who need ways of collecting qualitative data to understand the needs of people living with serious health issues or disabilities, who might be excluded by telephone, video or other 'live' interview methods.

In their self-described "serendipitous comparative opportunity" (p. 389), McCoyd and Schwaber Kerson (2006) explored women's experiences of decision-making around the bereavement process using telephone and face-to-face interview methods. During the course of their study, they found that some women preferred an e-mail interview for the sake of convenience, and also for a perceived anonymity. However Hamilton and Bowers (2006) suggest that such anonymity may lead to a form of 'data fraud' (p. 824), with participants able to take on alternate identities during the interview. However, we argue that any interview relies on the authenticity of participant responses whether face-to-face or electronically mediated. Like the studies described in this chapter, McCoyd and Schwaber Kerson used similar questions in e-mail interviews to other interview methods. They found that they were able to access a broader spectrum of respondents, including those who were geographically separated from the interview and those where were "socially-silenced" (p. 390). To recruit participants they used a 'listserv', an electronic mailing list that gave them access to a group of the possible target population who were already comfortable communicating electronically. The researchers carried out the interviews by sending batches of two or three questions, customised for each respondent. They concluded that, apart from the obvious practical advantage of having the interview already transcribed, "there seems to be a sense of privacy or safety that allows greater disclosure of intimate and stigmatizing information" (p. 397).

Participants' views about taking part in e-mail interviewing in two independent studies were summarised by James and Busher (2006). An advantage of the method perceived by their respondents was control of when they would respond, maybe after time for reflection. Disadvantages included difficulty in understanding a question or getting clarification, distractions of everyday life, lack of social signals and problems associated with receiving e-mail questions one at a time, including concerns about how many questions there would be in total. Methodological issues discussed by these researchers related to credibility of their interpretations of the e-mails, questions about the reflexivity of responses and consideration of the authenticity of the voices. Further, as an e-mail address identifies the respondent, James and Busher point out that issues of confidentiality and other ethical concerns need to be addressed with care. An unusual dilemma encountered by Illingworth (2001) in investigating sensitive women's issues

by e-mail was how to achieve closure for both researcher and respondent, as participants could – and did – continue to send e-mail communications to the researcher long after the conclusion of the investigation. Illingworth's report challenges the view that online research is an 'easy option' that automatically leads to success.

TOWARDS A METHOD FOR E-MAIL INTERVIEWS

First Attempts

Our first experiences with using e-mail for carrying out interviews came about by serendipity, when potential interviewees whom we were trying to contact were unavailable for a face-to-face meeting – Bampton and Cowton (2002) described a similar situation. In a project investigating mathematics students' and recent graduates' conceptions of mathematics (Reid *et al.*, 2003; Petocz & Reid, 2006), one of the graduates – Maya – who had agreed to be interviewed had recently moved from Sydney to London. The interview proceeded in much the same way as any live interview, starting from a list of predetermined questions and following threads based on the answers. There was an obvious awareness of distance and different time zones, as the following excerpt shows (Example 1), and we hoped that Maya's multitasking (work, TV, interview) did not affect the quality of the results!

Example 1

Interviewer: What do you think mathematics is about?

Maya: Was that your 1st question? I see what you mean by broad questions! Could you explain what you mean by that?

Int: Yes that was the first question. What do you think mathematics is about? It is, yes, very broad. Maybe, what do you think is important about mathematics? Or how would you want to explain mathematics to someone who is not an expert?

Maya: To explain it to someone who doesn't know about maths I'd say something along the lines of mathematics is the study of the measurement, properties, and relationships of quantities and sets, using numbers and symbols. I think mathematics is a way to train your mind to be more logical.

Int: Thank you. (How's it going there, if you start to feel that this is taking too long at any point please let me know and we could adjourn or something).

Maya: That's fine, I'm watching TV and doing work at the same time so your questions are a welcome break.

Int: I hope you got the email I sent about twenty minutes ago ... and this one too. It's going well, your answers so far have been very helpful. I'm going to have to go home now, because I'm falling asleep on the computer. I'll send you a few more questions now (we're a good way through what I wanted to talk about).

Maya: I got the one twenty minutes ago and I replied to it about ten minutes ago. If it hasn't arrived tomorrow, then please let me know and I'll resend it.

A trap with interviews carried out electronically is to formulate the potential exchange like a survey: the respondent answers the questions but the exchange does not invite any further questions or discussion. An early interview carried out in a project investigating business students' views of graduate dispositions such as creativity, ethics and sustainability (Reid *et al*., 2006) showed this problem (Example 2). Luke answered the series of questions that had been sent to him by e-mail, interleaving his responses with the questions (that originally had empty lines between them). There were no relation-building comments from the interviewer, and no invitation to further discourse

from the respondent: the result was a fairly sparse interview (though the responses were longer than the 10-word average quoted by Denham, 2004, for such situations).

Example 2

Interviewer: Thanks again for choosing to participate in our research project. I want to remind you that there are no right or wrong answers; I just want to know what you think, so reply at your own pace. Here are the questions:

Q1: What aspects of university study do you think will be of most use to you when you go to work?

Luke: The fact that I speak a language fluently will help me. The network I have built up. The courses attended. Pretty much everything I think.

Q2: How will that be useful in your future work?

Luke: I will have great understanding of teamwork. The fact of dealing with people from many different religions, cultures and countries. But also maybe a different approach to things compared to normal back home.

Q3: How do you understand the idea of creativity?

Luke: Creativity is one of the things I believe to be my greatest assets. To me creativity is all about being able to think, come up with new thoughts and ideas. Being innovative so to speak.

Q4: What role do you think creativity will play in your future professional work?

Luke: I think it will play very important part. In today's hyper competitive workforce, you will have a great advantage if you are able to be creative and come up with new solutions to problems.

Q12: How do you think these notions prepare you for professional work?

Luke: I believe that all of the issues above are issues you will come across in your worklife at one time or another. Maybe everyday even. So it is important to know what they are about and what you can do to solve it in the best ways possible.

In this project, around one-quarter of the 44 participants took up our offer of e-mail interviews. To get around the problems identified in the interview with Luke, in following interviews the interviewer sent questions in small batches, including follow-up questions based on the previous responses. This resulted in more interactive (and longer) interviews.

An Enhanced Approach

The first project in which we intentionally developed a method of e-mail interviewing was an investigation of international statistics educators' views on teaching and learning statistics as a service course (Gordon, Reid & Petocz, 2007). Participation was invited through an electronic request to the membership of the International Association for Statistics Education (IASE) and various Australian bulletin boards: interviews were conducted with 36 IASE members from 14 countries and with 9 Australian educators. We decided that the e-mail format would be familiar to the participating academics and that it would be convenient for disparate geographical locations and time zones.

The interview protocol, communicated in invitations to potential participants, consisted of an initial series of six questions with a maximum of two further rounds of questions. This sets a definite limit on the interview, a requirement from our ethics committee, and avoids the problems associated with completely open-ended plans (such as that of Kivits, 2005). The first question asked for details of participants' backgrounds, while the remaining five initial questions were posed in a deliberately open way to enable the participants to explore their own ideas rather than respond to direction from the researchers: they were all sent at the same time, and represented the formal start of the interview. After studying

the initial reply, we sent a second interview with questions that probed each participant's specific responses. Finally, a third interview allowed us to clarify previous responses. Examples of initial questions were: *What do you think makes a good statistics student? What are the attributes of a good statistics teacher at university?* Some follow-up questions were: *What advice would you give to a junior colleague starting to teach statistics as a servicing course? How do you teach students to evaluate statistics in the media?* We also requested in the final interchange feedback from participants about the process of e-mail interviewing from their perspectives. The interview process was a written version of the usual face-to-face interview, but at each point in the process participants had access to all previous parts of the interview, and both interviewers and respondents could continue the dialogue in their own time. The IASE study resulted in over 70 000 words of interview record, including questions and responses.

Example 3 shows an extract from our interview with Coach (his choice of pseudonym), who teaches upper division undergraduate and graduate students, most of whom are not statistics majors, in the life sciences at a large U.S. university. We conducted the interviews in the 'nested' format shown below: the first round of questions (Q3) and responses (R3) was followed by a second-round (Q3a, R3a) and then maybe a third-round (Q3a-i, R3a-i). At each stage, the e-mail was sent to respondents with the new questions inserted into the text in the appropriate place, and the replies were typed underneath them to produce a final document like the excerpt shown below. We pick up Coach's final interview at the third question.

Example 3

Q3: What do you think makes a good statistics student?

R3: Interest in learning to think rather than to memorize.

Q3a: Why do you think (some) students want to memorize?

R3a: I think students only want to memorize because that has been their conditioning in the past. That is all they were asked to do and they were conditioned that memorization = learning.

Q3b: What could you do with a group of students who seemed more interested in memorizing rather than thinking?

R3b: Dealing with students who only want to memorize is the biggest challenge and is a very common situation. I approach this situation by posing interesting questions from current events. For example, we examined the probability of six hurricanes hitting Florida in a given year if the average number of hurricanes per year is .5. Many statistical concepts can be incorporated into the discussion and it makes the ideas real for the students. Then they are motivated to move from memorization to thinking.

Q3a/b-i: In previous interviews that we have carried out, students have identified at least two other reasons for memorizing (rather than thinking/understanding) - first, it is sometimes a way of getting better marks; second, it is sometimes a way of handling a high workload (maybe an unreasonably high one). Would you have any comments on these reasons?

R3a/b-i: I certainly agree that those are among the reasons for the "memorization approach" to teaching and learning. That process is easy for the instructor and easy for the student. Therefore, it is used frequently. It is all driven by objectives and assessment. If the student's objective is to get a diploma with the least effort and the instructor's objective is to hand out diplomas with the least effort, then memorization pedagogy works for both. This will be acceptable as long as mastery of the material is measured by lower level cognitive skills. However, if higher levels of cognitive ability are measured, then neither the instructor nor the students will be satisfied.

This e-mail interview displays the discursive quality and the ability to explore issues in depth that are characteristic of a face-to-face interview. It is interesting to observe how the interview 'opens out': Coach's response to the main question looks like a standard quick response to an open-ended survey question, but by R3b he is writing in a much more open and personal style that indicates greater engagement with the questions. The discussion in the last question and response (labelled 3a/b-i, since it seemed to be equally appropriate as a follow-up to 3a and 3b) has become quite expansive. The format of the nested interview, with previous questions and responses available in each e-mail, allowed both Coach and the interviewer to recall and analyse previous interactions. In this important sense, it was quite *unlike* a face-to-face interview where *both* people rely on recall to pose and respond to questions.

A Mature Protocol

We used our experience and feedback from the IASE project to develop a mature protocol for carrying out research using e-mail interviews. We kept the successful features of the earlier study: sending potential participants' information about the interviewing process utilising a maximum of three cycles; starting with a small number of key initial questions and allowing the conversation to unfold according to the responses, directed by the interviewer; asking participants to choose their own pseudonym. We also followed previous logistical processes: sending a gentle reminder if responses had not been received in a reasonable time and setting a cut-off date for closure of interviews; sending participants a final e-mail thanking them for their participation, and then later, alerting them to any presentation or publication of the results.

We also included our format of 'nesting' or interleaving the questions and responses so that participants could review the thread of the conversation, despite the fact that a few respondents had found it difficult to navigate. However, we improved the format by using different coloured fonts for each level of question and response. This allows respondents to easily identify new or follow-up questions inserted into their previous responses, and becomes a useful analytic tool for helping the researchers understand the context of each response during later analyses.

We utilised this mature protocol in a project that we have called Teaching Approaches in Diverse Disciplines (TADD). Here, we interviewed university teachers, at both undergraduate and postgraduate levels, from a variety of professional areas, to investigate how they introduced students to their particular discipline and thence to the professions based on those disciplines. Most of the participants (22) were teacher educators working in Australia or overseas in a various disciplines including early childhood education, indigenous education, primary education, secondary education (disciplines included visual arts, environment, psychology, IT, science and language) and adult professional education. A smaller number of participants (12) represented a range of disciplines, including accounting, engineering, nursing, biology, mathematics and statistics. We have described the project more fully in Reid, Petocz, and Gordon (2010), investigating the range of ways in which lecturers introduce their field to students; and we have analysed participants' views of diversity in a later paper (Gordon, Reid, & Petocz, 2010).

The format of questions and responses was similar to the IASE project described earlier (though with entirely different questions). For example, two first-round questions were: *How do you go about introducing students to your discipline? How does student diversity influence learning and teaching in your classes?* Some

follow-up questions based on participants' responses were: *Could you give an example of a recent activity that you felt worked well? What are the pedagogical issues that are particularly important in teaching literacy for teachers? How does technology affect your teaching? How do you stimulate or challenge the more advanced students?* Again, participants – interviewer and respondent – were able to review previous parts of the interview, and continue the dialogue in their own time. The TADD study resulted in over 85 000 words of interview record, which includes questions as well as responses.

Below is an example of an interchange taken from the interview with Stark, who teaches academic practice and curriculum design at a university in the UK (Example 4). He is describing his approach to introducing his field of education. Our original questions and responses were in different colours: here we have indicated the three levels of questioning by indents. Only the first part of the interchange is shown here – there are more sub-questions and responses, and the full interview is almost 5000 words.

Example 4

Q3: What teaching approaches or methods do you use which are particularly helpful?

R3: Presentation of input ideas in a way, which should make them interesting, attractive – and fun. I warmed to the student recently who told me that he had responded to a challenge I suggested in his module design activity because he 'thought it would be fun to try it out'. It proved worthwhile – and I hope was fun. Questioning by me, and increasingly by peers and students, of what then emerges when they actively experiment with the input ideas.

Q3a: How do you encourage students to take risks in their learning?

R3a: (1) By making it safe to do so, (2) by making it an expectation of the course, (3) by valuing the way the risk is tackled, rather than the eventual success.

Q3a-i: Is risk-taking important for teachers in Higher Education too, and if so, how can this be encouraged?

R3a-i: Hey, you ask searching questions.

Of course it is important for teachers. If we don't try things we haven't done before, then we will never progress. Tackling the unknown is a risk; we can easily fail through lack of expertise or experience, or attempts to transfer the non-transferable. Even if someone else has done it before, then there are still these risks.

If it's not been done before, then the risks are massive. I think of two examples – sorry, examples again. When I negotiated with twelve students to run a 'course' (25% of their studies) in which they would each set their own aim, plan their own programme, set their own criteria, mark their own work – and submit the mark which would have a major influence on the class of degree they would receive – *that* was scary. Often.

Next we present a somewhat longer excerpt (Example 5) from our interview with 'Rfp' (as before, his choice of pseudonym), a lecturer in civil engineering and design at a university in the UK. Again, we have used indentation to show the level of questioning (our original use of colour is more immediately noticeable). Rfp's response to the original question 4 leads us to pose two further questions (4a and 4b), and his response to 4a generates two further questions (4a-i and 4a-ii). This is what the record looks like after the third and final round.

Example 5

Q4: How does student diversity influence learning and teaching in your classes?

R4: By promoting cooperation in small groups, using triads and peer review of work before

it is submitted, I hope to diffuse and share the strengths of the differences between students. I draw their attention to their diversity and suggest that this is a strength the class can use. Our teaching staff are also diverse, in their nationalities at least, (5 nationalities in 9 staff).

Q4a: We are interested in this idea of diffusing or sharing strengths. Could you expand on this or describe an experience (or experiences) of students' differences being a resource or strength the class could draw on?

R4a: Three areas of differences stand out. Mathematics, drawing, and use of English language. Group work usually enables people to use their strengths, and the need to check others' work enables skill sharing to take place.

Q4a-i: What do you see as the effects of skill sharing in groups where students have different mathematical backgrounds?

R4a-i: The strong students have their skills enhanced by having to explain it to the weaker students. The weaker students will at least see that something is achievable if they work at it. At this level, nobody has a mathematical ceiling that cannot be raised with the right attention, even if that is from fellow students.

Q4a-ii: And in groups where there are a range of skills in using English?

R4a-ii: Sometimes, in group work, the best writer takes charge of a group report, and the weaker students do not benefit so much.

Q4b: How do the diverse nationalities or backgrounds of staff influence the learning and teaching in the course?

R4b: Universities (like any institution) have enabling and well as disabling attributes. The differences enable variety and a spread of approaches, attitudes and values. The disabling aspect of that is the difficulty of the staff having a coordinated uniformity in their approach. In recent years, the university itself has at least established rules for assessment, etc., as have many others around the world, perhaps encouraged by the need for credit transfer systems.

Due to space limitations, we have used some of the shorter interchanges to illustrate our protocol. In our research, text around a question and its sub-questions sometimes resulted in well over 1000 words. In some cases participants included extra documents, such as curriculum outlines, in their interview records.

CRITIQUE OF A METHOD FOR E-MAIL INTERVIEWS

In this section, we present our evaluation of this approach to e-mail interviews and some reactions that we have gathered from our participants (as part of the interviews themselves). This critique could inform urban and planning studies researchers who may be considering whether to use this approach in their own research projects. While we have worked hard to hone our approach, it is very likely that improvements could be made, particularly to tailor the method to specific research projects and contexts.

We start with a brief discussion of important ethical issues: informed consent, transparency and confidentiality. All participants of our e-mail interview projects gave informed consent. This involved the researchers applying for ethics approval from the University of Sydney's Human Research Ethics Committee. A Participant Information Statement provided a clear statement of the aims of the research, and assured potential interviewees that they were not under any obligation to consent and – if they did consent – could withdraw at any time without affecting any relationship with the researchers or institution. Authenticity and credibility were enhanced by the opportunity for both participants and interviewers to reflect on the responses given, and to use them as a basis for constructing further questions and responses.

As part of the process to ensure trustworthiness (Lincoln & Guba, 1985), respondents were asked to choose their own pseudonyms: in this way confidentiality of individuals was protected in published reports on the project. In addition, respondents could identify and follow their own contributions from the interviews to the disseminated findings, which, we believe, increased participants' engagement with the project. Our process was that one researcher removed information identifying each participant (and moved responses into Word documents) before sharing the records with the team. The follow-up questions were then put together with researchers working only with respondents' pseudonyms; each member of the research team taking primary responsibility for some interviews. This partially addressed possible problems with researcher bias: if resources for an administrative assistant had been available, all interviewers could have been blinded to the identity of the participants.

Currently, one of the authors is involved in another research project using this e-mail interview protocol to investigate coordinators', teachers' and students' experiences of mathematics bridging courses (Gordon & Nicholas, 2010). In this project, issues of power and coercion are particularly sensitive, since some participating tutors are in an employer/employee relationship and some students are in a student/teacher relationship with the researchers, though it is clearly specified that the researchers have no role in students' assessments or grades for their degrees.

We now move to a consideration of our participants' critique of the interviews. As a final question, we asked all participants in the IASE project (and some of those in the TADD project) for their views on their participation in these e-mail interviews.

When we analysed their responses, several themes emerged (Reid *et al.*, 2008). Participants commented on the logistics of carrying out an e-mail interview, discussing the time it took versus the convenience of being able to pick up the interview when they chose. Many were positive about the opportunities for reflection on previous questions and responses, and even modification of earlier responses. Some of those with other-language backgrounds appreciated the time to formulate their comments in English. In comparison with face-to-face interviews, some participants noted that there was a lack of visual cues and a personal touch, but others felt that the interviews were more carefully structured and promoted less inhibited answers. In comparison to e-mailed (or paper-based) questionnaires, respondents appreciated the fact that their responses were not constrained to predetermined categories, and could be explored in depth in later rounds of questioning. Some noted the benefit that no transcription was required, and commented that the process works as long as the respondent is interested and motivated. Many participants felt (from their own inputs) that the researchers would collect detailed and useful information, and made positive comments on the quality of questions probing their responses. A representative selection of comments is given in Example 6 (in response to the question shown, which was identical for all participants in the IASE study).

Example 6

Question: We are interested in the process of carrying out such interviews using e-mails. Can you give us any comments about the interview from the point of view of a respondent?

Horace: It seems to me good, and efficient. I can reply in my own time, at whatever length I wish. You can get back to me if you wish… etc. I've carried out e-mail surveys on statistical topics, and a couple of internet-based studies in which participation was requested by e-mail. So I'd be interested to hear how this e-mail interviewing works out, for your research.

Ron Fisher: I certainly had no problem with using e-mail for the study. To be honest, it's hard for me to imagine how else it could have been done.

Andrew: I have found this exercise OK. It has taken a lot of time but I am interested to see what comes of your research and to see how some of my old-fashioned views differ from what others are doing now. … Before I returned my responses to you I did read through them and adapt my quickly written response where appropriate. I usually did this the following day.

Henry VIII: I think the idea is excellent, though it probably means a lot of work to you. You seem to invest a lot of thought in your follow-up questions.

Margaret: The fact that you provided my original responses and asked subsequent questions based on those was good. It gave me a chance to reflect on what I had said and think more fully about my original response. This is exactly what would be done in a face to face interview, except that the interviewee would not have a copy of what they said as additional questions were being asked.

Some of these comments are reminiscent of the participant in McCoyd and Schwaber Kerson's study (2006, p. 398) who commented: 'Actually, I prefer to continue the interview via e-mail since it gives me time to think and write.' In our studies, several participants commented that the process of interaction by e-mail was familiar to them from their own on-line teaching or electronic communication with students. Heintje, a teacher of statistics to psychology students in distance mode in the Netherlands, explains this point in Example 7.

Example 7

Just like in a CSCL [computer-supported collaborative learning] you're challenged to express yourself verbally without the support of gestures, mimics and so on. On the other hand, because of the time delay, you can think about the question more thoroughly and deeper and formulate the answers more exactly (especially, when English is your second language). In Holland it happens more often that interviews are carried out this way. Personally I feel very comfortable using this method of exchanging information and personal experiences or opinions.

Unexpectedly, several participants reported a range of benefits to themselves: some said that they were motivated to articulate and record their views, others mentioned that participation stimulated their interest in their own teaching, or even in conducting their own pedagogical research. John, a teacher of introductory statistics at a New Zealand university and a participant in the IASE project, wrote the response shown in Example 8 as the last part of a detailed interview of over 4000 words.

Example 8

I have just had a read over what I have sent to you on the two previous occasions – the act of writing down (albeit very raw, without editing and lacking any form of polish) of my views on some of this stuff has been good for me. I do little or no formal research as such, and hence do very little recording or writing about where I am at as an intro stats educator. Just as one of the main by-products of our in-house discussions about our teaching is that such activities act as a source of enthusiasm and motivation/inspiration juice, so I have felt that happen here with this activity. So, time consuming as this exercise has been, there has been that personal positive by-product involved here too (especially at this stage where I can re-read what I wrote last week/month).

Each of the last two sets of responses has taken about two to three hours and that is a bit of a demand especially for us at this time of the year. So mainly because of the time constraint I was restricted to the amount that I wrote and

then because of that restriction there is the risk of what I have written is not clear, or even worse, is incorrectly understood. I particularly felt this about Q2. Felt a real strong urge to write you and say "hey, give me a ring and I will talk with you about this for half an hour or so." Perhaps a combo of both – email the initial questions out so that we get a time to see them in advance and then a phone interview? I will be very interested to see what you people write about as a result of this process.

CONCLUSION

Our experiences with e-mail interviewing suggest that there are two dimensions of this methodology that are noteworthy. Firstly, e-mail interviews are an efficient and effective means of collecting and recording qualitative data – a useful way for researchers to communicate with participants. We note with Ison (2009) that an overwhelming benefit of this method remains its capacity to facilitate participation in research by individuals who are unable to participate in face-to-face interviews for any reason. Secondly, and equally importantly, the e-mail interviews provide respondents with a tool for structured reflection. In this latter respect the activity is similar to writing a journal, but unlike keeping a journal, participants are not constrained or even discouraged (Otienoh, 2010) by a sense of being assessed on their entries.

Our process of e-mail interviewing allowed us to construct a dialogue with our respondents: this notion of the interview as a (specific type of) conversation was explored by Kvale (1996, ch. 2) in his influential book *InterViews*. Here, he identified 'daily life' conversations, in which the attention is on the topic and the structure is unexamined, 'professional' conversations (such as a legal examination or a therapeutic interview), which have a specific purpose and explicit methodology, but also may have a power asymmetry, and 'philosophical' conversations in which the participants are on an equal footing and jointly commit to seek the truth. Kvale includes research interviews in the professional category, though it is the philosophical ones that he describes as 'ideal'. Our e-mail interviews certainly displayed some of the characteristics of 'professional' conversations, as we were directing the discussions, at least initially. However, we often felt that interviews were closer to 'philosophical' dialogues, as our respondents contributed to the direction and become, in effect, co-researchers in exploring the specific topic that we had put forward.

The final stage in each of our projects using e-mail interview methodology was the publication of academic papers in conference proceedings and academic journals. By alerting participants to these publications, we provided feedback and acknowledgement of respondents' contributions in time and insights. Almost all participants whom we were able to contact requested a copy of each publication or details on how to access it. Other feedback from participants included e-mailed informal comments about how respondents drew on the projects or publications in their own practices. In one case, this included developing an interview protocol for needs assessment in a college for teacher educators, based on our e-mail questions; in another case, we provided comments about a participant's contribution to our project and these were used in a promotion application. In turn, several participants sent us their own published papers as well as software and other resources that benefitted our teaching. Papers on the IASE project have been made available to members of bodies concerned with statistics education and statistics as a profession, and were welcomed as a resource. One example is the project summary published in a newsletter of the American Educational Research Association (AERA, 2007), which has resulted in ongoing feedback, discussion and presentations. The point here is that we – researchers and interview participants – are building a research sub-community who are interested in published results of the projects in which they participated,

with participants' own contributions marked by their self-chosen pseudonyms.

This research community can be inclusive of people whose preferred language is not English, a point that may be relevant in the field of Urban and Planning Studies where groups of interest may be predominantly from a different language background to that of the researcher. In the IASE project, one of our participants was César, a teacher of statistics at an Argentine university. He agreed to participate as long as he could write his responses in Spanish, though he was comfortable reading the questions in English. Supported by our modest abilities in Spanish (aided on occasion by reference to computer-based translations), we conducted a bi-lingual interview with him that resulted in a written record of almost 6000 words. Included in the discussion were asides about the exact meaning of various words that he had used, and references from him to some of our previously published writings on statistics education that he used to explain particular points. An extract from his final comments is included here as Example 9.

Example 9

Int: We would like to know your opinion about this method - any negative or positive features that you experienced while participating in the interview. (In your case, also, any comments about the problems or benefits of a bilingual interview would be very interesting.)

César: Participar de esta investigación ha sido para mí una excelente experiencia por diferentes razones que paso a resumir:
* Por la oportunidad de poder contar nuestras experiencias y problemas educativos a quienes los escuchan, analizan y comprenden. También la de poder intercambiar ideas con investigadores del prestigio que ustedes reúnen.
* Por la pertinencia y orientación de las preguntas que han permitido abarcar los

problemas centrales de la enseñanza y, en muchos casos, me han hecho reflexionar sobre cuestiones importantes. También por la posibilidad de ampliar-profundizar las respuestas.

* Por el medio (e-mail) utilizado que nos ha permitido trabajar prácticamente "on line" todo el tiempo. De no haber sido por esta fabulosa herramienta de las comunicaciones modernas, probablemente jamás hubieran entrado en contacto docentes de Australia con colegas de ¡Misiones -Argentina!.

… En consecuencia: ¡muchas gracias por haberme incluido en el panel!

Our translation:

Participating in this research has been a great experience for me for various reasons which I will summarise:

* For the opportunity to describe our experiences and educational problems to those who listen, analyse and understand. Also, to exchange ideas with researchers of the prestige that you represent.

* For the relevance and direction of the questions that have included the central problems of education and which have in many cases led me to think about important issues. Also for the possibility of exploring responses in depth.

* For the medium used (e-mail) that enabled us to work virtually on-line all the time. Without this wonderful tool of modern communication, we would probably never have Australian teachers coming into contact with colleagues from Misiones-Argentina.

… So, thank you very much for including me in the project!

We conclude that e-mail interviews provide a useful methodology to explore the experiences of an international group of participants, presenting opportunities to overcome barriers of language,

time and distance. While it has some limitations in terms of the lack of visual and auditory cues, it provides benefits in terms of confidentiality and record keeping. Further, the method enables respondents to participate in the process of collaborative knowledge building as co-researchers, by reflecting on and analysing their own responses in the e-mail interviews. We believe that such contemporary e-mail interviews represent a useful and practical balance between the traditional 'gold standard' of a live interview and high-tech alternatives such as recorded video interviews (live or at a distance), where every aspect of gesture and voice, as well as the actual verbal content, can be subjected to later analysis. Nevertheless, there will be situations where a live interview or a fully-recorded video interview will have benefits, and we would not claim that the e-mail interview is universally to be preferred. One of our respondents (Coach) succinctly summarised his experience with our e-mail interview approach with the comment: "It worked for me. I hope it worked for your research." We believe that it did work for us, and recommend it for interview-based projects in the field of Urban and Planning Studies.

REFERENCES

American Educational Research Association (AEEA) & Educational Statisticians (SIG). (2007). Research Synopsis: Statistics teachers' ideas about teaching and learning statistics at university. *Spring Newsletter, 4*(1), 8.

Bampton, R., & Cowton, C. (2002). The e-interview. *Forum: Qualitative Social Research, 3*(2). Retrieved August 25, 2010, from http://www.qualitative-research.net/fqs-texte/2-02/2-02bamptoncowton-e.htm

Denham, P. (2004). The impact of space and survey format on open ended responses. *Australasian Journal of Market and Social Research, 12*(2), 11–16.

Gordon, S., & Nicholas, J. (2010, September 29-October 1). Teachers' reflections on the challenges of teaching mathematics bridging courses. In M. Sharma (Ed.), *Proceedings of the 16th UniServe Science Annual Conference - Creating ACTIVE Minds in our Science and Mathematics Students,* Sydney, NSW, Australia (pp. 35–40).

Gordon, S., Reid, A., & Petocz, P. (2007). Teachers' conceptions of teaching service statistics courses. *International Journal for the Scholarship of Teaching & Learning, 1*(1). Retrieved August 25, 2010, from http://academics.georgiasouthern. edu/ijsotl/v1n1/gordon_et_al/index.htm

Gordon, S., Reid, A., & Petocz, P. (2010). Educators' conceptions of student diversity in their classes. *Studies in Higher Education, 35*(8), 961–974. doi:10.1080/03075070903414305

Gray, K., Chang, S., & Kennedy, G. (2010). Use of social web technologies by international and domestic undergraduate students: implications for internationalising learning and teaching in Australian universities. *Technology, Pedagogy and Education, 19*(1), 31–46. doi:10.1080/14759390903579208

Hamilton, R., & Bowers, B. (2006). Internet recruitment and e-mail interviews in qualitative studies. *Qualitative Health Research, 16*, 821–835. doi:10.1177/1049732306287599

Illingworth, N. (2001). The internet matters: Exploring the use of the internet as a research tool. *Sociological Research Online, 6*(2). Retrieved August 25, 2010, from http://www.socresonline. org.uk/6/2/illingworth.html

Ison, N. (2009). Having their say: e-mail interviews for research data collection with people who have verbal communication impairment. *International Journal of Social Research Methodology, 12*(2), 161–172. doi:10.1080/13645570902752365

James, N., & Busher, H. (2006). Credibility, authenticity and voice: dilemmas in online interviewing. *Qualitative Research, 6*(3), 403–420. doi:10.1177/1468794106065010

Kivits, J. (2005). Online interviewing and the research relationship. In Hine, C. (Ed.), *Virtual Methods: Issues in social research on the internet* (pp. 35–50). Oxford, UK: Berg.

Kvale, S. (1996). *InterViews: An introduction to qualitative research interviewing.* Thousand Oaks, CA: Sage.

Lincoln, Y., & Guba, E. (1985). *Naturalistic Enquiry.* Newbury Park, CA: Sage.

Martin, D. (2004). Reconstructing urban politics: neighbourhood activism in land-use change. *Urban Affairs Review, 39*, 589–611. doi:10.1177/1078087404263805

McCoyd, J., & Schwaber Kerson, T. (2006). Conducting intensive interviews using e-mail: a serendipitous comparative opportunity. *Qualitative Social Work, 5*(3), 389–406. doi:10.1177/1473325006067367

Myers, M., & Newman, M. (2007). The qualitative interview in IS research: examining the craft. *Information and Organization, 17*, 2–26. doi:10.1016/j.infoandorg.2006.11.001

Opdenakker, R. (2006). Advantages and disadvantages of four interview techniques in qualitative research. *Forum: Qualitative Social Research, 7*(4). Retrieved August 25, 2010, from http:// nbn-resolving.de/urn:nbn:de:0114-fqs0604118

Otienoh, R. (2010). Feedback on teachers' journal entries: a blessing or a curse? *Reflective Practice: International and Multidisciplinary Perspectives, 11*(2), 143–156.

Petocz, P., & Reid, A. (2006). The contribution of mathematics to graduates' professional working life. In P. Jeffery (Ed.), *Australian Association for Research in Education 2005 Conference Papers*. Melbourne: AARE. Retrieved August 25, 2010, from http://www.aare.edu.au/05pap/pet05141.pdf

Popkin, S., Leventhal, T., & Weismann, G. (2010). Girls in the 'hood': how safety affects the life chances of low-income girls. *Urban Affairs Review, 45*, 715–743. doi:10.1177/1078087410361572

Reid, A., Petocz, P., Braddock, R., Taylor, P., & McLean, K. (2006). *Professional formation: exploring students' understanding of creativity, sustainability, ethics and cross-cultural sensitivity* (Tech. Rep. GDN AP-EPRI No. 9). Seoul, Korea: Korean Education Development Institute (KEDI). Retrieved August 25, 2010, from http://eng.kedi.re.kr

Reid, A., Petocz, P., & Gordon, S. (2008). Research interviews in cyberspace. *Qualitative Research Journal, 8*(1), 47–61. doi:10.3316/QRJ0801047

Reid, A., Petocz, P., & Gordon, S. (2010). University teachers' intentions for introductory professional classes. *Journal of Workplace Learning, 22*(1-2), 67–78. doi:10.1108/13665621011012861

Reid, A., Petocz, P., Smith, G. H., Wood, L. N., & Dortins, E. (2003). Maths students' conceptions of mathematics. *New Zealand Journal of Mathematics, 32*, 163–172.

Selwyn, N., & Robson, K. (1998). Using e-mail as a research tool. *Social Research Update, 21*. Retrieved August 25, 2010, from http://sru.soc.surrey.ac.uk/SRU21.html

Wright, K. (2005). Researching internet-based populations: advantages and disadvantages of online survey research, online questionnaire authoring software packages, and web survey services. *Journal of Computer-Mediated Communication, 10*(3). Retrieved August 25, 2010, from http://jcmc.indiana.edu/vol10/issue3/wright.html

ADDITIONAL READING

Cohen, L., Manion, L., & Morrison, K. (2007). Research methods in education (6th Ed.). New York: Routledge. Chapter 16: Interviews pp. 349–383.

Denzin, N. K., & Lincoln, Y. S. (2005). *The SAGE handbook of qualitative research* (3rd ed.). Thousand Oaks, CA: SAGE Publications.

Dillon, L. (2010). Listening for voices of self. *Qualitative Research Journal, 10*(1), 13–27. doi:10.3316/QRJ1001013

Egan, J., Chenoweth, L., & McAuliffe, D. (2006). Email facilitated qualitative interviews with traumatic brain injury survivors: a new and accessible method. *Brain Injury : [BI], 20*(12), 1283–1294. doi:10.1080/02699050601049692

Hine, C. (Ed.). (2005). *Virtual Methods: Issues in social research on the internet*. Oxford: Berg.

Kvale, S., & Brinkmann, S. (2009). *InterViews: Learning the craft of qualitative research interviewing*. Thousand Oaks, CA: Sage Publications.

Lincoln, Y., & Guba, E. (1985). *Naturalistic Enquiry*. Newbury Park, CA: Sage Publications.

Padgett, D. (2008). *Qualitative Methods in Social Work*. Thousand Oaks, CA: Sage Publications.

Paul, M., Berger, R., Blyth, E., & Frith, L. (2010). Relinquishing frozen embryos for conception by infertile couples. *Families, Systems & Health, 28*(3), 258–273. doi:10.1037/a0020002

Chapter 6
The Story of Ethnochat:
Designing an Instant Messaging Program to Conduct Semi–Structured or Unstructured Interviews

Jason Zalinger
Rensselaer Polytechnic Institute, USA

ABSTRACT

Instant Messaging (IM) programs are powerful and unique tools for conducting semi-structured or unstructured online interviews. However, many unanswered questions exist surrounding the use of IM interviewing. This design chapter takes a storytelling approach to answer two specific research questions: (1) Do rich data collected via IM stand the test of time? (2) How can an IM program be built designed specifically for researchers? The chapter is organized into three parts. Part one reviews recent, related research. Part two takes a somewhat unusual approach to answer the research question regarding the long-term power of IM data by re-visiting the author's experience from 2007 using IM to interview female participants about their feelings using online dating sites. Part three is a detailed description of a prototype IM program, Ethnochat. There are many IM clients in existence, but nothing has been made specifically for professional researchers for semi-structured or unstructured interviews. Having the best tool available will help urban planners conduct their research more efficiently and at a significantly reduced cost.

INTRODUCTION

This is a design chapter that tells the story of Ethnochat, a prototype, instant messaging (IM) program created specifically for researchers conducting semi-structured or unstructured interviews. IM programs are powerful and unique tools for conducting online interviews. However, there are still many unanswered research questions surrounding the use of IM interviewing. For specific reasons, this chapter takes a kind of storytelling approach—organizing the paper into three sections so that each acts as a mini-chapter in a larger story. By linking existing research +

DOI: 10.4018/978-1-4666-0074-4.ch006

methodological experience + design, the reader/ future designer will receive a sense of the experience and rationale that led to my final design of Ethnochat. This story begins with a state-of-the-art on interviewing with IM. Next it puts the author's own methodological belief in IM interviewing to the test by reflecting back on interviews the author conducted in 2007 to see if the interviews still contain rich data. Finally, the paper dives into the specific design features of Ethnochat. This approach will hopefully offer value to both researchers and designers (who may never have conducted IM interviews). The ultimate goal of this "design story" chapter is an attempt to answer two specific research questions: (1) Do rich data collected via IM stand the test of time? (2) How can we build an IM program designed specifically for researchers? Design is an iterative process. This chapter is part of that process. It is yet another iteration of Ethnochat, another part of the larger dialog on designing tools for the 21st century researcher. If other researchers/designers are using or thinking of using IM, hopefully this chapter will inspire them to use IM for interviewing and/or to build upon the design of Ethnochat so that other researchers will have the best tool to do the best job.

STATE-OF-THE-ART

Conducting interviews through IM is a fairly recent phenomenon. Though there is, unfortunately, very limited research on IM interviews, much of the research done has had a self-reflective quality as the authors of various papers not only use IM but reflect on the experience of using it as a methodological tool. For example, Voida, Mynatt, Erickson, and Kellogg (2004) wrote:

Pragmatic challenges of interviews include the travel that may be required to meet face-to-face with a respondent or the time necessary to transcribe the exchange. As a tool for conducting

interviews, instant messaging presents some compelling potential benefits to mitigate challenges such as these. And yet, over the medium of instant messaging, the genre of the interview takes on a different character (Voida et al., 2004, p. 1344).

Voida et al., go on to write, "We have reflected on our own experiences interviewing over instant messaging, exploring the ways in which expectations about attention, timing, limited context, and persistence impact the genre of the interview" (Voida et al., 2004, p. 1347). Voida et al. identify, early on, some of the key elements in IM interviewing (timing, context, multi-tasking, etc.). They also explain that the medium of IM changes the genre. Fontes and O'Mahony (2008) chose important practical reasons for using IM interviews: It is cheap, if not free. As soon as you are done, the interview is transcribed, and you can conduct interviews with participants regardless of geography. Fontes and O'Mahony also discovered the benefits of the medium itself. For example, they write, "the lack of visual and auditory cues creates a level of detachment between the interviewers and the interviewees, which is particularly useful when conducting research on sensitive areas such as health, sexuality and so on" (Fontes & O'Mahony, 2008, p. 3). The authors also discuss the importance of the linguistic conventions (they may even be more like traditions than conventions at this point), such as, abbreviations or emoticons of which researchers should be aware. They write that if a researcher is not "*au fait*" with these aspects, they may not find the use of IM to be as rewarding" (Fontes & O'Mahony, 2008, p. 4).

Although the authors do explain that participants are open to explaining what *they* mean when they use an unknown abbreviation, it is critical to highlight this element for researchers using IM. Simply asking a participant what they mean by the use of an abbreviation or emoticon is not just to help the researcher, but it can create a stronger bond between both participant and researcher.

For example, I tend to use "lol" often in a kind of self-deprecating way when asking a participant what they mean. For instance, I might say something like, "what does tbh[1] mean? lol?!" Almost always, the participant responded with their own "lol" and an explanation, which tended to help solidify our collaboration. As Fontes and O'Mahony concluded, "We found IM to be indispensible to our research and strongly encourage its wider use as a valuable research instrument" (2008, p. 4). Others have even asked their participants if they enjoyed the experiences. For example, (Hinchcliffe & Gavin, 2008) found that all their participants, "felt comfortable and confident" using IM. In fact, they "enjoyed the experience" and "confirmed that they would be willing to use IM again" (2008, p. 97). Hinchcliffe and Gavin also noted some of the negative consequences of using IM. For example, bad internet connections, participants worried about their poor spelling, or even one participant who left the conversation to put some laundry in the machine. Still, these are relatively minor issues. Internet connections can be flaky, but an audio tape recorder could also break. A participant worried about spelling can and *should* be easily put at ease by telling them simply not to worry about spelling. As for a participant who leaves the conversation, even in face-to-face conversations a participant can "leave." During a face-to-face interview I once conducted, a participant received a phone call on their mobile and had to leave the interview temporarily. This is the equivalent of "leaving" a conversation, and it will require some patience on the part of the researcher.

Hinchcliffe herself kept a "daily reflective research diary" to record her thoughts about using IM for interviews. For example, she wrote in her research diary: *I am happy with the quality and utility of IM for online interviewing purposes… communication is immediate…the transcripts are visibly different from previous face to face interviews I have conducted in that there is less 'waffle', more succinct and pertinent answers*

(Hinchcliffe & Gavin, 2008, p. 100). Thus, using IM was a positive and *useful* experience. In another study, Hinchcliffe and Gavin (2009) specifically evaluated IM for its "quality and utility as an innovative research interviewing technique" (Hinchcliffe & Gavin, 2009, p. 322). They found that, "Quantitative and qualitative content analysis of respondent and researcher evaluation of IM positively enhanced knowledge concerning the quality and utility of using IM as a novel communication platform for research interviewing" (Hinchcliffe & Gavin, 2009, p. 333). Other work has focused on scientific studies using IM. Stieger and Görtiz (2006) concluded that "IM interviews are feasible, and that in some aspects they are superior to other methods of data collection. The risk of receiving false data in IM interviews is small" (2006, p. 558). Other researchers have used IM interviews to explore issues of gender stereotyping (Christofides, Islam, & Desmarais, 2009), and Stieger and Reips (2008) created, to my knowledge, the only custom IM client designed for *automated* interviewing.

Though the research on IM interviews is small, the existing literature all seems to indicate that IM interviews are extremely useful and capable of producing rich data. However, there are still unanswered questions. The next two sections of this chapter will attempt to define and offer solutions to these problems. One problem that has not been addressed in the literature is whether or not the rich data that can be produced by IM interviews will stand the test of time.

This section is based upon my own reflection of conducting IM interviews with six women in the fall of 2007. When I first did the interviews I was thrilled at what I considered the richness of data I was uncovering. After dusting off and re-visiting my transcripts are the IM interviews still as rich and interesting as I believed they were in 2007? Reflecting back on IM interviews is crucial right now for the social sciences in general and Urban and Planning Studies in particular because it is an emerging online method, and as time passes and

IM technology changes, it is critical to look back in order to move forward with new knowledge.

METHODOLOGICAL EXPERIENCE: REFLECTIONS ON MY IM INTERVIEWS

In the fall of 2007 for a PhD course in Ethnography, I conducted six, semi-structured interviews all via instant messenger. The topic of my study was on women's use of online dating sites.[2] I was interested in both their feelings about the sites as well as the technology of dating sites themselves. The youngest participant was 30, the oldest 50. Most lived on the east coast, one was in Texas and one in Canada. The shortest time spent on a dating site was three months (although they tended to go back after taking a break), and the longest was roughly two and a half years.

Revisiting my old transcripts was frightening and somewhat of a risk for this chapter (what if the data was not as rich as I initially thought? What if my participants were not as fascinating as I thought they were in 2007? Would this mean that IM interviews are not capable of providing data that is powerful and useful enough to continue the practice?). Luckily, looking back, I can report that what was uncovered three years ago is *still* rich data, still swirling, still palpable with emotion. In listening again to my participants, I can almost hear their excitement, frustration, disappointment, tension, and hope.

Many of my participants had gone through difficult breakups prior to trying dating sites. In some cases, the breakup drew users to the sites. In other cases, it caused participants to move at a more cautious pace. One participant had enjoyed a great success in her initial foray into online dating, so she "immediately" dove back in when her relationship failed. My participants described what it felt like to search dating sites after experiencing a breakup. The tension between breaking up and looking for someone new seems to have driven them towards the sites. Sara[3] told me she started looking on dating sites after she broke-up with her boyfriend in 1999. Gwen told me she and her new online potential partner had gone through "hard" divorces in the past, so they were "scared" to rush into anything, so they drew out their online discussions for a long time. Though Diane also had a "hard" breakup, she decided to give it another shot. When I asked Mary how long she took to sign up for a dating site after her breakup, she said, "immediately."

My participants expressed hope that they would find someone yet hopelessness that they would not. Sometimes they would take breaks from the dating sites, yet they came back. These opposing tendencies shaped their experiences as cyclical. For example, Sara told me that despite the depression and frustration of rejection, she always felt a sense of "tomorrowness," or hope that "tomorrow" she could get an email from someone perfect. Gwen told me that every email from a man contained "possibility." She said that Mr. Right could be the next person to send her a message. Michelle called online dating "addictive" because each time she checked her email there could be a "potential" date. I asked Jen if she thought she would find what she was looking for online. She said she went back to the site because she was still looking and "hoping." Mary was an extremely fascinating case. Mary lived a BDSM lifestyle as a sexual submissive, meaning she enjoyed being sexually dominated by men. She frequented a fetish dating site for people who live "the lifestyle." Maybe it was due to her submissive nature, but she told me many fascinating things. She had good luck the first time she tried the site, so when that relationship failed, she reactivated her account. When I asked her why she went back she said, despite the "mindfuckers," she had "faith" in humanity. Later in the transcript, Mary actually *gave me her username and password for the BDSM site*. She invited me to logon and read through her emails. Again, maybe this was due to her submissive tendency, but if this is not rich, powerful data exchanged *via* an IM interview then what is?

Another element in the constellation of contradictory feelings that my participants expressed was the challenge of acceptance versus rejection online. Rejection is not new, but rejection online adds a powerful plot twist in the ancient story of the search for connection. My participants experienced an emergent, evolving pattern of acceptance and rejection. Two elements seem to emerge as unique among online dating: (1) the sense of silent rejection, meaning, sending an email and not receiving a response, and (2) the rejection practice that at least one of my participants developed in order to cope with the guilt of rejecting people. An example of this latter practice is Diane's "form rejection letter" that she would send to men as a way of politely rejecting them and trying to minimize the guilt she felt when doing the rejection. My participants responded in various ways regarding the tension between connection and rejection online. For example, Sara told me that she tried to consider the first few dates with a man more like "interviews" as a kind of defense mechanism against the hurt associated with being rejected.

When I asked her if she had suffered specific rejections, she told me, yes, and some of them were "painful." She was especially hurt when she would email someone and receive a silent rejection. Gwen's response to the issue of rejection was complex and interesting. She first told me that she did not initiate emails to men because of the "risk" of being rejected. Then she told me that she did not initiate emails because she was raised in a time where it was the responsibility of the man to ask, not the woman. I asked her if she thought that online rejection hurt less than "real world" rejection. She said yes because, to her, online they are just rejecting her "words" and "pictures," which is merely a representation and not completely her. Michelle felt very bad when she did the rejecting. She told me she did not want to seem "shallow," but if the photograph of

the man was unattractive she would not respond or simply say no, thank you. I asked her if she felt guilty when she did not respond, and she said, yes, "definitely." She said it was rude not to respond, but it was also probably just as rude to respond and say no thanks. Michelle's conflict over appropriate ways to reject someone online is a reflection of the lack of clearly defined norms for online dating. Do you ignore someone, or do you send a rejection message? If you send a message, what should it say? Diane (who created a custom form rejection letter) told me she also had an excel spreadsheet for each man she met online. If she was not interested, she sent them her form rejection letter. Her response to doing the rejecting was to be polite. She respected the other person for taking the risk in sending her a message. Susan told me that online you can reject the other person without the guilt of looking into their "sad puppy-dog eyes." The practice of rejection frustrated her because it often led to men asking for an elaboration on her decision to reject them. This transformed rejecting strangers online into a practice fraught with anxiety. She said that feeling anxious over rejecting someone "sucks." Unlike Sara, Jen did not appear to feel unsettled over silent rejection. Possibly because she claimed to do most of the rejecting, Jen argued it was just as frustrating to feel rejected by someone she had not met in person then to have to look them in the eyes and reject them to their face. When Jen rejected someone it did not appear to be silently. Similar to Susan, those Jen rejected responded back. In fact, she received "rude" replies with some even calling her a "bitch" for rejecting them, which does not sound like they took it "easier."

Looking back, my interview transcripts suggest that what I discovered in 2007 is still very rich data now. My participants were engaged in a variety of practices used to negotiate the evolving, fluid nature of online dating sites and complementary technologies those sites provide such as email and IM. Many of the powerful emotions (e.g., hope and guilt) and experiences (e.g., rejection and binge dating) that my participants described seem just as thought-provoking now as they did back then: It's as if my transcripts were frozen for years. After I de-thawed them, I was both relieved and excited to find that the IM interviews worked, in that they produced data that, as I looked back, began to warm up, more and more. My participants seemed to lose themselves in the technological fog of hope and addiction. They disclosed a lot of very personal feelings to me over IM. The questions I asked and the feelings they revealed offer a new lens through which to understand not only how but *why* people use communications technology to connect to each other. Specifically, my research uncovered new ways to understand the complex dance of online dating, and *all* of this data was produced through IM. Despite the subject of this section (online dating) these examples are nevertheless illustrative of the potential usefulness of IM interviewing for Urban and Planning Studies. However, though my data is still rich, I encountered a lot of difficulty using IM, not because of the medium, but because no tool had been designed specifically for semi-structured or unstructured IM interviews. The next section details the design of my prototype, Ethnochat.

ETHNOCHAT[4]

This section is concerned with describing a *tool* rather than engaging in debates over the pros and cons of interviewing with IM. As noted above, to my knowledge, only one other IM client was built for interviewing, but it was used for *automated*, structured interviews, not semi-structured or unstructured interviews (Stieger & Reips, 2008). This section describes the design of Ethnochat, an IM program built for researchers who wish to conduct semi-structured or unstructured interviews. This is the first prototype of its kind. Online interview techniques are becoming a common method to investigate social interactions and settings in digital contexts, and this creates a demand for a *proper*

tool with which IM interviewers can practice their craft. The remainder of this chapter details the design and articulates how Ethnochat will have significant implications for online research methods in general and Urban and Planning Studies in particular.

Design Motivation

When I conducted my informal study on the topic of online dating, all the interviews were done via IM with one goal being that the form of the technology would allow for more open disclosure by the participants. The interviews were successful in that participants were open and willing to provide intimate details of their online behaviors and their feelings. The project produced a body of rich data, but the inadequacy of various IM clients used and the messiness of copying and pasting sections into Microsoft Word provided the motivation to begin work on designing Ethnochat in the spring of 2008. Qualitative analysis software, such as MAXQDA, ATLAS.ti and NVivo boast powerful annotation and analysis tools. Ethnochat, a work-in-progress, is not meant to be a replacement but rather an open-source, user-friendly *complement* to these programs that is filling a gap for researchers who conduct IM interviews. Ethnochat's design draws upon the first-hand knowledge of my experience using IM interviews. The immediate goals are that (1) programmers will build a rich and diverse set of plugins or extensions, and (2) Ethnochat will someday be able to export seamlessly to these existing qualitative programs.

Using IM for interviews can be cumbersome. For example, rather than having multiple windows and programs open at once, Ethnochat will act as a command center for everything the interviewer needs *during* the interview. Aside from the typical interview screen, the researcher can invoke separate panels inside Ethnochat for research questions, field notes and tagging. All notes and tags can be linked to any text that is highlighted in the transcript. Rather than copying and pasting questions, they can populate the chat field with one click, which is vital since interviews are fluid events. Tagged data can be viewed across interviews. If you make a tag for "Happy," you will be able to view every instance of that tag across one or all interviews, thus making it easier to visualize connections. The goal of Ethnochat is to create a one-stop shopping experience for researchers. In fact, Ethnochat might have more in common with creative software like Photoshop, rather than merely an IM program. Photoshop is designed to give users a creative canvas upon which they can perfect their craft. Likewise, I see Ethnochat as both academic and *creative* software.

Current State of Software

Ethnochat is currently in prototype form, but much of its functionality has been implemented[5]. Ethnochat allows for (1) chatting with automatic logging to a file, (2) creation and management of interview questions with one-click question copying into the chat window, (3) plug-in IM network service support, (4) cut-copy-paste to/from the question window and the conversation window, and (5) tag creation and management. With a better designed tool, IM interviews will become a more widely used approach in a variety of research domains, whether used as the sole method or in combination with other techniques. Ethnochat was meant to be similar to Zotero, a powerful bibliographic extension for Firefox that was built by academics, for academics (Zotero, n.d.). Urban planning researcher Giovanni Attili wrote, "New technologies transform ethnographic analysis into a different communicative tool that offers a surplus of meanings and interpretations. It does not exhaust itself. It is not univocally determined. It never finds a precise answer. Each view finds another richness" (2007, p. 94). Ethnochat is intended to provide researchers with a new tool to harness the richness of IM interviews.

Design Features

Multi-Protocol

Ethnochat (Figure 1) is built in Java allowing it to run across multiple platforms. I plan to distribute the code as an open-source project, enabling anyone to download the source code and redesign the program to fit his or her needs. Ethnochat is multi-protocol. The goal is to get it to connect with as many networks as possible (e.g., AIM, Yahoo!, Google, Jabber, MSN). Others have dealt with the frustrating issue of connecting to multiple networks when conducting IM interviews (Stieger & Göritz, 2006). When I conducted ethnographic interviews using the Adium client for the Mac OS, it worked well with most major IM networks. However, Microsoft's MSN network always seemed to be an obstacle. This led me to install MSN Messenger. Besides the hassle of an extra installed program, the other problem was that MSN Messenger formatted data in a different way, which made copying and pasting into Microsoft Word an awkward, time-consuming issue. This is why Ethnochat will work with all major networks. When conducting IM interviews it is vital that the researcher's client program works seamlessly with whatever networks *their participants prefer*, not the other way around.

Add-Ons

Like many extensible, open-source projects, the goal is to secure Ethnochat as the center of a vibrant community of programmers who create add-ons to support researchers. For example, a hypothetical extension for Ethnochat could be called Ethno-timeline, which could be used to help researchers visualize their data temporally.

Modular

Ethnochat is intended to give the interviewer the most flexible working space possible. The online

Figure 1. Ethnochat's main screen with interview, question, tags and contact windows visible

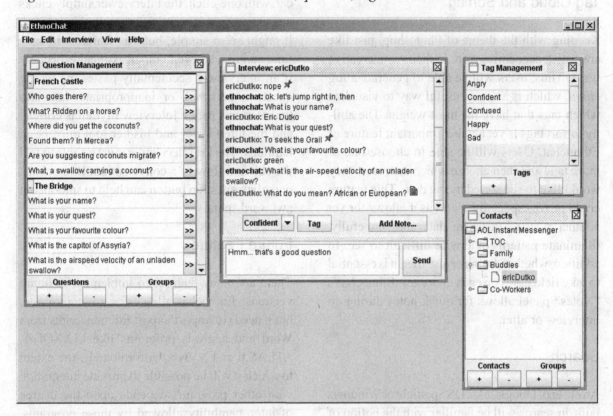

interview is a fluid process, and the researcher must have a workspace that is tailored to their needs. Photoshop is a great example in which the main "canvas" is completely customizable. Photoshop users can show and hide whatever windows they want to see. Similarly, interviewers need their own canvas in which all of their tools are ready at a click. Instead of using a variety of programs, users can have their main interview screen, as well as panels for their research questions, tags, and notes. Users will be able to drag the panels in whatever configuration they choose. The point is to give researchers a true canvass in order to practice the craft of IM interviewing.

Tagging

One of the most unique features of Ethnochat is the ability to tag data. Tagging allows users to mark their data with textual flags, which enables easier searching and organization. Ethnochat enables researchers to tag their data inside the interview window either during or after an interview. A user will highlight a specific line(s) directly from the interview window. Once the text is highlighted, the user simply clicks whatever tag is appropriate, or he or she can add a new one. The data and the tag are now linked permanently, unless the user specifies otherwise. All roads lead to Word, or at least some type of word processor. When interviewers begin to write, they will undoubtedly chop up their data and move it around as their ideas coalesce and organize around various themes. This cut-and-paste phase can lead writers to forget where their data originated. Kazmer and Xie echoed a similar problem of keeping IM transcripts complete and in order (2008). Ethnochat solves this problem. In Ethnochat, once you tag any piece of data, it is linked to that tag.

Tag Cloud and Sorting

Keeping with the theme of Photoshop, just like any artist, academics work in their own, creative ways. Thus, users will be able to generate a *tag cloud*, which is an easy, useful way to visualize which tags that have the most weight. The ability to sort tags is yet another important feature of Ethnochat. Users will be able to choose one or more tags and then choose which interview they would like to see sorted by tag data. This feature could prove especially useful as it allows for yet another way to visualize data and, hopefully, illuminate patterns otherwise difficult to see. In addition, whether during or just after, it is essential to take field notes on each interview. Ethnochat's "Notes" panel allows for quick notes during an interview or after.

Search

Any user of Google, Mac OS Spotlight or Windows built-in search will be familiar with the notion of a comprehensive search function. Ethnochat will include a search feature that will index across all interviews and all data. This allows the user to quickly find, say, a specific line from an interview, without having multiple documents for each interview. In other words, all your data is quickly accessible and centralized.

One-Click Questions

Interviews are fluid. The interviewer needs to pay attention to what the participant is saying and should not be distracted by tedious chores like cutting and pasting questions into the interview. Like a driver reaching into the back seat for a CD case, this can be fatal for the interview. The ethnographer cannot get lost in a momentary Word or browser ordeal. Thus, although it may seem trivial, it is vital that Ethnochat also include a *one-click question* function. Similar to having radio volume controls on the steering wheel of your car, with one-click, the interviewer simply clicks a question, and it populates the interview panel. It might seem simple, but this feature will save time and maybe even embarrassment especially if an interviewer accidentally pastes the wrong question, personal, or inappropriate data into the interview panel. Interview rhythm is critical, and the interviewer and his/her tool must be in harmony. The IM interviewer must be able to feel the ebb and flow of a conversation. Ethnochat's one-click question button can help to smooth out awkward spots.

Future Features

There are many features to implement in future versions: Ethnochat allows for cut-copy-paste, but it needs to import/export full transcripts from Word and analysis programs like MAXQDA, ATLAS.ti and NVivo. Unfortunately, the extent to which it will be possible to provide integration with other programs depends upon the degree of interoperability allowed by those programs. Photoshop and other creative software packages contain "libraries" of commonly used objects that make inserting media into their projects much more user-friendly. Ethnochat should contain an "Insert" panel. The reason for this is because not all interviews will be purely based on questions. It is possible that a researcher will want to show a participant images, video or audio. With a click, for example, a researcher could insert a picture into the main interview panel, thus eliminating the need to send a file via IM or email or even an external link. Another option would be a screen-sharing function, something Skype has already done successfully. Again, this feature will depend upon what mechanisms are supported by each IM service. Finally, Ethnochat will feature an auto-backup system. When the interviewer closes the program, they will be prompted to back up their data to an external source, for example, an external drive or ftp site.

CONCLUSION

Time, money and geography are constant challenges for interview-based research projects. In contrast, as others have noted, IM interviewing is cheap, convenient and self-transcribing. As more and more people grow up communicating using IM, conducting interviews via IM will feel more natural and routine. This paper asked if IM data would stand the test of time. Although my transcripts were only from 2007, I was both amazed and happy to report that the deeply personal emotions and stories my participants told me *through IM*, still ring true, still contain richness and power. Finally, this paper also noted that no custom designed IM program exists specifically for semi-structured or unstructured interviews. Thus, I described the details of Ethnochat, my prototype IM client to solve this problem. IM interviewing with Ethnochat may have significant implications for online research methods. With the right tool, interviews will run smoother because researchers will feel empowered. All creative and intellectual work is fundamentally about making connections, linking relationships, connecting the dots, so to speak. Poets connect words and make beautiful poems. Programmers connect code and produce elegant software. Interdisciplinary academics unite diverse ideas and forge new insights. Ethnochat is an attempt to take advantage of the new ways people communicate every day and help researchers connect new dots and make sense of our rapidly changing media ecology. New ways of communicating demand new ways of researching, which demand new tools. The goal is that Ethnochat will become not just a robust tool for online research methods but part of a larger conversation about how to make new academic tools for emerging media. This is a tool that does not exist and is long overdue. The more digital our world becomes, the more important it is for Urban and Planning Studies researchers to take advantage of the potential of new technology to help them gain new insights into why people do what they do. This chapter took an unusual design story approach in order to inspire researchers/designers to harness the power of IM to tell other people's stories and create new knowledge using a better tool.

REFERENCES

Attili, G. (2007). Digital ethnographies in the planning field. *Planning Theory & Practice*, 8(1), 90–97.

Christofides, E., Islam, T., & Desmarais, S. (2009). Gender stereotyping over instant messenger: The effects of gender and context. *Computers in Human Behavior*, 25(4), 897–901. doi:10.1016/j.chb.2009.03.004

Fontes, T. O., & O'Mahony, M. (2008). In-depth interviewing by instant messaging. *Social Research Update, 53*, 1-4. Retrieved from http://sru.soc.surrey.ac.uk/SRU53.pdf

Hinchcliffe, V., & Gavin, H. (2008). Internet mediated research: A critical reflection upon the practice of using instant messenger for higher educational research interviewing. *Psychology & Society*, 1(1), 91–104.

Hinchcliffe, V., & Gavin, H. (2009). Social and virtual networks: Evaluating synchronous online interviewing using instant messenger. *Qualitative Report, 14*(2), 318–340.

Kazmer, M. M., & Xie, B. (2008). Qualitative interviewing in internet studies: Playing with the media, playing with the method. *Information Communication and Society, 11*(2), 257–278. doi:10.1080/13691180801946333

Stieger, S., & Göritz, A. S. (2006). Using Instant Messaging for Internet-Based Interviews. *Cyberpsychology & Behavior*, 9(5), 552–559. doi:10.1089/cpb.2006.9.552

Stieger, S., & Reips, U.-D. (2008). Dynamic Interviewing Program (DIP): Automatic Online Interviews via the Instant Messenger ICQ. *Cyberpsychology & Behavior, 11*(2), 201–207. doi:10.1089/cpb.2007.0030

Voida, A., Mynatt, E. D., Erickson, T., & Kellogg, W. A. (2004). Interviewing over instant messaging. In *Proceedings of CHI '04: Extended Abstracts on Human Factors in Computing Systems,* Vienna, Austria (pp. 1344-1347). ACM Press.

Zotero. (n.d.). *Zotero*. Retrieved May 14, 2011, from http://www.zotero.org/

ADDITIONAL READING

Bampton, R., & Cowton, C. J. (2002). The e-interview. *Forum: Qualitative Social Research, 3*(2). Retrieved September 9, 2010, from http://www.qualitative-research.net/index.php/fqs/article/view/848/1842

Berg, B. L. (2008). *Qualitative research methods for the social sciences* (7th ed.). Boston: Allyn & Bacon.

Chen, P., & Hinton, S. (1999). Realtime interviewing using the World Wide Web. *Sociological Research Online, 4*(3). Retrieved September 9, 2010, from http://www.socresonline.org.uk/4/3/chen.html

Crichton, S., & Kinash, S. (2003). Virtual ethnography: Interactive interviewing online as method. *Canadian Journal of Learning and Technology, 29*(2).

Davis, M., Bolding, G., Hart, G., Sherr, L., & Elford, J. (2004). Reflecting on the experience of interviewing online: Perspectives from the Internet and HIV study in London. *AIDS Care, 16*(8), 944–952. doi:10.1080/09540120412331292499

Dourish, P. (2007). Responsibilities and implications: Further thoughts on ethnography and design. In *Proceedings of the 2007 conference on Designing for User eXperiences* (pp. 2-16). Chicago, Illinois: ACM Press.

James, N. (2006). Credibility, authenticity and voice: Dilemmas in online interviewing. *Qualitative Research, 6*(3), 403–420. doi:10.1177/1468794106065010

James, N. (2007). The use of email interviewing as a qualitative method of inquiry in educational research. *British Educational Research Journal, 33*(6), 963–976. doi:10.1080/01411920701657074

James, N., & Busher, H. (2009). *Online interviewing*. London: SAGE Publications.

Jones, S. (Ed.). (1999). *Doing internet research: Critical issues and methods for examining the net*. London: SAGE Publications.

King, N., & Horrocks, C. (2010). *Interviews in qualitative research*. London: SAGE Publications.

Kivits, J. (2005). Online interviewing and the research relationship. In Hine, C. (Ed.), *Virtual methods: Issues in social research on the internet* (pp. 35–49). Oxford, UK: Berg Publishers.

Kozinets, R. V. (2009). *Netnography: Doing ethnographic research online*. London: SAGE Publications.

Lazar, J., Feng, J. H., & Hochheiser, H. (2010). *Research methods in human-computer interaction*. West Sussex, UK: John Wiley and Sons.

Lenhart, A., Ling, R., Campbell, S., & Purcell, K. (2010). *Teens and mobile phones*. Pew Internet & American Life Project. Retrieved September 9, 2010, from http://www.pewinternet.org/Reports/2010/Teens-and-Mobile-Phones.aspx

Mann, C., & Stewart, F. (2000). *Internet communication and qualitative research: A handbook for researching online*. London: SAGE Publications.

Masten, D. L., & Plowman, T. M. (2003). Digital ethnography: The next wave in understanding the consumer experience. *Design Management Journal, 14*(2), 75–81.

Matthews, J., & Cramer, E. P. (2008). Using technology to enhance qualitative research with hidden populations. *Qualitative Report, 13*(2), 301–315.

McAuliffe, D. (2003). Challenging methodological traditions: Research by email. *Qualitative Report, 8*(1), 57–69.

Murthy, D. (2008). Digital Ethnography: An examination of the use of new technologies for social research. *Sociology, 42*(5), 837–855. doi:10.1177/0038038508094565

O'Connor, H., & Madge, C. (2001). Cyber-mothers: Online synchronous interviewing using conferencing software. *Sociological Research Online, 5*(4). Retrieved September 9, 2010, from http://www.socresonline.org.uk/5/4/o'connor.html

Sade-Beck, L. (2008). Internet ethnography: Online and offline. *International Journal of Qualitative Methods, 3*(2), 45–51.

Salmons, J. (2009). *Online interviews in real time.* London: SAGE Publications.

Wali, A. (2010). Ethnography for the digital age: http://www.YouTube/ Digital ethnography (Michael Wesch). *American Anthropologist, 112*(1), 147–148. doi:10.1111/j.1548-1433.2009.01204.x

Whitty, M. T. (2002). Liar, liar! An examination of how open, supportive and honest people are in chat rooms. *Computers in Human Behavior, 18*(4), 343–352. doi:10.1016/S0747-5632(01)00059-0

KEY TERMS AND DEFINITIONS

Ethnography: Broadly defined as a research technique used to illuminate individuals and cultures, usually through participant observation and interviews.

Instant Messenger: A software program that allows for real-time chats between two or more users.

Ethnochat: A prototype instant messenger program designed for professional researchers conducting online interviews.

Semi-Structured Interview: A flexible research method that allows the interviewer to explore themes rather than find answers to a rigid set of questions.

Un-Structured Interview: A research method where the interviewer comes to the interview with no predefined theories or questions. Rather, the interviewer engages in a dialog with the interviewee. Questions are generated through this dialog.

Self-Reflective: The ability in humans to exercise self-observation and a *willingness* to learn more about the self.

Tag Cloud: Similar to a word cloud, this is a way to easily visualize a large amount of text. In a word cloud, the more a word is used in the text, the larger it will show up in the visualization. Ethnochat's tag cloud will do the same thing except it will use the researcher's own tags rather than the raw text of the transcript. This will help researchers see at a glance which tags are most prominent in their transcripts.

ENDNOTES

[1] "tbh" means, "To be honest."

[2] As this was a class project, I unfortunately did not apply for IRB approval, so I will not be able to quote directly from my participants. Instead, I will paraphrase their words and feelings, and no real names will be used, so it will be impossible to identify any of my participants.

[3] For privacy concerns, all the names of my participants are fake.

[4]   The discussion of Ethnochat is based largely on Zalinger, J., Freier, N., & Dutko, E. (2009). Ethnochat: An instant messenger program for ethnography. In *Proceedings of the 27th International Conference Extended Abstracts on Human Factors In Computing Systems,* Boston, MA (pp. 3703-3708). ACM Press.

[5]   Special thanks to Eric Dutko for his incredible hard work programming Ethnochat.

Chapter 7
Video–Enhanced Self–Administered Computer Interviews

Joachim Gerich
Johannes Kepler University, Austria

ABSTRACT

In video-enhanced computer interviews, questions are presented by virtual interviewers by means of pre-recorded video sequences. To date, two strands of scientific interest in video-enhanced data collection are identifiable. On the one hand, video-enhanced data collection is employed for interviewing respondents with special needs (especially deaf respondents) and young respondents. On the other hand, research is focused on the impact on data quality. Following previous results on enhanced data quality with audio-enhanced computer interviews, video-enhanced surveys are seen as a logical extension. In this chapter, previous research on both strands of applications of video-enhanced computer interviews is summarized to gain insight into preliminary evidence about the impact of these methods.

INTRODUCTION

Turning from paper to computer-based questionnaires (regardless of whether administered offline or over the web) offers a multitude of communicative elements which can be implemented in self-administered data collection. Multimedia technology facilitates audio- and video-assisted computer-based self-administered interviews, where questions are asked with pre-recorded voice and video-sequences of a "virtual" human interviewer. Whereas there have been widespread applications as well as research about audio-enhanced methods within the last decade, this is still limited for video-enhanced methods. This chapter predominantly focuses on self-administered

DOI: 10.4018/978-1-4666-0074-4.ch007

computer based methods of (online as well as offline) data collection. Couper (2008) illustrates that offline and online trends of computer based data collection methods historically follow two different strands. On the one hand, online methods (web-surveys) are seen as the computerized extension of mail surveys to the internet. These methods (traditional paper-based mail surveys as well as web-surveys) are denoted as fully self administered methods in the sense that there is no direct contact between interviewer and respondent. In recent years, technological development also enabled the enhancement of web-surveys with multimedia elements (pictures, animations, audio- and video material)[1]. On the other hand, offline methods are seen as a development that follows a trend with its origin in face-to-face (FTF) interviews in that the interviewer is (partially or totally) replaced by self-administered paper-and-pencil (PP) questionnaires. Later on, paper questionnaires were replaced by computer-based questionnaires (computer-assisted self-interviewing, CASI).

Starting with text-based CASI methods (T-CASI), hardware development later on enabled audio-visual enhancement (AV-CASI) of purely text-based questionnaires especially by the use of audio (A-CASI) and video (V-CASI) material[2]. Self administered questionnaires (SAQ) in this strand of development were predominately used with sensitive topics to reduce response bias which are expected when answers have to be verbalized to interviewers. These methods differ from mailed and web surveys as interviewers are still present during the response process although the interviews are self-administered.

The motivation to utilize audio- and video enhanced computer methods (online or offline) in survey research again follows two strands. On the one hand, audio-visual computer questionnaires are suited to enable self-administered methods of data collection for special populations that are typically excluded when traditional (text-based only) questionnaires are employed. AV-CASI, for instance, has been used for respondents with

reduced literacy and special populations like young children and deaf respondents (Gerich & Bergmair, 2008; Gerich & Lehner, 2006; De Leeuw et al., 1997, 2003; Truman et al., 2003; Powell et al., 2002, Chan & Schmitt, 1997; Romer et al., 1997).

On the other hand, audio-visual methods are thought to be suited to improve data quality in survey research. This is mainly fuelled by previous research on A-CASI which has shown improved data quality compared to other modes of data collection (Couper, 2005; Turner et al., 1998; Lessler & O'Reilly, 1997; Tourangeau & Smith, 1996). It is argued along this line that the use of multiple channels of communication (textual, visual, and auditory channels) as well as the more human-like communication style (bringing social cues into self-administered interviews) helps to improve the understanding of questions and the support of respondents' cognitive processing (Fuchs, 2009a; Gerich, 2008a; Daft & Lengel, 1986). Furthermore, humanizing self-administered surveys is assumed to increase respondents' motivation and, hence, respondents' involvement during the question-answer process. Adding additional channels to interviews could help to make the communication more "natural" and emotionally satisfying (Sproull et al., 1996; Walker, Sproull, & Subramani, 1994).

However, human-like cues (e.g., voice or faces) and social presence are thought to evoke response bias like impression management, social desirability and reduced self-disclosure, which – in turn - would tend to negate the advantages of media richness regarding the processing of information (Cassell & Miller, 2008; Nass, Moon, & Green, 1997; Weisband & Kiesler, 1996).

In this chapter experiences and results of research on both strands of applications of audio-visual computer methods are summarized to give an overview of the current evidence regarding the possible impact of such methods for survey research.

AUDIO-VISUAL COMPUTER INTERVIEWS FOR SPECIAL TARGET GROUPS

Deaf Respondents

Besides other important strategies which mainly address aspects of question wording, adaptive technologies are one of the most important recommendations for the inclusion of disabled populations in social surveys (Parsons et al., 2000). Using multiple channels of communication is a principle consideration which includes the use of audio-assisted technologies to counteract communication problems induced by visual impairments or reduced literacy skills, as well (DeLeeuw et al., 1997). Of course, this is not conductive for persons with hearing deficiencies, like deaf or hard-of-hearing populations.

Most survey researchers that are not familiar with deafness would tend to underestimate methodological problems associated with this population due to the expectation that deaf people do not have problems with reading or writing in self-administered questionnaires or are able to read from the lips when face-to-face interviews are applied (Eckhardt & Anastas, 2007).

However, on the one hand, profound hearing-loss - especially in early childhood - also limits the acquisition of literal competences (Krammer, 2001). On the other hand, sign language is the preferred language of most prelingually deaf persons, which strongly differs from written language with respect to grammar and word-pool (Wilcox, 1989; Lucas, 1996). Hence, for instance, only ten percent of the Austrian deaf school graduates achieve a level of reading comprehension comparable to non-deaf pupils who finished primary school (Gelter, 1987).

This is the main reason why empirical and epidemiological research with deaf populations is rare, because classical survey methods are not appropriate (Lipton et al., 1996; Eckhart & Anastas, 2007). In addition to literacy problems, cultural differences between hearing and deaf persons also contradict the application of classical standardized methods, "which may be invalid or even unethical" (Cornes et al., 2006, p. 666). One has to assume reduced compliance of deaf respondents due to the resistance of deaf communities to disclose information to hearing persons especially in the case of sensitive questions and their fear of further stigmatization of deaf persons (Lipton, 1996).

Although Eckhardt and Anastas (2007) notice that web-based surveys have potential to reach hidden and disabled populations from a theoretical view, they argue, though, that this is contradicted due to the digital divide as well as literacy problems that raise the risk of biased samples. In reports from studies that applied written standardized methods for deaf populations, problems of data quality and biased samples are frequently reported. Hintermayer (2008), for instance, applied a text-based web survey for deaf and hard-of-hearing persons. 27 percent of the filled out questionnaires had to be excluded due to a high degree of item non-response. He also found evidence of strongly biased samples regarding the educational status and other demographic variables of the respondents, which leads to his conclusion that "this means that in this sample we were dealing with a comparatively privileged group within the whole group of deaf and hard-of-hearing people" (Hintermayer, 2008, p. 285). Bat-Chava (1993, 1994) reports that, due to the reduced reading skills, only brief questionnaires and mainly single item measures were used, which did not follow proper English syntax.

Also using signed questionnaires administered face-to-face would yield a series of problems. First, sign language has no written counterpart and has a lower level of standardization. Hence, interviewers would translate questions "on the fly", which introduces additional variability. Furthermore, recruiting interviewers with appropriate knowledge of sign language results in additional administrative work. Also, the high degree of institutionalization of deaf people significantly increases the probability that respondents and interviewers know each other. Therefore, together with the increased resistance of deaf communities to disclose information, face-to-face communication is expected to raise response bias.

Furthermore, things are complicated due to the heterogeneity of deaf populations. Language preferences and sign language skills differ with cultural group identification and the modalities of hearing loss (Hintermair, 2008; Bat-Chava, 2000). Prelingually deaf persons are more likely to use sign language compared to those with a later occurrence of hearing loss and hard-of-hearing populations (Parsons et al., 2000). Hence, researches have to account for different language preferences.

Due to these circumstances, video-based computer interviews are successfully applied in research with deaf respondents (Cornes et al., 2006; Gerich & Lehner, 2003, 2006; Fellinger et al., 2005; Goldstein et al., 2004; Lipton et al., 1996). In video-based computer interviews, signed and written versions of questions and response options are presented simultaneously so that respondents can choose their preferred language. The signed versions of the questions are pre-recorded and therefore additional interviewer variation due to different translations is avoided. Video sequences are selectable by a process of translation and back-translation to assure high validity and comparability with written versions. Finally, a video-based computer interview is the only mode of data collection which allows self-administration and the use of sign language at the same time. Besides the technical advantage, applications have shown that deaf respondents like the technology as well as the experience that is specially designed for deaf people. The advantage of the use of multiple channels is expressed by a respondent's statement cited by Lipton and colleagues: "I liked looking at the sentences and comparing them to the signs, and making sure it was consistent" (Lipton et al., 1996, p. 375).

Research which compared written and computer-assisted modes of data collection for broader deaf populations are rare, though, which is simply the case because written questionnaires are only applicable for highly educated deaf respondents (Gerich & Lehner, 2003, 2006)[3].

Cornes et al. (2006) compared prevalence estimations of psychopathology among deaf adolescents administered with written and computer-based signed questionnaires. They found higher non-response and lower prevalence estimates amongst written compared to signed questionnaires, which is mainly ascribed to comprehension problems with written questionnaires. Similarly, Zazove et al. (2006) report that a written compared to a signed version of a self-rated depression scale was less predictive for depressive symptoms in a deaf sample. Besides the literacy problem, they identified problems due to cultural differences regarding the acknowledgement of depression and partly missing analogons in sign language for idioms used in written speech (like "feeling blue").

In contrast to most video-assisted computer-based applications for other populations which are primarily thought to offer additional cognitive support by means of the use of visual cues, one has to ensure fully signed user interfaces. Field experience, for instance, has shown that it is useful to implement a function that gives feedback about the chosen response option in sign language. Furthermore, it is useful that buttons for the response categories are not only labelled with text versions of the corresponding answer, but also provide a logical association with the corresponding signed description of the answer categories[4]. One solution to this is to assign different colours to the response categories. A colour symbol is shown during the video-sequence where the answer category is shown in sign language as well as on the response button that corresponds to the answer category shown (Gerich & Lehner, 2006)[5].

To date, all video-based surveys for deaf populations were administered offline. Whether video web surveys for deaf respondents are promising seems doubtful. On the one hand, deaf persons are in need of communication and assistance to counter their skeptical attitudes towards surveys in general. On the other hand, due to low computer literacy – especially amongst elder deaf respondents – researchers have to keep certain requirements regarding the input devices in mind. In a recent survey for elder deaf respondents, most of the respondents expected that responses could be given via touchscreen functions. Touchscreens – when affordable – would be the optimal solution for deaf respondents. Only about one percent of elder deaf respondents used the mouse for response input. To enable input using the keyboard – which was most preferred when touch screens were not available – the keys had to be labelled with the corresponding symbols that were used in the survey. Considering these restrictions together, video web surveys for the broader deaf population seem to provide only little prospects for success to date.

Children as Respondents

In recent decades, young children have been increasingly addressed as respondents in standardized surveys although – due to the limited cognitive capacities of young respondents - doubts about data quality are frequently discussed issues (Fuchs, 2007; Fraser et al., 2004; Borgers & Hox, 2001; Scott, 1997). This is also underlined by the evidence for decreasing data quality with lower age of respondents (Fuchs, 2007). Although some authors argue that face-to-face interviews should be applied for young children. Others on the contrary argue that self-administration enables respondents for deeper question understanding and answer retrieval, which is "especially important when surveying special populations, such as children, adolescents, or elderly who need extra attention and time" (De Leeuw et al., 2003, p. 224). However, as Harter and Pike (1984) note, besides the literacy problem of young children, paper-based questionnaires are boring to young respondents and, hence, motivation and rapport is low. Romer

et al. (1997) were one of the first authors who argued that multimedia-enhanced computer interviews may be suitable to combining the benefits of both methods. They successfully used "talking computers" for children between 9 and 15 years and found evidence for enhanced data quality with sensitive questions compared to face-to-face interviews. Similarly, Trapl et al. (2005) report that later studies using A-CASI methods confirmed the findings with few exceptions that it increased reporting of sensitive behaviour compared to other modes (FTF, telephone and PP). The authors used audio-enhanced PDA-instruments for children with a mean age of 12 years and concluded that "with audio enhancement, students with a range of reading and language abilities were able to participate in data collection" and exhibited that only little fatigue occurred and children were highly motivated during the survey (Trapl et al., 2005, p. 303).

Powell et al. (2002) used a computer assessment for the child's understanding of different terms with an animated mouse ("Marvin"). They applied this method for children between 4 and 5 years and compared it to a verbal assessment. They see computer-administered tests as "child-centred" because they are enjoyed and stimulate empowerment: "whether their views are valid or not, children tend to consider the use of technology (such as computers or video recordings) as an indication that their statements are being taken more seriously" (Powell et al., 2002, p. 580). They confirmed the hypothesis of greater likeability by self-reported ratings as well as by behavioural responses, but found no differences regarding the performance of recall-tasks between the verbal and the computerized assessment. They further conclude that, as the self-administered computer assessment is more enjoyable and does not lead to higher distraction or to a reduction of honest answers compared to a verbal assessment, it has the potential to improve the quality of data collection with children.

Table 1. Percentages of positive ratings by mode of data collection

	V-CASI	Paper & Pencil	Face-to-face
Question comprehension	43.3	39.4	24.2
Low task difficulty	81.8	69.7	77.1
Fun	90.9	75.8	86.5
Would do it again	87.5	70.6	76.5
Duration of the survey	79.4	73.5	84.8
Not boring	96.8	88.2	75.7

Haines et al. (2004) report that children say that they are more willing to report truthful answers to sensitive questions with interactive computer-administered questionnaires compared to paper-based methods. Furthermore, answering computer questionnaires is reported to be "less onerous than filling in 'boring' paper questionnaires" (Haines et al., 2004, p. 29). Moreover, they argue that multimedia-enhanced computer interviews help to reduce literacy and comprehension problems even with older children. The authors, for instance, cite a 14-year-old respondent who said that "It helped if you couldn't pronounce a word. It read it to you. It took less time doing it that way. If you don't understand a word, when it reads it out to you, you clearly understand what it means" (Haines et al., 2004, p. 29). Similarly, Berger (2006) argues that, due children's increasing experience with computers and computer games, audio-visual computer interviews facilitate motivational benefits for interview situations which are potentially anxiety-provoking and boring.

Compared to direct interaction in face-to-face interviews, Doherty-Sneddon and McAuley (2000) argue that the greater social distance in video-mediated communication leads to a situation which is less stressful and intimating to children. For children between 6 and 10 years old, they found information benefits through increased resistance to misleading questions in video-mediated compared to face-to-face interviews (e.g., the question whether it was funny to come up with the lift when the children did not take a lift). They

especially report more mode-effects amongst younger children in the sense that their level of resistance equaled the level of older children in the video situation, whereas younger children showed lower levels of resistance compared to older in the face-to-face situation.

Gerich and Bergmair (2008) interviewed 106 children aged between 8 and 13 years who were randomly assigned to three different modes of data collection (V-CASI, PP and FTF). Similar to the results of other studies, it was found that the self-administered video-mode was rated more positively with respect to comprehension, task-difficulty, likeability, and attractiveness compared to the two other modes (Table 1).

On average, children in the video-mode rated 5.2 out of the six items in Table 1 positively. This mean rating of the video-mode is significantly larger (p=0.002) compared to the ratings of the paper-and-pencil (4.3 positive ratings) and the face-to-face mode (4.4 positive ratings).

The resulting data quality was compared with respect to reliability and response consistency. Whereas the study found no indications for mode differences with respect to reliability, differences with respect to response consistency were found. Response consistency was checked with four questions that were equally distributed through the questionnaire concerning the child's evaluation of pocket money. All questions asked about the same content, but the directions (positive and negative wording) were varied ("Do you think that it is fair (unfair) if other children get more (less)

Table 2. Response consistency across four questions ("pocket money" questions) per mode

	full consistency	partial inconsistency	maximal inconsistency
V-CASI (n=34)	47.1	38.2	14.7
Paper & Pencil (n=35)	31.4	34.3	34.3
Face-to-face (n=37)	48.6	40.5	10.8

Percentages (row-wise)

pocket money?"). The responses in the four questions were coded regarding their content-related consistency (Table 2)[6].

The most consistent (and least inconsistent) responses were observed for the face-to-face condition, closely followed by the video mode (the difference between the two modes is not significant). The consistency in the paper mode clearly revealed the least consistent responses. The proportions of fully consistent (p=0.028) and maximally inconsistent response pattern (p=0.009) in the paper version are significantly different compared to the other two modes.

Inspection of response consistency depending on the age of children shows that the consistency of the answers of older children (11 to 13 years) is highest in the video version (followed by the paper and the face-to-face mode), whereas the consistency of the answers of younger children (8 to 10 years) is highest in the face-to-face version (followed by the video and the paper mode). Hence, especially children elder than 10 years seem to benefit from the video-enhanced mode of data collection.

EFFECTS OF AUDIO-VISUAL COMPUTER INTERVIEWS ON RESPONSE BEHAVIOUR

To date, only a few studies have focused on mode effects of audio-visually enhanced web-surveys, which is especially due to the technical restrictions regarding audio-visual implementations in online research. Hence, most of the research on

mode effects of audio-visual computer interviews is based on offline methods (AV-CASI) and laboratory studies (Fuchs & Funke, 2009). When the impact of audio-visual methods on response behaviour is focused from a theoretical point of view, a first approach will be to locate these surveys within the classical spectrum of survey methods. The main differentiation in the methods of data collection is whether they are self-administered or interviewer-administered, which means face-to-face interviews.

Arguments in favour of FTF methods usually refer to a higher level of control over the interview situation. This includes opportunities for respondent's support (clarification of content and answer categories as well as skip and branch routines) and higher attention and motivation of respondents due to social interaction including the verbal and non-verbal cues of the interviewer and the social process of turn-taking (Anderson, 2008; Dykema et al., 1997; Sproull et al., 1996). These issues are sometimes subsumed under the concept of rapport[7], which seems to be a prerequisite in establishing trust and honest answers and is mainly achieved by non-verbal communication (Cassell & Miller, 2008; Groves et al., 2004).

On the other hand, interviewers are likely to exert social influence on a respondent's behaviour, which is usually seen as response bias. This bias may be due to the variability of interviewer behaviour, personal characteristics like age, gender, race, anticipated social class or political affiliation (Cassell & Miller, 2008; Dillman, 2000; Sudman & Bradburn, 1974) or simply due to the effects of "mere" social presence (Krysan & Couper,

2003; Sproull et al., 1996)[8]. Probably the most prominent biases associated with social presence are social desirability, impression management and reduced self-disclosure. Hence, especially with sensitive questions, SAQ's are recommended as a means of reducing response bias (Groves et al., 2004; Tourangeau & Smith, 1996; Sudman & Bradburn, 1974) due to the lack of social presence and enhanced privacy of the interview situation.

In addition, some authors, by contrast, assume that SAQ compared to FTF offers superior conditions in supporting cognitive retrieval during the response process: "The usually more leisurely pace of the self-administered procedure gives the respondent more time to understand the meaning of the question and retrieve and compose an answer, which improves the quality of answers" (De Leeuw et al., 2003, p. 224).

When applying previous knowledge about the characteristics of classical survey modes on audio-visual methods, one has to decide, whether they belong to self- or interviewer-administered methods. Of course, although audio-visual methods mimic social situations by the introduction of social cues like voice and facial expressions, it strongly differs from face-to-face communication due to the absence of co-temporality and mutual visibility. Also, unlike to the face-to-face condition, response is given via a classic communicative channel by keyboard (Fuchs, 2009b). On the other hand, the characteristics of SAQ are explicitly deduced by the absence of social cues during the question-answer process. This leads to the question asked by Cassell and Miller (2008) whether it is still "self-administration if the computer gives you encouraging looks". Hence, bringing social cues into self-administered modes of data collection disbands the classic dichotomy of FTF and SAQ.

Starting from these points of discussion, two – partly contradictory – strands of hypotheses about the effects of audio-visual elements in computer based data collection can be extracted from literature. On the one hand, previous findings of human-computer interaction research

and social interface theory are applied, which state that people tend to treat computers like real social actors, especially when they mimic some kind of subtle human-like elements (Couper et al., 2001). Nass et al. (1997), for instance, found that even minimal social cues like human voice implemented in computer interviews may provoke gender-specific stereotypes. Walker et al. (1994) found that different facial expressions (stern vs. pleasant mien) of artificial virtual faces could change response behaviour. Sproull et al. (1996) found that people respond differently and present themselves in a more positive light when interacting with a (synthetic) talking face compared to a text display.

Other studies (Nass, Moon, & Carney, 1999) found that people tend to be more polite to computers they have cooperated with – and hence found that respondents treat computers like real social actors. Also, studies have found evidence for virtual race-of-interviewer (Krysan & Couper, 2003) and gender-of-interviewer effects (Fuchs, 2009a) with video-enhanced computer surveys. Weisband and Kiesler (1996) conclude out of a meta analysis that differences in the psychometric properties of questionnaires may occur when multimedia elements are included which "partially mimic social situations". Hence, these results support the view that audio-visually enhanced interviews – although self-administered – have such properties that are more like those of face-to-face interviews. Therefore, it could be argued that audio-visually enhanced computer interviews – on the one hand – promote response bias induced by social presence, like social desirable responding or impression management.

This view of audio-visual methods however is partly contradicted by research on survey methodology. Many of the previous research studies have shown evidence for improved data quality with CASI compared to traditional methods (e.g., FTF or paper-and-pencil) of data collection (De Leeuw, 2002; De Leeuw, Hox, & Snijkers, 1995). For example, various studies conclude that CASI seems to offer a more private situation for the respondents than other forms of data collection, resulting in more self-disclosure compared to FTF and paper SAQ (Hewitt, 2002; Schneider & Edwards, 2000; Richman et al., 1999; Turner et al., 1998; De Leeuw et al., 1997; Nicholls et al., 1997; Weisband & Kiesler, 1996; O'Reilly et al., 1994).

Furthermore, the possibility of entry checks during the process of data administration, as well as computer-controlled skip and branch routines help to improve data quality and to reduce item non-response with CASI compared to traditional methods like paper-and-pencil or face-to-face (De Leeuw et al., 1995, 1997, 2003; De Leeuw, 2002; Turner et al., 1998; Nicholls et al., 1997; Ramos et al., 1998). Some authors highlight the special role of audio technology as a strategy to counter problems of substantial underreporting of sensitive behaviour (Turner et al., 1998; Lessler & O'Reilly, 1997; Tourangeau & Smith, 1996). A-CASI is seen as a well-established technology of data collection especially for sensitive questions (Couper, 2005). However, in sum, previous research provides only weak support for the higher data quality of A-CASI compared to simple text-based CASI (Couper, Singer, & Tourangeau, 2003). But even when there is no evidence for reduced social desirable responding in A-CASI compared to T-CASI, these results at least contradict the hypothesis of increased desirable responding with social interfaces as stated by human-computer interaction research.

Similar results are reported for visual social cues in surveys. Couper, Tourangeau, and Steiger (2001) used low intensity visual and interactive cues (pictures of researches, personalization with names of respondents and echoing back to earlier answers) and found no evidence for more socially desirable responding or impression management compared to simple text-based methods.

Katz et al. (2007) used A-CASI methods enhanced with pictures of interviewers and other illustrations for blood donor screenings to gain information about infections, risky sexual practices, drug use and risky health behaviour. They conclude that computer-assisted interviewing and especially audio-visual enhancement helps to increase the reporting of risk behaviour associated with transfusion-transmissible infections. In addition, it improves donor and staff satisfaction and leads to error reduction.

For those studies that found less than more desirable responding with audio-visually enhanced methods, different theoretical explanations were brought forward (Couper, Tourangeau, & Marvin, 2009; Fuchs & Funke, 2007, 2009; Fuchs, 2009a, 2009b; Anderson, 2008; Katz et al., 2007; Tourangeau & Smith, 1996). Some authors highlight the enhanced privacy of audio-visual modes also induced by the use of headphones, which are thought to support some kind of isolation from the surroundings. Joinson (2001), for instance, differentiates between private and public self-awareness, which he found to interact regarding their effect on self-disclosure in dyad-based computer-mediated communication. Private self-awareness (i.e., self-focused) combined with reduced public self-awareness (i.e., high anonymity or reduced identifiability) would heighten self-disclosure.

Furthermore, the cognitive argument of channel richness (Groves et al., 2004; Daft & Lengel, 1986) is brought forward, which states that using both audio and video channels improves reception and supports cognitive processing during the question-answer process and hence reduces satisficing[9]. Katz et al. (2007), for instance, conclude that the fraction of respondents with reduced literacy skills within a normal population sample is underestimated and hence using multiple channels for the presentation of questions and response options helps to improve data quality. Moreover, it is argued that using multiple communicative channels as well as the more human-like communication induced by social cues helps to increase respondents' motivation and involvement, which promotes question understanding und information retrieval and willingness to report even sensitive information.

Couper, Tourangeau, and Steiger (2001) suppose two reasons for the differences between the results of social interface and survey research. On the one hand, they argue that social interface research is typically conducted with laboratory experiments whereas survey research is typically conducted as field research where respondents are unaware of the experimental conditions. In addition, social interface research mostly focuses on performance measurement (e.g., task performance) as dependent variables whereas survey research mostly focuses on social desirability and impression management of self-reports.

In sum, however, De Leeuw (2005, p. 244) states as "information transmission and interviewer effects are related", it may well be that both effects of social presence and cognitive support are working, which results in a kind of trade-off between both. Anderson (2008, p. 105), for instance therefore speculates that "for very sensitive topics, however, it may be that a recorded video of the interviewer asking the questions with touchscreen responses may be the best mix for balancing rapport and privacy to maximize the accuracy of responses".

Fuchs and Funke (2007) hypothesize that this trade-off results in an advantage of audio-visual methods, because the positive effects of social cues on cognitive processing is contradicted by only small effects of social presence. The effects of social presence in video-enhanced modes are expected to be small because the behaviour of a virtual interviewer is more standardized and an interviewer cannot react to a specific respondent behaviour[10]. As responses are communicated through the keyboard, they expect that social presence is only active during the first cognitive stages of the question-answer process (i.e., question comprehension and retrieval), but not in the last stages where editing takes place. Hence, they conclude that audio-visual methods are suited to combine advantages of SAQ and FTF.

RESEARCH ON VIDEO-ENHANCED SELF-ADMINISTERED COMPUTER INTERVIEWS

Due to the technical limitations to date, only little research has been taken up on web-based surveys using video-material. For the display and transfer of videotaped questions over the web, some minimal technical requirements on client-side are still necessary. Hence, one has to assume higher dropout rates and potential sample bias when multimedia material is implemented into web surveys. Fuchs and Funke (2007), for instance, report higher unit non-response in a video-web survey compared to a randomized control group with a simple text-based web-survey. Whereas 51 percent of the respondents in the text-based survey entered the starting page of the survey, only 44 percent did so in the video-version. Also, they observed higher rates of break-offs in the video-version (17 percent) compared to the text-survey (1 percent).

These differences were partly attributed to the technical capabilities. One has to take into account that although most of the private computers of respondents are probably capable of playing multimedia elements, respondents frequently take access to web surveys out of home (e.g., via mobile devices or via public computers) which do not provide adequate technical requirements. However, the authors take into account that respondents are more reluctant to take part in a video survey when the privacy of surroundings is not guaranteed because of the fear that everyone could see or hear their answers to questions in the video-mode. The latter is supported by the circumstance that respondents in video-mode answered the survey more often in a private setting (at their own or a friend's or relative's computer) compared to text-mode. In addition, 14 percent of respondents in video-mode said that others could see or hear the questions while responding, but only five percent in text-mode said that others could see the questions. Hence, it is assumed that video- compared to text-based web surveys reduce the privacy of the interview situation. Also, contrary to a typically controlled interview situation with offline CASI-methods, it cannot be assumed that respondents use headphones to assure higher privacy. Indeed, only four percent of the respondents in this study said that they used headphones during the interview in the video-version.

Virtual interviewer-effects in video-enhanced computer interviews were found by Fuchs (2009a) and Krysan and Couper (2003). Fuchs (2009a) found gender-of-interviewer interviewer effects for questions regarding sexual behaviour when controlling for gender of interviewer and gender of respondent. However, the direction of these effects varied with different questions. Some questions showed same-gender, some questions showed opposite-gender effects. Krysan and Couper (2003) found race-of-interviewer effects in FTF Interviews as well as in V-CASI but with partly different directions.

As with every interviewer effect, where only a limited number of different interviewers are used, further possible confounded differences of the interviewers (for example, differences in voice, appearance, attractiveness) cannot be controlled. Hence, it cannot be concluded that the found interviewer effects are truly caused by gender or race. Nevertheless, both results show that – as stated by social interface theory – "virtual" interviewers (either because they "mimic" social presence or due to "mere presence") may also provoke interviewer effects.

Contrary to expectations, respondents in the video-mode said that they paid slightly less attention to the single question in the video- compared to the text-mode. However, it has to be noted that the authors used a video-only-mode in this study, which means that they did not provide a simultaneous text version of the question and the questions were only presented as video sequences. Hence the cognitive improvement using the video-

channel may have been reduced by omitting the text-channel.

In two studies, Fuchs and Funke found no differences in the scores of a desirability scale collected with a video-web survey compared to a text-based version (Fuchs & Funke, 2007, 2009). No significant differences regarding underreporting of sensitive behaviour (sexual behaviour) were found, either. Similarly, Gerich (2008a, 2008b) compared V-CASI with other modes (FTF, PP, T-CASI and A-CASI) within a randomized experimental design. Although, as expected, the highest scores on a social desirability scale were found in the face-to-face mode and the lowest scores in the V-CASI condition, none of the mode differences regarding social desirability proved to be significant. In addition, overall mode differences regarding self-reported norm deviation – which served as an indicator for underreporting of different types of sensitive behaviour – were not significant. However, the reported norm deviation in the video version was significantly higher compared to all other modes.

In another study (Gerich, 2009), smaller gender discrepancies regarding the reported number of lifetime sex partners were found in V-CASI with female and male interviewer compared to T-CASI. Gender discrepancies in the reported number of sex partners are frequently found in survey research with various cultures and samples. Predominately these gender differences are ascribed to result out of a gender specific response bias which is called the cultural double-standard (Wiederman, 1997; Catania, 1996; Wadsworth et al., 1996). Further it is assumed that male and female respondents apply different recall strategies for the processing of these questions, where men tend to apply rough estimation whereas women tend to apply count strategies (Brown & Sinclair, 1999; Wadsworth et al., 1996)[11]. Figure 1 shows the mean number of lifetime sex partners for a student-sample (n=300), randomly allocated on three modes of data collection. In all three modes, the mean number of reported sex partners

Figure 1. Mean reported number of lifetime sexual partners by interview-mode and gender of respondents (Means and standard deviation in brackets; r=point-biseral correlation between gender of respondents and number of sex partner; d=Cohen's d, n=number of cases)

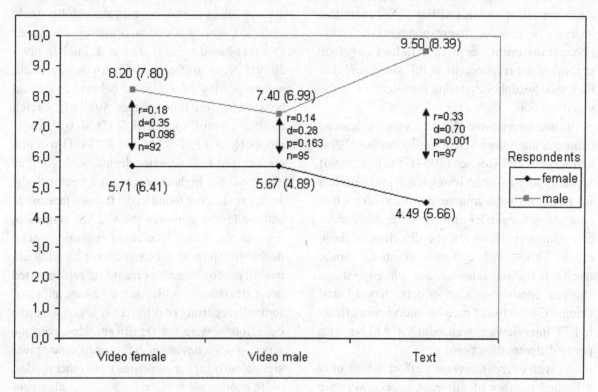

of male respondents was higher compared to the reported mean number of female respondents. However, the gender differences were stronger in the T-CASI mode (the correlation between the reported number of sex-partners and respondent's gender was 0.33; p=0.001) compared to the results in both V-CASI modes (non-significant gender differences). Hence, based on the results of the study, it was concluded, that response bias with respect to the number of lifetime sex partners is reduced in V-CASI.

A possible reason for this finding is that the video-enhanced mode of data collection does not lead to a higher degree of socially desirable responding, but to higher cognitive processing during the question-answer process, which supports the recall and estimation process.

In addition, results reported by Fuchs and Funke (2007, 2009) support the hypothesis of deeper cognitive processing with video-enhanced web surveys. They compared the impact of additional information that was given to respondents in a video-enhanced and a text-based web survey. They found that the additional information affected later response behaviour in the expected direction, but with larger effects in the video condition compared to the text condition. Similarly, they found that additional specifications within survey questions were more strongly recognized by respondents in the video- compared to the text-mode. Whereas additional specifications in the text-mode were primarily recognized when they were placed at the beginning of a question, it was also recognized when placed at the end of a question within the video mode.

Table 3. Influence of interview spots on desirability, self-control, and norm deviation by mode (ANOVA results)

	PP	FTF	A-CASI	V-CASI
Social desirability	0.010 (0.23)	0.004 (0.23)	0.979 (<0.01)	0.090 (0.13)
Self-control	0.395 (0.06)	0.031 (0.16)	0.323 (0.07)	0.400 (0.06)
Norm deviation	0.844 (0.02)	0.472 (0.04)	0.896 (0.01)	0.685 (0.03)

Results of ANOVAs for interview-spot on the three traits controlled for age and sex.

P-values for the main effect of interview spot, partial R^2 for interview spot in brackets.

PP=Paper & Pencil; FTF=Face-to-face; A-CASI=Audio-enhanced CASI; V-CASI=Audio and video-enhanced CASI.

Fuchs (2009b) compared the response behaviour with sensitive questions about sexual behaviour between text-based and video-enhanced mode more deeply. He found that underreporting of sensitive behaviour in the text-version was associated with higher scores on a social desirability scale and with higher perceived social presence. In the video-mode, underreporting of sensitive behaviour was not correlated with social desirability scores and – contrary to the text-based mode – higher degrees of perceived social presence promoted the reporting of sensitive behaviour. He concludes from the results that "while in the text-based Web survey condition the final survey response is promoted by question understanding and contradicted by social presence and social desirability, in the video-enhanced version social presence seems to facilitate the reporting of sensitive information" (Fuchs, 2009b, p. 12).

Similarly, Gerich (2008b, 2009) found that social desirability has the smallest effect on underreporting of norm deviation in V-CASI compared to other modes of data collection (PP, T-CASI and A-CASI). At the same time – using control theory (Pratt & Cullen, 2000; Gottfredson & Hirschi, 1990) as a theoretical framework for the explanation of norm deviation – he found the highest construct validity for responses collected with V-CASI compared to the other modes. Hence, as in the research of Fuchs (2009b) he concludes that social presence induced by the social cues

of video-enhanced surveys does not promote socially desirable responding, but helps to support respondents' cognitive work, which leads to higher data quality.

Gerich (2008a) analyzed four modes of data collection (PP, FTF, A-CASI, and V-CASI) with respect to the influences of the surroundings during interviews. 200 interviews were conducted by two interviewers each at four different locations at the university, where respondents were randomly assigned one of the four modes of data collection. Hence, the interviews can be grouped into four "spots." Each spot is characterized by the presence of two specific interviewers on a specific day of the week. All interviews were conducted in a public area but, because of the variation of the weekdays, the situation differed across the four spots as, for instance, the number of students present at university varied.

Table 3 displays the results of ANOVAs separately conducted for the four mode groups, with the interview spot as factor variable and social desirability, self-control, and norm deviation as dependent variables, respectively (control variables were the age and gender of respondents).

The results show significant main effects of the interview spot on social desirability scores and self-control in the FTF condition. In addition, a significant main effect for social desirability was found in the paper-and-pencil condition. Spot influence in the two CASI conditions does not reach a significance level of p<0.05. Hence, the results support the hypothesis of enhanced privacy of audio- and video-enhanced modes (which may be induced or amplified by the use of headphones), which help to reduce the effects of the social environment by the reduction of public self-awareness and enhancement of private self-awareness.

CONCLUSION

This chapter was aimed at summarizing previous research on the application of video-enhanced computer interviews. The text was organized around the two main strands of current research and applications, which are the utilization of video-enhanced methods of data collection for special target groups (namely deaf respondents and children) on the one hand and the mode effects of audio-visual computer interviews within standard survey applications on the other hand.

Video enhanced computer interviews clearly contribute benefit to survey research with deaf respondents. The method allows to reduce literacy requirements, allow deaf respondents to choose between their preferred language (sign language and text) or to employ both communicative channels to improve question understanding. Furthermore, the implementation of sign language helps to reduce the cultural distance between the deaf and the hearing world and hence contributes to respondents' motivation and compliance. However, due to special needs regarding assistance and interfaces for responding, web-based video applications for deaf respondents seem to provide only limited prospects for success.

Moreover, audio-visual computer interviews were successfully applied with standardized surveys for children. These methods can be characterized as child-centred, since they are able to attract children as well as reduce literacy requirements and cognitive load. It was found that children like these methods more than text-based interviews,

exhibit reduced fatigue, higher comprehension and produce higher data quality. Although especially for younger children (e.g., younger than 10 years) face-to-face interviews may still be the first choice regarding data quality, previous research shows that audio-visual computer interviews can be a promising trade-off between interviewer- and self-administered methods.

Regarding the general mode effects of video-enhanced surveys, two different views can be extracted from literature. From the viewpoint of social interface theory and human-computer interaction research, it is followed that respondents tend to treat computers like social actors. Hence, it is inferred that computer methods which include social cues (like human voice or faces) may enhance socially desirable responding comparable to face-to-face interviews.

Contrary to that view, previous results on research about audio-enhanced survey methods mainly stress the argument of channel richness and privacy. It is hypothesized that the implementation of different communication channels improves question understanding, fosters respondents' cognitive focus on processing the single question and simultaneously helps to suppress environmental influences.

As previous research about the effects of video-enhanced computer interviews on response behaviour is rare, evidence on the direction of mode effects is not conclusive yet. On the one hand, consistent with social interface theory, some studies found incidences for virtual interviewer effects (gender-of-interviewer and race-of-interviewer effects) comparable to face-to-face interviews. On the other hand, recent studies did not find evidence for enhanced socially desirable responding judged by the responses to social desirability scales and the reporting of sensitive behaviour. Consistent with the hypothesis of channel richness, some studies found indications for deeper cognitive processing regarding question comprehension and answer retrieval, higher construct validity, smaller amounts of social desirability contamination and reduced environmental influences on responses given with video-enhanced compared to other modes of data collection. However, for web-based surveys including virtual interviewers, one has to account for higher unit non-response and potentially biased samples. This is caused by the technical requirements on the client hardware, which has to be capable of playing multimedia elements, as well as by the fear of respondents that others could see or hear questions and answers in a video-web survey. In sum, it may well be the case that mode effects of video-enhanced online and offline interviews are different. Furthermore, it seems that video-enhanced methods have to be characterized as some kind of "hybrids" which combine properties associated with interviewer- and self-administered modes, as well. Further research is needed to explore the circumstances influencing the trade-off between both properties.

REFERENCES

Anderson, A. H. (2008). Video-mediated interactions and surveys. In Conrad, F. G., & Schober, M. F. (Eds.), *Envisioning the survey interview of the future* (pp. 95–118). Hoboken, NJ: John Wiley & Sons.

Bat-Chava, Y. (1993). Antecedents of self-esteem in deaf people: A meta-analytic review. *Rehabilitation Psychology, 38*(4), 221–234. doi:10.1037/h0080303

Bat-Chava, Y. (1994). Group identification and self-esteem of deaf adults. *Personality and Social Psychology Bulletin, 20*(5), 494–502. doi:10.1177/0146167294205006

Bat-Chava, Y. (2000). Diversity of deaf identities. *American Annals of the Deaf, 145*(5), 420–428.

Berger, M. (2006). Computer assisted clinical assessment. *Child and Adolescent Mental Health, 11*(2), 64–75. doi:10.1111/j.1475-3588.2006.00394.x

Borgers, N., & Hox, J. (2001). Item nonresponse in questionnaire research with children. *Journal of Official Statistics, 17*(2), 321–335.

Brown, N. R., & Sinclair, R. C. (1999). Estimating number of lifetime sexual partners: Men and women do it differently. *Journal of Sex Research, 36*(3), 292–297. doi:10.1080/00224499909551999

Cassell, J., & Miller, P. (2008). Is it self-administration if the computer gives you encouraging looks? In Conrad, F. G., & Schober, M. F. (Eds.), *Envisioning the survey interview of the future* (pp. 161–178). Hoboken, NJ: John Wiley & Sons. doi:10.1002/9780470183373.ch8

Catania, J. A., Binson, D., Canchola, J., Pollack, L. M., Hauck, W., & Coates, T. J. (1996). Effects of interviewer gender, interviewer choice, and item wording on responses to questions concerning sexual behavior. *Public Opinion Quarterly, 60*(3), 345–375. doi:10.1086/297758

Chan, D., & Schmitt, N. (1997). Video-based versus paper-and-pencil method of assessment in situational judgment tests: subgroup differences in test performance and face validity perceptions. *The Journal of Applied Psychology, 82*(1), 143–159. doi:10.1037/0021-9010.82.1.143

Cornes, A., Rohan, M. J., Napier, J., & Rey, J. M. (2006). Reading the signs: Impact of signed versus written questionnaires on the prevalence of psychopathology among deaf adolescents. *The Australian and New Zealand Journal of Psychiatry, 40*(8), 665–673.

Couper, M. P. (2005). Technology trends in survey data collection. *Social Science Computer Review, 23*(4), 486–501. doi:10.1177/0894439305278972

Couper, M. P. (2008). Technology and the survey interview/questionnaire. In Conrad, F. G., & Schober, M. F. (Eds.), *Envisioning the survey interview of the future* (pp. 58–76). Hoboken, NJ: John Wiley & Sons.

Couper, M. P., Singer, E., & Tourangeau, R. (2003). Understanding the effects of Audio-CASI on self-reports of sensitive behavior. *Public Opinion Quarterly, 67*(3), 385–395. doi:10.1086/376948

Couper, M. P., Tourangeau, R., & Marvin, T. (2009). Taking the audio out of Audio-CASI. *Public Opinion Quarterly, 73*(2), 281–303. doi:10.1093/poq/nfp025

Couper, M. P., Tourangeau, R., & Steiger, D. M. (2001, March 31-April 5). Social presence in web surveys. In *Proceedings of the Conference on Human Factors in Computing Systems,* Seattle, WA (pp. 412-415).

Daft, R. L., & Lengel, R. H. (1986). Organizational information requirements, media richness and structural design. *Management Science, 32*(5), 554–571. doi:10.1287/mnsc.32.5.554

De Leeuw, E. (2002). The effect of computer-assisted interviewing on data quality: A review of the evidence. In J. Blasius, J. Hox, E. de Leeuw, & P. Schmidt (Eds.), *Social science methodology in the new millennium.* Opladen, Germany: Leske + Budrich.

De Leeuw, E. (2005). To mix or not to mix data collection modes in surveys. *Journal of Official Statistics, 21*(2), 233–255.

De Leeuw, E., Hox, J., & Kef, S. (2003). Computer-assisted self-interviewing tailored for special populations and topics. *Field Methods, 15*(3), 223–251. doi:10.1177/1525822X03254714

De Leeuw, E., Hox, J., Kef, S., & Van Hattum, M. (1997). *Overcoming the problems of special interviews on sensitive topics: Computer assisted self-interviewing tailored for young children and adolescents.* Sequim, WA: Sawtooth Software Conference Proceedings.

De Leeuw, E., Hox, J., & Snijkers, G. (1995). The effect of computer-assisted interviewing on data quality: A review. *Journal of the Market Research Society. Market Research Society, 37*(4), 325–344.

Dillman, D. A. (2000). *Mail and internet surveys: The tailored design method.* New York, NY: Wiley.

Doherty-Sneddon, G., & McAuley, S. (2000). Influence of video-mediation on adult-child interviews: Implications for the use of the live link with child witnesses. *Applied Cognitive Psychology, 14*(4), 379–392. doi:10.1002/1099-0720(200007/08)14:4<379::AID-ACP664>3.0.CO;2-T

Dykema, J., Lepkowski, J. M., & Blixt, S. (1997). The effect of interviewer and respondent behavior on data quality: Analysis of interaction coding in a validation study. In Lyberg, L., Biemer, P., Collins, M., DeLeeuw, E., Dippo, C., Schwarz, N., & Trewin, D. (Eds.), *Survey measurement and process quality* (pp. 221–248). New York, NY: Wiley.

Eckhardt, E., & Anastas, J. (2007). Research methods with disabled populations. *Journal of Social Work in Disability & Rehabilitation, 6*(1-2), 233–249. doi:10.1300/J198v06n01_13

Fraser, S., Lewis, V., Ding, S., Kellett, M., & Robinson, C. (2004). *Doing research with children and young people.* London, UK: Sage.

Fuchs, M. (2007). Face-to-face interviews with children. Question difficulty and the impact of cognitive resources on response quality. In *Proceedings of the Survey Research Methods Section, American Statistical Association.* Retrieved from http://www.amstat.org/sections/srms/Proceedings/y2007f.html

Fuchs, M. (2009a). Gender-of-interviewer effects in a video-enhanced web survey. Results from a randomized field experiment. *Social Psychology, 40*(1), 37–42. doi:10.1027/1864-9335.40.1.37

Fuchs, M. (2009b, February 16-18). The video-enhanced web survey. Data quality and cognitive processing of questions. In *Proceedings of the Eurostat Conference on New Techniques and Technologies for Statistics,* Brussels, Belgium.

Fuchs, M., & Funke, F. (2007). Multimedia web surveys: Results from a field experiment on the use of audio and video clips in web surveys. In M. Trotman et al. (Eds.), *The Challenges of a Changing World: Proceedings of the 5th International Conference of the Association for Survey Computing* (pp. 63-80). Berkeley, CA: ASC.

Fuchs, M., & Funke, F. (2009). Die Video-unterstützte Online-Befragung: Soziale Präsenz, soziale Erwünschtheit und Underreporting sensitiver Informationen. In Jackob, N., Schoen, H., & Zerback, T. (Eds.), *Sozialforschung im Internet: Methodologie und Praxis der Online-Befragung* (pp. 159–180). Wiesbaden, Germany: VS-Verlag.

Gelter, I. (1987). Wortschatz und Lesefähigkeit gehörloser Schüler. *Der Sprachheilpädagoge, 3,* 37–42.

Gerich, J. (2008a). Real or virtual? Response behavior in video-enhanced self-administered computer interviews. *Field Methods, 39*(4), 985–992.

Gerich, J. (2008b). Effects of social cues on response behavior. In *Proceedings of the 7th International Conference on Social Science Methodology (RC33),* Naples, Italy.

Gerich, J. (2009). Multimediale Elemente in der Computerbasierten Datenerhebung. Der Einfluss Auditiver und Visueller Elemente auf das Antwortverhalten in Befragungen. In Weichbold, M., Bacher, J., & Wolf, C. (Eds.), *Grenzen und Herausforderungen der Umfrageforschung* (pp. 107–129). Wiesbaden, Germany: Verlag für Sozialwissenschaften.

Gerich, J., & Bergmair, F. (2008). Die Anwendung Videogestützter Selbstadministrierter Computerbefragungen in der Sozialforschung mit Kindern. *Zeitschrift fur Soziologie der Erziehung und Socialisation, 28*(1), 56–74.

Gerich, J., & Lehner, R. (2006). Video computer-assisted self-administered interviews for deaf respondents. *Field Methods, 18*(3), 267–283. doi:10.1177/1525822X06287535

Goldstein, M. F., Eckhardt, E. A., & Joyner, P. (2004). *HIV knowledge in a deaf sample: Preliminary results of a self-administered survey in American Sign Language.* Paper presented at the American Public Health Association Annual Meeting, Washington, DC.

Gottfredson, M. R., & Hirschi, T. (1990). *A general theory of crime.* Stanford, CA: Stanford University Press.

Groves, R. M., Fowler, F. J., Couper, M. P., Lepkowski, J. M., Singer, E., & Tourangeau, R. (2004). *Survey methodology.* Hoboken, NJ: John Wiley & Sons.

Haines, K., Case, S., Isles, E., Rees, I., & Hancock, A. (2004). *Extending entitlement: Making it real.* Cardiff, UK: Welsh Assembly Government.

Harter, S., & Pike, R. (1984). The pictorial scale of perceived competence and social acceptance for young children. *Child Development, 55*(6), 1969–1982. doi:10.2307/1129772

Hewitt, M. (2002). Attitudes toward interview mode and comparability of reporting sexual behavior by personal interview and audio computer-assisted self-interviewing. Analyses of the 1995 National Survey of Family Growth. *Sociological Methods & Research, 31*(1), 3–26. doi:10.1177/0049124102031001001

Hintermair, M. (2008). Self-esteem and satisfaction with life of deaf and hard-of-hearing people – A resource-oriented approach to identity work. *Journal of Deaf Studies and Deaf Education, 13*(2), 278–300. doi:10.1093/deafed/enm054

Katz, L. M., Cumming, P. D., & Wallace, E. L. (2007). Computer-based donor screening: A status report. *Transfusion Medicine Reviews, 21*(1), 13–25. doi:10.1016/j.tmrv.2006.08.001

Krammer, K. (2001). *Schriftsprachkompetenz gehörloser Erwachsener* (*Vol. 3*). Klagenfurt, Germany: Veröffentlichungen des Forschungszentrums für Gebärdensprache und Hörgeschädigtenkommunikation der Universität Klagenfurt.

Krosnick, J. A. (1991). Response strategies for coping with the cognitive demands of attitude measures in surveys. *Applied Cognitive Psychology, 5*(3), 213–236. doi:10.1002/acp.2350050305

Krysan, M., & Couper, M. P. (2003). Race in the live and the virtual interview: racial deference, social desirability, and activation effects in attitude surveys. *Social Psychology Quarterly, 66*(4), 364–383. doi:10.2307/1519835

Lessler, J. T., & O'Reilly, J. M. (1997). Mode of interview and reporting of sensitive issues: design and implementation of audio computer-assisted self-interviewing. *NIDA Research Monograph, 167*, 366–382.

Lipton, D. S., Goldstein, M. F., Fahnbulleh, F. W., & Gertz, E. N. (1996). The Interactive Video-Questionnaire: A new technology for interviewing deaf persons. *American Annals of the Deaf, 141*(5), 370–379.

Lucas, C. (1996). *Multicultural aspects of sociolinguistics in deaf communities*. Washington, DC: Gallaudet University Press.

Nass, C., Moon, Y., & Carney, P. (1999). Are respondents polite to computers? Social desirability and direct responses to computers. *Journal of Applied Social Psychology, 29*(5), 1093–1110. doi:10.1111/j.1559-1816.1999.tb00142.x

Nass, C., Moon, Y., & Green, N. (1997). Are machines gender neutral? Gender-stereotypic responses to computers with voices. *Journal of Applied Social Psychology, 27*(10), 864–876. doi:10.1111/j.1559-1816.1997.tb00275.x

Nicholls, W. L. II, Baker, R. P., & Martin, J. (1997). The effect of new data collection technologies on survey data quality. In Lyberg, L., Biemer, P., Collins, M., DeLeeuw, E., Dippo, C., Schwarz, N., & Trewin, D. (Eds.), *Survey measurement and process quality* (pp. 221–248). New York, NY: Wiley.

O'Muircheartaigh, C. (1997). Measurement error in surveys: A historical perspective. In Lyberg, L., Biemer, P., Collins, M., DeLeeuw, E., Dippo, C., Schwarz, N., & Trewin, D. (Eds.), *Survey measurement and process quality* (pp. 1–25). New York, NY: Wiley.

O'Reilly, J. M., Hubbard, M. L., Lessler, J. T., Biemer, P. P., & Turner, C. F. (1994). Audio and video computer-assisted self-interviewing: Preliminary tests of new technologies for data collection. *Journal of Official Statistics, 10*(2), 197–214.

Parsons, J. A., Baum, S., & Johnson, T. P. (2000). *Inclusion of disabled populations in social surveys: Review and recommendations*. Chicago, IL: Survey Research Laboratory, University of Illinois at Chicago.

Powell, M. B., Wilson, C. J., & Hasty, M. K. (2002). Evaluation of the usefulness of 'Marvin'; a computerized assessment tool for investigative interviewers of children. *Computers in Human Behavior, 18*(5), 577–592. doi:10.1016/S0747-5632(02)00003-1

Pratt, T. C., & Cullen, F. T. (2000). The empirical status of Gottfredson and Hirschi's general theory of crime: A Meta-Analysis. *Criminology, 38*(3), 931–964. doi:10.1111/j.1745-9125.2000. tb00911.x

Ramos, M., Sedivi, B. M., & Sweet, E. M. (1998). Computerized self-administered questionnaires. In Couper, M. P., Baker, R. P., Bethlehem, J., Clark, C. Z. F., Martin, J., Nicholls, W. L., & O'Reilly, J. M. (Eds.), *Computer-assisted survey information collection* (pp. 389–408). New York, NY: Wiley.

Richman, W. L., Weisband, S., Kiesler, S., & Drasgow, F. (1999). A meta-analytic study of social desirability distortion in computer-administered questionnaires, traditional questionnaires, and interviews. *The Journal of Applied Psychology, 84*(5), 754–775. doi:10.1037/0021-9010.84.5.754

Romer, D., Hornik, R., Stanton, B., Black, M., Li, X., Ricardo, I., & Feigelman, S. (1997). "Talking" computers: a reliable and private method to conduct interviews on sensitive topics with children. *Journal of Sex Research, 34*(1), 3–9. doi:10.1080/00224499709551859

Schneider, S. J., & Edwards, B. (2000). Developing usability guidelines for Audio-CASI for respondents with limited literacy skills. *Journal of Official Statistics, 16*(3), 255–271.

Scott, J. (1997). Children as respondents: Methods for improving data quality. In Lyberg, L., Biemer, P., Collins, M., DeLeeuw, E., Dippo, C., Schwarz, N., & Trewin, D. (Eds.), *Survey measurement and process quality* (pp. 331–350). New York, NY: Wiley.

Sproull, L., Subramani, M., Kiesler, S., Walker, J. H., & Waters, K. (1996). When the interface is a face. *Human-Computer Interaction, 11*(2), 97–124. doi:10.1207/s15327051hci1102_1

Sudman, S., & Bradburn, N. M. (1974). *Response effects in surveys.* Chicago, IL: Aldine.

Tourangeau, R., & Smith, T. W. (1996). Asking sensitive questions: The impact of data collection, question format, and question context. *Public Opinion Quarterly, 60*(2), 275–304. doi:10.1086/297751

Trapl, E. S., Borawski, E. A., Storck, P. P., Lovegreen, L. D., Colabianchi, N., Cole, M. L., & Charvat, J. M. (2005). Use of audio-enhanced personal digital assistants for school-based data collection. *The Journal of Adolescent Health, 37*(4), 296–305. doi:10.1016/j.jadohealth.2005.03.025

Truman, J., Robinson, K., Evans, A. L., Smith, D., Cunningham, L., Millward, R., & Minnis, H. (2003). The Strengths and Difficulties Questionnaire. A pilot study of a new computer version of the self-report scale. *European Child & Adolescent Psychiatry, 12*(1), 9–14. doi:10.1007/s00787-003-0303-9

Turner, C. F., Ku, L., Rogers, S. M., Lindberg, L. D., Pleck, J. H., & Sonenstein, F. L. (1998). Adolescent sexual behaviour, drug use, and violence: Increased reporting with computer survey technology. *Science, 280*(5365), 867–873. doi:10.1126/science.280.5365.867

Wadsworth, J., Johnson, A. M., Wellings, K., & Field, J. (1996). What's in a mean? - an examination of the inconsistency between men and women in reporting sexual partnerships. *Journal of the Royal Statistical Society. Series A, (Statistics in Society), 159*(1), 111–123. doi:10.2307/2983472

Walker, J. H., Sproull, L., & Subramani, R. (1994). Using a human face in an interface. In B. Adelson, S. Dumais, & J. Olson (Eds.), *Human Factors in Computing Systems: CHI'94 Conference Proceedings,* Boston, MA (pp. 85-91). ACM.

Weisband, S., & Kiesler, S. (1996, April). Self disclosure on computer forms: Meta-analysis and implications. In *Proceedings of the Conference on Human Factors in Computing Systems,* Vancouver, BC, Canada. Retrieved from http://www.acm.org/sigchi/chi96/proceedings/papers/Weisband/sw_txt.htm

Wiederman, M. W. (1997). The truth must be in here somewhere: examining the gender discrepancy in self-reported lifetime number of sex partners. *Journal of Sex Research, 34*(4), 375–386. doi:10.1080/00224499709551905

Wilcox, S. (1989). *American deaf culture*. Burtonsville, MD: Linstok Press.

Zazove, P., Meador, H. E., Aikens, J. E., Nease, D. E., & Gorenflo, D. W. (2006). Assessment of depressive symptoms in deaf persons. *Journal of the American Board of Family Medicine, 19*(2), 141–147. doi:10.3122/jabfm.19.2.141

ADDITIONAL READING

Conrad, F. G., & Schober, M. F. (Eds.). (2008). *Envisioning the survey interview of the future.* Hoboken: Wiley.

Couper, M. P., Baker, R. P., & Bethlehem, J. (Eds.). (1998). *Computer Assisted Survey Information Collection*. New York, NY: Wiley.

Lyberg, L., Biemer, P., & Collins, M. (Eds.). (1997). *Survey Measurement and Process Quality*. New York, NY: Wiley.

Trotman, M. (Ed.). (2008). The Challenges of a Changing World. Proceedings of the Fifth International Conference of the Association for Survey Computing. Berkeley, UK: ASC.

ENDNOTES

[1]   To date some web-survey tools (e.g., Global Park, http://www.globalpark.com, Instantsurvey, http://www.instantsurvey.com or Surveygizmo, http://www.surveygizmo.com allow to include video material into web-surveys.

[2]   Blaise (http://www.westat.com/statistical_software/blaise/), for instance, is a commercial Software which allows to construct A-CASI and V-CASI surveys. A software tool for non-commercial use may be requested from the author of this chapter.

[3]   Within pre-tests in a quality of life study for a deaf population (Gerich & Lehner, 2003, 2006), three modes of data collection (FTF, PP and V-CASI) were tested. Whereas self-administered processing was possible for all respondents in the computer version, only young and highly educated respondents were able to proceed with written questionnaires. In face-to-face interviews, most of the interviews led to extremely interactive communication styles which can be characterized more as some kind of bargaining than standardized interviews.

[4]   Lipton et al. (1996) also note the problem that it was difficult for respondents to keep the response options in mind and they were insecure whether they marked the correct response categories which were only text-labelled.

[5]   A software tool for non-commercial use that is capable of these features may be requested from the author of this chapter.

[6]   Responses were coded as fully consistent when the answers to all four questions were given in the same logical direction. They were coded as partially inconsistent when one out of four questions was answered in a different logical direction and maximally inconsistent when two questions were an-

swered in a different direction compared to the other two questions.

7   Rapport means that the interviewer is able to establish a communicative situation which is characterized by openness, honesty and mutual motivation (Groves et al., 2004). O'Muircheartaigh (1997, p. 15) explains the idea as "a variety of qualities that implied success on the part of the interviewer in generating satisfactory motivation for the respondent".

8   The term "mere presence" means effects due to the simple presence of another person during the interview, which does not necessarily imply social interaction. Krysan and Couper (2003), for instance, cite Hammonds (1966), who found response effects with a self-administered questionnaire distributed in a classroom situation which was dependant of the race of the person who simply distributed the questionnaire.

9   Satisficing means that "respondents may interpret each question only superficially and select what they believe will appear to be a reasonable answer to each question without referring to any internal psychological cues specifically relevant to the attitude, belief, or event of interest" (Krosnick, 1991, p. 215). Satisficing may provoke response-sets, random responses or socially desirable responses (in the sense of a "reasonable answer").

10   However, it should be noted that the reduction of interviewer variance does not necessarily mean that interviewer effects are reduced. Typically, in V-CASI or video-web surveys only videotapes of one or two different interviewers are used. These interviewers may well provoke interviewer effects and biased data which (due to missing interviewer variance) are difficult to detect within one study. Hence, this may be another reason for diverging results of the different studies using audio-visual methods.

11   Gerich (2009) found some indication for the latter explanation, as higher reported numbers of sexual partners was associated with higher response times of female respondents, but not for the male respondents. Hence, when it is assumed that a response strategy of counting is more time-consuming than rough estimation, the results support the hypothesis of different recall strategies of men and women.

Chapter 8
Unveiling Space by using Participatory Photo Interview

Bettina Kolb
University of Vienna, Austria

ABSTRACT

Using visual material in a participatory interview process allows for broadening communication with users and developing a deeper understanding of residents' perspectives. Photographs taken by respondents as part of a research and future planning process provide the opportunity to see local spaces from users' perspectives, thus allowing them to contribute to urban planning in a meaningful way. This chapter introduces the method of participatory photo interview, its use in social science, and its potential for urban and planning studies. It reviews literature on the topic, discusses opportunities for applying the method to spatial questions, and reviews the method's strengths and weaknesses, illustrated by an example taken from urban studies. In conclusion, the author considers the feasibility of using the method online and highlights possible pitfalls and advantages.

INTRODUCTION

The architectural and planning disciplines are strongly linked to visual approaches and the ability to create and interpret visual representations. Architects and planners regularly use visuals, sketches and photographs as well as digital visualizations in order to show future designs, obtain feedback from future residents and guide their expectations. During the planning phase, drawings, sketches and forms of digital visualization are valuable tools.

Similarly, the use of visuals in society is generally growing rapidly. Photos used in media and generated for personal use are available to nearly everyone, and can be used to observe and understand social life. Visual depictions in mass media and advertisements are ubiquitous. Thus,

DOI: 10.4018/978-1-4666-0074-4.ch008

both professionals and prospective residents of spaces that are being planned or designed are accustomed to working with photographs and applying visual analysis approaches in their daily lives and work. Therefore, one might ask: why not already bring the capacity of residents into the visual communication processes in architecture and the planning phase? Why not ask residents to use disposable or digital cameras to engage in an explicit visual process intended to communicate their wishes and desires for future planning?

This chapter introduces a method of respondent engagement called participatory photo interview, a form of photo elicitation, in which respondents take photographs of their environment in order to answer a research question posed by architects and planners, and to verbalize the images' importance and meaning in an interview. Using the participatory photo interview method, scientists and participants discuss participant photographs, share their insights and perspectives and develop a common understanding of local structures, processes, and possible solutions. From a methodological perspective, using visual media can be helpful to understand a spatial context from the residents' perspectives.

Photographs taken by residents can express connections between a place and local expectations regarding its use, and visualize participants' ideas and expectations. Visual data in the form of participant-generated photographs can support communication processes with groups of respondents through on-site focus groups or through communication via new media – web 2 or social networks. Participants' visual and interview data involve a lot of information for analysis, including the spatial analyses that reveal local opinions – positive and negative – of a place and the analyses of the local social context, grounded on subjective perspectives, and nested in a wider social and historical context.

This chapter offers examples taken from an interdisciplinary study of traditional Islamic baths in five Islamic cities, using the photo interview

method for studying hammams and their neighborhoods. The examples provided demonstrate examples of visual data interpretation with relevance for urban and planning studies, including neglected neighborhoods, attachment to place and familiar places that would otherwise remain hidden from an outsider's view. Finally, the chapter presents some of the advantages and risks of applying this method at the community level and through social media.

THE PARTICIPATORY PHOTO INTERVIEW

How to Characterize the Method of Photo Interview

Photo interview, also known as photo elicitation, introduces visual data into the interview process in order to stimulate verbal expression by the interviewees (Rose, 2007) and understand the world as defined by them (Harper, 2002). The participatory photo interview requires respondents to take photographs in the context of a research or planning process that is seen as a common or collaborative endeavor (Kolb, 2008). Taking photographs can be considered as a participatory activity intended to respond to questions posed by research or planning partners. In doing so, the participatory photo interview is part of a participatory research design. Taking photos and participating in the subsequent interviews invites residents to deepen their participation in a collaborative research process, as they explain notions to researchers or planners. Once the photo interview is completed, the photos and interview text are available as data for further research and sociological interpretation using different methods of scientific analysis.

How the Method of Photo Interview has Developed

The photo elicitation method has been used for many years in anthropology and later also in social science. Anthropologists and ethnographers used photographs to document and observe unknown cultures (Bateson & Mead, 1942). A first shift in the use of photos occurred when the anthropologist John Collier (Collier & Collier, 1991) used photos as prompts in interviews intended to explore changes occurring in the lives and environment of French Canadians in the 1950s. For Collier's study, a professional photographer took pictures of local living situations, and respondents (local residents) used the photos to introduce and explain their lives in an interview with the researcher. Collier found that single photos as prompts helped to stimulate respondent communication and memory in the interview situation. This method was called photo elicitation – an interview method developed from anthropological research, where photography is used to document cultural situations (Pink, 2001). With increasing societal visualization, photos were increasingly used in interview settings as photo elicitation, especially in the Anglican and American scientific communities. Visuals are widely accepted in social science, especially in organizational research and public health contexts (Warren, 2005; Knoblauch et al., 2008).

Within social science, many disciplines applies photo elicitation interviews in different research settings: First in psychological research, photo elicitation raises subjective intensions of feelings or explores specific psychological situations – e.g., the situation of recovery after an operation and disease, allowing people to allude to past traumatic events that might otherwise have remained hidden by using photographs (Radley & Taylor, 2003). Further, photos help investigate everyday life perceptions in familiar structures and motherhood (Mannay, 2010; Liebenberg, 2009), where visual methods assist researchers, healthcare providers,

and policymakers to "enter the worlds" of patients and residents.

Second, within the field of public health research, visual methods engage locals, whose voices might otherwise be ignored, or to adjust development efforts to reflect local realities (Wang et al., 1996; Wang & Burris, 1997). Visual methods are also applied to support specific target groups – e.g., patients (Lorenz, 2010), migrants (Holzwarth & Niesyto, 2008) or children (Jorgenson & Sullivan, 2010; White et al., 2010). In these research designs, photography and visuals used in photo elicitations support underprivileged members of society in expressing themselves in a thoughtful way.

Third, in sociological studies, photo elicitation explores subjective approaches to specific social situations: Douglas Harper introduced the use of photos in his sociological study of material and folk culture entitled "working knowledge" (Harper, 1987). For his study, he took the photographs himself. Harper started his study of a mechanic living and working in a remote rural area by recording field notes and taking photos of the mechanic as he worked. Harper then discussed his photos with the mechanic in order to understand his way of thinking and working as a research process. As with the work of Collier, a major difference between Harper's method and the one applied by the author is the role of the participant. For both Collier and Harper's studies, interviewees reviewed photos taken by professionals or researchers, and in their view photos should prompt a more intensive communication between researcher and interviewee. A step further into a participatory sociological research setting is Ulf Wuggenig work, applying the "Fotobefragung", the photo interview (Wuggenig, 1990). In this setting, respondents are both photographer and interviewee. In conducting a survey of people's living rooms, Wuggenig provided his respondents with an instant camera, asked them to take photos of important objects and artefacts in their living room and interviewed them immediately after taking the photos. In this pioneering study the importance of the space is evident, objects and artefacts and lifestyles within the living room should be detained on the photo, to document the spatial information for research (Wuggenig, 1990).

Photo elicitations studies were also applied to humanities and architectural research questions: visuals were meaningful in historical research designs, where photos helped to evoke memories and intension, e.g., of war experiences of soldiers (Kunimoto, 2004), and in the notion of architecture and public space. Visual methods, e.g., the photo-survey research method, helped to explore the perception of urban environment and public space, where photos are used by participants to document meaningful spaces (Moore et al., 2008). The "diary of the week", completed with photos, shows personal activities in the research of urban public life (Latham, 2003). Multiple methods like photographing and drawing also support studies of perceptions and experiences of space from children's perspective (Darbyshire et al., 2005).

Within the practical work of the author during the participatory photo interview, three phases of work with participants can be reported (Kolb, 2008). In the first or opening phase, researchers invite photo interview respondents to consider a general research question or planning effort. This starts a cognitive process on the part of the respondents, as they reflect on the influence or meaningfulness of the scientific question for their own life concepts and experiences (Lorenz & Kolb, 2009). In the second or active photo shooting phase, participants implement their reflections by taking photos of specific subjects in their social and material surroundings – for example, places, buildings, people, social networks or local activities and businesses that relate to the research or planning question and are meaningful to them. During this phase, the perspective of the outside research or planning team moves to the background, as participants use cameras to capture their ideas and determine relevant issues from their own perspectives. If possible, participants

should be involved in a participatory research process. Experience shows that a key factor in successful recruitment is to take as long as needed to explain and discuss the aims of that research project with potential participants in a detailed, participatory manner. It is during the opening phase that participants decide to commit to taking an active role in the process. Photo respondents often find this phase empowering, as they make their own perspectives explicit in their photos and gain new insights into their lives.

Although the application of photo interview does not intend to be an empowerment tool, it starts a process where people take on a more active role in their social environment. It is during the active photo shooting phase when respondents continue to reflect on the task and discuss it with family and friends. They locate places within the region, look at the backyards and explore neighbourhoods in order to show important aspects, facts and places. Participants' tacit knowledge about an issue emerges as they go through a process of visualizing the issue and producing images. In the third phase, the "reading" of the photo, participants discuss their photos and reflect their photo-taking strategies in an interview. It is recommended that respondents take responsibility for selecting which photos to discuss in the interview, as this allows them to frame the situation, determine the order of topics to be discussed, and feel valued for their work. The photos guide the interview thematically. The "readings" of the participants decode the visuals in the interview by describing their photos in their own words and personal values. In the adjacent interpretation phase, photos and interview transcripts are basic material for the scientist's readings. Before discussing this issue, we will focus on the challenges for an online use of visual methods.

Visual Face-to-Face Methods and Online Research

Face-to-face interviews are considered to be an important and efficient tool in qualitative social research because of the engagement and bodily presence of the respondent (Seymour, 2001). Qualitative online tools lack this important element, but other advantages become important, as discussed below.

Within the online use of photo elicitation, the contact between researcher and respondents changes and offers new possibilities: First, collecting photos on a specific topic can be done online by using a certain online tool – a website, album on a social network or a blog. The process is similar to the participatory photo interview, and participants deliver their photos to the researcher, who then compiles them by using the online tool. Second, participants are invited via online tools and participate by providing comments on photos and writing narrations. Third, the communication between researcher and participants can be extended. The photos can be used in an established forum, where a small number of users – researchers, the project team, participants or users – can access the images. They can read and write comments and narratives to selected uploaded photos, which is also a practical way in another form of online research: Studies in psychology show that web-based tools – like a web site – are a helpful way of collecting narrations. Sitting on the computer, participants feel freer to write narrations, although the topics are sensitive (Guy & Montague, 2008).

Seymour (2001) mentioned that in online research, the ongoing interaction between researcher and respondents via online tools can contribute to a more egalitarian research practice, because data can be discussed and questions clarified over a longer period of time. According to Seymour, research gives "people a voice" and the role of the researcher changes from a participant observation research to a participant researcher by communicating with online tools (Seymour, 2001). Within the online photo interview, the face-to-face situation is replaced by the interaction with the computer, and participants are able to assign selection and sequence of photos and their written comments and narrations. Formalised questions offered by the researcher can help to start a discussion; examples of structured interview questions could include: "What do you think is important on the photo? Please provide comments regarding the symbolic meaning, if there is one intended".

Some qualitative studies use web-based formats for narration, which respondents provide within a web- based survey. One of these studies claims that the written and anonymous format of the computer-based tool supports the quality of the data, given that participants voice their thoughts freely: Due to the medium of the computer, students felt safe enough to criticise and express their opinion honestly, and the web-based survey gave them a positive way of anonymity to voice unprivileged students (Shields, 2003). Transcending the photo interview approach and supporting its participatory aspects, a blog can also assist a participatory research design and integrate visual data, comments and discussion. Blogs support research endeavours, because they are publicly available, produce low costs and collect amounts of data without predating the interests of researcher (Hookah, 2008).

Using visuals in an online use, various borders, e.g., geographical and disciplinary distances, can be bridged: this form of web-based survey reduces restrictions to participation due to physical distance, and contributes to the transfer of knowledge and expertise on a global level. For example, residents of neighbouring communities or regions can take part in the discussion, or additional experts or researchers from other disciplines can also provide their perspectives. Literature gives several reasons for also applying photo interview in an online use. Expertise from the author could be verified and experience became obvious when looking at a project exploring youth culture: Adolescents took photos with their personal cameras and wrote individual narrations about personal life style. These photos and comments were collected in a photo album, and an exclusive community of peers living on another continent was invited to comment on the photos. This form of research participation was adequate for the age of the participants, although some participants were not at all familiar with the use of a computer.

Ethical Considerations

Participants should be informed of the process and intent of the research or planning activity. They should be free to agree to be part of this endeavour or to refuse to participate, and should know that their photos would be used for research activities such as publications. Anonymity of participants should be respected and considered. Ethical considerations on web-based online use include the respect of confidentiality of information shared on the internet. Access to the photos should be limited to a specific community with registered members. A more elaborated discussion on ethical considerations can be found in the British Sociology Association's "Statement of ethical practice" (2006), developed by the BSA visual study group and in the article "IVSA Code of Research and Ethics Guidelines" (Papademas & IVSA, 2009).

Using visual data brings along specific responsibilities, because the exchange between researcher and participants can be more intense than in traditional personal interviews, and brings out a greater number of private and subjective issues. Respondents' privacy and perspectives also need to be respected during the interpretation phase, when personal information has to be handled anonymously and with respect. Sometimes participants take photos but do not discuss them with researchers; the research team should then discuss whether including photographs without accompanying interpretation by the photographer is appropriate for their purposes or

not. Researchers will also have to discuss possible deviating interpretations among participants and research team members; ethical rules also need to be respected in this phase.

READING THE PHOTOGRAPHS: APPROACHES TO ANALYZING PHOTO CONTENT AND MEANING

Different disciplines approach the task of analysing photo material from different perspectives. The geographer and visual researcher Gillian Rose (2007) suggests analysing three aspects of visual images: "the production of images, the image itself and the audience" (Rose, 2007, p. 13), a distinction that brings out several strategies for visual interpretation. In sociological research, images and photos become a database of visual and social data. Photos are "supporting" research (Rose, 2007, p. 239), and the production processes resulting in the photos present information about specific socio-cultural situations. Other disciplines, including philosophy (Sontag, 1980) and art history (Panofsky, 2006), assess the qualities and characteristics of images (content and subject) and have developed strategies to include images in their disciplinary research context. With semiotics, images become representations and elements of a cultural expression (Eco, 1991). Disciplines such as biology, geography, and medical science use photos as documentation and an argument for objective evidence (Daston & Galison, 2007).

In European countries such as France, Germany and Austria, using photos for sociological interpretation is increasingly accepted, but the use of visual material is still unusual in academic research (Knoblauch et al., 2008). In English-speaking countries, visual data are commonly seen as representations of the current media society and research material for sociological analysis of society and the media. There are several content-oriented or linguistic procedures of interpretation, but also hermeneutic modes, analyzing the latent or manifest meaning of the data (Oevermann, 1993) in order to study a socio-cultural research question.

Overview – Categorizing the Visual Material

Focusing on the image itself, its subjects and motifs is an essential aspect of exploring patterns and social constructions represented in a photograph. A photo itself is meaningful for the photographer in a way that is not always explicit to other audiences (Becker, 1974). One task is to list the main contents of the image; this "fixing" of the photo identifies the visual content that the researcher is able to read and understand, and which becomes the basis for further interpretation.

The scientist's reading or "audiencing" of the image in turn also provides a valuable resource for understanding the cultural content of the photo expressed in visual codes. This task is a question of communication and fixing the content for the audience, and is not an ontological or philosophical question concerning the reality revealed in the photo. Fixing the content provides a guide for any observer of the photo as to how to read it, and forms the basis for the scientific interpretation. Following scientists who work with visual material a formal description of the visual content is helpful (Bohnsack, 2007; Rose, 2007).

Empirical Examples from the HAMMAM Study

Practical examples are provided from the HAMMAM (Aspects and Multidisciplinary Methods of Analysis for the Mediterranean Region) study, an intercultural, inter- and transdisciplinary study designing future scenarios to save the hammam as a cultural heritage, in order to show approaches for analyzing visual material. The project analyzed hammams in Islamic neighbourhoods in Fez (Morocco), Constantine (Algeria), Cairo (Egypt), Damascus (Syria) and Ankara (Turkey). Within this multidisciplinary study, architects and histori-

ans, town planners and restoration experts, social scientists and environmental experts, focused on the hammams with their complex urban and social relations and developed future scenarios that balance the desire of modernization with the needs of the environment. The team also studied how to preserve the typical architectural structure while meeting contemporary needs for sanitary and convenient places to bathe and socialize (Sibley, 2008). The multicultural team of social scientists sought to study the hammam as a cultural heritage and with its social functions for the neighbourhood (Kolb & Dumreicher, 2008).

The project design had a strong participatory approach and in each case country, a local interdisciplinary team of scientists, architects and other experts was responsible for supporting the field work. The photo interviews were part of the participatory research design, inviting local residents to have a "voice" in the research project and ensure that their viewpoint was incorporated into the future scenarios developed for the hammam architectural and restoration project. The local partners helped to recruit local residents to participate in the photo-elicitation portion of the study and functioned as gatekeepers. Within the investigations, the authors held five to eight photo interviews in each of the five case study cities, equal men and women and a child. Participants used a disposable camera to take 12–24 photographs each of positive and negative aspects of the hammam and their neighbourhood from their own point of view. The visual data were supplemented by interviews, field observations, and other disciplinary and interdisciplinary research carried out under the study. Results were presented in public presentations after the common field work and in interdisciplinary syntheses meetings, where all researchers discussed their preliminary results. In total, 562 photographs were taken by local residents representing the visual data material; some of them were discussed in an interview.

Results from the case studies were based on textual and visual material and were used to describe the social and spatial situation from the case study hammam within its urban neighbourhood. The theoretical approach of the "seven fields of encounter," a concept of socio-cultural and spatial conjunctions (Dumreicher & Kolb, 2006, 2008), helped to structure the visual material and identify spatial patterns. For this endeavour it was helpful to consider social and spatial qualities of the neighbourhood and city where the photos were taken: photos from several locations within the case study neighbourhoods in different countries showed similar topics, e.g., abandoned houses, neglected places, and renovated sites or houses. From case study to case study, more and more results from several disciplines, but also from various places were linked together. The empirical visual material suggested classification of the photos into four categories: (1) sites and famous places from a visitor's or tourist's perspective; (2) single renovated buildings, mostly shown as an example of good practice in taking care of the neighbourhood; (3) lively places such as shops and markets; and (4) neglected places, often ruined or abandoned buildings in the neighbourhood. These categories gave a first overview of the visual material.

Photo Motifs and Subjects

For the visual data collected in the HAMMAM project, the initial step in establishing a "scientific reading" of the photos involved formally describing the contents of the photo as fixed in three of the image's sectors: front (sector 1), middle (sector 2), and back (sector 3), and then focus on different aspects of photo quality. The elements of the spatial order focus on the space documented on the photo. Within a spatial question, grouping the photos gives hints regarding specific places and activities in the neighborhood. Similarities among the photos can be seen depicted in the places, their visual content or in the story being told. The standpoint of the photographer highlights participants' activities during the photo-taking process. The order of images on the film shows the sequence of places visited by participants, and one can reconstruct a certain way of walking through the neighbourhood. In order to document this process, places of the photos and perspectives can be recorded on a map. The combination of photo and text shows the interpretation of the photo in the interview, when participants explain their work and intention in taking a particular photo. Within the interview, the interviewee explains the meaning of the photo and how she/he is "reading" and interpreting the visual material. Researcher and participant share their knowledge and generate a common knowledge base. In a further step, the reading by the respondent can be supplemented by the researcher's reading.

To sum up, the interpretation steps are the following:

1. Fixing the content in sectors: front (sector 1), middle (sector 2), and back (sector 3);
2. Describing the elements of spatial order that can be seen in the photo;
3. Recognizing the activities of the photo taking process, and discuss the standpoint of the photographer;
4. Taking into consideration both photo and interview text.

The sections below set out these three different perspectives used to analyse photo material. This will be illustrated by specific examples from the HAMMAM project described above.

Photo A – A Focus on the Spatial Order

Fixing the Content in Sectors (1, 2, 3)

In the front (sector 1) of Figure 1, the photo shows the asphalt of the street wet from the rain, mirroring silhouettes of pedestrians. People cross this wide urban space and head to the center of the photo – the entrance and gateway. In the middle

Figure 1. PHOTO A, Entrance to the old town, HAMMAM Photo interview, Damascus 2007

part (sector 2), people are heading to the street in the dark entrance. Several persons on the photo pursue daily activities: walking (men, women), shopping (women) – they carry bags, sit in front of the shop (men), write (police men). The third part (sector 3) of the photo shows a gate which is made of white rectangular stones. There is a dark entrance in the back; one can see darkness and white little flags hanging in the center of the gate.

Documenting Elements of Spatial Order

The entrance shows a symmetric situation, with shops next to the gate on both the right and left side. Pedestrians cross the space in front, as they head towards the entrance of the gate. They are walking through different sectors of space. We can see a free space in the front, but nobody uses this space; people are heading to the center in the back. The gate usually designates an entrance to an important place, possible a city gate. Inside the gate there could be the medina, the market, the centre of the city. Everyone is heading to the center of the photo, the dark entrance, which seems to

be an attractive place, although it looks dark and especially women might feel anxious entering the dark place. All the persons on the photo seem to head to the gate crossing the empty street in front of the gate. Signs for the cars show the possibility for cars to drive on the street, although we can only see pedestrians on the photo.

Within an overall spatial research question, the photo helps to document a specific spatial situation: analyzing the photo, one can have a look at persons, buildings and arrangements on the streets. From a planning perspective, one might ask whether this space will be used for different purposes at different times of day, by different types of users. Are cars or trucks present at different times of the day? Are pack animals ever present, donkeys, camels? One can see a contradiction within the photo: the space is defined to function as a street, but in this situation of use, we can only see pedestrians on the street. The content of the photos contributes to an understanding of the problems and challenges faced by the neighborhood and town on a daily basis.

Figure 2. PHOTO B, Shopping Street, HAMMAM Photo interview, Constantine 2007

Photo B – The Standpoint of the Photographer

Photo B (Figure 2) provides an example of focusing on the standpoint of the photographer as a way of analyzing the photo. This focus of the photo can be used to document the activities that participants undertook during the photo-taking process. The standpoint of the photographer can be seen as a "mirror of activities", revealing places of positive or negative attitudes to researcher and planner. It is through the perspective of the photographer that experts perceive social activity, thus illuminating both the perspective of the photographer and the action before the camera. Reichertz (1994) suggests differentiating between "the action in front of the camera", where a situation is documented, and the "action with the camera", where the photographer is acting, e.g., exploring a forbidden space. The photographer's point of view reveals a social process and tells a story about the person who is taking the photo, within the larger context of the participatory photo interview process of several respondents who are taking photos for the study. Questions concerning the standpoint of the photographer can be the following: Is the photographer excluded from the scene below, and if so, how or why? Are there gendered aspects to exclusion, if any? Would the standpoint change at another time of the day, or another day of the week?

Photo B shows the participant's view onto a vivid street; there are houses and people walking on the street (front and middle sectors), shops are offering their goods, and the street is lined with houses and their facades, with balconies where viewers can look down onto the street life. Walking, selling, and observing are actions that can be seen in the photo. From the photographer's perspective, we start to imagine his or her standpoint. The photographer is standing on a higher place, looking down onto the street. He or she could be inside a house, leaning out a window or balcony, or could be outside on a bridge that is crossing the street. We do not know anything about the building that the photographer is using as a standpoint for this photo, but the photograph generates an overview over the street. One can observe the life on the street from a point that would be hidden from an outsider's view. No one on the street perceives the photographer. The standpoint describes itself within the view as a safe place and an outside perspective, and shows a distance between the photographer and the daily life on the street.

Looking at the other photos of the participant, one can try to understand the meaning of the exclusion. If this exclusion is a social one, it is supported by specific rules or habits, e.g., if women are not allowed to walk on the street without men. If this exclusion is an architectural one, a specific place is not attractive and "excludes" users, e.g., buildings are too narrow for carts or cars, or the street is busy and loud, with acoustic noise. The

Figure 3. PHOTO C, Courtyard, HAMMAM Photo interview, Damascus 2007

action with the camera opens up a new – perhaps quieter – space above.

Photo C – The Participant's Reading

Photo C shows the courtyard of a house (Figure 3). The front shows a fountain, which is white and could be made of marble. In the background one can see the wall of the building, with a mirror in the centre. On the right side of the building there is a corner, there are two windows in the vertical line and two windows in the horizontal line.

The following sentences are part of the interview, where the participant is explaining the subjective and personal meaning of the photo: *"This is our house; I think it is the best thing in our neighbourhood, so I took this photo to show that some of the houses, not all the houses in the neighbourhood are like this"* (HAMMAM Photo interview, Damascus 2007).

During the interview, the participant talks about the photo and points out the personal function and value of this place. *"This is our house; I think it is the best thing in our neighbourhood"*. The verbal text shows that there is a specific connection

between the resident and the place designated as *"our house"* and *"our neighbourhood."* Within these few lines, one can see the reference to the family and the connection with the neighbourhood. It ends with a comparison, mentioning the specific situation as follows: *"not all (houses) are like this"*.

Two points therein are worth highlighting: First, the meaning of the family for Damascenes residents and their connection with the *hara*, the nearest quarter and the neighbouring streets of the house. Second, the importance of the community, the neighbours embedded in the *hara*. Photo C shows a very valued, unique place – the courtyard of the photographer's own house. From a planning perspective, questions raised by the photographer's reading of the photo might include: Who has access to this space? Is it limited to family members and their servants and guests? Has this building always been the grandest in the neighbourhood, and if not, what has prompted deterioration of other formerly similar houses? What are the photographer's hopes for the future of this house?

PRACTICAL ADVICE FOR SUCCESS WITH PHOTO INTERVIEWS

One of the most important things when applying this method is to allow extra time throughout the process. This is due to several reasons: Participants sometimes need more time than expected to reflect on their perspective and take photos that will answer research questions and inform planning proposals. Their schedules may be busy, and they may not have time to take all the photos they want immediately. Moreover, participants may benefit from some simple technical photography training before they use the camera as a technical instrument and become observers of their community and lives.

The type of camera in use also needs consideration, as the cultural setting determines the type of camera: In a remote area, disposable cameras are practical for participants who have limited experience with modern technology. Furthermore, the cost of these cameras is low, and there is little harm if they get lost. In urban areas, respondents may prefer to use digital cameras and may own a personal camera.

In applying the method of photo interview to a research or planning process, the following steps are essential:

- Discussing information on research question or future planning an process (steps of photo interview or online tools) with participants;
- Taking enough time for taking photos;
- Developing photos (instant camera); upload photos (digital) to the online tool;
- Conducting the interview or discussion with participants; give time for comments and narration in online use;
- Preparing data (interview transcription, photo and text in one document, online material) for analysis;
- Analysing the data within a group of scientists/ planners/ research team;

- Integrating the resulting data and analysis within the research or future planning effort.

In order to best answer research questions or inform future planning, the participatory photo interview should be carried out with patience and should give time for answering respondent questions: it is essential that participants have a good understanding of the aims of the research or future planning. Once the photos are developed, the interview takes place. The interview should be conducted in a quiet location, where participants can talk without disturbances. After the interview, the work load of the researcher increases: different analyses can be carried out on the basis of written transcripts and photo descriptions. Having done that, the collection of expressions, opinions, visual subjects or presented places needs to be considered and integrated within the larger research or planning task.

Advantages and Limitations of the Method

The participatory photo interview has proven to be useful on several levels: first to collect visual material, second to integrate local knowledge in the scientific process, third to support the understanding between participants and researcher, and fourth to activate local residents to participate in working towards a common future. The photo interview allows research or planning endeavors to start with real places and real experiences. At the same time, visual data prove to be useful for envisioning and speaking about possible, desired futures. An important advantage of the photo interview method is its ability to engage and improve communication with participants from specific target groups such as disadvantaged groups, particularly the elderly, children, and those who are illiterate or have little education.

The limitation of the method is the time-consuming process during the survey and the interpretation phase. Also, results are sometimes difficult to integrate into the research questions because respondents hide personal voicing behind symbols. As participants speak about places shown in the photos, they present personal meaning and subjective functions of a certain place, and discuss the possibilities of change. At the same time, the researcher or planner needs to keep the identity of the participants in mind. Do they represent the community? Or people in power? As the method is based on subjective approaches, the sample of participants can constitute another limitation.

Moreover, planning experts have to consider their own role and contribution before using participatory visual methods: most importantly, the researcher needs to be open to new insights that he or she did not expect, and to sharing a common learning process with his or her "subjects." Ideally, the photo interview promotes mutual learning by both scientists or planners and residents in a conversation among equals. Photo analysis is an intensive process and, depending on the level of output and results, several discussion rounds will be necessary within the parameters of the research endeavour; for example, in case the research pertains primarily to spatial questions or to societal questions. For in-depth interpretation, the team should be supported by social scientists trained in qualitative research. Thereby, the intensive data management and interpretation work can also be considered as one of the limitations of the method.

CONCLUSION

The chapter discusses the method of participatory photo interview, and shows its use within a research or planning setting. This visual approach gives a certain measure of power to residents and includes inhabitants' perspectives within a planners approach. The method's participatory approach enlarges the planner's viewpoints and opinions, prompts discussion of broader meanings and complements the traditional verbal interview

with visual images. Hence, it facilitates cooperative planning between planners and users.

Efforts to involve residents may have different purposes, but one is to give them a voice within a process of future planning. Visual participatory methods provide an opportunity to address problems and resources from the view of residents and to ground the discussion on their subjective experience through the daily media of photography. The subjective visual views portrayed in their photos provide insights into possible stakeholder perspectives and decisions; the interview in turn allows for discussion of meaning, developments and possibilities.

The method has a big potential for online use. There are several possibilities of keeping the qualities of the face-to-face version and at the same time gaining the advantages of a qualitative online research. The computer as a medium for online research can support the democratic and honest way of expression of the participants, bridges geographical distances and disciplinary expertise on a global level.

The technological developments in online use mean that visual and verbal data can be combined with the technical help of the computer. Experiences gained in past projects show that participatory visual methods help to integrate the view of residents within a broader planning perspective. The method allows participants to add an emotional aspect to the planning process, which can be particularly useful for future planning, when ambiguity and unknown future developments can be difficult to identify and discuss. Moreover, photo interviews allow for integrating personal experience into planning and research. Sometimes participants come up with unexpected topics and open up an important discussion. For the architect or planner this process can help to adapt architectural designs to the reality of a particular place and allow for the integration of users' perspectives into future plans and visions.

ACKNOWLEDGMENT

Thanks to Dr. Laura Lorenz, Brandeis University, who is experienced in photo elicitation and photo voice and Mag. Marina Kolb for discussions and reflection. All the work described in this article would not have been possible without the financial support from the European Union for the study HAMMAM - Hammam, Aspects and Multidisciplinary Methods of Analysis for the Mediterranean Region" (2005-2008, FP6-2003-INCO-MPC-2, 517704). Thanks to Heidi Dumreicher, HAMMAM coordinator, and the partners in the case study teams for supporting photo interviews with selection, translation and transcription. Also thanks to the photo interview participants for contributing to the HAMMAM research project.

REFERENCES

Bateson, G., & Mead, M. (1942). *Balinese Character. A Photographic Analysis*. New York, NY: New York Academy of Sciences.

Becker, H. S. (1974). Photography and Sociology. *Studies in the anthropology of visual communication* 1974/ 1, 3-26.

Bohnsack, R. (2007). *Rekonstruktive Sozialforschung*, Einführung in qualitative Methoden. Opladen: Budrich UTB.

British Sociology Association (BSA). (2006). *Statement of ethical practice for the British sociological association – visual sociology group*, Retrieved September 15, 2010, http://www.visualsociology.org.uk/about/ethical_statement.php

Collier, J. Jr, & Collier, M. (1991). *Visual Anthropology: Photography as a Research Method*. Albuquerque, NM: University of New Mexico Press.

Darbyshire, P., MacDougall, C., & Schiller, W. (2005). Multiple methods in qualitative research with children: more insight or just more? *Qualitative Research, 5*, 417–436. doi:10.1177/1468794105056921

Daston, L., & Galison, P. (2007). *Objektivität*. Frankfurt, Germany: Suhrkamp.

Dumreicher, H., & Kolb, B. (2006). 'My house, my street', Seven fields of Spatial & Social Encounter. In D. Shehayeb, H. T. Yildiz, & P. Kellet (Eds.). *'Appropriate Home': Can we design 'appropriate' residential environments?* (pp. 97-108). Cairo, Egypt: Housing & Building National Research Centre (HBNRC).

Dumreicher, H., & Kolb, B. (2008). Place as a Social Space – Fields of Encounter Relating to the Local Sustainability Process. In *Journal of Environmental Management, Volume 87/2, Pages 201- 317*: Elsevier. doi: 10.1016/j.jenvman.2007.03.048

Eco, U. (1991). *Einführung in die Semiotik*. Munich, Germany: UTB.

Guy, L., & Montague, J. (2008). Analysing men's written friendship narratives. *Qualitative Research, 8*, 389–397. doi:10.1177/1468794106093635

Harper, D. (1987). *Working Knowledge, Skill and Community in a Small Shop*. Chicago, IL: The University of Chicago Press.

Harper, D. (1998). On the Authority of the Image: Visual Methods at the Crossroads. In N. K. Denzin & Y. S. Lincoln (Eds.), *Collecting and interpreting qualitative materials* (pp. 185-204). London, Uk: Sage

Harper, D. (2002). Talking about Pictures: a Case for Photo Elicitation. *Visual Studies, 17*, 13–26. doi:10.1080/14725860220137345

Holzwarth, P., & Niesyto, H. (2008). Representational and Discursive Self-expression of Young Migrants in the Context of Different (Media) Cultural Resources. *Forum: Qualitative Social Research, 9*(3). Retrieved September 15, 2010, from http://www.qualitative-research.net/index.php/fqs/article/view/1167

Hookway, N. (2008). Entering the Blogosphere: Some Strategies for Using Blogs in Social Research. *Qualitative Research, 8*, 91–113. doi:10.1177/1468794107085298

Jorgenson, J., & Sullivan, T. (2010). Accessing Children's Perspective through Participatory Photo Interviews. *Forum: Qualitative Social Research, 11*(1). Retrieved February 15, 2011, from http://nbn-resolving.de/urn:nbn:de:0114-fqs100189

Knoblauch, H., Baer, A., Laurier, E., Petschke, S., & Schnettler, B. (2008). Visual Analysis. New Developments in the Interpretative Analysis of Video and Photography. *Forum: Qualitative Social Research, 9*(3). Retrieved September 15, 2010, from http://www.qualitative-research.net/index.php/fqs/article/view/1170

Kolb, B. (2008). Involving, Sharing, Analysing—Potential of the Participatory Photo Interview. *Forum: Qualitative Social Research, 9*(3). Retrieved September 15, 2010, from http://www.qualitative-research.net/index.php/fqs/article/view/1155

Kolb, B., & Dumreicher, H. (2008). The Hammam - A living cultural heritage. *International Journal of Architectural Research, 2*(3). Retrieved September 15, 2010, from http://archnet.org/library/documents/one-document.jsp?document_id=10484

Kunimoto, N. (2004). Intimate archives: Japanese – Canadian family photograph, 1939-49. *Art History, 27*, 129–155. doi:10.1111/j.0141-6790.2004.02701005.x

Latham, A. (2003). Research Performances, and Doing Human Geography: Some Reflections on the Diary – Photograph, Diary Interview Method. *Environment and Planning, 35*, 1993–2017. doi:10.1068/a3587

Liebenberg, L. (2009). The visual image as discussion point: increasing validity in boundary crossing research. *Qualitative Research, 9*, 441–467. doi:10.1177/1468794109337877

Lorenz, L. S. (2010). *Brain Injury Survivors: Narratives of Rehabilitation and Healing*. Boulder, CO: Lynne Rienner.

Lorenz, L. S., & Kolb, B. (2009). Involving the Public through Participatory Visual Research Methods. In J. Tritter & K. Lutfey (Eds.), Bridging divides: patient and public involvement on both sides of the Atlantic" *Special Issue: Health Expectations, 12*, 262-274.

Mannay, D. (2010). Making the familiar strange: can visual research methods render the familiar setting more perceptible. *Qualitative Research, 10*, 91–110. doi:10.1177/1468794109348684

Moore, G., Croxford, B., Adams, M., Refaee, M., Cox, T., & Sharples, S. (2008). The photo survey research method: capturing life in the city. *Visual Studies, 23*(1), 50–62. doi:10.1080/14725860801908536

Oevermann, U. (1993). Die objektive Hermeneutik als unverzichtbare methodologische Grundlage für die Analyse von Subjektivität. Zugleich eine Kritik der Tiefenhermeneutik. In Jung, T., & Müller-Doohm, S. (Eds.), *Wirklichkeit" im Deutungsprozess: Verstehen und Methoden in den Kultur- und Sozialwissenschaften* (pp. 106–189). Frankfurt, Germany: Suhrkamp.

Panofsky, E. (2006). *Ikonographie und Ikonologie: Bildinterpretation nach dem Dreistufenmodell Erwin Panofsky*. Cologne, Germany: DuMont.

Papademas, D., & International Visual Sociology Association (IVSA). (2009). IVSA Code of Research Ethics and Guidelines. *Visual Studies, 24*(3), 250–257. doi:10.1080/14725860903309187

Pink, S. (2001). *Visual Ethnography*. London, UK: Sage.

Radley, A., & Taylor, D. (2003). Remembering One's Stay in Hospital: a Study in Photography, Recovery and Forgetting. *Health, 7*(2), 129–159. doi:10.1177/1363459303007002872

Reichertz, J. (1994). Selbstgefälliges zum Anziehen. In Schröer, N. (Ed.), *Interpretative Sozialforschung. Auf dem Weg zu einer hermeneutischen Wissenssoziologie* (pp. 253–280). Opladen, Germany: Westdeutscher Verlag.

Rose, G. (2007). *Visual methodologies: An Introduction to the Interpretation of Visual Materials* (2nd ed.). London, UK: Sage.

Seymour, S. W. (2001). In the flesh or online? Exploring qualitative research methodologies. *Qualitative Research, 1*, 147–168. doi:10.1177/146879410100100203

Shields, M. C. (2003). "Giving voice" to students: using the internet for data collection. *Qualitative Research, 3*, 397–414. doi:10.1177/1468794103033007

Sibley, M. (Ed.). (2008). Special Issue on Traditional Public Baths/Hammams in the Mediterranean *ArchNet-IJAR: International Journal of Architectural Research, (2)3*, ISSN 1994-6961. Retrieved September 15, 2010, from http://archnet.org/library/documents/one-document.jsp?document_id=10481

Sontag, S. (1980). *Über Fotografie*. Frankfurt, Germany: Fischer.

Wang, C., & Burris, M. A. (1997). Photovoice: Concept, Methodology, and Use for Participatory Needs Assessment. *Health Education & Behavior, 24*, 369–387. doi:10.1177/109019819702400309

Wang, C., Burris, M. A., & Ping, X. Y. (1996). Chinese Village Women as Visual Anthropologists: a Participatory Approach to Reaching Policymakers. *Social Science & Medicine, 42*, 1391–1400. doi:10.1016/0277-9536(95)00287-1

Warren, S. (2005). Photograph and Voice in Critical Qualitative Management Research. *Accounting, Auditing & Accountability Journal, 18*, 861–882. doi:10.1108/09513570510627748

White, A., Bushin, N., Carpena-Méndez, F., & Ni Laoire, C. (2010). Using visual methodologies to explore contemporary Irish childhood. *Qualitative Research, 10*, 143–158. doi:10.1177/1468794109356735

Wuggenig, U. (1990). Die Photobefragung als projektives Verfahren. *Angewandte Sozialforschung, 16*(1-2), 109–129.

ADDITIONAL READING

Barthes, R. (1985/1989). *Die helle Kammer. Bemerkung zur Photographie*, Frankfurt/M.: Suhrkamp.

Becker, H. S. (1986). Do Photographs Tell the Truth? In *Doing things together* (pp. 273–292). Evanston, IL: Northwestern University Press.

Bohnsack, R. (2008). The Interpretation of Pictures and the Documentary Method. *Forum Qualitative Sozialforschung / Forum: Qualitative Social Research, 9*(3). Retrieved May 12, 2011, from http://www.qualitative-research.net/index.php/fqs/article/view/1171

Breckner, R. (2010). *Sozialtheorie des Bildes. Zur Interpretation von Bildern und Fotografien*. Bielefeld: transcript.

Christmann, G. (2008). The Power of Photographs of Buildings in the Dresden Urban Discourse. Towards a Visual Discourse Analysis. *Forum Qualitative Sozialforschung / Forum: Qualitative Social Research, 9*(3). Retrieved May 12, 2011, from http://www.qualitative-research.net/index.php/fqs/article/view/1163

Dumreicher, H., & Kolb, B. (2010). Sieben Thesen zu Dorf und Stadt: Bemerkungen zur urbanen Nachhaltigkeit In A. Havemann & Selle K. (Eds): Plätze, Parks & Co. Stadträume im Wandel – Analysen, Positionen und Konzepte (pp329-347). Detmold: Rohn.

Englisch, F. (1991). Bildanalyse in struktur-alhermeneutischer Einstellung. Methodische Überlegungen und Analysebeispiele. In: Garz D. & Kraimer K. (Eds.): *Qualitativ-empirische Sozialforschung: Konzepte, Methoden, Analyse* (pp133-176). Opladen: WDV.

Harper, D. (1998). On the authority of the image: Visual methods at the Crossroads. In Denzin, N. K., & Yvonna, S. L. (Eds.), *Handbook of Qualitative Research* (pp. 403–412). Thousand Oaks: Sage.

Heinze-Prause, R. & Heinze, T. (1996). *Kulturwissenschaftliche Hermeneutik, Fallrekonstruktionen der Kunst-, Medien- und Massenkultur*, Opladen: WDV.

Heßler, M., & Mersch, D. (Eds.). Logik des Bildlichen. Zur Kritik der ikonischen Vernunft. Bielefeld: transcript

Jenks, C. (1995). *Visual Cultures*. London: Routledge. doi:10.4324/9780203426449

Kolb, B., & Dumreicher, H. (2008). The Hammam - A Living Cultural Heritage. In *ArchNet-IJAR: International Journal of Architectural Research vol. 2, issue 3*. Retrieved September 15, 2010, from http://archnet.org/library/documents/one-document.jsp?document_id=10484

Levine, R. S., Hughes, M. T., & Mather, C. R. (2008). The Medina, the Hammam and the Future of Sustainability. In *ArchNet-IJAR: International Journal of Architectural Research vol. 2, issue 3*. Retrieved September 15, 2010, from http://archnet.org/library/documents/one-document.jsp?document_id=10495

Mitchell, W. J. T. (2005). *What do Pictures Want? The Lives and Loves of Images*. Chicago: University of Chicago Press.

Müller-Doohm, S. (1995). Visuelles Verstehen - Konzepte kultursoziologischer Bildhermeneutik. In: T. Jung T.& Müller-Doohm S. (Eds.): *„Wirklichkeit" im Deutungsprozeß, Verstehen und Methoden in den Kulturwissenschaften* (pp458-481). Frankfurt/M: Suhrkamp.

Oevermann, U., Allert, T., & Konau, E. (1979). Die Methodologie einer „objektive Hermeneutik" und ihre allgemeine forschungslogische Bedeutung in den Sozialwissenschaften. In Soeffner, H. G. (Ed.), *Interpretative Verfahren in den Sozial- und Textwissenschaften* (pp. 352–434). Stuttgart: Metzler.

KEY TERMS AND DEFINITIONS

Photo Elicitation: Photo elicitation or photo interview is a special form of face-to-face interview, where visual material such as photos or drawings are introduced into the interview process in order to stimulate verbal expression by the interviewees.

Participatory Photo Interview: The participatory photo interview is based on a self-contained process, where respondents themselves take photographs of their daily life or spatial environment in order to answer a research question. Within the interview, respondents describe their photos and the images' importance and meaning. By applying the participatory photo interview, respondents can "voice" their subjective view in a research or planning process. The produced data material includes photos and interview texts.

Online use of Photo Elicitation or Participatory Photo Interview: Instead of face-to-face interviews, online tools - a website, album on a social network or a blog - are also used in order to collect visual and narrative interview statements. By using the online tool, participants themselves place photos or narrative comments. Researcher and respondents communicate via the online tool by providing visuals or written comments and narrations on photos.

Reading of Images: *Reading of Photographers:* Visuals and photos do not have one single meaning; there are several meanings in visual representations. Within the participatory photo interview, respondents point out their subjective perspectives and express a first interpretation of the photos. *Scientific Reading:* The scientific reading of a photo is based on a formal description of the visual content. There are several forms of scientific reading of a photo: content-oriented

modes (What is the visual content of the photo?), linguistic procedures of interpretation (What kind of story is told? What is the narrative expression of the photo?) or hermeneutic modes (What is the latent or manifest meaning of the data?).

Interpretation of Images: *Formal Description:* The interpretation of photos is based on the formal description of visual elements, colors and perspectives, and identifies the visual content the researcher is able to see and understand. This explicit form of reading becomes the basis for further interpretation and analysis. *Classifying Photos:* A useful first step in the analysis involves classifying photos from all participants into specific groups, categories, or themes of photos, irrespective of the individual photographer. *Interpretation:* The interpretation of visual material includes the scientific act of explaining the meaning of the photography. Based on individual subjects and motifs, the researcher explores general patterns and social constructions represented in the photo.

Chapter 9
Brainstorming in Virtual Teams

Mary T. Dzindolet
Cameron University, USA

Paul B. Paulus
University of Texas at Arlington, USA

Courtney Glazer
Cameron University, USA

ABSTRACT

Most research is conducted by teams rather than individuals, and due to a variety of technological advances many research teams do not work face-to-face; they work virtually. The creativity literature that explores how working as a member of a virtual team differs from working as a member of a face-to-face team or as an individual is reviewed in this chapter, with a focus on the idea generation phase of the research process. The chapter offers practical techniques to help researchers effectively and efficiently brainstorm in virtual teams. Specific techniques to guide researchers are offered based on laboratory and field research in electronic, face-to-face, and virtual brainstorming.

INTRODUCTION

Conducting a research project is such a complex and creative task that researchers often collaborate rather than working alone. Across a variety of disciplines, teams publish more papers and their papers are more frequently cited than individuals (Wuchty, Jones, & Uzzi, 2007). Finding collaborators close in physical proximity with the necessary skills, knowledge, ability, and motivation to complete the research project may be difficult. Forming virtual teams (VTs), researchers can

collaborate with others who are highly qualified, regardless of their location. The purpose of this chapter is to review the literature on brainstorming in VTs with the goal of providing urban and planning studies researchers with guidelines for effective VT brainstorming.

TEAM CREATIVITY

Although there are many techniques purported to increase creativity [e.g., attribute listing, morphological analysis, force field analysis, mind mapping, idea checklist; see Nemiro (2008) for

DOI: 10.4018/978-1-4666-0074-4.ch009

a review of each and how to apply the techniques in VTs], much of the laboratory research that has examined idea generation has relied on the brainstorming paradigm. Group or team members are instructed (a) to generate as many ideas as they can, (b) to say anything and everything that they think of, (c) to integrate ideas that have been presented into better ones, and (d) not to criticize their own or others' ideas (Bouchard & Hare, 1970; Osborn, 1957). Osborn found, as did others (Meadow, Parnes, & Reese, 1959; Parnes & Meadow, 1959), that brainstorming groups produce more ideas than other kinds of groups (e.g., critical groups or non-brainstorming groups), but he also believed brainstorming groups could generate more and better ideas than individuals working alone. In fact, Osborn (1957) predicted that if group members followed these brainstorming rules, they would generate twice as many ideas than if the members had worked alone, although alternating between individual and group brainstorming would yield the better results.

According to several models of brainstorming (e.g., Brown & Paulus, 2002; Nijstad & Stroebe, 2006,;Paulus & Dzindolet, 2008) in order to generate ideas, individuals must search their memories for a category of knowledge that is relevant to the problem. Ideas are generated within the selected memory category until that category is "tapped out" or attention is switched to a different category for some reason. New memory categories are searched for and ideas are created until they are "tapped out" or attention is diverted. Several models of brainstorming suggest that brainstorming in a group or team can stimulate people to search memory categories they might not otherwise have considered, and specific ideas that are shared by one member can stimulate related ideas or be combined with ideas that have been presented earlier (Brown & Paulus, 2002; Nijstad & Stroebe, 2006).

However, brainstorming groups do *not* always generate more ideas than the combined output of an equal number of people brainstorming separately (i.e., nominal groups: Mullen, Johnson, & Salas, 1991). Although other group members' ideas offer cognitive stimulation that can lead to synergy, there are a few negative forces that groups have to deal with. Brainstorming teams may not generate as many ideas as individuals due to production blocking, a consequence of the fact that only one member of a group can speak at a time (Diehl & Stroebe, 1987, 1991; Nijstad & Stroebe, 2006). While listening to others and waiting to speak, one may forget an idea one wanted to share or decide not to share it with the group because it may seem too similar to an idea that another group member has generated or too dissimilar from the current topic. Group brainstormers tend to generate ideas in a smaller set of topics than individuals, limiting the range of ideas they generate (Larey & Paulus, 1999). Waiting to speak may interrupt the flow of ideas one needs to be creative. Finally, evaluation apprehension (fear of being negatively evaluated; Camacho & Paulus, 1995) and social loafing (exerting less effort when performing a task as group than alone; Karau & Williams, 1993) may decrease the number of ideas generated by teams.

For urban and planning studies research teams to generate creative research hypotheses, models, and research designs, they should attempt to minimize evaluation apprehension (which the brainstorming rule directing members not to criticize ideas attempts to do), set up some degree of accountability to reduce social loafing, and encourage the exchange of ideas in an efficient manner with as little distracting material as possible (Paulus, Nakui, Putman, & Brown, 2006; Putman & Paulus, 2009). In addition, there is evidence that deconstructing the task into subtasks (Coskun, Paulus, Brown, & Sherwood, 2000) and providing brief breaks (Paulus et al., 2006) increases idea generation. Alternating between group and individual brainstorming sessions may also increase brainstorming production (Osborn, 1957; Paulus & Dzindolet, 1993). To eliminate production blocking, urban and planning studies research teams may want to communicate electronically; this form of communication allows team members to ignore the rule that only one person can "speak" at a time.

Electronic Brainstorming

To facilitate the exchange of ideas and decision making in groups, computer based group decision-support systems are often used (Kay, 1995). These computer based systems allow groups to exchange ideas, vote, and make decisions. Much of the research with these systems has involved co-located groups, although they can be used for distributed groups as well. Most research has focused on the idea sharing function of electronic brainstorming since this system is seen as a way of overcoming the limitations of the face-to-face paradigm such as production blocking and evaluation apprehension. Group members can submit ideas as they occur and see the ideas from other group members on another part of their screen. Electronic brainstorming does yield more ideas than face to face brainstorming with similar size groups (Gallupe, Dennis, Cooper, & Valacich, 1992). The ability to generate ideas without having to wait one's turn (reduced production blocking) appears to be a major factor in this enhanced performance (Gallupe, Bastianutti, & Cooper, 1991). However, whether the ideas are generated anonymously or with identification does not appear to have a consistent effect (DeRosa, Smith, & Hantula, 2007). It is possible that the benefit of reduced evaluation apprehension due to anonymity of responses is reduced by the tendency to loaf under such conditions (Karau & Williams, 1993).

The benefit of electronic brainstorming appears to increase with group size. In fact, the performance of electronic brainstorming groups with fewer than nine members can be worse than that of nominal groups. However, groups with 9 to 18 members often outperform similar size nominal groups in both number of ideas and the quality of the ideas (Dennis & Williams, 2005; DeRosa et al., 2007). Why larger groups benefit more from electronic

brainstorming than smaller groups is not clear. It could reflect the stimulating effect of the many ideas being shared, including presumably some relatively novel ones; but one study examining this possibility did not gain much support (Connolly, Routhieaux, & Schneider, 1993). To benefit from shared ideation, it is important that the group members do not become cognitively overloaded by the large number of ideas shared. Deconstructing the task so that participants only consider one sub-topic at a time seems to be helpful (Dennis, Valacich, Connolly, & Wynne, 1996). Also, the fact that the electronic brainstorming computer program used in most studies divides the ideas presented into subsets or folders for presentation during the session ensuring that participants do not see all the ideas that have been generated but only subsets at one time is helpful. If the number of folders increases with the number of group members, the cognitive overload can be minimized.

Thus, under certain conditions, urban and planning studies researchers may want to utilize electronic brainstorming. Reliance on electronic technology for communicating is one of the defining characteristics of a VT.

What is a Virtual Team?

Like other teams, VTs are comprised of multiple individuals, who have some degree of task interdependence, common goals, and shared values (Horvath & Tobin, 2001; Nemiro, 2001). Unlike other teams, VT members are sometimes geographically dispersed and rely on technology to communicate. Most researchers view virtuality (or the virtual-ness of the team) as a continuous rather than a dichotomous variable (Cohen & Gibson, 2003; Connaughton & Shuffler, 2007; Cordery & Soo, 2008; Leenders, Kratzer, & van Engelen, 2007; Webster & Staples, 2006). After all, it is common for co-located teams to use e-mail and other technologies, and many VTs meet face-to-face from time to time.

The dimensions that are used most often to define virtuality are geographic dispersion and electronic dependence (Gibson & Gibbs, 2006; Nemiro, 2001), national diversity (Gibson & Gibbs, 2006), the number of different work sites at which the team members are located, distance between sites, number of members per site (i.e., unevenness of membership across sites), the time zone overlap (Webster & Staples, 2006), the amount of time group members are apart while working on group tasks (Griffith, Sawyer, & Neale, 2003), and synchronicity of team interactions (Gibson & Gibbs, 2006). Virtual teams are more likely than face-to-face teams to interact asynchronously. However, some VTs will communicate at least some of the time electronically in-real-time and some face-to-face teams may choose to work asynchronously in subgroups some of the time.

Some researchers argue that VTs are unique and should not be conceptualized as modified co-located teams. Rather, VTs should be studied in their own right (e.g., Driskell, Radtke, & Salas, 2003). VTs may develop competencies in processes that do not exist in co-located teams. Nemiro (2002) studied actual VTs to discover VT processes not used by co-located teams. She concluded, "Much of what goes on when virtual teams create is similar to the process that occurs when any team creates" (p. 77). For example, the VTs tended to follow stages in the creative process: idea generation, development, finalization/closure, and evaluation. Like traditional teams, the VTs used various work approaches to accomplish their tasks (e.g., wheel approach, modular approach, and iterative approach). Members came "together" through technology and then would go apart and perform individual tasks. However, the VTs varied greatly in the way they balanced the "togetherness" and "apartness."

Nemiro (2002) identified two processes that did distinguish VTs from co-located teams: (1) archive capability, and (2) the ability to widen the creative pool of members through electronic links. Although members of traditional teams can listen to audiotapes of a team discussion, for the most part, the creative process is usually forgotten. However, VT members can easily review what each member said in the creative process. This archive capability gave VTs the ability to apply past approaches for resolving clients' problems more easily to current situations. One of the greatest benefits of VTs was that the team was able to bring individuals into the team who would not be able to work face-to-face with the team.

In addition, Nemiro (2002) found the VTs adjusted their communication strategy with the stages of creativity. For example, nearly every VT used face-to-face communication during the idea generation stage. However, during the development stage, nearly every VT performed the work electronically. Among the VTs that included an evaluation stage, the work was often done face-to-face. These preferences have practical implications for VTs (e.g., when in the creative process money should be spent on travel). Whether these communication strategy-task phase pairings led to optimal performance has yet to be explored empirically.

Research on electronic brainstorming in distributed or virtual teams has been very limited (Dornburg, Stevens, Hendrickson, & Davidson, 2009) and has not yet demonstrated its positive potential. The electronic brainstorming literature suggests that virtual brainstorming can be effective if it is structured appropriately and avoids cognitive load. Participants need to be able to process the shared ideas at a reasonable pace and be able to build on them. For asynchronous distributed teams this would involve mixing a range of activities—sharing ideas with the group, reading shared ideas, taking time to reflect on these ideas and build on them, and eventually selecting certain ideas for implementation. These activities would inevitably be coordinated with other work activities that can distract from the brainstorming process (Jett & George, 2003). So it is important either to have specific times that the group selects for synchronous brainstorming (all participate at once) or have members who interact asynchronously allocate a certain amount of time to this process within the time frame allotted for the virtual group interaction. This may require one of the urban and planning studies research team members to take a leadership role to insure that all members are contributing in a timely manner (Sosik, Kahai, & Avolio, 1998).

In summary, virtual urban and planning study research teams have the advantage of choosing members without having to consider where they live; other more important characteristics, such as the knowledge, skills, abilities (KSAs), and willingness to participate, can take top priority. In addition, virtual research team members can type their opinions and ideas whenever they want—even if other team members are posting their ideas. This eliminates the negative impact of production blocking in generating ideas. However, before an urban and planning study researcher decides to form a co-located or virtual research team and communicate face-to-face or electronically, synchronously or asynchronously, it is important he or she knows the variables that impact the creative performance of each team type.

VARIABLES THAT AFFECT VT BRAINSTORMING PERFORMANCE

Paulus and Dzindolet's (2008) model of team creativity organizes the VT brainstorming variables by highlighting how group, task, and situational variables influence and are influenced by the cognitive, social and motivational processes that underlie collaborative creativity. Although the model describes face-to-face brainstorming as well as VTs, we will focus on VT brainstorming (i.e., teams in which the structure involves communicating through an electronic medium) (Figure 1).

Brainstorming, or idea generation, is at its core a cognitive process. Individually, team members search their long term memories to generate ideas. However, as they attend to the ideas generated by others, VT brainstormers may generate ideas in a content area they had not considered or may combine ideas generated by themselves and others into better ideas. Deciding which ideas to share and whose ideas to attend to are regulated by social processes. For example, social comparison processes keep the number of ideas generated by group brainstormers similar to one another—rarely do brainstormers present many more or many fewer ideas than their team members. In addition, how well the VT manages conflict and allows for varied viewpoints has strong effects on the sharing of generated ideas. Both the cognitive and social processes affect and are affected by motivational processes. Intrinsic and extrinsic motivation affect how much effort group members will extend to generate ideas and how long they will persist in the task when idea generation is not easy or when group conflict exists. The three processes interact and affect one another and determine the creative output from the brainstorming VT.

The creative output affects group member variables, group structure, group climate, and external demands, which affect the cognitive, social, and motivational processes. It is important to note that the variables and processes interact with one another to affect VT brainstorming performance (i.e., the number and quality of the ideas generated), which in turn affect the variables and processes.

To provide an example of the interplay between various variables, processes, and the creative output, it is important to explore what the creative process of an urban and planning study virtual brainstorming team might entail. An urban and planning studies researcher, who has the task relevant knowledge, skills, and attitudes to complete the urban and planning studies research project and enough intrinsic motivation to focus on the task (group member variables) may search long term memory to generate ideas and solutions to the problem (i.e., engage in cognitive processes). The researcher will only share the generated ideas

Figure 1. Paulus and Dzindolet's (2008) Model of Team Creativity

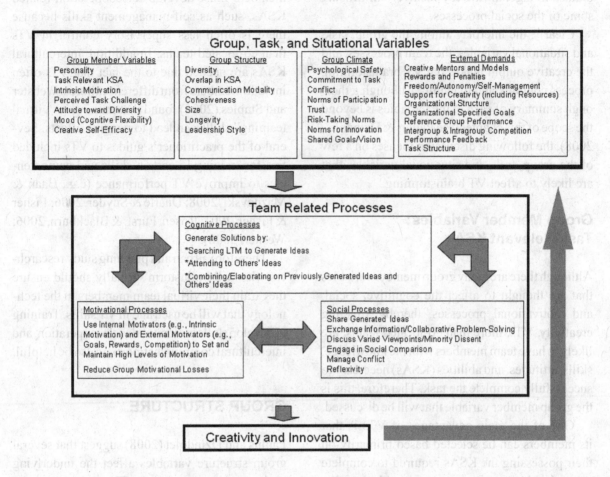

(i.e., engage in social processes) when motivated, which is influenced by external demands (e.g., a large gap in the urban and planning studies literature, university pressure on the team member to publish research in urban and planning studies) and group climate (e.g., a psychologically safe and participative group climate in which high levels of trust and support for full participation by all VT members will increase the researcher's likelihood of sharing generated ideas). Other VT members will only attend to the shared ideas (cognitive process) if they are motivated to do so. This attention is affected by how similar or diverse the researcher who shared the idea is perceived to be (group structure variable). If the researchers do pay attention to the shared ideas (cognitive

process), this exposure provides performance information, which may lead to social comparison (social process) to a referent within the group. The social comparison is influenced by group member variables (e.g., creative self-efficacy) and group structure variables (e.g., cohesiveness). If the researchers are rewarded for sharing ideas (external demand variable), the group's climate is perceived to be more psychologically safe (group climate variable) and the researcher's motivation to share future ideas is increased. Having created and shared a "successful" idea, the researcher's mood is likely to become more positive (group member variable), increasing cognitive flexibility (positively affecting cognitive processes). This may improve the creative output from the virtual brainstorming team, thereby positively influencing some of the social processes.

Clearly, the interplay among the group, task, and situational variables, the team processes, and the creative output makes the VT brainstorming process complex and dynamic. Although a thorough summary of each of the variables is beyond the scope of this chapter (see Paulus & Dzindolet, 2008), the following discussion focuses on a few of the group, task, and situational variables that are likely to affect VT brainstorming.

Group Member Variables: Task Relevant KSA

Although there are many group member variables that are thought to affect the cognitive, social, and motivational processes, thereby affecting creativity, VTs, more than co-located teams, are likely to have team members with the knowledge, skills, attitudes, and abilities (KSAs) necessary to successfully complete the task. Therefore, this is the group member variable that will be discussed.

One of the main advantages of VTs is that its members can be selected based primarily on their possessing the KSAs required to complete the task without regard to geographic location (Nemiro, 2002). Therefore, almost by definition, VTs should have members that are more likely to possess the appropriate KSAs to successfully meet the task demands. However, task KSAs are not enough. Not only must team members have the KSAs to meet the task demands, team members need to possess KSAs with regards to teamwork. Stevens and Campion (1994, 1999) have outlined specific team KSAs to help identify effective team members.

Not only do VT members need the same KSAs as their co-located counterparts, VT members must also have KSA competencies regarding the use of the technology. Training in the technology used for communication should alleviate this impediment (Rosen, Furst, & Blackburn, 2006). In addition, Hertel, Konradt, and Voss (2006) suggest that VT

members must develop telecooperation-related KSAs, such as self-management skills because there is often less supervisory control in VTs than co-located teams. In addition, intercultural KSAs are needed due to the fact that VTs often include members from different cultures. Webster and Staples (2006) found that training in "virtual teaming" skills can lead to positive effects. Several of the practitioner's guides to VTs included tips for training in certain skills and competencies to improve VT performance (e.g., Baan & Maznevski, 2008; Duarte & Snyder, 2006; Fisher & Fisher, 2001; Rosen, Furst, & Blackburn, 2006; Wesner, 2008).

Therefore, urban and planning study researchers who will brainstorm virtually should ensure they train their virtual team members in the technology that will be used and in VT skills. Training to develop skills in teamwork, telecooperation, and intercultural communication may also be helpful.

GROUP STRUCTURE

Paulus and Dzindolet (2008) suggest that several group structure variables affect the underlying brainstorming processes. Three that may be particularly relevant to VTs are communication modality, cohesiveness, and diversity. Each will be discussed in turn.

Communication Modality

Exchange of information has been extensively studied among VT and co-located teams. Because VTs must often rely on technology to exchange information, their information exchange patterns often differ from those of co-located teams. For example, Cooke, Gorman, Pedersen, and Bell (2007) compared 20 co-located and distributed teams of students as they performed seven different command and control type missions. Although the VTs and co-located teams did not differ in performance, co-located teams were significantly more likely to discuss each mission before they began it and assess their performance after the mission was over. In addition, VTs had fewer communication exchanges—both on- and off-task.

Cummings and Kiesler (2007) examined 491 research collaborations funded by the United States National Science Foundation. They found multi-university collaborations, which were more likely to be virtual than single university collaborations, produced less new knowledge and fewer new tools than single university collaborations. However, coordination, especially division of responsibilities and knowledge transfer mediated the relationship.

Based on these findings, urban and planning studies research teams that opt to work virtually should be careful to divide responsibilities clearly among team members and implement practices that encourage team members to exchange information.

Cohesiveness

Several meta-analyses focused on co-located groups and teams have found that group or team cohesion and performance affect one another and that the relationship becomes even stronger the more interdependent the task (e.g., Beal, Cohen, Burke, & McLendon, 2003; Gully, Devine, & Whitney, 1995; Mullen & Copper, 1994). Many VT researchers suggest that VTs have more difficulty in developing and maintaining cohesiveness than co-located teams (e.g., Hoefling, 2008), but few empirical studies have examined this claim (exceptions are Baltes, Dickson, Sherman, Bauer, & LaGanke, 2002; Warkentin, Sayeed, & Hightower, 1997). The cohesion-performance literature examining co-located teams suggests that group pride, attraction to group members, and task commitment are dimensions of cohesiveness; each dimension positively affects performance (Gully et al., 1995).

Group pride may be more difficult to develop in VT than co-located teams for several reasons.

Hinds and Mortensen (2005) hypothesize that spontaneous communication, which occurs less often among VTs than co-located teams, aids in the development of shared identity. Asynchronous communication and high levels of diversity may also hurt the development of shared identity (Mansour-Cole, 2001). In addition, group pride and attraction to group members may be more difficult to achieve in VTs relative to co-located teams due to less frequent communication (Hiltz, Johnson, & Turoff, 1986; Kiesler, Zubrow, Moses, & Geller, 1985; McGuire, Kiesler, & Siegel, 1987). Creating a team name or engaging in other activities to increase group pride may be beneficial to VTs.

In his review of literature, Walther (1992) cited Lim and Facciola's (1988) field study that compared an asynchronous virtual environment to a face-to-face environment and found that virtual group members rated each other more attractive and more credible. Walther proposed that although VTs may be slower to develop team cohesion, the research does not suggest that the same level of cohesion will not be reached over time.

Task commitment may be more easily achieved in VT than co-located groups. VT members are less likely to share off-task information and details; their communication focuses more on the task than the communication of co-located teams. Given the finding that task commitment is a better predictor of team performance than group pride or attraction (Mullen & Copper, 1994), VT members' cohesion may have a more positive effect on performance than the cohesion of co-located groups.

Although more research needs to be performed to examine the effect of cohesiveness on team effectiveness of VTs, it seems reasonable to suggest that urban and planning studies researchers should attempt to create group pride in their research teams, encourage positive relations among the research team members, and ensure the research team is committed to the research project.

Diversity

One of the identifying characteristics of VTs is that they are more likely to include members who are diverse in nationality. Theoretically, this diversity should increase VT members' exposure to diverse perspectives, which should increase creativity. Yet, two meta-analyses of co-located team performance (Bowers, Pharmer, & Salas, 2000; Webber & Donahue, 2001) did not find consistent evidence that diversity of team members improved performance and some researchers suggest that diversity can actually hinder team performance. Mannix and Neale (2005) conclude that diversity on surface level characteristics (e.g., race/ethnicity, gender, and age) among co-located teams can have negative effects on group processes leading diverse groups to be less cohesive, have higher turnover rates, lower levels of commitment, and experience more relationship conflict than more homogenous groups.

Salient differences among team members, according to social categorization theory and social identity theory (Abrams & Hogg, 1990; Tajfel & Turner, 1979), will lead team members to view themselves and others in terms of relevant stereotypes; in-group favoritism can cause friction between the sub-groups diminishing the perception of a psychologically safe environment and increasing relationship conflict. VTs may not have some of these deleterious effects of surface-level diversity because many of these differences may go undetected, especially if VT members never meet. Even among VTs that do meet face-to-face periodically, members' diverse surface level characteristics will not be as salient during interactions that are not face-to-face.

Given that urban and planning studies research teams that are high in national diversity are likely to be virtual rather than co-located and that highly diverse teams perform better virtually rather than face-to-face, urban and planning study researchers probably need not pay too much attention to its team members' diversity with respect to national-ity other than how it may affect trust, one of the group climate variables.

GROUP CLIMATE

When team members perceive that they agree as to the core mission or objectives the team is to accomplish, then team climate is strong and the team should be effective (Kozlowski & Ilgen, 2006). Given that VT members are often more diverse than co-located team members, reaching consensus may be more difficult. However, given the fact that VT's communication time has a higher on-task versus off-task ratio, VTs may actually have stronger team climates than co-located teams.

Nemiro (2001) has created a survey, the Virtual Team Creative Climate (VTCC), to assess the work environment for creativity in VTs. The survey includes eleven scales, two of which measure task connection: (1) Dedication/Commitment, and (2) Goal Clarity. Three of the eleven scales measure interpersonal connection: (1) Information Sharing, (2) Personal Bond, and (3) Trust. One of the eleven scales measures Sufficient Resources and Time. The remaining five scales measure management and team member skills: (1) Acceptance of Ideas and Constructive Tension, (2) Challenge, (3) Collaboration, (4) Freedom, and (5) Management Encouragement.

Urban and planning studies research teams might benefit from assessing their team's climate by administering the VTCC to its members periodically.

Psychological Safety

Team members must feel that the organization (e.g., the research community of urban and planning studies) and their research team is receptive to and supportive of the expression of new ideas. Unless there is this sense of psychological safety, VT brainstormers will not risk the potential ridicule or negative reactions that may accompany new ideas, especially radical ones. A number of research programs have provided strong evidence for the role of psychological safety in facilitating innovation (Edmondson & Roloff, 2009; West, 1990); Gibson and Gibbs (2006) identify psychological safety as important in VTs.

Conflict

Conflict can potentially *help* performance. Task conflict may increase exposure to diverse perspectives, which will increase creativity (Amabile, 1996) leading to the creation of better research ideas. However, conflict may require research team members to spend time managing the conflict rather than working on the tasks thus reducing the number of ideas generated. De Dreu and Weingart's (2003) meta-analysis of co-located teams found that both relationship conflict and task conflict hurt team performance.

Although much of the VT literature suggests that conflict is more likely to occur in VT than co-located groups and that this conflict will impair VT performance, only a handful of empirical studies have compared conflict and performance in VT and co-located teams. Griffith, Mannix, and Neale (2003) surveyed members of 35 teams and found that VT members had more process conflict when controlling for trust. However, they did not find VTs to have more (or less) task or relationship conflict than co-located teams. Similarly, Mortensen and Hinds (2001) found no significant differences in interpersonal or task conflict between VT and co-located teams. Hinds and Mortensen (2005) found the relationship between virtuality and conflict (both task and interpersonal) was mediated by shared identity and spontaneous communication, both of which may be more difficult to gain in more diverse teams.

Urban and planning studies researchers may be most creative if they work in teams in which there is enough conflict to expose members to varying ideas but not too much conflict as to distract the research team members from the task (for more

information on the 'balance' perspective see Paulus, Kohn, & Dzindolet, 2011).

Trust

Priest, Stagl, Klein, and Salas (2005) report that trust is important for VT performance. "Without sufficient trust, team members will expend time and energy protecting, checking, and inspecting each other's work as opposed to collaborating in facilitation of process gains" (p. 194). Additionally trust is important in disseminating information.

Duarte and Snyder (2006) in their practitioner's guide, *Mastering Virtual Teams,* suggest three factors that are important in developing trust: (1) performance competency, which can be enhanced by having a reputation for performance, demonstrating follow-through, and possessing the ability to obtain necessary resources for the group to succeed, (2) integrity, which is in a large part due to the consistency between what a person says and does, and (3) concern for the well-being of others, which means ensuring that each VT member is given the opportunity to perform relevant tasks, helping VT members transition to other teams as projects evolve, and knowing how the team impacts others. In addition, they suggest that leaders develop an "explicit trust plan for the team," and ask team members what they think could be done to build trust.

One of the problems in evaluating the importance of trust in VT and co-located team performance is that researchers do not consistently use one valid, reliable scale to measure team trust. This makes it very difficult to compare across studies. In addition, some scholars view trust as a unidimensional concept; others view it as having several subcomponents (e.g., Francovich, Reina, Reina, & Dilts, 2008; Peters & Manz, 2008). Clearly, future research needs to be done to measure trust and determine its effect on performance of co-located and virtual teams. Nonetheless, urban and planning researchers should attempt to develop and maintain trust among virtual brainstorming team members (for specific techniques see Duarte & Snyder, 2006).

External Demands: Rewards and Penalties

Consistent with the research on co-located teams, studies that focus on the effects of rewards and penalties on VT performance find that team based rewards can improve performance (Hertel, Konradt, & Orlikowski, 2004). Rewards rather than penalties should be the motivational focus due to the fact that several researchers hypothesize the importance of psychological safety to VT performance (e.g., Cordery & Soo, 2008).

Before concluding that urban and planning study researchers should develop reward structures for their team members, it is important to keep in mind that many studies have found that creativity can be *undermined* by external rewards (Amabile, 1985; Amabile, Hennessey, & Grossman, 1986; Kruglanski, Friedman, & Zeevi, 1971). Urban and planning studies research teams would be better off applying Paulus, Kohn, and Dzindolet's (2011) 'balance' perspective: research teams should be given enough autonomy to encourage psychological safety and creativity and enough external rewards to encourage persistence during dry spells.

CONCLUSION

It is clear that predicting the brainstorming performance among VTs is a complex process. Members of brainstorming VTs are sometimes geographically dispersed and must rely on technology to communicate. VT members are more likely to possess the necessary task KSAs and are often more nationally diverse than co-located teams. Geographical dispersion and reliance on technology affect the exchange of both task related and task unrelated information among members and the frequency and amount of spontaneous and planned communications. The communication

patterns of VTs are likely to be heavily influenced by the technology that is provided to the VT. The differing communication patterns are thought to affect the team's cognitive, social, and motivational processes that underlie brainstorming.

Each of the variables and processes discussed in the chapter must be considered when an urban and planning studies researcher is deciding to collaborate with a qualified colleague who lives miles away. Below are some suggestions that are likely to improve the brainstorming performance of virtual urban and planning studies research teams much of the time:

1. *Selecting the urban and planning studies VT members.* Select or train VT members so that they hold the task-necessary KSAs, team relevant KSAs, technology KSAs, and VT-specific KSAs. Make attempts to create group pride, encourage positive relations among the VT team members, and most importantly, keep the research members committed to the research project.

2. *Selecting the Technology.* The level of media richness required of the technology and the extent to which the technology needs to allow for synchronous communication will be determined by the research task the team will accomplish. Remember that one advantage of VTs and electronic brainstorming is that production blocking is eliminated.

3. *Setting the Stage.* Create an environment in which the urban and planning studies VT members feel psychologically safe. Virtual brainstormers should feel encouraged to freely express crazy, new, novel ideas trusting that the other urban and planning studies research members will not evaluate them negatively. There should be enough conflict to allow VT members to be exposed to varying ideas but not too much conflict as to distract the research team members from the task.

4. *Creating Carrots and Sticks.* Provide enough individual and group rewards to encourage urban and planning studies researchers to persist when the brainstorming becomes boring or difficult, being careful not to provide too many rewards as to undermine intrinsic motivation.

5. *Mixing It Up.* Alternate between working alone and working together (this should be easy for VTs). Decontruct the urban and planning studies research project into smaller parts. Be sure to take brief breaks.

Although virtual brainstorming is a complex process, following these guidelines should help urban and planning studies research teams generate many creative ideas.

REFERENCES

Abrams, D., & Hogg, M. A. (1990). *Social identifications: A social psychology of intergroup relations and group processes.* New York, NY: Routledge.

Amabile, T. M. (1985). Motivation and creativity: Effects of motivational orientation on creative writers. *Journal of Personality and Social Psychology*, *48*, 393–399. doi:10.1037/0022-3514.48.2.393

Amabile, T. M. (1996). *Creativity in context.* Boulder, CO: Westview Press.

Amabile, T. M., Hennessey, B., & Grossman, B. S. (1986). Social influences on creativity: The effects of contracted-for reward. *Journal of Personality and Social Psychology*, *50*, 14–23. doi:10.1037/0022-3514.50.1.14

Baan, A., & Maznevski, M. (2008). Training for virtual collaboration: Beyond technology competencies. In Nemiro, J., Beyerlein, M. M., Bradley, L., & Beyerlein, S. (Eds.), *The handbook of high-performance virtual teams: A toolkit for collaborating across boundaries* (pp. 345–365). San Francisco, CA: Jossey-Bass.

Baltes, B. B., Dickson, M. W., Sherman, M. P., Bauer, C. C., & LaGanke, J. (2002). Computer-mediated communication and group decision making: A meta-analysis. *Organizational Behavior and Human Decision Processes*, *87*, 156–179. doi:10.1006/obhd.2001.2961

Beal, D. J., Cohen, R. R., Burke, M. J., & McLendon, C. L. (2003). Cohesion and performance in groups: A meta-analytic clarification of construct relations. *The Journal of Applied Psychology*, *88*(6), 989–1004. doi:10.1037/0021-9010.88.6.989

Bouchard, T. J., & Hare, M. (1970). Size, performance, and potential in brainstorming groups. *The Journal of Applied Psychology*, *54*, 51–55. doi:10.1037/h0028621

Bowers, C. A., Pharmer, J. A., & Salas, E. (2000). When member homogeneity is needed in work teams: A meta-analysis. *Small Group Research*, *31*, 305–327. doi:10.1177/104649640003100303

Brown, V. R., & Paulus, P. B. (2002). Making group brainstorming more effective: Recommendations from an associative memory perspective. *Current Directions in Psychological Science*, *11*(6), 208–212. doi:10.1111/1467-8721.00202

Camacho, L. M., & Paulus, P. B. (1995). The role of social anxiousness in group brainstorming. *Journal of Personality and Social Psychology*, *68*(6), 1071–1080. doi:10.1037/0022-3514.68.6.1071

Cohen, S. G., & Gibson, C. B. (2003). In the beginning: Introduction and framework. In Gibson, C. B., & Cohen, S. G. (Eds.), *Virtual teams that work: Creating conditions for virtual team effectiveness* (pp. 1–14). San Francisco, CA: Jossey-Bass.

Connaughton, S. L., & Shuffler, M. (2007). Multinational and multicultural distributed teams: A review and future agenda. *Small Group Research*, *38*(3), 387–412. doi:10.1177/1046496407301970

Connolly, T., Routhieaux, R. L., & Schneider, S. K. (1993). On the effectiveness of group brainstorming: Test of one underlying cognitive mechanism. *Small Group Research*, *24*(4), 490–503. doi:10.1177/1046496493244004

Cooke, N., Gorman, J. C., Pedersen, H., & Bell, B. (2007). Distributed mission environments: Effects of geographic distribution on team cognition, process, and performance. In Fiore, S. M., & Salas, E. (Eds.), *Toward a Science of Distributed Learning* (pp. 147–167). Washington, DC: American Psychological Association. doi:10.1037/11582-007

Cordery, J. L., & Soo, C. (2008). Overcoming impediments to virtual team effectiveness. *Human Factors and Ergonomics in Manufacturing*, *18*(5), 487–500. doi:10.1002/hfm.20119

Coskun, H., Paulus, P. B., Brown, V., & Sherwood, J. J. (2000). Cognitive stimulation and problem presentation in idea-generating groups. *Group Dynamics*, *4*(4), 307–329. doi:10.1037/1089-2699.4.4.307

Cummings, J. N., & Kiesler, S. (2007). Coordination costs and project outcomes in multi-university collaborations. *Research Policy*, *36*(10), 1620–1634. doi:10.1016/j.respol.2007.09.001

De Dreu, C. K. W., & Weingart, L. R. (2003). Task versus relationship conflict, team performance, and team member satisfaction: A meta-analysis. *The Journal of Applied Psychology*, *88*(4), 741–749. doi:10.1037/0021-9010.88.4.741

Dennis, A. R., Valacich, J. S., Connolly, T., & Wynne, B. E. (1996). Process structuring in electronic brainstorming. *Information Systems Research*, *7*, 268–277. doi:10.1287/isre.7.2.268

Dennis, A. R., & Williams, M. L. (2005). A meta-analysis of group size effects in electronic brainstorming: More heads are better than one. *International Journal of e-Collaboration*, *1*(1), 24–42. doi:10.4018/jec.2005010102

DeRosa, D. M., Smith, C. L., & Hantula, D. A. (2007). The medium matters: Mining the long-promised merit of group interaction in creative idea generation tasks in a meta-analysis of the electronic group brainstorming literature. *Computers in Human Behavior*, *23*(3), 1549–1581. doi:10.1016/j.chb.2005.07.003

Diehl, M., & Stroebe, W. (1987). Productivity loss in brainstorming groups: Toward the solution of a riddle. *Journal of Personality and Social Psychology*, *53*(3), 497–509. doi:10.1037/0022-3514.53.3.497

Diehl, M., & Stroebe, W. (1991). Productivity loss in idea-generating groups: Tracking down the blocking effect. *Journal of Personality and Social Psychology*, *61*(3), 392–403. doi:10.1037/0022-3514.61.3.392

Dornburg, C. C., Stevens, S. M., Hendrickson, S. M. L., & Davidson, G. S. (2009). Improving extreme-scale problem solving: Assessing electronic brainstorming effectiveness in an industrial setting. *Human Factors*, *51*(4), 519–527. doi:10.1177/0018720809343587

Driskell, J. E., Radtke, P. H., & Salas, E. (2003). Virtual teams: Effects of technological mediation on team performance. *Group Dynamics*, *7*, 297–323. doi:10.1037/1089-2699.7.4.297

Duarte, D. L., & Snyder, N. T. (2006). *Mastering virtual teams: Strategies, tools, and techniques that succeed* (3rd ed.). San Francisco, CA: Jossey-Bass.

Edmondson, A. C., & Roloff, K. S. (2009). Overcoming barriers to collaboration: Psychological safety and learning in diverse teams. In Salas, E., Goodwin, G. F., & Burke, C. S. (Eds.), *Team effectiveness in complex organizations: Cross-disciplinary perspectives and approaches* (pp. 183–208). New York, NY: Routledge/Taylor & Francis.

Fisher, K., & Fisher, M. D. (2001). *The distance manager: A hands-on guide to managing off-site employees and virtual teams*. New York, NY: McGraw-Hill.

Francovich, C., Reina, M., Reina, D., & Dilts, C. (2008). Trust building online: Virtual collaboration and the development of trust. In Nemiro, J., Beyerlein, M. M., Bradley, L., & Beyerlein, S. (Eds.), *The handbook of high performance virtual teams* (pp. 153–176). Hoboken, NJ: John Wiley & Sons.

Gallupe, R. B., Bastianutti, L. M., & Cooper, W. H. (1991). Unblocking brainstorms. *The Journal of Applied Psychology*, 76(1), 137–142. doi:10.1037/0021-9010.76.1.137

Gallupe, R. B., Dennis, A. R., Cooper, W. H., & Valacich, J. S. (1992). Electronic brainstorming and group size. *Academy of Management Journal*, 35(2), 350–369. doi:10.2307/256377

Gibson, C. B., & Gibbs, J. L. (2006). Unpacking the concept of virtuality: The effects of geographic dispersion, electronic dependence, dynamic structure, and national diversity on team innovation. *Administrative Science Quarterly*, 51, 451–495.

Griffith, T. L., Mannix, E. A., & Neale, M. A. (2003). Conflict and virtual teams. In Gibson, C. B., & Cohen, S. G. (Eds.), *Virtual Teams that Work: Creating Conditions for Virtual Team Effectiveness* (pp. 335–352). San Francisco, CA: Jossey-Bass.

Griffith, T. L., Sawyer, J. E., & Neale, M. A. (2003). Virtualness and knowledge in teams: Managing the love triangle in organizations, individuals, and information technology. *Management Information Systems Quarterly*, 27, 265–287.

Gully, S. M., Devine, D. J., & Whitney, D. J. (1995). A meta-analysis of cohesion and performance: Effects of levels of analysis and task interdependence. *Small Group Research*, 26, 497–520. doi:10.1177/1046496495264003

Hertel, G., Konradt, U., & Orlikowski, B. (2004). Managing distance by interdependence: Goal setting, task interdependence, and team-based rewards in virtual teams. *European Journal of Work and Organizational Psychology*, 13(1), 1–28. doi:10.1080/13594320344000228

Hertel, G., Konradt, U., & Voss, K. (2006). Competencies for virtual teamwork: Development and validation of a web-based selection tool for members of distributed teams. *European Journal of Work and Organizational Psychology*, 15(4), 477–504. doi:10.1080/13594320600908187

Hiltz, S. R., Johnson, K., & Turoff, M. (1986). Experiments in group decision making: Communication process and outcome in face-to-face versus computerized conferences. *Human Communication Research*, 13, 225–252. doi:10.1111/j.1468-2958.1986.tb00104.x

Hinds, P. J., & Mortensen, M. (2005). Understanding conflict in geographically distributed teams: The moderating effects of shared identity, shared context, and spontaneous communication. *Organization Science*, 16(3), 290–307. doi:10.1287/orsc.1050.0122

Hoefling, T. (2008). The three-fold path of expanding emotional bandwidth in virtual teams. In Nemiro, J., Beyerlein, M. M., Bradley, L., & Beyerlein, S. (Eds.), *The handbook of high performance virtual teams* (pp. 87–104). Hoboken, NJ: John Wiley & Sons.

Horvath, L., & Tobin, T. J. (2001). Twenty-first century teamwork: Defining competencies for virtual teams. In M. M. Beyerlein, D. A. Johnson, & S. T. Beyerlein (Eds.), *Advances in Interdisciplinary Studies of Work Teams: Vol. 8. Virtual Teams* (pp. 239-258). Bradford, UK: Emerald.

Jett, Q. R., & George, J. M. (2003). Work interrupted: A closer look at the role of interruptions in organizational life. *Academy of Management Review, 28*(3), 494–507.

Karau, S. J., & Williams, K. (1993). Social loafing: A meta-analytic review and theoretical integration. *Journal of Personality and Social Psychology, 65*(4), 681–706. doi:10.1037/0022-3514.65.4.681

Kay, G. (1995). Effective meetings through electronic brainstorming. *Journal of Management Development, 14*(6), 4–25. doi:10.1108/02621719510086147

Kiesler, S., Zubrow, D., Moses, A. M., & Geller, V. (1985). Affect in computer-mediated communication: An experiment in synchronous terminal-to-terminal discussion. *Human-Computer Interaction, 1*, 77–104. doi:10.1207/s15327051hci0101_3

Kozlowski, S. W. J., & Ilgen, D. R. (2006). Enhancing the effectiveness of work groups and teams. *Psychological Science in the Public Interest, 7*, 77–124.

Kruglanski, A. W., Friedman, I., & Zeevi, G. (1971). The effects of extrinsic incentive on some qualitative aspects of task performance. *Journal of Personality, 39*, 606–617. doi:10.1111/j.1467-6494.1971.tb00066.x

Larey, T. S., & Paulus, P. B. (1995). Social comparison goal setting in brainstorming groups. *Journal of Applied Social Psychology, 26*(18), 1579–1596. doi:10.1111/j.1559-1816.1995.tb02634.x

Leenders, R. T. A. J., Kratzer, J., & van Engelen, J. M. L. (2007). Media ensembles and new product team creativity: A tree-based exploration. In MacGregor, S. P., & Torress-Coronas Lira, T. (Eds.), *Higher Creativity for Virtual Teams: Developing Platforms for Co-Creation* (pp. 75–97). Hershey, PA: Information Science Reference. doi:10.4018/978-1-59904-129-2.ch004

Mannix, E. A., & Neale, M. A. (2005). What difference makes a difference: The promise and reality of diverse groups in organizations. *Psychological Science in the Public Interest, 6*, 31–55. doi:10.1111/j.1529-1006.2005.00022.x

Mansour-Cole, D. (2001). Team identity formation in virtual teams. In M. M. Beyerlein, D. A. Johnson, & S. T. Beyerlein (Eds.), *Advances in Interdisciplinary Studies of Work Teams: Vol. 8. Virtual Teams* (pp. 41-58). Bradford, UK: Emerald.

McGuire, T. W., Kiesler, S., & Siegel, J. (1987). Group and computer-mediated discussion effects in risk decision making. *Journal of Personality and Social Psychology, 52*, 917–930. doi:10.1037/0022-3514.52.5.917

Meadow, A., Parnes, S. J., & Reese, H. (1959). Influence of brainstorming instructions and problem sequence on a creative problem solving test. *The Journal of Applied Psychology, 43*, 413–416. doi:10.1037/h0043917

Mortensen, M., & Hinds, P. (2001). Conflict and shared identity in geographically distributed teams. *The International Journal of Conflict Management, 12*, 212–238. doi:10.1108/eb022856

Mullen, B., & Copper, C. (1994). The relation between group cohesiveness and performance: An integration. *Psychological Bulletin, 115*(2), 210–227. doi:10.1037/0033-2909.115.2.210

Mullen, B., Johnson, C., & Salas, E. (1991). Productivity loss in brainstorming groups: A meta-analytic integration. *Basic and Applied Social Psychology, 12*(1), 3–23. doi:10.1207/s15324834basp1201_1

Nemiro, J. E. (2001). Assessing the climate for creativity in virtual teams. In M. M. Beyerlein, D. A. Johnson, & S. T. Beyerlein (Eds.), *Advances in Interdisciplinary Studies of Work Teams: Vol. 8. Virtual Teams* (pp. 59-84). Bradford, UK: Emerald.

Nemiro, J. E. (2002). The creative process in virtual teams. *Creativity Research Journal, 14*(1), 69–83. doi:10.1207/S15326934CRJ1401_6

Nemiro, J. E. (2008). Creativity techniques for virtual teams. In Nemiro, J., Beyerlein, M. M., Bradley, L., & Beyerlein, S. (Eds.), *The handbook of high performance virtual teams* (pp. 491–532). Hoboken, NJ: John Wiley & Sons.

Nijstad, B. A., & Stroebe, W. (2006). How the group affects the mind: A cognitive model of idea generation in groups. *Personality and Social Psychology Review, 10*(3), 186–213. doi:10.1207/s15327957pspr1003_1

Osborn, A. F. (1957). *Applied imagination; principles and procedures of creative problem-solving.* New York, NY: Scribner.

Parnes, S. J., & Meadow, A. (1959). Effects of 'brainstorming' instructions on creative problem solving by trained and untrained subjects. *Journal of Educational Psychology, 50*, 171–176. doi:10.1037/h0047223

Paulus, P. B., & Dzindolet, M. T. (1993). Social influence processes in group brainstorming. *Journal of Personality and Social Psychology, 64*(4), 575–586. doi:10.1037/0022-3514.64.4.575

Paulus, P. B., & Dzindolet, M. T. (2008). Social influence, creativity, and innovation. *Social Influence, 3*, 228–247. doi:10.1080/15534510802341082

Paulus, P. B., Kohn, N., & Dzindolet, M. (2010). Teams. In Runco, M., & Pritzker, S. (Eds.), *Encyclopedia of Creativity* (2nd ed.). Amsterdam, The Netherlands: Elsevier.

Paulus, P. B., Nakui, T., Putman, V. L., & Brown, V. R. (2006). Effects of task instructions and brief breaks on brainstorming. *Group Dynamics, 10*(3), 206–219. doi:10.1037/1089-2699.10.3.206

Peters, L. M. L., & Manz, C. C. (2008). Getting virtual teams right the first time: Keys to successful collaboration in the virtual world. In Nemiro, J., Beyerlein, M. M., Bradley, L., & Beyerlein, S. (Eds.), *The handbook of high performance virtual teams* (pp. 105–130). Hoboken, NJ: John Wiley & Sons.

Priest, H. A., Stagl, K. C., Klein, C., & Salas, E. (2005). Virtual teams: Creating context for distributed teamwork. In Bowers, C., Salas, E., & Jentsch, F. (Eds.), *Creating High-Tech Teams: Practical Guidance on Work Performance and Technology* (pp. 185–212). Washington, DC: American Psychological Association. doi:10.1037/11263-009

Putman, V. L., & Paulus, P. B. (2009). Brainstorming, brainstorming rules and decision making. *The Journal of Creative Behavior, 43*, 23–39.

Rosen, B., Furst, S., & Blackburn, R. (2006). Training for virtual teams: An investigation of current practices and future needs. *Human Resource Management, 45*, 229–247. doi:10.1002/hrm.20106

Sosik, J. J., Kahai, S. S., & Avolio, B. J. (1998). Transformational leadership and dimensions of creativity: Motivating idea generation in computer-mediated groups. *Creativity Research Journal, 11*(2), 111–121. doi:10.1207/s15326934crj1102_3

Stevens, M. J., & Campion, M. A. (1994). The knowledge, skill, and ability requirements for teamwork: Implications for human resource management. *Journal of Management, 20*, 503–530.

Stevens, M. J., & Campion, M. A. (1999). Staffing work teams: Development and validation of a selection test for teamwork settings. *Journal of Management, 25*, 207–228. doi:10.1016/S0149-2063(99)80010-5

Tajfel, H., & Turner, J. C. (1979). An integrative theory on intergroup conflict. In Austin, W., & Worchel, S. (Eds.), *The social psychology of intergroup relations* (pp. 33–48). Pacific Grove, CA: Brooks/Cole.

Walther, J. B. (1992). Interpersonal effects in computer-mediated interaction: A relational perspective. *Communication Research, 19*, 52–90. doi:10.1177/009365092019001003

Warkentin, M., Sayeed, L., & Hightower, R. (1997). Virtual teams versus face-to-face teams: An exploratory study of a web-based conference system. *Decision Sciences, 28*, 975–996. doi:10.1111/j.1540-5915.1997.tb01338.x

Webber, S. S., & Donahue, L. M. (2001). Impact of highly and less job-related diversity on work group cohesion and performance: A meta-analysis. *Journal of Management, 27*, 141–162.

Webster, J., & Staples, D. S. (2006). Comparing virtual teams to traditional teams: An identification of new research possibilities. *Research in Personnel and Human Resources Management, 25*, 181–125. doi:10.1016/S0742-7301(06)25005-9

Wesner, M. S. (2008). Assessing training needs for virtual team collaboration. In Nemiro, J., Beyerlein, M. M., Bradley, L., & Beyerlein, S. (Eds.), *The handbook of high-performance virtual teams: A toolkit for collaborating across boundaries* (pp. 273–294). San Francisco, CA: Jossey-Bass.

West, M. A. (1990). The social psychology of innovation in groups. In West, M. A., & Farr, J. L. (Eds.), *Innovation and creativity at work: Psychological and organizational strategies* (pp. 309–333). Hoboken, NJ: John Wiley & Sons.

Wuchty, S., Jones, B. F., & Uzzi, B. (2007). The increasing dominance of teams in production of knowledge. *Science, 316*, 1036–1039. doi:10.1126/science.1136099

ADDITIONAL READING

Amabile, T. M. (1996). *Creativity in context: Update to 'The Social Psychology of Creativity*. Boulder, CO: Westview Press.

Bell, B. S., & Kozlowski, S. J. (2002). A typology of virtual teams: Implications for effective leadership. *Group & Organization Management, 27*, 14–49. doi:10.1177/1059601102027001003

Beyerlein, M. M., Johnson, D. A., & Beyerlein, S. T. (eds.) (2001). *Advances in Interdisciplinary Studies of Work Teams: Vol. 8. Virtual Teams*. Oxford, UK: Elsevier Science Ltd.

Brown, V., & Paulus, P. B. (1996). A simple dynamic model of social factors in group brainstorming. *Small Group Research, 27*, 91–114. doi:10.1177/1046496496271005

Candy, L., & Hewett, T. T. (2008). *International Journal of Human-Computer Interaction: Special Issue. Investigating and cultivating creativity, 24(5)*. Taylor & Francis Group.

Chidambaram, L., & Tung, L. L. (2005). Is out of sight out of mind? An empirical study of social loafing in technology-supported groups. *Information Systems Research, 16*, 149–168. doi:10.1287/isre.1050.0051

Edmondson, A. (1999). Psychological safety and learning behavior in work teams. *Administrative Science Quarterly, 44*, 350–383. doi:10.2307/2666999

Farh, J. L., Lee, C., & Farh, C. I. C. (2010). Task conflict and team creativity: A question of how much and when. *The Journal of Applied Psychology, 95*, 1173–1180. doi:10.1037/a0020015

Gallupe, R. B., Cooper, W. H., Grise, M. L., & Bastianutti, L. M. (1994). Blocking electronic brainstorms. *The Journal of Applied Psychology, 77*, 77–86. doi:10.1037/0021-9010.79.1.77

Gibson, C. B., & Cohen, S. G. (Eds.). (2003). *Virtual teams that work: Creating conditions for virtual team effectiveness*. San Francisco, CA: Jossey-Bass.

Hennessey, B. A., & Amabile, T. M. (2010). Creativity. *Annual Review of Psychology, 61*, 569–598. doi:10.1146/annurev.psych.093008.100416

Jarvenpaa, S. L., Shaw, T. R., & Staples, D. S. (2004). Toward contextualized theories of trust: The role of trust in global virtual teams. *Information Systems Research, 15*, 250–267. doi:10.1287/isre.1040.0028

MacGregor, S. P., & Torres-Coronas, T. (Eds.). (2007). *Higher creativity for virtual teams: Developing platforms for co-creation*. Hershey, PA: Information Science Refernece/IGI Global. doi:10.4018/978-1-59904-129-2

Martins, L. L., Gilson, L. L., & Maynard, M. T. (2004). Virtual teams: What do we know and where do we go from here? *Journal of Management, 30*, 805–835. doi:10.1016/j.jm.2004.05.002

Nemiro, J., Beyerlein, M. M., Bradley, L., & Beyerlein, S. (Eds.). (2008). *The handbook of high-performance virtual teams: A toolkit for collaborating across boundaries*. San Francisco, CA: Jossey-Bass.

Offner, A. K., Kramer, T. J., & Winter, J. P. (1996). The effects of facilitation, recording, and pauses on group brainstorming. *Small Group Research, 27*, 283–298. doi:10.1177/1046496496272005

Osborn, A. F. (1953). *Applied imagination*. New York, NY: Scribner.

Paulus, P. B., & Brown, V. R. (2007). Toward more creative and innovative group idea generation: A cognitive-social-motivational perspective of brainstorming. *Social and Personality Psychology Compass, 1*, 248–265. doi:10.1111/j.1751-9004.2007.00006.x

Paulus, P. B., Dzindolet, M., & Kohn, N. (2011). Collaborative creativity-Group creativity and team innovation. In Mumford, M. (Ed.), *Handbook of organizational creativity* (pp. 325–354). Elsevier.

Paulus, P. B., & Nijstad, B. A. (Eds.). (2003). *Group creativity: Innovation through collaboration*. New York, NY: Oxford University Press.

Rice, D. J., Davidson, B. D., Dannenhoffer, J. H., & Gay, G. K. (2007). Improving the effectiveness of virtual teams by adapting team processes. *Computer Supported Cooperative Work, 16*, 567–594. doi:10.1007/s10606-007-9070-3

Runco, M., & Pritzker, S. (Eds.). (2010). *Encyclopedia of Creativity* (2nd ed.). Elsevier Publishing.

Shin, Y. (2005). Conflict resolution in virtual teams. *Organizational Dynamics. 34*, 331-345.

Staples, D. S., & Webster, J. (2007). Exploring traditional and virtual team members? 'Best Practices': A social cognitive theory perspective. *Small Group Research, 38*, 60–97.

Sternberg, R. J. (Ed.). (1999). *Handbook of creativity*. New York, NY: Cambridge University Press.

Ubell, R. (Ed.). (2010). *Virtual teamwork: Mastering the art and practice of online learning and corporate collaboration*. Hoboken, NJ: John Wiley & Sons. doi:10.1002/9780470615782

Wakefield, R. L., Leidner, D. E., & Garrison, G. (2008). A model of conflict, leadership, and performance in virtual teams. *Information Systems Research, 19*, 434–455. doi:10.1287/isre.1070.0149

KEY TERMS AND DEFINITIONS

Brainstorming Paradigm: Group members are given an idea generation problem and instructed (a) to generate as many ideas as they can, (b) to say anything and everything that they think of, (c) to integrate ideas that have been presented into better ones, and (d) not to criticize their own or others' ideas.

Electronic Brainstorming: A brainstorming group that communicates using a computer based group decision-support system.

Nominal Group Performance: The combined output (e.g., number of non-repetitive generated ideas) of individual brainstormers. Nominal group performance is often compared to the performance of face-to-face brainstorming groups.

Production Blocking: Due to the fact that only one member of a face-to-face group can speak at a time, each member's idea generation is blocked when group members brainstorm.

Psychological Safety: When team members feel the organization and the team is receptive to and supportive of the expression of new ideas, then the members feel psychologically safe and are likely to be creative.

Social Loafing: Group members sometimes exert less effort when performing a task as a group than when performing the task alone.

Virtual Team: Virtual teams are comprised of multiple individuals, who have some degree of task interdependence, share common goals, possess shared values, and rely on technology to communicate with one another.

Chapter 10

The use of Electronic Brainstorming for Collecting Ideas in Scientific Research Teams:
A Challenge for Future Online Research

Nicolas Michinov
University Rennes 2, France

ABSTRACT

The purpose of this chapter is to present an under-used technique for collecting ideas in scientific research teams, namely electronic brainstorming. This technique employs networked computer terminals and software designed to allow group members to communicate electronically during idea-generation tasks. A large number of studies have demonstrated that electronic brainstorming is a useful non-verbal technique for improving the efficacy of e-collaboration, but there are very few situations in which this technique has been used to collect ideas in scientific research teams. Writing articles, reports, white papers, and other scientific documents requires good ideas that can be generated through effective brainstorming. Brainstorming is also recognized as a problem-solving technique which can help researchers find solutions to complex problems by listing their potential causes. Although it is a simple technique that can gather ideas from a group of individuals rapidly by letting them express their ideas freely, it has not been widely used to collect ideas for complex research projects involving researchers working together or in geographically dispersed teams. After reviewing the literature in the field of (electronic) brainstorming, the challenges and opportunities for extending this technique to online research by scientific teams are discussed.

DOI: 10.4018/978-1-4666-0074-4.ch010

INTRODUCTION

With the development of the Internet over the last few decades, online research methods have gained increased recognition in fundamental and social sciences, providing new research opportunities not only for psychologists (e.g., Birnbaum, 2004a, 2004b; Kraut, Olson, Banaji, Bruckman, Cohen, & Couper, 2004; Skitka & Sargis, 2006), but also for other scientists in various disciplinary fields. The development of the Internet has considerably changed the way that research is conducted, allowing the use of new (online) scientific methods for optimizing the collection of data on a large scale, and promoting collaborative work.

A number of researchers from different disciplinary fields have begun to use the Internet and the World Wide Web as a medium for online research, thereby expanding traditional research in laboratory and field settings. For example, in psychology, a review of the publications in the main American Psychological Association journals for 2003-2004 revealed that 21% of these journals published at least one article that used the Web to collect data (Skitka & Sargis, 2006). In psychological research, online methods are often used to recruit large heterogeneous or specialized samples rapidly and to standardize experimental research procedures making it easier to replicate studies.

The Internet has also changed communication, business and learning, as well as many other activities of social and professional life, including scientific research. Scientific research is based on various practices, but researchers often work in teams, collecting and analyzing ideas for complex projects through collaboration and brainstorming. The Internet has notably changed the way scientists collaborate by making it easier to work with geographically distant partners and promoting e-collaboration practices (e.g., Finholt & Olson, 1997; Walsh & Maloney, 2002). This type of distance work in scientific research based on communication technologies may at least partly

explain the fact that the production of knowledge has increasingly become the domain of teams rather than sole authors (e.g., Levine & Moreland, 2004; Wuchty, Jones, & Uzzi, 2007). In addition to this trend toward collaboration in scientific research, it has become increasingly difficult to solve complex scientific problems in the social and human sciences based only on the advice of experts, including researchers.

Today, many research and innovation projects require the participation of several individuals, both experts and non-experts, who have to generate ideas, hypotheses or solutions to complex problems in the early stage of the project (e.g., Marín, Delgado, & Bachmann, 2008; Sengonzi, Demian, & Emmitt, 2009). The involvement of non-experts is important in the research process, because many problems challenge our conception of science and politics (e.g., Funtowicz & Ravetz, 1991; Ludwig, 2001). For example, conservation of forests and endangered species, climate change, nuclear energy, and urban overpopulation are complex issues that cannot be separated from governance, ethics and social justice, and thus involve more than the knowledge of researchers in a given specialized field. Nevertheless, it appears that there is very little collaboration between researchers and non-experts to solve complex problems, and little use of electronic brainstorming systems to facilitate the production and integration of ideas. Indeed, individuals are able to generate creative ideas (Hawkins, 1999), and it is a pity to be deprived of these ideas in scientific research projects and when developing new scientific proposals. Electronic brainstorming is one way of optimizing the collection of ideas.

The purpose of this chapter is to examine how electronic brainstorming can be used to collect ideas among experts, researchers and non-experts involved in collaborative projects, taking a participatory approach to solving complex problems. The first part introduces some examples of electronic brainstorming systems and then discusses the key advantages and disadvantages of these techniques for improving the efficacy of e-collaboration. The second part examines how electronic brainstorming can be used by research teams for gathering ideas for complex projects, and finally makes some recommendations for its use in this area.

FROM VERBAL BRAINSTORMING TO ELECTRONIC BRAINSTORMING: WHAT DOES RESEARCH TELL US?

Brainstorming is known to be a very useful technique for facilitating the generation of creative ideas or solutions on a specific topic in face-to-face interaction. From the outset, the goal of brainstorming has been to generate a long list of ideas, some of which will spark the imagination and facilitate the production of unique and original ideas. Brainstorming has been widely used in different fields such as advertising, marketing, policy-making, and management, but much less in scientific research. While groups of scientists often use brainstorming to develop their theories and models, this is not generally conducted in a formalized way (e.g., Dunbar, 1995, 1997). For example, it is well-known that Albert Einstein and his collaborators spent many years freely exchanging ideas and thoughts to establish the foundations of modern physics, without any formalization of brainstorming sessions (e.g., Michalko, 2001).

Research on Brainstorming

The advertising executive Alex Osborn is recognized as the "father" of the brainstorming technique, following the first edition of his book entitled "Applied Imagination" published in 1953. Since then, the technique has been commonly defined as a formalized method to think up solutions, ideas or new concepts, by listing all the ideas put forward by a group in response to a given problem or question.

The brainstorming technique is based on two principles, *deferment of judgment* and *quantity*

breeds quality. There are four rules that participants in a group session have to follow: (1) postpone and withhold judgment of ideas, (2) concentrate on quantity rather than quality, (3) build on ideas put forward by other participants, and (4) every person and every idea has equal worth. Osborn (1957) made some claims for the efficacy of group brainstorming when these rules are followed, such as "the average person can think up twice as many ideas when working with a group than when working alone" (Osborn, 1957, p. 229). Although brainstorming groups that observe the rules achieve better results than those with no rules (Parnes & Meadow, 1959), a large number of studies have demonstrated that brainstorming groups produce fewer (and often poorer quality) ideas than equal-sized identically instructed nominal groups, i.e., groups whose members work in isolation, pooling their ideas and eliminating any that are redundant (e.g., Diehl & Stroebe, 1987; Lamm & Trommsdorff, 1973; Mullen, Johnson, & Salas, 1991; Paulus, 2000; Paulus & Brown, 2003; Diehl, 1994; Stroebe, Nijstad, & Rietzschel, 2010).

A wide range of social and cognitive processes have been considered to explain this effect (e.g., Brown, Tumeo, Larey, & Paulus 1998; Connolly, Routhieux, & Schneider, 1993; Legett Dugosh, Paulus, Roland, & Yang, 2001; Nijstad & Stroebe, 2006; Paulus & Dzindolet, 1993). The most important concern the fact that expressing ideas verbally can lead to evaluation apprehension, i.e., fear of being judged by others (e.g., Camacho & Paulus, 1995) and to production blocking, i.e., the fact that only one person at a time can give an idea (e.g., Diehl & Stroebe, 1987, 1991; Mullen *et al.*, 1991; Taylor, Berry, & Block, 1958). Many procedural variations that neutralize productivity loss have been introduced to reduce the gap between nominal and brainstorming groups, such as including periods of pauses or breaks (e.g., Paulus, Nakui, Putman, & Brown, 2006), turn-taking (e.g., Diehl & Stroebe, 1987), structuring time and task (e.g., Dennis, Aronson, Heninger, & Walker,

1999), introducing standards of comparison (e.g., Larey & Paulus, 1995), delivering feedback of comparison (e.g., Jung, Schneider, & Valacich, 2010; Michinov & Primois, 2005; Roy, Gauvin, & Limayen, 1996; Shepherd, Briggs, Reinig, Yen, & Nunamaker, 1996), training facilitators (e.g., Kramer, Fleming, & Mannis, 2001), training groups on idea-generation tasks (e.g., Baruah & Paulus, 2008), using effective leadership styles (e.g., Offner, Kramer, & Winter, 1996; Sosik, Avolio, & Kahai, 1997), and combining group and individual sessions (e.g., Dunnette, Campbell, & Jaastad, 1963; Nagasundaram & Dennis, 1993). However, one of the best procedures for reducing the negative impact of productivity loss is undoubtedly electronic brainstorming. The extension of verbal brainstorming to online environments has generated a large number of studies demonstrating that electronic brainstorming is a useful technique for improving the efficacy of e-collaboration (e.g., Dennis & Valacich, 1993; Dennis & Williams, 2003; DeRosa, Smith, & Hantula, 2007).

A Brief Overview of some Electronic Brainstorming Systems

Electronic brainstorming is a non-verbal technique whereby participants produce their ideas via a computer, using *Group Support Systems* (e.g., Huber, 1980). These are computer-based network systems that support groups working on a common task, providing them with a shared interface (see Nunamaker, Briggs, & Mittleman, 1994). They were initially developed for commercial use, usually to support decision-making processes in business organizations and/or to improve productivity, for example, developing new competitive products (e.g., Rangaswamy & Lilien, 1997).

The most famous example of a pioneer Electronic Brainstorming system is Ventana Corporation's GroupSystems ThinkTank 4.0 (http://www.groupsystems.com/). This system contains modules for generating and categorizing ideas, outlin-

ing topics, commenting on ideas, evaluating and voting on proposals, producing reports summarizing a discussion, and maintaining records for future use (e.g., Nunamaker *et al.*, 1991; Rangaswamy & Lilien, 1997). Other applications have been developed to support electronic brainstorming, helping participants generate and manage ideas, including InnovationToolbox, Brainstorming Toolbox, BrainStorm, and Grouputer (cf. Rangaswamy & Lilien, 1997; Woerndl & Eicker, 2006). Another system derived from electronic brainstorming is Concept Mapping (e.g., Burke, O'Campo, Peak, Gielen, McDonnell, & Trochim, 2005). The main advantage of a concept map is that it displays the ideas of users and defines and manages the links between generated concepts. One example of this system is CmapTools, a digital concept-mapping program which can be downloaded free on a personal computer (http://cmap.ihmc.us/). Other free Web-based products such as Google.doc, EtherPad (or MeetingWords), Dabbleboard, Bubbl.us, Text2mindmap, and Mindmeister can also be used to generate and/or organize ideas collaboratively on conceptual maps. Google.doc (http://www.google.com/) and EtherPad or MeetingWords (http://www.meetingwords.com/) are web-based word processors enabling people to work together in real-time to list ideas on a shared space, whereas Bubbl.us (http://bubbl.us/), Dabbleboard (http://www.dabbleboard.com/), Text2mindmap (http://www.text2mindmap.com/), and MindMeister (http://www.mindmeister.com/) are online mind-mapping tools enabling people to build shared conceptual maps based on generated ideas. A simpler system can of course be used to lead an electronic brainstorming session using traditional web-based tools, either synchronous (chat room or Instant Messaging systems) or asynchronous (forums), including Web 2.0 technologies such as microblogging (http://twitter.com/), and online collaborative writing tools such as Wikis (http://www.wikispaces.com/, http://pbworks.com/, etc.).

Whichever electronic brainstorming system is used, they share a number of common characteristics:

- they are computer-based techniques for use by multiple participants;
- during the session, each participant generates ideas on a computer;
- participants present their ideas without having to wait for their turn;
- ideas are displayed electronically on a screen without identifying the source.

An electronic brainstorming session using one of these systems generally involves groups of various sizes whose members simultaneously (and sometimes anonymously) generate ideas about a specific issue on individual computers. The computers are generally located in the same electronic meeting room where group members communicate by exchanging typed messages instead of speaking (e.g., Dennis, Wixom, & Vandenberg, 2001; Nunamaker, Applegate, & Konsyski, 1987; Nunamaker, Dennis, Valacich, Vogel, & George, 1991; Valacich, George, Nunamaker, & Vogel, 1994). The individual computers are connected to a central computer which collects the generated ideas and displays them on a screen. Once an idea is entered, it becomes available for others to view in a shared space at the front of the room or on a designated section of the monitor at each workstation. With this technique, the ideas of group members can be displayed and re-read several times. It is widely acknowledged that ideas collected from electronic brainstorming are richer and easier to analyze than those produced in face-to-face brainstorming sessions (Shaw, 2003). The outcome is a ranked list of ideas which can then be subjected to a thematic content analysis (Shovlin, 2008) and/or reorganized in a conceptual map (Burke *et al.*, 2005).

After this brief overview of electronic brainstorming and some of the supporting systems, the next section describes the main social and psychological processes known to improve or impair group performance on an idea-generation task.

Electronic Brainstorming: Main Advantages and Disadvantages

Numerous studies have shown that electronic brainstorming improves group performance, particularly group productivity, i.e., the number of non-redundant ideas generated by group participants (e.g., Gallupe, Bastianutti, & Cooper, 1991; Nunamaker *et al.*, 1987; Pinsonneault, Barki, Gallupe, & Hoppen, 1999).

Reviews of the literature on electronic brainstorming suggest that this technique has a number of advantages over traditional brainstorming (e.g., Connolly *et al.*, 1990; Fjermestad & Hiltz, 1998; Kay, 1995). The main advantages are: removal of time and space constraints, parallel entry of ideas (participants express their ideas simultaneously), anonymity (participants are not worried about criticism), size (the number of participants is theoretically unlimited), memory (all sessions can be recorded for subsequent analysis), and focus on task (participants are more focused on the task than on the social aspects of interaction).

However, research suggests that one of the biggest advantages of electronic brainstorming is that it reduces or eliminates the detrimental blocking effects of verbal brainstorming (e.g., Diehl & Stroebe, 1987; Gallupe, Cooper, Grise, & Bastianutti, 1994; Valacich *et al.*, 1994); because nobody in the group has to wait for their turn to speak, it effectively eliminates production blocking, particularly in large groups (e.g., Gallupe *et al.*, 1991; Paulus, Leggett Dugosh, Dzindolet, Coskun, & Putman, 2002).

It has been found that large groups whose members share ideas through computers outperform both equivalent nominal groups whose members do not share their ideas, and groups whose members share their ideas verbally (e.g., Dennis & Valacich, 1993; Dennis & Williams, 2003; DeRosa *et al.*, 2007; Valacich *et al.*, 1994).

More specifically, large electronic brainstorming groups (> 8 people) outperform nominal groups, whereas small nominal groups (< 8 people) and very small verbal groups (< 4 people) outperform electronic brainstorming groups. These findings suggest a "process gain" whereby large electronic brainstorming groups are more productive than verbal brainstorming groups. These findings are crucial because, as pointed out by Kerr, Aronoff, and Messe (2000), there is very little evidence in the literature for this "process gain". Large electronic brainstorming groups have also been found to be more satisfied with the interaction process, and evaluation apprehension is reduced or eliminated when participants can produce their ideas anonymously (e.g., Connolly, Jessup, & Valacich, 1990; Cooper, Gallupe, Pollard, & Cadsby, 1998; Valacich, Dennis, & Nunamaker, 1992).

More recently, researchers have carried out experiments with new forms of electronic brainstorming for larger groups. For example, Vreede, Briggs, van Duin, and Enserink (2000) separated very large groups into sub-groups which had to generate ideas in serial mode. Once a sub-group had finished generating ideas, the next began, and so forth until all the sub-groups had performed the task. However, although this technique appeared to be more efficient than one in which sub-groups worked in parallel, the sub-group task involved synchronous electronic brainstorming in a traditional room-based context. Therefore, this technique still has time and space constraints, and there may also be more group members than there are computers in the electronic meeting room. To overcome these problems, asynchronous web-based systems have recently been developed, providing the opportunity for a large number of participants to work together without time constraints. Unfortunately, to date very few experiments have been conducted to test the efficacy of these asynchronous systems (e.g., Michinov & Primois, 2005; Vreede, Briggs, & Reiter-Palmon, 2010).

Despite the benefits of electronic brainstorming, there are also some disadvantages. First, one significant difference with traditional brainstorming is communication speed (e.g., Dennis & Williams, 2003). Ideas are expressed faster through oral communication than when written using a keyboard. Consequently, some participants may find it difficult to express themselves in writing. Secondly, participants who are unfamiliar with the layout of the keyboard will be slower than those with good keyboard skills, and they can be frustrated by their lack of typing skills. However, with the development of digital technologies and the extensive use of computers, these two disadvantages are becoming less of an issue. Other disadvantages include the fact that electronic brainstorming does not work well with small groups, i.e., less than four participants (e.g., DeRosa *et al.*, 2007), and that participants who give good ideas anonymously do not receive credit for them, producing a "social loafing" effect, i.e., individuals put less effort into group than individual tasks unless their individual contributions can be identified (e.g., Diehl & Stroebe, 1987).

Based on this selective review of the literature which suggests the efficacy of electronic brainstorming in e-collaboration, it can be assumed that the technique could be advantageously used by researchers working in teams either face-to-face or at a distance. With this in mind, an extension has been envisaged to facilitate the research process (e.g., Anson, Fellers, Bostrom, & Chidambaram, 1992), but unfortunately it has not been followed up by researchers, and formalized brainstorming for collecting ideas in research teams is still rarely used. The next section proposes recommendations for initiating and using (electronic) brainstorming techniques for collecting ideas from members of scientific research teams.

FROM VERBAL TO ELECTRONIC BRAINSTORMING AS A METHOD FOR GATHERING IDEAS IN SCIENTIFIC RESEARCH TEAMS

A number of studies have demonstrated that brainstorming has been used, formally or informally, to disseminate best practices in organizations (e.g., Bourhis, Dubé, & Jacob, 2005) and to adopt user innovations (e.g., Di Gangi & Wasko, 2009). Currently, a growing number of organisations use easily accessible electronic brainstorming systems where employees and other stakeholders can tap into a wealth of ideas and knowledge produced by others. Consequently, electronic brainstorming can be considered today as a non-intrusive technique allowing participants to produce their ideas in (online) groups. Unfortunately, many researchers appear to be unfamiliar with this technique (see Shovlin, 2008), even though electronic brainstorming has been recognized as a useful technique for reaching end-user groups in industrial settings by generating innovative ideas before the design phase (e.g., Dornburg, Stevens, Hendrickson, & Davidson, 2009).

To illustrate the benefits of electronic brainstorming, a recent study was carried out in a healthcare setting with the aim of designing the best possible facilities for the care of in-patients (Sengonzi *et al.*, 2009). The project involved collecting a large number of ideas from both hospital users and staff to develop a functional and effective care environment. In cases such as this, electronic brainstorming clearly provides a useful way of collecting interesting ideas in the early phase of the design process, which can have a beneficial impact on user satisfaction and project success.

To optimize its use for scientific research, electronic brainstorming sessions should be organized around a series of steps from the production of ideas to drawing up a conceptual map inter-linking the most important ideas. For maximum efficiency, the session should be rigorously structured and monitored by a project leader or facilitator. In a recent case study, Marín *et al.* (2008) tried to extend the brainstorming technique to scientific research teams. As far as we know, this is the first systematic attempt to use a formalized brainstorming technique to improve team-based scientific research. The study involved 15 people, including researchers (university professors and graduate students) and non-experts (undergraduate students and government officials), working on the management of ecological systems. Using a face-to-face brainstorming technique, the participants were invited to express their opinions. The authors tested what they called a "brainstorming strategy", organized in sequential steps from questioning to elaboration of a conceptual model, and demonstrated that all the participants generated fruitful ideas during the session. This "brainstorming strategy" could of course be transformed to an "electronic brainstorming strategy", although the authors did not envisage this possibility. This change from brainstorming to electronic brainstorming would be particularly relevant for interdisciplinary collaborative projects in which a wide range and number of participants are involved in solving complex scientific problems.

Figure 1 illustrates an adaptation of Marín *et al.*'s (2008) "brainstorming strategy" which starts by sending one or several question(s) about the topic. In the second step, a facilitator is selected to record ideas generated during the brainstorming session. In the third phase, the facilitator sets out the four brainstorming rules and records all the ideas, which are written down and pinned to the wall of the meeting room. The second and third steps are clearly not relevant for an electronic brainstorming session in which ideas are automatically recorded, and where the facilitator's role is to organize them into categories. In the fourth step, participants select ideas to construct a conceptual map during the final phase. In a room-based context, the facilitator uses a laptop computer equipped with a video projector to organize the ideas with the help of a conceptual mapping program or similar tool that displays

Figure 1. Stages in the production of a conceptual map in a brainstorming session (model adapted from the case study of Marín, Delgado, & Bachmann, 2008)

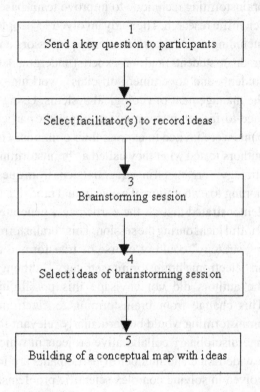

complementary electronic brainstorming systems. At the beginning of the session, twenty students sat round a horseshoe-shaped table facing a projection screen. One student was designated as facilitator and equipped with a laptop connected to a video-projector and the Internet. A web-based word processor allowed the participants to produce ideas in real-time for 20 minutes using the free web-based system EtherPad or MeetingWords (Figure 2).

Altogether, the group generated a list of 125 ideas. At the end of the session, the facilitator told the participants to eliminate redundant ideas and those judged uninteresting by the majority. They were then instructed to review the list of previously generated ideas and keep about 10 percent which were to be grouped using a minimum of categories. Finally, they were instructed to organize the categories and ideas in order to identify useful ways of promoting eco-citizenship behavior. To this end, a free web-based concept-mapping system (Cmap) was used to help participants establish links between ideas and propose a final map asynchronously over a 2-week period (see Figure 3 for the simplified concept map). This map represents the way students perceived sustainable development and eco-citizenship behaviors, the main concepts related to this topic, and ideas for promoting some of these behaviors.

Based on this simple illustration, it is reasonable to assume that electronic brainstorming can be advantageously used in the early stages of a scientific problem-solving task by facilitating the collection of verbal material and ideas in teams. Gathering a wide range of ideas may be one way of managing a project better, and electronic brainstorming might be useful for designing questionnaires, interviews and observation grids, and also help researchers collaborating remotely to formulate new research hypotheses. Although not an end in itself, electronic brainstorming provides not only a clearer view of the topic under study, but also useful material for further qualitative and/or quantitative analyses.

complex ideas. In their study, Marín *et al*. (2008) used the commercial modelling software Stella® which develops conceptual models using a simple set of icons for state variables, fluxes, parameters, and information flow.

The process of collecting ideas in groups using an electronic brainstorming technique can be illustrated by an example in an academic context where students had to use electronic brainstorming and concept-mapping systems for group projects. The topic concerned ways of promoting sustainable development and eco-citizenship behavior. Applying the scenario described above, verbal material was collected from Master's degree psychology students, who were informed that they would have to generate as many ideas as possible to identify eco-citizenship behaviors using two

Figure 2. Screen capture of the electronic brainstorming session with Etherpad

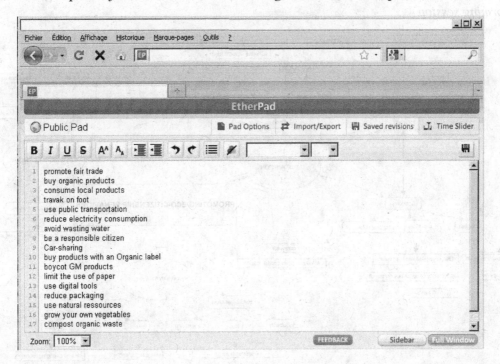

CONCLUSION

Although science is often considered as a social enterprise, it tends to be a "virtual collaborative enterprise" between scientists working in geographically dispersed teams, using digital environments, and calling on a wide variety of stakeholders (see Michinov & Michinov, 2009). Similarly, researchers today can use new tools for collecting data and, more particularly, for gathering verbal material such as ideas, concepts, hypotheses, proposals, solutions, and so on.

Based on the review of the literature about brainstorming and the recent development of this technique, it is very surprising that researchers have not used online research methods based on electronic brainstorming in teams to gather ideas for advancing scientific discoveries. Likewise, it is surprising that this technique has not been used more as an (online) research method *per se*. Although this technique could be useful for generating large quantities of data, its role as a research

tool has not been examined by psychologists, even in recent books in the field (e.g., Nestor & Schutt, 2011). It is clear that electronic brainstorming continues to be an under-used technique among researchers for collecting and organizing useful data for drawing up hypotheses, developing a theoretical background, treating a given scientific question, solving complex scientific problems, etc. Nevertheless, we have shown that this technique could be useful for members of scientific research teams. The role of a scientific project leader is to set out a time-frame for the project, which could include electronic brainstorming to collect a large quantity of ideas at a preliminary stage. The process of collecting ideas could be based on this technique, whereby participants have to draw up a list of factors, proposals, and solutions likely to contribute to the project. Like other research techniques, electronic brainstorming must be led and managed effectively by a facilitator to keep the participants focused on the task. After the collection phase, ideas can be categorized and linked

Figure 3. A simplified concept map produced from the verbal material gathered during the electronic brainstorming session

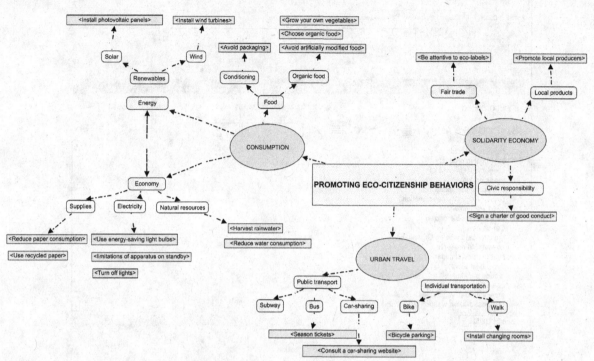

to each other with concept mapping in order to further a scientific research project.

The outlook for electronic brainstorming as an online research method is very promising, and this chapter may be considered as an incentive to develop its use in research, highlighting its advantages for gathering verbal materials such as creative ideas in a scientific project. Currently, electronic brainstorming is not commonly used, but it is reasonable to assume that it has considerable potential for future development. Finally, it is important to recognize that all techniques for collecting data for online research have limitations and scientists must be prepared to acknowledge them. This is equally true for electronic brainstorming, whose development is a challenge for future online research teams.

REFERENCES

Anson, R. G., Fellers, J. W., Bostrom, R. P., & Chidambaram, L. (1992). Using group support systems to facilitate the research process. In *Proceedings of the 25th Hawaii International Conference on System Sciences* (Vol. 4, pp. 70-79).

Baruah, J., & Paulus, P. B. (2008). Effects of training on idea-generation in groups. *Small Group Research, 39*, 523–541. doi:10.1177/1046496408320049

Birnbaum, M. H. (2004a). Methodological and ethical issues in conducting social psychology research via the Internet. In Sansone, C., Morf, C. C., & Panter, A. T. (Eds.), *Handbook of Methods in Social Psychology* (pp. 359–382). Thousand Oaks, CA: Sage.

Birnbaum, M. H. (2004b). Human research and data collection via the Internet. *Annual Review of Psychology, 55*, 803–832. doi:10.1146/annurev.psych.55.090902.141601

Bourhis, A., Dubé, L., & Jacob, R. (2005). The success of virtual communities of practice: The leadership factor. *Electronic Journal of Knowledge Management, 3*, 23–34.

Brown, V., Tumeo, M., Larey, T. S., & Paulus, P. B. (1998). Modeling cognitive interactions during group brainstorming. *Small Group Research, 29*, 495–526. doi:10.1177/1046496498294005

Burke, J. G., O'Campo, P., Peak, G. L., Gielen, A. C., McDonnell, K. A., & Trochim, W. M. K. (2005). An introduction to concept mapping as a participatory public health research method. *Qualitative Health Research, 15*(10), 1392–1410. doi:10.1177/1049732305278876

Camacho, L. M., & Paulus, P. B. (1995). The role of social anxiousness in group brainstorming. *Journal of Personality and Social Psychology, 68*, 1071–1080. doi:10.1037/0022-3514.68.6.1071

Connolly, T., Jessup, L. M., & Valacich, J. S. (1990). Effects of anonymity and evaluative tone on idea generation in computer-mediated groups. *Management Science, 36*(6), 689–703. doi:10.1287/mnsc.36.6.689

Connolly, T., Routhieux, R. L., & Schneider, S. K. (1993). On the effectiveness of group brainstorming: Test of one underlying cognitive mechanism. *Small Group Research, 24*, 490–503. doi:10.1177/1046496493244004

Cooper, W. H., Gallupe, R. B., Pollard, S., & Cadsby, J. (1998). Some liberating effects of anonymous electronic brainstorming. *Small Group Research, 29*, 147–178. doi:10.1177/1046496498292001

De Vreede, G.-J., Briggs, R. O., & Reiter-Palmon, R. (2010). Exploring asynchronous brainstorming in large groups: A field comparison of serial and parallel subgroups. *Human Factors, 52*(2), 189–202. doi:10.1177/0018720809354748

De Vreede, G.-J., Briggs, R. O., van Duin, R., & Enserink, B. (2000). Athletics in electronic brainstorming: Asynchronous electronic brainstorming in very large groups. In *Proceedings of the 33rd Hawaii International Conference on System Sciences.*

Dennis, A. R., Aronson, J. E., Heninger, W. G., & Walker, E. (1999). Structuring time and task in electronic brainstorming. *Management Information Systems Quarterly, 23*, 95–108. doi:10.2307/249411

Dennis, A. R., & Valacich, J. S. (1993). Computer brainstorms: More heads are better than one. *The Journal of Applied Psychology, 78*, 531–537. doi:10.1037/0021-9010.78.4.531

Dennis, A. R., & Williams, M. L. (2003). Electronic brainstorming. Theory, research, and future directions. In Paulus, P. B., & Nijstad, B. A. (Eds.), *Group creativity. Innovation through collaboration* (pp. 160–178). Oxford, UK: Oxford University Press.

Dennis, A. R., & Williams, M. L. (2005). A Meta-Analysis of group side effects in electronic brainstorming: More heads are better than one. *International Journal of e-Collaboration, 1*, 24–42. doi:10.4018/jec.2005010102

Dennis, A. R., Wixom, B. H., & Vandenberg, R. J. (2001). Understanding fit and appropriation effects in Group Support Systems via meta-analysis. *Management Information Systems Quarterly, 25*, 167–194. doi:10.2307/3250928

DeRosa, D. M., Smith, C. L., & Hantula, D. A. (2007). The medium matters: Mining the long-promised merit of group interaction in creative idea generation tasks in a meta-analysis of the electronic brainstorming literature. *Computers in Human Behavior, 23,* 1549–1581. doi:10.1016/j. chb.2005.07.003

Di Gangi, P. M., & Wasko, M. (2009). Steal my idea! User innovation community influence on organizational adoption of user innovations: A case study of Dell IdeaStorm. *Decision Support Systems, 48,* 303–313. doi:10.1016/j.dss.2009.04.004

Diehl, M., & Stroebe, W. (1987). Productivity loss in brainstroming groups: Toward the solution of a riddle. *Journal of Personality and Social Psychology, 53,* 497–509. doi:10.1037/0022-3514.53.3.497

Diehl, M., & Stroebe, W. (1991). Productivity loss in brainstorming groups: tracking down the blocking effect. *Journal of Personality and Social Psychology, 61,* 392–403. doi:10.1037/0022-3514.61.3.392

Dornburg, C. C., Stevens, S. M., Hendrickson, S. M. L., & Davidson, G. S. (2009). Improving extreme-scale problem solving: Assessing electronic brainstorming effectiveness in an industrial setting. *Human Factors, 51*(4), 519–527. doi:10.1177/0018720809343587

Dunbar, K. (1995). How scientists really reason: Scientific reasoning in real-world laboratories. In Sternberg, R. J., & Davidson, J. E. (Eds.), *The nature of insight* (pp. 365–395). Cambridge, MA: MIT Press.

Dunbar, K. (1997). How scientists think: Online creativity and conceptual change in science. In Ward, T. B., Smith, S. M., & Vaid, J. (Eds.), *Creative thought: An investigation of conceptual structures and processes* (pp. 461–493). Washington, DC: American Psychological Association. doi:10.1037/10227-017

Dunnette, M. D., Campbell, J., & Jaastad, K. (1963). The effect of group participation on brainstorming effectiveness for two industrial samples. *The Journal of Applied Psychology, 47,* 30–37. doi:10.1037/h0049218

Finholt, T. A., & Olson, G. M. (1997). From laboratories to collaboratories: A new organizational form for scientific collaboration. *Psychological Science, 8*(1), 28–36. doi:10.1111/j.1467-9280.1997. tb00540.x

Fjermestad, J., & Hiltz, S. R. (1998). An assessment of group support systems experiment research: Methodology and results. *Journal of Management Information Systems, 15,* 7–149.

Funtowicz, S. O., & Ravetz, J. R. (1991). A new scientific methodology for global environmental issues. In Costanza, R. (Ed.), *Ecological Economics: The science and management of sustainability* (pp. 137–152). New York, NY: Columbia University Press.

Gallupe, R. B., Bastianutti, L. M., & Cooper, W. H. (1991). Unblocking brainstorms. *The Journal of Applied Psychology, 76*(1), 137–142. doi:10.1037/0021-9010.76.1.137

Gallupe, R. B., & Cooper, W. H. (1993). Brainstorming electronically. *Sloan Management Review, 35,* 27–36.

Gallupe, R. B., Cooper, W. H., Grise, M. L., & Bastianutti, L. M. (1994). Blocking electronic brainstorms. *The Journal of Applied Psychology, 79,* 77–86. doi:10.1037/0021-9010.79.1.77

Hawkins, B. (1999). *How to generate great ideas.* London, UK: Kogan Page.

Huber, G. P. (1980). Organizational science contributions to the design of decision support systems. In Fick, G., & Sprague, R. H. Jr., (Eds.), *Decision support systems: Issues and challenges.* New York, NY: Pergamon Press.

Jung, J. H., Schneider, C., & Valacich, J. S. (2010). Enhancing the motivational affordance of information systems: The effects of real-time performance feedback and goal setting in group collaboration environments. *Management Science, 56*(4), 724–742. doi:10.1287/mnsc.1090.1129

Kay, G. (1995). Effective meetings through electronic brainstorming. *Journal of Management Development, 14*(6), 4–25. doi:10.1108/02621719510086147

Kerr, N. L., Aronoff, J., & Messe, L. A. (2000). Methods of small group research. In Reis, H., & Judd, C. (Eds.), *Research methods in social psychology: A handbook.* New York, NY: Cambridge University Press.

Kramer, T. J., Fleming, G. P., & Mannis, S. M. (2001). Improving face-to-face brainstorming through modeling and facilitation. *Small Group Research, 32*, 533–557. doi:10.1177/104649640103200502

Kraut, R. E., Olson, J., Banaji, M., Bruckman, A., Cohen, J., & Couper, M. (2004). Psychological Research Online: Opportunities and Challenges. *The American Psychologist, 59*(2), 105–117. doi:10.1037/0003-066X.59.2.105

Lamm, H., & Trommsdorff, G. (1973). Group versus individual performance on tasks requiring ideational proficiency (brainstorming). *European Journal of Social Psychology, 3*, 361–387. doi:10.1002/ejsp.2420030402

Larey, T. S., & Paulus, P. B. (1995). Social comparison and goal setting in brainstorming groups. *Journal of Applied Social Psychology, 25*(18), 1579–1596. doi:10.1111/j.1559-1816.1995.tb02634.x

Leggett Dugosh, K., Paulus, P. B., Roland, E. J., & Yang, H. C. (2001). Cognitive stimulation in brainstorming. *Journal of Personality and Social Psychology, 79*, 722–735. doi:10.1037/0022-3514.79.5.722

Levine, J. M., & Moreland, R. L. (2004). Collaboration: The social context of theory development. *Personality and Social Psychology Review, 8*(2), 164–172. doi:10.1207/s15327957pspr0802_10

Ludwig, D. (2001). The era of management is over. *Ecosystems (New York, N.Y.), 4*, 758–764. doi:10.1007/s10021-001-0044-x

Marín, V. H., Delgado, L. E., & Bachmann, P. (2008). Conceptual PHES-system models of the Aysén watershed and fjord (Southern Chile): Testing a brainstorming strategy. *Journal of Environmental Management, 88*, 1109–1118. doi:10.1016/j.jenvman.2007.05.012

Michalko, M. (2001). *Cracking creativity: The secrets of creative genius.* Berkeley, CA: Tenspeed Press Edition.

Michinov, N., & Michinov, E. (2009). Advantages and pitfalls of social interactions in the digital age: Practical recommendations for improving virtual group functioning. In Heatherton, A. T., & Walcott, V. A. (Eds.), *Handbook of social Interactions in the 21st Century* (pp. 83–96). Hauppauge, NY: Nova Science Publishers.

Michinov, N., & Primois, C. (2005). Improving group productivity and creativity in on-line groups through social comparison process: New evidence for asynchronous electronic brainstorming. *Computers in Human Behavior, 21*(1), 11–28. doi:10.1016/j.chb.2004.02.004

Mullen, B., Johnson, C., & Salas, E. (1991). Productivity loss in brainstorming groups: a meta-analytic integration. *Basic and Applied Social Psychology, 12*, 3–23. doi:10.1207/s15324834basp1201_1

Nagasundaram, M., & Dennis, A. R. (1993). When a group is not a group: The cognitive foundation of group idea generation. *Small Group Research, 24*, 463–489. doi:10.1177/1046496493244003

Nestor, P. G., & Schutt, R. K. (2011). *Research Methods in Psychology: Investigating Human Behavior*. Thousand Oaks, CA: Sage.

Nijstad, B. A., & Stroebe, W. (2006). How the group affects the mind: A cognitive model of idea generation in groups. *Personality and Social Psychology Review*, *10*, 186–213. doi:10.1207/s15327957pspr1003_1

Nunamaker, J., Briggs, B., & Mittleman, D. (1994). Electronic meeting systems: Ten years of lessons learned. In Coleman, D., & Khanna, R. (Eds.), *Groupware: Technologies Applications* (pp. 149–193). Upper Saddle River, NJ: Prentice Hall.

Nunamaker, J. F., Dennis, A. R., Valacich, J. S., Vogel, D. R., & Georges, J. F. (1991). Electronic meeting systems to support group work. *Communications of the ACM*, *34*(7), 41–61.

Nunamaker, T. I., Applegate, L. M., & Konsyski, B. R. (1987). Facilitating group creativity: experience with a group decision support system. *Journal of Management Information Systems*, *3*, 5–19.

Offner, A. K., Kramer, T. J., & Winter, J. P. (1996). The effects of facilitation, recording and pauses upon group brainstorming. *Small Group Research*, *27*, 283–298. doi:10.1177/1046496496272005

Osborn, A. F. (1953). *Applied imagination*. Oxford, UK: Charles Scribner's.

Osborn, A. F. (1957). *Applied imagination* (2nd ed.). New York, NY: Charles Scribner's.

Parnes, S. J., & Meadow, A. (1959). Effect of "brainstorming" instructions on creative problem-solving by trained and untrained subjects. *Journal of Educational Psychology*, *50*, 171–176. doi:10.1037/h0047223

Paulus, P. B. (2000). Groups, teams, and creativity: The creative potential of idea-generating groups. *Applied Psychology: An International Review*, *49*(2), 237–262. doi:10.1111/1464-0597.00013

Paulus, P. B., & Brown, V. (2003). Ideational creativity in groups: Lessons from research on brainstorming. In Paulus, P. B., & Nijstad, B. (Eds.), *Group creativity: Innovation through collaboration* (pp. 110–136). New York, NY: Oxford University Press.

Paulus, P. B., & Dzindolet, M. T. (1993). Social influence processes in group brainstorming. *Journal of Personality and Social Psychology*, *64*, 575–586. doi:10.1037/0022-3514.64.4.575

Paulus, P. B., Leggett Dugosh, K. L., Dzindolet, M. T., Coskun, H., & Putman, V. L. (2002). Social and cognitive influences in group brainstorming: Predicting production gains and losses. *European Social Psychology Review*, *12*, 299–325. doi:10.1080/14792772143000094

Paulus, P. B., Nakui, T., Putman, V. L., & Brown, V. R. (2006). Effects of task instructions and brief breaks on brainstorming. *Group Dynamics*, *10*, 206–219. doi:10.1037/1089-2699.10.3.206

Pinsonneault, A., Barki, H., Gallupe, R. B., & Hoppen, N. (1999). Electronic brainstorming: the illusion of productivity. *Information Systems Research*, *10*, 110–133. doi:10.1287/isre.10.2.110

Rangaswamy, A., & Lilien, G. L. (1997). Software tools for new product development. *JMR, Journal of Marketing Research*, *34*, 177–184. doi:10.2307/3152074

Roy, M. C., Gauvin, S., & Limayen, M. (1996). Electronic group brainstorming: The role of feedback on productivity. *Small Group Research*, *27*, 215–247. doi:10.1177/1046496496272002

Sengonzi, R., Demian, P., & Emmitt, S. (2009, April 1). Opportunities for e-brainstorming in pre-design processes of healthcare projects. In M. Kagioglou, J. Barlow, A. D. F Price, & C. Gray (Eds.), *Proceedings of the PhD Workshop of HaCIRIC's International Conference 2009: Improving Healthcare Infrastructures through Innovation* (pp. 32–41). Brighton, UK: HaCIRIC.

Shaw, D. (2003). Evaluating electronic workshops through analysing the 'brainstormed' ideas. *The Journal of the Operational Research Society*, *54*(7), 692–705. doi:10.1057/palgrave.jors.2601568

Shepherd, M. M., Briggs, R. O., Reinig, B. A., Yen, J., & Nunamaker, J. F. (1996). Invoking social comparison to improve electronic brainstorming: Beyond anonymity. *Journal of Management Information Systems*, *12*, 155–170.

Shovlin, C. (2008). *Harnessing social brainstorming for business decisions*. Paper presented at the Business Intelligence Group Conference.

Skitka, L. J., & Sargis, E. G. (2006). The Internet as psychological laboratory. *Annual Review of Psychology*, *57*, 529–555. doi:10.1146/annurev.psych.57.102904.190048

Sosik, J. J., Avolio, B. J., & Kahai, S. S. (1997). The impact of leadership style and anonymity on group potency and effectiveness in a GDSS environment. *The Journal of Applied Psychology*, *82*, 89–103. doi:10.1037/0021-9010.82.1.89

Stroebe, W., & Diehl, M. (1994). Why groups are less effective than their members: On productivity losses in idea-generating groups. *European Review of Social Psychology*, *5*, 271–303. doi:10.1080/14792779543000084

Stroebe, W., Nijstad, B. A., & Rietzschel, E. F. (2010). Beyond productivity loss in brainstorming groups: The evolution of a question. *Advances in Experimental Social Psychology*, *43*, 157–203. doi:10.1016/S0065-2601(10)43004-X

Taylor, D. W., Berry, P. C., & Block, C. H. (1958). Does group participation when using brainstorming facilitate or inhibit creative thinking? *Administrative Science Quarterly*, *6*, 22–47.

Valacich, J. S., Dennis, A. R., & Nunamaker, J. F. Jr. (1992). Group size and anonymity effects on computer-mediated idea generation. *Small Group Research*, *23*(1), 49–73. doi:10.1177/1046496492231004

Walsh, J. P., & Maloney, N. G. (2002). Computer network use, collaboration structures, and productivity. In Kiesler, S. (Ed.), *Distributed Work* (pp. 433–451). Cambridge, MA: MIT Press.

Woerndl, W., & Eicker, D. (2006). Creativity techniques meet the web. *International Journal of Web Based Communities*, *2*(1), 100–111. doi:10.1504/IJWBC.2006.008618

Wuchty, S., Jones, B. F., & Uzzi, B. (2007). The increasing dominance of teams in the production of knowledge. *Science*, *316*, 1036–1038. doi:10.1126/science.1136099

Ziegler, R., Diehl, M., & Zijlstra, G. (2000). Idea production in nominal and virtual groups: Does computer-mediated communication improve group brainstorming? *Group Processes & Intergroup Relations*, *3*(2), 141–158. doi:10.1177/1368430200032003

KEY TERMS AND DEFINITIONS

E-Collaboration: A form of collaboration among people or organizations made possible by means of electronic technologies such as the Internet.

Electronic Brainstorming: A technique to stimulate creativity through idea generation using the computer. This technique can also be used to share ideas or knowledge between participants throughout the world.

Facilitator: A person whose task is to ensure that members of a group can accomplish their goals during electronic meetings. During an electronic brainstorming session, the facilitator ensures a productive group process, stimulating idea generation.

Group Support Systems: A set of collaborative technologies designed to support group work on a common task and provide a shared interface for participating groups.

Production Blocking: A common problem in brainstorming groups where one individual tends to block or inhibit other participants during a group discussion.

Chapter 11
The Delphi Technique:
Use, Considerations, and Applications in the Conventional, Policy, and On-Line Environments

Chia-Chien Hsu
Kainan University, Republic of China

Brian A. Sandford
Pittsburg State University, USA

ABSTRACT

The Delphi research and investigation technique utilizes experts in any given field to generate information in greater abundance and specificity than what is currently known or available. The conventional and more widely used Delphi process strives for consensus so that target issues can be more fully investigated based on the feedback of the people who are most knowledgeable and involved. Policy Delphi differs in that it does not seek consensus but rather is meant to generate the strongest possible opposing viewpoints on an issue so that policy makers can consider divergent and opposing perspectives. Multiple iterations or rounds of data collection are the most unique aspect of both processes which allows the quality and relevance of the information concerning the target issue to become more precise and well defined. "Real-time or e-Dephi" uses the modern era of computers, electronic devices, and web-based communication to achieve the critical and unique group communication process utilized in a Delphi investigation.

INTRODUCTION

Delphi...operates on the principle that several heads are better than one in making subjective conjectures about the future, and that experts ... will make conjectures based upon rational judg-

ment and shared information rather than merely guessing and will separate hope from likelihood in the process (Weaver, 1971, p. 269).

Originated in the early 1950s and primarily developed by Dalkey and Helmer at the Rand Corporation (Ludwig, 1997), the Delphi technique

DOI: 10.4018/978-1-4666-0074-4.ch011

is a group communication process that solicits experts' opinions in order to specifically examine a particular issue or topic. The original source for the name of Delphi comes from the oracle at Delphi where the spirit of the Greek god Phoebus Apollo was asked for advice on critical issues associated with politics and questions of the unknown and social dilemmas. As the name indicated, the Delphi is initially designed as a method of predicting future events. The earliest application of the technique was for military purposes. Its first notable use was during the "Cold War" period involving a project funded by the U.S. Air Force. A group of experts was gathered to explore the possible bombing strategies from the viewpoints of Soviet strategic planners (Rowe & Wright, 1999; Novakowski & Wellar, 2008). The Delphi process was employed to generate and refine the list of strategies, probabilities, and consequences as perceived by the Soviet planners.

The Delphi technique gradually became popular in the early 1960s and was applied in various fields. For example, policy determination (Wilenius & Tirkkonen, 1997; Hahn & Rayens, 1999; Syed, Hjarone, & Aro, 2009), curriculum development (Reeves & Jauch, 1978; Stritter, Tresolini, & Reeb, 1994), resource utilization (Anderson & Schneider, 1993; Tsaur, Lin, & Lin, 2006), needs assessment (Brooks, 1979; Olshfski & Joseph, 1991; McGeary, 2009), business management (Mitchell, 1991; Grisham, 2009), nursing (Duffield, 1993; Gibson, 1998; Keeney, Hasson, & McKenna, 2001), environmental management (Green, Hunter, & Moore, 1989, 1990; Stubbles, 1992), and education in general (Wicklein, 1993; Tigelaar, Dolmans, Wolfhagen, & van Der Vleuten, 2004; Stitt-Gohdes & Crews, 2004; O'Neill, Scott, & Conboy 2009) were explored using the Delphi process to collect data concerning issues related to their respective disciplines. The popularity of the Delphi technique began to fade in the mid 1970s (Yousuf, 2007) but at present it is not uncommon that the Delphi technique is used as

a part or as the exclusive method of investigation in an evaluation or a research project.

The philosophical base of the Delphi technique is built on the Lockean idea that stresses the importance of human experience and agreement (Mitroff & Turoff, 1975; Powell, 2003). Therefore, the rationale of Delphi relies upon two presumptions. Foremost and simply stated, more minds are superior to one. More specifically, collective inputs should be better than individual judgments alone (Weaver, 1971; Dalkey, 1972). Second, ideas or comments produced by experts are based on their logical reasoning. The results generated by such reasoning are better than simple conjectures (Weaver, 1971). In essence, the Delphi technique involves a panel of experts in thorough examinations of a specific area of concern. The purposes of using Delphi can be benchmarking, policy investigation, and prediction of future events. In common survey practices, investigators attempt to identify "what is," but the Delphi is an effort to assess "what should/could be" (Miller, 2006; Hsu & Sandford, 2007a).

The purposes of this chapter are to describe the characteristics of the Delphi, to illustrate the Delphi process, to address strengths and limitations of the technique, to discuss different forms of the technique, to discuss its application in an online research environment, and to compare the electronic application with its paper-based counterparts. Following the discussion of the electronic application of the Delphi and policy Delphi, some examples are provided to help illustrate the research applications.

DISTINCT FEATURES OF THE DELPHI

The Delphi technique is characterized as a means of building consensus through the use of a series of questionnaires (Dalkey & Helmer, 1963; Dalkey, 1969; Linstone & Turoff, 1975; Lindeman, 1981; Young & Jamieson, 2001). As such, deploying multiple iterations or rounds of inquiry is the most distinctive feature of the Delphi technique. The iterations or rounds of inquiry denote a series of feedback processes. Such feedback enables researchers to gather more information about the area of concern during the data collection period as well as allowing participants the opportunities to see the input of other panel of expert members and to subsequently re-assess their responses (Ludwig, 1994; Hsu & Sandford, 2007a).

Other features of the Delphi technique are the ability to ensure subject anonymity, a controlled feedback process, and the suitability of using various statistical analysis techniques to interpret the collected data (Dalkey, 1972; Ludlow, 1975). These features help to counteract the drawbacks that can often affect face-to-face interactions imbedded within group data collection processes.

The advantage of subject anonymity can effectively reduce the influences of dominant individuals (Dalkey, 1972). This is because those selected subjects can be located in different geographic areas and may not know who else is invited to participate in the study. Controlled feedback helps to minimizing the effect of noise (Dalkey, 1972). Noise is a communication phenomenon in a group process in which the target issue(s) addressed by subjects is influenced by individual or group interests rather than centering on problem-solving. The information generated from this type of communication would be distorted and inevitably consist of bias which is unrelated to the purposes of the study. Basically, the controlled feedback process allows investigators to provide a structured summary of the previous round of data collection for the purpose of having subjects re-assess their and other experts' prior responses to produce more, and hopefully clearer, insights associated with the topics being examined. The capability of utilizing statistical analysis techniques is another Delphi characteristic addressed by Dalkey (1972) and is an application that attempts to reduce the group pressure for conformity. The tools of statistical analysis enable investigators to provide updated data and justified information to the participants. As a result, each subject would have no pressure, either perceived or real, to conform to others' responses as the data can be reported in aggregate or as a summary and can speak for itself rather than being considered anecdotal or opinion based.

THE DELPHI STUDY PROCESS

The process of conducting a Delphi study is unique. The iterative features of the Delphi technique raise a critical question; how many rounds are sufficient for a defensible Delphi study? In fact, no strict rule has yet been established in this regard. In the literature, researchers note that three rounds are usually enough to obtain the necessary data. The fourth or fifth round results may merely produce slight differences compared to the results of the third round (Cyphert & Gant, 1971; Brooks, 1979; Ludwig, 1997; Custer, Scarcella, & Stewart, 1999). In addition, when conducting a Delphi study, investigators need to be aware that instrument development, data collection, and questionnaire administration are interconnected between iterations or rounds (Figure 1). As such, following the sequential steps of the Delphi process is imperative and can help investigators plan and conduct a study using this technique. However, the total iterations or rounds needed in a Delphi investigation is predominantly, although not exclusively, determined by the purpose of the research, the logistics of time considerations, available resources, data collection and data analysis methods, and the complexity of the issue being studied.

Round One: Two different formats can be used in the first round of a Delphi study. First and conventionally, the Delphi subjects would receive an open-ended questionnaire and be asked to provide as many and as detailed as possible opinions or ideas for each open-ended question. After receiving responses from the participants, investigators must subsequently transform the qualitative data into a structured instrument which be-

Figure 1. The Delphi Process

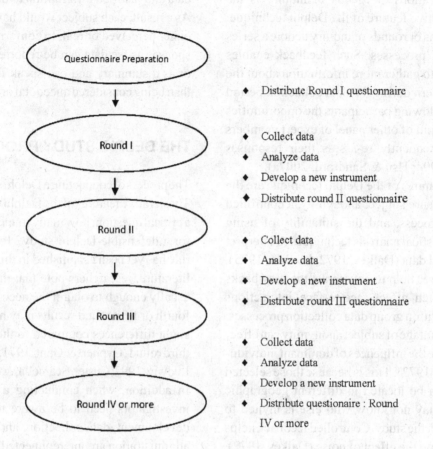

- Distribute Round I questionnaire

- Collect data
- Analyze data
- Develop a new instrument
- Distribute round II questionnaire

- Collect data
- Analyze data
- Develop a new instrument
- Distribute round III questionnaire

- Collect data
- Analyze data
- Develop a new instrument
- Distribute questionaire : Round IV or more

comes the questionnaire for the second round. An alternative method that can also be used to develop the first round questionnaire is for investigators to directly administer an already structured questionnaire. The sources of the questionnaire or the questionnaire development can be based upon individual interviews by the researchers and/ or an extensive review of the literature addressing the area of concern.

Round Two: In Round II, each subject is asked to review the information of the previous round in the newly developed questionnaire. The information consists of a statistical summary of the previous round of data as well as comments provided by participants which help to clarify the meaning or intended direction of the previous data or that assist in generating additional useful

reflection and in-depth participation of all the respondents. Additionally, it is the investigators' responsibility to facilitate subject responses by providing each participant with their previous response set. It is an unreasonable expectation that participants remember their previous responses and it also provides more thorough reflection and analysis of the individual's input in relation to the information and perspectives provided by other Delphi participants. Subjects are asked to rate/rank order the statements/items in the second round instrument and are encouraged to offer their justifications and inquiries related to any of the items.

Round Three: In Round III, subjects receive a third questionnaire. Again, they are asked to review their previous ratings, provide their justifications and/or inquiries, and rate/rank order those statements/items. This round gives subjects an opportunity to re-assess their judgments and to further clarify their points of view as well as contemplate the input of the other participants.

Round Four or Five: Under the discretion of investigators, a fourth or fifth round can be employed. The feedback process is repeated in the same manner as the previous iterations. Regardless of the number of rounds conducted by investigators, it should be noted that the essence of the Delphi is not only to fully disclose what each subject thinks and believes regarding the area of concern, but also to provide the opportunity of sharing their experiences and expertise to hopefully build a unified theme or defining concept of the topic for the researcher. In other words, the most important facts, perceptions, strongest opinions, informed experiences, and/or the widest held beliefs or relevant knowledge about a topic can and should surface through the successive review and ranking of the expert Delphi panel members. It is the investigator's decision concerning how many iterations are needed to produce the desired result(s) or those that meet the research objectives. The number of rounds could be based on the relative clarity or obscurity of the issue(s), the abundance or lack of information currently known by the respondents, as well as any other limitations or considerations imposed by the nature of the research.

Subjects

The core of the Delphi technique is to first seek, then solicit, and then sort through the possible ideas and/or insights from the selected participants. Therefore, how to appropriately choose the most qualified people to participate in a Delphi study becomes a significant issue. The quality of those who are selected subjects directly associates with the quality of the results produced (Judd, 1972; Taylor & Judd, 1989; Jacobs, 1996; Hsu & Sandford, 2007a).

The qualifications of Delphi subjects or panel members are widely discussed in the literature. Simply selecting those who are knowledgeable about the topic being investigated as well as being willing to respond to the data collection instrument is not enough to qualify as a participant nor is it recommended (Helmer & Rescher, 1959; Pill, 1971; Klee, 1972; Hsu & Sandford, 2007a). The subjects of a Delphi study not only should be highly trained, but also possess expertise and experience relevant to the area of concern. Delbecq, Van de Ven, and Gustafson (1975) suggest that qualified Delphi subjects should be top decision makers, professional staff members, and those people whose opinions are solicited. Hsu and Sandford (2007b) also recommend three approaches to establishing subjects' qualifications similar to Delbecq, Van de Ven, and Gustafson's suggestions. These approaches are to identify the positional leaders in the areas of investigation, to discover authors from a review of professional publications, and to verify those who have direct relationships with the target issue. In sum, investigators need to work diligently to find the most suitable persons to participate in a Delphi study. After gathering a pool of possible subjects, investigators can initiate a nomination procedure to determine the best or most appropriate people to join the study and subsequently distribute invitations to participate (Jones & Twiss, 1978).

There is no definite answer with regard to the optimal number of subjects engaged in a Delphi study. Although having a group of subjects of over 50 is not uncommon, Ludwig (1997) notes that the majority of subjects employed in Delphi are between 15 and 20. Delbecq, Van de Ven, and Gustafson (1975) recommend that 10 to 15 subjects should be enough to cover the issues addressed if the background of the members is homogeneous. However, more subjects become essential if a variety of groups or individuals that may have diverse views in the area of concern are considered imperative and thereby are invited to participate in a Delphi study. It should be noted that subjects may not be capable of dependably providing a representative pooling of judgments or opinions if the number of participants is too small. In contrast, the drawbacks of low response rate and excessive time requirements can take effect if there are too many subjects in a study. It is the investigators' responsibility to strike a balance in terms of an optimal number of Delphi subjects based on the needs and purpose of the study and the logistics encountered by the researcher.

Data Analysis

It is imperative at the onset of the Delphi process that decision rules based on the definition of consensus, the nature and type of research, the goals of the researcher, and any other justifiable criteria are established. Consensus in the area of concern can be determined when the ratings from subjects achieve an *a priori* or previously prescribed range. A common instance of consensus is that 80 percent of subjects cast their votes within two categories on a seven-point scale (Ulschak, 1983). However, depending on the scale(s) and measuring techniques used, the definition of consensus can vary. For example, some researchers note that a certain percentage of subject responses falling within a prescribed range are not an effective way of obtaining information. They propose using the indication of stability in subjects' response sets in successive rounds and further state that the stability measure is a preferable alternative to using the percent agreement method (Scheibe, Skutsch, & Schofer, 1975; & Dajani, Sincoff, & Talley, 1979). In other words, when participant feedback does not vary from one round to the next, consensus is assumed to be established and confirmed by the subjects.

In Delphi, both qualitative and quantitative data can be collected. Investigators must analyze qualitative data if the conventional Delphi, which uses open-ended questions to gather subjects' opinions in the initial iteration, is used. Investigators also need to provide the written comments

and opinions provided by other participants. The Delphi process encourages the participants to evaluate and respond to the comments of the other members in the study. It is strongly recommended that a panel of researchers and experts knowledgeable in instrument development as well as in the issues being discussed be used to analyze the written comments (Hsu & Sandford, 2010). Thematic alignment and summarizing the ideas and opinions of the respondents can be challenging and should be approached with the intent to provide valid and accurate data for each iteration.

Concerning the analysis and use of quantitative data, investigators need to provide summary descriptive statistics of member responses which are then distributed to all respondents. Statistical analysis in terms of quantitative data consists of the measures of central tendency (i.e., means, median, and mode) and level of dispersion (i.e., inter-quartile range and standard deviation). Investigators are obligated to provide information concerning subjects' collective responses (Hasson, Keeney, & McKenna, 2000). It is not uncommon in a Delphi study to see the use of nonparametric statistics to analyze data if the assumption of a normal distribution of the data is violated (Kalaian & Shah, 2006). The particular statistics employed in Delphi studies can vary depending on the level and method determined for achieving consensus defined by the investigators.

FORMS OF THE DELPHI TECHNIQUE

The Delphi technique can be broadly group into three categories; normative Delphi, forecasting Delphi, and policy Delphi (Novakowski & Wellar, 2008). The normative Delphi focuses on the explorations of "what should/could be" (Novakowski & Wellar, 2008). The research objectives of the normative Delphi concentrate on obtaining consensus about specific topics. It is usually used to generate evaluation frameworks, benchmark criteria, and/or indicators essential to a particular area of concern.

The forecasting Delphi centers on the predictions of future events (Novakowski & Wellar, 2008). This type of Delphi strives to obtain consensus by asking participants to use their knowledge and experiences for the purpose of delineating and identifying possible future scenarios associated with a particular area of interest. The study previously mentioned sponsored by the U. S. Air Force is a typical example.

The policy Delphi is a method frequently employed in the fields of system analysis, operations research, policy exploration, or urban planning. The options generated by this Delphi method would consist of a range of alternatives which may include both pro and con arguments, perspectives, and proposals. In other words, the policy Delphi seeks to generate the strongest possible opposing viewpoints on an issue to ensure that full disclosure and consideration by advocates of opposing perspectives is achieved. It is necessary to note that producing consensus is not the major goal of the policy Delphi (Turoff, 1975; Slocum, 2005). However, in the literature, some have used the term of policy Delphi as a method of gathering consensus for specific policy issues (Hahn & Rayens, 1999; Rayens & Hahn, 2000).

Specifics of the Policy Delphi

The policy Delphi originated in 1969 and its use was first reported in 1970 (Turoff, 1970). Turoff (1975) indicates that the policy Delphi is appropriate for the following objectives either by themselves or used in combination. First, the policy Delphi is an attempt to explore all of the possible alternatives to a topic and investigators attempt to ensure that those alternatives are exposed for the consideration of everyone involved or associated with the issue. Second, the technique enables involved persons to assess and address the impact(s) to both sides of a particular issue. Finally, this technique also allows investigators

to assess the acceptability of a particular issue to those who are affected, interested, or involved. The results of the policy Delphi serve as a benchmark or set boundaries for interested individuals or groups to give further consideration. Contrary to the conventional Delphi technique which attempts to achieve consensus, the policy Delphi aims at generating diverse options and resolutions for decision makers to consider related to policy and the possible outcomes and consequences generated by a particular policy or policies (Turoff, 1970, 1975; Turoff & Hiltz, 1995). Murry (1992) indicates that the aim of a policy Delphi study is to generate a "rich, meaty, stimulating body of opinion" (p. 18).

The process of conducting a policy Delphi study is basically identical to the conventional Delphi practice. However, since the policy Delphi attempts to explore various options at their "extremes", the process can be somewhat more demanding and complex. As such, a guideline involving six interactive phases among the investigators and subjects is delineated by Turoff (1975). The six phases are: (1) formulate the issues; (2) reveal various options; (3) decide initial positions on the issues; (4) explore and acquire the reasons for disagreements; (5) assess the underlying perspective and points of view; and (6) re-assess the options received (Turoff, 1975; Baker, Moon, & Bakowski, 2007).

Differences exist in both the conventional Delphi (i.e., normative Delphi, forecasting Delphi) and the policy Delphi practices. First, the purpose of conducting a policy Delphi and the conventional Delphi study is different (de Loe, 1995). As previously stated, the major objective of using the policy Delphi is to explore various options with both pro and con arguments whereas the conventional Delphi aims at generating a consensus with the target issues.

Second, the subjects involved in a policy Delphi may not necessarily be the experts linked to the areas of concern. "A policy issue is one for which there are no experts, only informed advocates and referees" (Turoff, 1975, p. 84). That is, experts of a particular field focusing on a particular policy may shift to the role of advocates who need to persuade or educate those having different views. Individuals who are invited to participate in a policy Delphi study can be the ones who are stakeholders or various interested groups related to the policy being examined but not necessarily those who are considered "experts." Turoff (1975) suggests that investigators may want to include a couple of liberal thinkers as subjects in order to possibly extend the coverage of the topic at hand. Diversity of thought, polarized positions, and oppositional viewpoints are sought rather than unification and consensus.

Third, the design of the questionnaire in the policy Delphi would be different from the conventional Delphi practice. Investigators need to pay special attention to the survey questions given to the subjects. Specifically, those questions or statements in the policy Delphi must aim at exploring all possible options and rationale related to that policy (Slocum, 2005). To facilitate subject responses, investigators should also provide the necessary and summarized factual materials to respondents to ensure that they have updated information and can subsequently assess the policy alternatives using the combination of facts, updated information, individual knowledge, and learned experience (Schneider, 1972; Turoff, 1975).

Examples: Application in Urban Planning

Both conventional Delphi and policy Delphi practices are employed by researchers in the field of urban planning. Masser and Foley (1987) used the conventional Delphi technique as an urban analysis tool to solicit the opinions of experts (leading public and private employers) and laymen (postgraduate students in Town and Regional Planning at Sheffield University) concerning the future development of Sheffield, Britain. The primary objective of the study was to predict the future of

the local economy. The results generated by the two groups were subsequently compared and led to better informed and defensible conclusions. Morgan, Pelissero, and England (1979) employed the conventional Delphi technique to identify the relative importance of development issues associated with the City of Norman, Oklahoma. The subjects of the study consist of community leaders and elected city officials. The primary objective of the study was to prioritize the development plans for the city. Decision makers were able to use the results of the study as an aid to decision making.

The policy Delphi is not a new concept and several examples of its use in urban planning exist in the literature. J. B. Schneider (1972) pioneered a study using the policy Delphi in the field of urban planning. The study involved three groups of people; individuals from the Seattle business district, the Bellevue business district, and faculty of the University of Washington. The major objectives of the study were to explore possible transportation alternatives concerning the development of the Seattle Central Business District and to identify the underlying information and assumptions that led to differing judgments concerning development in the area. Joel Goodman of the University of Delaware conducted a study on the issue of Costal Zone Land Use Planning by engaging a variety of individuals representing government agencies, businesses, public groups, and specialists. The topics of the study covered participant characteristics, attitudes, policy issues, strategic issues, and pro and con arguments (Turoff, 1975). Cravens, Woodruff, and Harper (1976) employ the policy Delphi to explore information concerning community transportation services and to assess the degree of agreement among respondents.

In summary, the applications of the conventional and policy Delphi in urban planning rest upon the research goals set by investigators. All in all, the conventional Delphi is thought of as a decision making tool, while the policy Delphi can be considered as a decision-facilitation tool (de Loe, 1995; Ali, 2005). Both Delphi methods used correctly and rigorously can be helpful in broadening knowledge in the profession of urban planning.

STRENGTHS AND SHORTCOMINGS OF THE DELPHI TECHNIQUE

When conducting a research or an evaluation project, a responsible researcher not only needs to understand the strengths of the approach and subsequently to fully exploit those strengths, but also to control the shortcomings of the approach as well. The Delphi technique is a unique approach and, like any research method, has its strengths and limitations. The following discussion will help the investigator to better choose and apply the Delphi process to align with the goals and objectives of a study.

Strengths of the Delphi

Several components of the Delphi technique are appropriate for use in research and evaluation efforts. First, the Delphi process is well suited for those issues and problems that are not previously documented or researched, are incapable of being analyzed thoroughly, do not possess updated benchmarking criteria, or do not have clear-cut indicators related to the target issue. In these situations the use of the Delphi technique enables investigators to obtain subjective judgments from selected experts on a collective basis (Yousuf, 2007). Second, the Delphi encourages innovative thinking, particularly for a study where the major purpose is to forecast a series of future events (Miller, 2006). Third, because of the series of feedback process or iterations, subjects have more time to reflect on their prior responses and thereby to modify or provide justifications for their judgments (Miller, 2006; Hsu & Sandford, 2010). Fourth, because small sample size is common in Delphi studies and there is no need for subjects

to have face-to-face interactions, conducting a Delphi study can be relatively inexpensive (Masser & Foley, 1987; Anderson & Schneider, 1993; van Teijlingen, Pitchforth, Bishop, & Russell, 2006). Lastly, subject anonymity enables investigators to eliminate the drawbacks (e.g., noise, influence of dominant individuals, the bandwagon effect) frequently encountered when a group process is utilized (Linstone & Turoff, 1975; Rainhorn, Brudon-Jakobowicz, & Reich, 1994). Therefore, each subject is free from conforming to the responses of other participants. Unlike other group communication processes (e.g., focus group interview, nominal group technique) which need to gather people together for face-to-face discussions, the Delphi technique can obtain thoughtful insights from experts without the group meeting in the same place or at the same time. Additionally, the issue of subject anonymity is also facilitated by geographic dispersion of the subjects as well as the use of electronic communication such as e-mail and the internet to collect information.

Shortcomings of the Delphi

There are, of course, some limitations with every research method and the Delphi technique is no exception. First, conducting a Delphi study can be time consuming (Cunliffe, 2002; Sandrey & Bulger, 2008). Although a minimum of 45 days for the administration of a Delphi study is recommended by many researchers (Delbecq, Van de Ven, & Gustafson, 1975; Ulschak, 1983; Ludwig, 1994), investigators need to be aware that the data collection process may take longer than expected or predicted. This is because data collection, data analysis and questionnaire development/administration are interconnected and sequential (Figure 1). The interconnected and sequential process can affect the capability of analyzing data, developing the next round questionnaire which relies on the responses of the previous iteration, and distributing the newly developed instrument in a timely manner (Ludwig, 1994;

Hsu & Sandford, 2007a). For example, after distributing the first round questionnaire investigators wait for responses from participants as well as answering any possible questions posed by subjects. Only 80 percent of the subjects have returned their questionnaires after the deadline for returning responses has passed. The investigators decide to pursue the non-respondents (20% of the participant population) and successfully motivate all of the non-respondents to return their questionnaires ten days after the original deadline has passed. At this point, the investigators need to analyze the Round I data, develop the second round questionnaire, and distribute the Round II questionnaire to subjects as soon as possible. However, the first to second round data collection process has been delayed for 10 days. The same or even greater delays may continue at each iteration until the end of the final round; as is the case in this illustration a compounded time elapse can be the result. Therefore, how to ensure the timely return of questionnaires is a concern for Delphi investigators and the issue of time management must be a primary consideration when using the Delphi technique.

Second, the Delphi technique is characterized by multiple iterations, but it is this very characteristic that can generate the possibility of a low response rate. "In the Delphi technique, [poor response rate] is magnified fourfold because a maximum of four surveys may be sent to the same panelists" (Witkin & Altschuld, 1995, p. 196). In fact, when conducting Delphi studies, investigators need not only to reach a high response rate in the initial round but also to ensure a favorable response rate in the subsequent iterations (Hsu & Sandford, 2007b). A risk of some or many subjects being unable, unsure, or unwilling to respond during the allotted time frame in each round is always a possibility. As such, how to motivate subjects to respond and how investigators play an active role in helping sustain a desirable response rate in each round is extremely important. Since the number of participants in Delphi is relatively

small, losing subjects in each round can lead to the results of a study being unreliable or invalid due to an insufficient and non-representative pooling of subjects and information.

Third, the process of summarizing and editing responses provided by subjects in a Delphi process enables investigators to, knowingly or unknowingly, impose their own perspectives on the data. This can have an influence on subsequent evaluations and responses by participants in the later iterations. Many researchers (Dalkey & Helmer, 1963; Cyphert & Gant, 1971; Scheibe, Skutsch, & Schofer, 1975; Witkin & Altschuld, 1995; Hsu & Sandford, 2007a) have documented such biased practices and encourage fellow Delphi investigators to exercise caution in this particular area.

Lastly, an assumption directly linked to Delphi subjects is that they are equally knowledgeable and experienced in the target issues. However, such assumptions are difficult to justify (Altschuld & Thomas, 1991). The reality could be that subject knowledge, expertise, and experience are unevenly distributed (Marchant, 1988; Altschuld & Thomas, 1991). Those statements and/or items identified as most important by subjects who have in-depth knowledge cannot be interpreted by those who do not possess the same depth of knowledge or experience. The findings in this kind of Delphi study could be the result of identifying a series of *general* or *middle-of-the-road* statements rather than an in-depth illumination of the target issues simply because the subjects can only offer mediocre knowledge concerning the target issue (Altschuld & Thomas, 1991; Yousuf, 2007; Hsu & Sandford, 2007a).

One additional limitation in the Delphi technique should also be mentioned. When conducting a conventional Delphi study, investigators must distribute a questionnaire with open-ended questions to subjects in the first round. Sometimes, those open-ended questions are not well constructed and, therefore, become ambiguous in nature and broad in scope. Submitting this kind of questionnaire to subjects can not only lead to skewed answers and/or responses unrelated to the objectives at of the study but also produce biased outcomes from then on (Marchant, 1988; Hsu & Sandford, 2007b). Consequently, how to accurately and precisely state open-ended questions is critical to conducting a successful Delphi study. Some researchers (Kerlinger, 1973; McCampbell & Stewart, 1992) suggest that the employment of the modified Delphi (using an already structured questionnaire) may be a better option if basic information concerning the topic area is already available and assumed valid and reliable. McCampbell and Stewart (1992) address the advantages of using the modified Delphi which helps assure that important statements/ideas are included in the questionnaire, time is saved between Round I and II implementations, and participant responses are facilitated. There is of course no definite answer regarding the superiority of using a traditional over a modified Delphi. In fact, when basic information is unavailable or limited, the use of the conventional Delphi becomes a necessity for researchers.

Strengths and Shortcomings of the Policy Delphi

The strengths of the policy Delphi are similar to that of the conventional Delphi. The three strengths of the policy Delphi specifically addressed by de Loe (1995) are: (1) cost efficiency; (2) generating effective and/or a substantial number of ideas; and (3) implementation flexibility. Also, Turoff's (1975) guidelines for the policy Delphi can be effectively and easily implemented in various ways by investigators making it a usable and useful investigative technique.

According to de Loe (1995), one shortcoming of the policy Delphi is likely to be the factor of time since the policy Delphi, like the conventional Delphi, is also characterized by multiple iterations. Second, the information generated can be difficult for some subjects to assimilate. This is because subjects may be overwhelmed by the amount and

depth of the information and may need to take a large block of time to process and respond accordingly. Certain participants may be unable to make sense of the comments of other participants or the statistics developed by the investigators because of differences in background, experience, and knowledge. Third, the results of a policy Delphi can be broad in scope but lacking in depth. This drawback is the direct consequence of the second shortcoming, lack of formal experience, education, or intimate knowledge in the content area. Considering that the primary objective of the policy Delphi is to generate diverse and sometimes opposing alternatives and that participants may lack expertise in the area of concern, certain responses which are criticized as "shallow" or "lacking in insight" can be a foreseeable consequence (de Loe, 1995). Additionally, the development of the first round questionnaire can be a real challenge for investigators to begin the policy Delphi process for the same reasons previously discussed for the conventional Delphi process concerning questionnaire design (Franklin & Hart, 2007). A considerable amount of time should be given to the development and pre-testing of the instrument for validity, reliability, and suitability prior to distributing the questionnaire to subjects (Jillson, 1975).

COMPUTER BASED APPLICATION OF THE DELPHI PROCESS

The use of the computer based Delphi process has been utilized since the 1970s (Price, 1975). At that time, the use was exclusively developed and employed on mainframe computers and narrowly designed networks (Colton & Hatcher, 2004). The present prevalence and use of electronic technologies greatly facilitates the implementation of the Delphi process using computer-based applications. Researchers, evaluation practitioners, businessmen, and decision makers in the public or private sector can and should take advantage of these electronic devices and applications.

The electronic application of the Delphi process, in comparison to paper-pencil implementation, has several advantages. First and foremost, when employing electronic methods in the Delphi process, subjects are able to have asynchronous interactions (Turoff & Hiltz, 1995; Colton & Hatcher, 2004). This means that each subject with internet access can participate in the group communication process at anytime and anywhere prior to the deadline set by investigators for the current iteration. Subjects are free to provide their contributions in the areas which they feel they are most qualified. That is, subjects can repeatedly access the online discussion forum, exchange their opinions more frequently, and receive more updated information while submitting their insights, skepticisms, and/or justifications to other participants without having to wait to receive edited summaries from investigators (Turoff & Hiltz, 1995; Katsioloudis, 2009). The technology induced Delphi process is less linear and/or structural and creates a more vibrant environment for subjects to discuss the target issues (Colton & Hatcher, 2004).

The electronic application in Delphi can also reduce the time required for questionnaire and feedback deliveries (Witkin & Altschuld, 1995; Kelbaugh, 2006; Skulmoski, Hartman, & Krahn, 2007; Hsu & Sandford, 2007a; Katsioloudis, 2009). Delphi investigators can speed up the feedback process and may shorten the entire data collection timeframe. Additionally, data collected via the electronic application can easily be converted into the needed forms of record keeping, data processing, and statistical analysis for both qualitative and quantitative responses (Kelbaugh, 2006; Katsioloudis, 2009). The readability of those converted forms, particularly the qualitative responses, can help investigators to not only easily read through those responses (e.g., some may have poor hand writing), but also to screen, manage, and distribute information more quickly and effectively.

E-Mail Version vs. Web Version

Since many researchers currently use e-mail as the primary tool of making contact with a study participant, ensuring that subjects' e-mail addresses are correct becomes a pre-requisite for conducting any study more effectively. While having subjects' agreements to participate in a Delphi study is advised, investigators should also obtain their permission to send study-related materials via e-mail and inform the recipients of the iterative nature of the study. In other words, participants should be advised about the amount of material and frequency of contact which they can expect as a member of the study.

Electronic application in Delphi is also named "e-Delphi" or "web-based Delphi" (Chou, 2002; Colton & Hatcher, 2004; Lindqvist & Nordanger, 2007) and is generally categorized into either the e-mail version or the Web version. The use of e-mails to collect information is an earlier method in which a questionnaire is typically embedded in or attached to an e-mail message. Subjects are asked to complete and return the questionnaire as an attachment or a modification of the initial message (Katsioloudis, 2009). The use of e-mails with attachments in the Delphi process is amenable to those investigators who want to replace the mail-in practice. The entire process is still sequential and linear. Questionnaire delivery becomes the biggest difference in implementation and its advantages can be notable when considering the cost and time efficiencies.

Currently, an increasing number of researchers directly embed a link in an e-mail to guide subjects to a webpage where they can provide insights, share information, and respond to a series of instruments (Nesbary, 1999; Katsioloudis, 2009). The degree of flexibility in web-based inquiry software can be a major concern. For example, subjects may write down a large amount of comments and supporting information to justify their point(s) of view. Therefore, the intentional design of how the web format and software accommodates word and space limitations (i.e., word limits, webpage layout) for all responses and, how the site directs individuals to navigate the webpage as effortlessly as possible is a primary consideration for researchers who conduct web-based Delphi studies.

Real-Time Delphi

Real-time Delphi (RT Delphi) developed by Articulate Software, Inc. is a new approach of performing a Delphi study without the involvement of a series of rounds or iterations. In 2004, the company received a Small Business Innovation Research grant from the U.S. Defense Advanced Research Projects Agency (DARPA) for the purpose of developing a Delphi-based approach to improve the speed and efficiency of collecting experts' opinions in situations where quick decisions are needed (Gordon & Pease, 2006; Gordon, 2007).

The RT Delphi is unique in that it is characterized by a "round-less" process of data collection. This approach enables participants to have not only asynchronous responses, but also synchronous interactions. That is, within a time frame set by the investigator(s), all invited participants have opportunities to submit their judgments or information at anytime and anywhere or they can join the study together at a designated time period to complete the entire data collection phase. Participants can view the group statistics and comments via direct or wireless computer connections. They are also asked to provide inputs if their responses fall out of a pre-determined range and are encouraged to revise or switch their responses. The appropriate computer software is required to facilitate the RT Delphi process, submissions, calculations, and to obtain results or conclusive information (Gordon & Pease, 2006).

Practical Notes on Computer-Based Delphi

Subject anonymity is one of the major characteristics in the Delphi study. However, when the feedback process becomes less structural and less linear, maintaining subject anonymous may possibly limit the possibility of subjects interacting with one another. Specifically, being able to reflect and review the information of other participants without fully knowing the source of the information can be a major premise in the Delphi process and may be a barrier to full disclosure in the computer-based Delphi. Turoff and Hiltz (1995) reveal that the feature of subject anonymity in Delphi can sometimes be carried too far. That is, a subject can contribute a set of insights and keeping that subject anonymous may hinder other subjects in obtaining greater understanding of the differing perspective or opinion. Therefore, the use of pen names or the assignment of specific codes which represent subject identities is recommended in order to ensure, as much as possible, subject anonymity while still encouraging and facilitating interaction when needed and beneficial to obtaining the best information possible. The faux identification can still provide for specific and intentional interaction between study members while maintaining each person's true identity or internet location.

The use of the computer and internet based Delphi may require investigators to make certain adjustments and take on different roles. In the traditional paper-pencil application, any responses provided by subjects are returned to the investigator(s). The investigator(s), sometimes referred to as moderators or facilitators, are responsible for screening, editing, and summarizing the feedback. Subsequently, investigators would then distribute the newly developed instrument to the subjects. Responses would be necessarily filtered and analyzed by the investigator(s) to use in the next iteration. However, because inputs offered by subjects in a computer or internet based Delphi are directly posted for other participants to review and everyone can access the designated website at their convenience, the issue of when to stop a particular round may become unclear. The iteration may possibly end in voting by the participants. This places some of the control of the study outcomes in the hands of the participants but may also be the only effective way for closure to occur. This is justifiable to a major extent in that participants are recognized as experts and would have the experience, knowledge, and background to reflect with authority on what is deemed conclusive concerning the topic of interest. Additionally, when subject discussions reach a dead end or feedback provided by subjects strays away from the target issues, it becomes the investigators' responsibility to help them re-focus and to screen information which is not helpful to the study. As such, the investigator in an online Delphi is engaged concurrently in the data collection process to ensure focus and relevance while a traditional Delphi investigator has only ex post facto involvement.

CONCLUSION

"The Delphi technique provides those involved or interested in engaging in research, evaluation, fact-finding, issue exploration, or discovering what is actually known or not known about a specific topic a flexible and adaptable tool to gather and analyze the needed data" (Hsu & Sandford, 2007a, p. 5). When conducting a Delphi study, researchers need to put forth diligent efforts in selecting the most qualified individuals to participate in their studies (also applicable to the policy Delphi), maximizing desirable response rates, offsetting the shortcomings of the Delphi, and efficiently managing the time required for the process of data collection. As Hasson, Keeney, and McKenna (2000) noted, researchers should never underestimate the administrative skills required for conducting a Delphi.

Of course, data collection in the Delphi process can be greatly facilitated using electronic applications. Researchers should take full advantage of the communication, storage, and processing abilities of computer based methodologies and devices. Shortening the turnaround time, while still being able to provide for subject anonymity, may be the most valuable asset for the electronic applications of the Delphi. The real-time Delphi is a new "round-less" innovation. Invited participants do not receive questionnaires in either printed or electronic form, but rather respond in a designated web-based environment within a pre-determined time frame. In the future, it is believed that more and more Delphi studies will be conducted using such applications.

REFERENCES

Ali, A. K. (2005). Using the Delphi technique to search for empirical measures of local planning agency power. *Qualitative Report, 10*(4), 718–744.

Altschuld, J. W., & Thomas, P. M. (1991). Considerations in the application of a modified scree test for Delphi survey data. *Evaluation Review, 15*(2), 179–188. doi:10.1177/0193841X9101500201

Anderson, D. H., & Schneider, I. E. (1993). Using the Delphi process to identify significant recreation research-based innovations. *Journal of Park and Recreation Administration, 11*(1), 25–36.

Baker, P. M. A., Moon, N. W., & Bakowski, A. (2007). *Access to wireless technologies for people with disabilities: Issues, opportunities, and policy options – Findings of a Policy Delphi (USDOE Grant: H133E060061 & H133E010804)*. Atlanta, GA: Georgia Institute of Technology, Rehabilitation Engineering Research Center for Wireless Technologies and Center for Advanced Communication Policy.

Brooks, K. W. (1979). Delphi technique: Expanding application. *North Central Association Quarterly, 54*(3), 377–385.

Chou, C. (2002). Developing the e-Delphi system: A web-based forecasting tool for educational research. *British Journal of Educational Technology, 33*(2), 233–236. doi:10.1111/1467-8535.00257

Colton, S., & Hatcher, T. (2004). *The web-based Delphi research technique as a method for content validation in HRD and adult education research.* Retrieved June 21, 2010, from http://www.mpc. edu/FacultyStaff/SharonColton/Documents/Establishing%20the%20Delphi%20Technique.pdf

Cravens, D. W., Woodruff, R. B., & Harper, J. F. (1976). *Urban public transportation goalsetting: A research approach.* Paper presented at the 54th Annual Meeting of the Transportation Research Board, Washington, DC.

Cunliffe, S. (2002). Forecasting risks in the tourism industry using the Delphi technique. *Tourism, 50*(1), 31–41.

Custer, R. L., Scarcella, J. A., & Stewart, B. R. (1999). The modified Delphi technique: A rotational modification. *Journal of Vocational and Technical Education, 15*(2), 1–10.

Cyphert, F. R., & Gant, W. L. (1971). The Delphi technique: A case study. *Phi Delta Kappan, 52*, 272–273.

Dajani, J. S., Sincoff, M. Z., & Talley, W. K. (1979). Stability and agreement criteria for the termination of Delphi studies. *Technological Forecasting and Social Change, 13*, 83–90. doi:10.1016/0040-1625(79)90007-6

Dalkey, N. C. (1969). An experimental study of group opinion. *Futures, 1*(5), 408–426. doi:10.1016/S0016-3287(69)80025-X

Dalkey, N. C. (1972). The Delphi method: An experimental study of group opinion. In N. C. Dalkey, D. L. Rourke, R. Lewis, & D. Snyder (Eds.). *Studies in the quality of life: Delphi and decision-making* (pp. 13-54). Lexington, MA: Lexington.

Dalkey, N. C., & Helmer, O. (1963). An experimental application of the Delphi method to the use of experts. *Management Science, 9*(3), 458–467. doi:10.1287/mnsc.9.3.458

de Loe, R. C. (1995). Exploring complex policy questions using the policy Delphi: A multiround, interactive survey method. *Applied Geography (Sevenoaks, England), 15*(1), 53–68. doi:10.1016/0143-6228(95)91062-3

Duffield, C. (1993). The Delphi technique: A comparison of results obtained using two expert panels. *International Journal of Nursing Studies, 30*(3), 227–237. doi:10.1016/0020-7489(93)90033-Q

Franklin, K. K., & Hart, J. K. (2007). Idea generation and exploration: Benefits and limitations of the policy Delphi research method. *Innovative Higher Education, 31*, 237–246. doi:10.1007/s10755-006-9022-8

Gibson, J. M. E. (1998). Using the Delphi technique to identify the content and context of nurses' continuing professional development needs. *Journal of Clinical Nursing, 7*(5), 451–459. doi:10.1046/j.1365-2702.1998.00175.x

Gordon, T. (2007). Energy forecasts using a "roundless" approach to running a Delphi study. *Foresight, 9*(2), 27–35. doi:10.1108/14636680710737731

Gordon, T., & Pease, A. (2006). RT Delphi: An efficient, "round-less" almost real time Delphi method. *Technological Forecasting and Social Change, 73*, 321–333. doi:10.1016/j.techfore.2005.09.005

Green, H., Hunter, C., & Moore, B. (1989). Assessing the environmental impact of tourism development: The use of the Delphi technique. *The International Journal of Environmental Studies*, *35*, 51–62. doi:10.1080/00207238908710549

Green, H., Hunter, C., & Moore, B. (1990). Application of the Delphi technique in tourism. *Annals of Tourism Research*, *17*(2), 270–279. doi:10.1016/0160-7383(90)90087-8

Grisham, T. (2009). The Delphi technique: A method for testing complex and multifaceted topics. *International Journal of Managing Projects in Business*, *2*(1), 112–130. doi:10.1108/17538370910930545

Hahn, E. J., & Rayens, M. K. (1999). Consensus for tobacco policy among former state legislator using the policy Delphi method. *Tobacco Control*, *8*, 137–140. doi:10.1136/tc.8.2.137

Hasson, F., Keeney, S., & McKenna, H. (2000). Research guidelines for the Delphi survey technique. *Journal of Advanced Nursing*, *32*(4), 1008–1015.

Helmer, O., & Rescher, N. (1959). On the epistemology of the inexact science. *Management Science*, *6*, 25–53. doi:10.1287/mnsc.6.1.25

Hsu, C. C., & Sandford, B. A. (2007a). The Delphi technique: Making sense of consensus. *Practical Assessment, Research, & Evaluation, 12*(10). Retrieved September 1, 2007, from http://pareonline.net/getvn.asp?v=12&n=10

Hsu, C. C., & Sandford, B. A. (2007b). Minimizing non-response in the Delphi process: How to respond to non-response. *Practical Assessment, Research, & Evaluation, 12*(17). Retrieved January 15, 2008, from http://pareonline.net/getvn.asp?v=12&n=17

Hsu, C. C., & Sandford, B. A. (2010). The Delphi Technique. In Salkind, N. J. (Ed.), *Encyclopedia of Research Design*. Thousand Oaks, CA: Sage.

Jacobs, J. M. (1996). *Essential assessment criteria for physical education teacher education programs: A Delphi study*. Unpublished doctoral dissertation, West Virginia University, Morgantown, WV.

Jillson, I. A. (1975). The national drug-abuse policy Delphi: Progress report and findings to date. In Linstone, H. A., & Turoff, M. (Eds.), *The Delphi method: Techniques and applications* (pp. 124–159). Reading, MA: Addison-Wesley.

Jones, H., & Twiss, B. C. (1978). *Forecasting technology for planning decision*. London, UK: Macmillan.

Judd, R. C. (1972). Use of Delphi methods in higher education. *Technological Forecasting and Social Change*, *4*, 173–186. doi:10.1016/0040-1625(72)90013-3

Kalaian, S. A., & Shah, H. A. (2006). *Overview of parametric and non-parametric statistical methods for analyzing*. Paper presented the 2006 Annual Meeting of the Mid-Western Educational Research Association, Columbus, OH.

Katsioloudis, P. (2009). Enhancing the collection process for the Delphi technique. In *Proceedings of the 2009 ASEE Southeast Section Conference*, Marietta, GA.

Keeney, S., Hasson, F., & McKenna, H. P. (2001). A critical review of the Delphi technique as a research methodology for nursing. *International Journal of Nursing Studies*, *38*, 195–200. doi:10.1016/S0020-7489(00)00044-4

Kelbaugh, B. M. (2006). *Using electronic systems to conduct a modified Delphi study*. Paper presented at the 2006 Annual Meeting of the Mid-Western Educational Research Association, Columbus, OH.

Kerlinger, F. N. (1973). *Foundations of behavioral research*. New York, NY: Holt, Rinehart, and Winston.

Klee, A. J. (1972). The utilization of expert opinion in decision-making. *AIChE Journal. American Institute of Chemical Engineers, 18*(6), 1107–1115. doi:10.1002/aic.690180604

Lindeman, C. A. (1981). *Priorities within the health care system: A Delphi study.* Kansas City, MO: American Nurses' Association.

Lindqvist, P., & Nordanger, U. K. (2007). (Mis-?) using the e-Delphi method: An attempt to articulate the practical knowledge of teaching. *Journal of Research Methods and Methodological Issues, 1*(1).

Linstone, H. A., & Turoff, M. (1975). General Applications: Introduction. In Linstone, H. A., & Turoff, M. (Eds.), *The Delphi method: Techniques and applications* (pp. 75–83). Reading, MA: Addison-Wesley.

Linstone, H. A., & Turoff, M. (1975). Introduction. In Linstone, H. A., & Turoff, M. (Eds.), *The Delphi method: Techniques and applications* (pp. 3–12). Reading, MA: Addison-Wesley.

Ludlow, J. (1975). Delphi inquires and knowledge utilization. In Linstone, H. A., & Turoff, M. (Eds.), *The Delphi method: Techniques and applications* (pp. 102–123). Reading, MA: Addison-Wesley.

Ludwig, B. G. (1994). *Internationalizing Extension: An exploration of the characteristics evident in a state university Extension system that achieves internationalization.* Unpublished doctoral dissertation, The Ohio State University, Columbus, OH.

Ludwig, B. G. (1997). Predicting the future: Have you considered using the Delphi methodology? *Journal of Extension, 35*(5). Retrieved November 6, 2005, from http://www.joe.org/joe/1997october/tt2.html

Marchant, E. W. (1988). Methodological problems associated with the use of the Delphi technique: Some comments. *Fire Technology, 24*(1), 59–62. doi:10.1007/BF01039641

Masser, I., & Foley, P. (1987). Delphi revisited: Expert opinion in urban analysis. *Urban Studies (Edinburgh, Scotland), 24*, 217–225. doi:10.1080/00420988720080351

McCampbell, W. H., & Stewart, B. R. (1992). Career ladder programs for vocational education: Desirable characteristics. *Journal of Vocational Education Research, 17*(1), 53–68.

McGeary, J. (2009). A critique of using the Delphi technique for assessing evaluation capability-building needs. *Evaluation Journal of Australasia, 9*(1), 31–39.

Miller, L. E. (2006). *Determining what could/should be: The Delphi technique and its application.* Paper presented at the 2006 Annual Meeting of the Mid-Western Educational Research Association, Columbus, OH.

Mitchell, V. W. (1991). The Delphi technique: An exposition and application. *Technology Analysis and Strategic Management, 3*(4), 333–358. doi:10.1080/09537329108524065

Mitroff, I., & Turoff, M. (1975). Philosophical and methodological foundations of Delphi. In Linstone, H. A., & Turoff, M. (Eds.), *The Delphi method: Techniques and applications* (pp. 17–35). Reading, MA: Addison-Wesley.

Morgan, D. R., Pelissero, J. P., & England, R. E. (1979). Urban planning: Using a Delphi as a decision-making aid. *Public Administration Review, 39*(4), 380–384. doi:10.2307/976215

Murry, J. P. (1992). Expectations of department chairpersons: A Delphi case study. *Journal of Staff, Program, & Organization Development, 10*, 13–21.

Needham, R. D., & de Loe, R. C. (1990). The policy Delphi: Purpose, structure, and application. *Canadian Geographer, 34*(2), 133–142. doi:10.1111/j.1541-0064.1990.tb01258.x

Nesbary, D. (1999). *Survey Research and the World Wide Web*. Boston, MA: Allen & Bacon.

Novakowski, N., & Wellar, B. (2008). Using the Delphi technique in normative planning research: Methodological design considerations. *Environment & Planning A, 40*, 1485–1500.

O'Neill, S., Scott, M., & Conboy, K. (2009). What's technology got to do with it? A Delphi study on collaborative learning in distance education. In *Proceedings of 17th European Conference on Information Systems*.

Olshfski, D., & Joseph, A. (1991). Assessing training needs of executives using the Delphi techniques. *Public Productivity & Management Review, 14*(3), 297–301. doi:10.2307/3380739

Pill, J. (1971). The Delphi method: Substance, context, a critique and an annotated bibliography. *Socio-Economic Planning Sciences, 5*, 57–71. doi:10.1016/0038-0121(71)90041-3

Powell, C. (2003). The Delphi technique: Myths and realities. *Journal of Advanced Nursing, 41*(4), 376–382. doi:10.1046/j.1365-2648.2003.02537.x

Price, C. R. (1975). Conferencing via computer: Cost effective communication for the era of forced choice. In Linstone, H. A., & Turoff, M. (Eds.), *The Delphi method: Techniques and applications* (pp. 497–516). Reading, MA: Addison-Wesley.

Rainhorn, J.-D., Brudon-Jakobowicz, P., & Reich, M. R. (1994). Priorities for pharmaceutical policies in developing countries: Results of a Delphi survey. *Bulletin of the World Health Organization, 72*(2), 257–264.

Rayens, M. K., & Hahn, E. J. (2000). Building consensus using the policy Delphi method. *Policy, Politics & Nursing Practice, 1*(4), 308–315. doi:10.1177/152715440000100409

Reeves, G., & Jauch, L. R. (1978). Curriculum development through Delphi. *Research in Higher Education, 8*(2), 157–168. doi:10.1007/BF00992116

Rowe, G., & Wright, G. (1999). The Delphi technique as a forecasting tool: Issues and analysis. *International Journal of Forecasting, 15*, 353–375. doi:10.1016/S0169-2070(99)00018-7

Sandrey, M. A., & Bulger, S. M. (2008). The Delphi method: An approach for facilitating evidence based practice in athletic training. *Athletic Training Education Journal, 3*(4), 135–142.

Scheibe, M., Skutsch, M., & Schofer, J. (1975). Experiments in Delphi methodology. In Linstone, H. A., & Turoff, M. (Eds.), *The Delphi method: Techniques and applications* (pp. 262–287). Reading, MA: Addison-Wesley.

Schneider, J. B. (1972). The policy Delphi: A regional planning application. *Technological Forecasting and Social Change, 3*, 481–497. doi:10.1016/S0040-1625(71)80035-5

Skulmoski, G. J., Hartman, F. T., & Krahn, J. (2007). The Delphi method for graduate research. *Journal of Information Technology Education, 6*, 1–21.

Slocum, N. (2005). *Participatory methods toolkit: A practitioner's manual*. Brussels, Belgium: King Baudouin Foundation and the Flemish Institute for Science and Technology Assessment.

Stitt-Gohdes, W. L., & Crews, T. B. (2004). The Delphi technique: A research strategy for career and technical education. *Journal of Career and Technical Education, 20*(2), 1–10.

Stritter, F. T., Tresolini, C. P., & Reeb, K. G. (1994). The Delphi technique in curriculum development. *Teaching and Learning in Medicine, 6*(2), 136–141. doi:10.1080/10401339409539662

Stubbles, R. (1992). Economic and environmental futures of the Black Hills: A Delphi study. *Great Plains Research, 2*(1), 97–108.

Syed, A. M., Hjarone, L., & Aro, A. R. (2009). The Delphi technique in developing international health policies: Experience from the SARS Control project. *The Internet Journal of Health, 8*(2).

Taylor, R. E., & Judd, L. L. (1989). Delphi method applied to tourism. In Witt, S., & Moutinho, L. (Eds.), *Tourism marketing and management handbook*. Upper Saddle River, NJ: Prentice Hall.

Tigelaar, D. E. H., Dolmans, D. H. J. M., Wolfhagen, I. H. A. P., & van Der Vleuten, C. P. M. (2004). The development and validation of a framework for teaching competencies in higher education. *Higher Education, 48*, 253–268. doi:10.1023/B:HIGH.0000034318.74275.e4

Tsaur, S. H., Lin, Y. C., & Lin, J. H. (2006). Evaluating ecotourism sustainability from the integrated perspective of resource, community, and tourism. *Tourism Management, 27*, 640–653. doi:10.1016/j.tourman.2005.02.006

Turoff, M. (1970). The design of a policy Delphi. *Technological Forecasting and Social Change, 2*, 149–171. doi:10.1016/0040-1625(70)90161-7

Turoff, M. (1975). The policy Delphi. In Linstone, H. A., & Turoff, M. (Eds.), *The Delphi method: Techniques and applications* (pp. 84–101). Reading, MA: Addison-Wesley.

Turoff, M., & Hiltz, S. R. (1995). Computer based Delphi processes. In Adler, M., & Ziglio, Z. (Eds.), *Grazing into the oracle: The Delphi method and its application to social policy and public health* (pp. 56–88). London, UK: Jessica Kingsley.

Ulschak, F. L. (1983). *Human resource development: The theory and practice of needs assessment*. Reston, VA: Reston Publishing Company.

van Teijlingen, E., Pitchforth, E., Bishop, C., & Russell, E. (2006). *Delphi method and nominal group techniques in family planning and reproductive health research*. Retrieved June 7, 2010, from http://eprints.bournemouth.ac.uk/10152/1/The_Delphi_method_revised_final.pdf

Weaver, W. T. (1971). The Delphi forecasting method. *Phi Delta Kappan, 52*(5), 267–273.

Wicklein, R. C. (1993). Identifying critical issues and problems in technology education using a modified-Delphi technique. *Journal of Technology Education, 5*(1), 54–71.

Wilenius, M., & Tirkkonen, J. (1997). Climate in the making: Using Delphi for Finnish climate policy. *Futures, 29*(9), 845–862. doi:10.1016/S0016-3287(97)00061-X

Witkin, B. R., & Altschuld, J. W. (1995). *Planning and conducting needs assessment: A practical guide*. Thousand Oaks, CA: Sage.

Young, S. J., & Jamieson, L. M. (2001). Delivery methodology of the Delphi: A comparison of two approaches. *Journal of Park and Recreation Administration, 19*(1), 42–58.

Yousuf, M. I. (2007). Using experts' opinions through Delphi technique. *Practical Assessment, Research, & Evaluation, 12*(4). Retrieved June 28, 2007, from http://pareonline.net/getvn.asp?v=12&n=4

KEY TERMS AND DEFINITIONS

Computer-Based Delphi: An electronic application of the Delphi technique characterized by shortened feedback turnaround times and asynchronous interactions between participants.

Delphi Process: The data collection procedure in Delphi studies which is characterized by multiple iterations, anonymity, and controlled feedback.

Delphi Technique: A communication process which strives to establish consensus so that target issues can be more fully investigated based on the feedback of those who are most knowledgeable and involved.

Forecasting Delphi: A type of Delphi which strives for obtaining consensus concerning the prediction of future events.

Normative Delphi: A type of Delphi which strives for generating consensus and focuses on the explorations of "what could/should be."

Policy Delphi: A communication process which strives to collect divergent opinions on an issue so that policy makers can consider opposing perspectives.

Real-Time Delphi: An electronic application of the Delphi technique characterized by both asynchronous and synchronous interactions which enable panelists to participate in a Delphi study without using multiple iterations for data collection.

Chapter 12
Designing Online Laddering Studies

Thorsten Gruber
Manchester Business School, UK

Alexander E. Reppel
Royal Holloway, University of London, UK

Isabelle Szmigin
Birmingham Business School, UK

Rödiger Voss
HWZ University of Applied Sciences of Zurich, Switzerland

ABSTRACT

Laddering is a well-established research technique in the social sciences which provides rich data to help understand means-end considerations otherwise hidden from quantitative research. It does this through revealing relationships between the attributes of individuals, objects or services (i.e., means), the consequences these attributes represent for the respondent, and the values or beliefs that are strengthened or satisfied by the consequences (i.e., ends). This chapter describes how qualitative researchers can successfully apply laddering in an online environment. Through an explanation of the different stages of the online laddering process, the authors hope to encourage researchers to use this technique in their urban planning research projects. To illustrate the benefits of the technique, the authors describe a research study that successfully used the laddering technique in an online environment. The chapter concludes with the discussion of the limitations of using laddering online and suggests avenues for future research.

INTRODUCTION

Urban marketing is concerned about changing people's perceptions of a place with regard to urban regeneration (Skinner, 2008). Negative perceptions can have a damaging impact on the success

DOI: 10.4018/978-1-4666-0074-4.ch012

of urban regeneration and "destroy the confidence of local communities, leading to the notion of a 'lost' city with no clear identity or brand" (Trueman, Cornelius, & Killingbeck-Widdup, 2007, p. 20). As urban places increasingly compete for resources, visitors, investors and residents, it is crucial for them to offer an excellent environment to attract new users and activities but also "to keep existing ones happy with their place" (Kavaratzis, 2005, p. 329).

To find out what place users value in the "place product" which is co-produced by a large number of autonomous public and private organisations (Hankinson, 2007), researchers can use qualitative research methods to get a deep understanding of social phenomena in context and interpret "phenomena in terms of the meanings people bring to them" (Denzin & Lincoln, 2003, p. 5). In this regard, Laddering is a well-established qualitative research technique, which has been used successfully in several disciplines (Reynolds & Gutman, 1988). This technique enables researchers to reveal the "reasons behind the reasons" (Gengler, Mulvey, & Oglethorpe, 1999, p. 175) and has been frequently used especially in exploratory qualitative phases of research projects (e.g., Botschen, Thelen, & Pieters, 1999; Denzin & Lincoln, 2003; Zanoli & Naspetti, 2002).

The aim of the chapter is to describe in detail how qualitative researchers can apply the established qualitative laddering technique to an online environment. To counter criticism that qualitative researchers produce unclear or ambiguous reports, we will describe the online laddering process thoroughly. Common difficulties include, not explaining how the research was conducted, why a certain research method was selected, how respondents were recruited, how data analysis was carried out, and conclusions reached (Bryman, 2008). Even though qualitative research is less structured and rule driven than quantitative research, this does not prevent the standardisation of data collection and analysis such that it is comprehensible to other researchers who may want to replicate the study in a different context. Reynolds, Dethloff, and Westberg (2001) distinguish the laddering method from typical qualitative research methods because the technique has a definite structure using standard probing questions and following an explicit agenda. They contrast the typical qualitative structure as shallow and broad while results from laddering are deep and focused. Thus, the

laddering method can be described as a structured qualitative method that leads to deep and focused results. By explaining the different stages of the online laddering process thoroughly, we hope that fellow researchers will become interested in using this technique and apply it to their urban planning projects to find out what place users value in a place.

To illustrate the benefits of the technique better, we describe a research study that used the laddering technique successfully in an online environment. This case study (see also Gruber, Szmigin, Reppel, & Voss, 2008; Reppel, Szmigin, & Gruber, 2006) aimed at getting a deeper understanding of the preferred product attributes of the lifestyle product "Apple® iPod®" by revealing underlying consumer benefits of and preferences for this innovative brand. The chapter concludes with the discussion of the limitations of using the laddering technique online and suggests some fruitful avenues for future research.

BACKGROUND

The laddering technique has been described as "one of the most promising developments in consumer research since the 1980s" (Grunert, Beckmann, & Sørensen, 2001, p. 63). While qualitative in terms of its focus on the individual consumer, it also produces quantitative results. Through laddering researchers discover the salient meanings that individuals associate with products, services and behaviours to reveal so-called means-end chains. The focus is on the associations in the individual's mind between the attributes of products, services or behaviours, which are the "means", the consequences of these attributes for the individual, and the personal values or beliefs, the "ends", which are satisfied by the consequences. While the attributes are the characteristics of a product or service, the consequences are the reasons why an attribute is important. They are the psychological or physiological aspects, which motivate an individual to use a product or service (Gutman, 1982). Values are a more universal concept and may be considered as life goals; personal and general consequences individuals are striving for in their lives (Rokeach, 1973). The linkages between attributes, consequences and values produce the means-end chains (Peter, Olson, & Grunert, 1999). Knowledge is assumed to be hierarchically organized in the individual's memory spanning different levels of abstraction (Reynolds, Gengler, & Howard, 1995); the higher the level of abstraction, the stronger the connection to the self. In this hierarchy attributes (low level of abstraction) are less relevant to the self than consequences (mid level of abstraction) and values are of most relevance (high level of abstraction) (Olson & Reynolds, 1983).

Laddering is based on two premises (Manyiwa & Crawford, 2002): First, that values have a significant impact on (buying) behaviour, and secondly that individuals cope with the huge diversity of products (or services or behaviours) by classifying them into classes or sets to make the choice-making process easier. The approach also parallels the expectancy-value theory (Rosenberg, 1956), which proposes that actions have consequences and that individuals learn to relate certain consequences to certain product attributes (Reynolds & Gutman, 1988). Consumers will seek attributes that produce desirable and relevant consequences, and a consequence fulfils this requirement if it helps the individual to attain his or her personal goals. Correspondingly, individuals learn to avoid certain attributes that produce consequences, which prevent them from reaching their goals or from justifying their beliefs and/or behaviour.

Laddering has its roots in Kelly's (1955/1991a, 1955/1991b) Personal Construct Psychology. According to Kelly, individuals have their own view of the world and are probably capable of reflecting on and controlling their behaviour by creating rules or developing theories. The laddering technique emerged in the clinical psychology area introduced by Dennis Hinkle (1965) to model the concepts and beliefs of people (cf., Bannister & Mair, 1968). In a market research context, the technique was first used for product or brand positioning issues and to link the consumer's product knowledge to his/her self-knowledge (Gutman, 1982; Olson & Reynolds, 1983). Early work in this area helped to resolve product-or brand positioning problems and to link the consumer's product knowledge to his/her self-knowledge (Gutman, 1982; Olson & Reynolds, 1983). More recently, the laddering technique has been applied successfully to domains such as relationship marketing (Paul, Hennig-Thurau, Gremler, Gwinner, & Wiertz, 2009), sales management (Deeter-Schmelz, Goebel, & Kennedy, 2008), buyer-seller interactions (Reppel & Szmigin, 2010), business-to-business relationships (Gruber, Henneberg, Ashnai, Naudé, & Reppel, 2010; Henneberg, Gruber, Reppel, Ashnai, & Naudé, 2009), higher education (Voss, Gruber, & Szmigin, 2007), and services marketing (Gruber, Szmigin, & Voss, 2006, 2009a, 2009b).

TWO LADDERING METHODS: HARD AND SOFT LADDERING

Two approaches to laddering, soft and hard have been distinguished (Botschen & Thelen, 1998; Grunert et al., 2001). Soft laddering refers to in-depth interviews where respondents are restricted as little as possible in their natural flow of speech. The researchers have to be able to understand the meaning of the given answers and to link them to the means-end model (Grunert et al., 2001). Hard laddering, by contrast, uses a structured approach with interviews and questionnaires where respondents will be led to "produce ladders one by one and to give answers in such a way that the sequence of the answers reflects increasing levels of abstraction" (Grunert et al., 2001, p. 75).

Principles of Soft Laddering

Here semi-standardized qualitative in-depth interviews are used, digging deeper by asking probing questions to reveal attribute-consequence-value chains by taking the subject up a ladder of abstraction (Reynolds & Gutman, 1988). Prior to laddering, an elicitation stage derives preference based distinction criteria (Grunert & Grunert, 1995; Reynolds & Gutman, 1988). While techniques such as triadic sorting, direct elicitation or free sorting may be used, research shows that such complex and time consuming methods do not outperform free sorting techniques such as direct questioning and ranking (Bech-Larsen & Nielsen, 1999). These derived criteria form the opening for the laddering probes to uncover the complete means-end structure, which will reveal cognitive relationships of personal relevance to the respondent (Gengler & Reynolds, 1995). For this purpose, the interviewer repeatedly questions why an attribute/consequence/value is important to the respondent. The answer acts as the starting point for further questioning.

Recognizing the repetitive nature of the technique, Reynolds et al. (2001, p. 105) suggest the following examples of questions that could be used instead of just constantly asking "Why is that important to you?":

- "How does that help you out?"
- "What do you get from that?"
- "Why do you want that?"
- "What happens to you as a result of that?"

For higher-level consequences and values, Reynolds, et al. (2001) suggest questions such as "How does that make you feel?" This is called "laddering up" as the interviewer pushes the respondent up a ladder of abstraction, starting with concrete attributes and ending with abstract values (Gutman, 1997; Manyiwa & Crawford, 2002; Reynolds & Gutman, 1988; Valette-Florence & Rapacchi, 1991). Occasionally, respondents may skip less abstract attributes. Then the interviewer has to "ladder down" asking questions like "how is that outcome achieved?" to reveal the skipped category (Manyiwa & Crawford, 2002).

During the laddering interview, two problems can occur (Reynolds et al., 2001; Reynolds & Gutman, 1988):

- The respondent really does not "know" the answer: The respondent may be unable to articulate the reason why a specific attribute or consequence is important to him. The interviewer can then try to rephrase or change the question to "unblock" the respondent.
- Issues are too sensitive: As the respondent is forced up the ladder of abstraction, the questions become increasingly personal. Respondents may circumvent the topic or say that they don't know, remain silent or evade the question. Interviewers may then try to make the respondent feel more comfortable by revealing something personal about himself or herself. This has to be cone with care and in such a way as not to lead the respondent. Alternatively, the interviewer can take a note of the sensitive question and return to it at a later stage.

Principles of Hard Laddering

While the majority of published means-end use soft laddering based on interviews, some researchers also use questionnaires to collect laddering data. Walker and Olson (1991) developed a paper-and-pencil version of the laddering interview (hard laddering) where respondents fill in a structured questionnaire identifying up to four attributes that are of relevance to them and then provide reasons why each attribute is of importance to them (Botschen & Hemetsberger, 1998). An example for a typical laddering questionnaire is presented in Figure 1.

Figure 1. Paper-and-pencil version of laddering (adapted from Pieters et al., 1998, p. 760; Botschen & Hemetsberger, 1998, p. 154)

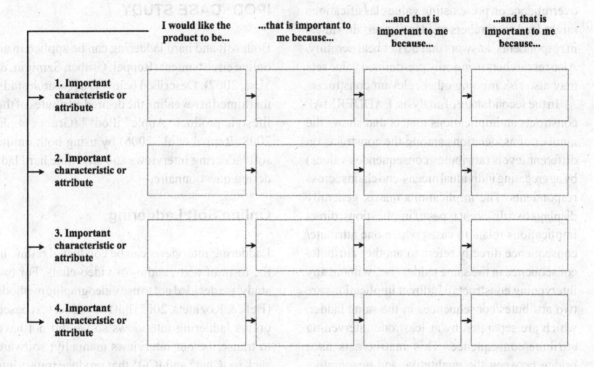

The paper-and-pencil version has been successfully used by a number of researchers (e.g., Botschen & Hemetsberger, 1998; Botschen & Thelen, 1998; Goldenberg, Klenosky, O'Leary, & Templin, 2000; Pieters, Baumgartner, & Allen, 1995). Botschen and Hemetsberger (1998) suggest that the advantage of hard laddering is that it reduces interviewer bias and minimizes social pressure on the respondents who can decide for themselves when they want to end the laddering process. Furthermore, in comparison to soft laddering, it is a much more cost- and time-efficient and is easier to manage. Data collection and analysis are also quicker.

Laddering Data Analysis

Following Reynolds and Gutman (1988), laddering data is analysed in three stages. First, sequences of attributes, consequences and values (the ladder) are coded to make comparisons across respondents. The decision-support software program LADDERMAP (Gengler & Reynolds, 1993; Peffers & Gengler, 2003) helps researchers categorise each phrase from the questionnaire as an attribute, a consequence, or a value. At this stage meaningful categories must be developed so that comparable phrases and data points can be grouped together. Coding is an iterative process of recoding data, splitting, combining categories, generating new or dropping existing categories, in line with content analysis techniques (Strauss & Corbin, 1998), specific codes for the first analysis are developed and then combined until a manageable number is reached (approximately fifty) (Gengler & Reynolds, 1995). To classify categories, phrases and key words used by respondents used in the online laddering interviews or questionnaires are identified, as well as concepts from a current literature review and from value lists such as Schwartz (1992) and Rokeach (1973). However, this need to be used with caution as overreliance on pre-existing value classifications might lead researchers to identify certain values in respondents' answers that do not bear scrutiny. Also researchers using only pre-defined value sets may also risk missing other relevant constructs.

In the second stage of analysis, LADDERMAP constructs an implications matrix that shows the number of associations among the constructs on different levels (attributes/consequences/values) by aggregating individual means-end chains across respondents. The implications matrix generally displays two different types of implications: direct implications relate to cases where one attribute/consequence directly refers to another attribute/consequence in the same ladder (i.e., without any intervening constructs). Indirect implications are two attributes/consequences in the same ladder, which are separated by at least one intervening attribute/consequence. This matrix acts as a bridge between the qualitative and quantitative elements of the laddering technique by showing the frequencies with which one code (construct) leads to another (Deeter-Schmelz et al., 2008).

LADDERMAP then generates a hierarchical value map (HVM) consisting of the nodes representing the most important attributes/consequences/values, and lines indicating links between concepts (Claeys, Swinnen, & Abeele, 1995). The HVM normally consists of three different levels relating to the three concepts of meaning: attributes, consequences, and values. Frequently, the lower section of the map is crowded and cluttered with a large number of attributes identified in the laddering process (Gengler, Klenosky, & Mulvey, 1995). Avoiding several crossing lines (i.e., overlapping ladders) is important in enabling easier interpretability of the HVM for this reason.

USING SOFT AND HARD LADDERING ONLINE: THE IPOD® CASE STUDY

Both soft and hard laddering can be applied to an online environment (Reppel, Gruber, Szmigin, & Voss, 2007). Described below is a research study that aimed at revealing the desired attributes of the lifestyle product "Apple® iPod®" (Gruber et al., 2008; Reppel et al., 2006) by using both online soft laddering interviews and an online hard laddering questionnaire.

Online Soft Laddering

Laddering interviews can be conducted online in the form of text-, audio- or video-chats. For our study, we decided not to use videographic methods (Belk & Kozinets, 2005) but to conduct text based online laddering interviews so we did not have to transcribe our interviews manually; software such as iChat® and ICQ® that produce transcripts automatically. Text-based online soft laddering interviews are conducted in rounds: After some introductory words (thanking the respondent for taking part in the interview, introducing oneself and the aim of the research project, and assuring anonymity and confidentiality) the interviewer begins the interview by typing the first question in a small text box of the chat software. By clicking a "send button", the question is then immediately sent to the interviewee who can read the question in a larger text box. The interviewee can then respond to the interviewer the same way.

We conducted online soft laddering interviews with iPod® users to learn more about the iPod® phenomenon and the preferred attributes of the iPod® player in particular. Apple® iPod® users were invited to fill in a web survey, through invitations on several websites that iPod® users frequently visit. We also advertised in the search results of a well known search site. The purpose was to make potential respondents aware of the website which hosted the project questionnaire. The web survey included an opinion leadership scale that was originally constructed by Flynn, Goldsmith, and Eastman (1996) consisting of six items to identify the desired homogeneous group of opinion leaders. Our scale was adjusted by including a 'no answer' option to exclude those participants who would otherwise only consider the end points of the scale. We also scaled the six items from 1 to 5, with a higher number meaning stronger agreement. The Cronbach's alpha reliability coefficient for our opinion leadership scale was .73.

We focused on opinion leaders as they exercise informal influence upon other peoples' behaviours and attitudes through product-related conversations (Goldsmith & De Witt, 2003). Moreover, opinion leaders are considered attractive targets for marketing communication (Stern & Gould, 1988), as well as for the adoption and diffusion of newly developed products (Chan & Misra, 1990). As the information or advice they provide is perceived to be more credible than mass advertising, opinion leaders can informally influence others' attitudes and behaviours (Stern & Gould, 1988). Opinion leaders are particularly important for the success of innovative products when they are among the early adopters themselves as they pass on important information to opinion seekers (Flynn et al., 1996). Finally, we believed that opinion leaders would be highly motivated and willing to invest sufficient time in taking part in the online interviews.

The web survey also covered the following topics: satisfaction with the iPod® in general and with its product attributes in particular (e.g., design, usability, etc.), importance of iPod® product attributes, and the reasons for choosing the iPod®. Respondents were also asked how much time they would spend daily listening to music. We also included a question concerning usage of direct messaging software (e.g., iChat®, ICQ®). Finally, we asked respondents whether they would be interested in being contacted for another research project and we gave them the

possibility of creating an anonymous e-mail for the research project purpose only.

Cobanoglu and Cobanoglu (2003) suggest that researchers using web surveys should use incentives to achieve good response rates. They recommend that researchers should offer a small prize to all respondents and also enter them into a raffle for a bigger prize. Following these recommendations, all respondents who filled in the web survey could download two exclusive chapters (78 pages in total) of an iPod® book. They were also included in a draw for prizes such as a computer, audio books, sound systems, and personalised protective covers for the iPod®.

A total of 2,472 respondents participated in our web survey and 2,178 (88% out of 2,472) of them provided complete answers to the opinion leadership scale. From the 317 respondents that scored highest on this scale (i.e., scores of 26 or higher with a possible score range between 6-30), 273 (86% out of 317) agreed to be contacted for a further study and 198 of them were not only opinion leaders but also owners of an iPod® and regular users of instant messenger software. From this group, participants for both our online soft and hard laddering interviews were randomly selected and were asked whether they would prefer to fill in a questionnaire or be interviewed.

For our online interviews, we then contacted respondents by email and thanked them for having taken part in the web survey and for being interested in the new research project. We then informed them that this new project was concerned with identifying the attributes of the iPod® that they valued the most. We told respondents that we were particularly interested in their views as opinion leaders with regard to digital music players. We then informed them that the new project would be conducted in the form of an online interview that would last for approx. 60 minutes. We also promised participants an issue of an iPod® magazine and a protective cover for their iPod® as a further reward for taking part in the research study.

Respondents were able to schedule their own interview appointment via our homepage. For this purpose we used an online appointment scheduling software that allowed respondents not only to view and edit their own appointments online but also to change or cancel appointments if necessary. Participants had to provide the following information: email address, chat name, date and time of online interview and the name of the preferred chat software (e.g., iChat®, ICQ®, etc.).

We originally planned to conduct as many interviews as possible and analyse the results after every ten interviews. After twenty interviews, however, it became evident that our categories had reached theoretical saturation, i.e., no new or relevant data concerning categories were emerging and the categories and linkages between categories were well established (Strauss & Corbin, 1998). We therefore decided that no additional interviews were necessary, so the laddering process was completed with 22 interviews.

The Three Stages of the Online Soft Laddering Process

In the following, we explain the online laddering interviewing process thoroughly. In order to understand the laddering process better we divided it into three stages: a pre-online soft laddering phase, an online soft laddering phase, and a post-online soft laddering phase.

The Pre-Online Soft Laddering Phase

Based on the information gathered from the web survey, we prepared "participation cards" of all respondents, which contained e-mail addresses, age, and gender of the respondents, their current iPod® models, favoured music groups, and recommended new iPod® special editions, preferred circumstances for using the iPod®, and the time they spent daily listening to music and using their iPod®. The day before an online interview we reminded participants by e-mail and told them that

we were looking forward to meeting them online. In this e-mail we also mentioned the scheduled interview appointment, the chat name of the interviewer, and the name of the chat software that the respondent selected.

Before an online laddering interview started, we studied the respondent's participation card to be better prepared for the interview. We then knew for example which music group the interviewee favoured and how much time he or she spends on their iPod®. We also opened a word document with prepared standardised text modules such as "My name is..." for the opening of each interview and modules such as "Please follow the link to download your issue of the iPod® magazine" for the conclusion of the interview. As soon as respondents were online and ready for the online interview, we immediately contacted them by typing "Hello Mr/Ms..." in a small text box of the chat software. By clicking a "send button", our message was immediately sent to the interviewees who could read it in a larger text box. Interviewees could then send an answer back to us the same way. We then thanked respondents for taking part in the interview and introduced ourselves and the aim of the research project. Following that, we promised all interviewees that we would use the information for research purposes only, it would not be used commercially, and we assured confidentiality.

Collen and Hoekstra (2001) emphasise the need to create a non-threatening interview environment so that respondents can talk freely about their motivations. Respondents should get the impression that their opinion is important and that there are no right or wrong answers. The interviewer should only act as a facilitator "who has to keep the respondent talking" (Collen & Hoekstra, 2001, p. 296). Thus, we assured respondents that they could not give any wrong answers, that we would not judge their answers, and that they could use colloquial language or even slang to tell their stories. We also told them that we would be particularly interested in their expert opinions on this topic.

Reynolds et al. (2001) recommend that interviewers should start with warm-up questions to put interviewees at ease before the actual laddering interview begins, this we did at the beginning of each interview. As our study combines a quantitative web survey with the qualitative laddering process, we were able to refer to information from the initial questionnaire such as respondent's answers to questions like "For which music group or person should Apple® introduce an iPod® special edition?" and "When and in what circumstances do you like to use your iPod® the most?" The idea behind this 'small-talk' was to break the ice and create rapport so that respondents felt comfortable and were prepared for the following interview. By having this informal chat, we not only tried to establish a relationship with the respondents and to encourage them to take part in the interview but we also helped us to 'warm up'.

The Online Soft Laddering Phase

After the warm up session, the actual laddering interviewing process began. First, we asked all 22 interviewees to tell us three or four attributes of the iPod® that was relevant to them and that distinguish the iPod® from its competitors. The derived criteria were then used as the starting point for the laddering probes. For this, we began with the attribute of the iPod® that respondents considered to be the most important and asked: "Why is attribute x important to you?" The answer to this question served as the starting point for further questioning. We continued with the laddering process until respondents gave either circular answer, were incapable or reluctant to answer or reached the value level. As the laddering interview is semi-structured it allows for flexibility, for example, interviewees occasionally mentioned new attributes, which we also addressed during the interview.

Although all respondents were able to climb the ladder of abstraction, which means they were all capable of associating attributes with consequences and consequences with values, they sometimes had difficulty climbing the ladder of abstraction any further during the interview. In these cases, we applied several of the techniques recommended by Reynolds and Gutman (1988) to facilitate the interview. For example, we asked them how they would feel if the iPod® was not easy to use or if the design was not attractive. We also asked respondents to imagine how they feel when they use their iPod®.

If interviewees did not give sufficient answers, we employed probes to gather additional and/or more detailed information. We also asked respondents to clarify certain answers, particularly if their responses were ambiguous. We related respondents' answers to their previous answers and asked if these connections were valid. In applying these techniques, we tried not to push respondents but to accompany them on their way up the ladder of abstraction. It was important for us to find a balance between helping respondents and avoiding influencing their answers.

To maintain rapport during the interview, we attempted to adapt interpersonally using language that was comprehendible and relevant to our respondents, for example using emoticons if they did or being chatty if they were. Similarly, if interviewees seemed to be in a rush, we tried to complete the laddering process as quickly as possible. We believe that a personal connection can only develop online if a genuine interest is shown by the interviewer. We therefore tried to listen as actively as possible to what respondents were saying and attempted to remain focused and pay attention during the entire interviews.

The Post-Online Soft Laddering Phase

After each interview, we thanked respondents again for their participation. We then gave them a web address to download the promised issue of the iPod® magazine and we informed respondents that we could send them the study results if interested. Finally, we asked them to give us a delivery address to ship the iPod® protective cover and to visit another website to fill in a feedback form.

Thirteen respondents gave us constructive feedback. They particularly enjoyed the friendliness of the interviewers, the relaxed atmosphere, and the interesting and appropriate questions. They also liked the idea of having a personalised interview in a normally impersonal online environment preferring it to a telephone or face-to-face interview. Respondents also enjoyed the fact that the online interview did not focus on the preferred attributes of iPod® solely but was concerned with broader topics to get a deeper understanding of the iPod® phenomenon. Only two respondents mentioned drawbacks of the online interviewing experience, they criticised the length of the interview and the long interval between questions and answers. Respondents also suggested that interviewers should be quicker typists and that the whole interview should be shorter. Some suggested that they should be informed at the beginning of the chat how long the interview would take and what issues would be discussed. The online laddering interviews lasted between 50 and 140 minutes in comparison to traditional laddering interviews that normally last between 45 to 120 minutes (Reynolds et al., 2001).

Finally, respondents were asked to mark the online laddering interviewing experience according to a six-point scale running from 1 (very satisfactory) to 6 (very unsatisfactory). The overall average grade was 1.6 (very good).

Online Hard Laddering

The paper-and-pencil version of laddering can also be conducted in web-based form as an online laddering questionnaire. Respondents were asked to write down the three most important attributes of the iPod®. They were urged to be as specific as possible. Respondents were presented with three text boxes on the computer screen to type in their chosen attributes, which were then referred to in the following laddering questions. On the next computer screen, respondents then had to type in a large open text box why the first attribute they had just identified was important to them. They were, for example, asked "You have stated that one of the most important attributes or characteristics of your iPod® is "DESIGN" Could you please explain to us what you mean by this and why exactly this attribute is important to you? In a third text box, respondents then had to specify why what they indicated in the second box was important to them. Respondents were then asked to complete a fourth and any additional boxes (if they wanted to elaborate further on their previous answers) in the same way. After having completed the laddering process for the first attribute, respondents then had to fill in text boxes for the second and third most important product attributes as well. Alternatively, a laddering questionnaire could also have been attached to an email. We decided not to use this approach as it has several disadvantages: Potential respondents could decide not to download the attached questionnaire fearing that they could get a virus from doing so. Further, respondents may not possess the necessary programme to open and fill in the document. Finally, respondents would have had to send back the filled in document, which they could consider too demanding or time consuming (Gunter, Nicholas, Huntington, & Williams, 2002).

Analysis, Results and Discussion

First, we used the decision-support software program LADDERMAP (see Gengler & Reynolds, 1993; Peffers & Gengler, 2003) to enter up to ten chunks of meaning per ladder with the categorization of each phrase as either an attribute, consequence or value. We then identified and grouped meaningful categories. After 22 interviews and 26 questionnaires, it was evident that our categories

Table 1. Characteristics of sample

	All iPod® Opinion Leaders	Online Laddering Questionnaire Participants	Online Laddering Chat Participants
Average Age	28.8	30.4	28.3
Gender • Male • Female	97% 3%	92.3% 7.7%	95.7% 4.3%
In employment	63.6%	69.2%	58.7

had reached theoretical saturation, i.e., no new or relevant data concerning categories was emerging and the categories and linkages between categories were well established (Strauss & Corbin 1998). We therefore decided that no additional interviews and questionnaires were necessary. This sample size is sufficient for exploratory research studies and Reynolds et al. (2001) recommend that laddering studies should, as a rule of thumb, include at least 20 respondents. This sample size could already give a significant understanding of the main attributes, consequences, and values of products, services or people. Details regarding our sample are summarised in Table 1.

Codes for individual means-end chains were then aggregated and expressed in an implications matrix, which details the associations between the constructs. A graphical representation of the aggregate chains was presented in a Hierarchical Value Map (HVM). A hierarchical value map only displays associations beyond a specific "cut-off" level, which means that associations have to be mentioned by a certain number of respondents in order to be graphically represented.

Two resulting HVMs detailing the online laddering interviews and questionnaires are described below. They only display concepts of meaning (attributes, consequences, and values) and associations beyond cut-off level 2, meaning that concepts and linkages had to be mentioned by at least 2 respondents to be represented.

The size of the circles in Figure 2 stand for the frequency respondents brought up a certain concept. The most important attribute is labelled "control elements (n=20)", this includes aspects such as the menu navigation. The thickness of lines represents relative frequency of association between the concepts of meaning, so for example, the attribute "control elements (n=20)", the consequence "simplicity (n=18)" and the value "feeling good (n=10)" are strongly linked. Of the eleven attributes mentioned by respondents, the two most frequent were "control elements (n=20)" and "design (n=16)". This result is not surprising as both attributes of the iPod® are frequently discussed as being responsible to a large extent for distinguishing the iPod® from competitor's products. Secondly, both attributes represent a variety of aspects. For example, "control elements" subsumes hardware aspects, such as the 'click wheel' control, software aspects, such as the menu navigation, as well as the ease with which an iPod® can be connected to additional accessories through a standard connection 'dock connector'. A key attribute of importance for iPod® users is clearly its design. The iPod® is not only easy to use but it also makes its users feel proud, which, in turn, helps them to feel good. The iPod®'s design satisfies users' desire for beauty and helps them to feel individual. This is in line with the three dimensions of product design outlined by Norman (2005), namely the visceral, behavioural and reflective components, which are interwoven in any product design. While visceral design is concerned with appearance, behavioural design is related to the effectiveness of use and the pleasure related to the product. Finally, reflective design "considers the rationalization and

Figure 2. HVM of online soft laddering (attributes=dark, consequences=medium dark and values=light) (adapted from Reppel et al., 2007, p. 522)

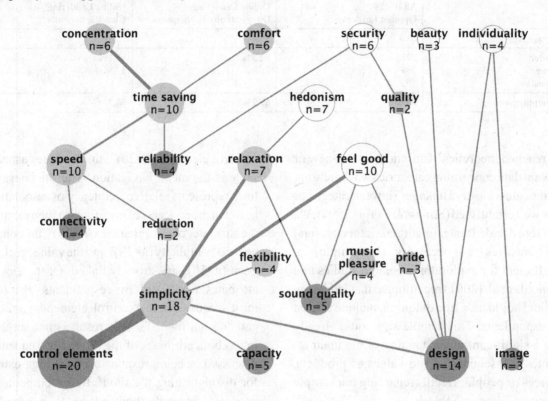

intellectualization of a product" (Norman, 2005, p. 5). The direct linkages between the attributes "design" and "image" and the values "beauty" and "individuality" support findings by Mort & Rose (2004) who discovered that for hedonistic products (products that consumers purchase for pleasure only) direct attribute-value connections are more common than indirect attribute-conse-quence-value linkages. Respondents also value the iPod®'s good sound quality that allows them to enjoy music and to relax. The iPod®'s ease of use and simplicity also helps users relax and enjoy life and have fun ("hedonism"). In addition, users can then save time, which allows them to devote attention to other issues ("concentration"). Further, the iPod®'s reliability creates a feeling of security.

The HVM in Figure 3, which is based on 26 online laddering questionnaires, is less complex than the HVM of the online interviews: While the interview HVM displays 23 concepts of meaning (seven attributes, eleven consequences, and five values), the questionnaire HVM only reveals 16 concepts (six attributes, seven consequences, and three values). The interview HVM displays more associations between concepts than the HVM based on the questionnaires (25 associations in comparison to 16).

Two concepts "handiness" and "mobility", appear in the questionnaire HVM but not in the interview HVM. Although mentioned during the online interviews they do not appear in the cor-responding HVM due to the chosen cut-off level. As stated, the HVM only displays associations that a certain number of respondents mentioned. Thus, only a few respondents mentioned these concepts during the interviews. Similarly, the concepts that appear in the interview HVM but not in the questionnaire HVM were also mentioned

Figure 3. HVM of online hard laddering (attributes=dark, consequences=medium dark and values=light) (adapted from Reppel et al., 2007, p. 522)

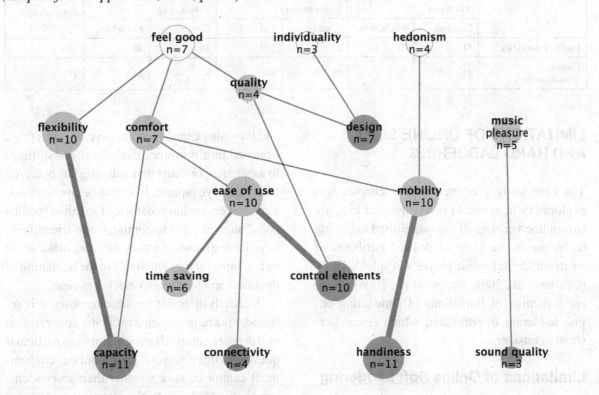

in the questionnaires but are not displayed in the HVM due to the cut-off level. Apart from these differences; however, the results from both laddering techniques are generally similar.

Table 2 shows that far more concepts of meaning (attributes, consequences, and values) were elicited during online laddering interviews than in the online laddering questionnaires. For example, respondents mentioned twice as many values during the online interviews as in the questionnaires. It seems to be more difficult for respondents to climb the ladder of abstraction and to elicit associations at the highest value of abstraction without the presence of an interviewer.

Table 3 shows that a total of 71 ladders were collected from the chats and the 22 respondents provided between two and five ladders each, with an average of 3.25 ladders per respondent. The longest ladder consisted of six concepts of mean-

ing (attributes, consequences, and values) and the shortest two, with an average of 3.2 concepts of meaning per ladder.

By comparison, a total of 70 ladders were collected from the online laddering questionnaires and the 26 respondents provided between one and four ladders each, with an average of 2.7 ladders per respondent. The longest ladder consisted of four concepts of meaning (attributes, consequences, and values) and the shortest two, with an average of 2.6 concepts. These results suggest that more ladders (in total and per person) and concepts of meaning can be collected during personal online soft laddering interviews than with the online application of the paper and pencil version of laddering. The ladders collected from the online interviews are also on average longer than the ladders from the online questionnaires.

Table 2. Comparison of attributes, consequences, and values

	Attributes		Consequences		Values		Concepts of Meaning
	Concepts	# in ladders	Concepts	# in ladders	Concepts	# in ladders	
Online Interviews	11	73	23	109	10	48	230
Online Questionnaires	14	70	18	88	8	24	182

LIMITATIONS OF ONLINE SOFT AND HARD LADDERING

The case study presented in this chapter was exploratory in nature as it was the first to apply two online versions of the established laddering technique to the issue of desired attributes of an iconic digital music player – Apple®'s iPod® (Gruber et al., 2008; Reppel et al., 2006). There are a number of limitations of conducting online laddering in particular, which researchers should consider.

Limitations of Online Soft Laddering

A major disadvantage of text based online laddering interviews is the loss of all non-verbal communication cues making it difficult for interviewers to create rapport (Chen & Hinton, 1999; Folkman Curasi, 2001; O'Connor & Madge, 2003). Rapport, however, is important to establish a relationship with respondents in order for them to share information (Bryman, 2008). Interviewers cannot receive and interpret respondents' non-verbal cues (e.g., body language, facial expressions)

and they also cannot send non-verbal cues (e.g., head nodding, murmurs of approval, and smiling) to assure respondents that listening has occurred and to achieve rapport. In an online environment, interviewers are limited to use of so called "emoticons" such as " ☺ " to communicate friendliness or other responses but they can also make some online introductory small talk at the beginning of the interview to put respondents at ease.

Similarly it is not possible to observe if respondents are losing interest in the conversation or if they are annoyed or unclear about a particular question. Interviewers in an online environment cannot be sure whether their respondents remain focused during the interview or become distracted (Comley, 2002; O'Connor & Madge, 2003) and so it may be difficult for researchers to control the success of online interviews (Folkman Curasi, 2001).

Online soft laddering interviews require motivated respondents who have to invest a significant amount of time and money for an online interview. These interviews are also physically more demanding than traditional face-to-face interviews as respondents continuously have to type, look at a

Table 3. Comparison of number (#) and length of ladders

# of ladders		# of ladders (per respondent)			# of concepts (A/C/V)	# of concepts per ladder (=length of ladder)		
		Min	Max	Avrg.		Min	Max	Avrg.
Online Interviews	71	2	5	3.2	230	2	6	3.2
Online Questionnaires	70	1	4	2.7	182	2	4	2.6

computer monitor, and think about their answers before typing (Chen & Hinton, 1999; O'Connor & Madge, 2003). Therefore online soft laddering interviews may not be suitable for respondents who do not possess good typing skills as they may feel under constant time pressure to give quick answers and may decide to shorten answers and not think carefully about their answers. Similarly, interviewers need to type quickly or work together with a second interviewer (O'Connor & Madge, 2003; Sweet, 2001) to ensure respondents do not have to wait too long for the next question to appear. These problems may be of particular relevance for certain respondents who are not used to an online environment or have difficulty typing. Higher incentives may be used to compensate for some of the issues discussed above (Tse, 1999) but clearly participating in and conducting online interviews will not suite everyone and reduces the applicability of this method.

Researchers using the laddering technique should also be aware of the fact that departures from the "ideal" laddering interview exist (Grunert & Grunert, 1995). Some respondents may not always give simple answers to the standard laddering probe "Why is attribute/consequence/value xyz important to you?" but tell little stories ("The last time I went shopping I found…", and "I always wondered if, and then", etc.), add details, or jump around from one category to another. Some other respondents may be unable to climb the ladder of abstraction any higher even if they are only at the attribute or consequences level. In this connection, Veludo-de-Oliveira, Ikeda, and Campomar (2006, p. 303) suggest that interviewers should ask respondents "to give examples and to make analogies. It will help them to go up to different levels of abstraction". These issues raise a number of important questions for the interviewer: Should they press respondents to give an additional answer? When should they stop probing? This is one of the most difficult aspects of conducting laddering interviews as it is not always clear for the interviewer when to stop the laddering process.

Ultimately interviewers have to find a balance between helping respondents to climb up the ladder while avoiding influencing their answers.

Limitations of Online Hard Laddering

Botschen et al. (1999) pointed to the fact that the paper-and-pencil laddering questionnaires provide hardly any contextual information. As a consequence, researchers may have difficulties developing meaningful categories during content analysis, especially if the researcher's pre-laddering knowledge about their respondents' cognitive categories is rather limited (Grunert & Grunert, 1995).

In addition, Botschen et al. (1999, p. 55) maintain that "little is known about the validity and reliability of the procedure and the comparability of results obtained from traditional laddering interview (soft laddering) and paper-and-pencil laddering". Finally, the researcher has no control over the laddering process (e.g., who really fills in the questionnaire).

The results of the iPod® study also indicate that, without the guidance of interviewers most respondents were not able climb the ladder of abstraction as only a few respondents were able to reach the highest level of abstraction (value level). However, in comparable paper-and-pencil laddering studies by authors, such as Pieters, Botschen, and Thelen (1998), Botschen et al. (1999), and Botschen and Hemetsberger (1998), respondents were also only able to come up with few values like "feeling good", "harmony with yourself", and "satisfaction". In this regard, Banister, Burman, Parker, Taylor, and Tindall (1994) point out that many people may have difficulties with verbalizing their experiences and reflecting on their behaviors and attitudes. This may explain why only few respondents, who filled in the online laddering questionnaires, mentioned values. Alternatively, respondents may not have climbed the ladder to the value level as they didn't want to spend too much time on the interview length and in an online hard laddering context it is much easier to terminate a ladder as there is no interviewer present that could help respondents climb up the ladder.

FUTURE RESEARCH DIRECTIONS

Despite the promise of our study results, more research and development are needed to refine and improve the online laddering process. For example, there is a relatively small number of constructs at the highest level of abstraction (values) produced by online hard laddering. One explanation for this deficit is that textual instructions take the place of the interviewer- respondent interactions in explaining the online laddering procedure. Some respondents in our study seemed to have difficulties with the design of the online laddering questionnaire. After having stated the three most important attributes of the iPod®, they wrote all they wanted to express about the first attribute in the first text box provided without realising that they should have just mentioned why the attribute is important to them. In the next text box they should then have described the reasons why what they indicated in the first box is important to them. They did then the same for the other two attributes they had specified.

Thus, further research should address this issue by designing a new version of an online laddering questionnaire that reduces potential ambiguity or provides respondents with more detailed instructions on how to fill in the online questionnaire. Future research could test the relative performance of four ways of implementing laddering online tutorials differing in the levels of presentation of information (i.e., text only, text and image, video and audio, screencast with audio) at the start of the study to assist participants of non-interviewer based online laddering studies. The rationale for these four conditions is provided from two streams of literature explaining the usefulness of various media, 'media richness theory' (Daft & Lengel,

1986) and research on the use of text, graphics, video and audio in instructional design (Anglin, Vaez, & Cunningham, 2004; Dillman, Smyth, & Christian, 2009; Levie & Lentz, 1982; Moore, Burton, & Myers, 2004): The first tutorial would be text only based and would serve as a base line.

The addition of graphics to text has advantages for attracting and directing attention (Levie & Lentz, 1982). Hence, tutorial two would introduce images showing screenshots of completed parts of the actual questionnaire. This condition is expected to have advantageous effects. Tutorial three would introduce animated text to the screening of example quotes with some additional audio comments. The addition of moving images was suggested by research showing that animations focus attention and can increase learning of complex processes, which seems applicable to these tutorials. However, adding animation is not always beneficial; the animation must be a "critical aspect" of the task and not merely to "enhance the realism". The addition of a voice could be made in consideration of media richness theory. Media richness theory proposes that a message sender should use the richest possible mix of cues (such as text, verbal or nonverbal cues, see Dennis & Kinney, 1998) to support communication of task information. This supposition that richer media, particularly those that support the use of natural language, can help clarify ambiguity and promote understanding is relevant to the idea of adding voice when transmitting information to participants of non-interviewer based qualitative research studies. In this context, supplementing text and graphics with audio instructions or introducing film of a person completing the questionnaire should result in better understanding and retention of the information. In tutorial three, audio could be used to read out the short text instructions and in tutorial four, a continuous voice-over could be used. Tutorial four could show an actual film of someone completing the survey and so, theoretically, would have the highest media richness. In contrast, other research suggests that providing too much information in too many modalities can be counter-productive. Misanchuk, Schwier, and Boling (1999) caution that high realism introduces irrelevant information that makes learning more difficult and Moore et al. (2004) advise that people find difficulty in processing both text and audio at the same time.

Further research should also contrast different hard laddering techniques with soft laddering applications (Botschen & Thelen, 1998) to clarify "under which circumstances it may be safe to perform hard laddering, and when it appears necessary to employ soft laddering" (Grunert et al., 2001, p. 76). Our results show the depth of insight that can be achieved using an online laddering approach, but there is clearly room for more work in the future examining the validity of different laddering approaches in particular.

CONCLUSION

This chapter has shown how the established laddering interviewing technique can be applied successfully to an online environment. While the online soft laddering interviews produced significantly more depth in understanding, the results of the two online laddering methods are broadly similar. In addition to displaying the most important attributes of the iPod®, the two hierarchical value maps also showed why they are important. In this way, the HVM offered a deeper understanding of the attributes of the iPod® that users desire by graphically illustrating the underlying benefits that users look for.

Both online laddering techniques allowed an inexpensive and fast collection of qualitative data. There was no need to tape and transcribe online interviews as transcripts were automatically generated, which allowed for quick data analysis. This was similar for the filled in online questionnaires, which were also available in electronic form. Moreover, applying the laddering technique to an online environment allows researchers to gather information from an interesting group of respondents that would have been difficult to contact otherwise. Respondents came from diverse backgrounds (e.g., politicians, actors, musicians, professors, and business people) and would probably not meet each other in real life. All respondents, however, had one thing in common: they were all opinion leaders with regard to the Apple® iPod® and interested in sharing their views with us.

The whole online laddering process was convenient for respondents who did not have to leave their homes and offices for the interviews and questionnaires. Following the principles of a new approach of conducting research termed "permission research" (Bronner & Kuijlen, 2007), we tried to treat respondents as 'customers' by asking them whether they would be interested in participating in the laddering study, rewarding their participation, allowing them to choose the laddering method, and by respecting their privacy.

The laddering technique is a valuable research method especially for the exploratory stages of market research projects (van Rekom & Wierenga, 2007). After having shown that the qualitative laddering technique can be combined successfully with a quantitative web survey to reveal the personal relevance of the preferred attributes of an iconic brand and market leader for Apple® iPod® users we hope that urban marketing researchers will use the two online versions of the laddering technique to investigate interesting urban planning phenomena. Even though there already exist a significant number of case studies looking into several important aspects such as city marketing (e.g., Griffiths, 1998), city tourism (e.g., Maitland, 2007), and retail environments in cities (e.g., Bennison, Warnaby, & Medway, 2007), the laddering technique could provide urban marketing researchers with a deeper insight and understanding of why certain attributes of places matter to place users. In particular, they could for example use laddering to find out the attributes of places that place users desire the most and to understand the underlying motives and benefits sought by them. These in-depth studies would reveal the "reasons behind the reasons" (Gengler et al., 1999, p. 175), which would then improve our knowledge of this important topic significantly.

REFERENCES

Anglin, G. J., Vaez, H., & Cunningham, K. L. (2004). Visual message design and learning: The role of static and dynamic illustrations. In Jonassen, D. H. (Ed.), *Handbook of Research for Educational Communications and Technology* (2nd ed., pp. 865–916). Mahwah, NJ: Lawrence Erlbaum Associates.

Banister, P., Burman, E., Parker, I., Taylor, M., & Tindall, C. (1994). *Qualitative Methods in Psychology – A Research Guide*. Maidenhead, UK: Open University Press.

Bannister, D., & Mair, J. M. M. (1968). *The evaluation of personal constructs*. London, UK: Academy Press.

Bech-Larsen, T., & Nielsen, N. A. (1999). A comparison of five elicitation techniques for elicitation of attributes of low involvement. *Journal of Economic Psychology*, *20*(3), 315–341. doi:10.1016/S0167-4870(99)00011-2

Belk, R. W., & Kozinets, R. V. (2005). Videography in marketing and consumer research. *Qualitative Market Research: An International Journal*, *8*(2), 128–141. doi:10.1108/13522750510592418

Bennison, D., Warnaby, G., & Medway, D. (2007). The role of quarters in large city centres: a Mancunian case study. *International Journal of Retail & Distribution Management*, *35*(8), 626–638. doi:10.1108/09590550710758612

Botschen, G., & Hemetsberger, A. (1998). Diagnosing means-end structures to determine the degree of potential marketing program standardization. *Journal of Business Research*, *42*(2), 151–159. doi:10.1016/S0148-2963(97)00116-1

Botschen, G., & Thelen, E. M. (1998). Hard versus soft laddering: Implications for appropriate use. In Balderjahn, I., Mennicken, C., & Vernette, E. (Eds.), *New developments and approaches in consumer behaviour research* (pp. 321–339). Stuttgart, Germany: Schäffer-Poeschel.

Botschen, G., Thelen, E. M., & Pieters, R. (1999). Using means-end structures for benefit segmentation. *European Journal of Marketing*, *33*(1-2), 38–58. doi:10.1108/EUM0000000004491

Bronner, F., & Kuijlen, T. (2007). The live or digital interviewer. A comparison between CASI, CAPI, CATI with respect to differences in response behaviour. *International Journal of Market Research*, *49*(2), 167–190.

Bryman, A. (2008). *Social research methods* (3rd ed.). Oxford, UK: Oxford University Press.

Chan, K. K., & Misra, S. (1990). Characteristics of the opinion leader: A new dimension. *Journal of Advertising*, *19*(3), 53–60.

Chen, P., & Hinton, S. M. (1999). Realtime interviewing using the World Wide Web. *Sociological Research Online*, *4*(3). doi:10.5153/sro.308

Claeys, C., Swinnen, A., & Abeele, P. V. (1995). Consumers' means-end chains for "think" and "feel" products. *International Journal of Research in Marketing*, *12*(3), 193–208. doi:10.1016/0167-8116(95)00021-S

Cobanoglu, C., & Cobanoglu, N. (2003). The effect of incentives in web surveys: application and ethical considerations. *International Journal of Market Research*, *45*(4), 475–488.

Collen, H., & Hoekstra, J. (2001). Values as determinants of preferences for housing attributes. *Journal of Housing and the Built Environment, 16*(3-4), 285–306. doi:10.1023/A:1012587323814

Comley, P. (2002). Online survey techniques: Current issues and future trends. *Interactive Marketing, 4*(2), 156–169. doi:10.1057/palgrave.im.4340174

Daft, R. L., & Lengel, R. H. (1986). Organizational information requirements, media richness and structural design. *Management Science, 32*(5), 554–571. doi:10.1287/mnsc.32.5.554

Deeter-Schmelz, D. R., Goebel, D. J., & Kennedy, K. N. (2008). What are the characteristics of an effective sales manager? An exploratory study comparing salesperson and sales manager perspectives. *Journal of Personal Selling & Sales Management, 28*(1), 7–20. doi:10.2753/PSS0885-3134280101

Dennis, A. R., & Kinney, S. T. (1998). Testing media richness theory in the new media: The effects of cues, feedback, and task equivocality. *Information Systems Research, 9*(3), 256–274. doi:10.1287/isre.9.3.256

Denzin, N. K., & Lincoln, Y. S. (2003). The Discipline and Practice of Qualitative Research. In Denzin, N. K., & Lincoln, Y. S. (Eds.), *The Landscape of Qualitative Research – Theories and Issues* (pp. 1–45). Thousand Oaks, CA: Sage.

Dillman, D. A., Smyth, J. D., & Christian, L. M. (2009). *Internet, mail, and mixed-mode surveys: The tailored design method* (3rd ed.). New York, NY: John Wiley & Sons.

Flynn, L. R., Goldsmith, R. E., & Eastman, J. K. (1996). Opinion leaders and opinions seekers: Two new measurement scales. *Journal of the Academy of Marketing Science, 24*(2), 137–147. doi:10.1177/0092070396242004

Folkman Curasi, C. (2001). A critical exploration of face-to-face interviewing vs. computer-mediated interviewing. *International Journal of Market Research, 43*(4), 361–375.

Gengler, C. E., Klenosky, D. B., & Mulvey, M. S. (1995). Improving the graphic representation of means-end results. *International Journal of Research in Marketing, 12*(3), 245–256. doi:10.1016/0167-8116(95)00024-V

Gengler, C. E., Mulvey, M. S., & Oglethorpe, J. E. (1999). A means-end analysis of mothers' infant feeding choices. *Journal of Public Policy & Marketing, 18*(2), 172–188.

Gengler, C. E., & Reynolds, T. J. (1993). *LADDERMAP: A software tool for analyzing laddering data (Version 5.4)*. Camden, NJ: Means-End Software.

Gengler, C. E., & Reynolds, T. J. (1995). Consumer understanding and advertising strategy: Analysis and strategic translation of laddering data. *Journal of Advertising Research, 35*(4), 19–33.

Goldenberg, M. A., Klenosky, D. B., O'Leary, J. T., & Templin, T. J. (2000). A means-end investigation of Ropes course experiences. *Journal of Leisure Research, 32*(2), 208–224.

Goldsmith, R. E., & De Witt, T. S. (2003). The predictive validity of an opinion leadership scale. *Journal of Marketing Theory & Practice, 11*(1), 28–35.

Griffiths, R. (1998). Making sameness: Place marketing and the new urban entrepreneurialism. In Oatley, N. (Ed.), *Cities, economic competition and urban policy* (pp. 41–57). London, UK: Paul Chapman.

Gruber, T., Henneberg, S. C., Ashnai, B., Naudé, P., & Reppel, A. E. (2010). Complaint resolution management expectations in an asymmetric business-to-business context. *Journal of Business and Industrial Marketing, 25*(5), 360–371. doi:10.1108/08858621011058124

Gruber, T., Szmigin, I., Reppel, A. E., & Voss, R. (2008). Designing and conducting online interviews to investigate interesting consumer phenomena. *Qualitative Market Research: An International Journal, 11*(3), 256–274. doi:10.1108/13522750810879002

Gruber, T., Szmigin, I., & Voss, R. (2006). The desired qualities of customer contact employees in complaint handling encounters. *Journal of Marketing Management, 22*(5-6), 619–642. doi:10.1362/026725706777978721

Gruber, T., Szmigin, I., & Voss, R. (2009a). Developing a deeper understanding of attributes of effective customer contact employees in personal complaint handling encounters. *Journal of Services Marketing, 23*(6), 422–435. doi:10.1108/08876040910985889

Gruber, T., Szmigin, I., & Voss, R. (2009b). Handling customer complaints effectively - a comparison of the value maps of female and male complainants. *Managing Service Quality, 19*(6), 6636–6656. doi:10.1108/09604520911005044

Grunert, K. G., Beckmann, S. C., & Sørensen, E. (2001). Means-end chains and laddering: An inventory of problems and an agenda for research. In Reynolds, T. J., & Olson, J. C. (Eds.), *Understanding consumer decision making - the means-end approach to marketing and advertising strategy* (pp. 69–90). Mahwah, NJ: Lawrence Erlbaum Associates.

Grunert, K. G., & Grunert, S. C. (1995). Measuring subjective meaning structures by the laddering method: Theoretical considerations and methodological problems. *International Journal of Research in Marketing, 12*(3), 209–225. doi:10.1016/0167-8116(95)00022-T

Gunter, B., Nicholas, D., Huntington, P., & Williams, P. (2002). Online versus offline research: Implications for evaluating digital media. *Aslib Proceedings, 54*(4), 229–239. doi:10.1108/00012530210443339

Gutman, J. (1982). A means-end chain model based on consumer categorization processes. *Journal of Marketing, 46*(2), 60–72. doi:10.2307/3203341

Gutman, J. (1997). Means-end chains as goal hierarchies. *Psychology and Marketing, 14*(6), 545–560. doi:10.1002/(SICI)1520-6793(199709)14:6<545::AID-MAR2>3.0.CO;2-7

Hankinson, G. (2007). The management of destination brands: Five guiding principles based on recent developments in corporate branding theory. *Journal of Brand Management, 14*(3), 240–254. doi:10.1057/palgrave.bm.2550065

Henneberg, S. C., Gruber, T., Reppel, A. E., Ashnai, B., & Naudé, P. (2009). Complaint management expectations: An online-laddering analysis of small versus large firms. *Industrial Marketing Management, 38*(6), 584–598. doi:10.1016/j.indmarman.2009.05.008

Hinkle, D. (1965). *The change of personal constructs from the viewpoint of theory of construct implications.* Unpublished doctoral dissertation, Ohio University, Athens, OH.

Kavaratzis, M. (2005). Place Branding: A Review of Trends and Conceptual Models. *Marketing Review, 5*(4), 329–342. doi:10.1362/1469347057751868 54

Kelly, G. A. (1955/1991a). The psychology of personal constructs: *Vol. 2. Clinical diagnosis and psychotherapy.* London, UK: Routledge.

Kelly, G. A. (1955/1991b). The psychology of personal constructs: *Vol. 1. Theory and personality*. London, UK: Routledge.

Levie, W. H., & Lentz, R. (1982). Effects of Text Illustrations: A Review of Research. *Educational Communication and Technology, 30*(4), 195–232.

Maitland, R. (2007). Marketing National Capital Cities [Special Issue]. *Journal of Travel & Tourism Marketing, 22*(3-4).

Manyiwa, S., & Crawford, I. (2002). Determining linkages between consumer choices in a social context and the consumer's values: A means-end approach. *Journal of Consumer Behaviour, 2*(1), 54–70. doi:10.1002/cb.89

Misanchuk, E. R., Schwier, R. A., & Boling, E. (1999). *Visual design for instructional multimedia*. Paper presented at the World Conference on Educational Multimedia, Hypermedia and Telecommunications (EDMEDIA), Chesapeake, VA.

Moore, D. M., Burton, J. K., & Myers, R. J. (2004). Multiple-channel communication: The theoretical and research foundations of multimedia. In Jonassen, D. H. (Ed.), *Handbook of Research for Educational Communications and Technology* (2nd ed., pp. 979–1005). Mahwah, NJ: Lawrence Erlbaum Associates.

Mort, G. S., & Rose, T. (2004). The effect of product type on value linkages in the means-end chain: Implications for theory and method. *Journal of Consumer Behaviour, 3*(3), 221–234. doi:10.1002/cb.136

Norman, D. A. (2005). *Emotional design - why we love (or hate) everyday things*. New York, NY: Basic Books.

O'Connor, H., & Madge, C. (2003). "Focus groups in cyberspace": using the Internet for qualitative research. *Qualitative Market Research: An International Journal, 6*(2), 133–143. doi:10.1108/13522750310470190

Olson, J. C., & Reynolds, T. J. (1983). Understanding consumers' cognitive structures: Implications for marketing strategy. In Percy, L., & Woodside, A. G. (Eds.), *Advertising and Consumer Psychology* (pp. 77–90). Lexington, MA: Lexington Books.

Paul, M., Hennig-Thurau, T., Gremler, D. D., Gwinner, K. P., & Wiertz, C. (2009). Toward a theory of repeat purchase drivers for consumer services. *Journal of the Academy of Marketing Science, 37*(2), 215–237. doi:10.1007/s11747-008-0118-9

Peffers, K., & Gengler, C. E. (2003). How to identify new high-payoff information systems for the organization. *Communications of the ACM, 46*(1), 83–88. doi:10.1145/602421.602424

Peter, J. P., Olson, J. C., & Grunert, K. G. (1999). *Consumer behaviour and marketing strategy*. London, UK: McGraw-Hill.

Pieters, R., Baumgartner, H., & Allen, D. (1995). A means-end chain approach to consumer goal structures. *International Journal of Research in Marketing, 12*(3), 227–244. doi:10.1016/0167-8116(95)00023-U

Pieters, R., Botschen, G., & Thelen, E. M. (1998). Customer desire expectations about service employees: An analysis of hierarchical reslations. *Psychology and Marketing, 15*(8), 755–773. doi:10.1002/(SICI)1520-6793(199812)15:8<755::AID-MAR3>3.0.CO;2-4

Reppel, A. E., Gruber, T., Szmigin, I., & Voss, R. (2007). *Conducting qualitative research online – an exploratory study into the preferred attributes of an iconic digital music player*. Paper presented at the European Advances in Consumer Research Conference, Milan, Italy.

Reppel, A. E., & Szmigin, I. (2010). Consumer-managed profiling: A contemporary interpretation of privacy in buyer-seller interactions. *Journal of Marketing Management*, *26*(3-4), 321–342. doi:10.1080/02672570903566383

Reppel, A. E., Szmigin, I., & Gruber, T. (2006). The iPod phenomenon: Identifying a market leader's secret through qualitative marketing research. *Journal of Product and Brand Management*, *15*(4), 239–249. doi:10.1108/10610420610679601

Reynolds, T. J., Dethloff, C., & Westberg, S. J. (2001). Advances in laddering. In Reynolds, T. J., & Olson, J. C. (Eds.), *Understanding consumer decision making - the means-end approach to marketing and advertising strategy* (pp. 91–118). Mahwah, NJ: Lawrence Erlbaum Associates.

Reynolds, T. J., Gengler, C. E., & Howard, D. J. (1995). A means-end analysis of brand persuasion through advertising. *International Journal of Research in Marketing*, *12*(3), 257–266. doi:10.1016/0167-8116(95)00025-W

Reynolds, T. J., & Gutman, J. (1988). Laddering theory, method, analysis, and interpretation. *Journal of Advertising Research*, *28*(1), 13–33.

Rokeach, M. (1973). *The nature of human values*. New York, NY: Free Press.

Rosenberg, M. J. (1956). Cognitive structure and attitudinal affect. *Journal of Abnormal and Social Psychology*, *53*(3), 367–372. doi:10.1037/h0044579

Schwartz, S. H. (1992). Universals in the content and structure of values: Theoretical advances and empirical tests in 20 countries. In Zanna, M. P. (Ed.), *Advances in experimental social psychology* (pp. 1–65). San Diego, CA: Academic Press. doi:10.1016/S0065-2601(08)60281-6

Skinner, H. (2008). The emergence and development of place marketing's confused identity. *Journal of Marketing Management*, *24*(9-10), 915–928. doi:10.1362/026725708X381966

Stern, B. B., & Gould, S. J. (1988). The consumer as financial opinion leader. *Journal of Retail Banking*, *10*(2), 43–52.

Strauss, A., & Corbin, J. (1998). *Basics of qualitative research - techniques and procedures for developing grounded theory*. Thousand Oaks, CA: Sage.

Sweet, C. (2001). Designing and conducting virtual focus groups. *Qualitative Market Research: An International Journal*, *4*(3), 130–135. doi:10.1108/13522750110393035

Trueman, M. M., Cornelius, N., & Killingbeck-Widdup, A. J. (2007). Urban corridors and the lost city: Overcoming negative perceptions to reposition city brands. *Journal of Brand Management*, *15*(1), 20–31. doi:10.1057/palgrave.bm.2550107

Tse, A. C. B. (1999). Conducting Electronic Focus Group Discussions among Chinese Respondents. *Journal of the Market Research Society. Market Research Society*, *41*(4), 407–415.

Valette-Florence, P., & Rapacchi, B. (1991). Improvements in means-end chain analysis: Using graph theory and correspondence analysis. *Journal of Advertising Research*, *31*(1), 30–45.

van Rekom, J., & Wierenga, B. (2007). On the hierarchical nature of means-end relationships in laddering data. *Journal of Business Research*, *60*(4), 401–410. doi:10.1016/j.jbusres.2006.10.004

Veludo-de-Oliveira, T. M., Ikeda, A. A., & Campomar, M. C. (2006). Laddering in the practice of marketing research: barriers and solutions. *Qualitative Market Research: An International Journal*, *9*(3), 297–306. doi:10.1108/13522750610671707

Voss, R., Gruber, T., & Szmigin, I. (2007). Service quality in higher education: The role of student expectations. *Journal of Business Research, 60*(9), 949–959. doi:10.1016/j.jbusres.2007.01.020

Walker, B. A., & Olson, J. C. (1991). Means-end chains: Connecting products with self. *Journal of Business Research, 22*(2), 111–118. doi:10.1016/0148-2963(91)90045-Y

Zanoli, R., & Naspetti, S. (2002). Consumer motivation in the purchase of organic food - a means-end approach. *British Food Journal, 104*(8), 643–653. doi:10.1108/00070700210425930

KEY TERMS AND DEFINITIONS

Laddering: A research technique in the social sciences that helps to reveal relationships between the attributes of individuals, objects or services (i.e., means), the consequences these attributes represent for the respondent, and the values or beliefs that are strengthened or satisfied by the consequences (i.e., ends).

LADDERMAP: A decision-support software program originally developed by Charles Gengler that allows researchers to generate graphical representations of laddering data, referred to as Hierarchical Value Maps (HVMs).

Hard Laddering: A paper-and-pencil version of the laddering interview technique where respondents fill in a structured questionnaire identifying attributes that are of relevance to them and then provide reasons why each attribute is of importance to them.

Hierarchical Value Map (HVM): A graphical representation of laddering data, consisting of the nodes representing the most important attributes/consequences/values, and lines indicating links between concepts. A HVM normally consists of three different levels relating to the three concepts of meaning: attributes, consequences, and values.

Means-End Chains: The linkages between attributes, consequences and values identified through the laddering research technique.

Online Laddering: Adaptation of soft laddering or hard laddering data collection methods to an online environment. Soft laddering interviews can be applied online as text, audio or video chats and hard laddering versions as online questionnaires.

Soft Laddering: A semi-standardized qualitative in-depth interview technique where respondents are asked probing questions to reveal attribute-consequence-value chains.

Chapter 13
Search Conferences and Future Search Conferences:
Potential Tools for Urban Planning in an On-Line Environment

Rosalind Hurworth
The University of Melbourne, Australia

ABSTRACT

This chapter examines the potential of the Search Conference (SC) and a later version, the Future Search Conference (FS), as useful participatory methods that contribute to urban and other types of planning. An unusual feature of these approaches is that participants are expected to contribute to the implementation of any action recommended. The chapter begins with a definition and history of these conferences before outlining how traditional, face-to-face conferences are implemented. As an illustration, the Future Search Conference 'Bendigo +25' (carried out in a regional Australian city to determine ways forward for the next 25 years) is discussed. The same case study is then re-examined in the context of attempting to run such an exercise in a Web-based environment. Both advantages and challenges of this mode of delivery are considered.

INTRODUCTION

A Search Conference (SC), and its later offshoot the Future Search Conference, (FS) can be excellent qualitative research tools for urban or other types of planning, as they use participatory techniques involving interested groups (such as experts, clients and residents) in order to find solutions and set priorities for future action.

Both techniques constitute a form of strategic planning run by a facilitator. However, after the event, desired outcomes are achieved not by those in power, but rather by the delegates working together to implement agreed-upon solutions

DOI: 10.4018/978-1-4666-0074-4.ch013

Copyright © 2012, IGI Global. Copying or distributing in print or electronic forms without written permission of IGI Global is prohibited.

or recommendations that have been determined during the conference.

In order to understand the approach further, this chapter sets out to define the terms 'Search Conference', and 'Future Search Conference', their derivation and how they have been applied in a variety of settings. This is followed by details of how to set up and run such an event, illustrated by a case study of a FS that was organized to assist town planning for the next 25 years. Having presented the case, it is then reassessed in the context of running such an activity on-line.

BACKGROUND

What Are Search Conferences and What Are Their Origins?

A Search Conference has been defined as a: "… social event convened to create a collaborative picture of probable and desirable futures and to develop plans to move towards that desirable future" (Williams, 1984, p. 29), or a "…carefully planned, custom-designed, participative event embedded in a longer process of planning and improvement. Its main focus is to create ideas for future action that are to be implemented by the participants" (Hurworth, 2006, 2007). As Large adds: "This approach can lead to learning, purposeful action, commitment, creative involvement and ownership because people are working together on what matters to them" (Large, 1998a, p. 63).

Origins and History of the Search Conference

The Search Conference was originally conceived in the late 1950s by Fred Emery and his wife Merrelyn (both from Australia) working in conjunction with Eric Trist (from the Tavistock Institute in London). This trio's work in socio-technical systems, open systems theory and participative planning made an important contribution to management

thinking. Their ideas came at a time when organisations were finding it difficult to drive changes from the top and were seeking to engage larger stakeholder groups in future planning.

Fred and Eric first implemented a Search Conference to assist with the merger of the Bristol and Siddely Aircraft Companies. The SC process allowed the two companies to merge successfully, as well as the creation of new engine ideas and the concept of an airbus (Emery, 1995; Weisbord, 1992). Next, Fred experimented and worked further on the rationalization of conflict, which involved working to find common ground, rather than tackling conflict head on.

The SC approach then 'took off' in places such as Scandinavia, Australia and North America where is it was used by companies such as Microsoft and Hewlett Packard. Back in Australia, Fred and Merrelyn continued to develop the SC further, and applied the method within a variety of planning contexts, such as local communities, the public service and companies.

Meanwhile, Marvin Weisbord and Sandra Janoff developed their own version of the technique called the Future Search Conference (FS) (Weisbord & Janoff, 1995) which tends to involve larger numbers and leaves less time for action planning. For instance, during the 1970s the latter authors assembled as many as 300 people in order to work with a vertical slice of an entire community.

Since then, various other types of Search Conferences have evolved (see Crombie, 1984, who describes four versions). Also, in Australia and elsewhere, the terms 'Search Conference' and 'Future Search Conference' have become blended, or at least blurred, so that conferences often contain elements of both approaches.

Main Features of Search Conferences Held Face-to-Face

Some particular features of traditional search conferences held face-to face are that they:

- act as an agent of social change;
- are held in a retreat-like atmosphere, usually away from the participants' normal environment
- last two to three days;
- involve 20-50 people for a Search Conference (but can be as many as several hundred for Future Search Conferences);
- the majority attending should be those who are less powerful and would be most affected by any decisions made (e.g., citizens, recipients of services/programs, factory workers or marginalised groups). The remainder may be those who can contribute useful opinion, such as those with related interests, policy makers or government representatives. However, selection is dependent on the nature and purpose of the task;
- involves a democratic process where there is planning for the people by the people;
- expects participants to learn from the process and to act on the outcomes;
- comprises a mixture of small group and plenary sessions;
- starts and ends with a plenary session;
- involves a variety of processes such as small group discussion, drawing and plenary group work;
- generates material used in later reports;
- results in collective action planning with decisions made about who is to do what, when and with what resources. This work may result in the setting up of sub-groups to work on any following actions that have been determined.

The Role of the Search Conference Facilitator

Another key feature of Search Conferences is that the event requires a facilitator. This person has a number of roles to perform before, and during, the conference. Indeed, the facilitator needs to be involved from the outset and to possess certain qualities. S/he needs to:

- work with the planning group beforehand;
- help to design the conference structure;
- run activities within the conference;
- manage and ensure an optimal learning environment;
- manage large group dynamics;
- be able to build up a strong sense of trust between all those involved;
- possess strong time management skills.

However, quite often the facilitator takes along an assistant to help with general organisation or with small group activities. Importantly, though, a facilitator needs to manage all aspects of the conference environment (such as physical and emotional aspects, as well as coping with any emergence of conflict) while not intruding on the content. Another key aspect of the facilitator role is that s/he should be an 'outsider' with no vested interests and so is truly independent.

Tasks within Search Conferences

Within any search conference there are several major tasks to accomplish, but basically it starts with a wide perspective to explore possibilities and then narrows to produce key strategic visions. Therefore, whatever time has been allocated is usually split into three components:

(Day) 1. *Discovery of current trends in the environment and any recent changes*. This is often dealt with first, as participants are likely to find the present relatively easy to deal with. Common questions at this stage are: Where are we now? What are our existing goals, resources and constraints?

(Day) 2. *A review of the past*. Typical questions posed at this point are: What has shaped the present? What has made us what we are? What do we need to preserve?

(Day) 3. *The creation of visions for the future and determining actions about how to reach the vision.* Questions at this final stage might be: What do we want to achieve? What do we want to become? These are then tested against existing constraints before the group determines: how to implement strategic goals; who is going to implement them; and who is going to undertake any associated work.

Through scanning the broad environment holistically in this way (including examining historical, political, economic and technological factors, as well as values), those involved learn about their environment and, when informed, can make judgments and generate recommendations for the future.

Search Conference Applications

Applications for Search Conferences have been wide-ranging but have often been set in a planning context. For instance, SCs and FSs have been run to address issues in: regional; health system; corporate; public sector; and environmental planning. However, they have also been employed: for product development; to solve industrial issues; to plan for economic development; and to assist with policymaking. So, for example, over the last fifteen years or so, they have been used within the domains of:

- *Community development*: as a way to make communities work better (Large, 1998a);
- *The Environment*: as a means to engage local Canadian communities in wildlife management planning (Schusler, 2002) and to address environmental issues in a rapidly growing town (Shweitz, 1996);
- *Business*: as a participative approach to: plan a merger (Large, 1998b); enable company strategic planning (Cabana, 1995); and to redesign work practices (Axelrod, 1993);

- *Education:* as a way to involve a local community in college planning (Casolara, Haynes, & McPheeters, 1999; Quereau, 1995); effect educational change (Bailey, 1992); explore how the Aboriginal community and TAFE (Technical and Further Education) sector might work together better (Hurworth, 2007); and to plan school library services across a state (Baldwin, 1995);
- *Health*: to establish community food security (McCullin, 2002); find common ground and action in relation to repetitive strain injuries (Polanyi, 2001); improve the health and situation of homeless men (Hurworth, 2007); build healthier communities; and to determine the future of dietetics education and credentialing (Parks, 1995).

Having presented some background in relation to both Search Conferences and Future Search Conferences I would now like to present a detailed example of a Future Search that is linked to urban planning. First of all there will be a description of what actually happened face-to-face.[1] Then I progress to consider how such an activity might be replicated using information technologies.

A CASE STUDY OF A FACE-TO-FACE FUTURE SEARCH CONFERENCE: 'BENDIGO +25'; INVOLVING CITIZENS TO PLAN THE FUTURE OF A REGIONAL CITY

Context and Rationale

The case presented below describes a community Future Search Conference, held over two and a half days, in Bendigo, Australia. Bendigo, lies 150 kms North of Melbourne and is the second largest regional municipality in the State of Victoria. It is also the fastest growing regional city with a population of over 100,000. Consequently, it is making the transition from being a large rural town to a nationally recognised, provincial city.

The reason for holding the FS was that the City of Greater Bendigo Council had moved from perceiving the local population merely as rate payers to valuing them as customers with rights and ideas. So, up until then (2005), most strategic planning had occurred behind the scenes, in Council offices; the results of which were then sent out for comment. The latter way of operating, therefore, had largely been about the 'inside directing the outside', leaving the community feeling that it hadn't been consulted enough. With its new way of viewing their local community, the Council now wished to find a way of bringing residents and Council together, in order to strengthen connections and find ways forward for the City.

The idea of running a Future Search Conference was introduced by Council's Chief Executive Officer (CEO) because he knew of the technique and had contacts with experienced, potential facilitators. The aim of the event was to consider the future of the city over the next 25 years; hence the title; *'Bendigo +25'*. As the CEO emphasised it was to be "all about giving everyone a chance to get involved in the development of a vision and values that will guide future directions and decision-making for the region" (Rance, 2005).

Planning the Future Search Conference

Setting Up a Steering Committee

A small Steering Committee was set up by Council to plan the Search Conference. Those asked to sit on this Committee were some of those who could be affected by the outcomes (such as members of the Council, a water company, local businesses and residents from the local community). So, it became an important way of engaging initial interest from a variety of community agencies.

The Committee held four meetings over several months, where they discussed which groups from

the community needed to attend the FS. They also developed a strategy for recruiting citizens for the event, as well as determining the brand name (Bendigo +25).

Determining Areas of Interest to be Covered at the Conference

Areas of interest to be talked about within the FS were to reflect the whole community system. These were determined by the Steering Committee and comprised:

* Health
* Education and Training
* Community Safety and Wellbeing
* Business and Economic Wellbeing
* Sport and Recreation
* Culture and Lifestyle
* Built Environment
* Natural Environment
* Rural and Regional Matters
* Governance

The Budget

The Council allocated $25,000 (Australian) for the task.

Appointment of a Facilitator

An independent facilitator was required to lead and manage the conference (i.e., it was not to be someone influenced by local issues or who might have a hidden agenda). Council looked at a number of possibilities before making the final selection but it was recognised that:

There's an art to letting people have discussion and if they get stuck not to step in and 'unstick them'. That's the thing with the Search Conference – allowing people to get stuck and providing a safe space for people to work through it. However, at the same time the facilitator has to keep the ball rolling unobtrusively — this needs someone particularly skilled (Council Officer, personal communication).

The person appointed was eminently appropriate as he had a background in community development, been a former general manager of a City Council and was experienced in the Future Search Conference process. He had also been the chairman of 'Tasmania Together', a project that provided Tasmanians with a say in the island's long-term future. As a consequence, he was described as being able to: "help groups move from uncertainty to purpose" (Rance, 2005).

He attended some of the final meetings where he outlined how the FS event itself could be organised and also put forward various activities that could be introduced to create and maintain interest for participants over several days.

The facilitator also said that he would bring along an assistant to act as a scribe (so there would a daily record of events which could be referred to for a report that had been requested by Council) as well as to assist delegates during exercises.

Advertising and Initial Recruitment

In order to determine who should attend the conference, Council used a database of community groups and leaders. These people were contacted by mail and enclosed was a printed flyer that explained about: *Bendigo +25*; the advantages of working together to create a shared direction for the future; and the need for community feedback.

In addition, there was support from ABC (Australian Broadcasting Commission) radio which ran daily stories and interviews about Bendigo's future, for six weeks. Interested listeners were also urged to sign up for the event on the Council's web site and to watch out for brochures about the project around the town.

The Council also undertook a community survey, in which they asked people to take part in the FS and explained that it was open to all. In addition, the Steering Committee contacted potential attendees through their personal networks.

Selecting 100 People to Attend

As this was a Future Search Conference which can accommodate large numbers, it was determined that there should be 100 in the group so that there would be ten people in each of the interest groups listed earlier. This was because Council wanted all systems and major sub-systems to take part (i.e., not just 'Health' but all aspects of health from primary care to cancer services). They also wanted to involve a wide range of ordinary citizens.

In the end, about 150 people registered, but this was considered too many. Thus the Steering Committee and others helped determine the best mix of people to attend, in order to arrive at the desired number. This was achieved by creating an applicant matrix upon which demographic details (such as age) and particular area of interest were noted. Drawing this up showed where there were gaps or oversubscription. So, for example, it became clear that there were too many in the over 50 age-group, while there were difficulties filling some of the particular interest groups. Any people that could not be accommodated were then invited to workshops which were to be held after the conference.

Finding a Venue

Decisions about where to hold the event were made by Council, guided by the facilitators who provided a set of criteria. Although in many conferences people are taken right away from their usual environment, it was decided to hold the event within the City. This was so the venue would be accessible to everybody and not become a barrier to attendance. Furthermore, to encourage participation, the Council were happy to provide transport and child care.

Eventually, a sports club's hall was chosen for the SC site, as Council were looking for somewhere that:

- was large enough for 100 people to sit in a circle;
- possessed good acoustics;
- felt informal;
- was airy and full of light;
- contained plenty of wall space, so that several displays could be mounted simultaneously'
- possessed an external area so that people could sit outside during breaks;
- had car parking facilities; and
- had a community feel about it, as the project was about community and grassroots activity.

Catering

Local shops were asked to provide refreshments each day. Meanwhile, members of Rotary International served the food and cleaned up afterwards. This was considered appropriate because it allowed other volunteers from the community to be involved.

Resources to Support the Conference

Some pre-conference reading was sent out to conference delegates. This included:

- A message from the Mayor;
- Community survey results (In just over 6 weeks replies had come in from more than 500 respondents. Residents were asked about what they liked most about the region and what concerned them about the locality);
- An overview of the *Bendigo +25* project which explained the need to achieve a development plan for the next 25 years.

The Conference Process

Overall Activity

As described earlier, citizens with particular interests worked through the Future Search Conference process over a three-day period. However, the order suggested earlier was changed a little in that there was more emphasis on the past at the beginning, before moving on to the present.

In order to achieve conference aims, participants took part in: a mix of exercises within their own interest group; activities in plenary sessions; and finally worked in action planning teams. Specifics of how activities were organised day-by-day are set out below:

Day 1

As delegates arrived they were given coloured name tags (gold, red, blue, orange, black, yellow, brown, pink, green and purple) in order to identify their special interest group.

They then assembled in these interest groups and the ice was broken by discussing an artefact that each had been asked to bring along to symbolise the past or future of Bendigo. Next, they were asked to select one item from each group to present to the entire conference. Examples included: a set of scales from the goldfields (which reflected the past Gold Rush in the 1850s and balance for the future); a twig of an iron bark tree (which needs a great deal of water to grow so it becomes problematic in times of drought); and a traditional Chinese costume (a souvenir from the Chinese working on the goldfields but which also reflected the City's ethnic diversity today). These items were then displayed in the 'Gallery'—a wall area where items could be stored and people could see them throughout the FS.

The conference then went on to focus on the past, during which a joint picture of values and history was developed. To assist with this, notes on past key personal, local and global events, as well as major turning points, were kept. These were discussed in groups before being transferred to timelines drawn on a 'Past Wall'. From this, it was possible to identify common themes while enabling participants to find common ground. Consequently, by means of such an activity, delegates could see that they shared much in common.

Those attending the FS had also been asked to bring a newspaper article, which dealt with a current issue or trend affecting Bendigo. First, these were talked about in the special interest groups before a particularly pertinent one was presented to the entire conference. Each selected article was then pasted on a wall to create a 'mind map'. After that, people met in their groups to discuss emerging trends before identifying three issues of particular importance to their group. Discussion then progressed to what could be done to overcome each issue.

Interestingly, issues raised were not only associated with the special interest group themes but included matters associated with: population change; housing development; the arts; tourism; embracing diversity; climate change; rural living; ecological issues; IT; community services; energy; and community safety. So, the first day ended with a series of trends and issues to be resolved.

Day 2

On the second day, people were given seven dots to 'vote' on the key issues indicated on the mind map. Through such an activity, delegates could see that decisions and priorities were starting to emerge.

Back in their interest groups, participants next had to determine three hard questions raised by the mind map that might have to be answered by the end of the conference. This was followed by being asked to make a list of; 'prouds and sorries'—i.e., positive things that had been occurring in the region or what could have been done better. This was a way to acknowledge that some poor decisions and choices had been made

in the past. It also enabled people to 'let go' and to move beyond complaining and blaming.

In the afternoon, those attending the conference moved to thinking about the future. They had to visualise an ideal Bendigo, 25 years hence, that would be feasible, desirable and motivating, and that they would be proud to pass on to future generations. This resulted in some 'creative dreaming' with the result that presentations entailed skits, poetry and songs.[2]

At the same time, participants were still noting trends related to the future. These were written on small pieces of paper and stuck on the wall according to themes. Again, this activity revealed the common ground shared by the whole conference, for the future of the town.

The previous activity was repeated with respect to values needed to underpin future directions. Again ideas were posted on the wall, grouped, named and voted on. Themes included: care for environment; community spirit; creativity; democracy; innovation; trust; liveability; inclusion'; pride; tolerance; spirituality; family values; and leadership. These were then prioritised once more. By this time there was some tension, as the choices were likely to affect outcomes.

Day 3

By the third day all the data had been collected and priority lists had been drawn up. But now delegates were asking: *'Are these the right things? Should certain things go ahead?'*

The major part of the morning was allocated to working on vision statements and these were created from the themes that encapsulated desired future directions and values. This work was carried out in the small interest groups, and again the results were presented to the entire conference in a plenary session.

The final activity was to devise a set of action plans. First the key directions were laid out on the floor and for each, certain questions were posed such as:

What could be advanced in the area?

What could be achieved in one year?

What could be achieved in 20 years?

What would need to change?

Which participants would commit to particular issues?

The last question was the hardest aspect—to get attendees to commit to follow-up action. Nevertheless, many people volunteered and names were collected for each area of interest.

Results were then fed back to the conference, actions were set and work groups formed for the following areas: youth; governance; education; transport; health and well being; the arts; tourism and hospitality; the museum; heritage; renewable energy; industry and innovation; water; diversity; environment; leisure and recreation; primary production; and the disadvantaged.

The day ended with everyone sitting in a circle so that they had the chance to make some concluding remarks. Some had learned a great deal (one of the major aims of a Search Conference) with the result that people made comments such as:

- *I found the views of others eye opening.*
- *I'm amazed at the number of issues involved in running a community.*

while others affirmed the need to work together post-conference:

- *This is the start, not the end of the process*
- *Everyone needs to take the plan forward.*

Yet others had altered their point of view as:

- *I arrived sceptical and am leaving optimistic!*

Post Conference

A week after the SC, detailed notes were sent to each delegate and then Council worked with interested parties to draw up plans.

In addition, a series of workshops was run for those who could not be accommodated at the conference. They were run at various times of day (morning, afternoon and evening) in order to attract different types of resident. Eighty people attended one of the four, two-hour sessions and in the process confirmed many of the conference outcomes. They also discussed contentious issues that would need to be noted by the action groups later.

Another workshop was held for Council staff—as they had not been allowed to take part in the Search Conference.

The Benefits of the Bendigo + 25 Search Conference

Benefits of the FS were articulated by both Council staff and the facilitators. They felt it:

..got people to think what is really important, so it was powerful. It united people round common ground and nothing came out of left field. It was also really amazing to see how committed people were to their community (Council Officer, personal communication).

Meanwhile, the facilitators felt that by running a FS, one can:

- obtain a better understanding of what's important to the local population;
- understand trends and issues and how they affect the community;
- use community values to develop a consistent approach to future planning;
- make long-term decisions using a big picture; and
- work together towards the future.

After the conference, Council members considered that the event had been a success as it:

- led to improved good will and community pride;
- resulted in greater understanding and respect between parties attending;
- brought together a broad-cross section of the community representing all walks of life and each had an equal voice;
- empowered the community as the ensuing Community Plan provided a powerful mandate for the community, business and council to act together;
- allowed the community a sense of ownership of the Project as they had all contributed to the City of Greater Bendigo's Council Plan;
- created new relationships, partnerships and networks between community members, groups, businesses and organisations.

THE POTENTIAL FOR CONDUCTING A SEARCH CONFERENCE THROUGH THE WORLD WIDE WEB (WWW)

As we have seen from the detailed case study, a Search Conference can be a huge undertaking. So might it be worthwhile considering running one using the World Wide Web? If so, what advantages could be gained, what would need to be considered and how could it be achieved? With these questions in mind, the next section goes on to consider the possibilities and challenges that such queries present, before thinking about how the *Bendigo +25* project could be tackled via an on-line environment.

A Rationale for Using the Web as a "Space" to Run a Conference

As far as can be ascertained, no-one has attempted to run a Search Conference on-line; yet in many ways it seems a potentially exciting forum, pregnant with possibility. Introducing the use of the Web environment for such an exercise would also bring to fruition Berners-Lee's (the originator of the WWW in the late 1980s) dream of "making it a collaborative medium where we all meet and read and write" (Carvin, 2005). He foresaw the potential to build a vast web of linked information so that data, experience and talents can be shared (which is needed during Search Conferences).

At that time though, users of the Web tended to be mere readers/consumers of information. However, this is no longer the case, because we can all be "collaborators in the creation of large storehouses of information. In the process we can learn much about our world and ourselves" (Richardson, 2010, p. 3), and this is what is meant to occur during an SC or FS. Indeed, this seems to be quite feasible as the Pew Internet and American Life Project (Lenhart, Fallowas, & Horrigan, 2004) found that 44% of adult Internet users had used it to publish their thoughts, respond to others, post pictures and share files (all potential tasks within Search Conferences). Furthermore, the ability to mount text, photos and video is also opening doors for interaction. Participants can comment on material, ask further questions or even edit what is written. By including people in these processes, the Web opens up all kinds of opportunities for widespread participation, which is exactly what a Search Conference demands. It also brings a new transparency—where clients or service recipients can communicate their experiences and ideas with one another. Shirky (2008) also notes that the Web allows interest sub-groups to form (again a requirement of the SC structure): "Newly capable groups are assembling ...These changes will transform the world everywhere, with groups coming together to accomplish something" (Shirky, 2008, p. 3).

POSSIBLE SOFTWARE/TOOLS THAT COULD ALLOW A SEARCH CONFERENCE TO BE RUN ON-LINE

Web Conferencing

Options are growing in relation to how we can communicate and share information via the Web. As yet, there is no one tool that can do everything. However, if dealing with groups such as the public (who will have varying levels of computer literacy) whatever is employed will need to be simple and require minimal support.

So, what is available that fits the bill? One idea could be to use a Web Conferencing package. A good example is Adobe *Acrobat Connect Pro* (ACP). This program is particularly accessible because it is: a) based on a certain technology (Flash) that is installed on 98% of internet-connected computers; and b) boasts an exceptionally low bandwidth consumption rate.

ACP also combines features that allow organizations and individuals to discuss or collaborate in a secure, virtual environment. Thus it is able to integrate audio, video, and collaborative features so that you can: telephone and video conference (so participants can see and hear each other); present material through 'whiteboards'; keep notes; lead sessions; interact with delegates; (through streaming); instigate and manage breakout groups; and move between the breakout group and the whole group. As a reviewer elucidated:

Adobe Connect Pro creates a conference room that audiences, hosts and participants can access through a unique URL. There, slideshows and presentations can be given with hosts leading audio commentary. You can also delegate different responsibilities and tasks to designated parties

in order to answer particular questions (http://web-conferencing-servicecs.toptenreviews.com).

Other attractive features, when considering running Search Conferences, are that ACP has a registration page and the system keeps full logs of meetings including data, time and source of information. As noted above, it also possesses a 'whiteboard' feature where people can draw and compile images. It also offers a mechanism whereby people can vote (for as we have seen, voting was used several times during the case study FS).

Another useful attribute of ACP is that it can be used synchronously (where all are on-line together) or asynchronously (which allows individuals time for reflection) or a mixture of both modes of operation.

Supplementary Tools

Web conferencing software can also be supplemented or supported by other tools available on-line such as:

- *Weblogs (Blogs)*. These are easily created and updated Websites that permit author(s) to create written material on the Internet from any Internet connection. Blogs allow an individual or a group to post text, hyperlinks, images and multimedia. This medium can also be interactive, so would allow the conference facilitator and participants to hold conversations or to add information forming a highly interactive discussion board. It would also, for example, be possible for individuals to present information or ideas.
- *A Wiki*. This is a collaborative Web space where anyone can add or edit content that has been contributed. For example, in reference to the case described, this could be used to maintain facts about Bendigo and its region, e.g., demographic information;

Table 1. Benefits and Issues Associated with Planning a Search Conference On-Line

PLANNING		
Face-to-Face	**Advantage On-Line**	**On-Line Issue**
Steering Committee Comes Together to Discuss Planning	Can meet via Web-conferencing Can be located at dispersed sites Don't have to travel Can fit in with working day Can write ideas, e.g., for determining areas of interest on the ACP 'whiteboard'	
Decision on SC Length (2-3 days)	Could still be carried out on consecutive days Time more flexible—can be organised over a number of days/weeks	If 2-3 days, concentrating on screen for long periods would be difficult for some Difficult keeping people on task
Selection of Facilitator		Not only has to have ability to run a SC but has to possess extra IT skills to deal with Web conferencing
Number of Participants	Potentially limitless theoretically	Probably needs to be 20-50, otherwise difficult to manage
Venue, Catering, Provision of transport / child care	Unnecessary, so more cost-effective	
Resources	Can put up PDF documents on ACP or mount on a Wiki or send as Email attachments. Saves on postage	

business matters; arts and cultural events; history, etc. Information could be added by any of the conference delegates under the areas of special interest. It can also form a 'display area'. So the virtual gallery of artefacts and newspaper articles (referred to in the face-to-face SC description) could be stored and displayed here. A Wiki can also be password protected if desired.

- *Really Simple Syndication (RSS).* This is a technology that allows people to subscribe to "feeds" of content that is created on the Internet, i.e., the content is sent to the reader instead of the reader seeking information. So, when considering the case presented, material about Bendigo from either Blogs or traditional media such as newspapers or magazines could be obtained. It might also be possible to receive alerts from the Greater Bendigo Council regarding recent reports or statistics.

The advantage of these three tools is that material can be added to at any time and remain available post-conference.

COMPARISON BETWEEN CARRYING OUT A SEARCH CONFERENCE FACE-TO-FACE AND ON-LINE

Next, I am going to imagine how the face-to-face SC elements already described, might be translated into an on-line environment. I also point out some of the issues that could arise.

Planning Comparison

First, let us look at a comparison of the planning component; both face-to-face and on-line while noting some of the advantages and disadvantages when undertaking this task via web-conferencing (Table 1).

As we know, a Steering Committee has to be set up and in a conventional scenario, meets at a central location. This is unnecessary in an on-line version, as meetings can be held via ACP and the Committee can join in from their homes or offices, making it much more convenient for (often) busy people. Also, any ideas can be recorded on the whiteboard.

Furthermore, a great advantage of an on-line SC is that there is no need to find a venue or provide refreshments—so both time and money are saved. This is in contrast to a face-to-face SC, where an inordinate amount of resources can be spent dealing with these aspects.

The Committee also has to determine the length of the conference. Normally, in a face-to-face conference, the event runs over two or three days in order to follow Search Conference structure. This length of time would probably be too long to remain engaged on-line. However, for Web-based SCs there can be greater flexibility regarding how long the SC can run for. For instance, the 'event' could occur over an increased number of days or take place week-by-week for a certain period. Such arrangements also allow both the facilitator and delegates to work in a number of ways, i.e., synchronously or asynchronously. However, with any breaks between 'meetings' the facilitator is likely to have to send regular reminders in order to keep people engaged. Also 'attendance' is likely to dwindle if computer tasks take place over too long a period, or if tasks begin to feel repetitive. It may also be difficult to keep up momentum.

Another job for the Steering Committee to carry out during the planning stage is to choose a facilitator. This may be more difficult than for a face-to-face SC, because not only will the person selected require knowledge about how to run such an event, but needs extra computer facilitation skills to cope with any difficulties that may arise with the software.

The number of people to be involved in the SC also has to be determined. While theoretically, any number of people can come into a virtual confer-

ence, the reality is that large numbers working/meeting on-screen could be very difficult to manage. Therefore, it is probably advisable to have a maximum of 50 people.

Lastly, resources and reading to inform participants before the SC begins normally have to be packed up and sent out to delegates in advance. In an on-line situation this becomes much simpler because you can mount PDF files on ACP or create a Wiki using any information that is to be shared. This makes material available to all those to be involved and saves on postage. It also has the advantage of allowing extra items to be added at any time during or after the conference.

Implementation Comparison

Next, all the FS tasks outlined earlier would need to be implemented on-line. When trying to replicate face-to-face activities, useful features of the ACP and Web tools come into play (Table 2). For example in connection with Bendigo+25 you could:

- use the whiteboard facility to create/draw a 'Past Wall', a vertical timeline and a mind map;
- introduce the breakout mechanism for special interest discussion in small groups
- open up discussion to the whole conference;
- keep notes on ideas during the event;
- create lists, e.g., of those who volunteer to implement action plans;
- use the voting facility (e.g., to vote on major issues/trends);
- mount documents on a Wiki or a Blog, e.g., the newspaper articles or pictures of artefacts;
- maintain a Wiki to store a record of the all ACP sessions to reflect upon later; or use a Wiki or a blog to debrief post conference (Table 2).

Table 2. A Comparison of Search Conference Implementation Face-to Face and On-Line for the Bendigo +25 Project

FACE-TO FACE TASKS	ON-LINE EQUIVALENT
(DAY 1)	
Given coloured name tags	Allocate colours which would be used for all interest group written entries
Discussion of Artefacts in Special Interest Group	Take pictures of artefacts and mount them on a 'Past Wall' on the whiteboard ACP or on a Wiki for people to see Discuss in ACP breakout groups
Choose one Item	Use voting facility in ACP
Present to whole group	Open ACP site to whole group to discuss
Recording a) the past b) values	Keep notes in ACP Draw timeline on the ACP whiteboard
Work on newspaper articles depicting trend or Issue	Mount documents on a Wiki or Blog for discussion
Choose an Item from each area of Interest	Use voting facility in ACP
Present to whole group and create a Mind Map	Open ACP site for whole group to discuss Use whiteboard facility to create a 'mind map' and create themes
Choose 3 trends of importance to each group	Discuss in ACP breakout group and use voting facility
(DAY 2)	
Vote on key issues	Use voting facility in ACP
Work in interest groups to determine 'Hard Questions to be Answered' by the end of the SC	Use breakout facility for area of interest discussion Keep notes in ACP
Interest groups make lists of 'Prouds' and 'Sorries'	Make list in ACP
Interest groups list key features of an Ideal City in 25 years	Make list in ACP Use creative ways to depict results, e.g., poems, cartoons Create PDF documents for others to see and discuss
Future trends and value statements	Note trends on ACP whiteboard and vote on using voting facility
DAY 3	
Interest groups work on vision statements	Create from list noted on the whiteboard
Presentation of statements to whole group	Create document and discuss
Devise action plans	Write key directions on ACP whiteboard Discuss key questions about what could be changed/improved
Create list of names of those committed to particular action	Facilitator to use attendance list facility
POST CONFERENCE	
Conference notes sent out a week later	Record whole ACP session and store in a Wiki so participants can reflect on the event later

Summary of Advantages and Disadvantages of Using the Web for a Search Conference

Some advantages regarding the use of the World Wide Web have been outlined earlier. However, there are a number of other pragmatic reasons for

using on-line software and tools to run Search Conferences. For example, an on-line environment:

Deals with geographic barriers so that it:

- overcomes the wide dispersal of some populations;

- removes the need for travel or the acquisition of a venue;
- allows participants to interact over large distances at a fraction of the cost.

Enables certain members of the population to take part when they might not otherwise be able to so that it:

- has the potential to expand the pool of project participants;
- enables the richness of ideas that comes with group interaction to emerge from people who are unable to come together easily face-to-face, e.g., the ill, disabled, frail, carers or the housebound;
- encourages busy professionals (such as GPs, bankers, CEOs, judges, etc.) to take part in group exercises.

Allows activities to take place at any time with the result that many activities can be:

- fitted into a working day;
- carried out beyond working hours such as during weekends, early mornings or late at night.

Can operate in various ways so that:

- activities/discussions can take place synchronously (live) or asynchronously (giving people time to reflect), or both modes can be used.

However, there are a number of issues to be considered. First, using conferencing software presumes that potential delegates have access to computers. This may not always be the case. For instance, it would be very difficult if SCs were to be held to improve the lives of the homeless, remote rural populations or the elderly, as these are groups less likely to have access to technology. Furthermore, for packages such as ACP, a

fast Internet connection is needed and this is not always available.

Closely aligned to access is the degree of computer literacy possessed by individuals. Those taking part on-line need to know how to use the technology and be able to respond to facilitator requests to carry out tasks using the features within a software package. For those that possess little, or no, computer literacy, such requirements remove the possibility of taking part. Indeed, even those who are quite 'computer savvy' may find using a new system involves a steep learning curve (as the technology is not always easy to use).

In regard to aspects of Search Conferences themselves, there is another set of issues to consider. For instance, will it be possible for a sense of trust to be built up between participants when they are contributing from afar? Can a sense of cohesion be formed?—especially if the exercise is carried out over a period of time. Certainly, it would require a great deal of hard work on the part of the facilitator to achieve this.

Therefore, those contemplating running a Search Conference or a Future Search Conference will have to consider the advantages and disadvantages of each mode of implementation and make a choice, based on the particular context. One possibility of course, is that there could be a combination of the two, i.e., both face-to-face or on-line. For instance, you could undertake the planning on-line and then hold the event face-to-face, or run the conference face-to-face and then use technology to keep in touch with, and encourage, those who are planning and implementing future actions.

CONCLUSION

This chapter has discussed the potential for using a Search Conference as an urban planning tool. Using a case study of the project *Bendigo +25*, we have seen that a traditional face-to-face event could occur entirely, or partly, on-line, as there are many advantages including: greater flexibility; the ability to overcome geographic barriers; and greater cost-effectiveness.

Nevertheless, currently, there are still issues associated with computer access, computer literacy and the level of software sophistication — as well as the ability of the facilitator to manage the technology, maintain cohesion and build up trust. As time progresses, however, many of these issues are likely to be overcome and then running or participating in a (Future) Search Conference on-line is should become simpler and more commonplace.

REFERENCES

Axelrod, D. (1993). Using the conference model for work redesign. *Journal for Quality and Participation, 16*(7), 58–62.

Bailey, D. (1992). The future search conference as a vehicle for educational change: A shared vision for Will Rogers Middle School, Sacramento, California. *The Journal of Applied Behavioral Science, 28*(4), 520–534. doi:10.1177/0021886392284005

Baldwin, M. (1995). A future search conference: The future of information services in K-12 schools in Washington State. *Emergency Librarian, 22*(5), 20–22.

Cabana, S. (1995). Motorola: Strategic planning and the search conference. *Journal for Quality and Participation, 18*(4), 22–31.

Carvin, A. (2005). *Tim Berners-Lee: Weaving a semantic web*. Retrieved from http:www.digitaldivide.net/articles/view.php?ArticleID=20

Casolara, W. M., Haynes, C. E., & McPheeters, J. (1999). Involving the community in college planning: The future search conference. *Community College Journal of Research and Practice, 23*(2), 193–205. doi:10.1080/106689299265016

Crombie, A. (1985). The nature and types of search conferences. *International Journal of Lifelong Learning, 4*(1), 3–33.

Flower, J. (1995). Future search: Power tool for building healthier communities. *The Healthcare Forum Journal, 38*(3), 34–42.

Green, T. D., Brown, A., & Robinson, L. (2008). *Making the most of the Web in your classroom*. Thousand Oaks, CA: Sage.

Hurworth, R. (2006, September). *The use of (future) search conferences as a tool for two community development type exercises in Victoria*. Paper presented at the Australasian Evaluation Society International Conference, Darwin, NT, Australia.

Hurworth, R. (2007). The use of (future) search conferences as a qualitative improvement tool. *Qualitative Research Journal, 7*(2), 52–62. doi:10.3316/QRJ0702052

Large, M. (1998a). Using search conferences for building, learning, planning and implementing communities that work. *The Learning Organization, 4*(3), 190–114.

Large, M. (1998b). Using the search conference for planning a merger participatively. *Career Development International, 3*(2), 62–66. doi:10.1108/13620439810207554

Lenhart, A., Fallows, D., & Horrigan, J. (2004). *Online activities and pursuits*. Retrieved from http://wwwpewtrusts.org/our_work_detail/aspx?id=50

McCullum, C. (2002). Use of a participatory planning process as a way to build community food security. *Journal of the American Dietetic Association, 102*(7), 962–967. doi:10.1016/S0002-8223(02)90220-8

Parks, S. C. (1995). Challenging the future of dietetics education and credentialing—dialogue, discovery and directions: A summary of the 1994 Future Search Conference. *Journal of the American Dietetic Association*, 95(5), 598–606: doi:10.1016/S0002-8223(95)00165-4

Polyani, M. (2001). Towards common ground and action on repetitive strain injuries: An assessment of a future search conference. *The Journal of Applied Behavioral Science*, 37(4), 465. doi:10.1177/0021886301374005

Quereau, T. (1995). *Creating our future together: A summary report from the future search conference series for Austin Community College* (ERIC Document Reproduction Service ED396791).

Rance, C. (2005, April 30). In Bendigo the people have spoken (p. 24). The Age.

Richardson, W. (2010). *Blogs, Wikis, Podcasts and Other Powerful Web Tools for Classrooms* (3rd ed.). Thousand Oaks, CA: Corwin Sage.

Schusler, T. M. (2002). Engaging local communities in wildlife management area planning: An evaluation of the Lake Ontario Islands search conference. *Wildlife Society Bulletin*, 30(4), 1226–1237.

Schweitz, R. (1996). Searching for a quality environment. *Journal for Quality and Participation*, 36–40.

Shirky, C. (2008). *Here comes everybody: The power of organizing without organizations*. New York, NY: Penguin.

Williams, P. (1984). Consulting the aged—A search conference approach. *Australian Journal of Adult Education*, 24(3), 29–40.

ADDITIONAL READING

De Nitish, R. (1981). Search conference and conscientization process in building institutions. In *R. de Nitish, Alternative designs of human organizations*. New Delhi: Sage.

Emery, M. (1994). *The search conference in the USA today: clarifying some confusions*. Available from: www.sustainablefutureplanning.com.au/adapter/item/id/9

Emery, M. (1995). The power of community search conferences. *Journal for Quality and Participation*, (December): 1–10.

Emery, M. (1999). *Searching: The theory and practice of making cultural change*. Amsterdam, Philadelphia: John Benjamin.

Emery, M., & Purser, R. E. (1996). *The search conference*. San Francisco: Jossey Bass.

ENDNOTES

[1]   At this point it should be recognised that all search conferences vary in their content and organisation. They do not always follow the 'pure' form as described by the originators. Consequently, they vary in the order of events and in the tasks decided upon. These vary according to the time available, the abilities of the participants and the needs of those organising the conference

[2]   This is not a common feature of FSs but was appropriate for this group of people

Chapter 14
Netnography:
An Assessment of a Novel Research Approach and its Underlying Philosophical Assumptions

Guido Lang
The City University of New York, USA

Stanislav Mamonov
The City University of New York, USA

Karl R. Lang
The City University of New York, USA

ABSTRACT

The advent of the Internet has facilitated many new forms of communication and thus has laid the foundation for new forms of interaction and social organization. The challenges of gaining insight into the social processes that occur in these newly emerging digital spaces require the development of new research approaches and methodologies. Netnography, or Internet ethnography, is one such example. It focuses on gaining cultural insights from virtual community environments and was originally developed for consumer research in the field of marketing, but has since been used in a number of other fields, including urban planning. This chapter examines the philosophical assumptions and specific methods of netnography as a newly emerging research approach. Findings from a qualitative analysis of ten cases of published netnography studies reveal differences in both philosophical assumptions and uses as a research methodology, including the subject of research – community – and the role of the researcher. The chapter closes with some recommendations and a call for future research.

DOI: 10.4018/978-1-4666-0074-4.ch014

INTRODUCTION

The Internet has been transformational with introducing new methods of communication and collaboration. The Internet has brought about numerous new forms of communication – including instant messaging, online forums, blogs, massively multiplayer online gaming environments, and online social networks. The new communication channels show new communication patterns and also lead to the formation of new types of online communities. These communities are enabled and empowered by the new technology, but they also have to wrestle with technology limitations. In many cases the communities evolve language and culture that help manage the tensions and the limitations of electronic communication, which tends to strip most non-verbal cues (posture, tone, eye contact, etc.) from communicative exchanges.

The evolution of new forms of communication, online communities, as well as the associated cultural and linguistic artifacts offers an opportunity to learn about a broad spectrum of research questions, covering a wide range of online communities, from product co-creation in sports oriented online communities to peer-support in plastic surgery related online discussion forums. The development of online communities and new online cultures creates a need for new research methods that are specifically suited for research in this new environment.

Netnography, or online ethnography, is such a new research approach, with its own methodological issues, that is growing in popularity. It was originally developed by Robert Kozinets for consumer research in the field of marketing (Kozinets, 1998), but has since been used in a number of other fields, including urban planning. Netnography applies and adopts traditional ethnographic techniques to the online context, with a particular focus on gaining cultural insights from virtual community environments. Kozinets is frequently cited by studies employing netnographic methodology as a definitive reference on the proper

methodological procedure. However, netnography is not a stand-alone approach but an interpretive research methodology that inherits many philosophical assumptions from ethnography.

The present work examines the origins, critical philosophical assumptions, and specific methods of netnography for the study of cultural issues in online communities. In particular, we report the findings of a qualitative multi-case study using content analysis of published netnographic studies, highlighting the similarities and differences arising from varying philosophical viewpoints. The remainder of the chapter is organized as follows. The next section reviews the genesis of netnography, including the philosophical inheritance from ethnography, as well as recent developments relevant to netnography. The following section explains the method used in our own analysis, including sample case selection and qualitative content analysis. Then we present the results for each study separately, followed by a broader cross-case discussion. Finally, we offer some conclusions and recommendations.

THE GENESIS OF NETNOGRAPHY

The Philosophical Roots of Ethnography

Ethnographies seek to gain insight into communities and cultures. The outcome of an ethnographic study is typically a rich description of the culture under study emphasizing the unique patterns of communications, behavior, and cultural artifacts that are present in the target community. Ethnographies are inherently interpretive from the philosophical point of view. In order to conduct an ethnography, a researcher must immerse herself in the community and become an integral part of it in order to gain an inside view (Tedlock, 2000). Immersion occurs following a cultural entry by the researcher and through prolonged membership that leads to the researcher's acceptance into the community by other members. The acceptance gives the researcher an opportunity to observe and learn about the community and culture without the hindrance of being perceived as an outsider and being treated with distrust and caution. Immersion is central for a researcher's ability to conduct an ethnographic study and one of the criteria for evaluation of ethnographic studies is in fact proof of immersion.

The researcher plays a pivotal role while conducting ethnographic research in that participant-observation is the principle method underlying ethnographic studies. A researcher identifies a community of interest, enters the community and then observes the community from inside in order to gain an understanding of community fabric and culture. The goal of an ethnographic study is in fact twofold. The first is to develop a rich description of the community under study. The second is to conceptualize key observations from a broader perspective in order to offer an integrated account and theoretical perspective of the observations that are derived from the collected data and observed patterns. The following discussion focuses on Kozinets' original (1998) work on netnography because it has been the most widely applied. However, more recently there have been some updates on issues and recommendations, discussed in Kozinets (2010).

The Origins of Netnography

Kozinets (1997) was among the first researchers to conduct an ethnographic study online and is credited with the development of the methodology. The initial study was a part of a broader offline ethnographic study that focused on exploring the culture surrounding avid fans of *The X-Files* television series. While studying the consumer culture centered on key themes developed by the TV show, Kozinets discovered that a significant amount of the community interaction was happening online and thus the researcher followed the community members online and in the process had to adapt

and evolve the traditional ethnographic methodology. Kozinets (1998) presents a methodological summary of lessons learned through the experience of conducting several netnographic studies by the author. Despite his more recent works on netnography (Kozinets, 2002, 2007, 2010), these are still among the most frequently cited references in published netnographic studies.

Kozinets (1998) defines netnography as the process of producing a "written account resulting from fieldwork studying the cultures and communities that emerge from online, computer mediated, or Internet-based communications, where both the field work and the textual account are methodologically informed by the traditions and techniques of cultural anthropology". Consistent with the traditional ethnographic methodology, the netnographic method requires "immersive combination of cultural participation and observation, resulting in a researcher becoming for some period of time, in some unpredictable ways, an active part with "full participation in the culture being studied, as a recognized cultural member".

According to Kozinets (1998), data collected in netnographic studies consist of "researcher's field notes about her cyber-cultural experiences, combined with the artifacts of the culture and community". Researcher's reflective field notes emphasize the similarity between ethnographic and netnographic methodology and the central role played by the researcher in both. Kozinets reminds us that a researcher needs to be aware of constrains imposed by computer-mediated communications that "eliminate and simulate physicality and body, privilege verbal-rational states and skills over nonverbal-emotional ones, and allow 'pre-editing' of expressed thoughts and thus more opportunities for strategic self-presentation efforts". To mitigate the issues of potential self-presentation bias in netnographic studies, Kozinets (1998) advocates the use of "adjunct methods of inquiry, such as in-person or telephone interviews with person participating as members of the virtual community open interpretive scrutiny of details." The use of adjunct methods should be "based on a foundation of direct participation and immersion in the relevant cyber-cultures and virtual communities".

To further illustrate the inherent similarity between ethnography and netnography, Kozinets points out that cultural entree is the first step in the process. He recommends conducting research on relevant online resources and communities prior to making an entree, observing (lurking) in online communities prior to announcing presence, and then establishing relationships with the community members through direct interactions. The guiding principle is "to fit in as a cultural insider, and gain the perspective and experience of a member of the virtual community".

Cyber culture is more narrowly conceptualized as the patterns of behavior and their associated symbolic meanings expressed primarily through computer-mediated communication. Netnography investigates the specific instances in which community is built through computer-mediated communications. In general, culture and communities are created through communication, whether traditional or electronic. Virtual communities indicate more than just electronic transmission of information. It is the task of the researcher to define and conceptualize what constitutes culture and community. Indicators used by Kozinets include "(1) individuals who are familiar with one another, (2) communications that are identity-specific, and thus not anonymous, (3) group-specific language, symbols and norms, and (4) the maintenance and enforcement of in-group/out-group boundaries." Application of netnography is most defensible when the phenomenon exists primarily online.

Integrity of research is guided through adherence to a recommended method – prolonged engagement, persistent observation, gaining rapport and trust, triangulating across sites and sources, good interview techniques, researcher introspection and member checks. Evaluation of qualitative research is based on "verisimilitude (providing a lifelike simulation of the culture), reflexivity (consciously recounting the inevitable effects of

the researcher participating in the culture), and authenticity (giving proof that one was actually accepted as, and felt oneself to be, a culture member)" (Kozinets, 1998, p. 370).

In summary, Kozinets (1998) presents netnography as the adaptation of traditional ethnographic methodology to the online setting, implicitly inheriting the relativist perspective associated with traditional ethnographic research, but also keeping in mind that the advantages offered by netnographic studies in gaining easier access to online communities are counter-balanced by the need for awareness of limitations imposed by computer-mediated communication. As presented, netnography is a qualitative research methodology that carries relativist philosophical assumptions.

Recent Developments in Netnography

In the years following the publication of the initial guidelines on conducting netnographic studies, the Internet has continued to evolve and as web 2.0 technologies and social media tools have been leading the recent growth of online communities that offer members a platform for sharing user-generated content. The netnographers have kept up with the evolving online communications and increasingly study discussion forums and content-based online communities. Kozinets (2010) offers a slightly revised and updated perspective on netnography as a methodology. But since currently published netnographies rely foremost on Kozinets earlier work (1998, 2002), we focus our review on Kozinets original work.

According to Kozinets (2002) "netnography, or ethnography on the Internet, is a qualitative research methodology that adapts ethnographic research techniques to the study of cultures and communities emerging through computer-mediated communications." While the methodological relationship with ethnography is still present in the definition, there is – compared to Kozinets (1998) – much more emphasis on differentiating netnography and ethnography by focusing netnographic studies on computer-mediated communication spaces. Netnography typically uses publicly accessible information (on the Internet), and thus it is often less time consuming than a traditional ethnography, and the methodology also offers another potential benefit -- studies can be conducted unobtrusively.

Kozinets (2002) focuses the discussion on market-oriented netnography to extend the market-oriented ethnography methodology. Market oriented ethnography sounds very similar to ethnography in name, but is in fact a rather distinct methodology. Developed in the context of investigating consumer behavior in the field of marketing, market-oriented ethnography advocates the use of content analysis as a methodology for developing rich contextual insights into issues and themes present in specific consumer groups (Arnould & Wallendorf, 1994). Market-oriented ethnography was developed to tackle issues relevant to understanding consumer behavior and thus is greatly affected by the pragmatic philosophical ontology that is dominant in consumer behavior studies. As mentioned previously pragmatic philosophy accepts the subjective nature of reality, but recognizes useful conceptual frameworks that reveal limitations imposed by reality.

The meaning of netnography changes rather dramatically from Kozinets (1998) to Kozinets (2002). Kozinets (1998) presents netnography as an exploratory methodology rooted in traditional ethnographies and inheriting ethnographic relativist philosophical assumptions. Netnographic studies are appropriate for the study of communities that are defined through language and cultural artifacts and the researcher is the primary instrument in conducting the study delivering a contextual rich interpretive narrative as the research outcome. Kozinets (2002), on the other hand, presents netnography as an extension of market-focused ethnography, which is quite different from a traditional ethnography. Market-oriented ethnography has an implicit pragmatic stance and far less restrictive requirements of what constitutes a community. According to the market-oriented ethnographic methodology any group of consumers that share a consumption pattern can serve as a target community. There is no requirement for a prolonged immersion on the part of the researcher in order to gain access to the community (Lincoln & Guba, 1985) and a much broader perspective is taken on what are the appropriate research methods to be used for data collection and analysis. Methodologically market-oriented ethnographies are arguably closer to content analysis than they are to ethnographies.

Although there are substantial differences between Kozinets (1998) and Kozinets (2002, 2010) in what points are emphasized in relation to ethnography as a methodology, they are not necessarily in conflict with each other. Kozinets (1998) notes "netnography can be applied (1) as a methodology to study pure cyber-cultures, (2) as a methodological tool to study "derived" cyber-cultures and virtual communities, and (3) as an exploratory tool to study general topics." This is an important point because it illustrates that the netnographic approach in itself is not exclusively associated with any particular philosophical viewpoint. The philosophical position taken up by individual researchers in fact shapes the choice of the specific methods employed and the presentation of the findings that are obtained from a netnographic study. There is in fact a broad spectrum of philosophical points of view and methodological variants that are captured under the netnographic umbrella. On the one hand, there are netnographic studies that emphasize netnographic heritage from ethnographies and the requisite focus on community and researcher immersion as a factor in gaining access to the communities. But on the other hand, there is the market-oriented pragmatic approach to conducting netnographic studies that applies much less stringency in defining the communities and in essence resembles the content analysis method that is used to inductively gain insight into practical issues in consumer behavior.

Given the broad range of studies that are referred to as netnographies it is of interest to examine how different studies appropriate the methodology to different contexts. Specifically, we examined whether and how the netnographies differed in their use of the notions of community, researcher immersion, and explicated philosophical assumptions. In order to gain such an understanding of the practice of netnography we conducted a qualitative content analysis of a sample of netnographies. The following section presents the sample selection and method of content analysis.

METHOD

In order to evaluate how netnography as developed by Kozinets (1998, 2002) is being used in research practice, a multi-case study (Yin, 2008) using qualitative content analysis (Krippendorff, 2004) of a selection of published papers, representing cases of netnograpy studies, was conducted. The case selection of studies ranged from publications from back in 1997 to 2009 and came from two top-rated business journals that have developed a tradition of publishing netnographic studies, namely the Journal of Business Research (JBR) and Advances for Consumer Research (ACR). We limit the case selection to business research because netnography originated from marketing and also because business research is our own area of expertise. Excluding articles that used netnography primarily as a method to gain preliminary or supplemental insights, for example in combination with a large-scale survey, we selected six articles published in Journal of Business Research and four articles published in Advances for Consumer Research. The obtained sample size of ten cases falls well within the range of six to twelve that is usually recommended for multi-case studies (Yin, 2008). The final sample of netnography cases was

then subjected to a qualitative content analysis (Krippendorff, 2004), focusing particularly on the notions of community, researcher immersion, and philosophical assumptions. The following section presents the results of our analysis.

RESULTS (SINGLE CASE ANALYSES)

In Tables 1 through 10, we present an overview of the state of netnography and describe the specific approaches to netnograhy research as currently practiced in the field, summarizing the results from our single case analyses that we applied to the ten individual studies that were included in our sample. Specifically, for each individual table and study case, the following concepts are discussed:

1. *Summary* of the content of the study, including research objectives and contributions.
2. *Methodology*, as cited in the methods section of each study,
3. *Site* of the netnographic fieldwork,
4. *Methods* employed by the authors,
5. *Community* as defined and examined in the study.
6. *Researcher immersion* into the community and corresponding evidence provided,
7. *Philosophical assumptions* explicitly stated or implied by the authors.

DISCUSSION (CROSS-CASE ANALYSIS)

Comparing the results from the individual study cases presented above, it becomes clear that there is no single type of netnography in current research practice. In fact, based on our cross-case analysis, it becomes apparent that topics as diverse and far-reaching as cross-cultural wedding planning, X-Files fandom, and Napster file-sharing seem

Table 1. Summary of Netnography Approaches in the Sample—Study Case 1: Cromie & Ewing (2009)

Study Case 1: Cromie & Ewing (2009)	
Summary	The authors present a netnographic study that explores the motivations behind member participation in open source software projects. The authors tackle the topic of whether and how brand dominance in a particular market is related to consumer efforts to undermine the brand. Specifically, the researchers were interested in how Microsoft's dominance in the software industry affected the motivation of participants in the open source software community.
Methodology	Kozinets (1998, 2002)
Site	The researchers setup a new open source software project for the study (without an actual software being developed) and invited members of the OSS community to participate in the study. An effort was made to engage a broad demographic basis of participants through theoretical sampling. The participants were asked to fill out an extensive biographic survey (an average response included over 6000 words) and participate in the forum discussions related to the study.
Methods	The authors employ grounded theory methodology of data analysis, transcribed content is coded through the open and axial coding to categories participants responses on motivations for participation. The classification produced three core categories – positive, negative and environmental motivations. The authors present a thorough literature review in accordance to guidelines for grounded theory development.
Community	Although the authors engaged in an artificial online community-building exercise, no direct evidence of the participants' feeling of belonging to that community is provided.
Researcher immersion	Apparently, the researchers did not deeply immerse themselves into the online community, but rather administrated and managed it. Thus, no direct participation or member-to-member interaction took place.
Philosophical assumptions	None explicated. The study follows a pragmatic approach to research, starting with a research question, explicating awareness of prior research on the topic and then constructing a classification of motives from the ground up. This is a qualitative exploratory study.

all equally "fit" for netnographic exploration. All of the studies cite either Kozinets (1998) or Kozinets (2002) as a reference for the employed methodology. In terms of sites, most researchers rely on data collected from forums (or message boards), with two notable exceptions using online blogs (Hsu et al., 2009; Tynan et al., 2010). The methods used in the 10 netnographies differ, although content analysis and grounded theory emerged as the two most important ones.

Community

The existence of a community is seen as a key requirement for any netnographic study (Kozinets, 1998). Despite this fact, very few studies actually address and verify whether or not their object of study really constitutes a new form of (online) community. Kozinets (1998, p. 368) provided concrete examples for verifying the existence of an online community by looking for (1) individuals that are familiar with one another, (2)

communications that are identity-specific, and thus not anonymous, (3) group-specific language, symbols, and norms, and (4) the maintenance and enforcement of in-group/out-group boundaries. The majority of studies, however, did not provide evidence that the group under study represents an online community (Cromie & Ewing, 2009; Fong & Burton, 2008; Hsu et al., 2009; Tynan et al., 2010; Kozinets & Handelman, 1998).

In contrast, Füller et al. (2007) do provide an excellent example of addressing community formation. In addition to providing a precise definition of what constitutes an online community, the authors provide evidence from member postings clearly supporting the notion of felt community and membership. Similarly, Kozinets (1997) provides insight and empirical evidence for the existence of a unique X-Philes community through shared culture. Nelson and Otnes (2005) in turn state that message boards on wedding websites constitute an online community by shared ritual, camaraderie, and information exchange (p. 90). However,

Table 2. Summary of Netnography Approaches in the Sample—Study Case 2: Fong and Burton (2008)

Study Case 2: Fong & Burton (2008)	
Summary	The authors "investigate cross-cultural differences in eWOM, by conducting an ethnographic and textual analysis of discussion boards based in the U.S. and China over a two-year period" (p. 234). The authors develop four hypotheses on the types of behavior and statements expected on U.S. versus Chinese discussion boards. The hypotheses are based on Hofstede's (1980, 1991) dimensions of culture as well as the country-of-origin effect (Johansson, 1989). Quantitative and qualitative measures support the hypotheses.
Methodology	Kozinets (1998, 2002)
Site	The authors select six discussion boards "based on the recommendations by Kozinets (2002) that study sites should have a high level of interaction and a sufficient amount of web traffic" (p. 236).
Methods	Online observations over two periods of three months, each period one year apart. Information from each posting was recorded into a database and subsequently content analyzed. Specifically, each posting was "coded for a number of measures" (p. 236).
Community	No direct mentioning of an online community. In fact, the researchers state that "the study investigated the behavior of individuals who visited six discussion boards" (p. 236), suggesting that an understanding of the online community was not a core part of the study.
Researcher immersion	The researchers conducted pure "online observation" (p. 236) and did not engage in any participatory immersion into the online community.
Philosophical assumptions	Implicit, but positivist. The development of hypotheses clearly suggests that the authors assume fixed relationships to exist in the phenomena under investigation.

they fail to provide actual empirical evidence that would support this assertion. Similarly, the two studies by Giesler and Pohlmann (2003a, 2003b) both state that Napster constitutes an online community, but fail to provide empirical evidence supporting their claim.

Table 3. Summary of Netnography Approaches in the Sample—Study Case 3: Füller et al. (2007)

Study Case 3: Füller et al. (2007)	
Summary	The authors investigate the phenomenon of user-innovations within online basketball communities. Specifically, the study aims to provide deeper insights into "(1) the quality and quantity of ideas innovated by consumers on the Internet, (2) the reasons that drive individuals to jointly innovate in online communities, (3) the process through which innovations emerge, and (4) the community members' willingness to share their ideas with inquiring companies" (p. 61). Findings suggest that "online consumer groups are a promising source of innovation" (p. 69)
Methodology	Kozinets (2002)
Site	Five basketball message boards were selected based on "quality of content, posting frequency, professionalism, and member profile" (p. 63).
Methods	The researchers observed all five communities over a period of six months and filed all innovation-related content electronically. Subsequent content analysis followed a grounded theory approach (Glaser & Strauss, 1967). In addition, four "experienced product managers checked the trustworthiness of the findings and interpretations and evaluated the quality and variety of user ideas" (p. 63).
Community	The authors specifically address the issue of community in the study, providing evidence that members do in fact feel like being part of a larger community (in the respective message board).
Researcher immersion	Despite the fact that one of the authors "possesses profound knowledge in the field of basketball footwear, indispensible in understanding the conversation among community members" (p. 62), it is not clear whether and how the author actually immersed himself into the community through active participation or social interaction.
Philosophical assumptions	Implicit, but pragmatic. This is indicated by the reliance on quantitative measures (in addition to qualitative content) and a pre-determined set of research questions including theoretical concepts.

Table 4. Summary of Netnography Approaches in the Sample—Study Case 4: Giesler and Pohlmann (2003a)

Study Case 4: Giesler & Pohlmann (2003a)	
Summary	The authors present a netnographic study that examines file sharing on Napster – a peer-to-peer file sharing network. The study was conducted in over a five month period from October 2000 to February 2001 when Napster was growing rapidly, having already attracted over 10 million members.
Methodology	Kozinets (1997), Sherry & Kozinets (2000)
Site	Data includes observations using Napster.com
Methods	Cyber-interviews, emails, board postings, homepages, functional and historical writings, as well as authors' observations. 40 cyber-interviews form the bulk of the data.
Community	Defining Napster as a community – "a distinct subgroup of society that self-selects on the basis of a shared commitment to a particular product class, brand or consumption activity". Further indirect evidence to support identification of Napster is drawn from Irwin (1973) that proposed that "a subculture of consumption exhibits a life cycle consisting of four stages: articulation, expansion, corruption, and decline". The authors deduce that since Napster appears to have transitioned through all the stages, the progression classifies Napster as a community. This is a case of fallacy involving affirmation of the consequent that occurs when an argument is made by following the logic exemplified in the next sentence. "If she's Brazilian, then she speaks Portuguese. Hey, she does speak Portuguese. So, she is Brazilian".
Researcher immersion	The authors participated in the community to a degree, "in order to find potential informants the authors occasionally entered Napster's instant messaging system as ordinary subscribers" (p. 274). However, apparently no deep immersion through active member-to-member interaction took place.
Philosophical assumptions	Implicit, not explicated. The authors in fact engaged in a mixed form of theory development, employing prior theories on gift giving and parasitic behaviors and inductive reasoning. The researchers propose a framework of motives that underlie "gift-giving" on Napster. It is not clear whether the research began with a positivist research question – "is there evidence that Napster community could in fact be explained by theories on gift-giving?" or if interviews with Napster users lead to integration of prior theories on gift-giving as a legitimate synthesis of qualitative observations with prior theory through the process of grounded theory development (no reference to grounded theory is made).

Researcher Immersion

Researcher immersion in an online community refers to the combination of cultural participation and observation, resulting in "the researcher becoming for a time and in an unpredictable way, an active part of the face-to-face relationships in that community (Van Maanen, 1988, p. 9, as cited in Kozinets, 1998, p. 366). Full immersion is achieved when the researcher becomes a "recognized cultural member" (Kozinets, 1998, p. 366), which needs to be adequately addressed in a netnography by "giving proof that one was actually accepted as, and felt oneself to be, a culture member" (Kozinets, 1998, p. 370). Again, despite the fundamental importance of researcher immersion for netnography, the majority of studies did not address this issue (Cromie & Ewing, 2009; Fong & Burton, 2005; Hsu et al., 2009; Nelson

& Otnes, 2005; Tynan et al., 2010; Giesler & Pohlmann, 2003b).

However, Kozinets (1997) does provide an excellent example of researcher immersion in the community of X-Philes. In addition to collecting data in three venues (both online and offline), he actively participated in panels and discussions at conventions, in fan club meetings, and further typical fan activities – amounting to approximately 350 hours of researcher immersion. With such immersion, Kozinets clearly became a recognized member of the X-Philes community. Several other studies address the issue of researcher immersion at best peripherally. Giesler and Pohlmann (2003a) address the issue of immersion into the Napster online community by occasionally entering Napster's instant messaging system as ordinary subscribers. However, it is highly questionable whether this activity alone would suffice

Table 5. Summary of Netnography Approaches in the Sample—Study Case 5: Giesler and Pohlmann (2003b)

Study Case 5: Giesler & Pohlmann (2003b)	
Summary	The authors published a second netnographic study that in fact offers an alternative theoretical conceptualization of Napster as "a particular social form of emancipation". The study overlaps with (Giesler & Pohlmann, 2003a) in the time frame – the data are gathered during the same period. It is not clear if the data overlap between the two studies.
Methodology	Kozinets (1997)
Site	Observations using the music file-sharing site Napster.com.
Methods	Cyber-interviews, emails, board postings, homepages, functional and historical writings, as well as authors' observations. 80 cyber-interviews form the core of the data.
Community	Thin evidence and faulty logical arguments are put forward to conceptualize Napster as a community. It would seem that in fact the only common theme that links Napster users is the primary activity of file sharing, while the researchers themselves in fact offer two very different theoretical frameworks to explain motivations behind user participation in Napster. It would appear that Napster user base of ten million users and the broad geographic distribution of the user base would in fact serve as significant barriers to effective acculturation. The community is simply too large and too diverse to represent a single community and if communities did in fact exist within Napster they would be much smaller.
Researcher immersion	The authors provide no information as to whether and how they immersed themselves through active participation in the online community.
Philosophical assumptions	Implicit, not explicated. Similarly to the previous study, the authors combine discussion of prior research and a brief summary of Napster history to launch into theorizing about Napster while providing only minimal evidence supporting the proposed theories. The authors propose that "consumer emancipation is the reassurance of social difference through communication, and the implicit self-paradoxification of centering into the cultural crosshairs those entities one wishes to emancipate from."

Table 6. Summary of Netnography Approaches in the Sample—Study Case 6: Hsu et al. (2009)

Study Case 6: Hsu et al. (2009)	
Summary	Findings of a netnography to "learn how consumers implicitly and explicitly enact brand myths" (p. 1224) are presented. Based on online blog posts written by first-time visitors to China, "the stories visitors tell themselves and others about their visits" as well as "the iconic myths implied by first thoughts" (p. 1224) are explored. Balance theory (Heider 1958) is applied as a theoretical lens to analyze the individual stories. Implications for building a destination brand icon are derived.
Methodology	Kozinets (2002)
Site	The netnography is based on a purposive sample of 12 online blog posts written by first-time visitors to China. By their own account, the "sampling strategy used does not offer representativeness or transferability, but focuses on building theory through analytic depth and insights into lasting iconic impressions" (p. 1225).
Methods	Qualitative content analysis of blog posts. The authors map the concepts found in each of the twelve stories "according to relationships from one concept to the next that appear in the stories" (p. 1225), followed by content analysis based on Heider's (1958) balance theory.
Community	The study does not provide any information with regards to whether or not the individual blog posters are seen as part of a larger online community.
Researcher immersion	No information is provided on whether or not the authors immersed themselves or interacted with the individuals in the study.
Philosophical assumptions	Implicit, but pragmatic. The researchers assume that the individuals construct their own subjective view of the world around them in and through their blog posts. A deeper understanding of the phenomenon as it occurs naturally is sought. However, the application of balance theory suggests that the authors assume an objective reality to exist outside of the individual subjective interpretation.

Table 7. Summary of Netnography Approaches in the Sample—Study Case 7: Kozinets (1997)

Study Case 7: Kozinets (1997)	
Summary	The study titled "I Want to Believe": A Netnography of the X-Philes subculture of consumption is the first study that defined and exemplified netnography as a methodology. The reported study was a part of a larger study on consumer behavior focused on the fans of a TV show called The X-Files. Kozinets followed the community of X-Philes ("the 'phile' is derived from the Greek word philos, meaning 'to love'") who represented the most avid fans of the show among the reported audience of over 14 million TV viewers.
Methodology	Based on (Arnould & Wallendorf, 1994)
Site	The present study is in fact among the first to use online data as a major source of data in an ethnographic study. (The suggestion of calling the methodology a netnography came from an anonymous reviewer.) In addition to conducting the research online, the author had also attended two live events in which the X-Philes gathered – a media convention and a media fan club. The site triangulation is emphasized as an important component of the study. The author further emphasizes the importance of observation of participation critical to ethnographic research that was done at the live events.
Methods	An extension of traditional ethnographic techniques to analysis of data gathered in online forums. Gathered data was "read 9 times, and analyzed using the constant comparative method, categorization, abstraction, and the holistic search for unifying themes". The findings of the study were shared with 9 members and 6 provided feedback that was incorporated in the final draft of the manuscript.
Community	Definition of the community of X-Philes is based on Schouten and McAlexander (1995) definition of the "sub-culture of consumption" as "a distinct subgroup of society that self-selects on the basis of a shared commitment to a particular product class, brand or consumption activity". The X-Philes community is defined not just by affinity for viewing the TV show, but at a deeper level through shared culture, "based on shared aesthetic tastes, shared experience of awe and mystery and a shared drive to consume the symbols related to the X-Files".
Researcher immersion	In addition to collecting data in the three venues over a seven-month period, the author actively participated in the studies culture. Specifically, "participation in several panels and discussions at conventions, at fan club meetings, during informal interviews with media fans, combined with X-Phile fan activities such as viewing and reviewing the show and reading X-Files related materials constitutes a prolonged engagement of approximately 350 hours in duration" (p. 471).
Philosophical assumptions	Implicit, but interpretive. The author deliberately assumed the role of participant-observer in order to understand the attitudes and behavior as subjectively perceived by a member of the community.

to make the researcher a recognized member of the Napster community. Similarly weak attempts are put forth by Kozinets and Handelman (1998), who post requests for interviews in observed Internet newsgroups. This obviously made their presence in the community public. However, it seems highly unlikely that such behavior made the researcher become a recognized member of the community. Lastly, Füller et al. (2007) argue that one of the researchers possessed profound knowledge of the Basketball community due to personal involvement with the product (basketball shoes), which was "indispensable in understanding the conversation among community members" (p. 62), but do not provide any insight into whether and how this researcher participated in the online community under investigation.

Philosophical Assumptions

The philosophical assumptions underlying the examined netnographies vary from interpretive to pragmatic and positivistic. However, none of the studies in the sample specifically explicates their philosophical assumptions. Judging by the authors' approach to the research, theory development, and data analysis, out of the ten studies we categorized only one as interpretive (Kozinets, 1997) and one as positivistic (Fong & Burton, 2008). The remaining eight were within the pragmatic paradigm, driven by a clear research question with pre-determined theoretical frameworks. Interestingly, although the very first published netnography (Kozinets, 1997), as well as the following methods paper written by the

Table 8. Summary of Netnography Approaches in the Sample—Study Case 8: Kozinets and Handelman (1998)

Study Case 8: Kozinets & Handelman (1998)	
Summary	The authors present a netnographic study of consumer boycotting behavior by examining the content of Internet news groups seeking examples of boycotting behavior. Iterative exploratory analysis identified several unexpected themes that were not captured in prior theories concerning boycotting behavior. While much of theory focused on advantages gained through collective bargaining as a theoretical frame in understanding boycotting behavior, the ethnographic study revealed that in fact much of the boycotting behavior that was evident in the news groups was driven by individuals and individual need for emotional self-expression and moral self-realization.
Methodology	Kozinets (1997)
Site	11 different Internet newsgroups observed for a two month period.
Methods	Content analysis of newsgroups, email interviews, 3 phone interviews.
Community	The authors do not provide direct evidence of the existence of an online community among the members of the 11 Internet newsgroups.
Researcher immersion	In addition to observing the community, the first author posted a request for interviews about boycotts in a newsgroup. However, no direct immersion through active participation was reported.
Philosophical Assumptions	Not explicated. Implicit assumptions indicate a pragmatic approach. The study is motivated by research questions, employs qualitative approach to data collection, interpretive approach to data analysis. Triangulation is employed to support trustworthiness of findings, although the insight is severely limited by a very short duration of the study (2 months) and relatively few data sources (only 3 phone interviews).

Table 9. Summary of Netnography Approaches in the Sample—Study Case 9: Nelson and Otnes (2005)

Study Case 9: Nelson & Otnes (2005)	
Summary	The authors examine cross-cultural ambivalence and how it influences brides-to-be while they plan cross-cultural weddings. Specifically the research questions addressed are "(1) What roles do wedding message boards play for brides as they plan cross-cultural weddings? (2) How do brides use these Internet communities to cope with the cross-cultural ambivalence they experience?" (p. 90). Findings suggest different roles of the virtual community in resolving cross-cultural ambivalence, as well as different coping strategies employed by brides for managing ambivalence.
Methodology	Kozinets (2002)
Site	Three wedding-related websites were selected based on the "prevalence of communications related to cross-cultural weddings" (p. 90). However, since "messages observed across the three sites were similar, [the authors] collapsed them into one large data set" (p. 90).
Methods	Messages were content analyzed by the first author through constant comparative method (Glaser & Strauss, 1967), "reading the postings several times, moving from the specific to the general, and devising categories" (p. 90). The second author "audited these themes and made suggestions" (p. 90).
Community	The authors define following (Rheingold, 1993). They state that with regards to message boards on wedding websites, "such communities focus on shared ritual and offer camaraderie and information exchange" (p. 90). However, in their analysis, the author collapsed the data collected in the three communities into one large data set. Hence, it is not clear whether and how each of the sites individually constitute an online community.
Researcher immersion	Messages from relevant forums were archived, but no direct participation or interaction with members of the online community took place.
Philosophical assumptions	Implicit, but pragmatic. The specific research questions in conjunction with the content analysis approach suggest that authors are not necessarily assuming a purely subjective view of reality.

Table 10. Summary of Netnography Approaches in the Sample—Tynan et al. (2010)

Study Case 10: Tynan et al. (2010)	
Summary	The authors "seek to explore conceptually the meaning of value for luxury brands, and empirically investigate how firms and consumers co-create value in the luxury market" (p. 1). Consequently, the authors develop and extend a theoretical framework of types of value for a luxury brand, based on existing literature and reported empirical findings.
Methodology	Kozinets (2002)
Site	Three brands were selected based on their "global iconic status" (p. 4). Numerous brand-related blogs (not further specified) were used for the netnography.
Methods	Face-to-face interviews with senior practitioners and customers outside flagship stores; Retail observations at each store; Analysis of official brand websites; Netnography of online market-oriented communities (blogs)
Community	Albeit stating that the netnography aimed "to explore the attitudes and behavior of online market-oriented communities" (p. 4), no definition or verification of the existence of an online community is provided.
Researcher immersion	The authors do not provide any information as to whether and how they immersed themselves and participated in the online community.
Philosophical assumptions	Implicit, but pragmatic. The researchers are clearly informed by theoretical frameworks suggesting an assumed objective reality. At best, the study represents a positivistic-descriptive stance in that comments are used to support quasi-factual statements.

same author (Kozinets, 1998), were both part of the interpretive paradigm, all following studies in our set were either pragmatic or positivistic.

Obviously, given the nature of case studies, with a necessarily small sample size, it would be pre-mature to conclude that netnographies in general fall mostly within the pragmatic paradigm. However, it is interesting to note that a methodology originally developed in the interpretive paradigm finds such wide-spread acceptance in other paradigms. At the same time, one could question whether the use of netnography in anything but an interpretive paradigm represents a faithful and rigorous use of the methodology. In the absence of verification of community existence and researcher immersion, as apparently commonly practiced (see above), one might ask whether and how netnography actually differs from plain content analysis of data collected on the Internet.

Limitations

Several limitations prohibit the generalizability of the study's findings. First and foremost, the purpose of case studies is not to generalize beyond the cases selected for analysis, but rather to discern interesting conditions and patterns that help understand the complexities of the researched phenomenon. To what extend these patterns transfer to other cases must be determined with follow up research, which may be based on larger and more representative samples of netnography cases. We focused on business journals as the main source of sample studies, in particular, the *Journal of Business Research* and *Advances for Consumer Research*. Many more netnographies have been published in other journals and in other research areas, including urban planning, and thus we cannot generalize to this broader population. On the other hand, it is not the intent of this qualitative study to generalize to a broader population, but rather to develop some in-depth knowledge of the selected group of netnographic studies and reveal interesting patterns across studies that help us better understand how researcher have adopted and applied netnography as newly emerging research approach.

FUTURE RESEARCH DIRECTIONS

Since we study the emerging body of netnography research in practice, which is referring primarily to the original Kozinets methodology, the present study does not consider in depth Kozinets more recent work (2007, 2010), which presents a more evolved and detailed explication of netnography than the original Kozinets (1998) paper. Certainly, one could further build on the present chapter by following these more recent developments and also by adding more and newer netnography studies to the analysis and selecting more studies from areas beyond business research and perhaps also by examining netnography in the specific context of urban planning research.

The more recent work on the netnography research approach (e.g., Kozinets, 2010) presents a somewhat evolved and more detailed perspective on netnography and it would be interesting to follow up this study with a broader analysis in future research and see if the netnography research community cannot just establish clear guidelines on how to do quality netnograhpy but also adhere to them more rigorously in research practice. While most of the issues discussed in the chapter are relevant beyond business research, it would also be desirable to examine the netnography research practice in urban planning, specifically, to find out if there are any significant differences in using this approach that are unique to urban planning research.

CONCLUSION

The advent of the Internet and the introduction of new forms of electronic communication and collaboration among members of private and public communities have opened new areas for academic research. With this opportunity comes a need for new, or newly adapted, online research methods. In this context, netnography (Kozinets, 1998), or online ethnography, is one such approach that has been offered as a viable option for the study of online communities in research areas that include marketing in business, sociology, anthropology, and urban planning, among others. Numerous studies have employed this rather new methodology and have offered new insights into online communities concerning topics as diverse as, for example, cross-cultural weddings (Nelson & Otnes, 2005), tourism experiences (Hsu et al., 2009), luxury brands (Tynan et al., 2010), and basketball shoes (Füller et al., 2009), just to name a few. However, netnography is inherently an interpretive methodology that shares many philosophical assumptions from ethnography. Importantly, it requires the existence of a community, determined by a number of factors relating to a shared culture, as well as the immersion by a researcher.

Findings suggest the majority of published netnographies do not rigorously follow the philosophical assumptions inherent in the originally proposed netnography methodology. Specifically, the majority of studies are found not to systematically verify whether or not the group studied in fact constitutes a community. Moreover, the majority of studies were done by researchers who did not truly immerse themselves in the community by means of prolonged interaction with the members of the community. Certainly, netnography is a novel research methodology and the current study can only highlight some of the most obvious concerns arising from the philosophical assumptions and implications inherent in netnography.

Due to the small and biased sample, no general conclusions should be drawn from this study. Therefore, future research should further investigate the commonalities and differences between the apparent schools of thought in netnography that were partially uncovered by the present study.

REFERENCES

Arnould, E. J., & Wallendorf, M. (1994). Market-Oriented Ethnography: Interpretation Building and Marketing Strategy Formulation. *JMR, Journal of Marketing Research, 31,* 484–504. doi:10.2307/3151878

Cromie, J., & Ewing, M. (2009). The rejection of brand hegemony. *Journal of Business Research, 62*(2), 218–230. doi:10.1016/j.jbusres.2008.01.029

Fong, J. (2008). A cross-cultural comparison of electronic word-of-mouth and country-of-origin effects. *Journal of Business Research, 61*(3), 233–242. doi:10.1016/j.jbusres.2007.06.015

Füller, J., Jawecki, G., & Muhlbacher, H. (2007). Innovation creation by online basketball communities. *Journal of Business Research, 60*(1), 60–71. doi:10.1016/j.jbusres.2006.09.019

Giesler, M., & Pohlmann, M. (2003a). The Anthropology of File Sharing: Consuming Napster as a Gift. *Advances in Consumer Research. Association for Consumer Research (U. S.), 30,* 273–279.

Giesler, M., & Pohlmann, M. (2003b). The social form of Napster: cultivating the paradox of consumer emancipation. *Advances in Consumer Research. Association for Consumer Research (U. S.), 30,* 94–100.

Hsu, S., Dehuang, N., & Woodside, A. G. (2009). Storytelling research of consumers' self-reports of urban tourism experiences in China. *Journal of Business Research, 62*(12), 1223–1254. doi:10.1016/j.jbusres.2008.11.006

Kozinets, R. V. (1997). "I want to believe": A Netnography of the X-Philes' Subculture of Consumption. *Advances in Consumer Research. Association for Consumer Research (U. S.), 24,* 470–475.

Kozinets, R. V. (1998). On Netnography: Initial Reflections on Consumer Research Investigations of Cyerculture. *Advances in Consumer Research. Association for Consumer Research (U. S.), 25,* 366–371.

Kozinets, R. V. (2002). The Field behind the Screen: Using Netnography for Marketing Research in Online Communities. *JMR, Journal of Marketing Research, 39*(1), 61–72. doi:10.1509/jmkr.39.1.61.18935

Kozinets, R. V. (2007). Netnography 2.0. In Belk, R. W. (Ed.), *Handbook of Qualitative Research Methods in Marketing* (pp. 129–142). Northampton, MA: Edwards Elgar.

Kozinets, R. V. (2010). *Netnography: Doing Ethnographic Research Online.* Thousand Oaks, CA: Sage.

Kozinets, R. V., & Handelman, J. (1998). Ensouling Consumption: A Netnographic Exploration of the Meaning of Boycotting Behavior. *Advances in Consumer Research. Association for Consumer Research (U. S.), 25*(1), 475–480.

Krippendorff, K. (2004). *Content Analysis: An Introduction to Its Methodology* (2nd ed.). Thousand Oaks, CA: Sage.

Lincoln, Y. S., & Guba, E. G. (1985). *Naturalistic Inquiry.* Newbury Park, CA: Sage.

Nelson, M., & Otnes, C. (2005). Exploring cross-cultural ambivalence: a netnography of intercultural wedding message boards. *Journal of Business Research, 58,* 89–95. doi:10.1016/S0148-2963(02)00477-0

Tedlock, B. (2000). Ethnography and Ethnographic Representation. In Denzing, N., & Lincoln, Y. (Eds.), *The Handbook of Qualitative Research* (2nd ed., pp. 455–486). Thousand Oaks, CA: Sage.

Tynan, C., McKechnie, S., & Chhuon, C. (2010). Co-creating value for luxury brands. *Journal of Business Research, 63*(11), 1156–1163. doi:10.1016/j.jbusres.2009.10.012

Yin, R. (2008). *Case Study Research: Design and Methods* (4th ed.). Thousand Oaks, CA: Sage.

ADDITIONAL READING

Clemons, E. K. (2009). The Complex Problem of Monetizing Virtual Electronic Social Networks. *Decision Support Systems, 48*(1), 46–56. doi:10.1016/j.dss.2009.05.003

Hemetsberger, A., & Reinhardt, C. (2006). Learning and Knowledge-building in Open-source Communities: A Social-experiential Approach. *Management Learning, 37*(2), 187–214. doi:10.1177/1350507606063442

Hewer, P., & Brownlie, D. (2007). Cultures of Consumption of Car Aficionados. *The International Journal of Sociology and Social Policy, 27*(3/4), 106–119. doi:10.1108/01443330710741057

Lang, R., & Le Furgy, J. (2007). Boomburb "Buildout": The Future of Development in Large, Fast-Growing Suburbs. *Urban Affairs Review, 42*(4), 533–552. doi:10.1177/1078087406295893

Muñiz, A. M., & Schau, H. J. (2005). Religiosity in the Abandoned Apple Newton Brand Community. *The Journal of Consumer Research, 31*, 737–747. doi:10.1086/426607

Muñiz, A. M., & Schau, H. J. (2007). Vigilante Marketing and Consumer-Created Communications. *Journal of Advertising, 36*(3), 35–50. doi:10.2753/JOA0091-3367360303

KEY TERMS AND DEFINITIONS

Community: A collection of like-minded people who share some common interests or goals and who are organized in a formal or informal way is referred to as a community. When the organization of the community is primarily Internet-based they are also called online community. Community culture is the focus in ethnographic community research.

Ethnography: A research methodology, developed in the social sciences, that is designed to study human cultures. The research outcome includes a rich narrative description of the studied culture.

Multi-Case Analysis: A research method that collects qualitative and/or quantitative data from several cases. It usually includes an analysis of the individual cases as well as a cross analysis that aims to find interesting patterns. Typically, a sample size of 6 to 12 cases is recommended where cases should represent different categories.

Netnography: A new research approach that is based on the principles of ethnography but is specifically designed to study the behavior and culture of communities that form and develop on the Internet.

Qualitative Content Analysis: A research method that uses textual data and applies inductive reasoning to obtain interesting categories. It is different from quantitative content analysis, which relies on deductive reasoning and uses quantitative techniques like frequency measures to identify categories.

Researcher Immersion: A key principles of ethnographic research that refers to the participation of the research in the community that he or she is studying. It typically involves explicit or implicit acceptance into the community and some form of active participation.

Chapter 15
Citizens on YouTube:
Research–Method Issues

Stefano Pace
Bocconi University, Italy

ABSTRACT

Videos on YouTube can be analysed at two connected levels: (1) the content of the video, and (2) its context, which comprises viewers' comments and replies, tags, and related videos, and is both visual and textual. In order to comprehend the meanings of a video, researchers should focus on both levels and on all contextual facets. This chapter provides some suggestions on how to plan research pertaining to YouTube videos, with reference to videos focused on urban and planning issues.

INTRODUCTION

The Web 2.0 represents a key evolutionary step in the lifecycle of the Internet and, more generally, of the media. The Web 2.0 has two main characteristics: creative platform and networked interactivity. The Web has experienced a noteworthy shift from a platform of learning and consumption to a platform of creation (Kozinets, Hemetsberger, & Schau, 2008). In the past, Web users read articles online, downloaded files, and consulted the Internet as a limitless encyclopaedia.

DOI: 10.4018/978-1-4666-0074-4.ch015

This behaviour still exists, but it coexists with a more creative activity. Today, the Web 2.0 is a creative platform where individuals can create; this creation can take the form of posting of texts on forums or in the Wikipedia, photos on Flickr, and videos on YouTube, among others. Some of these creations are generated through collective rather than individual effort. Even companies have acknowledged the creative force of individuals, both offline and online, by allowing customers to participate actively in the co-creation of products or services (Vargo & Lusch, 2004). The creativity inherent in the Web 2.0 can radically change entire sectors. The most famous TV shows are usually re-edited by active viewers and posted online as new creations that can draw further attention and further creation from other viewers. A question arises: Where does the creation of the original producer (the media company) end, and where does that of the consumer start? There are no clear boundaries, and any creation eventually becomes a collective creation. This thinking is in line with the 'culture of remix' that characterises the Web 2.0 (Lessig, 2008).

The second feature of the Web 2.0 is its networked interactivity. Users are connected to each other not in a linear form (as with telephone or e-mail connections), but rather in a networked context (Venkatesh, 1999). Any contribution to a forum or social network, for instance, is not addressed to specific other individuals, but rather to a mass of users who can collectively react to the contribution. Networked interactivity in the Web 2.0 can be seen at two levels. First, there are interactions in the forms of messages, instant messages, chat exchanges, 'likes', 'pokes', and so on. Second, interactions can be silent—namely, a never-ending exchange of gazes among profiles. Facebook, for instance, represents a virtual place where people look at other people, update each other, seeing what is going on in others' lives, and share their own daily lives. Facebook and similar social networks establish a panopticon of gazes where anyone can freely subscribe to the idea of being watched and being able to watch others. Critics of these systems highlight the social control that social networks could exert over us by impinging upon our privacy. On the other hand, still others stress the free participation of people and the friendly environments involved, emphasising the novelty and advantages of Web 2.0 human communication. Creativity and interactivity allow citizens to debate common concerns, create and share possible solutions, and even develop some forms of e-democracy.

These two dimensions—namely, creative platform and networked interactivity—also characterise YouTube. YouTube is both a media outlet

where portions of mainstream TV programmes or self-made videos are broadcasted and a social network where comments, replies, and interactivity take place. In particular, YouTube is a place where the second form of interactivity—that is, a gazing interactivity—takes place: people look at other people's creations.

This chapter seeks to suggest possible approaches to exploring YouTube videos that deal with citizenship and urban issues. First, this chapter provides an overview of YouTube, and then proceeds to provide some research-method suggestions that are viable to the study of YouTube videos. A preliminary case study is then briefly illustrated. The final section draws some conclusions and suggests future research paths. The background question addressed in this chapter, therefore, is "How can one optimally study urban-related videos on YouTube?" This question will be of interest to city officials, urban planners, researchers, and whoever wishes to inform themselves about issues of a given city. With its huge repertoire of videos and comments, YouTube can serve as an interesting part of any research that focuses on a city or territory; however, as with most research materials, it must be approached critically and with caution.

YOUTUBE: BROADCASTING CITIZENS

Issues, Controversies, Problems

Since its origins, YouTube has been a topic of debate and even conflict among observers of the social-media phenomenon. Videos on YouTube can be posted by traditional media companies or be user-created; in fact, extensive research by Burgess and Green (2009) shows that around 60% of the most popular videos in YouTube are posted by users and not by traditional media companies. These videos can be parts of video-blogs, completely new videos, or television programmes that are re-edited by users to create new media content. For instance, it is common to see videos on YouTube where passionate users edit episodes of the most famous movies or TV series (such as Lost, Dr. House, and Twilight) as a tribute to their favourite show. An interesting conclusion reached by Burgess and Green (2009) is that while user-generated videos generally receive fewer views compared to videos posted by traditional media companies, they are the ones that garner the most discussion and the greatest number of responses on YouTube. User-generated videos can create an aggregation of fellow users who reply with their own videos and comments, to share ideas and emotions. These user-generated videos can thus create a sort of community that allows individuals to share common interests and passions. Sometimes, the core of the community is a person: some YouTube users are celebrities with thousands of video-blog subscribers.

YouTube hosts a peculiar balance of private and public expressions. Lange (2008) suggests that YouTube videos can be 'publicly private' or 'privately public'. Users willing to be identified post publicly private videos, allowing the video to circulate among a relatively small circle of friends and acquaintances. The user can thus decide to hide partially his or her video by employing tags that are uncommon and unknown to the wider audience, but known among his or her friends. Privately public videos, on the other hand, do not reveal the identity of the user, and they circulate widely among many viewers who do not belong to the poster's personal network. This typology of videos shows the fractalisation of the private–public dichotomy (Gal, 2002, as cited in Lange, 2008). 'Private' and 'public' become relative terms, and their meanings shift according to the perspective adopted. The example cited by Lange (2008) relates to the private–public territory: compared to a neighbourhood, a home is private space; at the same time, a home has public spaces inside it (Lange, 2008).

In the same vein, issues touching a local community may be private matters, compared to issues at a national level; whether a local issue can escalate and become a national matter depends on a number of different factors. The main factor, however, is whether the issue has some symbolic power that can be extended to other communities. A worker losing her job in a remote village, for example, can be symbolic of a declining economy across the whole of a country. Usually, media outlets are the links that connect local issues and debates to a broader level of interests. During the current economic crisis, the MSNBC news staff created the Elkhart Project in an editorial office in the town of Elkhart, Indiana, to cover the effects of the crisis in that corner of America. Other media companies planned similar extensive coverage of local communities. Such examples show that matters relating to small communities are both local and particular issues, and a symbol of wider phenomena to which they are connected. Thanks to this connection, local matters are found to be similar to those that happen elsewhere, and thus they can serve as a source of reflection. YouTube allows for an emergence of the same effect: local and even very personal perspectives can be read as individual expressions or as symbols that are more public. The difference is that with traditional media, the editorial staff members select what can be considered a newsworthy fact; with social media like YouTube, however, there is no central filtering or selection, and so a private video can escalate and become a viral in a matter of days, often through no design of the user. The dynamics that dictate which videos become famous or even viral are detached, at least partially, from individual or organisational intentions and strategies.

Spatial phenomena can be framed under four different theoretical lenses: territory, place, scale, or network (Jessop, Brenner, & Jones, 2008). The territory frame stresses boundaries and enclosures; place focuses on issues such as spatial differentiation and proximity; scale deals with hierarchisation; and network focuses on interconnectivity and interdependence (Jessop, Brenner, & Jones, 2008). YouTube videos that refer to spatial phenomena may synthesise any of these four levels. For instance, a video can stress how a given urban issue is linked to a national problem, while referring to the scale of the issue. A video from a tourist, in another instance, can exalt the beauty of a city, thus adopting the place framework. The same location can thus be seen from different angles, by different users, thus giving rise to the production of different videos. By fully comprehending the meanings conveyed by these perspectives, researchers can answer their specific research questions, such as how people perceive a given place or what type of reactions are caused by a new city service. We can expect YouTube videos referring to urban issues to be read as being connected to larger issues and drivers that are distinct from individual circumstances; these videos can also depict a location or spatial phenomenon from different perspectives. The researcher that uses YouTube has the opportunity to understand this complex, user-created system of meanings.

YouTube Citizens: Research Methods

The researcher who works in an online environment can rely on a rich repertoire of methods. Some of these methods have been translated from the offline environment and applied to the virtual realm, including surveys, interviews, journals, focus groups, and social network analysis (for an overview of these methods, see Kozinets, 2010). One method, however, is peculiar to the Web: netnography (Kozinets, 2010). The founder of netnography, Robert V. Kozinets, defines netnography as a 'participant-observational research based in online fieldwork', and says that 'It uses computer-mediated communication as a source of data to arrive at the ethnographic understanding and representation of a cultural or communal phenomenon' (Kozinets, 2010, p. 60).

YouTube is part of the online world, and so methods devised for the online realm are readily applicable there. However, as mentioned, YouTube also presents some peculiarities: a video on YouTube can have a trail of comments, replies, and ratings that are given by unknown passers-by or by regular subscribers of the user who uploaded the video. The researcher should analyse both the video and the context of comments on it, to fully comprehend the meaning of the video.

The previous section outlined two relevant features of YouTube videos: 1) user-generated videos represent a substantial proportion of all YouTube uploads, and they also comprise the most debated and lively portions of this platform; and 2) by posting a video, a subject implicitly selects the audience that will watch it, whether a small circle of people or an undefined, open audience. In focusing on user-generated videos, this second characteristic in particular presents researchers with an epistemological challenge. If a tourist posts a video of her London trip, for instance, this video can be addressed to friends—like a private album to share—or it can serve as a tutorial of which places one should visit when in London. The difference can be clear or, as in most cases, more nuanced. What if the video is not self-made, but a mere posting of an official tourism video? In doing so, is the user advocating a London trip, or is she hinting at the sites she actually visited? Determining the user's intention is essential to comprehending the true and intended meaning of the video; the researcher cannot simply refer to the video itself and adopt a content-based approach. Research of this variety really needs to integrate analysis with an understanding of the overall context in which the video was posted. These two dimensions (i.e., the video itself and the context of its comments) are discussed in the two subsections that follow.

Watching YouTube: Analysis of Uploaded Videos

Visual materials can be analysed using a rich set of methods and techniques, such as content analysis, psychoanalytical approaches, semiotics, and discourse analysis (Rose, 2007). The first step to take in the study of YouTube videos is to focus on the content of the video itself. As with other visual materials, various research methods may be applied to YouTube videos: theatre theory, since the YouTube video is often a performative act (Goffman, 1959); visual analysis (Schroeder, 2002, 2007; Heisley, 2001), rooted in semiotics; videography, as an interpretive research method (Belk & Kozinets, 2005, 2007); and mass media approaches (Gunter, 2000), given that YouTube is a form of broadcasting to an audience. (The YouTube slogan is, after all, 'Broadcast Yourself'.)

Among these different methods, narrative analysis can have an especially interesting application (Pace, 2008). YouTube videos show an implicit narrative nature: the basic structure of a video posted on YouTube is that of a story. It can be a very original story, an edit of a television show, or a portion of a show posted online with no changes whatsoever. In any case, the YouTube user uploads a narrative entity that is deciphered by the audience as a story; for this reason, narrative analysis can be a useful research method with respect to YouTube videos (see Pace, 2008).

Another fruitful methodological approach is visual analysis. A visual element can be considered the historically situated manifestation of some intelligible meaning (Floch, 1995/2000); the visual itself is a concrete rendition of a more abstract idea. Visual analysis attempts to connect these two levels, thus drawing the abstract idea contained in the concrete visual. Videos on YouTube seem particularly akin to the idea of bricolage (Floch, 1995/2000), an enunciative praxis where pre-existing elements are selected by the actor and put together to convey his or her personal meaning. As with other visual expressions (Schirato & Webb, 2004), the YouTube user combines different signs to form his or her own text. The acts of selecting and editing are, in themselves, steps in meaning making. As suggested by Floch (1995/2000), semiotic analysis applied to visual elements can take place by segmenting the object of study. In applying this procedure to a YouTube video, it becomes clear that the video contains three main dimensions: the narrative, the visual frames that form the video, and sound or music. The visual-analysis and narrative-analysis methods are complementary and interconnect. The story is one of the segments that constitute the video. In the analysis of a Waterman's print advertisement, for instance, Floch (1995/2000) adopts narrative analysis to understand the written text of the ad. As Schirato and Webb (2004, p. 9) note, one 'of the important ways to make sense of visual texts is through *narrative*, or stories that are organised visually'. Indeed, one cannot draw a decisive boundary between narrative analysis and visual analysis.

The visual part can be further segmented, following the technique suggested by Schirato and Webb (2004). One should first focus on what is selected in the video, as well as in what is omitted. Any image has both a foreground subject and a background; the creator of the image produces this distinction, or at least hints at it. For instance, a video showing a famous monument surrounded by tourists may have the monument as the main subject in the foreground and thus imply that the tourists are unimportant (or even disruptive) details. On the other hand, another video might have the tourists as the main subject and the monument as the background—to show, perhaps, the perils of crowds amassing around delicate monuments or signify the notoriety of the monument. The differences between the two videos depend on the attention of the video producer, and whether it focuses on the monument or on the crowd. Other elements of the video, like the voice of the camera operator, can provide clues that can lead to the correct interpretation of the video; one can also refer to contextual clues, such as comments on the video or its tags.

Rose (2007) provides a useful scheme for framing a visual analysis. She distinguishes three sites where the meanings of an image are created: production, which refers to the techniques, methods, and circumstances of the actual production of an image; the image itself, including its compositional features; and the audience that is watching the image and interpreting it. Each of these sites can be analysed along three modalities: the technology used to produce the image; the compositional elements of the image; and social modality, or the system of social relations and practices used to produce and interpret an image. A YouTube video can be analysed along the same three modalities; let us examine each of them, within this context, in detail.

Technology. A key difference between YouTube videos and other images resides in the networked interactivity that YouTube allows. Any watcher can leave his or her comments or reply to a video, and thus contribute to the formation of a network of interactions. A second difference between YouTube videos and another image technology is that a video is usually watched individually, often while looking at the screen of one's own computer. There is no collective watching, as seen with paintings in a gallery. Finally, videos on YouTube are part of a very large collection of very different videos, and they are searchable through an internal search engine. This gives the user the freedom to decide when and how to watch a video. Other images surrounding us—such as television programmes, paintings, print advertising in a magazine, billboards—are provided through different technologies, and they imply different consumption methods.

Composition. A video can be considered part of a certain genre—an agreed-upon categorisation of creative material. By understanding the genre to which a video belongs, the watcher can contextualise its meaning. For instance, by recognising that a video about a celebrity is a parody, one can

understand the hyperbole within the video. Such hyperbole would be meaningless, or left unnoticed, without the frame provided by the genre.

The composition of the moving images can then be analysed by adopting the technique suggested by Monaco (2000, as cited in Rose, 2007). Any film or video has a *mise-en-scéne* and a montage. *Mise-en-scéne* refers to the spatial arrangements of elements, where the frame of the screen and the shots (i.e., angle, perspective, distance, and movement) form the spatial rendition of the story. The montage addresses the flow along time of the different scenes, as well as their spatial coherence. Different cuts link the shots and form the unfolding story. Sound is a further compositional element of the video. A video can be commented with music, voices, or other sounds. The source of the sound can be internal or external to the scene. The sound can run parallel to the images—that is, a sound that accompanies the images and proceeds with them in a synchronous fashion. Alternatively, it can be contrapuntal, meaning a sound provides commentary on the images, independent of them.

Social modality. Any visual element is embedded in a society and in its net of social forces. Social aspects represent the system of practices that shape not only how an image is created, but also how the audience interprets it. One example is the genre of female nude painting in older Western art (Berger, 1972; Rose, 2007)—a genre that makes social assumptions regarding gender roles. The beauty to be seen was that of a woman, while the implicit watcher admiring that beauty is a man. That genre and the paintings within it are thus part of a wider social discourse about masculinity and femininity.

Rose (2007) also provides a general orientation on how to choose a specific method of analysis—be it content, discourse, compositional, or some other variety of analysis—according to the visual material at stake. However, she warns that there are no predefined or fixed reasons as to why one should study a particular visual material with a given method. She wonders why, for example, audience studies are predominantly used in research pertaining to television programmes, rather than other methods.

YouTube: Relating Videos to Their Contexts

Once the content of the video has been assessed and analysed, the researcher can proceed with the second step: relating a video to its peculiar context. Any video is part of a network that comprises

- Comments: text-based responses with reference to the video
- Video responses: other users can post their own videos as a reply
- Suggested videos: on YouTube, these appear in a column on the right side of the page.

This column lists videos that are similar in terms of subject matter. YouTube automatically generates the video suggestions based on the content of the focal video.

Any video is also characterised by

- Its number of views
- Its rating, measured in terms of the 'likes' and 'dislikes' provided by viewers
- Tags, provided by the posting user

Researchers can consider all these components and characteristics and follow a considerable number of related videos and profiles from people posting comments; by also analysing the content of these further videos and their respective contexts, researchers can create a useful and relevant database of videos related to the specific topic under study. This method is useful in covering aspects that are of interest to YouTube users, as well as in generating hypotheses and research questions.

Here, the topic under study comprises videos that address urban issues—videos that do seem to take a peculiar position. A video camera can be used to show faulty public services, the state of a neglected neighbourhood, or other critical urban issues. In this way, a video camera can become a tool in performing an act of citizen journalism. Another possible use of YouTube among citizens is to show the hidden value of their city; in this case, the user can adopt a marketing posture, advocate the value of his or her city, and thus attract visitors, or the user can simply indicate that he or she belongs to the local community. In the former, the story resembles a self-made tourism advertisement; in the latter, the video would resemble a public expression of a sense of citizenship. Other video forms concerning spatial phenomena may emerge, and a video can spark a discussion and incite further reactions. The presence of a rich network of video-based responses and comments would indicate the relevance of an issue.

To explore videos regarding a city or territory, researchers should clarify their aims. For instance, a study can aim to assess the image of a tourism city. In such a case, research can follow a number of different research paths:

- Verify whether the videos examined focus on the main monuments of a city, or on its tiny details (e.g., traffic, shops displays, and unknown corners). In the first case, the image of the city as conveyed by travel guides probably aligns with what visitors upload to YouTube. In the second case, the hypotheses can be made that the city is appreciated for its overall atmosphere or that visitors should establish a personal path outside the canonical suggestions made by tourism guides.
- Verify whether a video's comments reinforce, praise, or criticise the video. Comments can also point out other towns and peripheral areas to visit, and they can allow residents a voice in talking about their respective cities' issues.
- The related videos can be useful in understanding the associations that the city

elicits. For instance, related videos can refer to historical facts, exceptional events, street entertainment, or urban development projects, among other elements. If most of these related videos discuss a specific topic, one can consider that topic as being a sort of association linked to the city's image.

In summary, an overall analysis of YouTube videos must take into account the complex nature of this platform and its three dimensions, at two different levels: 1) the visual, represented by the videos themselves, and 2) the contextual, comprising the system of comments and reactions to a video. The contextual level is often overlooked, despite the fact it can define the true and intended meaning of a video. In this sense, YouTube is not only a broadcast platform but also a nomological net comprising a web of interlinking tags and comments.

YOUTUBE CASE STUDY: FLASH MOBS

Flash mobs are temporary and sudden gatherings in a public space of a city (such as squares, train stations, or supermarkets) of an organised and large crowd of people who engage in some collective action (like dancing or pillow-fighting) or even inaction (like in the 'frozen' flash mobs) for a short period of time, with no outwardly apparent purpose. When a flash mob takes place, a very large group of coordinated strangers suddenly occupies a public space.

Although flash mobs may have some roots in the collective activist happenings of the 1960s, flash mobs represent a recent phenomenon in the cityscape. According to some reports, the first flash mob was organised in 2003 in New York City by the senior editor of *Harper's Magazine* (Gore, 2010). A group of a few hundred people gathered at Macy's Department Store and, for some

minutes, they had a surreal discussion with the sales personnel about rugs to buy for their alleged community. After those few minutes, they disappeared. Flash mobs represent a reappropriation of public space using a spectacular subversion of the daily rules and practices of using a space: the space is reserved not for single individuals for their own tasks (i.e., catching a train, doing shopping, taking a walk), but for a collective entity. The non-place (Augé, 1992), populated by single strangers, becomes a meaningful place occupied by a self-organised collective of strangers. The link between flash mobs and social media is strong, because flash mobs are usually organised via the Internet and mobile phones. In addition, flash mobs are recorded and shown in social media, and the resulting videos sometimes 'go viral'. As a result, YouTube has become a repository of videos of flash mobs: in fact, the search term 'flash mob', when used in YouTube, produces more than 68,000 results. Flash mobs are thus an interesting example of the possible ways in which research methods can be applied to YouTube and urban studies. What follows briefly illustrates a preliminary study that could be conducted vis-à-vis representations of flash mobs in YouTube videos. The findings are exploratory rather than final, and no specific research questions are analysed; rather, what follows is meant only to illustrate a possible path of research.

The researcher can select a sample of the thousands of videos that refer to flash mobs. It would be advisable to sample videos from different periods, to notice any evolution in the ways in which flash mobs are represented.

A visual analysis of flash mob videos shows a clear distinction between professional and amateur videos. This distinction is noteworthy, because it may suggest the transformation of some flash mobs from spontaneous events involving the humorous reappropriation of public space into a commercial tool used to promote products or a corporate brand. In fact, some companies employ flash mobs as a form of unconventional marketing and use videos to record the event. Flash mobs organised by advertising agencies or other commercial organisations are usually represented through professional videos that are produced as reports and promotional materials.

Among the most viewed flash mob videos, a sizeable proportion are of professional videos. In a professional video, a careful montage is used to convey the three stages of a flash mob: the normal atmosphere of the place prior to the event; the event itself, with the lively presence of an odd and very large crowd; and the celebration at the end of the flash mob. The sound in the video comprises a mixture of music and sounds taken from the scene. The producers of the video select the best scenes from the flash mob, and sometimes add interviews with individuals who were participants or passers-by caught in the middle of the event. What is also noteworthy in professional videos is the omitted content. For instance, professional videos usually do not focus on a single participant preparing him or her for the flash mob; this omission can imply that the event, although highly and centrally coordinated, is similar to an impromptu event based on the instantaneous teamwork of strangers. The attempt is to preserve or otherwise portray some sense of spontaneity. The genre adopted by flash mob videos is often inspired by the genre of hidden-camera television shows, where people are unaware of being filmed as they are caught in strange situations staged by the show's producer. In flash mob videos, the camera often focuses on the amazed expressions of passers-by. Other genres employed include music video-clips (for flash-mob dancing) or the typical television advertisement.

Some flash mobs are organised to address specific social issues, by a non-profit organisation or by private citizens. For instance, in different cities around the world, mothers have organised 'breastfeeding flash mobs' to sensitise the public opinion to this issue. Other flash mobs with social aims strongly resemble some forms of protest, such as strikes or picketing. In all these cases, some

visual cues show that the form of the flash mob has been changed and applied to suit the final aim. For instance, some videos reserve more space for comments and interviews, both before and after the event, and merely for the flash mob itself. Such accommodations are essential to providing a full explanation of the social issue at stake.

Amateur videos are technologically limited, due to the use of a single camera (sometimes using the camera integrated into a smartphone) and no editing. An amateur video can represent the equivalent of the surprised glance of a casual passer-by. The shots taken focus solely on the flash mob and its unfolding action, and no attention is paid to the reactions of other people. In this case, the genre is more akin to a TV 'reality' show, where extraordinary facts are recorded as they happen. If the amateur producer of the video is part of the organisation, a more complex video can be expected. For instance, the perspective of the shooting is wider, to allow for an appreciation of the group as a whole.

To understand the comments garnered by a video, we can consider posts in the long series of more than 21,000 comments garnered by one of the most famous flash mobs, organised in London by a mobile operator as a commercial communication. This thread of comments was long enough to form a conversation that included many aspects of the network of reaction to the video. Many comments were expressions of appreciation for the video (e.g., 'Like it!', 'haha, heartwarming', 'London...the greatest city in the world', and 'flash mobs are awesome').

Although there were also negative comments, the overall discussion mainly centred on the event and its extraordinary occurrence. Many comments pinpoint specific minutes of the video to indicate a brilliant dancer or a funny person (e.g., '0:43 LOL priceless how the woman in the right corner with the black bag dances XD XD' and 'oldman 0:52 WIN!'). Others emphasised the commercial aim of the video, and how it spoiled the magical atmosphere of the video (e.g., 'somehow it's not nearly as cool when it's a large corporation doing it for a commercial' and 'Corporations... what will they make people do next?'). However, the commercial intent was also seen in positive terms (e.g., 'That's advertising done right' and 'I LOVE this advert...one of the best I have ever seen...MAGIC!').

This preliminary analysis of flash mob videos shows how the flash mob movement has evolved from a spontaneous means of reappropriating city spaces to a tool that can be organised by corporations or non-profit organisations to help fulfill commercial or social agendas. In particular, the use of flash mobs as marketing tools can be considered fair by some segments of the population, or as a sort of exploitation by marketers of a spontaneous trend. While non-commercial flash mobs organised just for fun are still vital and relevant, flash mobs can be integrated into commercial practices. The amusing subversion of public space rules is, in many ways, restricted and controlled. Further analyses could address other, more nuanced research questions.

FUTURE RESEARCH DIRECTIONS

The current evolution of the Web 2.0 has blurred the boundaries among social network platforms. For example, is Facebook a textual or visual platform? No one answer is possible, since videos, pictures, text, and other forms of expression are combined there by users to convey rich and complex meanings. Further complexity is added by the interface devices used by the subject, be it a computer or a handheld device; the types of interaction and content often change according to the device employed. The increasing richness of the content that a user can upload is a feature of the Web 2.0. Facing these increasingly complex multimedia entities, future researchers should refrain from adopting just a single research methodology; indeed, the challenge for researchers in the online environment is to become familiar

with a wide array of methods, both quantitative and qualitative. Another interesting consideration in future research will be the use of software and systems that can automatically gather large sets of data for analysis.

Finally, researchers should consider ethical concerns, such as privacy and online users' rights. It is likely, given present trends that in the future more and more private facts and data will be made available online; such circumstances call for careful attention vis-à-vis ethical concerns in online research. Researchers should always be mindful of the fact that the public nature of Web content does not necessarily imply that researchers can freely use the content. The ethical issues rose by text-based virtual communities and the debates therein (Langer & Beckman, 2005) are even more relevant in the social media age of multimedia.

CONCLUSION

Research that necessitates the use of YouTube videos requires that one consider both the content of the videos and their respective contexts. Narrative analysis, the visual analysis of videos, or other viable methods can be applied to video, and research must focus on the rich context comprising comments, replies, related videos, and tags. Any video represents part of an ongoing debate of which any researcher should be mindful, if he or she wishes to reach a full understanding of the true and intended meanings behind a single video. In other words, any study of YouTube videos must consider the complex nexus of intertwined meanings created by the video and the reactions to it. Among the different methods, netnography (Kozinets, 2010) seems both suitable and sufficiently comprehensive in achieving the goals of research that involves YouTube content. Under netnographic criteria and planning, other methods can be applied according to the specific object: social network analysis, for the network of comments; content analysis, for textual comments; and narrative and visual analysis for videos.

REFERENCES

Augé, M. (1992). *Non-lieux: Introduction à une anthropologie de la surmodernité*. Paris, France: Seuil.

Belk, R. W., & Kozinets, R. V. (2005). Videography in marketing and consumer research. *Qualitative Market Research: An International Journal, 8*(2), 128–141. doi:10.1108/13522750510592418

Belk, R. W., & Kozinets, R. V. (2007). Camcorder society: Quality videography in consumer and marketing research. In Belk, R. W. (Ed.), *Handbook of qualitative research methods in marketing* (pp. 335–344). Cheltenham, UK: Edward Elgar.

Berger, J. (1972). *Ways of seeing*. London, UK: British Broadcasting Corporation, Penguin Press.

Burgess, J., & Green, J. (2009). *YouTube. Online video and participatory culture*. Cambridge, Malden, MA: Polity.

Floch, J. M. (1995/2000). *Visual identities* (van Osselaer, P., & McHould, A., Trans.). London, UK: Continuum.

Gal, S. (2002). A semiotics of the public/private distinction. *Differences: A Journal of Feminist Cultural Studies, 13*(1), 77–95. doi:10.1215/10407391-13-1-77

Goffman, E. (1959). *The presentation of self in everyday life*. New York, NY: Doubleday Anchor Books.

Gore, G. (2010). Flash mob dance and the territorialisation of urban movement. *Anthropological Notebooks, 16*(3), 125–131.

Gunter, B. (2000). *Media research methods*. London, UK: Sage.

Heisley, D. D. (2001). Visual research: Current bias and future direction. *Advances in Consumer Research. Association for Consumer Research (U. S.), 28*(1), 45–46.

Jessop, B., Brenner, M., & Jones, M. (2008). Theorizing sociospatial relations. *Environment and Planning. D, Society & Space, 26*, 389–401. doi:10.1068/d9107

Kozinets, R. V. (2010). *Netnography. Doing ethnographic research online*. London, UK: Sage.

Kozinets, R. V., Hemetsberger, A., & Schau, H. J. (2008). The wisdom of consumer crowds. Collective innovation in the age of networked marketing. *Journal of Macromarketing, 28*(4), 339–354. doi:10.1177/0276146708325382

Lange, P. G. (2008). Publicly private and privately public: Social networking on YouTube. *Journal of Computer-Mediated Communication, 13*, 361–380. doi:10.1111/j.1083-6101.2007.00400.x

Langer, R., & Beckman, S. C. (2005). Sensitive research topics: Netnography revisited. *Qualitative Market Research, 8*(2), 189–203. doi:10.1108/13522750510592454

Lessig, L. (2008). *Remix: Making art and commerce thrive in the hybrid economy*. New York, NY: Penguin Press.

Monaco, J. (2000). *How to read a film*. Oxford, UK: Oxford University Press.

Pace, S. (2008). YouTube: An opportunity for consumer narrative analysis? *Qualitative Market Research: An International Journal, 11*(2), 213–226. doi:10.1108/13522750810864459

Rose, G. (2007). *Visual methodologies: An introduction to the interpretation of visual materials*. Thousand Oaks, CA: Sage.

Schirato, T., & Webb, J. (2004). *Understanding the visual*. Thousand Oaks, CA: Sage.

Schroeder, J. E. (2002). *Visual consumption*. London, UK: Routledge.

Schroeder, J. E. (2007). Critical visual analysis. In Belk, R. W. (Ed.), *Handbook of qualitative research methods in marketing* (pp. 303–321). Cheltenham, UK: Edward Elgar.

Vargo, S. L., & Lusch, R. F. (2004). Evolving to a new dominant logic for marketing. *Journal of Marketing, 68,* 1–17. doi:10.1509/jmkg.68.1.1.24036

Venkatesh, A. (1999). Postmodern perspectives for macromarketing: An inquiry into the global information and sign economy. *Journal of Macromarketing, 19*(2), 153–169. doi:10.1177/0276146799192006

ADDITIONAL READING

Bal, M. (1997). *Narratology: Introduction to the theory of narrative*. Toronto, Canada: University of Toronto Press.

Bauer, B., & Gaskell, G. (Eds.). (2000). *Qualitative researching with text, image and sound: A practical handbook*. London, UK; Thousand Oaks, CA: Sage.

Burns, A. C., Williams, L. A., & Maxham, J. (2000). Narrative text biases attending the critical incidents technique. *Qualitative Market Research: An International Journal, 3*(4), 178–186.

Cova, B., & Cova, V. (2009). Faces of the new consumer: A genesis of consumer governmentality. [English Edition]. *Recherche et Applications en Marketing, 24*(3), 81–99.

Cova, B., Kozinets, R. V., & Shankar, A. (2007). *Consumer tribes*. Oxford, UK: Elsevier.

Elliott, J. (2005). *Using narrative in social research: Qualitative and quantitative approaches*. London, UK; Thousand Oaks, CA: Sage.

Emmison, M., & Smith, P. (2000). *Researching the visual: Images, objects, contexts and interactions in social and cultural inquiry*. London, UK: Sage.

Evans, J., & Hall, S. (Eds.). (1999). *Visual culture: The reader*. London, UK; Thousand Oaks, CA: Sage Publications, in association with the Open University.

Füller, J., Mühlbacher, H., Matzler, K., & Jawecki, G. (2009). Consumer empowerment through internet-based co-creation. *Journal of Management Information Systems, 26*(3), 71–102. doi:10.2753/MIS0742-1222260303

Hall, S. (Ed.). (1997). *Representation: Cultural representations and signifying practices*. London, UK; Thousand Oaks, CA: Sage Publications, in association with the Open University.

Heath, C., Hindmarsh, J., & Luff, P. (Eds.). (2010). *Video in qualitative research: Analyzing social interaction in everyday life*. London, UK; Thousand Oaks, CA: Sage.

Hopkinson, G. C., & Hogarth-Scott, S. (2001). 'What happened was …': Broadening the agenda for storied research. *Journal of Marketing Management, 17,* 27–47. doi:10.1362/0267257012571483

Kozinets, R. V. (2001). Utopian enterprise: Articulating the meanings of *Star Trek*'s culture of consumption. *The Journal of Consumer Research, 28,* 67–88. doi:10.1086/321948

Merz, M. A., Yi, H., & Vargo, S. L. (2009). The evolving brand logic: A service-dominant logic perspective. *Journal of the Academy of Marketing Science, 37*(3), 328–344. doi:10.1007/s11747-009-0143-3

Muñiz, A. M., & O'Guinn, T. C. (2001). Brand community. *The Journal of Consumer Research, 27,* 412–432. doi:10.1086/319618

Propp, V. (1968). *Morphology of the folk tale*. Austin, TX: University of Texas Press.

Scott, L. (1994). The bridge from text to mind: Adapting reader-response theory to consumer research. *The Journal of Consumer Research, 21*, 461–480. doi:10.1086/209411

Van Leeuwen, T., & Jewitt, C. (Eds.). (2001). *Handbook of visual analysis*. London, UK; Thousand Oaks, CA: Sage.

Vargo, S. L., & Lusch, R. F. (2008). Service-dominant logic: Continuing the evolution. *Journal of the Academy of Marketing Science, 36*, 1–10. doi:10.1007/s11747-007-0069-6

Worth, S. (1981). *Studying visual communication*. Philadelphia, PA: University of Pennsylvania Press.

KEY TERMS AND DEFINITIONS

E-Democracy: Web applications and platforms that facilitate the application, in an online context, of the criteria and methods of democracy. It can be promoted by public institutions and government bodies, or by everyday citizens.

Facebook: An online social networking platform (www.facebook.com). Users can create and update their personal profile and connect with other users or groups.

Netnography: Research method created by Robert V. Kozinets. This method applies the criteria of ethnography to online contexts, such as virtual communities and forums.

User-Generated Content (UGC): Any content that is produced by an individual, rather than by a company or organisation.

Web 2.0: An evolutionary stage in the Web life-cycle characterised by interactivity, user-generated content, and social/collaborative networks.

YouTube: An online platform for uploading and sharing videos (www.youtube.com). Most of the videos are either user-generated or posted by users.

Chapter 16
Online Opportunities for Mobile and Visual Research

Lesley Murray
University of Brighton, UK

ABSTRACT

The recent surge in interest in both mobile and visual methodologies reflects an increasing awareness of mobility and visualization in shaping our social worlds. The 'mobilities turn' in social science draws attention to the significance of a range of mobilities, from everyday to global. In tandem, visualization of virtual and lived spatial and social contexts is increasingly central to daily life and wider social processes. Both mobile and visual methods have evolved to reflect the epistemological changes that accompany these realizations, leading to a mobility of method as approaches draw from a range of disciplines. Online resources present particular opportunities for the expansion of these methods. For example, video methods can be adapted for online use in collecting visual data; this data can then be disseminated in video form through the Internet. However, this interrelationship between online, mobile, and visual methods has not been fully explored. This chapter explores the ways in which these methods can be combined to create knowledge in a unique way. It assesses the efficacy of these methodologies and methods by reviewing existing research and draws out key themes for analysis and further development.

INTRODUCTION

The urban landscape is shaped by mobility, through the movement of people, objects, information and ideas, as well as the meanings ascribed to these

mobilities in everyday life. The city is increasingly mobile and increasingly visual. The visual cacophonies that are negotiated in cities situate our experience of the urban in a global as well as local context. Glimpses of worlds beyond the city are available through static devices such as television and computers that give access to a world beyond;

DOI: 10.4018/978-1-4666-0074-4.ch016

and mobile devices such as mobile phones, laptops as well as a growing range of handheld devices. These technologies are both visual and mobile, and are productive of the social world. Much of the increased mobility and visualization is therefore 'online' as the virtual world acts as a conduit for textual and pictorial information and ideas, as well as a 'place of being'. It is considered that this increased virtuality could threaten the notion of cities as we know them. It is therefore critical that we develop a way of knowing the mobile, visual and virtual aspects of urban life.

Acknowledgment of these changes, and the theories that seek to make sense of them, gives rise to new epistemologies. For example, the 'mobilities turn' (Urry, 2007; Cresswell, 2006) in social science suggests that we cannot create knowledge about the social world without recognizing the centrality of mobility, including virtual mobility. Mobile methodologies represent a 'new approach to excavate and access the meaning of human constructions of the world' (Anderson, 2004, p. 254). Similarly, visual epistemologies incorporate an understanding of distinct forms of knowledge that can be created through visual methods, including online visual methods. However, this does not necessarily imply a disregard of previous methodological approaches, but rather presents opportunities to mobilize and visualize existing ones. This means that we may not be able to adhere strictly to any singular established paradigm but instead need to draw from a number of research traditions and philosophical approaches, in a 'bricolage' (Denzin & Lincoln, 1994, p. 4).

Along with a rethinking of methodological approach, research methods and tools need to be developed to adequately explore these changes, some of which will necessarily be online. Mobile and visual methods allow the creation of knowledge of both the global implications of changes in mobility, and the everyday lived experiences of mobile practices and cultures. Although it is argued that this necessitates a divergence from more traditional research methodologies and

methods (Sheller & Urry, 2006), this chapter approaches this as a mobilization of current more static research such as existing ethnographic approaches (Fincham, McGuinness, & Murray, 2010; Murray, 2009a).

BACKGROUND

There is a vast array of research tools available to the mobile researcher, and the complexity of the social world often necessitates a multi-pronged approach that mixes a number of methods (e.g., Freudendal-Pedersen et al., 2010). As discussed, the virtual realm is an important aspect of this complex social world, particularly in urban contexts. In order to explore virtual spaces, we need online tools. The recent surge in interest in the field of mobile methodologies and methods (Fincham, McGuinness, & Murray, 2010; Büscher, Urry, & Witchger, 2010; Adey, 2010), has not yet fully embraced this notion. This chapter therefore seeks to explore the capacity both to continue the development of online and mobile methods, and to examine nuanced ways of integrating them. There are already clear intersections, as online methods inhabit a virtual and inherently mobile realm. Online methods are already on the move.

Mobile and online methods are also needed to explore virtual spaces as significant spaces of mobility. Social networking sites, blogs, micro blogs, internet discussion forums, e-mails and list serves can be used to investigate both virtual and imagined mobilities as well as other forms of mobility. Other more established methods could also be said to be, to a degree, 'mobile', and present similar opportunities in exploring urban experiences. The application of visual methods, which have witnessed a similar but more established surge in interest, in unison, can further enrich the research process and outcomes. These methods are not only complementary but together provide a toolkit of methods, both tested and innovative, for the study of urban spaces.

This chapter seeks to address some of the methodological challenges presented by new ways of being in urban space, including the increasingly important reliance on online spaces in negotiating everyday life. This includes the growth of the 'virtual city' with its implications both for the physicality of cities, and theoretical debates on the relevance of this physicality (e.g., Castells, 1996; Massey, 2005). It argues for an appreciation of these challenges, as well as presenting methods that are best suited to create knowledge of increasingly online, mobile and visual, urban spaces.

The chapter therefore presents an exploration of the mobility of methods by examining the possibilities and rationale for the development of research methods that combine the mobile, visual and online. It begins with a review of debates in mobile methodologies moving on to examine the ways in which mobile and visual methods can be integrated and the implications for knowledge creation. Video, an example of a mobile and visual method is then explored before discussing the application of methods that are online, mobile and visual. The potential for these methods is then illustrated through my own research on aspects of everyday mobility.

Finally, although there is no specific section dedicated to ethical issues in research, it should be noted that such concerns are particularly pertinent in the fields of mobile, visual and online research as due to their nature, such methods can potentially intrude on everyday lives and often require a 'going with' participants that can jeopardize researcher integrity. Existing ethical codes can often be interpreted in a way that incorporates these methods, with the recognition that their ethical application requires negotiation between participants, researchers and others inadvertently incorporated into the research, through, for example, appearing in a research video. Debates on the ethical use of images are more established in the field of visual methods (Wiles et al., 2008) and these can be used to inform the application of the methods set out in this chapter.

MOBILITY OF METHODS

As urban studies are necessarily interdisciplinary, so too are the fields of mobilities and visual studies. Of course these fields are diverse, and so aspects of the study of urban areas, of mobility and of the visual have become associated with particular disciplinary perspectives. Nevertheless, as burgeoning approaches to an understanding of the social world, both mobile and visual methods have attracted attention from across academia. New insights and practical developments in mobile and visual methodologies and methods are emerging across a number of disciplines in the social sciences, including geography (Anderson, 2004; Barker & Weller, 2003; Lashua, Hall, & Coffey, 2006; Laurier, 2010; Rose, 2007), sociology (Büscher, 2006; Emmison, 2004; Emmison & Smith, 2000; Germann Molz, 2010), psychology (Reavey & Johnson, 2008), anthropology (Banks, 2001; Pink, 2007a) education (Prosser, 2007) and urban studies (Jirón, 2010; Latham, 2004). Online methods similarly intersect disciplines. As Madge and O'Connor (2005, p. 84) argue, 'cyberspace is the interdisciplinary research arena par excellence'. Research methods are thus becoming increasingly mobile by moving between disciplines resulting in new ways of creating knowledge of a changing social world.

It is apparent that, to some extent, mobility of methods is inevitable, and that it is more difficult to retain a purity of methods. However, there is also an argument that we need to ensure that we are mobile by considering a range of methods that may be appropriate to the investigation (e.g., Freudendal-Pedersen et al., 2010). Neyland (2006) alerts us to the perils of immobilizing ourselves as researchers by adhering to one particular view or standpoint. He examines a number of examples of mobility and immobility through different analytical lenses, including ethnographic re-telling, surveillance approach; ethnomethodological approach and an Actor-Network-Theory approach. He argues that an ethnographic account of a particular scenario based on a chronology of events can immobilize the story. He illustrates this with the example of the study of CCTV footage of a group of young people. When viewed as a sequence of images, disconnected from discourses and practices of surveillance, he argues, the story is immobilized. He contends that, in effect, there is a closing off of the story, like a 'closed circuit'. Instead he proposes a 'textual nomad' approach, with different methodological perspectives, which mobilize the research.

The relatively new field of 'mobile methodologies and methods' is emerging, partly as a response to this mobility of methods, as well as from the 'mobilities turn' in social science (Adey, 2010; Cresswell, 2006; Sheller & Urry 2006; Urry, 2007), which places mobile practices and cultures at the centre of social processes. This is founded on a reconsideration of sociological theories, such as Georg Simmel's, which recognizes the spatial significance of urban social relations and mobile place-making (Urry, 2007). In this contemporary analysis, mobility is considered to be produced by, and productive of, social relations (Creswell, 2006). This is particularly critical in urban areas where *hyper*mobility is considered to pose significant risks to society (Urry, 2007; Adams, 1999). The polarization of urban society, however, leads to a significant level of *hypo*mobility (Murray, 2009b), as particular sections of society are unable to access their needs and wants, remaining permanently or intermittently disconnected (Massey, 1994). A lack of transport has a part to play in this (Church et al., 2000). Researchers must be equipped with the appropriate tools to create understandings and offer solutions.

A number of forums with a specific focus on mobile methods such as the well attended session at the 2007 Royal Geographical Association with the Institute of British Geographers Annual International Conference, UK and the Mobile methods workshop at the Centre for Mobility and Research at Lancaster University, UK, have subsequently produced published collections (Fincham, McGuinness, & Murray, 2010; Büscher, Urry, & Witchger, 2010), which set out both a mobile methodological rationale, and an array of research tools that are mobile and contingent on a mobile world. These contribute to the toolkit of methods (Urry, 2007) required to create knowledge within the context of a complex mobile society. Other developments include the application of existing approaches, such as ethnomethodology (Laurier, 2010) and autoethnography (Fincham, 2006), to the exploration of mobile contexts as well as a range of specific techniques that produce knowledge of mobile relations including: go-alongs (Kusenbach, 2003), soundwalking (Lashua, Hall, & Coffey, 2006), travel diaries (Watts & Lyons, 2010) and GPS tracking (Gong & Mackett, 2009). There are also methods that explore spaces of 'in-betweenness' (Bissell, 2010), photo-diaries (Latham, 2004) and a large amount of work devoted to developing research methods that are specific to particular travel modes such as commuting by car (Edensor, 2004), walking in the city (Anderson, 2004; Lashua, Hall, & Coffey, 2006), driving practices (Dant, 2004; Laurier et al., 2008), and cycling (Fincham, 2006; Brown & Spinney, 2010). Much of this work is premised on the notion of researching 'in place' and 'on the move', with an acknowledgment of the contexts of research, which will be outlined in the following.

Researching in Place

One of the key aspects of researching 'in place' is the gathering of data whilst moving along or making journeys with participants. A number of research studies have used mobile interviewing to explore both movement in space and the significance of particular spaces and places. Lashua, Hall, and Coffey (2006) studied young people's movement and spatiality in areas undergoing regeneration and found that the mobile interviews provided a 'three-way conversation' involving participants, researchers and place. In his study of radical environmentalism, Anderson (2004,

p. 254) emphasizes the 'inherently socio-spatial' nature of the walking interview and argues that this provides a unique means of accessing human knowledge. He argues that the spatial context of the interview is often ignored despite the relationship between spatial identity, human action and knowledge formation. Recognition of the 'co-ingredience' of people and place, Anderson argues, enables a full understanding of spatialized practices as well as providing spatial cues for prompting lifecourse memories. Much of the research on corporeal mobility and the production of social space, has focused on these aspects of researching in place; talking and moving with participants in a way that creates knowledge in a distinctive way.

Researching in place or 'being there' is therefore a key element of mobile methods. This contextualization in space is a critical element of methodologies that encompass the centrality of mobility in everyday life and societal structures (Urry, 2007; Cresswell, 2006). Such a methodological approach is considered to enhance our knowledge of the world in two ways. Firstly, being in place is always relative to another place. A specific spatial context can only be given meaning in relation to another, and these spatial contexts are then linked by mobility, be it corporeal, visual, audial, imagined or virtual. Secondly, researching in situ requires consideration of the research methods that make this possible. It can both demonstrate the need for mobile methods and produce the methods themselves. It is this that makes methods that may not purport to be 'mobile', such as narrative interviews, nevertheless 'mobile'. It also means that we often need to look across disciplines to find the right mix or toolkit of methods.

VISUALIZING THE MOBILE AND MOBILIZING THE VISUAL

Following on from urban theorists, such as Simmel (1971), De Certeau (1984), and Lefebvre (1996), it is argued that using both mobile and visual explorations of urban areas produces distinct forms of knowledge, particularly of the co-construction of social interactions and urban space. In turn, visual and mobile practices are themselves generative. Büscher (2006) argues that 'mobility is mediated through material and narrative resources'. In her exploration of visual practices in shaping place, Büscher explores the ways in which we navigate space using maps and talking with other people. Mobility is therefore produced through visual and discursive practices (Cresswell, 2006). Like mobile methods, visual methods encompass a toolkit of techniques that utilize the visual image in the exploration of the social world. Methods can be based on the analysis of existing visual images or the production of images by participants through, for example, drawings, photography and video. A full analysis of the range of visual methods is available elsewhere (Pink, 2007a; Rose, 2007). The concern in this chapter is the juxtaposition of visual and mobile methods, where the methodological approaches and methods intersect.

One of the main debates within the field of visual methods, and one that is relevant here, concerns the nature of the knowledge produced. Where previously a positivist approach used the image as a representation of truth, without questioning its social, spatial and historical context and subjectivity, more recent approaches (Banks, 2001; Emmison, 2004; Pink, 2007a; Rose, 2007) have recognized these contextualities from a critical and therefore reflexive perspective. As Rose (2007, p. 12) argues 'cultural practices like visual representations both depend on and produce social inclusions and exclusions, and a critical account needs to address both those practices and their cultural meaning and effects'. Rose (2007) explores three sites of visualization:

the production of images, the image itself and the audiencing of the image. Visual images can be used as a form of mediation between researcher and participant; 'images or material objects implicated in the interview mediate the relationship between researcher and informant' (Pink, 2007a, p. 33). Taking a reflexive and therefore ethical approach therefore assumes recognition of the positionality of researcher and participant in a process of co-construction of knowledge (Latham, 2004; Pink, 2007; Rose, 2007).

Visual methods are contextualizing in that they can visually situate a subject in a particular place. At the same time, the role of the visual image is always contingent on both the context in which the image was captured, and the context in which it is audienced. Emmison (2004, p. 250) contextualized the image in space, arguing for an understanding of its dimensionality, contesting that 'objects, places and locales carry meaning through visual means just like images'. Citing Simmel's visual analysis of the city, he argues for critical visual methodologies that are spatially situated and 'lived'. Of course, this contextualization in space, which the visual image both allows and is necessary for its analysis, is highly significant in terms of mobile research. As Latham (2004, p. 119) argues, 'the sequence within which people and materials pass through and inhabit particular locales, as well as the frequency and intensity with which they do so, is a fundamental element of contextuality'. Latham (2004, p. 126) used a visual diary method, with participants representing their everyday experiences in urban space through photographs and argues that visual methods allow a capturing of the intensity of everyday mobile life in the city, a 'sense of mood and ambience – of the colour and energy – of a particular moment'.

There are already a number of examples of methodological approaches to research that explicitly use both mobile and visual methods. Indeed, it can be argued that any research that incorporates explorations of the social world through a sensory lens can be considered neces-

sarily mobile (Murray, 2008). Pink's (2007b) project 'Walking With Video', which is discussed later, is a good example of this. In turn, many of the innovations taking place within the field of mobilities employ visual methods. For example, Laurier et al. (2008) attached a video to a car dashboard and recorded the 'inhabitation' of the car in their exploration of automobile culture. Recognition of the co-construction of knowledge between participant, researcher and mobile space is a necessary element of a critical approach to mobile and visual methods. So too is the recognition of the series of interpretations that visual and mobile data undergoes.

As discussed, the critical application of mobile and visual methods requires contextualization in time and space, with the recognition that both are socially constructed and 'like all sensory experience the interpretation of sight is culturally and historically specific' (Banks, 2001, p. 7). Although visual methods provide this context, there is almost always a need to further contextualize through text or dialogue. Investigations of the social world are often only possible from a perspective that incorporates more than one dimension, or more than one sensory element.

The application of visual and mobile methods facilitates the capture of the discrete interplay between people, material objects and space, contingent on prevailing meanings and beliefs, whilst recognising that these meaning and beliefs are co-constituted with practices of mobility and visualization. One of the research methods that best epitomizes the way in which mobile and visual are complementary is the moving image. This method also illustrates the trans-disciplinary development of a research tool that meets the needs of mobile research.

CAPTURING, INTERPRETING, AND RE-INTERPRETING THE MOVING IMAGE

The advantages of using video as a central tool in a toolkit of methods are numerous. Firstly, the use of video is premised on the value of contextualized moving, visual and audial data (Dant, 2004; Pink, 2007a; Rose, 2007). Both the process of filming and the video footage put social and material interactions 'in place' and, in doing so, allow an understanding of the production of space. The video permits a capture of the moment-ness of everyday life (Murray, 2008; Pink, 2007b). In Pink's (2007b, p. 250) 'Walking With Video', the process of filming the act of walking is seen as a way of place-making, 'a more involved approach to the question of how place and identities are constituted'.

Secondly, video enables the capture of multisensory engagement with space. It captures experiences through a range of senses, as Pink (2007a) illustrates in her study of housework, in which participants used metaphors to illustrate their particular housework strategies. This notion is developed in a special edition of *Visual Studies* (Pink et al., 2010) on walking, ethnography and the arts, looking at walking as a multisensory ethnographic tool. As Pink et al. (2010, p. 4) argue, 'when we study visual forms and practices we need to account for the other senses and, when we study corporeal practices, we need to account for how vision and visual forms are inextricable from these experiences'. The capture of multisensory experiences is central to Brown and Spinney's (2010) mobile video ethnography of cycling in London (UK) and rural Scotland. They contend that video allows a 'place travel' that engages with the mobile practices of cycling in a way that incorporates the embodied sensory and emotional aspects of being mobile in this way, 'an intertextual evocation of inhabiting and attaching meaning to the bodily experience of riding, with its accompanying feelings and thoughts, through

the entwining of moving image and language' (Brown & Spinney, 2010, p. 150).

Thirdly, video methods promote a reflexive approach to research and, in some ways, enable this. They present the opportunity to reflect visually on the research process as a video recording can be watched and watched again; but there is also the opportunity to re-interpret and negotiate the data as it is audienced again and again (Rose, 2007). This reflexivity also involves the awareness of, and reflection on, the impact of performance on the data collected. The notion of performance to the camera is one that is often used as a critique of video and other visual methods. The cultural meanings surrounding being photographed and filmed are considered to detract from the ability of the visual data to represent everyday life. However, proponents of these methods argue that performance is an intricate part of everyday life, and should be both understood and embraced within the research process (Holliday, 2004; Loescher, 2005). Using video methods to explore children's use of an adventure playground, Loescher (2005) found the children performances for camera problematic as they created particular identities through this process. However, this representation of identity through performance became an integral part of the research as it became recognised that this identity is informed by the children's interaction with the urban space, which was the subject of Loescher's research. This then became a distinct finding in the research as 'visual language [became] the language of research rather than its tool' (Loescher, 2005, p. 63).

Similarly in Morel and Licoppe's study of the use of mobile video calls they found that 'it may be the case with mobile methods we have to consider mobile-capture technologies not just as recording apparatus, but as part of the phenomena we want to study' (Morel & Licoppe, 2010, p. 180). In their research they used either video glasses that give partial access to a mobile screen, or direct recording on mobile phones that had a video output with a wireless microphone, which allowed ongoing interaction on the move.

Of course, as in all research, there is always significance in the data that was not recorded and that remained unseen by the video camera (Dant, 2004). This absence must be incorporated into the analysis as part of the reflexive process, with an understanding of the mediation of events through the interpretation of data by the researcher. This interpretation continues through the analysis process and during dissemination of the visual data as it is audienced in different ways (Rose, 2007). Through this process of interpretation and re-interpretation, the visual data becomes more and more distorted from its original context and meanings as it is further and further removed from its original context. Of course the researcher can seek to reduce this distortion by ensuring that film subjects become part of the interpretation process. In addition, 'self-filming' can be used to enable participants to decide what is included and what is left out. This method has a long history in visual research, having been used extensively in anthropology, and can be traced back to Sol Worth and John Adam's 1966 film 'Navajo Film Themselves' (Pink, 2007a). Holliday (2004, p. 509) contends that this method allows participants to self-represent their 'performativities of identity' in specific socio-cultural contexts.

Finally, using video methods allows reflection on elements of everyday lives that might otherwise be taken for granted. As Latham (2004, p. 122) argues, it enables both 'spatially dispersed' and routine social interactions to be investigated in a meaningful way. However, again, this visual data must be interpreted by the researcher and this will often involve textualizing the visual data during analysis (Pink, 2007a; Rose, 2007). Nevertheless, the use of video allows a capturing of the moment-to-momentness of life, and the study of the representation of social and material interaction in space and time that other methods neglect.

So far this chapter has set out the development of mobile methods as an emerging field, and argued that we need to approach research with a transdisciplinary approach in a way that enables the 'right' mix of methods. One approach to this is to combine mobile and visual methods, and the benefits of this have been illustrated using video - one of the most mobile of visual methods. This discussion illustrates the characteristics of mobile and visual methods, which blend well with online methods. The chapter will now focus more directly on this combination.

COMBINING ONLINE, MOBILE, AND VISUAL

The virtual realm, in its enormity, presents endless opportunities for social researchers with an interest in mobility. Online tools are themselves mobilizing; from facilitating corporeal travel through route information and GPS based applications to the movement of ideas, information, and identities that is possible in the virtual realm. However, the possibilities presented have been adopted inconsistently by mobile researchers. There are distinct possibilities for dissemination and knowledge exchange in particular, which have, to a greater extent, been taken up by visual researchers. Pink (2010) has developed a web-based forum on the use of hypermedia, including the Internet, to disseminate visual ethnographic research. Pink describes the use of the Internet in visual anthropology and visual sociology, signposting to a number of useful sites that themselves have links to hypermedia representations of visual research. This webpage provides an analysis of the potential for hypermedia representation of visual research since then, including the University of Kent's Centre for Social Anthropology and Computing (CSAC), Visual Anthropology Net and Visione Reciproche. The webpage also includes original hypermedia resources. Pink also discusses the journal AV-Materiali and archiving sites such as Marcus Banks Haddon site at Oxford, and the Lacuna project at Edinburgh and the IWF Knowledge and Media site in Goettingen (Germany). These online and off-line hypermedia projects are considered to be significant developments in ethnographic methods.

Online methods offer significant potential for mobile ethnographies. They can be used to respond quickly to events and enable social researchers to lead the way in analyzing critical events. Researchers can make use of web-based questionnaires and use mobile and online communications to stimulate interest. Such an online questionnaire was posted following the eruption of the Icelandic volcano, Eyjafjallajökull, in April 2010, causing major disruption to air traffic worldwide. Its composer, Jo Guiver from the Institute of Transport and Tourism at the University of Central Lancashire (2010), sums up the temporal mobility of experience of such events: 'Once the dust has settled, literally, the story about what happened and how people felt about it will change'. Online methods make researching immediate responses possible before this dust has settled.

With these opportunities come challenges in negotiating this 'excessive proliferation of information' (Germann Molz, 2010, p. 97). However, as the 'production of knowledge is always social' (Germann Molz, 2010), it is left up to social researchers to manage and interpret this information in innovative ways. Both online technologies and mobility are both generative of the social world and, at the same time, are producers of knowledge. In turn, the production of knowledge through mobility and online technologies is itself productive of the social world. The mobility of online methods deems them an ideal accompaniment to mobile and visual methods in exploring our changing social world.

Another challenge for researchers is maintaining the ability to keep pace with the range of technologies that allow large-scale explorations. Büscher, Urry, and Witchger (2010) suggest that such technologies are being exploited commercially, and that social researchers need to compete with their capabilities. They argue that 'other

social forces [are] also developing powerful mobile computer-based methods and these may win out in part because of their interconnections with forms and forces of monitoring and surveillance' (Büscher, Urry, & Witchger, 2010, p. 2). However, the extent to which this competition restricts social researchers, particularly those concerned with everyday mobilities, is questionable. For example, technologies that track social practices are being applied to everyday mobilities. Research carried out at University College London (Gong & Mackett, 2009) to explore children's mobility used questionnaires, interviews, and GPS (global positioning satellite) devices and RT3 physical activity monitors as well as and asking participants to keep diaries. From these methodologies, the following became known about the children in the study: where they went, what they did when they were there, who accompanied them (adult, other children or nobody), and how active they were. Children were fitted with GPS (global positioning system) monitors as well as using the activity monitors and diaries, so that it was possible to establish where the children went for various activities. Data was recorded on the trackers, and analysed afterwards, but there is potential here to build in online methods of data transport and analysis.

As we use mobile methods to explore mobile practices, we can use online and mobile methods to explore online and mobile practices. The advantages of this approach seem obvious; and they appear to be right tools for the task. However, the most interesting aspect of this approach is perhaps the intersection of methods and social practices. Earlier in the chapter, we discussed the challenges to knowledge creation presented by an increasingly online world and, in particular, in negotiating the boundary between the physical and virtual worlds. Germann Molz (2010) argues that this challenge can be met, in part, through exploring how particular groups of people negotiate these boundaries in their everyday lives. She argues that mobile researchers have much to learn from interactive travellers and the way they create knowledge as they 'make sense of their online practices and mediated social interactions through a matrix of electronic and social connectivity' (2010, p. 89).

Germann Molz looks at the relationship between mobility, technology and knowledge, and the creation of knowledge through mobility and technology, contending that mobilizing technologies such as laptops, MP3s, GPS devices and mobile phones can create distinctive knowledge of the mobile world. Her research explored interactive travel using methods that included following blog updates, watching online videos, using emails and discussion forums, as well as meeting participants in person. In particular, Germann Molz is interested in where 'online, on-the-phone and face-face socialities intersect with the technical materiality, visual and narrative representations and embodied practices of interactive travel' (Germann Molz, 2010). The remainder of this chapter focuses, to some extent, on this intersection by illustrating a number of applications of methods that are online, mobile and visual.

ONLINE, MOBILE, AND VISUAL APPLICATIONS

Having drawn from a range of research studies, the following discussion is premised on themes that emerged from my own research of aspects of everyday mobility. The research explored the co-construction of risk, mobility, motherhood and childhood in determining mothers' and children's mobilities in a specific urban mobile space, the space between home and school. This space is considered distinctive in that, for children, it offers the opportunity for independent travel outside the constraints of school and home; and for mothers (who make the majority of escort trips in the UK) it represents an often highly social and emotional space of 'letting go' (Murray, 2009b). The research employed mobile and visual methods primarily,

with online methods playing a minor role but, nonetheless, one that illustrates their potential.

One of the aims of the research was to enable children and young people to play an active role in the research process. In total twenty five young people from a range of social backgrounds, and in different urban contexts, filmed their journey to or from school, and took part in film-elicitation interviews afterwards. The children's mothers took part in narrative interviews, which mapped out mobility experiences through the lifecourse. Through the videos and interviews the children and young people represented their mobile experiences, the socialities of the journey, their emotions attached to different aspects of their journey, and their construction of the risks they encountered. Following this first stage of research, the footage from the children's videos was edited into a short film (Figures 1 and 2), in collaboration with a professional filmmaker. The film was produced on DVD, which was distributed widely to transport policy-makers and practitioners. A clip of the film has now been made available online by the filmmaker (http://www.youtube.com/marielenclos) and this has lead to further audiencing.

A number of themes emerged from this methodological approach that are relevant here, such as demonstration of the production of urban space through mobile practices and the overall enrichment of data through multi-context, and therefore mobile and visual research, and these are described in detail elsewhere (Murray, 2010). More importantly here are the key themes that emerged from the research in relation to online, mobile and visual methods: virtual space as a space of 'being' that tells us about other spaces, the opportunities offered by the liminality of virtual space; and the potentials of online methods in enhancing the inclusivity of mobile and visual methods.

'Being There' Virtually

As the discussion of mobile methods set out, exploring the mobile world often involves mobiliz-

Figure 1. Filming a school journey, still from video Through our Eyes

ing the research methods, with the argument that it is only possible to know by 'being there'. The virtual world represents a place of being that is of great interest to the mobile and visual researcher. Research studies have illustrated that as well as being a place in itself, the virtual world can enhance our understanding of other places. For example, in Clarke's (2010) study of British working holiday makers the virtual realm provided a 'home' that could be revisited regardless of location; a virtual place of being. The ways in which holiday-makers inhabited this place, however, provided insights into the concept of home, which is more often associated as a corporeal place of being. Travellers visited particular websites, accessed particular forms of media, and communicated online in ways that connected them virtually with their physical home. The mobile practices of the British working holiday makers in Clarke's study were based on 'travelling-in-dwelling': returning 'home' from time to time through online means; and dwelling-in-travelling: creating traveller communities using a range of mobile technologies

such as web-based e-mail accounts and mobile telephones, alongside more traditional social practices that were face-to-face.

Following on from the earlier discussion of the importance of mobile and visual methods in enabling contextualization, of placing subjects during the research process, the virtual world can provide a new context for the research, an additional place of being. This can be illustrated through the various research spaces created by participants in my research. In filming their journeys to school the children and young people contextualized it in time and space, capturing the moment-to-momentness (Büscher, 2006) of their journeys, and often providing a commentary on it. Using video facilitated the capture of the moving context of the children and young people's material and social interactions. The participants were then able to explore this moving context further through watching the videos afterwards in the film-elicitation interviews, and re-visiting and re-making their mobile experiences. In addition, the video was audienced and interpreted by the

Figure 2. Opening titles of video Through our Eyes

children and young people's families, adding another dimension to the data. The film was also sent to participants who viewed it, along with their friends and families (Figure 3). They responded to it via a short questionnaire either using a form provided or via email.

These different contexts provided different layers of data to be interpreted and made sense of. In doing so they produced a rich set of data. This data was contingent on the particular social and material interactions and the emotions evoked in different settings. This meant that particular elements of this interaction were given a greater significance than others, as children and young people drew attention to particular parts of their journeys, or particular people along the way. They mentioned particular fears they had when they were alone in particular parts of the journey. However, when they were re-visiting the same journey in another space, their home, the journey was constructed in a different way. The participants drew attention to different parts of the journey

and either did not mention, or denied, fears that were evident during filming, when removed from direct and multi-sensory interaction with particular mobile spaces. The two-dimensionality of the viewing experience produced another set of responses and emotions.

This is particularly evident in two of the young people's experience of bullying on the school journey. Lily and her sister Jasmine were threatened with a BB gun on their way home from school a few months before they were interviewed. However, as they passed the place where the incident occurred they said the following:

That's the big house at the end of the road then you've got to cross the main road, which is absolutely horrible. I like running across it. It gets warmer up here than down there. One of my friends lives in one of these houses (Lily, video).

Figure 3. On the school bus, still image from the video Through our Eyes

There was no reference to the incident at all. However, during the film-elicitation interview Lily explains:

Somebody threatened us with a gun, a BB gun, to shoot us. We phoned the police. It was near [our friend's] house...We stayed near Jade's house and phoned the police from a mobile. The police came and me and my friend walked down further and the police came and they were jumping fences and everything. But they never caught them but they have now and they've put them on a list so that if they do another thing wrong... They go to our school...When we went back to school I had pictures of it shooting 'cause they put the gun to our head. I had a picture of the gun. We walked to school on the Monday. (Lily, young person, interview)

As discussed, participants were contacted by email and asked to respond to a series of questions two years later, the third research context

they encountered. By this time, the visual data had been re-visited a number of times, and audienced by a range of people. It is surprising that Lily did not mention this incident earlier in the research, when she videoed her journey, particularly, as it emerged later, she associated it with the friend's house she pointed out in the video. Lily again discusses the incident in her email:

A few months after we made the video these boys were messing around and pointed a fake gun at my sister's head and were so frightened for a week we walked with my mum. (Lily, two years after original research in email)

Lily's recollection of the event has become distorted. She remembers the event occurring after the research rather than before it. She also has a stronger reaction and uses more emotive language. The online communication with Lily reflects her 'being' in online space, a space in which young people create particular identities (e.g., Hodkin-

Figure 4. Watching the video Through our Eyes

(a)   (b)

son & Lincoln, 2008) (Figure 4). For some, this distinct space can represent an in-between space that allows them to discuss issues that they feel less able to discuss in other contexts.

A Liminal Space of Escape

For Madge and O'Connor (2005) virtual space is not a place in itself but can be constructed as liminal, or in-between space. In Clarke's (2010) study of the construction of this space a 'home', it can also be seen as a place that was between 'home' and 'away'. Whether the virtual realm represents a distinct place of being or is a liminal space between worlds, there is evidence to suggest that it can be a place of refuge. Hence, in presenting an additional research context that enables a particular discourse, virtual space can be a rich source of data for researchers. Madge and O'Connor argue that the liminality of the space makes it a mobile space as it is on the way to somewhere else. As a mobile space it becomes a place of escape. Often spaces that are mobile are constructed in this way. The journey to school, for example, is considered to be a space in which young people can 'be', which is beyond the confines of home and school (Murray, 2009b).

Similarly, Internet forums represented a liminal space for mothers in Madge and Connor's (2005) study. They used a web-based questionnaire survey and semi-structured virtual group interviews in their research exploring mothers' use of mothering-related Internet forums. Their focus is on the assumed dichotomies of online and offline space as real and unreal, embodied and virtual. They use the concept of liminality to make sense of cyberspace as a space of inbetween-ness, both a metaphorical space and practical space where mothering roles developed. In doing so they argue that this liminal space is both a virtual and corporeal space in which mothers interact through their bodies. Similarly for Holt (2011, p. 8), in her study of the 'hidden' issue of parent abuse, the liminality of online message boards provides a 'space where parental powerlessness can be articulated (and heard) without censure'. Online spaces, therefore, often provide an anonymous space where particular marginalized groups are able to convey their life experiences in a way that circumvents many of the barriers encountered in other spaces.

This theme emerged in my research in which mothers discussed their mobility histories and their experiences of mobility through their lifecourse in more than one research context. One of the key issues in this research was the emergence of critical incidents in the participant's pasts that had a major impact on their current mobility and the mobility of their children. When Kim was asked about particular memorable experiences in mobile space, it appeared at first that she had not encountered anything specific. Kim's first response during the narrative interview suggested that, although there may have been a minor incident, it did not impact on her mobility.

No accidents at all. No I don't think so. I don't really want to go into it (looks at children) but there was one incident in the park when I was at college and there was someone lurking a bit...but that didn't affect how I travelled after. Only being more cautious of what was around me, of what I was doing but I would still have gone through the park. (Kim, Interview)

However, Kim responded to the same question very differently in her email response two years after her interview:

I think one or two experiences from when I was younger have affected how I treat the way the children travel. When I was a teenager I helped at a playschool and got to know lots of the children. Several years later after I had left home the teenage sister of one of those children was raped and murdered on her way home from the school that had been my secondary school. Although I hadn't known her, I had known her sister and mum, and the area was so familiar to me. Also my sister was still a pupil at the school. At the time I felt quite deeply affected and know that I had some bad dreams. The second incident was at college. I had to walk across a park every morning usually meeting my friend and going together. One wintery morning was quite misty; my friend wasn't there so I went on my own. As I walked along I became aware of someone walking quite close to me. It was a teenage boy. I was scared but thought a bit of bravado and staring at him might work. It did

because he ran away. My friend eventually arrived at college telling us that she had been flashed at in the park - from her description it was the same boy. (Kim, email, one year later)

Kim's experiences seem highly emotive ones, which she felt unable to detail in the original interview. However, she was able to provide a detailed account in her email and send it through cyberspace. Drawing from this and the studies discussed previously (Fay, 2008; Holt, 2011; Madge & O'Connor, 2005), there appears to be a particularly gendered occupation of virtual space that constructs it as a place of security, away from the constraints of everyday gendered life. Kim may have been similarly occupying the liminal cyberspace described by Madge and O'Connor, as she responded on the second occasion. This is therefore a space where certain groups can escape their (gender) roles including those associated with childcare in Kim's case and occupy a less bounded and more flexible space in which to take part in research.

This gendered virtual space is also evident in Fay's (2008, p. 70) study of a virtual university forum for women set up to debate issues of gender and mobility. She adopted 'cyber-ethnographic research' including online questionnaires and analysis of mailing list and website content. In 'depart[ing] from a concrete localized example' Fay (2008, p. 67) uses the boundless possibilities of online methods in capturing the boundless possibilities of virtual mobilities. She found that the space had been constructed in a particular way, as a gendered liminal space in which contributions to the forum had a 'confessional air' whilst, at the same time, resisting gender constraints associated with mobility. Online methods in these contexts are mobile and can facilitate discussions relating to the marginalization of certain groups, particularly groups that may be considered less mobile than others.

The Inclusivity of Virtual Space

Mobile and visual methods are premised on the understanding that to create knowledge about a world that is increasingly understood on an everyday basis in mobile and visual ways, we need to develop methods that capture these mobile and visual practices, beliefs, meanings, cultures and emotions. The adoption of a methodology that incorporates a range of mobile and visual methods can indeed broaden the participant base by ensuring that participants, who may otherwise be excluded from the research process, are included.

Including a group of people often marginalized by the research process was one of the decisive factors in the adoption of mobile and visual methods in my research. As well as evidence from other research with children and young people (Barker & Weller, 2003) that similar research methods appealed to children as a 'difficult to reach' social group, the majority of children taking part in my research said that they volunteered because the research involved them videoing their journey. Following on from this, it is not difficult to appreciate the possibilities for developing online research with children and young people using similarly attractive online tools. Social networking sites, such as *Facebook*, and micro blog sites, such as *Twitter*, offer possibilities to capture data on the move and in visual form. As discussed, virtual spaces can represent a research space that allows an articulation of experience that may not otherwise be possible. In this way it enables a range of experiences to be included in the research process. Madge and Connor (2005) found that online methods similarly allow research with groups less likely to become involved with research.

At the same time, researchers should proceed with caution and consider the myriad ethical, epistemological and logistical issues associated with the mixing of methods. Research that adopts any untried methods needs to be reflexive in approach. For example, in Fay's (2008) study of the interplay between theory, feminism and mobility,

although the virtual space was envisaged as a 'lived-in' and 'being together' space, she argues that it developed into a more traditional university setting for discussion, which was simply facilitated by technology. The emphasis on creating an innovative space raised tensions as the virtual space continued to be structured by existing rules of discussion.

It is also necessary to understand the wider role of technology in society and the inclusions and exclusions that result from its complex interrelationships. The technologies behind virtual mobilities have become embedded in society with substantial increases in mobility for a proportion of the population. However, just as some become virtually hypermobile, others are virtually hypomobile. It could be argued that the technology designed to relieve the pressure of hypermobility has simply increased the pace of modern life and magnifies the polarization of mobility (for a discussion of the relationship between virtual and social exclusion, see Kenyon, 2006). Social inequalities are intensified by the unevenness, the crumpling of time and distance as specific forms of mobility are available to specific populations (Massey, 1994). This can be exacerbated when those without access to mobile communications or who are generally less mobile social groups are excluded from research. Whilst numerous studies have explored this (e.g., Church et al., 2000), few studies have emphasized the methods best applied for its fuller understanding. However, as illustrated in the research studies discussed, there is potential in mixed method approaches that use online, mobile and visual tools, to overcome some of the problems associated with involving groups that are both marginalized and mobility excluded.

CONCLUSION

This chapter has considered the opportunities for the integration of a number of methodological approaches and methods that incorporate the specificities of an increasingly online, mobile and visual world. Such methods are already being used by a number of social researchers across the social science disciplines, including urban studies, and provide a distinctive approach to knowledge creation. Mobile, visual and online methods are transdisciplinary, in that the continuing innovation of these methods takes place where disciplines intersect. Such an approach promotes a mobility of method, which in some ways is an inevitable consequence of the exploration of increasingly complex social world. At the same time, it is a notion that needs to be actively embraced. Visual methodologies are an already established field of research, in which key issues have been debated, while it continues to evolve. Mobile methodologies are an emerging field in research, but nonetheless one that in recent times has witnessed a surge in interest. As a result, both visual and mobile methods have established toolkits of methods. In addition, these methodological approaches, and especially visual methodologies, have established ethical guidelines. The flourishing field of online methods can benefit from the work that has been carried out to date. In addition, mobile, visual and online are good companions, they work well together. To some extent online methods are already mobile. As discussed, in adopting methods that recognize the spatiality of social and material interaction in different spaces, the methods are mobilized. Mobile methods are predicated on the embedding of everyday activities in space and place, the generative nature of space, and the separation of different spaces and places that requires movement between them, be it corporeal/material, imagined or virtual.

Merging mobile, visual and online methods has a number of advantages. In particular they allow the contextualized production of knowledge, a knowledge based on the co-constituted relationship between mobilities, visualizations and cyberspace; and mobile, visual and online research. Online methods enrich data as they provide another context in which to research; a virtual context that can be detached from the materiality of everyday life, providing an alternative in its liminality (Madge & O'Connor, 2005). This may be due to the less bounded nature of the space, although cyberspace can also be constrained in similar ways to other research spaces as demonstrated in Fay's (2008) study of a university discussion forum. This researching in context is inherently mobile as it recognizes the spatial and mobile production of the social world. For this reason, because online methods are mobile methods, they will remain a key element of debates on mobile methodologies and methods. Online methods can also provide a liminal space in which marginalized groups in particular can inhabit as a place of escape. For example virtual space can present women with a secure space that lies outside of gender constraints. These methods, therefore, offer possibilities for extending research with groups often excluded from the research process, but who may feel able to engage with research in the virtual sphere. This is a significant advantage in a world that for some, at certain times and in certain spaces, is becoming increasingly hypermobile and for others, at certain times and in certain spaces, increasingly hypomobile.

REFERENCES

Adams, J. (1999). *The social implications of hypermobility*. Paris, France: OECD.

Adey, P. (2010). *Mobility*. London, UK: Routledge.

Anderson, J. (2004). Talking whilst walking: a geographical archaeology of knowledge. *Area*, *36*, 254–261. doi:10.1111/j.0004-0894.2004.00222.x

Banks, M. (2001). *Visual methods in social research*. London, UK: Sage.

Barker, J., & Weller, S. (2003). Is it fun?' Developing children centred research methods. *International Journal of Sociology*, *23*(1), 33–58.

Bissell, D. (2010). Narrating Mobile Methodologies: Active and Passive Empiricisms. In Fincham, B., McGuinness, M., & Murray, L. (Eds.), *Mobile Methodologies* (pp. 53–68). Basingstoke, UK: Palgrave Macmillan.

Brown, K., & Spinney, J. (2010). Catching a glimpse: the value of video in evoking, understanding and representing the practice of cycling. In Fincham, B., McGuinness, M., & Murray, L. (Eds.), *Mobile Methodologies* (pp. 130–151). Basingstoke, UK: Palgrave Macmillan.

Büscher, M. (2006). Vision in motion. *Environment & Planning A, 38,* 281–299. doi:10.1068/a37277

Büscher, M. Urry, J., & Witchger, K. (2010). *Mobile methods*. London, UK: Routledge.

Castells, M. (1996). *The rise of the network society*. Cambridge, MA: Blackwell.

Church, A., Frost, M., & Sullivan, K. (2000). Transport and social exclusion in London. *Transport Policy, 7,* 195–205. doi:10.1016/S0967-070X(00)00024-X

Clarke, N. (2010). Writing mobility: Australia's working holiday programme. In Fincham, B., McGuinness, M., & Murray, L. (Eds.), *Mobile Methodologies* (pp. 118–129). Basingstoke, UK: Palgrave Macmillan.

Cresswell, T. (2006). *On the move*. New York, NY: Routledge.

Dant, T. (2004). Recording the 'habitus. In Pole, C. (Ed.), *Seeing is believing? Approaches to visual research* (pp. 41–60). Oxford, UK: Emerald. doi:10.1016/S1042-3192(04)07004-1

De Certeau, M. (1984). *The practice of everyday life*. Berkeley, CA: University of California Press.

Denzin, N. K., & Lincoln, Y. S. (1994). *Handbook of qualitative methods*. London, UK: Sage.

Dwyer, C., & Davies, G. (2010). Qualitative methods III: animating archives, artful interventions and online environments. *Progress in Human Geography, 34,* 88–97. doi:10.1177/0309132508105005

Edensor, T. (2004). Automobility and National Identity: Representation, Geography and Driving Practice. *Theory, Culture & Society, 21*(4-5), 101–120. doi:10.1177/0263276404046063

Emmison, M. (2004). The conceptualisation and analysis of qualitative research. In Silverman, D. (Ed.), *Qualitative research: theory, method and practice* (pp. 246–265). London, UK: Sage.

Emmison, M., & Smith, P. (2000). *Researching the visual*. London, UK: Sage.

Fay, M. (2008). Mobile belonging: exploring transnational feminist theory and online connectivity. In Priya Uteng, T., & Cresswell, T. (Eds.), *Gendered mobilities* (pp. 65–83). Aldershot, UK: Ashgate.

Fincham, B. (2006). Back to the Old School: Bicycle Messengers, Employment and Ethnography. *Qualitative Research, 6*(2), 187–205. doi:10.1177/1468794106062709

Fincham, B., McGuinness, M., & Murray, L. (Eds.). (2010). *Mobile Methodologies*. Basingstoke, UK: Palgrave Macmillan.

Freudendal-Pedersen, M., Hartmann-Petersen, K., & Drewes Nielsen, L. (2010). Mixing methods in the search for mobile complexity. In Fincham, B., McGuinness, M., & Murray, L. (Eds.), *Mobile Methodologies* (pp. 25–42). Basingstoke, UK: Palgrave Macmillan.

Germann Molz, J. (2010). Connectivity, collaboration, search. In Büscher, M., Urry, J., & Witchger, K. (Eds.), *Mobile methods* (pp. 88–103). London, UK: Routledge.

Gong, Y., & Mackett, R. (2009). Visualizing Children's Walking Behaviour Using Portable Global Positioning (GPS) Units and Activity Monitors. In Lin, H., & Batty, M. (Eds.), *Virtual Geographic Environments* (pp. 295–310). Beijing, China: Science Press.

Guiver, J. (2010). *UCLan transport institute surveys on volcano crisis for lessons learned*. Retrieved August 12, 2010, from http://www.uclan.ac.uk/schools/ssto/uclan_transport_institute_surveys_on_volcano_crisis_for_lessons_learned.php.

Hodkinson, P., & Lincoln, S. (2008). Online journals as virtual bedrooms? Young people, identity and personal space. *Young, 16*(1), 27–46. doi:10.1177/110330880701600103

Holliday, R. (2000). We've been framed: visualizing methodology. *The Sociological Review, 48*(4), 503–521. doi:10.1111/1467-954X.00230

Holt, A. (2011). 'The terrorist in my home': teenagers' violence towards parents – constructions of parent experiences in public online message boards. *Child & Family Social Work, 16*(4), 454–463. doi:10.1111/j.1365-2206.2011.00760.x

Jirón, P. (2010). Mobile borders in urban daily mobility practices in Santiago de Chile. *International Political Sociology, 4*(1), 66–79. doi:10.1111/j.1749-5687.2009.00092.x

Kenyon, S. (2006). Reshaping patterns of mobility and exclusion? The impact of virtual mobility upon accessibility, mobility and social exclusion. In Sheller, M., & Urry, J. (Eds.), *Mobile Technologies of the City* (pp. 102–120). London, UK: Routledge.

Kusenbach, M. (2003). The Go-Along as Ethnographic Research Tool. *Ethnography, 4*(3), 455–485. doi:10.1177/146613810343007

Lashua, B., Hall, T., & Coffey, A. (2006). *Soundwalking as research method*. Paper presented at the Institute of British Geographers Annual International Conference, London, UK.

Latham, A. (2004). Researching and writing everyday accounts of the city: an introduction to the diary-photo diary-interview method. In Knowles, C., & Sweetman, P. (Eds.), *Picturing the Social Landscape: Visual methods and the sociological imagination* (pp. 117–131). London, UK: Routledge.

Laurier, E. (2010). Being there/seeing there: recording and analyzing life in the car. In Fincham, B., McGuinness, M., & Murray, L. (Eds.), *Mobile Methodologies* (pp. 103–117). Basingstoke, UK: Palgrave Macmillan.

Laurier, E., Lorimer, H., Brown, B., Juhlin, O., Nobel, A., & Perry, M. (2008). Driving and passengering: notes on the natural organization of ordinary car travel. *Mobilities, 3*(1), 1–23. doi:10.1080/17450100701797273

Lefebvre, H. (1996). *Writings on cities* (Kofman, E., & Lebas, E., Trans.). Oxford, UK: Blackwell.

Loescher, M. (2005). Cameras at the Addy: speaking in pictures with city kids. In Grimshaw, A., & Ravetz, A. (Eds.), *Visualizing Anthropology*. Bristol, UK: Intellect. doi:10.1386/jmpr.3.2.75

Madge, C., & O'Connor, H. (2005). Mothers in the making? Exploring liminality in cyber/space. *Transactions of the Institute of British Geographers, 30*(1), 83–97. doi:10.1111/j.1475-5661.2005.00153.x

Massey, D. (1994). *Space, place and gender*. Cambridge, UK: Polity Press.

Massey, D. (2005). *For space*. London, UK: Sage.

Morel, J., & Licoppe, C. (2010). Studying mobile video telephony. In Büscher, M., Urry, J., & Witchger, K. (Eds.), *Mobile methods*. London, UK: Routledge.

Murray, L. (2008). Motherhood, risk and everyday mobilities. In Priya Uteng, T., & Cresswell, T. (Eds.), *Gendered mobilities* (pp. 47–63). Aldershot, UK: Ashgate.

Murray, L. (2009a). Looking at and looking back: visualization in mobile research. *Qualitative Research*, *9*(4), 469–488. doi:10.1177/1468794109337879

Murray, L. (2009b). Making the journey to school: The gendered and generational aspects of risk in constructing everyday mobility. *Health Risk & Society*, *11*(5), 471–486. doi:10.1080/13698570903183889

Murray, L. (2010). Contextualizing and mobilizing research. In Fincham, B., McGuinness, M., & Murray, L. (Eds.), *Mobile Methodologies* (pp. 13–24). Basingstoke, UK: Palgrave Macmillan.

Neyland, D. (2006). Moving Images: The Mobility and Immobility of 'Kids Standing Still'. *The Sociological Review*, *54*(2), 363–381. doi:10.1111/j.1467-954X.2006.00618.x

Pink, S. (2007a). Walking with video. *Visual Studies*, *22*, 240–252. doi:10.1080/14725860701657142

Pink, S. (2007b). *Doing Visual Ethnography: images, media and representation in research* (2nd ed.). London, UK: Sage.

Pink, S. (2010). *Visualizing ethnography*. Retrieved June 20, 2010, from http://www.lboro.ac.uk/departments/ss/visualising_ethnography/

Pink, S., Hubbard, P., O'Neill, M., & Radley, A. (2010). Walking across disciplines: from ethnography to arts practice. *Visual Studies*, *25*(1), 1–7. doi:10.1080/14725861003606670

Prosser, J., & Burke, C. (2007). Childlike perspectives through image-based educational research. In Knowles, J. G., & Cole, A. (Eds.), *Handbook of the arts in qualitative research: perspectives, methodologies, examples and issues* (pp. 407–421). Oxford, UK: Oxford University Press.

Reavey, P., & Johnson, K. (2008). Visual methodologies: using and interpreting images in qualitative psychology. In Willig, C., & Stainton-Rogers, W. (Eds.), *Handbook of Qualitative Research in Psychology*. London, UK: Sage. doi:10.4135/9781848607927.n17

Rose, G. (2007). *Visual methodologies: an introduction to the interpretation of visual materials* (2nd ed.). London, UK: Sage.

Sheller, M., & Urry, J. (2006). The new mobilities paradigm. *Environment & Planning A*, *38*, 207–226. doi:10.1068/a37268

Simmel, G. (1971). The metropolis and mental life. In Simmel, G., & Wolff, K. H. (Eds.), *The Sociology of Georg Simmel* (Wolf, K. H., Trans.). New York, NY: Free Press.

Urry, J. (2007). *Mobilities*. London, UK: Sage.

Watts, L., & Lyons, G. (2010). Travel remedy kit: interventions into train lines and passenger times. In Büscher, M., Urry, J., & Witchger, K. (Eds.), *Mobile methods*. London, UK: Routledge.

Wiles, R., Prosser, J., & Bagnoli, A. Clark, A., Davies, K., Holland, S., & Renold, E. (2008). *Visual Ethics: Ethical Issues in Visual Research*. Southampton, UK: NCRM.

ADDITIONAL READING

Anderson, J. (2004). 'Talking whilst walking: a geographical archaeology of knowledge'. *Area*, *36*, 254–261. doi:10.1111/j.0004-0894.2004.00222.x

Banks, M. (2001). *Visual methods in social research*. London: Sage.

Büscher, M., Urry, J & Witchger, K. *Mobile methods*. London: Routledge.

Cresswell, T. (2006). *On the move*. New York: Routledge.

Fay, M. (2008). Mobile belonging: exploring transnational feminist theory and online connectivity. In *T. Priya Uteng and T. Cresswell, Gendered mobilities*. Aldershot: Ashgate.

Fincham, B., McGuinness, M., & Murray, L. (Eds.), *Mobile Methodologies*. Basingstoke: Palgrave Macmillan.

Freudendal-Pedersen, M., Hartmann-Petersen, K., & Drewes Nielsen, L. (2010). Mixing methods in the search for mobile complexity. In Fincham, B., McGuinness, M., & Murray, L. (Eds.), *Mobile Methodologies*. Basingstoke: Palgrave Macmillan.

Graham, S. (Ed.). (2004). *The Cybercities Reader*. London: Routledge.

Grimshaw, A., & Ravetz, A. (eds.) (2005). *Visualizing Anthropology* Bristol: Intellect.

Holliday, R. (2000). We've been framed: visualizing methodology. *The Sociological Review*, *48*(4), 503–521. doi:10.1111/1467-954X.00230

Murray, L. (2009). Looking at and looking back: visualization in mobile research. *Qualitative Research*, *9*(4), 469–488. doi:10.1177/1468794109337879

Pink, S. (2007). *Doing Visual Ethnography: images, media and representation in research. Revised and expanded* (2nd ed.). London: Sage.

Pink, S. (2009). *Doing Sensory Ethnography*. London: Sage.

Pink, S. Hubbard, P., O'Neill, M. Radley, A. (2010). Walking across disciplines: from ethnography to arts practice, *Visual Studies*.

Prosser, J. with Burke, C (2007). Childlike perspectives through image-based educational research. In: J. G. Knowles & A. Cole (Eds.) *Handbook of the arts in qualitative research: perspectives, methodologies, examples and issues*. Oxford University Press.

Reavey, P., & Johnson, K. (2008). 'Visual methodologies: using and interpreting images in qualitative psychology' in C. Willig and W. Stainton-Rogers (Eds.) *Handbook of Qualitative Research in Psychology*. London: Sage.

Rose, G. (2007). *Visual methodologies: an introduction to the interpretation of visual materials* (2nd ed.). London: Sage.

Rose, G. (2010). *Doing Family Photography: The Domestic, The Public and The Politics of Sentiment*. Aldershot: Ashgate.

Sheller, M., & Urry, J. (2006). The new mobilities paradigm. *Environment & Planning A*, *38*, 207–226. doi:10.1068/a37268

Urry, J. (2007). *Mobilities*. London: Sage.

KEY TERMS AND DEFINITIONS

Audiencing: Used by Gillian Rose (2006) to capture the way in which visual images are interpreted and re-interpreted as they are viewed by different people.

Film Elicitation Interviews: Interviews that make use of film footage to frame the process and provide a point of reference for discussion.

Hypermobility/Hypomobility: Concepts used to illustrate the negative impacts of an increasingly mobile world where, at certain times, some people are required to be too mobile and others not mobile enough.

Mobile Methodologies: Ways of researching that incorporate an understanding of the importance of mobility in exploring the social world and allow mobility to be captured.

'Mobilities Turn': A shift in thinking in the social sciences that recognizes the centrality of mobile space and mobile social relations.

Researching in Place: Research that recognizes the need to capture data about the social world in appropriate settings as social experience is contingent on its context. For example, mobile interviews involve the researcher moving along with the research participant in a process that allows the exploration of experience in situ.

Social Inclusion/Exclusion: These terms are used here in relation to a process whereby certain people lack power to access and shape opportunities available to others.

Visual Methods: Ways of researching that embrace the idea that the visual image can create knowledge of the social world in a distinctive way.

Chapter 17
Using Digital Tools in Qualitative Research:
Supporting Integrity, Simplicity, Deep Insight and Social Change

Susan Crichton
University of British Columbia, Canada

ABSTRACT

Digital tools can help simplify qualitative researchers' work. They can also add depth and richness by capturing data in a way that can be viewed and reviewed without preliminary transcription. This chapter shares an approach to working with digital data that honors participant voice and the lived experiences of those under study. The chapter also suggests new tools and common software applications. Further, it suggests a workflow to guide researchers as he or she begins to work to incorporate digital data into their studies.

INTRODUCTION

In 2005 I wrote my first article on the use of digital tools to support qualitative research (Crichton & Childs, 2005). In that paper, coauthored with my doctoral student, we described an approach I developed and that she used to work with primary source data (in that case digital recorded interviews) and minimize the need for transcription. Our argument was, by clipping and coding the digital files, using simple editing software, the vitality and integrity of the participants' voices and lived experiences were retained throughout the data analysis process. Further, we described a process of maintaining tables within Microsoft Office that would help researchers to organize

DOI: 10.4018/978-1-4666-0074-4.ch017

themes and codes as well as references and digital data to determine when a research theme had become saturated.

Since that time, researchers and graduate students (Childs, 2004; Shervey, 2005; Bremner, 2007) have contacted me about the approach, and I have presented it at various conferences (Hawaii International Conference on Education; International Advances In Qualitative Methods Conference) – typically receiving great enthusiasm and interest. I have used this approach extensively in my own work – often with unexpected impacts such as those described later in this paper (see A Case in Support of the Point). Existing and emerging technologies are helping to make this approach easier and appropriate to different approaches to qualitative research.

Einstein's statement "Everything should be made as simple as possible but not simpler" helps frame the discussion in this paper of how and why we might use digital tools for qualitative research.

BACKGROUND

In 2005 we wrote "Qualitative researchers have been attempting to make sense of the world around them since armchair anthropologists and sociologists left the confines of their familiar environments and ventured into the field (Crichton & Child, 2005; Crichton, 1997). Little has changed about the nature of the work and the challenges of working in the field. What have changed are the rapid development of digital tools and the increased availability of rich digital sources of data.

Typically, qualitative research, in particular ethnography and case study attempt "to construct in-depth depictions of the everyday life events of people through active re-searcher participation and engagement" (Crichton & Kinash, 2003, p. 102). Therefore, the biggest challenges of the work is managing the sheer quantity of data captured and the need to develop an elastic yet rigorous structure in which to organize and analyze it. Further, this management structure has to be nimble enough to allow the researcher to "read" and "re-read" the data, and organize and share it in a way that is accessible and ethical. The researcher has the added challenge of representing and maintaining the integrity of the firsthand experiences, in a narrative form that allows a reader, not familiar with the field, to gain insight and make personal sense from the rich description. As Genzuk (2004, p. 10) notes, it is through the narrative that "readers … understand fully the research setting and the thoughts of the people represented . . . [stopping] short, however, of becoming trivial and mundane" (Genzuk, 2004, p. 10).

With a bounty of rich digital data, the researcher is challenged to determine the balance between the essential description required to set the context and the critical analysis and interpretation that is necessary to help the reader come to an understanding of the findings. When that balance is achieved, the reader is able to interpret and understand the work and make relevant links that might extend the work and generalize the findings.

Typically, research findings that have been reached using qualitative methods will include thick descriptions of the experiences, contexts, and general environment of the site, individuals, and/or phenomenon under study. These descriptions are critical for the reader to understand the details of what has happened and the various viewpoints of the participants. They help to create a holistic picture, so that the findings do not lose their credibility and impact. Traditionally, these findings have been reached through the analysis of transcribed data or using [complicated and expensive] qualitative analysis software (Crichton & Kinash, 2003).

SUPPORTING A DIGITAL PROCESS

Many researchers (Creswell, 2003; Merriam, 1998; Hammersley, 1990; Stake, 1995) would agree that qualitative research is, at its core, social research involving the study of people and events within everyday rather than experimental conditions. It is an attempt to collect data from a range of sources, including formal and informal conversations and observations as well as tangible and intangible artifacts. Although it might appear that the approach to the data collection is unstructured and at times chaotic and eclectic, it does not suggest that the collection of data has not been considered and planned. On the contrary, qualitative research encourages the ongoing collection of raw data from the widest and richest range of possible sources, continuing the collection until the field is either saturated or the data becomes repetitive.

Merriam (1998) suggests the "emergence of regularities" serves as the indicator that a sufficient amount of data had been collected, noting further "data collection in a case study is a re-cursive, interactive process in which engaging in one strategy incorporates or may lead to subsequent sources of data" (p. 134). Put simply, qualitative research is the way many of us make sense of events in our daily lives. Typically, data are collected from structured or semi structured interviews, formal and informal observation, and the analysis of various documents developed by or found at the site under study. From these data, the researcher is able to analyze, interpret, and share direct quotations, thick descriptions, and selected excerpts (Hammersley, 1990), merging them into a rich narrative that forms a complex narrative quilt that covers the essential aspects of the study.

Management

One of the blessings, and challenges, of qualitative research concerns the amount of data typically collected. Finding ways to manage it and review it can be daunting. However, new tools are emerging that makes this task easier and more intuitive. One tool, the LiveScribe pen (http://www.livescribe.com/en-us/), will be discussed later in this paper.

It comes with its own management system for both online and computer resident file naming and sorting.

I tend to use very simple tools in my work, adapting existing software programs that I am familiar with and already own for data management. Because I work primarily with Apple hardware, I use iPhoto to organize, edit, and manage my short, simple videos and photo collection. If the videos are longer and require more complete editing, I use iMOVIE. I use iTUNEs to manage my audio files. When I am ready to compile various data pieces for sorting / categorizing, I simply import them into a table in MS WORD. I also upgraded to QuickTIme Pro – which is an inexpensive software application that provides an easy way to cut relevant content from longer audio and video clips.

The value of working in this manner is multifold:

- The Apple software comes already installed on the computer – with the exception of MS Office and the Quick Time Pro upgrade
- The interoperability of the software makes editing / integrating the various media formats simpler. Each application has its own file management system
- The learning curve is nil for research use as I am already using the applications for other purposes, and the support for the various applications is excellent (both online tutorials and course availability to Apple retail stores)
- MS Word is a standard for word processing and editing, and to save costs one could use Open Office just as effectively
- Time capsule, another Apple application, makes backing up data automatic, so it is easy to store copies of the data and draft publications on external storage devices.

This paper is not meant to be an advertisement for Apple – I think they are doing just fine without my endorsement. However, it is the operating system / hardware I have chosen to make my research process easier. Other than the Livescribe pen and video and still cameras, I use only the software suggested above. This makes my work easier, less expensive, and allows me to focus on the parts of the process I enjoy most … the actual data from the field. The actual workflow that I use will be described later in this paper.

Analysis

Analyzing the rich data sources starts the narrative process. Typically, the researcher starts the process by labeling and sorting items into a type of order – an attempt to make sense of what is there and group items into categories into initial categories. Through this process, the researcher gains a sense of what is there, what is missing, and whether the data-gathering phase is nearing completion. Further, this process allows the researcher to see the patterns emerging. The possible themes, often coming from the literature or the researcher's previous work, can be confirmed, modified or rejected. While many researchers interpret and analyze their data collections and begin to manage them from transcribed data, I would argue that transcription is NOT only unnecessary, but on some levels is almost unethical as it degrades the quality and integrity of the participants' lived experiences.

SELECTING THE RIGHT DIGITAL TOOLS

A challenge in case study, and many other types of qualitative research, is managing the sheer quantity of data collected. As the data collection process draws its strength from accumulating raw data and making sense of it without a set of preconceived hypotheses, the analysis process is labor intensive and time consuming. Researchers wishing to use a qualitative approach usually do so because they wish to honor and record the participants' lived experiences in situ, allowing them to speak for themselves without misinterpretation (Crichton & Kinash, 2003).

Since I started using digital tools in my research in 2001, I have taken the stance the best way to enter the field under study is to become the unobtrusive observer suggested in the literature (Kellehear, 1997). This involves using the least intrusive photography and recording devices and attempting to engage with the participants authentically and with as little disruption as possible. Further, by using simple technologies such as the FLIP video camera (http://www.theflip.com/en-ca/), the prosumer Canon G10, and the Livescribe pen, I can record participants, analyze their words and actions, clip the relevant segments, and organize those segments into a series of frames and codes (Goffman, 1959, 1974). Prosumer suggests a middle ground between consumer quality equipment and professional quality equipment. This blend has come about thanks to advances in simple yet high quality editing and publishing applications that started with the desktop publishing revolution in the 1984.

By not transcribing or altering the original format of the digital data, researchers can keep those images and/or recordings intact for as long as possible. This method allows them to hear and see the gestures, intonation, passion, pauses, and inflections throughout the analysis process. It reduces the impact the transcription process has on the content, given that the principal researcher, due to time constraints and efficiency, often is not the person doing the transcription. Further, "researchers have traditionally spent large proportions of their budgets on interview transcription, [which, in turn, has influenced] the number and extent of interviews based on cost (time and money) projections" (Crichton & Kinash, 2003, p. 104). Further, I would argue the transcription process tends to flatten the rich, three-dimensional quality of the original footage, reducing it into a two-dimensional text format.

Among the researchers and graduate students to have used this approach was Barb Bremner (2007), who used the open source software Audacity in the Windows environment. In the final chapter of her dissertation, Bremner notes: the process for analysis provided a rich experience that the researcher never thought possible. Audio recordings of the interview data were collected using *Audacity©*, an audio recording and editing software. The researcher listened to each audio file, and relevant audio clips were copied, exported, named using key words applicable to the content, placed in the appropriate frame and code, and saved as a hyperlink in a *MicroSoft© Excel* file. Following the advice of Crichton and Childs (2005), each code was set up in its own spreadsheet with information about related documents and literature, and salient quotes. The process was simple and time efficient.

In the process of analysis, the researcher listened to key quotes many, many times and the researcher became familiar with each quote, who said it, and how it was said. This process ensured the caution of Kvale (1995) was heeded, 'Do not conceive of the interviews as transcripts: the interviews are living conversations' (p. 182). The process also allowed the researcher to relive the interaction as advocated by Crichton and Childs (2005). As a result of using this process and at the time of the writing of this final chapter, the researcher could still hear the intonation, the excitement, the frustration, the awe, the surprise, the disappointment, the enthusiasm, the aggravation, and the satisfaction of each participant's voice – an exceptionally rich experience that will not soon be forgotten (pp. 272-273).

Working with primary data, and delaying transcription for as long as possible, the images and/or voices stay intact. The participants' voice and the field in which they live and work stay rich and multifaceted. As suggested in the title of this paper, working with primary source digital data

allows the researcher to maintain the integrity of the data and, therefore, allows continued reflection / review of the content and the development of deeper insight. Further, it:

- Keeps the interviews alive and vibrant – Kvale's (1995) notion that "… interviews are living conversations" rather than data that has been transcribed;
- Maintains the gestures, intonations, passion, pauses so the researcher can remember and revisit the passion, manner and intangible aspects of the interview and the field;
- Provides visual evidence;
- Enables the researcher to code clips and arrange them in tables for ease of categorizing and sorting;
- Reduces transcription error and helps with more "honest" interpretation of the data. Because the audio / video files are clipped into smaller pieces, they can be sent to the participant to further questions or verification. This is so much more manageable than sending a participant multiple pages of transcribed data from an hour or so interview;
- Allows the researchers to relax more in the field, knowing that the activities and interactions are being "recorded" in audio, video, and photos as well as with field notes; and
- Allows the research to scan the data before leaving the field to see what other questions / concerns have arisen.

HAVING IT ALL IN THE BAG

A common question I get asked is "What do you take into the field?" Of course there is a risk in suggesting hardware, as there is nothing more consistent than change and upgrades when discussing computer technology. Having said that, the list below has served me for the last three years with only the occasional software upgrade.

My equipment list includes the following items - all of which fit within my backpack:

- Journal for field notes (including pens and pencils)
- MacBook Pro laptop – 13 inch model with standard memory and hard drive
- Western Digital external hard drive for backing up my laptop
- LiveScribe Pen which charges via USB from my laptop
- LiveScribe Pen notebook
- FLIP video camera
- Canon G10 still camera with video capability and camera to laptop cable
- Mini tripod for both still and video camera

The FLIP has a built in USB plug, and the LiveScribe pen has its own USB dock that synchronizes the data with the laptop. Using this collection of hardware, I can be set up and ready to work within minutes, it doesn't appear to be threatening or intimidating for participations, and it is not particularly onerous for me to manage. Typically, my laptop stays in my backpack until I synch my data at the end of a working session.

My backpack is my mobile office. I rarely unpack it. It also includes miscellaneous stationary supplies, a few granola bars, and a small bit of duct tape rolled around an old pencil. Not too sure why I include that, but somehow duct tape always comes in handy for something.

CONSIDERING WORKFLOW

I started talking about workflow rather than steps or "How to Tips" a few years ago when I realized that working with digital tools should enrich the core work rather than hijack it to accommodate the technology. Typically, the two aspects (the actual task and the technology to support it) have been considered in separate silos. The concept of workflow unites the two into almost a recipe:

1 part research design
1 part ICT enhanced research methodology
1 part appropriate technology

The focus of this paper has been the rationale for the use of digital tools for qualitative research – ICT enhanced research - one part. Previously in this paper I shared my thoughts on appropriate technologies – a second part. The reader brings his/her own research design to the process and work with the technology to enhance their practice – a final part. Workflow varies by data type and application, and I offer examples for the most common types (audio, video, and still images – pictures and pdf).

Audio Workflow: Using the LiveScribe Pen

1. Prepare ethics application / consent forms noting that you will be digitally recording interviews, conversations, and / or focus group interactions.
2. Prepare semi-structured interview / conversation prompts. These help focus the conversations and make sure similar questions are asked for each participant / group.
3. Meet with participants, inform them of their right to withdraw from the study, review their comments, and approve their contributions prior to their use in papers / reports.
4. Explain how the pen works and the fact that you are making notes and sketches that will be used in the study.
5. Attach the earphone to the pen and test for sound quality. Following the directions described in the Livescribe tutorial, click on the Livescribe paper and record a test conversation.

6. Listen to the recording to ensure you are close enough to your participant and there is little or no disruptive background noise.

7. Begin the interview. There is no need to write copious notes on the Livescribe paper. The notes you do write will link directly to the recorded sections, so these will act as an index to the complete recording.

8. You can allow the participant to use the pen to sketch ideas or show diagrams. All marks on the paper will link to the specific location within the recording.

9. During the interview, it is wise to listen through at least one of the earphones as this lets you "hear" exactly what the pen is "hearing."

10. Conclude your interview / interaction and thank the participants. Ask them if they would like to review any comments attributed to them that you might use in your write-ups or presentations. Ask them if you might send audio clips to them via email for elaboration or confirmation.

11. When it is convenient, synch your pen to your computer using the dock provided with the Livescribe equipment. When you initially installed your Livescribe pen, a directory and management structure was set up.

12. As you synch the pen / data with your computer, you are able to name the page. At this point it is wise to archive it within the name of the larger study (PAGES), and then name the individual interview (NOTEBOOK) with a unique identifier.

13. You will note that you can navigate the interview content from either your paper notebook or the software version. They are identical by both look and feel. When you click on the actual word, corresponding audio will play.

14. Depending on the number of sketches / visual information you have recorded, it is easier to work with the AUDIO segments. Individual files are compiled by page reference and session name and time stamp.

15. Open the AUDIO → Sessions area in the Livescribe desktop (Figure 1). My clicking on a Session Name, you can re-name the segment to match your coding / research design.

16. Export the segment you want to "clip" and code onto your desktop.

17. Using either QuickTime Pro (QT Pro) (Figure 2) or Audacity, listen to the clip and cut the parts you wish to use as evidence in your research.

18. Rename the smaller clip, and save it. This clip can then be placed into your table as evidence to support your frames and codes for your data analysis (Table 1).

19. The table allows the researcher to see whether the field is saturated - Merriam's (1998) benchmark for when enough data has been collected, and if the pre-selected frames and codes are holding up during the data analysis process. If there is no evidence to support a frame or code, it can be deleted, and if other frames or codes are needed, they can be added and related literature can be found to explain them. The actual data can be played directly within the table. This allows the researcher to hear the short clip (for example 45 seconds) that has been cut from the longer interview. For more details on the actual

Table 1. Sample table

FRAME & REFERENCES	CODE	GENERAL DESCRIPTION	EVIDENCE
Trust (Author, date; Author, date; Author, date)	Trusting, risk taking, collegial	o Willing to support o Suspend disbelief	Sally_disbelief.mov

Figure 1.

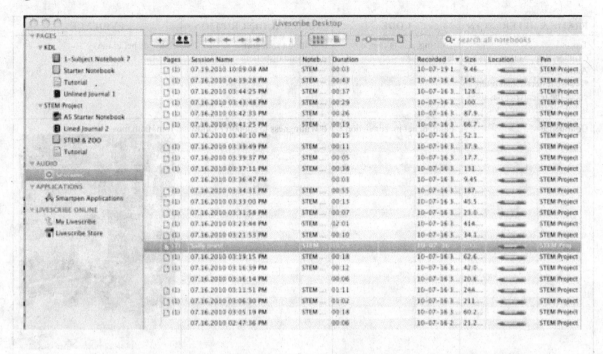

process of Clipping and Coding, please see Crichton and Childs (2005) and Crichton (2010).

20. Once the entire table is filled, and all the frames and codes relevant to the research design have been addressed and the data analyzed, the researcher can begin the writing process. At that point, the researcher can transcribe exactly what is required, insert the actual video into conference presentations, and consider submitting the paper to an online journal / publication that accepts multimedia. Transcript time and costs are reduced considerably and the integrity and poignancy of the data has been retained.

Video Workflow – Using iPhoto for Management

1. Many of the Audio Workflow steps are similar for video files. Participants need to be made aware of the fact that video recordings are more than just complete recordings of events with images and sound. They might be short clips that set a scene, capture a unique activity, and show a way of working / interacting.

2. Using either a FLIP recorder or the video option on a still camera, video files can be stored and organized using the Album option in iPhoto.

Figure 2.

Table 2. Expanded sample table using Workflow #18

FRAME & REFERENCES	CODE	GENERAL DESCRIPTION	EVIDENCE
Trust (Author, date; Author, date; Author, date*) * These reflect actual references the researcher has used in her/his literature review.	Trusting, risk taking, collegial	o Willing to support o Suspend disbelief	Sally_disbelief.mov
Confidence	Faith, belief in, conviction	o Willingness to support / follow	Tom_faith.mov

3. Follow Audio Workflow step #16 above to export the clip and crop it using QT Pro or Audacity.
4. Follow Workflow #18 to insert the clip into the table (Table 2).

Image Workflow: Using iPhoto for Management

1. The first steps are similar for AUDIO and Video. Participants need to be made aware of the fact that image collection is more than just pictures of them doing things. Images can be photos of documents, working places, tools, and bulletin boards. It also can be pictures of hands workings, groups taken from the back rather than full front photos. It can also be pdf documents and other media in various formats.
2. Folders can be created within iPhoto (or windows Media Center). It is there that im-

ages are cropped, sorted, labeled, and made ready for export.
3. Exported images should be in the smallest format available. This will help to keep the file size small. Images can then be placed directly into the table as evidence of specific frames and codes (Table 3).
4. Researchers can click on the image and enlarge it to see details. Using the hyperlink function in WORD, you can create links to .pdf files or images / resources stored on the web.

ISSUES, CONTROVERSIES, PROBLEMS

I have use the approach described in this paper for almost a decade. It has made my work easier and richer. Of course, it is not without its challenges – especially in the area of ethics and publishing options for digital media.

Table 3. Expanded sample table with images

FRAME & REFERENCES	CODE	GENERAL DESCRIPTION	EVIDENCE
Trust (Author, date; Author, date; Author, date*) * These reflect actual references the researcher has used in her/his literature review.	Trusting, risk taking, collegial	o Willing to support o Suspend disbelief	Sally_disbelief.mov
	Risk taking	o Willing to follow a trusted leader o Willing to do something new	 SUSAN compiled 8-07/Desktop items/ To Read/tust_factors.pdf
Confidence	Faith, belief in, conviction	o Willingness to support / follow	Tom_faith.mov

While camera and recording devices are increasingly common, if not ordinary in data collection, some participants are uneasy being audio recorded, videoed, or photographed, but rarely in my experience with all three. The University of Calgary has addressed this concern by creating a layer consent form. Participants can select the option they are comfortable with, and whether they wish to review it before it is used (http://www.ucalgary.ca/research/cfreb).

The second concern is a tricky one. While there are more and more publishing options with online journals and electronic publication (ePub) format books, often they do not command the status of the more mainstream presses and format. This will probably change in the future, but currently, researchers have limited options in terms of publishers willing to print in color or incorporate multimedia and larger format video in their editions.

An interesting smaller concern about using the approach described in this paper is the issue of what to do with all the rich data one can collect. As Genzuk (2004) cautioned, "Endless description becomes its own muddle. [The] . . . purpose of analysis is to organize the description in a way that makes it manageable" (p. 10). This caution became quite real during the defense of a recent doctoral dissertation. Because the student has digital recorded, and not transcribed her interviews until the last possible moment, the participant voices were so vibrant and live, it was hard to ignore them and limit their inclusion in the findings chapter. This prompted one of the examiners to note that while he was certain the student had been more than rigorous in her data collection, he found the amount of evidence presented to be almost boring. Almost a sense of "death by richness."

RECOMMENDATIONS

Working with primary source research data as described in this paper is incredibly valuable. Not only does it use the power of emerging, readily available technologies, it also allows the research to see deeply and really explore the data beyond the obvious; it allows us to delve into the margins of the media – the quieter voice, the subtle pause, the inflection. It allows us to question where our eye was directed when we filmed a particular sequence or snapped an image; to puzzle what caught our gaze and what didn't; and to question what was going on just beyond our reach.

A CASE IN SUPPORT OF THE POINT

Those new to the use of digital data to support their research might tend to dismiss photos and conversations as "not" being real data or simply pretty or an extra. I share the following situation from my work as support for digital media.

Background

From 2003 – 2007 I participated in a Canadian International Development Project (CIDA) – Strengthening Capacity in Basic Education in Western China (SCBEWC). SCBEWC was a bi-lateral project (Government of the People's Republic of China and Canada)[1] with the goal of improving the quality of basic education (grades 1 – 9) in three poor provinces in Western China[2] through teacher education and distance education. During those years, I had many memorable roles (researcher, workshop facilitator, content developer, and distance education consultant), but the one that lingers most vividly concerns the use of digital data collection in the field.

As I traveled to project schools, I took still and video cameras with me, capturing site-specific examples for research and curriculum resources. This was a change in practice as much for the respected research was quantitative and the majority of the instructional resources were developed using studio scripted controlled production. The proposed change caused much concern among my Chinese colleagues who felt their professional reputations might be impacted by narrative data and images and media that were not studio quality.

WORKING IN THE FIELD

Taking technology on the road is always interesting. From issues of power supply to merely transporting the equipment, nothing is ever easy and in small, remote areas, the technology itself, along with a collection of "outsiders" always manages to attract a crowd. Whenever possible I tried to avoid using large, bulky professional equipment, but occasionally, especially for better production values it was necessary (Figure 3).

Achieving the balance between production value and unobtrusive photography became a major focus of my work, and I attempted to use small, more prosumer (Prosumer, 2008) quality equipment, arguing that content quality was more important than production quality (Figure 4).

It is within this contested space of the prosumer realm that this story takes place. Much to the humor and often surprise of the schools we visited, it was the foreign "expert" who carried the "poorest" equipment but often captured the most sought after pictures. Typically this opened the conversation concerning knowing what to take and when it might occur rather than attempting to control lighting and sound values.

During a school visit in a spectacular mountainous region in rural western Sichuan province, I wandered into the central playground area. People in this region tend to be poor as the area is challenging to farm and many are Tibetan, a

Figure 3.

Figure 4.

minority group in China. Mandarin, the official language for commerce and schooling, is not their first language. It was lunchtime, and the children had left their classrooms to enjoy the sunshine and get their lunches from the walls outside their rooms. We all were basking in the warmth like a collection of cats, when I decided to film the children as they enjoyed their lunches and chatted happily on chairs surrounding the play area. I had time to spend as a group for graduate students and their supervisor, who had traveled with us from Beijing, were conducting interviews with community members concerning the impact of poverty on schooling and regional development. Sitting back down, I scrolled through the pictures I had just taken, ensuring that I had what I wanted when I noticed a group of children in one image who were sitting just on the margins of one the photo – these children were just outside the actual frame, but it was something about the freeze frame of the photograph that allowed me to notice something that I had not been able to observe when I watched the children earlier.

I showed the picture to my colleague who, fortunately for me, spoke enough English as I spoke no Chinese. In wonderfully descriptive yet thoughtfully selected English she explained,

"Those children are pretending to eat lunch. Those children are too poor to bring food from home." Literally they were the children in the margins of more than my photograph. They were ones who typically formed the large numbers of minority children who dropped out of rural schools after their compulsory Basic Education (grades 1-9) was completed – if not earlier. In an odd drama, these children sat off to the side, with their empty lunch boxes, pretending to eat, taking the same amount of time and effort as their classmates with actual food.

Ironically, immediately after this observation, we were taken to lunch; a lovely meal in nearby hotel. While nothing fancy, the fact that it was warm and nourishing immediately took away the chill of the cold morning in the unheated school.

Needless to say, the topic of children pretending to eat lunch dominated our conversation. Through my translator I asked about subsidized lunch programs, explaining the role they played in many North American schools. The principal of the school was quite interested, both in the fact that Canadian schools needed food programs, but also in the mechanics of these programs – whose responsibility it was, who paid, how they were managed, etc. Our consensus was that it was wrong for children to drop out of school because they were hungry, but the professor, an expert in educational policy, noted there was nothing in school fees or government policy that allowed for lunch programs. It was then that the Lunch for Learning idea was born. I asked the principal if there was anything wrong with a grass roots initiative to start a lunch program. I proposed asking the Canadian experts to contribute small amounts of money to the program, donating left over Chinese currency or making periodic contributions. I explained that grass roots projects NEVER paid overhead or administrative costs, but local people should be paid for make and distribute simple hot lunches each school day. We discussed the plan for the next two days, and when I left, I gave the principal all the foreign cash I had (about $150 CDN) and 300 RMB (about $40). This was enough to start the program and feed the students for the first few months.

Over the next year, SCBEWC project administrators, both Canadian and Chinese, regularly sent money out to the principal. As expected, Canadian consultants donated rather than converted their remaining RMB, and the lunch program grew. Eventually, almost a year to the day it started, the principal emailed me (via the original interpreter) that I no longer needed to send money; the teachers at the school had taken over the program as they felt they needed to be ones responsible.

The Long Legs of Kind Acts

During the next year of the SCBEWC project I forgot about Lunch for Learning, However, near the end of the work, I attended a meeting with a Chinese expert on educational policy, and, of course, it was the professor from the Sichuan trip. This man had the ear of government, and when he saw me again, he explained how much the trip to Sichuan had impacted him. Further, he explained that he put the issue of lunch programs on the agenda for government meetings, encouraging that it be entrenched in policy and the images became part of his research reports and findings – something very new within the Ministry of Education.

The following year, as part of the project's concluding activities, three of us from the original teacher education content team were invited to Beijing to conduct a four-day case study workshop.

Teachers and administrators from project schools across the three provinces were invited to learn how to conduct case study research as it was felt that evidenced based reporting was critical to promote and sustain innovative practice.

As we planned the workshop, it was decided the use of digital media for research should be included, and that we use the photograph that had prompted the Lunch for Learning program as an example. On the second day of the workshop we presented our case. The participants actively discussed its structure, the photographs, and the content. When participants from another province asked in which school the case had taken place, the three administrators from that school's regional office erupted. They denied that there was poverty in their schools, the lunch program has taken place, and explained that somehow I had gotten all the information wrong – the interpreter had made a mistake. Needless to say, there was tension in the air and the three of us pictured our multi-year, highly successful project ending as an international incident. Ironically, we had to break for lunch. During lunch I sat with the upset participants trying to smooth the situation. They stated they had been embarrassed in front of their colleagues and that the events had never really happened in the way they had been projected in the case we presented.

After lunch the workshop resumed. We decided to follow our agenda and not specifically address the concerns expressed before lunch unless participants brought them up. However, one of the participants defused the situation by suggesting that even though people might forget the details of actual events years after they had occurred, digital media served an important role by providing photographs that stood testament to events, recording them in ways that prompt description and bear witness in ways that memories may tend to dim or ignore. Significant to this statement was that the woman who made it was, in fact, a video producer who had wrestled early on in the project with production values of raw content collected in the field, using prosumer technologies.

CONCLUSION

As researchers work on the front lines of the human experience, digital data offers rich ways to consider the situation, invite others into the work, and confirm ideas and assumptions. Transcribing digital data and working with text rather than media is unnecessary and almost unethical. We now have the tools to enhance our research, understanding and publications in significant ways, and engage in practice that supports the tradition of social research and social change – enhanced with digital media.

REFERENCES

Bremner, B. (2007). *Facilitating online learning adoption.* Unpublished doctoral dissertation, University of Calgary, Calgary, AB, Canada. Retrieved from http://ucalgary.summon.serialssolutions.com/search?s.q=bremner+%2B+dissertations

Childs, E. (2004). *Impact of online PD on teaching practice.* Unpublished doctoral dissertation, University of Calgary, Calgary, AB, Canada.

Creswell, J. (2003). *Research Design: Qualitative, Quantitative, and Mixed Methods Approaches* (2nd ed.). Thousand Oaks, CA: Sage.

Crichton, S. (2010). Use of Digital Data. In Mills, A., Durepos, G., & Wiebe, E. (Eds.), *Encyclopedia of Case Study Research* (pp. 950–954). Thousand Oaks, CA: Sage Reference.

Crichton, S., & Childs, E. (2005). Clipping and Coding Audio Files: A Research Method to Enable Participant Voice. *International Journal of Qualitative Methods*, *4*(3). http://www.ualberta.ca/~ijqm/backissues/4_3/pdf/crichton.pdf

Crichton, S., & Kinash, S. (2003). Virtual ethnography: Interactive interviewing online as method. *Canadian Journal of Learning and Technology*, *29*(2), 101–115.

Januszewski, A., & Molenda, M. (Eds.). (2008). *Educational technology: A definition with commentary.* Mahwah, NJ: Lawrence Erlbaum Associates.

Merriam, S. (1998). *Qualitative Research and Case Study Applications in Education.* San Francisco, CA: Jossey-Bass.

Shervey, G. (2005). *Pre-service teachers and online teaching.* Unpublished master's thesis, University of Calgary, Calgary, AB, Canada.

Stake, R. (1995). *The art of case study research.* Thousand Oaks, CA: Sage.

ADDITIONAL READING

Goffman, E. (1974). *Frame Analysis: An Essay On The Organization Of Experience.* New York: Harper Colophon.

Pink, S. (2007). *Doing Visual Ethnography.* Thousand Oaks, CA: Sage Publications.

Stanczak, G. C. (Ed.). (2007). *Visual Research Methods: Image, Society, and Representation.* Los Angeles, CA: Sage Publications.

KEY TERMS AND DEFINITIONS

Appropriate / Simple Technologies: "A tool or practice that is the simplest and most benign solution to a problem" (Januszewski & Molenda, 2008, p. 10). The phrase was coined by E. Schumacher in his book Small Is Beautiful.

Primary Source Data: Research data collected by a researcher directly from the field and that has not be translated, altered or interpreted.

Prosumer: A middle ground between consumer quality equipment and professional quality equipment. The phrase was coined by Alvin Tofler.

Studio Quality: Refers to the high production values for media that can best be obtained in a controlled setting where light, sound, and other conditions can be controlled.

Unobtrusive: An approach used by observers to maintain a "low" profile when they are in the field. As much as possible, researchers attempt to blend into their setting and therefore avoid moving furniture, bringing in lighting or microphones, etc. to record events.

Workflow: Steps or process for integrating software and hardware application into the actual work that is being done.

ENDNOTES

[1] SCBEWC. Project Partners included: National Center for Educational Technology (NCET), an agency of the Chinese Ministry of Education and a consortium of Canadian organizations lead by Agriteam Canada Ltd. and including Alberta Learning, the University of Calgary, Athabasca University and the University of Alberta.

[2] Project Counties: Yuanzhou (in Ningxia Hui Autonomous Region), Xiji (in Ningxia Hui Autonomous Region), Tianquan (in Sichuan Province), Kangding (in Sichuan Province), Shanshan (in Xinjiang Uygher Autonomous Region), Altay (in Xinjiang Uygher Autonomous Region).

Chapter 18
Empirical Research Methods in Virtual Worlds

Travis L. Ross
Indiana University, USA

Edward Castronova
Indiana University, USA, & German Institute for Economic Research (DIW Berlin), Germany

Gert G. Wagner
German Institute for Economic Research (DIW Berlin), Max Planck Institute for Human Development, & Berlin University of Technology (TUB), Germany

ABSTRACT

This chapter summarizes current empirical methods in virtual world research. Since 2001, virtual worlds have become an important form of social media and a new forum for human interaction. Researchers have begun to study virtual worlds both for their inherent interest, as well as for insights about broader human behavior. This chapter addresses the quality of data obtained, as well as early experience with surveys, experiments, ethnography, and direct observation in virtual worlds. The conclusions are that virtual worlds are a valid location for empirical research and many methods from the "real" world are suitable for deployment. Virtual worlds also present challenges in terms of technology and the nature of society, and researchers must not overlook these challenges.

INTRODUCTION

Over the last few hundred years the social sciences have pursued a variety of methods, which attempt to explain, understand, and predict human behavior at both the individual and societal level. Experimental economics, historical analysis, game theory, computation, and mathematical modeling are just a few of a wide range of techniques

DOI: 10.4018/978-1-4666-0074-4.ch018

and tools that have been applied. As science has progressed these methods have been refined, and retooled each providing its own piece to the puzzle of social science theory.

Occasionally, a new tool or technique comes along that promises to provide researchers with access to information about the world that was previously unobtainable or intractable. In doing so, it provides new perspectives and insights into biological processes and social interactions. The microscope, calculus, probability theory, game theory, computer, and fMRI, are all examples of this type of tool. We argue that a virtual world is also such a tool. This chapter will explore key developments in virtual world research. In doing so it will examine two different methodological approaches (experimental and observational), and two different data collection techniques (survey and dataveillance) that share a common theme. They free the researcher from the burden of data collection and take advantage of large-scale databases and the computational power of virtual worlds to provide huge datasets that can be generalized to the real world.

BACKGROUND: VIRTUAL WORLDS - REAL PEOPLE

One of the chief criticisms of virtual world research is that virtual worlds are simply not real. That the players in them are interacting in a contrived environment and so a virtual world is not suited for providing generalizable information to the real world. Williams (2010b) identifies this criticism as what he calls a mapping problem. The implications are strait forward. If human behavior mirrors real world behavior then virtual worlds are suitable environments for drawing conclusions about individual and group behavior in the real world. If no fidelity exists to the real world, then they are not.

The evidence suggests that virtual worlds lie somewhere in between. That even in play-acting environments, human behavioral theories continue to hold water. The Stanford Prison Experiment and its follow-ups strongly suggest that people who are consciously play-acting a role nonetheless behave as if the role was real (Zimbardo, 2007). The fact that players of virtual worlds have committed murder and suicide over events within them certainly suggests that these events matter to those involved despite the fact that the worlds are fanciful by design.[1]

This evidence is all indirect, and so the question of whether virtual world behavior maps onto "true" human behavior remains open. However, researchers in communications have tackled this question directly. Byron Reeves and Clifford Nass (1996) summarize a long series of experiments targeting cognition showing that people seem to treat media as real, apparently because of the simple fact that the brain evolved before media existed. More recently, Nick Yee and Jeremy Bailenson (2007) have coined the term "Proteus Effect" to describe the phenomenon of a person treating his or her virtual body as if it were a real body. In one example from their studies, they found that people given a taller avatar in the virtual world act, in that world, more confidently. A result that maps to the real world as observations have shown that height predicts social confidence. From their studies, Yee and Bailenson demonstrate that many features of human behavior in the real world map onto virtual behavior. Furthermore, traditional experiments applied by behavioral economists underscore these conclusions. As it is accepted that experiments, which place subjects in a more or less artificial laboratory or survey environment that is conceptualized as a game, map onto real world behavior (e.g., Fehr et al., 2002; Dohmen et al., in press).

Mappings from the virtual world have been studied in other contexts. Recent research seems to indicate that macro-economic behavior and collective outcomes map into the real world. Castronova, Cummings, et al. (2009) constructed a small-scale virtual world to conduct an experiment which mapped the theory of supply and demand. On a larger scale and using player data provided directly by Sony Online Entertainment, the makers of the virtual world *Everquest II*, Castronova et al. (2009) found that the aggregate economic behavior of *Everquest II* was slightly more unstable than one would expect, but in general tended to follow the real world.

Determining where virtual world behavior mimics real world behavior is quite important for methodological reasons. If virtual world behavior can be treated as a model of human behavior in general, it will allow the virtual world to be a powerful tool for empirical social science. Although the jury is still out, from Williams suggestions and the evidence above, we conclude virtual behavior does, to a considerable degree, map onto real world behavior. With this assumption in place, the remaining sections of this paper will detail means by which virtual worlds can be used to study generalizable human behavior.

TYPES OF DATA COLLECTION

Researchers who wish to examine behavior in virtual worlds have quite a few methods available to them for collecting data. Some of these require researchers to play a significant role in the actual data collection while others do not. This paper will examine several of these methods and then focus specifically on two further techniques. The additional techniques allow researchers to collect very large datasets about the population of a virtual world, yet do not require a team of researchers to do so. Such methods are more common among social scientists and form a core element in game industry analytics, "Game Telemetry". Telemetry is emerging as a key technique in game design and commercialization, as companies like Zynga have used extensive large dataset analysis to propel their corporate valuation into the billions of US dollars.

Probably the most common method used by researchers in virtual worlds is direct observation. The individual scholar enters the world as a player and records experience. Like an anthropologist among the aboriginals, she gains direct insight into the normal lives of the people who play. The great benefit of this method is that it can come to grips with concepts that are typically difficult to operationalize. The drawbacks are that the findings are hard to generalize and it often relies on subjective interpretation.

Another method is the small-scale experiment. Researchers can send teams of collaborators into a virtual world to conduct some sort of intervention, and then track the result. The benefit here is some degree of causal explanation, although the cost is again that a small scale makes generalization difficult and the available manipulations are limited by an inability to alter the environment outside the rules of the game.

A third important method is to conduct in-world surveys. Here the benefit is that you achieve some generalizability, since the scale is larger. The drawback is that such surveys break immersion and require teams of researchers to conduct.

Beyond these methods, two further methods, dataveillance and automated survey, can provide researchers with insights into the beliefs, desires, and direct behavior of individuals in a virtual world at both the individual and collective level. Both methods are automated; therefore, they free researchers from having to be on hand during data collection.

Measurement error is an issue in all forms of data collection in the natural and social worlds, but in the social sphere, it is particularly acute. Those who wish to collect reliable data from human populations must deal with many problems caused by the simple fact that the subject of study is a human person. It is possible to record many things about an atom without asking for the atom's help, which is not so with a human person. This makes it very hard to get some of the most important data that we might want to have about people.

Take for example time-use data. In the offline world, an effort to record the time use of a person – which is an extremely important and useful bit of data – requires researchers to ask a person to carry some sort of recording device around and enter their activities into it at frequent intervals (Riediger, 2011). There are at least three huge problems with this. First, this approach will limit the sample to people who do not really care about walking around recording every moment of their time; this is probably not a representative sample of humans. Second, even among those people, they are likely to be annoyed during much of the survey; negative mood and associated crabbiness errors will therefore be more common than they would be usually. Third, the cost of the recording device and the hassle of getting people to use it must limit the number of people in the study, further increasing the likelihood of error.

Considering these problems, the ideal time-recording tool would be something that the subject could completely ignore; that automatically recorded everything necessary (and nothing unnecessary); and that did so perfectly, without measurement error. This is impossible in the offline world, but can be implemented easily in a virtual world. Thus, because automated data methods enhance our ability to obtain important information, dataveillance and automated survey seem well poised to become important methods of research in virtual worlds.

Dataveillance

The term 'Dataveillance', coined by Roger Clark (1988), is particularly well suited for describing the ability of a virtual world to track the behavioral data of a population. As players move through the world and interact with each other specific data such as movements, communications, resources collected, market transactions, and quests and achievements are recorded in a large database. Once the data has been collected, researchers can gain access to a longitudinal dataset that describes the actions of the all of the players in the world.

In modern society, dataveillance has been identified as something that exists all around us, and that is not just a product of virtual worlds. Credit cards, Facebook information, customer discount cards, and online shopping are all examples of how companies monitor information and consumption in day-to-day life (Deuze, 2007). However, what is unique about dataveillance in a virtual world is that almost all behavior can be recorded in one large database. If a researcher wants to understand

to what degree individuals will cooperate in a given institutional setting, he can ask for permission from players to access their behavioral data through hooks in the code and analyze the results. In fact, as we will demonstrate in a later section, if researchers can be involved in the design of the environment dataveillance becomes and even more powerful tool.

Imagine the following scenario. A player sits down in front of the computer to enter a virtual world. Perhaps she wants to spend some time with friends, or finish a series of quests in an ongoing story where she is a key protagonist. She begins by simply signing into the world with a unique ID and as she does, her time and location are stored in a database. Next, she checks her social networks to see if any of her guild members or friends are online. Each network is stored and organized in the database. At any time a researcher could view this information to see how individuals are socially connected in the virtual world. She chats with her friends for a bit, but they are busy or don't have time to organize any activities that she finds particularly interesting, so she decides that she will participate in her ongoing story. This particular segment of the story involves building a community center for a group of villagers. In order to accomplish this she must solicit the help of the villagers and harvest wood in the forest. As the story unfolds, her decisions and actions with the villagers are recorded and stored.

For a single player dataveillance may not seem that remarkable; however, when every player's actions, networks and changes to the world are recorded in an online database it becomes a very powerful tool. Network structures, path finding behavior, preferences, and the economic conditions of the world are just a few of the structures that can be examined for insights into both individual and collective behavior. Since the state of the world is recorded in a database, researchers have a lens into the dynamic and contextually situated nature of human activities.

By taking a step up to the collective level of behavior in the story of our player, we see that the forest has actually been designed as a common-pool resource – a good that is rivalrous and non-excludable. While the individual player toils over the creation of the community center, other members of the virtual world also harvest from the forest in order to accomplish a wide variety of tasks. If too many players harvest from the forest in a short period without a collaborative scheme for sustainment then the forest becomes depleted and takes time to grow back. In this scenario, across a variety of servers and hundreds of thousands of players researchers could implement different institutional structures to examine how contextual variables influence forest consumption. This example paints a compelling picture of how a virtual world with dataveillance could provide a powerful tool for researchers to collect and analyze large-scale collective behavior.

It is important to remember that dataveillance is still in its early stages, and although the possibility of researchers and game designers working together to design games and build a database is exciting, it is not – a least for now – how virtual worlds are developed. A typical game is designed to attract players. The database is designed to allow the world to function in an efficient and cost effective manner. Unfortunately for researchers wishing to examine this data it means less than transparent access, and sometimes, intractable data. In fact, Williams (2010a) who was recently the recipient of a very large data set – over 50 terabytes from the virtual world *Everquest II* – has dealt with this this problem first hand. Williams notes that the sheer amount of data that was made available to him requires a multidisciplinary team of social scientists, computer scientists, and statisticians to analyze, which made it extremely challenging and expensive to conduct research.

Does this mean that the benefits obtained from dataveillance must be accompanied by formidable and costly data analysis? Not necessarily. The *Everquest II* dataset was never intended for use by researchers, making formatting and management a challenge. If researchers can demonstrate that commercial interests can run parallel to researcher interests then perhaps the developers of virtual worlds will be more open to collaboration.

Another option is for researchers to design and control their own virtual worlds. By creating a database that has been designed for their needs, and developing tools that allow them to observe the state of the world as it progresses, researchers do not have to sacrifice tractability for the power of dataveillance. Early forays into mining virtual data have demonstrated the power of large-scale data analysis packages (Bohannon, 2010). Additionally, depending on the theory being tested a virtual world does not need to be populated by hundreds of thousands of players – as is the case with *Everquest II* and other commercial virtual worlds. In fact, depending on the theory a few thousand or hundred players could be sufficient.

Even if researchers can design their own databases, there is another potential hurdle in the use of dataveillance. The problem being that dataveillance does not work particularly well with qualitative data that has not been carefully categorized. Both nominal and ordinal data are acceptable for storage and retrieval in databases so long as the research carefully plans how the categories will be useful to them. However, a problem arises in situations where the researchers do not know in advance. The nature of large databases is that they are most easily queried when data is numeric or has distinct categories. Simple non-numeric categories such as NPCs that that character visited that day, achievements that they have accomplished, or the types of items that a character uses are definitely useful, in fact they can be sorted into interesting categories by large scale data collection software. However, it is important that these are grouped beforehand based on what researchers believe are the key distinctions. If not, the thousands, millions, or even billions of records that are generated as behavior is recorded can become impossible to organize post-hoc. For example, a researcher who wants to evaluate the number of characters in the world who have used a consumable item in the past should hope that the items are flagged as consumable or non-consumable, otherwise they will have to sort each item individually.

Finally, pure dataveillance only records behavioral data, and so assumptions must be made about the beliefs and desires of the individual based on their observable actions. Some of the most useful insights into human behavior have been uncovered by comparing the perceived beliefs and desires of individuals directly against actual behavior (Dohmen et al., in press). The next section presents a means by which researchers can begin to examine perceived beliefs and desires alongside the behavioral data collected via dataveillance.

Automated Survey

Traditional methods of survey research require that individuals be contacted through some means – websites, mail, face to face or phone – and then actually answer survey questions. However, in recent years, computer technology has begun to alleviate this problem by providing a means to target specific populations and incentivize individuals participate in survey research. One particularly interesting example is Amazon.com's Mechanical Turk (Mason & Suri, 2010). Mechanical Turk allows individuals to submit surveys and target a specific demographic of individuals. When researchers submit a survey they also pay a small fee to Amazon.com, between 1 to 10 cents per survey they wish to collect. Individuals who are signed into Mechanical Turk and match the target demographic are then paired with the survey, can agree to any necessary human subjects agreements, and upon completion are paid directly into an Amazon account.

Mechanical Turk provides an example of how online surveys can target a specific population in an online environment, and encourage participation through the use of relatively small incentives. The same type of targeted research can be applied to virtual worlds. Surveys have been done that target the demographic information and motivations of players in virtual worlds, but these studies have generally been accessible from forums and splash screens and they can't, or don't, provide incentives for participation. More recently, Bell, Castronova, and Wagner (2009, in press) constructed a survey tool for use in second life, and found results similar to Mechanical Turk. With the inclusion of a small incentive – about 250 Linden Dollars ($.97 US) – they found that the community in Second Life was very receptive to the survey (N=2094). The large N and the validity of the Second Life results provides evidence that researchers can collect survey data in virtual worlds, and that by providing a small extrinsic incentive for doing so they can collect a large amount of responses.

Survey tools are an important component of the virtual world research paradigm because they provide a window into the beliefs and desires of the players. These data can be compared with behavioral data to tell a more robust story of perceived and actual motivations. Surveys also allow for the collection of demographic data about players, especially information about what players are doing outside the virtual world which is important for expanding motivations and generalizing to real world populations. By comparing behavioral data from dataveillance to that gained from surveys researchers can look for anomalies, identify self-deception, and begin to understand why individuals believe they are performing certain actions. The survey tool and dataveillance are powerful tools when combined.

If we return to the example of our player above we can imagine how she might navigate through the virtual world and encounter opportunities to participate in survey research. Remember that our player has just finished performing the line of quests that had her working with villagers to construct a community center. Dataveillance provided us with insights into her actions. We know whether she harvested wood, what other players she talked to during the process, and if she participated in any activities that would help the forest regenerate. However, with dataveillance there was still a lack of understanding regarding her beliefs, desires, and motives. By having our player interact with a survey that is embedded within the environment and that rewards her with some in game currency, or a useful item, we can gain some insights into her internal motivations.

TWO RESEARCH METHODS

Up to this point we have hinted that researchers can design their own virtual worlds for study. However, games are difficult to make. *World of Warcraft* currently dominates the popular MMO market and after six years there are still no real competitors. Entry into the MMO market is just that difficult. On other hand, the recent popularity of Facebook and browser-based gaming provides researchers with a much more attainable goal of creating a simple game that attracts a few hundred players. However, even if researchers can build a game, it is still difficult to attract subscribers, as there are simply a huge variety of games available to players. The market for online games is a very competitive market, and building virtual worlds is just not always the best means for answering research questions. In the next two sections, we will discuss two research methods that can be used when asking questions about the populations that inhabit a virtual world. Direct observation is a method for researchers who do not have the power to build or edit the code of a virtual world, or are interested in questions about the behavior of players in established worlds. While the experimental method is a technique that allows researchers to ask questions about the impacts of design in virtual worlds and infer causation from carefully controlled changes.

Method: Observation

Direct observation is the earliest from of virtual world research, and has been employed by a wide variety of scholars from anthropologists to lawyers (Lastowka & Hunter, 2004; Malaby, 2006; Steinkuehler & Williams, 2006; Taylor, 2006; Turkle, 1997), and it simply means observing players or the data that they generate and looking for patterns in behavior.

Direct observation is used most effectively when actually attempting to observe a specific theoretical phenomenon in virtual worlds. "Are players in virtual worlds engaging in communities of practice?" or "What is the Gross National Product (GDP) of Norrath?" are just the kind of questions that direct observation is suited to answer. Using a method of direct observation, virtual worlds can be compared and contrasted against one another, in a fashion similar to the comparative analysis that a political scientist might use, when observing the influence of different government structure on a battery of countries.

Although it has considerable power, direct observation is less suited for asking questions of causation. Attempting to understand if an institutional change will stimulate the virtual economy, or cause more sharing among players requires direct manipulation of the virtual environment, and therefore is not suited to direct observation.

One reason to prefer direct observation to experimental manipulation is that it can capture concepts that are difficult to operationalize and it is simply easier. Developers of virtual worlds seem open to the idea of sharing data with researchers (Szell, Lambiotte, & Thurner, 2010; Williams, 2010a), and even without collaboration with developers, researchers can use web services to gather limited datasets about virtual world behavior. Both dataveillance and survey can be implemented in worlds were developers can only act as observers. However, survey research is more problematic because it cannot be embedded within the game unless the researcher can agree with the developer to allow it. Providing incentives for participation becomes difficult when the survey is not situated in the world, and reaching an actual representative sample of the world can be difficult if the survey is located somewhere off-site such as a community website. For these reasons, dataveillance is the more powerful of the two methods in an observational research setting; however, it is also the most complex.

Even though observation is not as powerful as direct experimental manipulation, researchers have only explored the tip the iceberg. There are still many questions about behavior that can be investigated only in virtual environments simply because dataveillance is so powerful. For researchers who do not have the opportunity to conduct experiments inside of virtual worlds large-scale data analysis via virtual world is still offers many great opportunities for generalizable insight.

Method: Experiment

The idea of using virtual worlds as experimental environments is not a new one. Castronova, Bell, et al. (2009) and others have observed that virtual worlds could be used as "petri-dishes" for social science (Castronova & Falk, 2009, 2011; Ross, 2009; Ross & Cornell, 2010). The analogy is often that of a petri-dish. As multiple copies of a virtual world could be constructed with all elements in the world being identical. Depending on the nature of the experiment, the world could be framed and designed in a variety of ways. Once the world was constructed it would behave like the ager of the petri-dish, and populations could be "inoculated" into multiple instances of the virtual world. After running the virtual worlds for a time sufficient to establish that they were behaving in a similar fashion, controlled changes to a variable of interest could be made – similar to how a microbiologist might expose the bacterial in a petri-dish to various environmental conditions.

This analogy works for virtual worlds because they are software environments that run on com-

puters. Common practice for commercial virtual world management is to run multiple instances of virtual worlds on what are known as servers or shards. Each shard has the same exact starting features except that they feature different populations. The starting populations of virtual worlds may be individually different, but random sampling can easily create environments that are normally distributed at the macro-level, resulting in a set of servers with populations that are qualitatively the same.

Lab experiments often have practical size constraints when dealing with groups, preferring to keep them small and manageable. Virtual worlds can be designed to accommodate dozens to tens of thousands of participants. Virtual worlds are also persistent, the players who inhabit them participate for very long periods, and players who are invested in a particular world can find it difficult to leave. Researchers who have wrestled with this problem in the past have generally assumed that it would be impossible to conduct experiments that are truly macro-level and persistent. In the words of the Nobel Prize winning economist Robert Lucas, "The problem involved in convincing a collection of experimental subjects that they are in an infinite-horizon environment seems to me insurmountable" (1986, p. S421). Such a problem may have been insurmountable in 1986, but virtual worlds provide a potential solution.

With virtual worlds, the experimental environment can be made to persist quite literally forever. Already, in commercial versions such as Blizzard Inc.'s *World of Warcraft,* we have millions of people, over the course of years, pursuing rewards of such value that they can even motivate some people to kill themselves or others. In such an environment, it would be possible to conduct controlled experiments at the macro level. Natural experiments that have already occurred seem to demonstrate the feasibility of this approach (Castronova, 2006).

Such a method overcomes the difficulties faced by social researchers in establishing large-scale causation. In typical macro-level social science research, one uses independent variables to attempt to isolate the direct relationship between the variable of interest and the dependent variable. However, even a lengthy list of independent variables and sophisticated analytical tools like regressions are insufficient to completely isolate the effect of interest. Moreover, most regression analyses must make use of quite a bit more artillery – multiple equation systems, adjustment for unobserved variables, different functional forms, and so on. However, none of this, of course, is sufficient to establish causation; it merely isolates the direct correlation between a specific independent variable and the dependent variable. This isolated relationship is then assessed for whether or not it is consistent with a casual theory. Contrast this complex and indirect method of inference with the far simpler method of controlled experimentation, on which the natural sciences are based. Place two equivalent Petri dishes on the counter. Insert the same yeast in each one. Expose one of the dishes to fire. Observe that the no yeast grows in the burned dish. Conclude: "Fire causes yeast to die." Causation is directly identified, in a method that is simple, replicable, and persuasive. This is the method that social science might be able to use on a large scale, in place of regressions and classical statistical inference, if virtual worlds are found to induce behavior that generalizes to the real world.

So far the use of virtual worlds as experimental environments has been met with limited success the construction *Arden: World of William Shakespeare* provided a means for testing the law of supply and demand, yet could not sustain momentum or interest past the initial experiment (Castronova, Cummings, et al., 2009). Another online virtual world developed by Castronova named *Greenland* successfully attracted hundreds of players, but suffered from problems with implementation and design (Ross, 2009).

Creating virtual worlds for experimental research – even ones that are simple and web based – is a difficult task and one that researchers should not take lightly. It is probable that as more researchers take to the challenge of creating virtual worlds designed for research that even more hurdles to the method will become apparent. However, the use of virtual worlds as experimental environments, or even as platforms for observation, coupled with dataveillance and survey tools has such powerful implications that we hope researchers will continue to work toward making their use a reality.

Method: Survey plus Experiment

In certain large-scale surveys, it is now possible to conduct experiments. For example, the German Socio-Economic Panel has recently included quasi-experimental questions as part of its normal survey, resulting in unique new ways of generalizing experimental results (Fehr et al., 2002; Naef & Schuepp, 2009; Dohmen et al., in press; Siedler & Sonnenberg, 2011).

CONCLUSION

Empirical research in virtual worlds is in its infancy. To date, scholars have not had direct control over large virtual worlds in the way that, for example, physicists have control over their supercolliders and astronomers have control over their telescopes. The situation is rather more like one in which the private sector had decided that telescopes were wonderful things for having fun and thus built hundreds of hugely expensive ones on its own. As commercial applications dominate the technology, the astronomers must take their place in line, using cheap, barely-adequate scopes while waiting for technology and time to make nice machines available for scientific use.

This survey has suggested, however, that virtual worlds are a research technology well worth waiting in line for. They offer extremely high data quality at extremely low cost per observation. They offer the opportunity for extreme flexibility in terms of experimental design, as well as a persistent and potentially very large sample.

Virtual worlds are the only research tools for social scientists that would allow controlled experiments on the macro scale. Moving to the macro scale would solve many critical problems in social science inference, including but not limited to:

- The tendency of governments to deploy massive policy changes without any tests, at the macro scale, of possible consequences
- The reliance on ideology, in the absence of fact, in debates about large-scale and long-time-period evolution of society
- The dearth of policy innovation for dealing with truly global problems, such as climate change, religious extremism, the aging society, and the demographic implosion.
- The reliance in current research on WEIRD samples – Western, Educated, Industrial, Rich, Democratic (Henrich, Heine, & Norenzayan, 2010)

For all of these reasons and more, having a cheap virtual world toolkit would improve research as well as society.

While virtual worlds are undoubtedly an interesting new tool, it must be borne in mind that they are unique in many ways. As Williams (2010b) has pointed out, determining where and when a virtual world finding maps onto the real world is an important research agenda. Nonetheless, given the prospects of virtual worlds as research tools, this agenda would seem well worth pursuing and many large research organizations have already begun to show interest. For example, the German Data Forum (2011) which give advice on research policy to the German government explicitly names virtual world research as an interesting new development in behavioral and social sciences. It is our hope that other organizations and researchers will continue to realize the power of virtual worlds and push the current research trajectory further along.

REFERENCES

Bell, M. W., Castronova, E., & Wagner, G. G. (2009). *Surveying the virtual world: A large scale survey in second life using the Virtual Data Collection Interface (VDCI)*. Berlin, Germany: German Institute for Economic Research (DIW Berlin)

Bell, M. W., Castronova, E., & Wagner, G. G. (in press). Virtual Assisted Self Interviewing (VASI): An expansion of survey data collection methods to virtual worlds by means of VDCI. *Journal of Virtual Worlds Research*.

Bohannon, J. (2010). Game-miners grapple with massive data. *Science, 330*(6000), 30–31. doi:10.1126/science.330.6000.30-a

Castronova, E. (2006). On the research value of large games: Natural experiments in Norrath and Camelot. *Games and Culture, 1*(2), 163–186. doi:10.1177/1555412006286686

Castronova, E., Bell, M. W., Cornell, R., Cummings, J. J., Falk, M., & Ross, T. (2009). Synthetic Worlds as Experimental Instruments. In Perron, B., & Wolf, M. J. P. (Eds.), *The Video Game Theory Reader 2* (pp. 272–294). New York, NY: Routledge.

Castronova, E., Cummings, J., Emigh, W., Fatten, M., Mishler, N., & Ross, T. (2009). Case Study: The economics of Arden. *Critical Studies in Media Communication, 26*(2), 165–179. doi:10.1080/15295030902860286

Castronova, E., & Falk, M. (2009). Virtual worlds. *Games and Culture, 4*(4), 396–407. doi:10.1177/1555412009343574

Castronova, E., & Falk, M. (2011). Virtual worlds as petri dishes for the social and behavioral sciences. In German Data Forum (Ed.), *Building on Progress – Expanding the Research Infrastructure for the Social, Economic and Behavioral Sciences* (pp. 595-606). Opladen, Germany: Budrich UniPress.

Castronova, E., & Wagner, G. G. (in press). Virtual Life Satisfaction. *Kyklos*.

Castronova, E., Williams, D., Shen, C., Ratan, R., Xiong, L., & Huang, Y. (2009). As real as real? Macroeconomic behavior in a large-scale virtual world. *New Media & Society, 11*(5), 685–707. doi:10.1177/1461444809105346

Clarke, R. (1988). Information technology and dataveillance. *Communications of the ACM, 31*(5), 512. doi:10.1145/42411.42413

Deuze, M. (2007). *Media Work*. Malden, MA: Polity Press.

Dohmen, T., Falk, A., Huffman, D., Sunde, U., Schupp, J., & Wagner, G. G. (in press). Individual risk attitudes: Measurement, determinants, and behavioral consequences. *Journal of the European Economic Association*.

Fehr, E., Fischbacher, U., van Rosenbladt, B., Schupp, J., & Wagner, G. G. (2002). A Nation-Wide Laboratory – Examining trust and trustworthiness by integrating behavioral experiments into representative surveys. *Schmollers Jahrbuch, 122*(4), 519–542.

German Data Forum. (2011). Recommendations. In German Data Forum (Ed.), *Building on Progress – Expanding the Research Infrastructure for the Social, Economic and Behavioral Sciences* (pp. 17-40). Opladen, Germany: Budrich UniPress.

Henrich, J., Heine, S. J., & Norenzayan, A. (2010). The weirdest people in the world? *The Behavioral and Brain Sciences, 33*(2), 1–23. doi:10.1017/S0140525X0999152X

Lastowka, F., & Hunter, D. (2004). The laws of the virtual worlds. *California Law Review, 92*(1), 1–73. doi:10.2307/3481444

Lucas, R. E. (1986). The behavioral foundations of economic theory. *The Journal of Business, 59*(4), S401–S426.

Malaby, T. (2006). Parlaying value: Capital in and beyond virtual worlds. *Games and Culture, 1*(2), 141–162. doi:10.1177/1555412006286688

Mason, W., & Suri, S. (2010). Conducting behavioral research on Amazon's Mechanical Turk. *Behavioral Research Methods*.

Naef, M., & Schuepp, J. (2009). *Measuring Trust: Experiments and surveys in contrast and combination* (SOEPpaper No. 167). Retrieved from http://www.diw.de/de/diw_02.c.240038.de/soeppapers.html

Reeves, B., & Nass, C. (1996). *The Media Equation: How People Treat Computers, Television, and New Media like Real People and Places*. Cambridge, UK: Cambridge University Press.

Riediger, M. (2011). Experience Sampling. In German Data Forum (Ed.), *Building on Progress – Expanding the Research Infrastructure for the Social, Economic and Behavioral Sciences* (pp. 581-594). Opladen, Germany: Budrich UniPress.

Ross, T. (2009). Constructing a virtual world as a research tool: Lessons learned from the first iteration in the development of Greenland. In *Proceedings of the International Conference on Computational Engineering (CSE 2009)*, Vancouver, BC, Canada (pp. 1163-1168).

Ross, T., & Cornell, R. D. (2010). Towards an Experimental Methodology of Virtual World Research. In *Proceedings of the 2010 Second International Conference on Games and Virtual Worlds for Serious Applications* (pp. 143-150).

Siedler, T., & Sonnenberg, B. (2011). Experiments, Surveys, and the Use of Representative Samples as Reference Data. In German Data Forum (Ed.), *Building on Progress – Expanding the Research Infrastructure for the Social, Economic and Behavioral Sciences* (pp. 547-562). Opladen, Germany: Budrich UniPress.

Steinkuehler, C., & Williams, D. (2006). Where everybody knows your (screen) name: Online games as "Third Places". *Journal of Computer-Mediated Communication*, *11*(4), 885–909. doi:10.1111/j.1083-6101.2006.00300.x

Szell, M., Lambiotte, R., & Thurner, S. (2010). Multirelational organization of large-scale social networks in an online world. *Proceedings of the National Academy of Sciences of the United States of America*, *107*(31), 13636–13541. doi:10.1073/pnas.1004008107

Taylor, T. (2006). *Play between Worlds: Exploring Online Game Culture*. Cambridge, MA: MIT Press.

Turkle, S. (1997). *Life on the Screen: Identity in the Age of the Internet*. New York, NY: Simon and Schuster.

Williams, D. (2010a). *The promises and perils of large-scale data extraction*. Chicago, IL: MacArthur Foundation.

Williams, D. (2010b). The mapping principle, and a research framework for virtual worlds. *Communication Theory*, *20*(4), 451–470. doi:10.1111/j.1468-2885.2010.01371.x

Yee, N., & Bailenson, J. (2007). The Proteus Effect: The effect of transformed self-representation on behavior. *Human Communication Research*, *33*(3), 271–290. doi:10.1111/j.1468-2958.2007.00299.x

Zimbardo, P. (2007). *The Lucifer effect: Understanding How Good People Turn Evil*. New York, NY: Random House.

ADDITIONAL READING

Bartle, R. (2003). *Designing Virtual Worlds*. Indianapolis, IN: New Riders.

Bell, M. W., Castronova, E., & Wagner, G. G. (2009). Surveying the virtual world: A large scale survey in second life using the Virtual Data Collection Interface (VDCI). *SSRN eLibrary*.

Bell, M. W., Castronova, E., & Wagner, G. G. (2011). (forthcoming). Virtual Assisted Self Interviewing (VASI): An expansion of survey data collection methods to virtual worlds by means of VDCI. *Journal of Virtual Worlds Research*.

Bohannon, J. (2010). Game-miners grapple with massive data. *Science*, *330*(6000), 30. doi:10.1126/science.330.6000.30-a

Castronova, E. (2005). *Synthetic Worlds: The Business and Culture of Online Games*. Chicago, IL: The University of Chicago Press.

Castronova, E. (2006). On the research value of large games: Natural experiments in Norrath and Camelot. *Games and Culture*, *1*(2), 163–186. doi:10.1177/1555412006286686

Castronova, E., Bell, M. W., Cornell, R., Cummings, J. J., Falk, M., & Ross, T. (2009). Synthetic Worlds as Experimental Instruments. In Perron, B., & Wolf, M. J. P. (Eds.), *The Video Game Theory Reader 2* (pp. 272–294). New York, NY: Routledge.

Castronova, E., Cummings, J., Emigh, W., Fatten, M., Mishler, N., & Ross, T. (2009). Case Study: The economics of Arden. *Critical Studies in Media Communication*, *26*(2), 165–179. doi:10.1080/15295030902860286

Castronova, E., & Falk, M. (2009). Virtual worlds. *Games and Culture*, *4*(4), 396–407. doi:10.1177/1555412009343574

Castronova, E., & Falk, M. (2011). Virtual worlds as petri dishes for the social and behavioral sciences. In German Data Forum (Ed.), *Building on Progress – Expanding the Research Infrastructure for the Social, Economic and Behavioral Sciences* (pp. 595-606). Opladen & Farmington Hills, MI: Budrich UniPress.

Castronova, E., Williams, D., Shen, C., Ratan, R., Xiong, L., & Huang, Y. (2009). As real as real? Macroeconomic behavior in a large-scale virtual world. *New Media & Society*, *11*(5), 685–707. doi:10.1177/1461444809105346

Gotts, N. M., Polhill, J. G., & Law, A. N. R. (2003). Agent-Based Simulation in the Study of Social Dilemmas. *Artificial Intelligence Review*, *19*(1), 3–92. doi:10.1023/A:1022120928602

Mason, W., & Suri, S. (2010). Conducting behavioral research on Amazon's Mechanical Turk. *SSRN eLibrary*.

Reeves, B., & Read, L. J. (2009). *Total Engagement: Using Games and Virtual Worlds to Change the Way People Work and Businesses Compete*. Boston, MA: Harvard University Press.

Ross, T. (2009). Constructing a virtual world as a research tool: Lessons learned from the first iteration in the development of Greenland. *CSE*, *4*(1), 1163–1168. doi:doi:10.1109/CSE.2009.405

Ross, T., & Cornell, R. D. (2010). *Towards an Experimental Methodology of Virtual World Research*. Paper presented at the Proceedings of the 2010 Second International Conference on Games and Virtual Worlds for Serious Applications. doi:10.1109/VS-GAMES.2010.16

Szell, M., Lambiotte, R., & Thurner, S. (2010). Multirelational organization of large-scale social networks in an online world. *Proceedings of the National Academy of Sciences of the United States of America*, *107*(31), 13636–13541. doi:10.1073/pnas.1004008107

Williams, D. (2010). The mapping principle, and a research framework for virtual worlds. *Communication Theory*, *20*(4), 451–470. doi:10.1111/j.1468-2885.2010.01371.x

Williams, D. (2010a). *The promises and perils of large-scale data extraction. MacArthur Foundation*. Chicago, Illinois, USA: TBA.

KEY TERMS AND DEFINITIONS

Automated Survey: A survey that uses automatic data collection so that no intervention on the part of the researcher is required. In virtual worlds these can take the form of kiosks or non-player characters. Automated surveys often offer incentives such as money to a target population for participation.

Dataveillance: The systematic use of personal data systems (discount cards, credit cards, hooks in online data) in the investigation or monitoring of the actions or communications of one or more persons. The term was coined in 1988 by Dr. Roger A. Clarke.

Experiment: A major approach to social research that entails the manipulation of the independent variable and researcher control over the events to which the research participants are controlled. Experiments are often used to examine if a causal direction exists between two variables.

The Mapping Problem: Do players in a virtual world exhibit the same behavior as players in the real world? Early results suggest that many behaviors are similar, however, designing a game that corresponds on a one to one basis with the external feature under investigation can be difficult.

Shard: An instance of a virtual world. A single virtual world can have multiple shards. Each is generally an exact copy of the original virtual world with the only difference being the player population.

Virtual World: Crafted places insides computers that are designed to accommodate a large number of people. They are replicable and often have a degree of persistence.

ENDNOTE

[1] "Ill Hudson Man Took His Own Life After Long Hours On Web," Milwaukee Journal Sentinel, March 31, 2002. "'Game Theft' Led to Fatal Attack," BBC News, March 31, 2005.

Chapter 19
Monitoring Pedestrian Spatio-Temporal Behaviour using Semi-Automated Shadowing

Alexandra Millonig
Austrian Institute of Technology, Austria

Markus Ray
Austrian Institute of Technology, Austria

Helmut Schrom-Feiertag
Austrian Institute of Technology, Austria

ABSTRACT

Mobility and orientation behaviour research often requires the monitoring of pedestrian spatio-temporal behaviour. A number of different empirical methods have been developed to investigate specific aspects of pedestrian behaviour. However, each method has certain drawbacks, which aggravate the collection and analysis of relevant data. This chapter describes a new method which combines the advantages of simple observation and technological data collection. Pedestrian trajectories are collected by observing and annotating spatio-temporal tracks using a semi-automated shadowing tool. In this chapter, the authors describe the background and related work in pedestrian spatio-temporal behaviour research as well as most commonly applied methods and their respective advantages and drawbacks. The authors then present a shadowing approach with specific characteristics and implementation. Additionally, three case studies are described to illustrate potential fields of application. Finally, ongoing efforts to enhance the method through the use of additional sensors and features, as well as potential future developments, are described.

DOI: 10.4018/978-1-4666-0074-4.ch019

INTRODUCTION

Pedestrian spatio-temporal behaviour is a particular phenomenon of interest to researchers of many different fields. Comprehensive knowledge about the way people use space, how they move around and what influences their motion behaviour is, for example, necessary for designing infrastructures, developing simulation models, and optimising the spatial distribution of services and facilities. In the field of mobility and orientation behaviour research the scientific interest is focussed on the routes pedestrians choose, the way they interact with the environment (other pedestrians, obstacles, etc.) as well as the places where people stop and why they do so. Various methods have been developed for collecting pedestrian spatio-temporal data in order to analyse their motion behaviour. First attempts mainly used direct observation applying paper maps and pencils for recording and analysing pedestrian movements. With advancing technological progress, several technology-based methods are now available for localising pedestrians and collecting trajectory data. Hence, nowadays researchers can choose from a variety of different methods each providing specific advantages. However, there are still several drawbacks which have to be accepted when adopting a particular method. Especially when pedestrian motion behaviour is to be analysed in larger environments and both indoor and outdoor, there is a lack of methods which are applicable, low priced, and providing sufficient accuracy.

Facing these difficulties, we developed a technology-enhanced variant of the classical observation method for annotating pedestrian trajectories and location-related activities in medium scale environments (public buildings, urban quarters). This "shadowing" method does not require any installations on site, nor do the participants need to be equipped with any devices. Here semi-automated shadowing denotes observations conducted by using a digital map on a tablet PC instead of paper maps, which facilitates data

collection in large and/or multi-storey environments and allows a more precise temporal and spatial annotation of events. It can be used in a non-disguised manner or unobtrusively and is applicable in indoor and outdoor areas.

In this chapter we introduce this semi-automated shadowing method and explain its advantages in comparison with other methods of tracing pedestrian spatio-temporal behaviour. The chapter is structured as follows: firstly, a general overview about the most commonly applied methods for monitoring pedestrians is given. Subsequently, we describe the characteristics of the semi-automated shadowing method, the data collection and analysis process and the method's advantages and limitations in comparison with common methods. Next, we present three case studies of recent applications of the method, focusing on the specific benefits in empirical data collection the shadowing method provided. We further describe current ideas and efforts to enhance the method and combine it more effectively with supplementary sensors. The chapter ends with final conclusions and a summary of the main characteristics and advantages of semi-automated shadowing.

BACKGROUND: EXPERIENCES IN PEDESTRIAN SPATIO-TEMPORAL BEHAVIOUR RESEARCH

The investigation of walking behaviour has usually focused on the analysis of motion behaviour within a specific environment and/or a specific context. First attempts to record and analyse human spatial behaviour have been made for studying the movements of visitors of museums and exhibitions (Bechtel, 1967; Weiss & Boutourline Jr., 1962; Winkel & Sasanoff, 1966). Other research topics focusing on the investigation of pedestrian motion behaviour include for example tourism research, design principles for pedestrian facilities, evacuation behaviour, or the development of navigation and guiding systems (Helbing, Molnár, Farkas,

& Bolay, 2001; Millonig & Schechtner, 2007; O'Connor, Zerger, & Itami, 2005).

Human walking patterns and spatial decision processes show high complexity. Pedestrians have a unique capability for flexible and small scale movements. Consequently, this poses a number of challenges when measuring and investigating pedestrian spatio-temporal behaviour especially in real world environments. Researchers have to carefully choose suitable empirical methods for monitoring walking behaviour. For a general overview about different empirical methods used in social science data collection, see Burgess (1995), Hay (2005), or Kitchin and Tate (1999). Usually, one of the following methods is applied (Borgers et al., 2008; Millonig, Brändle, Ray, Bauer, & Spek, 2009): survey techniques (interviews, questionnaires), observations, localisation technologies (satellite-based localisation using GPS, land-based localisation techniques using, e.g., mobile phone cells, Bluetooth, WLAN, laser scanning, RFID, sensor mats), and video-based data collection. The selection of the most appropriate method (or a combination of methods) for a specific research focus is additionally determined by several limiting factors, e.g., available resources (person power, financial resources), investigation area (indoor, outdoor), unobtrusive or non-disguised form of data collection, required accuracy, required completeness of trajectories, or general conditions on the site (e.g., practicality of installing technological equipment in the investigation area). Another determining factor of which method to choose depends on whether the aim is rather to investigate *how* people are moving through space (quantitative-statistical methods, e.g., for calibrating simulation models, calculating capacities), or *why* they are behaving in a specific way (qualitative-interpretative methods, e.g., for understanding behaviour and identifying influence factors, developing measures to motivate different behaviour). Numerous scholars suggest the combination of several appropriate methods in order to hedge against potential drawbacks,

increase external validity and gain comprehensive insight into the subject of interest (Bouchard, 1976; Denzin, 1970; Jick, 1979; Stone-Romero, 2002).

Many investigations concerning the collection of data on pedestrian route choice use questionnaire survey techniques. Inquiries represent one of the most important data collection techniques in transportation studies and belong to the first methods of data collection that have been applied in human spatio-temporal behaviour research (Hill, 1984; Keul & Kühberger, 1997). The advantages are obvious: firstly, questionnaires can be easily distributed and no expensive equipment is needed, making it possible to collect large samples. Secondly, questionnaires (and any other form of inquiry, such as interviews) provide the chance to collect additional information such as intentions, preferences, aversions, attitudes and any other information which cannot be reliably concluded from motion tracks but need to be reported by the pedestrians (Blivice, 1974; Borgers et al., 2008; Kurose, Borgers, & Timmermans, 2001; Lorch, 2005). The popularity of questionnaires rests on its utilisation of language as the most powerful form of communication (Bouchard, 1976): if someone is willing and able to give information, it saves an enormous amount of time and effort to simply ask that person. However, this major advantage also causes the method's most significant drawback. The validity of responses is not always given: respondents may not be able to correctly report all their routes or activities (Borgers et al., 2008; Brown, 1992). Moreover, human behaviour is never fully determined by verbalised structures (Nisbett & Wilson, 1977) and spatio-temporal behaviour is mainly based on subliminal decisions. As a consequence, responses may be incorrect and constructed ex post, and people tend to adapt their answers – consciously or subconsciously – to what they expect to be socially desired behaviour (Esser, 1993). The limited response rate of questionnaires (about 50% on average) also aggravates efficient data collection; significant distortions in the sample of respondents (uneven distribution of people belonging to different groups) need to be taken into account (Baruch, 1999).

Personal interviews (either face-to-face or via telephone) provide the same advantages as questionnaires, but are more labour intensive. The analysis of data collected in personal interviews with "open" questions is more complex than data collected by standardised questionnaires, as answers have to be categorised (Babbie, 2010; Bouchard, 1976; Denzin & Lincoln, 2005). However, this technique is especially useful if a survey aims at including persons who belong to so-called "hard-to-reach" groups, such as individuals who either usually refuse to participate, do not understand all the questions, or cannot fit into categories of answers designed for the average citizen (Corbetta, 2003). Still, interviews face the same difficulties as described above and the validity of collected data may not be sufficiently given.

Another frequently used method in human spatio-temporal behaviour research is the time-space budgets technique comprising, for example, recall diaries in questionnaire or interview form, face-to-face interviews and self-administered diaries (Lorch & Smith, 1993; Shoval & Isaacson, 2007; Thornton, Williams, & Shaw, 1997). This method can also provide detailed additional information like intentions and motivations, but is just as dependant on the subject's memory, or – if written in real-time as in the case of self-administered diaries – requires the subjects' cooperation to a very large extent. Large samples are hard to achieve and the reliability and completeness of data will decrease with the duration of data collection (Pearce, 1988).

While questionnaires, interviews and similar methods involve the pedestrians directly and require their active participation, other empirical methods focus on the investigation and interpretation of the visible motion behaviour by observing or tracking an individual's path. One of the earliest and most commonly applied methods in pedestrian behaviour surveys is direct observation, also known as behavioural mapping, tracking, or

shadowing. This method has first been used for studies concerning the movement behaviour of visitors of museums and exhibitions (Hill, 1984). Tracking involves following the subject at a distance and recording the observed movements by drawing a line corresponding to the subject's path on a map of the investigation area (Chang, 2002; Millonig & Gartner, 2008; Zacharias, 1997, 2000). This method yields information concerning the exact routes and activities of pedestrians in urban environments in time and space. One of the main advantages of this method is the reliability of the collected data: pedestrians can be traced during an entire route in an investigation environment; also, activities can be recorded (Borgers et al., 2008). In contrast to interview or questionnaire techniques, observations can also provide richer information. Especially regarding the unconscious nature of spatio-temporal behaviour and decision processes, observers often see things that respondents take for granted or have not consciously noticed (Bouchard, 1976). Yet, this method is very time-consuming and labour intensive, and the observer's presence may also influence the pedestrians' behaviour. Finally, data quality (accuracy and completeness) strongly depends on the researcher's observation and recording abilities, and uncontrollable impacts of the situational context (high crowd densities, limited visibility) will also influence data quality for the worse (Millonig & Maierbrugger, 2010).

With advancing technological developments, localisation technologies have gained increasing importance for tracking pedestrians. Among these methods, the use of the satellite-based positioning technology GPS (Global Positioning System) has become widely spread due to low prices of commercial GPS devices and publicly available signals (Raper, Georg Gartner, Karimi, & Rizos, 2007). GPS has been used in a number of research projects for investigating pedestrian behaviour in mid- or large-scale urban environments, e.g., for tracking tourists (Shoval, 2008; Shoval & Isaacson, 2007; Spek, 2008), investigating the use of space of residents in a certain area (Bohte, Maat, & Quak, 2008), or for tracking visitors of parks or recreation areas (Hovgesen, Nielsen, Bro, & Tradisauskas, 2008; Schechtner & Schrom-Feiertag, 2008). Although GPS is frequently used and the accuracy can reach up to three metres with highly frequented positioning (e.g., every second), its applicability for pedestrian motion behaviour research is still limited. Accurate positioning requires unobstructed satellite signals, and multipath effects in "urban canyons" can aggravate data collection. Furthermore, participants have to be equipped with GPS devices, and unobtrusive tracking is not possible. Indoor data collection cannot be performed by using GPS. An alternative positioning technology for monitoring individual motion behaviour is cell-based positioning relying on mobile telecommunication technology (GSM/UMTS). Cell-based positioning primarily benefits from its indoor availability and the high market penetration of mobile phones. However, the position quality is restricted (especially in rural areas) and high accuracy is not achievable. This method is more appropriate for tracking people using different transportation modes over larger distances than for tracking pedestrians only (Ray & Schrom-Feiertag, 2007).

Other localisation technologies applying, e.g., Bluetooth, WLAN, or RFID require the installation of beacons or readers for recording the position of a person carrying a device with corresponding technologies. Hence, larger samples and the investigation of "natural" behaviour and additional information can hardly be achieved (Borgers et al., 2008). Video-based data collection enables obtaining pedestrian trajectories with high spatial and temporal resolution both in outdoor and indoor environments covered by cameras (Bierlaire, Antonini, & Weber, 2003; Millonig, Brändle, Ray, Bauer, & Spek, 2009). The method currently works best for scenarios with isolated individuals and loose groups of people. However, studies using video captured data are usually limited to a small observation field, as many built

environments might require too many cameras to cover the whole area. The majority of the existing automatic video surveillance techniques can only claim robustness and reliability for limited scenarios (Remagnino, Velastin, Foresti, & Trivedi, 2007). Although visual data contains richer information than mere spatio-temporal data, it is still only visible behaviour that can be investigated, leaving the subjects intentions and motives as well as most other personal characteristics in the dark.

SEMI-AUTOMATED SHADOWING

Traditional shadowing is widely used in the field of motion behaviour analysis due to the fact that this method only requires a paper map and pencil for recording pedestrian routes. Depending on the map scale and the observed area, accurate spatial information can be gathered. This method is applicable for both indoor and outdoor environments and does not have the same context restrictions compared to various technology based approaches like GPS, RFID, Cell-Positioning and Bluetooth. However, there are also several drawbacks which have to be accepted when adopting shadowing. Routes on a paper map only contain spatial information and hence without gathering additional timing information only limited behaviour analysis methods can be applied. Gathering extensive additional information like timestamps and additional events of interest (e.g., longer stays) often overloads the cognitive abilities of the observer and therefore may result in inaccurate and/or intermittent data. Moreover, observing large scale areas using traditional shadowing requires either multiple paper maps or one map of unmanageable dimensions. Correcting wrongly marked routes without the loss of information in an interpretable way is challenging. However, if shadowing is used in a suitable way it provides a simple and accurate method to collect route information of pedestrians. While the costs for collecting route information are low compared to alternative technology-based

Figure 1. Semi-automated shadowing using a tablet PC with carrying strap

solutions, the additional expenditure for digitalisation and data preparation for subsequent motion behaviour analysis causes excessive costs. Hence, considering the whole process chain of shadowing, the main cost factor takes effect after the collection phase is finished. In the following, requirements on and characteristics of semi-automated shadowing are discussed in more detail.

Requirements and Characteristics

Semi-automated shadowing is an approach which combines the advantages of traditional shadowing with features of modern mobile computers. Here, instead of drawing on paper maps, a tablet PC is used for drawing the observed route on a digital map using the provided digital pen and a special software tool. This method requires no post-digitalisation of the drawn route and hence overall costs of observations are reduced while ac-

curacy of information can be increased depending on the provided software functionalities. Figure 1 illustrates how shadowing is applied using a tablet PC and a digital pen instead of paper map and pencil. Adopting this method the following parts are required: a tablet PC with digital pen as human interface (hardware) and a software tool for:

- handling digital maps (import and pen),
- recognising observers' drawings,
- adding timing information automatically, and
- providing manual annotation ability and analysis.

However, before applying semi-automated shadowing some recommendations should be considered when choosing a tablet PC and developing a reliable software tool. In the following, hardware and software requirements for reliable data collection are discussed. Furthermore, the system components which have been applied for the studies described in this chapter are presented in more detail.

Requirements on the Tablet PC

Numerous restrictions have to be considered when choosing hardware for reliable und usable semi-automated shadowing. Nowadays, various tablet PCs are available on the market but the range of applicable hardware in the context of shadowing is limited to a few devices. Particularly, it is strongly recommended not to use a touch sensitive screen for the reasons that finger drawings might be inaccurate and unintended touches of the screen cause route artefacts during data collection. Therefore, some manufactures offer tablet PCs with touch insensitive screens and provide an active digital pen instead. These systems are more convenient in drawing accurate routes because only contacts between screen and digital pen are recognised and therefore the observer's hand can touch the display without influencing the collection. This system's behaviour is more similar to drawing on a paper map using a pencil. However, operating time of the tablet PC in general is only sufficient for a few hours, dependent on both the system configuration and the capacity of the battery. Some systems support double batteries which are hot-plug able and hence one battery can be charged and replaced during operation without the need to shutdown the PC and interrupt shadowing for long time periods. More powerful battery packs with more capacity are heavier than typically supplied batteries and hence put an additional strain on users. Sunny days and particularly direct sunbeams on the tablet's screen often make the digital map unrecognisable for observers and useless for outdoor applications. Here, special screens are offered which are more suitable in such situations. It is also recommended to use industrial hardware for shadowing by reason that the case is more robust against damages and the electronic is better protected towards temperature variations.

However, it has to be considered that industrial hardware weighs more than commercial products and therefore might reduce device handling. In general it is recommended to buy or construct a carrying strap to lower the user's affliction, particularly when two battery packs are used simultaneously (see Figure 1). A USB interface should be provided to transfer shadowing data to a workstation and at least 2 GB main memory are recommended to process multiple large-scale digital maps. Although computational power and disk space of modern computers definitely fulfill shadowing requirements, the cost for applicable hardware in the context of shadowing is significantly higher than the cost for consumer hardware. The following list summarises the main requirements and recommendations:

- Touch-insensitive screen with active digital pen,
- Dual battery system or high capacity battery pack,
- 12.1" high resolution screen, e.g., (S)XGA,
- Special screen for outdoor applications,
- Carrying strap,
- Min. 2 GB main memory,
- USB interface for data transfer.

As an example of a tablet PC that fulfils all the given requirements, we list the hardware and the price of the system used for the investigations presented in this chapter. The tablet PC was bought in 2008 for an overall cost of about 2300 EUR excl. taxes.

- Motion Computing LE1700 Tablet PC,
- 12.1" SXGA Ultra View Anywhere Display,
- 4 GB Main memory,
- 80 GB Hard disk space,
- Extended battery,

- LS Series bump case (carrying strap included).

Requirements on Software

The main idea of semi-automated shadowing is to replace traditional paper map and pencil with digital map and digital pen. As far as we know, no commercial drawing software solution covering the required functionality can be adopted mainly for the reason that timestamp collection is not supported. Hence, a customised tool had to be developed for this purpose. Here we outline the development of the application and the tool that was developed for the investigations presented in this chapter.

The software for semi-automated shadowing should be able to import and display digital maps on the screen. Numerous map formats exists and it is not necessary to support all of them within the shadowing application which would require an enormous programming effort. Instead, it is recommended to use existing software for converting the given map material to a lossless image format like BMP or PNG. Here, image libraries for all common programming languages are available to handle such maps in a high-performing way. When developing a shadowing tool, usability aspects with respect to the provided human interface of the chosen hardware have to be considered. The digital pen only provides limited possibilities to interact with the software tool. The minimal requirements are fast access to functionalities like panning the map, drawing a route as well as undoing and redoing. Furthermore, if multi-floor shadowing within buildings is required usability and complexity issues increase vastly and therefore well-conceived software and usability concepts are necessary. Often it is desirable to make additional annotations when observing pedestrians (e.g., person is entering a specific shop), which also has to be considered. In the following we give an impression of our solution to these requirements through a description of the functionality of our Graphical User Interface (GUI).

In Figure 2 the GUI of our software developed for semi-automated shadowing is illustrated. After the application has been started, digital maps can be loaded using the "add layer…" button on the left in the tool's menu bar. Here, it is possible to import standard image formats like BMP, PNG or JPEG. After importing the map, the user is asked to label the chosen layer (e.g., "Level 1"). The tool supports multi-floor functionality, which means that multiple layers can be added to the workspace. The import sequence defines the order of the layers and cannot be changed afterwards. Tab pages are used to switch between the layers during observation (as shown in Figure 2 as "Multi-Floor support"). After importing all layers required for shadowing, the user can draw the observed route on the digital map using the tablet PC's digital pen. For each point on the map, timing information is stored automatically in the background. Large scale maps with high resolutions do not fit in the application window and therefore panning has to be supported. In general, digital pens also provide right-click functionality similar to a wheel mouse. Here, by holding the right-click button while moving the digital pen on the screen, users can pan the map in the same direction, which enables them to deal with large scale maps during the observation.

For annotating pedestrian events an annotation dialog is used. A text file containing an event type per row is automatically loaded at program start. This is used to customise the annotation dialog. The dialog appears when the user performs a right-click on the screen without panning the map (a single right click on one point of the map) and hides after annotating one event or continuing shadowing. Each annotated event is marked as "EVENT" on the map. The route options in the menu bar are used to save, load or clear recorded routes. For correcting routes an undo/redo slide bar was implemented. Here, the user can drag the slide bar to the left for stepwise undoing and to

Figure 2. Graphical User Interface (GUI) of the semi-automated shadowing tool developed for investigations described in this chapter

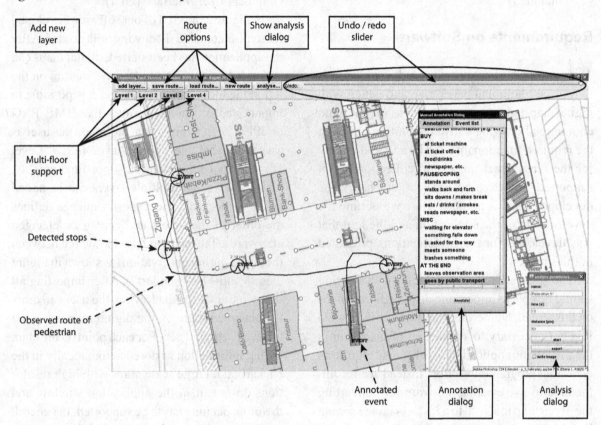

the right for redoing. Finally, a stop detection algorithm and velocity calculator is provided (see Figure 2 "Analysis dialog"). The dialog appears when the "analysis…" button in the menu bar is clicked by the user. Considering that only pixel information of the digital map is used, all spatial parameters and information are given in pixel values.

Built-in Export and Analysis Functionality

Once the data has been collected the tool allows exporting of both, the recorded route (*A*) and the annotated events (*B*) to a semicolon-separated text file. For *A*, the file contains the whole multi-floor route information in the way that each drawn point on the map is stored in one line with additional

floor and timing information. For *B,* each line contains information about time, place and type of one annotated event. Hence, the text files give the possibility for simple post-processing. To provide additional data sets for further analyses we implemented two simple methods analysing the drawn route. The stop detection algorithm searches for stops within the recorded route. The user has to define one time (*t*) and pixel distance (*d*) parameter, before the analysis can be applied (see Figure 2 "Analysis dialog"). A stop is detected when the pedestrian spends at least time *t* within a distance *d*. Here, each row of the resulting text file contains information about when, where, how long and within which distance the pedestrian stopped. The results are presented on the digital map (see circles in Figure 2) to check if the chosen parameters are reasonable for the purpose. The second algorithm segments the route in constant short time periods. For each segment the mean velocity is calculated and coloured on the map (due to greyscale not illustrated in Figure 2). Here, the resulting file includes a sequence of duration and velocity of the route segments.

Shadowing Accuracy and Map Scale

The digital map provided for shadowing strongly impacts the quality of the recorded route. On the one hand high resolution maps are required for detailed spatial-route information. On the other hand the observer requires enough context information on the map to follow one person in a reliable and accurate way. Hence, a trade-off between context information and map accuracy has to be found and it is recommended to test some settings in practice before observation starts. However, this trade-off also has to be fulfilled when using paper maps. By using the concept of semi-automated shadowing gives the observer more flexibility in choosing an applicable map (scale and level of detail) and in handling multi-floor observations and therefore provides a framework for higher spatial accuracy. Due to the fact that accurate timing-information is automatically gathered in the background more detailed timing information is provided than using paper maps. In general, the digital map should only contain details which are required for shadowing for the reason that information overload (e.g., dimensions) could impede orientation tasks in the observation area. However, if the investigation area is composed of multiple floors, the digital maps must be prepared for same pixel size and exact overlapping. Furthermore, the digital map should be equalised in dimensions in the *x* and *y* directions if the built in stop detection and velocity calculation is used. The tool does not include translation functionality between pixel and real-world coordinates. Hence, the transformation equation has to be determined and applied in post processing tasks.

Case Studies

The semi-automated shadowing approach has been used in several recent research projects in combination with complementary techniques, following the recommendation to "carefully choose as many supplementary methods as necessary in order to conduct meaningful tests of his hypotheses and thereby draw robust conclusions" (Bouchard, 1976, p. 368). We present three case studies where semi-automated shadowing has been combined with other methods for exploring the behaviour of pedestrians in shopping environments, of public transport passengers under time pressure in a station, and of passengers facing specific mobility barriers in a public transport infrastructure. The demand for accessible transport infrastructures comes as a result of the rapid growth in the number and proportion of older persons having reduced physical abilities. This has made it increasingly important that simulation models are built to assess schemes for pedestrians with mobility impairments. Available simulation software does not reflect behavioural characteristics of pedestrians with mobility impairments and the impact their impairments might have at stations. Shadowing provides the possibility to investigate and understand how people move and make use of the environment. The insights gained provide a basis for accurate modelling of all types of pedestrians and adequately estimate the effects of infrastructure design to calculate flow rates and congestion delays to pedestrian movement.

Identifying Spatio-Temporal Behaviour Patterns in Shopping Areas

As part of the recently completed research project UCPNavi, spatio-temporal behaviour patterns of shopping pedestrians and corresponding influence factors have been investigated in order to identify typical classes of motion behaviour in shopping environments. The main objective was to develop a typology which can be used for personalising information provided by mobile navigation and information services for pedestrians. Additionally, the motion patterns and type-related behaviour characteristics are to be used for defining parameters for pedestrian simulation models.

The study comprised a multi-stage approach combining qualitative-interpretative and quantitative-statistical methods. The selection of appropriate methods had to fulfill several requirements. Firstly, we aimed at collecting data of sufficient quality and accuracy in larger environments (indoor and outdoor). Secondly, as it is assumed that people might change their behaviour when knowing that they are being observed, an unobtrusive form of monitoring was to be included. Thirdly, measurable behaviour patterns had to be combined with interview data in order to allow identifying relevant underlying intentions, preferences and lifestyle-related factors. Therefore, we applied the following methods during two phases of empirical data collection:

- Unobtrusive observation (semi-automated shadowing),
- Non-disguised observation (tracking with localisation technologies),
- Interviews.

The semi-automated shadowing approach has been used to perform unobtrusive observations in order to hypothesise and identify basic types of pedestrian spatio-temporal patterns solely based on visible motion behaviour. The unobtrusive form of observation may raise ethical concerns. In this case the potential threat of violating privacy was avoided by only recording the path of individuals in public environments outside of shops and some visible features (gender, estimated age, fashion style). The data does not allow drawing conclusions concerning individual persons. The data collection procedure started with the random selection of an unaccompanied walking person. The researcher then followed the individual as long

as possible while mapping the path on the digital map. The accuracy of trajectories obtained in this study reached approximately 1 to 3 metres. The observations have been terminated if the observed person left the investigation field, stayed inside a shop more than 20 minutes, or if the observer lost sight of the individual or felt that the person might notice the observation.

In total trajectories of 111 individuals with a balanced gender and age ratio have been collected (57 outdoor, 54 indoor). Analytical categories/classes have been derived inductively by a coherent and systematic approach (hierarchical clustering, k-means clustering). We used velocity histograms showing the proportional amount of time an individual walked at a velocity within a specific time interval for clustering. Figure 3 shows the speed histograms compiled from each trajectory. The analysis resulted in three behaviour clusters for the shopping mall and three similar clusters plus one additional behaviour cluster for the outdoor environment. For more information on the project and the shadowing results, see Millonig and Gartner (2010).

Analysing Stress-Induced Motion Behaviour of Passengers in Public Transport Infrastructures

In the course of the scientific project IANUS we examined the impacts of stress on the physical and psychological condition of passengers in train stations in order to identify relevant determinants and to develop recommendations for reducing stress-inducing factors in public transport infrastructures. We conducted experiments with participants of four different target groups (young and elderly people, both either experienced in using public transport or not) in a laboratory environment and during field tests. We applied a combination of different complementary methods such as physiological measurements of heart rates, visual field analysis based on eye-tracking data, interviews, and semi-automated annotation of trajectories

Figure 3. Histograms of all indoor (left) and outdoor (right) observations. Rows present individual observations, columns present speed intervals of 0.1 m/s ranging from 0 to 3 m/s. Lighter areas represent higher histogram bin values.

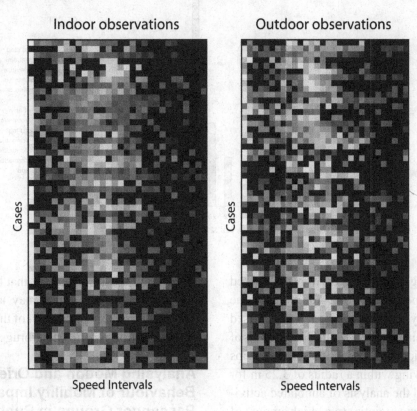

and activities for identifying potentially stress-influenced behaviour.

Observing and analysing the spatio-temporal movement patterns of the test subjects was a main part of the field tests. Several potential indicators for stress-induced behaviour can be identified through observation. For our study, we specifically focused on motion-related indicators such as:

- unusual speed levels (hurrying or hesitating),
- frequent stops and specific activities (e.g., gathering information), or
- uncertainties in route choice (e.g., turning back).

For each participant, two datasets were produced: trajectories of the path a participant fol-

lowed (with data collected in several layers for the different levels of the multi-storey infrastructures) and a list of annotated activities the person performed on the way through the station (e.g., gathering information, buying a ticket, waiting) including time and place of each activity. For identifying potentially stress-induced behaviour, we selected datasets with noticeable behaviour in one or more categories (velocities, stopping behaviour, or routes) for a subsequent detailed interdisciplinary analysis.

To detect unusual speed patterns, we compiled speed histograms of each trajectory, which have been classified using a self-tuning clustering algorithm from the family of spectral clustering (Zelnik-Manor & Perona, 2004). The cluster comprising the majority of initial histograms was assumed to be the "normal" speed behaviour type.

Figure 4. Amount of time spent for specific activities for each participant

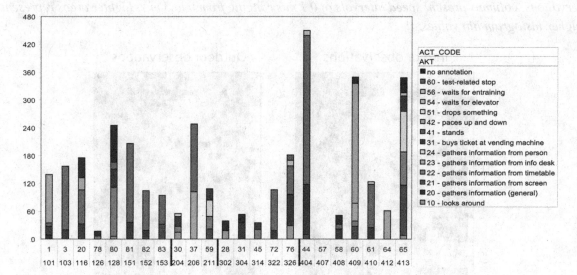

Cases belonging to other clusters were interpreted as "unusual" speed behaviour. Additionally, the average velocity of each participant has been used for identifying unusual behaviour. The analysis of stopping behaviour included the detection of stops (defined as staying within a radius of 3.25 m for at least 5 s) and the analysis of annotated activities indicating uncertainties (e.g., high amount of time for gathering information) and stress coping activities (e.g., pacing up and down). Figure 4 shows the list of annotated activities and gives an impression of time spent on each activity. To identify unusual route choice, we qualitatively compared the routes of all participants and selected examples of differing paths or changes in direction that were obviously due to previous incorrect decisions.

The results of the analyses provided a useful basis for selecting specific participants for integrative analysis with results from the complementarily applied methods (psychological interviews, heart rate measurements). See Figure 5 for an example of the comparison of the walking route and the corresponding heart rate of one participant. The observed person turned back twice on his search of the correct way. At that time, the heart rate also increased, which may indicate stress. More information on this part of the study can be found in Millonig and Maierbrugger (2010).

Analysing Motion and Orientation Behaviour of Mobility Impaired Passenger Groups in Public Transport Infrastructures

Over the last few years, many advances have been made in the field of pedestrian simulation modelling. For a recent review, see Bierlaire and Robin (2009). To enhance the understanding of parameters and their influence on individuals' route choice and of measures providing a basis for simulation model calibration on a tactical level, an empirical data collection was performed. The main focus of this empirical data collection was the evaluation of group specific walking, orientation, and navigation behaviour in relation to features of the built environment such as the guidance system, advertising and architectural features. Therefore, several empirical methods were combined in order

Figure 5. Individual trajectory on level 3 of the station building (above) and heart rate measurements of the participant collected during his entire stay at the station (below)

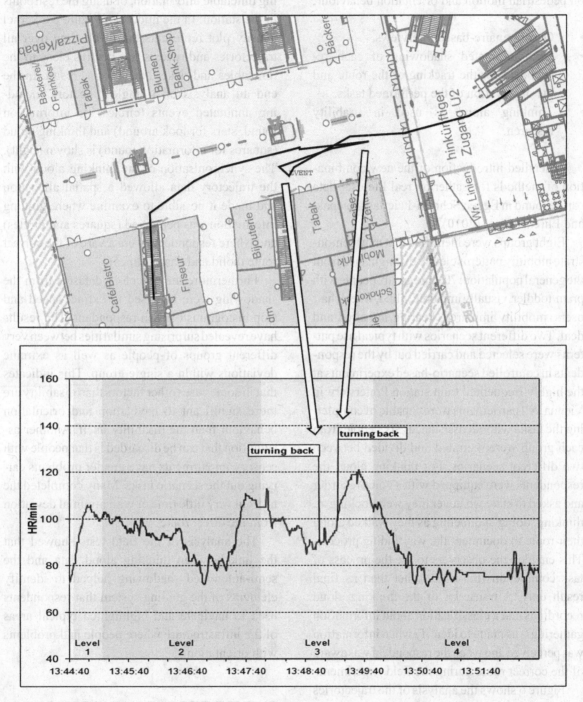

to gain relevant qualitative and quantitative data on pedestrian motion and orientation behaviour:

- Questionnaire-based interviews,
- Semi-automated shadowing of each respondent for the tracking of the route and the observation of the performed tasks,
- Thinking aloud as used in usability research.

A detailed introduction of the new combination of methods for gathering real life user data can be found in Egger, Schrom-Feiertag, Telepak, and Ehrenstrasser (2010).

Eight groups were identified that may demonstrate mobility patterns clearly distinguished from the general population: 70+ age group, people with pram/toddler, visually impaired, blind, wheelchair users, mobility impaired, hearing impaired and deaf. Two different scenarios with typical use patterns were selected and carried out by the respondents in controlled scenario-based experiments at the highly frequented train station Praterstern in Vienna. All participants were capable of completing the tasks without assistance. Six people from each group were recruited and divided between two different scenarios. For thinking aloud the respondents were equipped with a voice recorder and asked to state whatever they were looking at, thinking, doing and feeling as they walked along their route to document the wayfinding process. This enabled the observers to see the process of task completion first-hand rather than its final result only. A transcript of the thinking aloud recordings and a classification about information gathering was made to identify when information was perceived and when the respondent was aware of the correct route during the field experiment.

Figure 6 shows the analysis of the trajectories from semi-automated shadowing and the combination with thinking aloud. First all the 22 recorded trajectories of the respondents from scenario 2 are plotted over the layout of the infrastructure (left). The scenario contains user tasks such as buying a ticket or a drink for the journey, locating timetable information, or using the restrooms in the station. In the middle of Figure 6 a kernel density plot represents the dwell time over all trajectories and reveals two centres close to the timetables and ticket machines as result. In the end an analysis of a single trajectory including annotated events (circles for information found, stars for look around) and thinking aloud (squares for information found) is shown (right). The synchronisation of the thinking aloud with the trajectory data allowed a spatial allocation and made it possible to examine where guiding information was perceived (squares and circles) and where respondents were aware of the correct route (solid and dashed lines).

Furthermore the trajectory datasets from the shadowing were analysed to extract speed and stop histograms of each respondent. The results have revealed surprising similarities between very different groups of people as well as extreme deviations within a single group. This indicates that in some cases other factors than disability are more significant to navigation and orientation behaviour than the disability itself. Another assumption that can be discarded is that people with sensory impairments have greater problems carrying out the scenario tasks. Many completed the tasks in very little time or with minimal deviation from the direct route.

The analysis of the field tests showed that the link between thinking aloud data and the semi-automated shadowing helped to identify elements of the guiding system that respondents used to navigate and highlighted typical areas of the infrastructure where people had problems with orientation.

FUTURE RESEARCH DIRECTIONS

Future research in mobility and orientation behaviour research directs to the development of a multisensory platform for an improved estimation

Figure 6. Trajectories from the 22 respondents of scenario 2 (left), the kernel density showing the dwell time (middle) and a single route analysis including annotated events and thinking aloud (right)

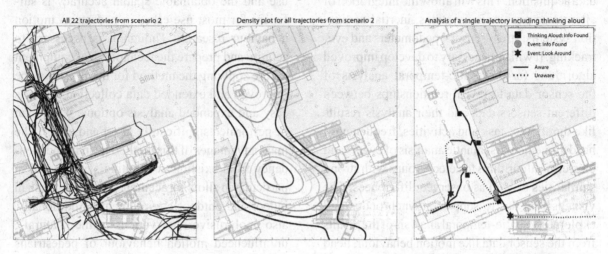

of attention, position, orientation and navigation of people. Semi-automated shadowing has already been used in research projects and was combined with different sensors for different motivations and objectives to provide a more comprehensive view into human spatio-temporal behaviour. In all field studies there was a tremendous effort to combine the insights and results from different data sources especially in the spatio-temporal mapping of the findings. Semi-automated shadowing combined with automated image analysis and multi-sensor measurements that are synchronised in time will enable an improvement in the spatial allocation of perception and behaviour and allow a reduction in time and effort. Trajectories of passengers can be associated with the user's perception of information in the built environment and the results can be projected onto a 3D model for exploratory analysis. Therefore the distribution of attention on objects in the environment can be visualised via 3D heat maps and help to identify prominent landmarks. The resulting automatisms will enable the annotation of large amounts of data in order to receive statistically significant results in social studies.

As desired, such a quantitative evaluation system is currently neither on the market nor in development. The research focus for such a system does not lie in the integration of sensors with the shadowing tool but rather by the sensors and algorithms themselves. For example the key elements in eye-tracking are the automated annotation of video eye-tracking data and automated positioning of the line of sight. This will identify the objects perceived in the video stream and locate them in the environment. The state of the art eye-tracking annotation allows the evaluation of areas of interest in videos but is done semi-automated and requires extensive manual review which does not represent a practical solution. In research for automated annotation a vision based object detection approach is used and tested prototypically in laboratory environments only. Furthermore the integration of image-based extraction of visual objects and multi-sensor-positioning including GPS-based positioning or inertial navigation systems finally will allow a geo-referenced analysis of eye tracking studies. For the application of such methods in field studies many improvements have to be made to overcome existing hurdles and to provide the desired data quality.

Future development of the semi-automated shadowing tool aims at the redesign of the application using a plug-in architecture to enable the integration of additional sensors for synchronous data acquisition. This will allow the integration of alternative positioning systems, inertial navigation systems, stress sensors, pedometers and eye-tracking. It will be necessary to develop improved algorithms for the spatio-temporal analysis of the sensor data to reveal relationships between different sensors data and their analysis results like duration of task and activities, frequency of head movements, semantic analysis of events and clustering algorithms to detect groups with strong similarities as well as observed differences. The visualisation has to support a synchronous and exploratory spatio-temporal analysis of the results from the sensor data like motion behaviour, head movements, semantics and events.

A final issue for future research is that psychological factors are currently absolutely neglected and are not observed during the experiments, but play a major role in motion behaviour and route choice.

CONCLUSION

Many empirical methods are available for monitoring pedestrian motion patterns. Each method usually has a number of drawbacks which have to be accepted or compensated by combining several complementary methods. Shadowing is one of the oldest and most commonly used methods for investigating pedestrian spatio-temporal behaviour, because it is easily applicable, sufficiently accurate for mid-scale investigations, and does not require expensive equipment. Still, its major drawback lies in the fact that it is very difficult to add additional useful information such as time and duration of certain events or the kind of activities that are performed by an observed person.

We therefore developed a new shadowing approach in order to technologically enhance traditional observations. Semi-automated shadowing provides a profound basis for tracking and the analysis of pedestrian motion behaviour

and for the annotation of activities. It is easy to use and the obtainable spatial accuracy is sufficient for most use cases in pedestrian motion behaviour research. Though it is necessary to acquire and prepare the technological equipment before applying the method for the first time, the improved and extended data collection supports easy and expanded analysis options, which can be performed significantly faster and easier. The main advantages of this method lie in its independency from existing positioning systems and in particular in allowing accurate positioning both in indoor and outdoor environments. Additionally, also unobtrusive observations of the "natural", uninfluenced motion behaviour of pedestrians with adequate accuracy can be performed in mid-scale environments, which is not possible with other localisation techniques as they require participants to carry a device.

The method has already been successfully applied in several research projects following different research emphases. The main application for semi-automated shadowing is to improve the understanding of individuals' walking and route choice behaviour. It is particularly advantageous when combined with other methods for a more profound investigation of motion patterns and influence factors. Semi-automated shadowing provides an essential link between different empirical methods in pedestrian spatio-temporal behavioural research.

Currently, simultaneous collections of trajectories and events can still be a challenge for the observer in complex situations. Also the comparison of shadowing results with results obtained from other methods can still be simplified. Therefore, we currently examine the potential extension of the system by synchronising additional sensor data to further improve the comprehensive and integrative analysis of pedestrian spatio-temporal behaviour.

REFERENCES

Babbie, E. R. (2010). *The Practice of Social Research*. Independence, KY: Cengage Learning.

Baruch, Y. (1999). Response rate in academic studies--a comparative analysis. *Human Relations*, *52*(4), 421–438. doi:10.1177/001872679905200401

Bechtel, R. B. (1967). *Human movement and architecture*. Washington University.

Bierlaire, M., Antonini, G., & Weber, M. (2003). *Behavioral dynamics for pedestrians*. Retrieved from http://infoscience.epfl.ch/record/86990

Bierlaire, M., & Robin, T. (2009). Pedestrian Choices. In Timmermans, H. (Ed.), *Pedestrian Behaviour: Models, Data Collection and Applications* (pp. 1–26). Bradford, UK: Emerald.

Blivice, S. (1974). *Pedestrian Route Choice: A Study of Walking in Munich*. Ann Arbor, MI: University of Michigan.

Bohte, W., Maat, K., & Quak, W. (2008). A Method for Deriving Trip Destinations and Modes for GPS-based Travel Surveys. In Schaick, J. V., & Spek, S. V. D. (Eds.), *Urbanism on Track* (pp. 129–145). Amsterdam, The Netherlands: IOS Press.

Borgers, A., Joh, C., Kemperman, A., Kurose, S., Saarloos, D., Zhang, J., et al. (2008). *Alternative Ways of Measuring Activities and Movement Patterns of Transients in Urban Areas: International Experiences*. Paper presented at the 8th International Conference on Survey in Transport, Annecy, France.

Bouchard, T. J. (1976). Field research methods: Interviewing, questionnaires, participant observation, systematic observation, unobtrusive measures. In Dunette, M. D. (Ed.), *Handbook of industrial and organizational psychology* (pp. 363–413). Chicago, IL: Rand McNally.

Brown, S. (1992). *Retail location: a micro-scale perspective*. Aldershot, UK: Avebury.

Burgess, R. G. (Ed.). (1995). *Computing and Qualitative Research*. Greenwich, CT: JAI Press.

Chang, D. (2002). Spatial Choice and Preference in Multilevel Movement Networks. *Environment and Behavior*, *34*(5), 582–615. doi:10.1177/0013916502034005002

Corbetta, P. P. (2003). *Social Research: Theory, Methods and Techniques*. Thousand Oaks, CA: Sage.

Denzin, N. (1970). *The research act: a theoretical introduction to sociological methods*. New Brunswick, NJ: Transaction Publishers.

Denzin, N. K., & Lincoln, Y. S. (2005). *The SAGE handbook of qualitative research*. Thousand Oaks, CA: Sage.

Egger, V., Schrom-Feiertag, H., Telepak, G., & Ehrenstrasser, L. (2010). Creating a Richer Data Source for 3D Pedestrian Flow Simulations in Public Transport. In *Proceedings of the 7th International Conference on Methods and Techniques in Behavioral Research*.

Esser, H. (1993). Response Set: Habit, Frame or Rational Choice? In Krebs, D., & Schmidt, P. (Eds.), *New Directions in Attitude Measurement* (pp. 293–314). Berlin, Germany: Walter de Gruyter.

Hay, I. (2005). *Qualitative Research Methods in Human Geography* (2nd ed.). New York, NY: Oxford University Press.

Helbing, D., Molnár, P., Farkas, I. J., & Bolay, K. (2001). Self-organizing pedestrian movement. *Environment and Planning. B, Planning & Design*, *28*(3), 361–383. doi:10.1068/b2697

Hill, M. R. (1984). Stalking the Urban Pedestrian. *Environment and Behavior*, *16*(5), 539–550. doi:10.1177/0013916584165001

Hovgesen, H., Nielsen, T., Bro, P., & Tradisauskas. (2008). Experiences from GPS tracking of visitors in Public Parks in Denmark based on GPS technologies. In J. V. Schaick & S. V. D. Spek (Eds.), *Urbanism on Track* (pp. 65-77). Amsterdam, The Netherlands: IOS Press.

Jick, T. D. (1979). Mixing Qualitative and Quantitative Methods: Triangulation in Action. *Administrative Science Quarterly, 24*(4), 602–611. doi:10.2307/2392366

Keul, A., & Kühberger, A. (1997). Tracking the Salzburg Tourist. *Annals of Tourism Research, 24,* 1008–1024. doi:10.1016/S0160-7383(97)00038-8

Kitchin, D. R., & Tate, D. N. (1999). *Conducting Research in Human Geography: Theory, Methodology and Practice* (1st ed.). London, UK: Longman.

Kurose, S., Borgers, A. W. J., & Timmermans, H. J. P. (2001). Classifying pedestrian shopping behaviour according to implied heuristic choice rules. *Environment and Planning. B, Planning & Design, 28*(3), 405–418. doi:10.1068/b2622

Lorch, B. (2005). Auto-dependent induced shopping: exploring the relationship between power centre morphology and consumer spatial behaviour. *Canadian Journal of Urban Research, 14*(2), 364–383.

Lorch, B. J., & Smith, M. J. (1993). Pedestrian Movement and the Downtown Enclosed Shopping Center. *Journal of the American Planning Association. American Planning Association, 59*(1), 75–86. doi:10.1080/01944369308975846

Millonig, A., Brändle, N., Ray, M., Bauer, D., & Spek, S. V. D. (2009). Pedestrian Behaviour Monitoring:Methods and Experiences. In Gottfried, B., & Aghajan, H. (Eds.), *Behaviour Monitoring and Interpretation - BMI - Smart Environment: Ambient Intelligence and Smart Environments* (*Vol. 3*, pp. 11–42). Amsterdam, The Netherlands: IOS Press.

Millonig, A., & Gartner, G. (2008). *Shadowing - Tracking - Interviewing: How to Explore Human Spatio-Temporal Behaviour Patterns (Tech. Rep.).* Bremen, Germany: TZI.

Millonig, A., & Gartner, G. (2010). Show Me My Way: The Use of Human Spatio-Temporal Behaviour Patterns for Developing Ubiquitous Wayfinding Systems. In Wachowicz, M. (Ed.), *Movement-Aware Applications for Sustainable Mobility: Technologies and Approaches* (pp. 157–174). Hershey, PA: IGI Global. doi:10.4018/978-1-61520-769-5.ch010

Millonig, A., & Maierbrugger, G. (2010). Using semi-automated shadowing for analysing stress-induced spatiotemporal behaviour patterns of passengers in public transport infrastructures. In A. Spink, F. Grieco, O. Krips, L. Loijens, L. Noldus, & P. Zimmerman (Eds.), *Proceedings of the 7th International Conference on Methods and Techniques in Behavioural Research* (pp. 314-317).

Millonig, A., & Schechtner, K. (2007). Developing Landmark-based Pedestrian Navigation Systems. [IST]. *IEEE Transactions on Intelligent Transportation Systems, 8*(1), 43–49. doi:10.1109/TITS.2006.889439

Nisbett, R., & Wilson, T. (1977). Telling more than We can Know: Verbal Reports on Mental Processes. *Psychological Review, 84,* 231–259. doi:10.1037/0033-295X.84.3.231

O'Connor, A., Zerger, A., & Itami, B. (2005). Geo-temporal tracking and analysis of tourist movement. *Mathematics and Computers in Simulation, 69*(1-2), 135–150. doi:10.1016/j.matcom.2005.02.036

Pearce, D. G. (1988). Tourist time-budget. *Annals of Tourism Research, 15*(1), 106–121. doi:10.1016/0160-7383(88)90074-6

Raper, J., Gartner, G., Karimi, H., & Rizos, C. (2007). A critical evaluation of location based services and their potential. *Journal of Location Based Services, 1*(1), 5–45. doi:10.1080/17489720701584069

Ray, M., & Schrom-Feiertag, H. (2007). Cell-based Finding and Classification of Prominent Places of Mobile Phone Users. In *Proceedings of the 4th International Symposium on Location Based Services & TeleCartography*.

Remagnino, P., Velastin, S. A., Foresti, G. L., & Trivedi, M. (2007). Novel concepts and challenges for the next generation of video surveillance systems. *Machine Vision and Applications, 18*(3-4), 135–137. doi:10.1007/s00138-006-0059-6

Schechtner, K., & Schrom-Feiertag, H. (2008). Understanding and influencing spatiotemporal visitor movement in national parks based on static and dynamic sensor data. In *Proceedings of the 6th Conference on Pervasive Computing (Pervasive 2008), Workshop on Urban Atmospheres* (pp. 95-99).

Shoval, N. (2008). Tracking technologies and urban analysis. *Cities (London, England), 25*(1), 21–28. doi:10.1016/j.cities.2007.07.005

Shoval, N., & Isaacson, M. (2007). Tracking tourists in the digital age. *Annals of Tourism Research, 34*(1), 141–159. doi:10.1016/j.annals.2006.07.007

Spek, S. V. D. (2008). Spatial Metro: Tracking pedestrians in historic city centres. In Schaick, J. V., & Spek, S. V. D. (Eds.), *Urbanism on Track* (pp. 79–101). Amsterdam, The Netherlands: IOS Press.

Stone-Romero, E. F. (2002). The relative validity and usefulness of various empirical research designs. In Rogelberg, S. G. (Ed.), *Handbook of research methods in industrial and organizational psychology* (pp. 77–98). Cambridge, MA: Blackwell. doi:10.1002/9780470756669.ch4

Thornton, P., Williams, A., & Shaw, W. G. (1997). Revisiting Time-Space Diaries: An Exploratory Case Study of Tourist Behavior in Cornwall, England. *Environment and Behavior A, 29*, 1847–1867.

Weiss, R. S., & Boutourline, S., Jr. (1962). *A summary of fairs, pavilions, exhibits, and their audiences* (Tech. Rep.).

Winkel, G. H., & Sasanoff, R. (1966). An approach to an objective analysis of behavior in architectural space. In Proshansky, H. M., Ittelson, W. H., & Rivlin, L. G. (Eds.), *Environmental Psychology* (pp. 619–631). New York, NY: Holt, Rinehart & Winston.

Zacharias, J. (1997). The impact of layout and visual stimuli on the itineraries and perception of pedestrians in a public market. *Environment and Planning. B, Planning & Design, 24*(1), 23–35. doi:10.1068/b240023

Zacharias, J. (2000). Shopping behavior at the Alexis-Nihon Plaza in Montreal. *Journal of Shopping Center Research, 7*(2), 67–79.

Zelnik-Manor, L., & Perona, P. (2004). Self-Tuning Spectral Clustering. In *Advances in Neural Information Processing Systems* (pp. 1601-1608).

ADDITIONAL READING

Bandini, S., Federici, M. L., & Manzoni, S. (2007). A Qualitative Evaluation of Technologies and Techniques for Data Collection on Pedestrians and Crowded Situations. *Summer Computer Simulation Conference 2007 (SCSS 07), San Diego, California (USA)*.

Bauer, D., Brändle, N., Seer, S., Ray, M., & Kitazawa, K. (2009). Measurement of pedestrian movements - a comparative study on various existing systems. *Pedestrian behaviour: Models, data collection and applications, ed. H. Timmermans* (pp. 301-319). Emerald Group Publishing.

Bauer, D., Ray, M., Brändle, N., & Schrom-Feiertag, H. (2008). On Extracting Commuter Information from GPS Motion Data. *Proceedings International Workshop on Computational Transportation Science (IWCTS08)*.

Bohte, W., & Maat, K. (2009). Deriving and validating trip purposes and travel modes for multi-day GPS-based travel surveys: A large-scale application in the Netherlands. *Transportation Research Part C, Emerging Technologies, 17*, 285–297. doi:10.1016/j.trc.2008.11.004

Boltes, M., Seyfried, A., Steffen, B., & Schadschneider, A. (2008). Automatic Extraction of Pedestrian Trajectories from Video Recordings. *Proceedings of the 4th PED conference*. Wuppertal, Germany.

Brändle, N., Bauer, D., & Seer, S. (2006). Track-based Finding of Stopping Pedestrians – A Practical Approach for Analyzing a Public Infrastructure. *Proceedings of the ITSC2006 Conference*. Toronto, Canada.

Daamen, W., & Hoogendoorn, S. (2003). Research on pedestrian traffic flows in the Netherlands. *Proceedings Walk 21 IV, Portland, Oregon, United States* (pp. 101-117).

Diogenes, M., Greene-Roesel, R., Arnold, L., & Ragland, D. (2007). Pedestrian Counting Methods at Intersections: A Comparative Study. *Transportation Research Record: Journal of the Transportation Research Board, 2002*(-1), 26-30. doi:10.3141/2002-04

Golledge, R. G., & Stimson, R. J. (Robert J. (New York : Guilford Press, c1997.). *Spatial behavior : a geographic perspective / R. G. Golledge & R. J. Stimson*. New York : Guilford Press.

Hartmann, R. (1988). Combining Field Methods in Tourism Research. *Annals of Tourism Research, 15*, 88–105. doi:10.1016/0160-7383(88)90073-4

Hoogendoorn, S. P., & Bovy, P. H. L. (2004). Pedestrian Route-Choice and Activity Scheduling Theory and Models. *Transportation Research Part B: Methodological, 38*, 169–190. doi:10.1016/S0191-2615(03)00007-9

Johansson, A., & Helbing, D. (2008). Analysis of empirical trajectory data of pedestrians. *Proceedings of the 4th PED conference*. Wuppertal, Germany.

Koike, H., Morimoto, A., Inoue, T., & Kawano, T. (2003). Studies on the Characteristic Differences of Pedestrian Behaviors among Cities and Between City Districts auch as Downtown and Suburban Shopping Centers. *Proceedings Walk21 IV, Portland, Oregon, United States*.

Millonig, A., & Brändle, N. (2009). What Type of Pedestrian are You? Walking Patterns and Route Preference of Shoppers. *Proceedings of the Walk 21 10th International Conference on Walking and livable Communities*. Presented at the Walk 21 10th International Conference on Walking and livable Communities.

Millonig, A., & Gartner, G. (2007). *Monitoring Pedestrian Spatio-Temporal Behaviour*. (B. Gottfried, Ed.). TZI Technologie-Zentrum Informatik (No. 42), Universität Bremen.

Millonig, A., & Gartner, G. (2011). Identifying motion and interest patterns of shoppers for developing personalised wayfinding tools. *Journal of Location Based Services, 5*(1), 3–21. doi:10.1080/17489725.2010.535029

Millonig, A., & Maierbrugger, G. (2010). Identifying Unusual Pedestrian Movement Behaviour in Public Transport Infrastructures. *Proceedings of the 1st Workshop on Movement Pattern Analysis, MPA'10*, CEUR Workshop Proceedings (Vol. 652, pp. 106-110). Presented at the 1st Workshop on Movement Pattern Analysis, MPA'10, Zurich, Switzerland, September 14, 2010, CEUR-WS.org.

Millonig, A., Maierbrugger, G., & Favry, E. (2010). Classifying trip characteristics for describing routine and non-routine trip patterns. *Intelligent Transportation Systems (ITSC), 2010 13th International IEEE Conference on* (pp. 149-154). Presented at the Intelligent Transportation Systems (ITSC), 2010 13th International IEEE Conference on. doi:10.1109/ITSC.2010.5625222

Pearce, L., Powell, P., Duff, R., & Kerr, A. (2008). Passengers with reduced mobility: modelling their behaviour in underground stations. *European Transport Conference*. Presented at the European Transport Conference.

Schaick, J. V. (Ed.). (2008). *Urbanism on track: application of tracking technologies in urbanism.* IOS Press.

Schneider, R., Patton, R., Toole, J., & Raborn, C. (2005). *Pedestrian and Bicycle Data Collection in United States Communities: Quantifying Use, Surveying Users, and Documenting Facility Extent.* U.S. Department of Transportation, Federal Highway Administration.

Sidla, O., Lypetskyy, Y., Brändle, N., & Seer, S. (2006). Pedestrian Detection and Tracking for Counting Applications in Crowded Situations. *Proc. IEEE Intl. Conf. on Avanced Video and Signal based Surveillance (AVSS2006)*. Sydney, Australia.

KEY TERMS AND DEFINITIONS

Digital Map: A digitalised map processable with computers. A digital map can be stored in different digital file formats.

Digital Pen: Electronic input device for Tablet-PCs for direct pen-display interaction. Often used with touch insensitive displays.

Image Format: Defines how the image information is organised and compressed in a digital file.

Image Libraries: Application Programming Interface (API) providing methods for processing digital images.

Industrial Hardware: Hardware built for more reliability and robustness than standard hardware as often required in industrial applications.

Observation: Watching and registering activities of individuals and groups (e.g., pedestrians).

Pedestrian Spatio-Temporal Behaviour: Motions and activities of walking individuals in time and space.

Semi-Automated Shadowing: Shadowing conducted by using a digital map on a tablet PC instead of paper maps.

Shadowing: (Unobtrusive) following of pedestrians in medium scale environments (public buildings, urban quarters) and annotating trajectories and location-related activities; a form of pedestrian observation.

Stop Detection Algorithm: A mathematic algorithm for finding stops defined by specific parameters in spatio-temporal trajectories like stays of pedestrians in GPS data.

Survey Techniques: Self-report instruments (e.g., questionnaires or interviews); in the context of pedestrian behaviour research these techniques are used for gathering information about habits and preferences based on the participants' self-assessments.

Trajectory: The path a moving object follows through space.

Chapter 20
Mobile Phones as a Lens into Slum Dynamics

Amy Wesolowski
The Santa Fe Institute, USA & Carnegie Mellon University, USA

Nathan Eagle
The Santa Fe Institute, USA & Massachusetts Institute of Technology, USA

ABSTRACT

The worldwide adoption of mobile phones is providing researchers with an unprecedented opportunity to utilize large-scale data to better understand human behavior. This chapter highlights the potential use of mobile phone data to better understand the dynamics driving slums in Kenya. Given slum dwellers informal and transient lifetimes (in terms of places of employment, living situations, etc.), comprehensive longitude behavioral data sets are rare. Working with communication and location data from Kenya's leading mobile phone operator, the authors use mobile phone data as a window into the social, mobile, and economic dimensions of slum dwellers. The authors address questions about the functionality of slums in urban areas in terms of economic, social, and migratory dynamics. In particular, the authors discuss economic mobility in slums, the importance of social networks, and the connectivity between slums and other urban areas. With four years until the 2015 deadline to meet the Millennium Development Goals, including the goal to improve the lives of slum dwellers worldwide, there is a great need for tools to make development and urban planning decisions more beneficial and precise.

INTRODUCTION

For the first time in history, more people live in cities than in the countryside. Our world is no longer simply going through the experience of urbanization. Our world has become urban-

ized. One billion people - or one in every three urban residents - now live in an urban slum, the vast majority of them in developing nations (Kramer, 2006).

The United Nations Secretary-General Ban Ki-moon stated, "with more than half of the world's population now living in urban areas1, this is

DOI: 10.4018/978-1-4666-0074-4.ch020

the urban century" (UN-Habitat, 2008, 2009). By 2015, there will be at least 500 cities whose population is over one million (UN-Habitat, 2002, 2003). It is estimated that by 2050, the world population will reach ten billion, with the majority of those people living in urban areas (Davis, 2002). The brunt of this population growth will occur in developing countries. Ninety-five percent of the growth of the human population will occur in the urban areas of developing countries, whose population is expected to double to nearly four billion over the next generation (Yeung, 1997). In particular, Africa's urban population is expected to triple in the next 20 years (Kaplan, Wheeler, & Holloway, 2009). As cities continue to grow at such an alarming rate, the level of inequality continues to rise. Africa is experiencing the largest urbanization force without a stable economic basis to sustain this growth. The push of rural landlessness and poverty are driving more individuals, at a rate of 5% per year, to cities. Likewise, there is less correspondence between urban growth and overall economic growth than in other developing countries. As a result, urbanization in Africa will continue to go hand in hand with slum growth and formation. For example, between 1990 and 2000 slum in Africa areas grew at a rate of 4.53%, while overall urban growth rates were 4.58% in the same period (UN-Habitat, 2006). These figures imply that the vast majority of new urban migrants are settling into slums.

While there is no universally agreed upon definition of a slum2, the UN designates an area as a slum if it meets a majority of the following characteristics: lack of basic services, substandard housing or illegal and inadequate building structure, overcrowding and high density, unhealthy living conditions and hazardous locations, insecure tenure, irregular or informal settlements, poverty and social exclusion, and minimum settlement size. The operational definition is restrictive to physical and legal characteristics of slums including: inadequate access to safe water, inadequate access to sanitation and other infrastructure, poor

structural quality of housing, overcrowding, and insecure residential status. Given the complexity, relative nature, and informality of slums, any finer definition is difficult to achieve (UN-Habitat, 2002, 2003).

Currently, almost a billion individuals, or one in every three urban dwellers, lives in a slum. It is estimated that by 2030 there will be two billion individuals living in slums, with a total of 45% of the total urban population living in slums (Ravallion, 2001). In sub-Saharan Africa the statistics are even more staggering. There, nearly two-thirds of city dwellers (or 62%) live in a slum (UN-Habitat, 2008, 2009). Since, urban areas, in particular slums, provide a means for individuals to improve their quality of their life, their growth is inevitable. Slum play a number of roles in a city as a first stopping point for immigrants, a key source of local enterprise and industry, and the most obvious source of low-cost labor. They are the easiest access point for new migrants to a city with affordable housing. Many argue their growth is an inevitable consequence of urbanization. Cities cannot provide housing or social support for the large influx of migrants during rapid periods of growth. Slums are able to ease the housing burden for cities since they provide shelter in an incredibly small area for a large group of people without any governmental aid. With a lack of governmental infrastructure and plans for urban growth, it is unsurprising that slums continue to prosper. Moreover, in many parts of the world local and central authorities do not recognize this large and growing population. This "invisible" population and unplanned part of most cities desperately needs better policy and planning strategies to alleviate the suffering of slum dwellers.

Although slums serve an important role in growing urban areas, the high density of people, low-cost infrastructure, and lack of organization and social support typically cause poor living conditions. Most of the humanitarian issues with slums concern the detrimental effect living in a slum has on one's health and safety. The majority of slums lack health facilities, sanitation, or clean water. These factors contribute to the high prevalence of disease. For example in Kenya, one fifth of the 2.2 million Kenyans living with HIV live in Kibera, the largest slum in Nairobi. In Quito, Ecuador, infant mortality is thirty times higher in slums than in the wealthier neighborhoods. Mike Davis said, "Today's mega-slums are unprecedented incubators of re-emergent diseases that can travel across the world at the speed of a passenger jet." In addition crime is often more prevalent in slums than other parts of the city. The Zambian president Kaunda stated in 1986 that "the majority of crime perpetrators find refuge in unauthorized townships (slums) because by virtue of their existence, they lack proper monitoring systems" (Mulwanda & Mutale, 1994, p. 311). In addition, the poor land quality, often swamps, flood-plains, volcano slops, unstable hillsides, rubbish mountains, chemical dumps, railroad sidings, and desert fringes, make this population more prone to environmental hazards and more susceptible to natural disasters. Aside from the living conditions slum provide, slum life is notorious difficult. With a lack of stable work, secure housing, food, water, and security, living in a slum is a constant struggle.

For decades, researchers from nearly every social science discipline have studied slums. The majority of this work has been aimed at understanding the role of slums in cities, the social dynamics of slum communities, possible avenues to improve living conditions in slums, and health related issues. Slums are the most obvious of contemporary urban stratification in terms of economic, political, cultural, social, ethnic, and spatial separation. Therefore, it is incredibly difficult to understand and quantify the many-layered dimensions that interplay to form the workings of a slum. In one of the most comprehensive studies to date, *The Challenge of Slums*, the UN employed more than a hundred researches conducting case studies of poverty, slum conditions, and housing policy. They produced governmental reports citing the importance of understanding slums, poverty, and their effects on urban areas. This invaluable field and policy work has begun to change government priorities in dealing with slums and the growth of cities.

While a large body of theory has been developed to understand cities, these theories cannot be scaled to better understand slums. The current slum growth and formation does not fit the traditional Chicago School or Alonso-Muth Mills models. To better understand the current state of the world's slums, empirical evidence is necessary to build more accurate models. In particular, to truly understand the dynamics driving the growth and proliferation of slums, large longitudinal data sets are necessary. Since slums are temporary, informal, and commonly ignored from censuses, this type of data is difficult to get. The majority of work has been conducted using survey data, mostly collected by NGOs and health-related organization. Typically, this type of information provides a very detailed snapshot of a group in a slum and is invaluable to conducting research. However, this data often lacks longer time frames and large sample sizes.

The characteristics of slums and typical slum residents make overarching patterns about dynamics difficult to quantify. From temporary work situations, unstable tenure housing, and a lifestyle driven by available work, slum residents live extremely transient lives. As a result we see the potential of using mobile phone data to aid traditional techniques to further enrich the current literature while providing new opportunities to better understand this population.

Currently, there are over four billion mobile phone subscribers around the world. However, the majority of these are in the developing world, where the rate of adoption greatly outpaces that of the developed world. Many developing countries are skipping the land phone stage of development and instead jumping into the mobile phone market. In 2008, the number of mobile phone subscribers in Africa passed the number in North America with over 280 million subscribers. More importantly, the penetration of mobile phones in urban African enables researchers to look at previously understudied populations, such as slums. Mobile phone penetration is over an estimated 35% in Nairobi's slums allowing researchers to look at social, economic, and locational variables for a population historically left out of census or other government demographic programs (UN-Habitat, 2007).

As a result, mobile phones are providing enormous behavioral data sets, especially for underrepresented populations in the developing world. Using mobile phone call logs, we can track human movement, infer socioeconomic status, and better understand human dynamics. As opposed to self-reported surveys or anecdotal evidence from field work, human behavior can be quantified using these data sets without the same type of human bias inherent in field work. Recently, work has been done to use mobile phones to increase our insight into human movement and behavior (Gonzales, 2008; Calabrese, 2006). While mobile phone data cannot replace traditional methods, such as survey data, this source of data provides dynamic information for incredibly large sample sizes. The important sampling issues in traditional data sources are minimized and by looking at the dynamics of an entire country, comparative analyses are obtainable.

Our research focuses on two slums in Kenya, Mathare and Kibera, with the goal of better understanding their dynamics and benefits arising from living in slums. Ultimately, we hope to utilize our behavioral analysis to inform urban planning and aid strategies. Currently, most of our research has been in investigating the possible uses of mobile phone data to see if it can enlighten slum dynamics to better understand and serve this growing population.

Our research uses mobile phone data to understand the role of slums in urban areas to better guide policy and planning protocols to better serve the slum population. The scope and ubiquitous nature of mobile phone ownership enables researchers to quantitatively understand these previously difficult to quantify human establishments. Mobile phones provide a unique opportunity to obtain behavioral data about human populations that have traditionally been under represented in national surveys. The remainder of the chapter first introduces our data set and explains the slums studied. Then we present research looking at socio-economic status, the economic, and social dynamics of slums quantified through mobile phone call data. Finally, we put our results in context of designing better urban planning strategies for slums.

DEVELOPING AN UNDERSTANDING OF SLUM DYNAMICS

Although many western European countries and the US are no longer experiencing a large percentage of their urban population living in slums, this was not always the case. As these countries urbanized, many of their poorest urban dwellers experienced living conditions not unlike current slum dwellers. Many researchers agree that urban conditions were at least as bad and as widespread, relative to the population, as today. Eventually, affluence, high rates of industrialization, and effective interventions eliminated a vast majority of slums while reducing inequality. Even though we can learn valuable lessons from these historical strategies, the current political, economic, and social climate of most developing countries makes it very difficult and uninformative to translate plans directly. The current issue is growing on a scale and an order of magnitude than any previously seen. Instead, a new theory and understanding of the dynamics driving slum formation and proliferation is needed. In particular, our research focuses on economic, social, and tribal dynamics of slum residents. Our goal is to develop an understanding of current dynamics, based on behavioral data sets, in particular successful aspects of slums. Instead of attempting to relate historical policy to the current situation, we are focusing on developing a policy based on and better suited for the current population, social, economic, and political climate.

While much of our research focuses on positive aspects of slums and successful slum dwellers, our research is not intended to glamorize the life of slum dwellers. Slums are often the refuge for the city's externalities: noxious industry, waste materials, ill health, crime and social dysfunction, and fragile, dangerous, or polluted land that no one wants (UN-Habitat, 2003). However, out of these unhealthy, crowded and dangerous environments emerge high economic productivity, cultural movements, and strong internal social support networks not found in other parts of the city. Already slum dwellers represent the largest urban demographic in many countries. As slums continue to become the dominant portion of the city in many developing countries, there are attributes of slums that are beneficial to a city and as a result should no longer be ignored as an invisible population.

Data

For this research, we are mostly utilizing mobile phone data provided through one of the leading mobile phone operators in Kenya. Using communication data over one year, we analyze over 12 billion calls from over 10 million mobile phone subscribers. With each call we are able to infer a number of attributes about an individual's social network, socio-economic status, and location.

- Location Data: For every call, two of the over 11,000 cell towers are registered for the caller and receiver. These towers correspond to geographic coordinates and we can infer the location of both individuals. Moreover, based on the location of cell towers an individual calls from, we can

calculate an approximate movement value (movement score/MS) for a given time window. Also, we are able to associated individuals with a living tower based on the tower they most commonly call from.

- Social Data: Every subscriber is associated with a hashed caller ID. From this, we can look at an individual's mobile phone contacts and infer the degree of their social network.

- Economic Data: With nearly all mobile phone subscribers in Kenya using pre-paid plans, economic variables can be inferred. An individual's call volume corresponds to an economic amount of Ksh spent on calling cards. Moreover, to add more airtime to an individual's phone, Top-Up cards are bought. We have all Top-Up card activations and can also infer economic status based on this marker. In addition, the mobile phone provider allows individuals to transfer airtime as a form of payment. These transfers, Sambaza, are recorded financial transactions. Finally, we have developed an inferred socio-economic status based on a number of mobile phone characteristics that will be described in a later section.

Let x be a caller, identified by an unique hashed caller ID. Consider $T = \{t_1, t_2, ..., t_n\}$, the set of towers the individual has called from, $TU = \{tu_1, tu_2, ..., tu_m\}$, the set of Top-Up cards activated, $S = \{samb(c_1), samb(c_2), ..., samb(c_j),\}$, the set of outgoing Sambaza transfers to a subset of x's contacts, and $C = \{c_1, c_2, ..., c_k\}$, the set of an individual's contacts.

- MovementScore: $ms(x) = \sum_{i=1}^{n-1} d(t_i, t_{i+1})$ where $d(t_i, t_{i+1})$ is the distance between towers t_i and t_{i+1}.

Figure 1. This image of Kibera in Nairobi, Kenya (courtesy of Google Earth) shows the high density of settlements in the slum. Moreover, the cell tower locations are marked in yellow. For our analysis, we focus on the main cell tower location in the center of Kibera.

- Living Tower: $lt(x) = \max_{t_i \in T} \ddot{a}(t_i)$ where $\ddot{a}$ is the total amount of time spent calling from tower t_i.
- Degree: $\deg(x) = |C|$
- Call Volume: $cv(x) = \sum_{t_i \in T} \ddot{a}(t_i)$
- Top-Up: $top(x) = average\ (\{tu_{m-12}, tu_{m-11}, \dots tu_m\})$ if $m-12 < 1$, we consider the average of TU.
- Sambaza - Outgoing: $samb_{out}(x) = \sum_{i=1}^{j} samb(c_i)$

In Kibera, there is one cell tower location (associated with six unique cell tower IDs) in the center of the slum (Figure 1). We define an individual as living in Kibera if their living tower is one of those six unique cell tower IDs.

While mobile phone data provides a wealth of information, this cannot replace traditional social science methods. Detail survey data, fieldwork, and case studies are critical to understand any population of individuals. Mobile phone data cannot replace these traditional and valuable

methods. We are utilizing a number of traditional research projects in Kenya to guide, inform, and validate our research questions.

Slums Studied

Our research focuses on slums in Nairobi, Kenya. Since UN-Habitat, one of the largest international organizations focused on aiding slum dwellers, is located in Nairobi, Kenya's slums are some of the most studied worldwide. In the capital alone, nearly 2 million people live in its informal settlements and slums. Representing around half of the total population of Nairobi, these individuals live in one of 134 uniquely identified settlements. In Kibera, the largest slum, population estimates vary, with most agreeing the population is well over 600,000 or around one-fifth of Nairobi's population (Kramer, 2006). These residents live in only 5 percent of the total residential area without basic necessities, such as sanitation, water, healthcare, or education (Amnesty International, 2009). Most slums are located on land unsuitable for building with population densities as high as 2300 person per hectacre. However, even with these conditions, the population of Kibera grows at an annual rate of 12 percent (Kramer, 2006). However, the Kenyan government excludes slums from city authority planning and budgeting and treats these regions as if they do not exist. We have also begun to analyze Mathare slum, located in the northern part of Nairobi. Mathare's population is estimated to be near 200,000 individuals and is one of the older, larger slums in the city.

Inferring Status

Our measure of status is not a traditional socio-economic variable looking at factors such as income, education, occupation, etc. Instead, we are utilizing contact, location, and economic variables from mobile phones to develop an inferred measure of status. For a given individual x, our inferred measure of status $SES(x)$ is a combination of Top-Up value, $top(x)$, call volume, $cv(x)$, degree, $deg(x)$, Sambaza transferred out, $samb_{out}(x)$, and movement score, $ms(x)$.

$$SES(x) = a'top(x) + \hat{a}cv(x) + \tilde{a}\deg(x) + \ddot{e}samb_{out}(x) + o'ms(x)$$

Where $a', \hat{a}, \tilde{a}, \ddot{e}, o'$ are normalization constants.

In order to assess if our measure accurately reflects the economic level of Kenyans, we used the *Geographic Dimensions of Well-Being in Kenya: Who and Where are the Poor? Volume II* by the Central Bureau of Statistics, World Bank, Swedish International Development Cooperation Agency, and Society for International Development. This document ranks constituencies by level of poverty incidence (percentage of the population living under the poverty line). We analyzed the average SES for individuals living at: estates in Nairobi, slums in Nairobi, providences with the highest level of poverty, and providences with the lowest level of poverty. The results are shown in

Figure 2 and accurately reflect the known level of poverty. This measure will be regularly used in the remaining analysis.

Economic Dynamics of Slums

In our research, we tested if cities enabled individuals to increase their status faster than rural areas, thus providing evidence for cities are providing better opportunities than rural areas. Second, we investigated the effect slums had on individuals increasing their status. For every cell tower, we determined the SES for individuals living at that tower in a given month. We then determined the percent change in SES for each living tower. This value, referred to as a springboard score, allows us to compare living towers to identify towers where individuals increase or decrease their SES.

For every tower in Kenya, we consider the set of all callers living at tower t_k during month k, $P_{k,i} = \{x_i, ..., x_n\}$. For every caller $x_m \in P_{i,k}$ consider

$$\Delta SES_i(x_m) = \frac{SES_i(x_m) - SES_{i-1}(x_m)}{SES_i(x_m) + SES_{i-1}(x_m)}$$

We then sum over all $\Delta SES_i(x_m)$ for all $x_m \in P_{i,k}$ to calculate a tower's springboard score.

In order to determine individuals who have moved, we divided Kenya into 280 Voronoi Cells. We assume an individual has moved if their living tower has moved between Voronoi Cells and they have remained in the new cell for at least two months. We analyzed towers in Nairobi, Kenya. As Figure 3 shows, most towers in Nairobi have a very low springboard score, with the mean value less than 50. However, towers in Kibera have an average springboard score of 83. This shows that when individuals move to Kibera, they are able to increase their status to a greater degree than other parts of Nairobi.

Figure 2. Average SES scores for a number of different locations in Kenya. The solid lines represent regions with the lowest rates of poverty, the dashed lines represent two known slums, the dotted lines represent regions with the highest rates of poverty, and the dashed dotted lines represent known estates in Nairobi. As one can see, SES scores correspond nicely with known economic ranking.

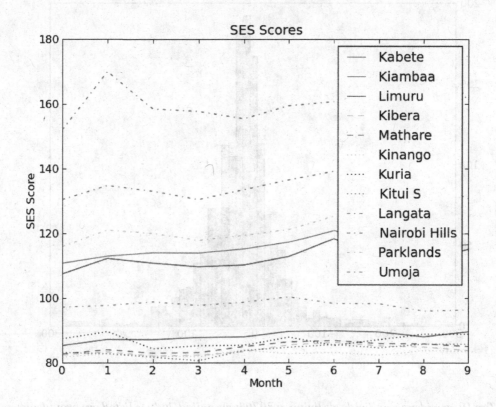

Tribal Affiliations

Aside from employment, rural-urban migration is greatly affected by tribal affiliations. It is widely accepted that people are more likely to move to a slum where they know others from their tribe already reside. The continued salience of tribalism or ethnic affiliation is a defining characteristic of African cities. Tribal relationships are a prime determinant where an individual will move to, and thus rural-urban migration patterns have a strong political underpinning. Furthermore, identifying with a particular tribe helps new migrants navigate the social landscape of the city. Tribal identification is often the most effective pathway to find jobs and housing. These ties provide an extraordinary service to new migrants in the form of shelter and food.

We wanted to determine regions of Kenya that have strong tribal ties to Kibera. Using call volume to different locations in the country, we are able to weight the connection of different regions as well as how these connections change over time. As Figure 4 shows, the majority of Kibera residents communicate with the Eastern Providence, followed by the Nyanza and Western Providences. In Figures 5 and 6, we can again see the relationship between different parts of the country and Kibera. Here, we notice that Kibera is most connected to other poorer parts of the country. Likewise, we have analyzed the trends in call volume to different providences over the course of the year to see if

Figure 3. Average cumulative springboard score based on individuals who have moved to Nairobi. Towers in Kibera have an average score of 83.

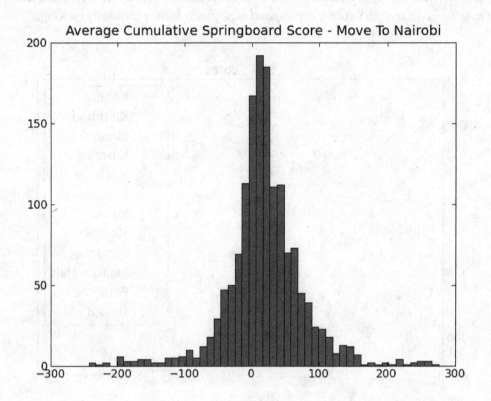

Figure 4. Top 10 providences individuals living at 3070 have called. Values listed are providence, percent of total call volume to providence, region, and poverty ranking.

Percent Call Volume to Providence - 3070			
Providence	Percent Call Vol	Region	Poverty Ranking
Sabatia	0.10308889212	Western	76
Mwala	0.103582282982	Eastern	43
MwingiSouth	0.105241159192	Eastern	59
Butere	0.118749016835	Western	46
Mutito	0.121939987887	Eastern	28
Emuhaya	0.127027328407	Western	78
Moyale	0.140896667536	Eastern	64
KituiCentral	0.141682530872	Eastern	8
Westlands	0.182830987681	Nairobi	195
Dagoretti	0.292507862759	Nairobi	141

Figure 5. Distribution of call volume from the Kibera cell tower 3070 to other regions in Kenya. Here regions are broken by the providence

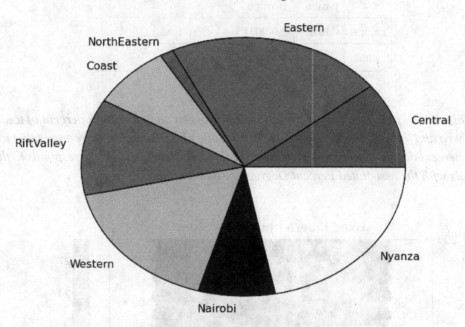

Figure 6. Providences called with calls originating at Kibera cell tower 3070. The size of each dot corresponds to the call volume and the color corresponds to ranking based on poverty level (200 = lowest incidence of poverty, 0 = highest incidence of poverty).

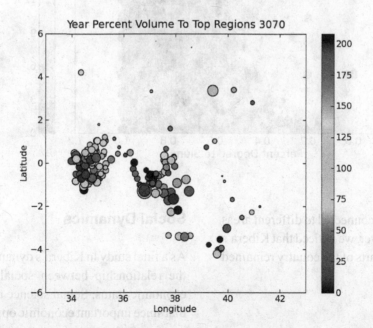

Figure 7. Kibera Corrcoef percent degree and SES (June 2008)

Kibera - June 2008 - Corrcoef Percent Degree and SES			
	r-value	p-value	
capital	.1628	< 0.0001	
slum	-.1323	< 0.0001	

Figure 8. This density plot represents the relationship between an individual's percent of total contacts living in Kibera and their SES value. Based on their mobile phone contacts, one can see that individuals with a high percent degree to Kibera have a lower SES value. Here the color corresponds to the number of individuals with the associated Percent Degree to Slum and SES.

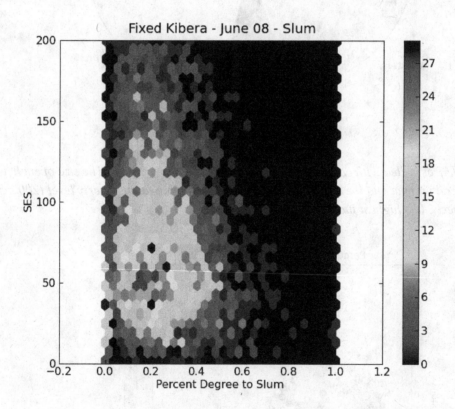

Kibera became more connected to different areas of the country. However, we noticed that Kibera's connection to other parts of the country remained mostly stable.

Social Dynamics

As a final study in Kibera's dynamics, we studied the relationship between social insularity and economic status. Social science theories suggest that since important economic opportunities arise from contacts outside of a small local contact group, insular communities would be less prone to experiencing these opportunities. Historically, poorer communities experience higher rates of social isolation (Woolcock, 1998). This further feeds the loop of poverty as limited access to outside social and economic networks increases poverty. This study compares measures of diversity of communication between cell towers and locational economic data (Eagle et al., 2010).

By analyzing resident's of Kibera degree to other regions of Kenya and inferred status, we see that individuals who are highly connected to Kibera have a lower status. We looked at the relationship between SES and the percent of one's contacts also living in Kibera versus Nairobi us-

ing a Pearson's correlation coefficient. Moreover, those individuals who were highly connected to Nairobi, outside of Kibera, overall had a higher SES (Figures 7 through 9). We also analyzed the percent degree to other urban areas or rural parts of the country and did not see a statistically significant correlation. This provides evidence for the effect of social insularity and the negative effect it has on an individual's status. Moreover, this result emphasizes the importance of forming stronger bonds between Kibera and the neighboring city to help increase the status of slum residents.

Figure 9. Relationship between an individual's percent of total contacts living in Nairobi, with Kibera excluded, and their SES value. As opposed to the previous plot showing the relationship between Percent Degree to Slum and SES, here a higher Percent Degree to Capital and higher SES value are not negatively correlated.

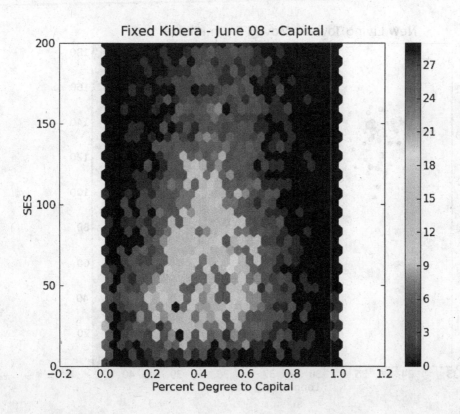

URBAN PLANNING AND POLICY APPLICATIONS

While the previous section focused on understanding a number of dynamics in Kenya's slums, as an illustration of the potential use of mobile phones as a research tool for data collection in Urban and Planning Studies, in this section we turn out attention to better aiding current and future policy and planning strategies. We examine Kenya's slums as an example of how to use mobile phones data in urban policy formulation. The Kenyan government has officially committed to improving the livelihood of their nearly 2 million slum dwellers to join the rest of the international community in meeting many of goals listed in the Millennium Declaration. Currently, projects in Kenya can be divided into two broad categories: slum upgrading and resettlement programs. Our research is focused on the topic of resettlement programs by improving our understanding of current trends in resettlement by slum dwellers to create new programs that are the least disruptive to the current lives of Kibera and Mathare's residents. Resettlement is a broad term encompassing a wide array of strategies designed to enhance the use of the land and property upon which slums are located or housed. Strategies range from building temporary housing close to the slum in order to upgrade the slum to little better than forced eviction. One of the most profound shifts in Kenya's government practices is from mass evictions to resettlement strategies.

While almost all experts agree that new housing opportunities need to be close to the current slum, due to land limitations this is not always possible. Most slums in Nairobi are located near

Figure 10. New living providences for individuals who have moved from Kibera. The size of each point corresponds to the number of movers.

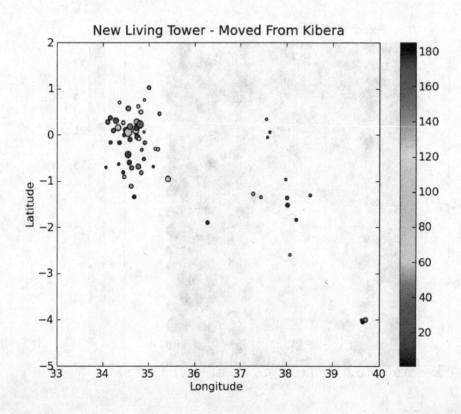

Figure 11. New living providences for individuals who have moved from Mathare. The size of each point corresponds to the number of movers.

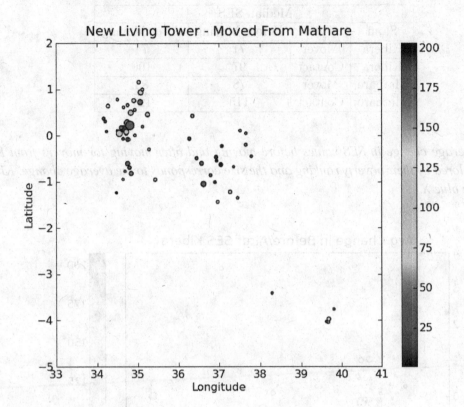

either highly industrialized areas or extremely wealthy estates. Both situations do not provide ample opportunities for the Kenya government to allocate land to these housing establishments. The current plans and locations for resettlement cannot scale to accommodate the entire slum population. Therefore, it will most likely become necessary to search for areas outside of the general vicinity of the slum to begin resettlement housing.

We are using mobile phone data to look at individuals who have moved from Kibera and Mathare slums. The main goal is to identify places where a large number of individuals have moved and determine places where individuals have moved and then asses the changes in SES. Since it has been shown the importance of social networks for low-income groups, ideally new resettlement locations will enable movers to connection with

previously slum dwellers as a form of social support. Moreover, we are trying to determine current migration trends where individuals have been economically successful. For Kibera and Mathare, we are considering around 4000 movers over the course of the year.

First, we analyzed what providences individuals move to after leaving Kibera or Mathare. Figures 10 and 11 show the distribution of providences individuals have moved to with size of the points corresponding to the number of individuals now living in this providence. Overall, individuals are moving to other densely populated area, with very few moving back to rural parts of Kenya.

Next, we analyzed the differences in SES between individuals who have moved out of Kibera and Mathare and their contacts who have remained living in the slum. For every mover, we calculate

Figure 12. Median SES value of individuals before moving and after moving -- for individuals who have moved (Movers) and their contacts who have remained in the slum (Contacts)

Median SES			
Slum	Type	Before Moving	After Moving
Kibera	Mover	71	74
Kibera	Contact	97	100
Mathare	Mover	78	83
Mathare	Contact	115	121

Figure 13. Average change in SES values before moving and after moving for movers from Kibera. Each dot is colored by their poverty ranking and the size corresponds to the average change. Kibera is marked with a blue X.

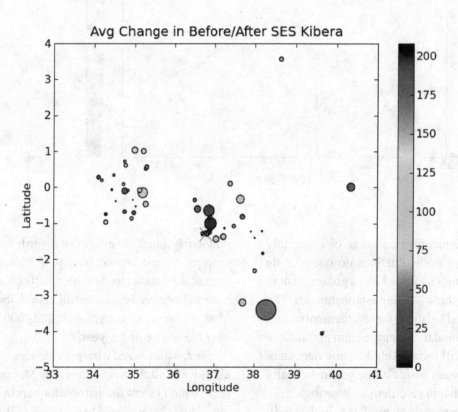

their average SES before moving out of the slum and their average SES after moving out of the slum. We also calculate the average, based on their slum contacts average SES value before and after moving. Overall, individuals and their contacts experience a positive change in SES, how-

ever movers experience a smaller change than their contacts. Moreover, we have correlated the average change in SES with individuals who have moved to certain providences. As Figures 12, 13, and 14 show, there are certain areas outside of

Figure 14. Average change in SES values before moving and after moving for movers from Mathare. Each dot is colored by their poverty ranking and the size corresponds to the average change. Mathare is marked with a blue X.

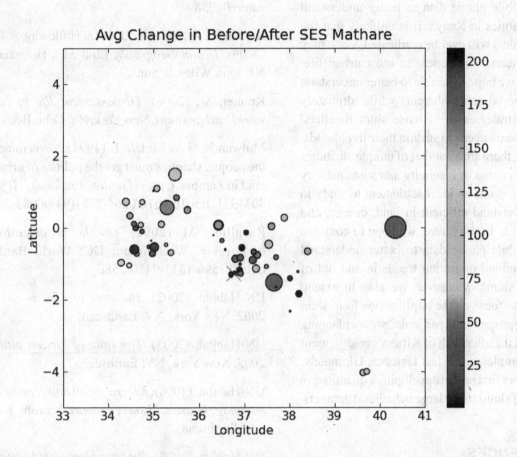

Nairobi where individuals experience a greater increase in SES.

FUTURE RESEARCH DIRECTIONS

As the worldwide adoption of mobile phones continues to increase and their usage becomes more representative of human behavior, data generated by mobiles can continue to be utilized to quantify human settlements. Our analysis presented one possible direction for research using mobile phone call data, which is only a small analysis in comparison to the possibilities for research. A

clear direction for the utilization of mobile phone data is to better understand human mobility and social networks to understand the probability of disease introduction in slums. Given the poor health conditions, access to health care, and low incomes, slums are incredibly vulnerable to disease outbreaks. Mobile phone data can be utilized to understand not only the population mobility elements of the problem but also for contact tracing using degree.

CONCLUSION

In this chapter we focused on preliminary work to use mobile phone data to better understand slum dynamics in Kenya. It is unlikely that the issue of slums will ever be eradicated, since they are an inherent component to most urban life. However, we hope to be able to better understand these informal establishments while ultimately devising strategies to increase slum dwellers' access to basic needs to sustain their livelihoods. Moreover, there are a number of unique attributes to slums in terms of ingenuity and sustainability that makes slums an ideal settlement to study to better understand efficient in land, energy, and resource use. In the future, we hope to continue to use mobile phone data to better understand the longitudinal migration trends in and out of Nairobi's slums. Moreover, we plan to extend our work to focus on the implications from slum upgrading programs. In particular, we are planning to analyze the aftermath of Kibera's resettlement program implemented last October. Ultimately, this work is a first pass at developing a quantitative analysis of slums using large behavioral data sets.

REFERENCES

Amnesty International. (2009). *The unseen majority: Nairobi's two million slum-dwellers*. London, UK: Author.

Calabrese, F., & Ratti, C. (2006). Real time Rome. *Networks and Communication Studies*, *20*(3-4), 247–258.

Davis, M. (2002). *Planet of slums*. London, UK: Verso.

Eagle, N., Macy, M., & Claxton, R. (2010). Network diversity and economic development. *Science*, *328*(5981), 1029–1031. doi:10.1126/science.1186605

Gonzales, M., Hidalgo, C., & Barabasi, L. A. (2008). Understanding individual human mobility patterns. *Nature*, *453*, 779–782. doi:10.1038/nature06958

Kaplan, D. H., Wheeler, J. O., & Holloway, S. R. (2009). *Urban Geography* (2nd ed.). Hoboken, NJ: John Wiley & Sons.

Kramer, M. (2006). *Dispossessed: life in our world's urban slums*. New York, NY: Orbis Books.

Mulwanda, M., & Mutale, E. (1994). Never minds the people, shanties must go: the politics of urban land in Zambia. *Cities (London, England)*, *11*(5), 303–311. doi:10.1016/0264-2751(94)90083-3

Ravallion, M. (2001). *On the urbanization of poverty*. Washington, DC: World Bank. doi:10.1596/1813-9450-2586

UN-Habitat. (2002). *The state of African cities 2002*. New York, NY: Earthscan.

UN-Habitat. (2003). *The state of African cities 2003*. New York, NY: Earthscan.

UN-Habitat. (2006). *Kibera social and economic mapping: household survey report*. Nairobi, Kenya: Earthscan.

UN-Habitat. (2008). *The state of the world's cities 2008*. New York, NY: Earthscan.

UN-Habitat. (2009). *The state of the world's cities 2009*. New York, NY: Earthscan.

Woolcock, M. (1998). Social capital and economic development: toward a theoretical synthesis and policy framework. *Theory and Society*, *27*, 151–208. doi:10.1023/A:1006884930135

Yeung, Y. (1997). Geography in an age of megacities. *International Social Science Journal*, *49*(151), 91–104. doi:10.1111/j.1468-2451.1997.tb00008.x

ADDITIONAL READING

Bauder, H. (2002). Neighbourhood effects and cultural exclusion. *Urban Studies (Edinburgh, Scotland)*, (39): 85. doi:10.1080/00420980220099087

Begg, I. (2004). *Urban competitiveness: policies for dynamic cities*. Policy Press.

Brown, Lawrence A. (1974). The intra-urban migration process: a perspective, series B. *Human Geography* (1), p. 1-13.

Byerlee, D. (1974). Rural-urban migration in Africa: theory, policy, and research implications. *The International Migration Review*, (4): 543–566. doi:10.2307/3002204

Dafe, F. (2009). No business like slum business? The political economy of the continued existence of slums: a case study of Nairobi. *Working Paper Series: Destin Development Studies Institute, LSE.* (09-98), p. 1-38.

Lall, S. V., Lundberg, M. K. A., & Shalizi, Z. (2008). Implications of alternative policies on welfare of slum dwellers: evidence from Pune, India. *Journal of Urban Economics*, (63): 56–73. doi:10.1016/j.jue.2006.12.001

Macharia, K. (1992). Slum clearence and the informal economy in Nairobi. *The Journal of Modern African Studies*, (30): 221–236. doi:10.1017/S0022278X00010697

Neuwirth, R. (2006). *Shadow cities: a billion squatters, a new urban world*. New York, New York: Routledge.

Obudho, R. A., & Aduwo, G. O. (1989). Slum and squatter settlements in urban centres of Kenya: towards a planning strategy. *Journal of Housing and the Built Environment*, (1): 17–30.

Odhiambo, W., & Manda, D. K. (2003). Urban poverty and labour force participation in Kenya. *World Bank Urban Research Symposium*.

Plane, D. A. Henrie and Perry, M. J. (2005). Migration up and down the urban hierarchy and across the life course. *Proceedings of the National Academy of Sciences of the United States of America*, 43.

Preston, V., & McLafferty, S. (1999). Spatial mismatch research in the 1990s: progress and potential. *Papers in Regional Science*, (78): 387–440. doi:10.1007/s101100050033

Todaro, M. P. (1997). Urbanization, unemployment, and migration in Africa: theory and policy. *Policy Research Division Working Paper.*

Ullah, Akm A. (2004). Bright city lights and slum of Dhaka city: determinants of rural-urban migration in Bangledesh. *Migration Letters* (1), p. 26-41.

UN-Habitat. (2003). *The challenge of slums – global report on human settlements*. London: Earthscan.

Van der Ploeg and Poelhekke. (2008). Globalization and the rise of mega-cities in the developing world. *CESifo Working Paper No. 2208.*

Vaquier, D. (2010). The impact of slum resettlement on urban integration in Mumbai: the case of the Chandivali Project. *Society for Economic Dynamics Working Papers* (2428).

Varela-Michel. Manuel. (1997). Cultural adaptation and rural migrant housing. *Masters of Architecture Thesis*. Retrieved July 28, 2009, from http://digitool.Library.McGill.CA:80/R/-?func=dbin-jump-full&object_id=27983&current_base=GEN01.

World Bank. (2000). *World development report 1999/200: entering the 21st century*. New York: Oxford University Press for the World Bank.

KEY TERM AND DEFINITION

Slum (Squatter Settlement): Area which meets a majority of the following characteristics: lack of basic services, substandard housing or illegal and inadequate building structure, overcrowding and high density, unhealthy living conditions and hazardous locations, insecure tenure, irregular or informal settlements, poverty and social exclusion, and minimum settlement size.

ENDNOTES

[1] In this chapter, we use city and urban area interchangeably. Although there are legal

and political characteristics that designate a city separate from an urban area, for our purposes we can ignore the differences.

[2] Legally, slums are differentiated from squatter settlements. However, in this chapter we are using the term 'slum' to represent the broader class of housing establishments with squatter settlements a subset of slums.

Chapter 21
Archiving Audio and Video Interviews

Almut Leh
FernUniversität in Hagen, Germany

Doris Tausendfreund
Freie Universität Berlin, Germany

ABSTRACT

This chapter explores developments in and prospects for the online archival storage and retrieval of oral history interviews—with a focus on experiences and projects in Germany. The introductory section examines the contemporary history research method, oral history, which has led to extensive collections of interviews with witnesses of different historical periods, including survivors of Nazi persecution. To characterize the nature of oral history interviews, attention is given to their narrative form and the biographical dimension. Emphasizing the specific value of this material, the authors discuss the demands involved in archiving such material framed by the expectations on both sides, witnesses as interview partners and researchers and other interested persons as archive users. A German example for state-of-the-art online archiving strategies called the "Forced Labor 1939-1945. Memory and History" archive, is presented, outlining the technical challenges and research features as well as research functionality and further enhancements. Possible avenues for further development within the field are outlined: a meta-search engine covering multiple databases and an open online archive. A crucial ethical question is also presented in this chapter: How can a responsible online access policy ensure the protection of the contemporary witnesses' personal rights?

DOI: 10.4018/978-1-4666-0074-4.ch021

A BRIEF INTRODUCTION INTO THE HISTORY OF ORAL HISTORY IN GERMANY

Research based on interviews with witnesses to historical events and the interest in biographical processes and subjective personal information have a long tradition in the social sciences and humanities. In the field of sociology, the study "The Polish Peasant in Europe and America" by the Chicago sociologist Isaac Thomas and his Polish colleague Florian Znaniecke, published in 1918-1920, is regarded as the starting point of biographical methods. In historiography oral testimonies based on the subjective memory of events have been used as a source since antiquity.

However, in Germany, as in various other Western European countries, it was in the 1970s and 1980s that research based on interviews with contemporary witnesses, or life-story interviews with people who lived through a certain period or event, really boomed in almost all areas of the humanities: biographical research emerged in sociology and pedagogy, ethnography and ethnology, historical and literary studies, as well as in psychoanalysis and psychology.

For all the differences among the various academic disciplines, in terms of their research questions, terminology, methods, and research strategies, all these fields emphasize the subjectivity or/and the relationship of the individual to society. This attitude has developed against a background of increasing doubt about the explanatory claims of grand historical narratives or large-scale theoretical frameworks. As a result, biographical research has increasingly claimed its own independent research approach and has asserted the efficacy of individual action in relation to the determinative power of structural conditions.

In German historiography, research based on interviews with contemporary witnesses has become known as oral history. The USA and Great Britain had a pioneering role in this field, and it was some time before other countries followed suit.

As it was adapted and developed further, the oral history method was enhanced by different national scientific and political traditions. [1] In Germany this branch of research initially encountered a great deal of resistance from established historians, while from the outset oral history enjoyed great popularity in the non-academic context, in local historical associations (*Geschichtswerkstätten*) as well as school and non-school based educational programs. Indeed, in the 1980s a virtual movement emerged dedicated to researching "history from below" and the history of the "little people." This was reinforced by a democratic impulse to include the people such as women or laborers who had been notoriously ignored by historiography up until this point.

In Germany this research was focused above all on the period of National Socialism and the Second World War. However, interview-based research has also come to include many other topics and historical periods, and as a result the past thirty years have seen a multitude of witnesses to a wide range of historical events interviewed by researchers.

As this practice has developed over the years a process of normalization and professionalization can be discerned in the attitude toward oral history interviews. We can speak of normalization in the sense that, where it is appropriate, the use of interviews as a historical source in scholarly research has now become largely uncontroversial. The historical profession has largely abandoned its initial reservations, and today it is hard to imagine the presentation of historical information in exhibitions, documentations and films without the use witness accounts of the relevant events.

The process of professionalization relates to the development of a specific methodological approach. Whereas in the early years of oral history, it seemed that anyone capable of operating a tape recorder considered themselves qualified to conduct an interview, subsequent years have seen the development and establishment of the narrative interview method developed by the sociologist and biographical researcher Fritz Schütze (Schütze, 1976).

This method is characterized by the fact that rather than structuring the interview around questions, the interviewer encourages the interviewee to freely narrate his or her life story. In terms of biographical research, the outcome is qualified as a narrative life-story interview. This approach is based on the assumption that the narrative will inevitably accord with the sequence of past events and that narratives are thus the appropriate linguistic form for the recollection of past realities—whereas the linguistic forms of the report and explanation exhibit a greater distance to the material under discussion. The three basic principles of narration identified by Schütze—the obligation to fit parts into a larger whole that gives some form of closure to the story as a whole, the obligation to increase the density of a story, and the obligation to give detailed background information—are regarded as creating a framework in which the narrator relates events as they happened.

The interview should ideally proceed in three phases. In the first phase the interviewee is asked to narrate his life story in detail and according to his own determination of what is relevant. During this phase the interviewer intervenes as little as possible and motivates the interviewee to continue his narrative solely through attentive listening. At the conclusion of this free-wheeling phase the interviewer asks questions designed to clarify what he has heard. In a third phase the interviewer can address themes and asks question that are of interest to him but have not as yet been addressed. In all phases the conduct of the interview should be oriented to eliciting the impromptu narration of events in which the narrator was actively or passively involved.

Schütze's so-called homology assumption, the idea that there is a direct correspondence between biography as narrated life-story and biography as lived experience, has been the target of trenchant criticism and dismissed by many. Nevertheless, new research on memory and recollection suggest that narration, especially in the context of a life story, is particularly suited to activating recollective capacity (Plato, 2000). Furthermore, the narrative form of conducting interviews has the advantage of a degree of openness. The more scope the interviewee is granted, the less the danger that the interview will be burdened by presuppositions on the part of the interviewer that may prejudice the result.

It is easy to conceive of such an interview as representing a highly individual testimony in which the interviewee has presented large parts of his life story and his world view in a way that is often unguarded and sometimes contradictory. Moreover, the result is also one in which the interviewer has played a part not only as an initiator but also as an interested and sympathetic listener. At the same time, every interview is unique and irreproducible in as far as it is tied to the life of the interviewee and the historical moment of the interview itself. Given this framework, it is also easy to appreciate that the archiving of such subjective, sophisticated sources presents particular challenges.

ARCHIVING ORAL HISTORY INTERVIEWS

It was and still is typical for German oral history that, in the academic field, interviews were and are conducted almost exclusively as part of research projects. There are also local oral history projects conducted by lay researches. There are no archival oral history programs where interview projects are initiated and conducted mainly for archival purposes by archiving institutions.[2] Thus the archiving of oral history interviews was not regarded as a mission initially, but instead followed as second thought to interview projects for research. Whereas the early oral history research projects preserved their interviews largely for reasons of thoroughness or inertia, it soon became clear that these sources could be of value beyond the initial project and that for this reason they needed to be safeguarded and made accessible for future research. This change in attitude was also motivated by a new appreciation of the time and effort required to gather such material and of the material's complexity, the potential of which can hardly be exhausted by a single analysis. Each interview is unique and irreproducible and may even become more valuable for future scholars since in most cases a new interview is no longer possible. And even in cases where a second interview is possible, it is more than likely that the political, historical and personal circumstances that shape memory and the presentation of a life story will have changed so fundamentally that a second interview will produce quite different results.

In addition, it is basically sensible and good scholarly practice to retain empirical research data, to document the research process and allow results to be reviewed. In fact many such interviews are indeed retained by the institutions that originally conducted them. They are stored on the premises of historical associations and memorials, in research institutes, and in company and municipal archives. Some, however, are not archived at all and lie, all but forgotten, in the desk drawers of individual scholars. On the other hand, in Germany archives specializing in oral history interviews are rather rare, and a number of those that do exist are limited to very specific themes. This situation creates difficulties for researchers both in terms of locating relevant sources and finding archives willing to store interview material they have compiled.

The reluctance of archives to move quickly to store and process interviews can be explained not least by the time and effort required to ensure the suitable "disclosure"—the cataloging and description—and long-term preservation of interviews. Making such interviews a usable source requires at least a classification of the material according to predefined thematic characteristics or keywords, or, better still, the indexing of individual sequences in order to ensure they are searchable. This in

turn requires the formulation of keywords and indices that refer to the content of the interview as comprehensively as possible. In addition, such indices need to function for search requests that can change from one research generation to the next.

Another form of disclosure entails the transcription of interview material so that it can be subject to a full text search, a search strategy that does not always meet all user requirements but is nevertheless highly effective. Unfortunately both the indexing and the transcription itself require a big personnel investment.

The most technically demanding aspect is the long-term preservation of audio and video recordings, which requires digitization of analog recordings. This is demanding because it means dealing with both historical and current recording technologies and because decisions regarding formats and storage media must take into account both current and future technological developments. All this can quickly overtax archives that lack special expertise regarding audio and video material in general and interviews in particular. In this regard the British and Austrian examples are instructive: there sound archives manage oral history collections.[3]

Another problem is the lack of certainty when it comes to the legal aspects of archiving life-story interviews. In many countries, the kind of personal data revealed in oral history interviews are subject to long blocking periods. In Germany this period is thirty years, during which the interview may be archived but not released for use. It is for this reason that interviewees are usually asked to sign a declaration allowing for immediate access to the content of the interview. Although this means that the blocking period is rendered null and void, the interviewee and in some cases his relatives and descendants can retract their permission at any time.

The early release of interviews is highly sensitive because more often than not they are not anonymized: In the case of a transcript, obscuring the names of people and places can be done using a simple command but for audio material this procedure is very complicated. In fact, in many cases effective anonymization would require the deletion of entire passages, which is certainly not desirable if further use is to be made of the material. If it is not possible to locate the source in terms of place, time and personalities, it becomes useless for many avenues of inquiry.

In order to ensure the interviewee's personal rights, the access to oral history interviews has until now usually been confined to the archives in which they are held. Here archive users are required to sign an agreement that they will not make use of personal data and in the case of publication ensure that the interviewee and other featured persons are adequately anonymized. The archiving of interviews with contemporary witnesses is thus a complex undertaking with an insecure legal foundation. As a result, it is difficult for users to locate appropriate interview material, and actually using the material tends to be time-consuming and bound to a particular physical location.

Nevertheless, for some years now, relevant archives have been registering a growing interest in oral history interviews. Whereas the main focus of archives when it came to this material used to be compilation and storage, advisory services and retrieval are now demanding an equal amount of time and effort.

There are a number of reasons for this increased interest. On the one hand, the use of interviews with contemporary witnesses is now accepted practice within historical disciplines. Today it has become indispensible in certain areas of serious historical study not only to evaluate relevant written sources but also to consider the perspectives of witnesses—in so far as relevant sources such as audio and video interviews are available in archives.

A second reason probably has to do with the large number of interviews that have been carried out in recent decades. In fact, we have now reached something like a "critical mass" of

archived interviews that can provide a resource for researchers on a range of themes. In the context of a large number of projects, different groups of witnesses have been questioned on a wide range of aspects of twentieth-century history. And due to the open way in which interviews based on life stories have been conducted, these documents usually lend themselves to the consideration of many questions beyond their original focus. It is therefore often not even necessary for researchers to conduct interviews themselves. Indeed, in many cases this is not even possible. Research into National Socialism and the Second World War are good examples in this respect. While the interest of historians and the political public sphere in these themes remains unabated, there are few surviving witnesses to this period of history. Archived interviews will therefore soon constitute an essential form of access to the experiences and memories of this generation.

Interviews on the theme of National Socialism and the Second World War are indeed requested with conspicuous frequency. However, what is also noticeable is the enormous thematic range of the requests. Whereas some themes are very closely connected with the original research interests, we are now seeing many requests for material linked with groups of people and themes that were not the direct focus of the original investigation—and this places particular demands on archival research. In addition, while historians constitute the largest group of users, scholars from other disciplines are increasingly using oral history archives, including sociologists, educators, ethnographers and ethnologists as well as linguistic and literary scholars. Users also include filmmakers, exhibition curators and journalists. The emergence of new kinds of questions and the development of new user groups are underscoring their enduring value and the importance of archiving these testimonies.

However, along with this increased user interest, relevant archives are also registering a change in user expectations. Accustomed to rapid access to all types of information on the Internet, users of archives now expect at least the possibility of online research in databases and preferably the online provision of the sources themselves. A number of archives are technically equipped for such possibilities. For some years now, demands for long-term preservation have been met in part with the digitization of analog media in so far as this is permitted by the limited financial means available to the (often poorly equipped) archives. As a result, not only transcriptions but also significant numbers of audio and film recordings are now available in digital form.

Nevertheless archives tend to still be hesitant to go online and continue to expect users to engage in what is often very time-consuming work on the archival premises. While it is undeniable that modern and user-friendly forms of the provision of interview material need to be developed, including utilization of the possibilities presented by the Internet, we must not lose sight of the sensitive character of the material and the personal rights of interviewees. The responsibilities of archives include both protecting the interests of interviewees and responding as far as possible to the need of archive users for a service that takes advantage of modern technologies.

The following discussion of experiences with an online archive in the field of oral history should be seen against this background. What types of documents are being offered in this context? How are they presented in technological terms and how are they described in thematic terms? Are the use of the archive and/or the provision of materials subject to particular limitations? What provisions are there to ensure the interviewee's personal rights? What are the dangers that need to be countered and where does the potential lie for further development?

EXPERIENCES WITH AN ONLINE ARCHIVE

The "Forced Labor 1939-1945. Memory and History" archive holds over 390 audio- and 190 video-interviews with people forced to labor for Nazi Germany. The interviews were conducted in 2005 and 2006 within the framework of "Documentation of Life Story Interviews with Former Slave and Forced Laborers," a project involving 32 research institutions and project groups and coordinated by the Institute for History and Biography at the FernUniversität Hagen.[4]

The archive contains interviews with survivors of Nazi forced labor in 25 languages; interviews were conducted in 26 countries, above all in Central and Eastern Europe. The interviewees were free to choose the interview language. Interviewees include former concentration camp inmates, prisoners of war and members of victimized groups that are often "forgotten" such as Roma and victims of forced Germanization.

The interviews in the "Forced Labor 1939-1945" archive are narrative life-story interviews and begin with an open question. They follow a structure that begins with the stating the time, date, location and participants of the interview (in text form on an opening slide, and often verbally as well), followed by the narration of the witness's life story, and concluding with the presentation of documents and artifacts. The interviews are unedited.

Each interview is accompanied by a short report by the interviewer (which is not made public), along with biographical questionnaires and a brief biography of the interviewed person. In this project, transcripts and translations of the interviews have been produced, and these allow for the provision of particularly detailed research options and a user-friendly environment.

From the analog audio and video collection the Center for Digital Systems of the Freie Universität Berlin – in cooperation with the Foundation Remembrance, Responsibility and Future – created an online archive. The interview archive is available for education and research and embedded in a Web site which provides contextual information about the collection, the project, oral history, forced labor, compensation of forced laborers and activities for education, teaching and exhibits. Thematically related links are available as well as literature references.

The original tapes have been archived by the Deutsches Historisches Museum, where they are stored under optimal conditions. However, it is still unclear whether transfer to other digital formats will be possible in twenty or thirty years without quality losses. High-quality (albeit lossy in comparison to the original) digital reference copies in DV Pal format has been made of the interviews. Copies of the video recordings were also transcoded for the internet into Flash and MPEG 4 end-user formats. MPEG 3 copies have been made of the audio recordings. The reference copies are intended to provide a basis for generating other up-to-date formats for end-use in the future.

Access to the online archive is open to registered users only. Potential users must apply for registration and provide not only personal details but also precise information about their interest in the material. This information is checked, and within two days applicants either receive personal access data or are informed that their application has been declined. Users must also agree to abide by the comprehensive conditions of use.

The issue of confidentiality for interviewees has been approached with great care. Access to the documents is controlled in a similar way to that used in traditional, physical archives that the user must visit in person. This indicates that the concerns repeatedly raised about confidentiality in the context of digital or online archives can, in fact, be adequately dealt with.

The uncut interviews have been processed by the CeDiS team in such a way as to make possible a number of navigation and search tools for archive users. One popular, standard option is the combination of biographical search criteria. For each interview, the following information is recorded: persecuted group, labor deployment area (e.g., mining, private household, agriculture, etc.), internment conditions (e.g., prison, concentration camp, private lodgings), interview language, (current) place of residence (country). The user can select for certain categories to, for example, identify everyone who gave his/her interview in Polish and belonged to the group of "politically persecuted". In this case, 32 interviews from the archive would be immediately found. Such a search can be refined in various ways to get more and more specific (and fewer) results. For example, the search above can be refined to include only those who labored in the field of "industry": for which 13 results can be found in the archive. This search possibility identifies complete interviews (rather than particular segments in the interviews).

The "Forced Labor 1939-1945" archive also offers users the possibility of targeting concrete passages in the interviews. For this purpose interviews have been transcribed and translated into German, and divided into individual segments, with each segment corresponding to a sentence. The text-based segments are linked with the video and audio time codes with the result that a full-text search shows the individual segments as well as the corresponding sequences in the video and audio files. This type of linking has the additional function of allowing for the synchronous presentation of image/sound and the accompanying text, which is shown in subtitles.

The full-text search, which is made possible by the transcription and translation of the interviews, offers the advantage of allowing every word to be searched and found. The disadvantage is that these words are not weighted. For instance, a place name can refer to somewhere an interviewee stayed for several years or to one of many cities through which someone traveled en route to a camp; the latter result is unlikely to be interesting for the researcher.

In order to counteract such irrelevant search results and to provide archive users with tools in addition to the full-text search, headings have been written and a register was set up. The headings provide the user with a quick overview of the interview structure and the main points covered. They can also be used to locate more abstract connections, even if the familiar terminology does not appear in the spoken text. For instance, an interviewee might speak vividly about the riots during the November Pogrom without using this term or one of the other common synonyms for it (e.g., "Kristallnacht"). A full-text search would thus not locate this thematic segment. Headings are a great help to users in such cases, as they link familiar, technical terms to the segment in question. The headings are located right next to the player and are therefore easy to access.

The registers include all geographical locations of relevance to the interviewees' biography, the names of companies connected to the labor years, sites of persecution, as well as any individual whose full name was mentioned in the interview. The registers build the foundation for additional functionalities of the archive, which are currently being developed. In general, it is important to note that the archive is being constantly expanded and improved upon. A first version went online in January 2009, and a second version with new functionality was released in June 2010. More modifications are planned or already in progress. This process reflects a compromise between making the interviews available to research and education as soon as possible and advancing interview processing or "disclosure" and technical research capabilities. Thus, some of the archive's interviews do not (yet) offer the full variety of search functionalities described. Information regarding the processing stage is displayed with the interview so that a user can see which of the consecutive steps (proofreading, segmenting, translating, and register/heading processing) the interview has been through.

The register will also allow for maps to be generated in the future. In response to a user's queries, these collection maps will display, for example, birth place, location of deportation or forced labor, or the post-war residence of all interviews. Users will be able to select a particular location on the collection map and be taken to a list of interviews that mention that location in the particular connection (as birth place, for example). Similarly, information from the register can be used to make and display individualized maps for each interview; they would display and designate (e.g., by color code) the most relevant locations (birth place, internment location) of that interviewee's biography.

In sum, the archive offers a highly user-friendly interface and helpful research tools. The capacity to locate thematically relevant segments, or particular names and terms within the interview has been made possible by an immense input of time and personnel, which has produced, among other things, the complex indexing of the content of every interview, including producing transcripts and translations as well as registers and headings. The archive online platform also required complex programming, which includes an editing system, documentation and indexing system, a search engine, and an interactive user-interface with multimedia elements. Furthermore, digitization and archiving also represent a substantial challenge in terms of navigating the prevailing technical parameters and financial constraints. Thus the Forced Labor 1939-1945 archive had to find a pragmatic solution that guarantees the preservation of the interviews without astronomical costs; this entailed a loss in terms of quality compared with the original recordings.

The archive is designed for use in research and education. The user interface features comprehensive search functions that are particularly suited to researchers and teachers at the university level. The archive is used by teachers and students from a diverse range of disciplines. Apart from the more obvious fields of history and cultural studies, the testimonies are being used, for example, in seminars run by departments of sociology, political science, English philology, East European studies, Jewish studies, film studies and educational science. Some seminars focus completely on the interviews, while others use them as supplementary sources.

The use of such testimonies in the school context has proved particularly effective, since pupils respond very well to accounts by witnesses to historical events and direct encounters with the few surviving witnesses are seldom possible due to their advanced age. However, the use of these archives in their existing form without a didactic framework and contextualization is unsuited to the 13-20 year-old target group. In particular, the vast number of interviews seems to confuse pupils and quickly overtaxes them. For this reason, a number of approaches have been devised for using the interviews with school students.

Educational materials based on the testimonies have been developed. A project team at Freie Universität Berlin has used the interviews to produce a multimedia application on DVD that allows for independent learning. The learning software is based on abridged, video graphed life stories, which are accompanied by specially prepared questions. The DVDs also include additional materials such as images of original documents or photographs, animated and navigable time lines, maps, musical sources, etc. (Pagenstecher, 2009). The software is also supplemented with a printed teacher handbook that includes in-depth historical, contextual background to the interviews' content. The material is being distributed by the German Federal Agency for Civic Education (Bundeszentrale für politische Bildung).

Finally, plans are underway to create partial collections for the Forced Labor 1939-1945 archive that are particularly suited to school work. These collections are to be compiled in collaboration with memorial centers and will include, for example, interviews and additional material designed to prepare pupils for visits to memorial centers.

Due to the special nature of the materials it holds and the aids it provides, the Forced Labor 1939-1945 archive is of particular interest for the field of historical-political education. For scholars, online access to interviews relevant to their research provides a real advantage that will lead to greater utilization of the interviews. Whereas previously time-consuming and costly visits to archives were reserved for scholars involved in projects with adequate financing, online offerings now also enable students and pupils, as well as lay researchers, to make use of interviews with witnesses to historical events. The increased visibility and use of their holdings is also of benefit to the archives, since it enables them to acquire greater significance and recognition, which could in turn lead to more resources in terms of staff and financing. Finally, for the interviewees, the improved access to and increasing use of the material they have provided represents a recognition of their role as witnesses and a confirmation that their memories and experiences will continue to be appreciated by future generations.

PERSPECTIVES AND POTENTIALS

Apart from the interviews in the archive discussed here, there are many other collections of interviews with contemporary witnesses focusing on life stories during the Nazi period.[5] Each of these collections has its own guidelines regarding the conduct of interviews, the interview focus, the archiving and, where relevant, indexing of the interviews, the storage and safekeeping of tapes, etc.

These collections represent extremely valuable resources for researchers. However, as yet no comprehensive directory exists that researchers can use to locate individual holdings. Producing such a directory would be a first step towards making all interviews available to scholars. Even more worthwhile would be the implementation of a meta-search engine that could search through the directories of the different holdings. However, such a project has to confront certain difficulties.

On the one hand, due to the differences in the forms interviews take, it is difficult to find data fields that are congruent across the individual holdings. The fields "first name" and "surname" may seem unambiguous, but even in this simple case there is no uniform approach. Sometimes the first name is equated with the name by which a person is usually known, different spellings are used, and in the case of women the "surname" field sometimes contains the individual's birth name and sometimes the name later adopted through marriage.

Geographical entries represent a further problem. If a search request is to be successful, then some form of standardization is required. For example, the field "place of birth" in one collection needs to be correlated with the field "origin" in another. Moreover, the degree of specification in the fields differs greatly. The information provided in the field "origin" (e.g., Germany) is far more general than the information in the field "place of birth" (Dresden). We are thus confronted with a difference in order. To allow for entries to be systematically called up by way of a controlled allocator, such as a listing according to country names, the most general term has to be selected. This can lead on the one hand to the loss of important information and, on the other, to transmission errors if, for example, it is mistakenly assumed that the Dresden referred to is located in Austria and not in Germany.

A further difficulty lies in differences in the extent to which those managing collections are prepared to make the interviews and information about them available online. In particular, the desire to protect the confidentiality of interviewees often results in a refusal to place content online. One possible solution would entail anonymizing certain data fields or only allowing selected data fields to be searched. As a result, researchers would still be provided with at least rudimentary

help, since having access to the information, for instance, that a certain number of interviews with survivors of a particular camp could be found in a particular collection would still be valuable.

It would be meaningful in this context to semantically connect the different data holdings and their use as Linked Data. This system not only facilitates searches for individual text fragments and keywords. It also allows for the transfer of the meanings of terms into expandable ordering systems on the basis of which computer systems can draw logical conclusions according to predefined rules. Such a system would allow more complex relationships to be revealed. For example, the relationship of one surviving witness to another could be identified and supplemented by additional information. Inquiries relating to people who were born in Berlin, incarcerated in Sachsenhausen and survived a death march could be provided with targeted answers.

In such systems, open standards are applied such as the *Resource Description Framework* (RDF). These standards facilitate a constant expansion of attributes, something that is not possible using more static meta-data schemata. They support connections with constantly renewed, open data sources. In addition, data fields can be displayed overlapping one another without any loss of quality. Remaining with the previous example, the specific information pertaining to Dresden as the place of birth would be retained and subsumed under the more general relationship indicated by "place of origin." The information provided would thus indicate that Dresden is the place of birth but also the place of origin.

The semantic processing of information relating to biographical interviews will also make them compatible with the databases of larger initiatives designed to safeguard our digital cultural heritage that are also developed for the differentiated use of large numbers of media digitization using future-oriented technologies and concepts related to the Semantic Web and Web 2.0.[6] The selected open standards, which can constantly be developed and supplemented, will ensure the preservation and thus usability of the data for future generations.

Apart from the need for metadata search engines covering different collections, the preservation and utilization of smaller, "neglected" collections is also something that requires attention in the near future. Particularly relevant here are the individual interviews conducted by scholars in the context of research projects that are not further utilized and tend to be, as it were, deposited in drawers and forgotten. This group also includes local initiatives such as history associations that have conducted interviews with surviving witnesses but have not had the know-how or technical and financial means to do further work with the material, as well as film makers who have used only extracts from interviews and not made any further use of the interview material.

These small stocks of material are extremely difficult to locate and thus not available for use by researchers. Particularly worrying in this context is the fact that the quality of tapes will progressively decline. (Van Bogart, 1995) If they are to be preserved and made available for research and education, digital copies certainly need to be made. These digital interviews could then be placed in an "open" online archive, which would not have to be restricted to a certain historical phase but could be used to store interviews relating to various themes. However, because of privacy rights and copyright issues, it would be necessary to ensure that use of such an archive was subject to registration procedures.

Should individual proprietors of interview material nevertheless be reticent to make their material available online, it would also be possible to impose a hold-back period before interviews could be accessed or to only make meta-data available on the platform so that researchers would at least know that the interview exists and could contact the proprietor directly with their requests.

In the ideal case, the interview should be accessible through the platform and, where appropriate, supplemented by transcripts, interview reports,

etc. The proprietor would post the interview and, in accordance with the concept developed by the Freie Universität Berlin, would be responsible for all the tasks necessary to make the interview available for use. Proprietors would use software tools made available to them to process their interview for better use online and supplement it with further material. Such an approach would have a number of advantages. The costs involved in the disclosure process would be kept low and interview proprietors would be able to bring their specialized knowledge to bear. In addition a well conducted interview made available for easy use could, like a well-written article, promote the scholarly reputation of the researcher involved.

It is also conceivable that other individuals could be involved in the disclosure process. Interested parties with the appropriate knowledge could be allowed to assume certain tasks in this regard on the condition that they used the tools made available for this purpose. Such individuals could also make their versions and interpretations available online, thereby opening up further avenues of access to the sources and drawing attention to their own research.

Both the meta-search engine and the open online archive would contribute to making the many smaller and larger collections of interviews that have been accumulated over recent decades secure and visible in the longer term and thereby available for future research. In addition, increased use of interview documents would provide an opportunity to encourage users to improve the availability of content through transcriptions and indexing, something which is hardly possible under current conditions. Efficient disclosure strategies are ultimately the most important precondition for ensuring that interviews retain their role as historical sources and are opened up to the kind of questions future generations of researchers will be seeking answers to.

REFERENCES

Pagenstecher, C. (2009). Zwangsarbeit 1939-1945. Erinnerungen und Geschichte. Ein digitales Interviewarchiv und seine Bildungsmaterialien. In D. Baranowski (Ed.), *Ich bin die Stimme der sechs Millionen. Das Videoarchiv im Ort der Information* (pp. 192-198). Berlin, Germany: Stiftung Denkmal für die ermordeten Juden Europas.

Perks, R. (2010). The Roots of Oral History: Exploring Contrasting Attitudes to Elite, Corporate, and Business Oral History in Britain and the U.S. *The Oral History Review, 37*(2), 215–224. doi:10.1093/ohr/ohq049

Plato, A. v. (2000). Zeitzeugen und die historische Zunft. Erinnerung, kommunikative Tradierung und kollektives Gedächtnis in der qualitativen Geschichtswissenschaft – ein Problemaufriss. *BIOS. Zeitschrift für Biographieforschung und Oral History, 13*, 5–29.

Plato, A. v., Leh, A., & Thonfeld, C. (Eds.). (2010). *Hitler's Slaves. Life Stories of Forced Labourers in Nazi-Occupied Europe*. New York, NY: Berghahn Books.

Schütze, F. (1976). Zur Hervorlockung und Analyse von Erzählungen thematisch relevanter Geschichten im Rahmen soziologischer Feldforschung – dargestellt an einem Projekt zur Erforschung von kommunalen Machtstrukturen. In *Arbeitsgruppe Bielefelder Soziologen: Kommunikative Sozialforschung* (pp. 159–260). Munich, Germany: Fink.

Van Bogart, J. (1995). *Magnetic Tape Storage and Handling. A Guide for Libraries and Archives.* Retrieved August 19, 2010, from http://www.clir.org/pubs/reports/pub54/4life_expectancy.html

ADDITIONAL READING

Baranowski, D. (Ed.). (2009). *"Ich bin die Stimme der sechs Millionen." Das Videoarchiv im Ort der Information*. Berlin: Stiftung Denkmal für die ermordeten Juden Europas.

Boyd, D. (2011). Achieving the Promise of Oral History in a Digital Age. In Ritchie, D. A. (Ed.), *The Oxford Handbook of Oral History* (pp. 285–302). New York: Oxford University Press.

Charlton, T. L., Myers, L. E., & Sharpless, R. (Eds.). (2006). *Handbook of Oral History*. Lanham, MD: AltaMira Press.

Edmondson, R. (2009). Sunrise or Sunset? The Future of Audiovisual Archives. *IASA Journal, 34*, 30–35.

Klingenböck, G. (2009). "Stimmen aus der Vergangenheit." Interviews von Überlebenden des Nationalsozialismus in systematischen Sammlungen von 1945 bis heute. In D. Baranowski (Ed.), *"Ich bin die Stimme der sechs Millionen." Das Videoarchiv im Ort der Information* (pp. 27-40). Berlin: Stiftung Denkmal für die ermordeten Juden Europas.

Leh, A. (1999). La entrevista de historia oral como material de archivo. *Historia, Antropología y Fuentes Orales, 1*(21), 171-176. (English: (2000). Problems of Archiving Oral History Interviews. *Forum Qualitative Social Research, 1*(3). Retrieved September 15th, 2010, from http://www.qualitative-research.net/fqs/fqs.htm.)

Leh, A. (2009). Ethical Problems in Research Involving Contemporary Witnesses. *Oral History Forum d'histoire orale, 29*. (Spanish: (2003). *Historia. Antropología y Fuentes Orales, 3*(29), 155–165.

Leh, A. (2010). Biographieforschung. In Gudehus, C., Eichenberg, A., & Welzer, H. (Eds.), *Gedächtnis und Erinnerung. Ein interdisziplinäres Handbuch* (pp. 299–311). Stuttgart: J.B. Metzler.

Lyons, B., Salsburg, N., & Lomax Wood, A. (2009). Sharing resources, Sharing Responsibility: Archives in the Digital Age. *IASA Journal*, *34*, 36–40.

Medjovic, I., & Witzel, A. (2010). *Wiederverwendung qualitativer Daten: Archivierung und Sekundärnutzung qualitativer Interviewtranskripte*. Wiesbaden: VS Verlag. doi:10.1007/978-3-531-92403-8

Perks, R. (2009). The Challenges of Web Access to Archival Oral History in Britain. *IASA Journal*, *32*, 74–82.

Perks, R. (2011). Messiah with a Microphone? Oral Historians, Technology, and Sound Archives. In Ritchie, D. A. (Ed.), *The Oxford Handbook of Oral History* (pp. 315–332). New York: Oxford University Press.

Perks, R., & Thomson, A. (Eds.). (2006). *The Oral History Reader* (2nd ed.). London, New York: Routledge.

Plato, A. v. (2010). Interview Guidelines. In Plato, A. v., Leh, A., & Thonfeld, C. (Eds.), *Hitler's Slaves. Life Stories of Forced Labourers in Nazi-Occupied Europe* (pp. 401–408). New York: Berghahn Books.

Ritchie, D. A. (2003). *Doing Oral History: A Practical Guide* (2nd ed.). New York: Oxford University Press.

Ritchie, D. A. (Ed.). (2011). *The Oxford Handbook of Oral History*. New York: Oxford University Press.

Schrum, K., Brennan, S., Halabuk, J., Leon, S. M., & Scheinfeldt, T. (2011). Oral History in the Digital Age. In Ritchie, D. A. (Ed.), *The Oxford Handbook of Oral History* (pp. 499–516). New York: Oxford University Press.

Thompson, P. (2000). *The Voice of the Past: Oral History* (3rd ed.). Oxford: Oxford University Press.

KEY TERMS AND DEFINITIONS

Biographical Research: Biographical research is a branch of research that is now being conducted in almost all areas of the humanities and social sciences, particularly in sociology, pedagogy and history. Across all disciplines such research is characterized by its use of life stories as a source of base data (or as one source among others), a life story being understood as the presentation of the conduct of a life and life experience from the perspective of the individual living that life.

Digital Oral History Archive: Digital oral history archives provide a platform for the differentiated and flexible use of interviews with contemporary witnesses that for the most part have a thematically uniform focus. The majority of such archives are web-based, although not all of them are freely accessible online. The archives enable users to replay interviews and view additional material such as photos, short biographies and short reports. Digital oral history archives provide a wide range of search options and auxiliary tools that enable search results, for instance, to be stored and annotated.

Digitization: Digitization involves the conversion of the analog signals on a magnetic tape (video or audio) into digital signals. Digital master formats provide the basis for generating user formats for different purposes (e.g., the web). Digital signals have the advantage that they can be transferred and copied without any loss of quality.

Disclosure: The "disclosure" of digitized oral history interviews is based above all on the cataloging of material. However, in context of the current discussion it also involves the identification and definition of individual segments within a report by contemporary witness, for instance through the use of keywords and subheadings. These are linked to time codes so that individual passages in the interview can be located and retrieved at any time. Disclosure in this sense thus entails providing access not only to the entire interview, as in the classic archival context, but also to individual elements within the testimony.

Long-Term Preservation: Long-term preservation refers to the compilation, storage and maintenance of information to ensure its availability on an enduring basis. Such preservation is the task of archives, museums and libraries and involves both physical objects and electronically stored information. Effective long-term preservation requires the responsible development of strategies to respond to the constant process of change generated by the information market.

Narrative Interview: The narrative interview is the most common form of interview in the field of biographical research and was originally developed by Fritz Schütze. It essentially involves encouraging the interviewee to narrate his or her life story by asking open questions and keeping interventions to a minimum. This approach is based on the assumption that the narrative will inevitably accord with the sequence of past events and that narratives are thus the appropriate linguistic form for the recollection of past realities. The method is geared to encouraging interviewees to speak ad hoc about events in which they were actively or passively involved.

Oral History: Oral history is a method employed in historical research and is based on interviews with witnesses to historical events. As a rule, the interview takes the form of a narrative account of the interviewee's life history, which is recorded using audio or video technology. The method is used within the framework of historical biographical research. The interviews are structured around questions regarding the history of everyday life and experience.

Transcript: A transcript is a transcribed version of a spoken interview. In the process of transcription the spoken language is "translated" into the written form of the language used in the interview and identified as the utterance of the respective speaker. Transcriptions are based on literal rather than phonetic accuracy and follow the rules of orthography and punctuation associated with the respective language in order to produce a readable, comprehensible text. They are produced in accordance with mandatory, uniform guidelines designed to meet scholarly standards.

ENDNOTES

[1] With respect to the different origins and traditions of oral history in Great Britain and the USA see Perks, 2010.

[2] Like for example the National Life Stories Collection, an independent charitable trust within the British Library Sound Archive, which was established in 1987 to "record first-hand experiences of as wide a cross-section of present-day society as possible". See: http://www.bl.uk/nls. Retrieved March 5, 2011.

[3] In Great Britain the British Library Sound Archive is leading in the field of archiving oral history collections. In Austria several oral history collections are archived by the Österreichische Mediathek (Austrian Media Center) at the Technisches Museum Wien.

[4] Both authors are engaged in the project at different stages. Almut Leh as part of the coordinating team was responsible for the conducting of the interviews and building up a consistent collection. Doris Tausendfreund as project manager at Center for Digital Systems is in charge of the creation of the multimedia archive "Forced Labour 1939-1945". For reports on the interview project see Plato/Leh/Thonfeld, 2010.

[5] A good overview of European oral history collections in memorial centers can be found in the online catalog of the United States Holocaust Memorial Museum: http:www.ushmm.org/research/collections/oralhistory/search. Retrieved October 20, 2010. See also: Klingenböck, G. (2009). "Stimmen aus der Vergangenheit." Interviews von Überlebenden des Nationalsozialismus

in systematischen Sammlungen von 1945 bis heute. In D. Baranowski (Ed.), *"Ich bin die Stimme der sechs Millionen." Das Videoarchiv im Ort der Information* (pp. 27-40). Berlin: Stiftung Denkmal für die ermordeten Juden Europas.

[6] See the initiatives CONTENTUS (http://theseus-programm.de/anwendungsszenarien/contentus/default.aspx) and EUROPEANA (http://www.europeana.eu/portal/) as well as Deutsche Digitale Bibliothek (http://www.deutsche-digitale-bibliothek.de/). Retrieved October 20, 2010.

Chapter 22
Addressing Legal Issues in Online Research, Publication and Archiving:
A UK Perspective

Andrew Charlesworth
University of Bristol, UK

ABSTRACT

This chapter provides background to, and a broad understanding of, the legal (and ethical) risks that researchers face in their utilisation of online mechanisms, in terms of the collection and analysis of research data, the communication of research results, and the retention and archiving of data generated by researchers and third parties. While researchers may understand the legal rules in the off-line research environment, research, dissemination and archiving on the Internet can pose more complex, and sometimes entirely novel, issues. The highly visible and accessible nature of the medium also means that existing legal risks may be significantly magnified in comparison to the off-line environment. Researchers should always seek advice specific to those jurisdictions they are targeting with their research, and particularly the jurisdiction in which they are located. Practical advice may be obtained from fellow researchers, institutional research support officers, or legal professionals. This chapter identifies activities that are likely to raise legal issues, or which are likely to require consideration of appropriate means of review, oversight and audit by researchers and ethical committees. Reference is thus primarily made to the law in the author's home jurisdiction, with some comparative references to other jurisdictions.

DOI: 10.4018/978-1-4666-0074-4.ch022

INTRODUCTION

It is a truism that, over the last 25 years, innovations in information technologies have significantly changed the:

- environments in which research can take place, e.g., the Internet, mobile communications;
- tools that are available to conduct that research and to collect data; e.g., e-mail, social networking tools; and,
- ways in which resulting data can be presented and preserved, e.g., web journals, blogs, digital archives.

Equally, the speed of change in information technologies has often outpaced the law's ability to assimilate and adapt to the social and economic consequences that stem from those changes, e.g., intellectual property in digital works, privacy and data mining.

The first of these issues, technological innovation, can provide researchers with significantly expanded abilities for accessing and collecting traditional and new forms of research data, and presenting them to an international audience. By doing so, however, it also potentially exposes researchers to an expanded range of legal risks, a greater number of legal and regulatory authorities and, in some cases, to cross-jurisdictional liability, i.e., exposure to the legal systems of countries other than their own. Detailed knowledge of such issues has tended to be, and often still remains, the province of legal specialists. Non-specialist researchers may struggle to interpret the implications of particular laws for their research; to successfully navigate the restrictions and requirements of those laws to ensure their research is in compliance; and to understand the nuances of, and utilize effectively, legal or administrative processes and guidance.

A consequence of the second issue, pressure on legal systems to adapt to the consequences of new technologies, is that laws relating to, or affected by, information technologies are in a constant state of flux. Legislators and judges are called upon to provide new legal solutions to perceived problems, in relative haste, often under pressure from vocal interest groups, and without time to ponder on the wider-reaching consequences. The impact such new jurisprudence might have upon the practices and methodologies of academic researchers is rarely, if ever, going to be a significant consideration to those making and interpreting the law. However, whether those solutions take the form of the adaptation and re- interpretation of old laws and judgments, or the creation of *sui generis* laws, designed specifically to handle new developments, they constitute an evolving body of rules of conduct with which researchers will have to engage.

Thus, researchers seeking to engage in online research and publication find themselves in a position where, more than ever, they must be cognisant not just of an increasing body of national (and possibly foreign) laws, but also of the on-going development of such laws, and their likely impact on research strategies and methodologies. Equally, as online publication and access to electronic resources increases, researchers' methodologies, data and outputs have become increasingly publicly accessible, and open to greater peer scrutiny, public criticism and legal oversight/regulation. In the UK, this process is likely to be given greater impetus by freedom of information legislation, which treats UK universities as 'public authorities' with an obligation to disclose information that they hold, including research data, to members of the public on request (subject to certain exemptions). While FOI requests relating to research remain rare at present, it is not hard to envisage areas of scientific and social research where journalists and public interest groups will be interested to scrutinize not just the research data generated, but also researchers' methodologies and practices.

Of course, from a research dissemination perspective, such broadening of access to research processes and outputs is to be welcomed, but it inevitably requires that researchers develop a more pragmatic and proactive approach to identifying and addressing legal risks. Open source software developers often like to say that "With enough eyeballs, all bugs are shallow," meaning that the more developers you have looking at software source code, the more likely mistakes in that code are to be identified. The underlying principle in that statement also applies to research: the more public scrutiny there is of research methodology, processes and outputs, the more likely it is that legal and ethical breaches will be identified and publicly exposed.

Ethics and Law

The work of many academic and commercial researchers will already be subject to scrutiny, prior to, during, and after the research takes place. That scrutiny will usually take the form, not of an assessment of conformity with legal rules *per se*, but of conformity with a set of ethical standards. These are usually defined by the prevailing views of researchers in the particular field of research, and often prescribed and/or codified by their representative bodies, e.g., the Association of Internet Researchers (Ess & AoIR, 2002) and the British Psychological Society (BPS, 2007), or by funding bodies, e.g., the UK Economic and Social Research Council (ESRC, 2010).

In academic research circles, ethical guidelines and standards have achieved a higher profile than legal rules (the literature survey undertaken for this chapter in 2010 produced well over a hundred books, book chapters and journal articles discussing the ethical issues of online research and approximately twelve directly addressing the legal issues). Therefore, where legal rules are discussed in the literature, that discussion is frequently structured by relation to wider ethical considerations: data privacy laws are often considered under general privacy issues (e.g., Eynon et al., 2008); and intellectual property law,

notably copyright, as part of a wider 'ownership of research data' debate (Kastman & Gurak, 1999). For many researchers, the line between ethical requirements and legal requirements is thus a blurred one. While they may have access to documented ethical standards and guidance, and other researchers or institutional ethical review bodies can advise on institutional ethics practices, there is often less institutional capacity for the provision of accurate and up-to-date advice on legal issues. It is suggested that this is a state of affairs that researchers and their institutions need to reconsider across the board, but in particular with regard to online research and publication.

There are several points to consider with regard to the relationship between ethics and the law, and its implications for online academic research. The key element is that ethical standards and legal rules, while clearly overlapping in effect, serve different purposes. In broad terms, ethical standards in research seek actively and explicitly to:

- preserve the research environment (e.g., by precluding practices which might impede or reduce the effectiveness of future research);
- create trust in both researchers and research outcomes (e.g., by endorsing or rejecting practices which affect the actual or perceived reliability or trustworthiness of research data); and,
- protect the rights and interests of the subjects of research (e.g., requiring informed consent in human research).

In contrast, general laws, such as data privacy laws, or intellectual property laws, are drafted to regulate broader spheres of human activity, within which academic (and commercial) research is a minor dimension. Thus, while laws may seek to achieve similar goals to ethical standards (e.g., protecting the rights and interests of individuals, including research subjects), they are often not sensitive to either ethical practices in, or the practicalities of, research. This makes it difficult for researchers to assess and interpret the impact of the law upon their existing methodologies and practices. Occasionally, the gap between what a general law provides or permits, and what the conduct of effective research requires, may be so large that legislators are forced to provide explicit provisions to enable research to take place. Both UK copyright law and data protection law contain provisions specifically designed to permit research activities which might otherwise expose researchers to civil or criminal liability.

The motivations for, and the speed of changes to, legal rules and ethical standards and guidelines relating to the online environment also demonstrate divergences. While information technologies and the online environment have sparked rapid and continuing changes in national laws, the pace of change in ethical standards appears more sedate. In part, this is because the ethical standards tend to be principle-based, community-mediated and aspirational. Thus development of ethical guidelines for online research have tended to come from the 'grassroots', usually driven by researchers seeking not just to adopt cutting-edge research tools and techniques, but also to legitimise that adoption by demonstrating that those tools can be utilised within the existing ethical paradigms (or at least without causing undue violence to them).

Ethical standards and guidelines, when faced with new developments, may be more flexible than legal rules, but that very adaptability may sometimes be problematic. While, as the AoIR Guidelines note, there is usually sufficient agreement on the parameters of ethical behaviour that 'ethical relativism' can be avoided, there remains the risk that ethical standards and guidelines may, when exposed to new developments or social/cultural challenges, fail to adapt appropriately or expeditiously. For example, community-mediated ethical standards in certain types of research may prove vulnerable to special interest influences: consider the history of tobacco research. In such circumstances, the fact that adherence to ethical standards and guidelines is rarely mandatory may be problematic. While breaching ethical standards and guidelines will attract peer disapproval and may ultimately attract sanctions, e.g., loss of external funding, or disciplinary action by an employer; such sanctions are largely discretionary, and discussion of the behaviour sanctioned may be kept internal to the organisation(s) involved.

Legal rules, whether derived directly from legislation, via judicial decisions, or through regulatory interventions, are mandatory, and failure to observe them will result in enforceable public or private sanctions. Processes for determining whether a breach of legal rules has occurred are also normally carried out in the public gaze, where there is much less scope for avoiding unwanted publicity. Legal rules can therefore be considered to form the baseline of ethical requirements—in that they set a standard below which the actions of researchers may not fall (Charlesworth, 2008). Thus, a UK researcher may fail to complete her ethical obligations with regard to acquiring ethical clearance or adequately completing informed consent processes without triggering legal sanction, but if she processes personal data without meeting the basic requirements of the Data Protection Act 1998, then data subjects may request the Information Commissioner to take action against her, including imposing monetary penalties; if they have suffered damage or distress, they may sue her for damages themselves.

The relationship between legal rules and ethical standards and guidelines is thus a complex and interactive one. New legal developments may spark valuable debate about whether existing ethical practices, as opposed to ethical standards, are adequate to meet researchers' legal obligations. Engagement with new modes of research, or new research environments, may identify weaknesses in legal protections provided to research subjects, and suggest that the ethical researcher should aspire to, or actively provide, more effective safeguards. These are certainly issues which online researchers have had to face and can expect to grapple further with in the future.

The vital component of both these elements – knowing where proposed research activities will cross from legality into illegality and identifying where the mere observance of laws is insufficient to meet ethical standards – is an adequate understanding of the letter and spirit of those laws, and their applicability to particular forms of research (Charlesworth, 2008).

International and Cross-Jurisdictional Issues

While international research is hardly a new issue, use of internet research tools has enabled researchers to engage in cross-border research at considerably lower cost. It is now possible to carry out a range of traditional, but expensive, research methodologies such as field observation, interviewing, focus groups, posted questionnaires, etc., via online technologies such as video-conferencing, voice and video over IP communications, internet surveys, wiki-based focus groups and observation in chat rooms, via social networking tools, and in virtual worlds. Internet-based publishing, through open access web journals, institutional repositories, and even personal web-pages, also permits research data and analysis to be disseminated globally, and potentially to achieve a much greater audience than via traditional publication venues, such as monographs, journals articles and conference papers. These developments mean that engaging in international research and dissemination is financially viable for a larger range of researchers, and it has become considerably easier and cost-effective to establish and co-ordinate international research collaborations.

There are, however, negative aspects to this technology-mediated expansion of research reach and capacity. The declining cost of international research reduces the need to seek funding at levels previously required: international travel

costs can be reduced or avoided, international communication costs cut virtually to nil, the cost of producing, distributing and collecting survey materials, and the time needed to process them significantly reduced. Paradoxically, this may lead to a reduction of legal and ethical oversight of international research (or indeed national internet-based research). There are three reasons for this. First, low-cost projects are less likely to be subjected to significant scrutiny and oversight by internal review processes, and external funding bodies, than costly projects. Second, when even undergraduate students have the facility to conduct international online surveys or interviews, institutions may find it difficult, for reasons of cost and time, to apply appropriate scrutiny to research proposals, or to engage in meaningful oversight of research projects. Third, in the short to medium term, there is likely to be a knowledge gap within scrutiny bodies with regard to the legal and ethical issues raised by online research, particularly internationally-focused research.

If traditional models of research oversight and scrutiny cannot adequately address the legal and ethical risks posed by the expansion of international research, researchers must take on greater responsibility for understanding the potential legal liabilities that may arise from their research when it is undertaken in, or has impacts upon, jurisdictions other than their own. Such legal liabilities might permit third parties to take legal action in other jurisdictions, or via the researcher's own national legal system. For example:

- A UK researcher carries out an internet survey across Europe, obtaining information from senior civil servants about their attitudes to the construction of new nuclear power plants in their countries. As the topic is controversial, respondents are told that responses obtained will be anonymised after collection. However, the survey software is insecure, and a hacker uses a known 'exploit' to access and download the survey responses, which are then post-ed on Wikileaks. After their unanonymised responses are made public, two civil servants in France are fired, and another, in Germany, is attacked by anti-nuclear pro-testors. They complain to their respective national data privacy commissioners and to the UK Information Commissioner's Office, and bring a legal action in the UK alleging they have suffered damage and distress due to a breach of UK data protection law, and should be awarded compensation.

- A UK university researcher joins a research consortium with colleagues from India and China to run a longitudinal study of the effectiveness of techniques for reclaiming sites contaminated with hazardous substances by measuring the health of individuals living around such sites. Researchers in all three countries are to exchange data collected in their respective countries. The nature of the study means that the data cannot be anonymised, but has been coded, i.e., the names of the research subjects are known only to the researchers in their country. Because the data is not anonymised, it is subject to UK data protection law. Since the EU Member States do not regard either India or China as having 'adequate' data protection laws, any personal data transferred to those countries must be subject to specific contractual provisions in the agreement between the members of the research consortium. Failure to incorporate such contractual provisions will breach UK data protection law.

- A Spanish researcher carries out an internet survey across Europe on government corruption in large infrastructure projects. Several respondents from Belgium state in their responses that former Belgian politician, X, was involved in corrupt dealings concerning road building. A preliminary

paper is based on the responses is published in a web journal in the UK. While X is not identified by name, information provided in the article clearly refers to him. Shortly after the article is published several European governments decide not to support him in his bid for an EU Commission position. X brings legal action for defamation (libel) in the UK courts against the researcher and the journal.

These three hypotheticals demonstrate not just that international online research may result in risks in more than one jurisdiction, or that different jurisdictions may have varying attitudes towards particular legal claims, e.g., the right to data privacy; but also that it may be possible for third parties to take action in more than one jurisdiction, or to choose the jurisdiction in which they have the best chance of obtaining a favourable result – 'forum shopping'. For example, the UK courts will accept jurisdiction in libel cases where there is a significant link with the UK jurisdiction, even if neither of the parties are themselves UK citizens, or present in the UK. Indeed, in the hypothetical, even if the journal had been published in Germany, if X could show sufficient people had read it in the UK, and his reputation was thereby diminished, he would be able to bring an action in the UK courts.

National laws do not just vary widely in terminology and coverage, their practical application is also influenced heavily by political policies or cultural understandings. While most countries have some form of copyright law, usually based on the Berne Convention for the Protection of Literary and Artistic Works, their copyright laws may be very different. This makes it risky to assume that if a particular activity is legal in one jurisdiction, it will also be legal in another.

For example, in Canada, the Copyright Act s.80 explicitly allows individuals to make copies of sound recordings on an audio recording medium for their own private, non-commercial use.

In the UK the same action would technically be a breach of copyright without a licence from the copyright holder. With regard to defamation law, the UK's broad approach to accepting jurisdiction over issues involving foreign parties has led the United States to pass the SPEECH Act of 2010, which prevents U.S. courts from enforcing libel judgments issued in foreign courts against U.S. residents, if the speech would not be libellous under American law. Finally, in terms of data protection law, particularly relevant to much internet-based empirical research, U.S. law is rather different from that of the EU Member States: there is no overarching data protection framework; rather, there is a patchwork of federal and state privacy laws covering various sectoral activities, and a set of privacy rights derived from judicial interpretation of the U.S. Constitution. In the EU Member States, by contrast, there are overarching data protection frameworks based on the EU Directive. Even within the EU the Member States have differing definitions in their national legislation for such key terms as "data controller," "data processor," "sensitive data," "anonymous data," "consent," "third party," "establishment," and "equipment" (Charlesworth 2003a). The reason for the differences between EU Member States and the U.S. in their approaches to privacy law (and, of course, which is the 'right' approach) is a matter of debate, but the outcome is that the U.S. has largely adopted a teleological (consequentialist or market-based) approach, and the EU a deontological (rights-based) approach. This inevitably impacts not just upon their respective legal systems, but also upon the approaches that researchers in those countries, and the bodies tasked with research governance, take to ethical issues surrounding the handling of data concerning individuals (Ess & AoIR, 2002; Charlesworth 2008).

LAW AND THE ONLINE RESEARCHER

The discussion above has outlined the key reasons why online researchers should seek to familiarise themselves with the legal issues pertinent to the type of online research and/or publication they are engaging in. This section considers some of the common legal issues that arise with online research.

Access Issues

While the online environment may seem, at first sight, to be a cornucopia of potential research information, collecting and utilising that information requires consideration of the legal rights of potential research subjects, as well as the owners of particular works, websites, and online services. There is sometimes a misperception amongst academic researchers that, because they are undertaking 'research', this somehow exempts them from the normal legal rules pertaining to online access and data collection. While there are some exceptions and exemptions available to *bona fide* researchers, e.g., in UK copyright law (copying for non-commercial research purposes) and EU data privacy law (exemptions for use of personal data for research), these are usually limited in scope, and subject to compliance with particular conditions (see below).

Harvesting of online research data, including personally identifying information (PII), from online sources, such as the Web, is a common phenomenon, e.g., the 'scraping' of websites, or access to and downloading from online data sources. Sometimes data harvesting is actively encouraged by websites and services, e.g., web archives using the Open Archives Initiative Protocol for Metadata Harvesting (OAI-PMH) (Hunter & Guy, 2004; Tonkin, 2010). However, much material which is made publically accessible online by individuals or organisations is not intended to be collected and reused by third parties without notice or permission. Scraping a website for personal information, or joining a Social Networking Service (SNS) as a developer in order to gain access to its users' personal data, may be plausible technical mechanisms for obtaining data and, in some circumstances, may be legal. However, such techniques are usually viewed unsympathetically by online services and their users. In large part, the negative response to such techniques stems from their association with various unwelcome or illegal online activities, such as phishing or spamming. Hostility towards data gathering may also stem from perceived breaches of politeness – spidering or scraping a website may impact upon the performance of the website and/or affect the experience of other users, or otherwise affect the business of the website. Clauses such as the following are not uncommon in website and SNS terms and conditions of use:

You agree that you will not use any robot, spider, other automatic device, or manual process to monitor or copy our web pages or the content contained herein without our prior express written permission. You agree that you will not use any device, software or routine to bypass or to interfere or attempt to interfere with the proper working of the <website>. You agree that you will not take any action that imposes an unreasonable or disproportionately large load on our infrastructure. (KinkSpace Terms of Service - http://www. kinkspace.com/help_tos.php)

Websites and services may also seek to place conditions or restrictions on the collection of information from their users by third parties using their systems:

5. Protecting Other People's Rights
…

7. If you collect information from users, you will: obtain their consent, make it clear you (and not Facebook) are the one collecting their informa- *tion, and post a privacy policy explaining what information you collect and how you will use it. (Facebook Statement of Rights and Responsibilities - http://www.facebook.com/terms.php)*

Such clauses may impact the researcher's ability to collect, observe or otherwise lurk in virtual spaces. Although the risk of the website/ SNS owner, or another user taking legal action may be low (for example, if the parties are in different jurisdictions), the website/SNS owner may legitimately refuse researchers access to their systems, delete researchers' user accounts without warning or recompense, and take action to block the use of automatic tools.

Even where there are no contractual terms or end user licence agreements (EULAs) requiring researchers to seek permission before conducting research on publicly accessible online information, or where researchers are in compliance with such terms or EULAs, ethics review bodies may still require that permission is sought from research subjects prior to research beginning, for example:

1. Just because a researcher comes across a support group's conversation online doesn't give him the automatic right to conduct research on that conversation. Technology alone (access) cannot be used as a legitimate justification for use of the information as if it were intended to be public.

2. As most on-line groups allow persons to join and not participate, the investigator should not attempt to justify not obtaining permission because of concern that the investigator's presence will affect the behaviour. Permissions must be obtained from the list/group/community manager, and an announcement should be made to the list/group/community that an observation is taking place for research purposes (after IRB approval and PRIOR to collecting ANY research data) (VCU, 2006).

This would also be relevant for research in wider communities, such as SNS users, e.g., the survey of personal information of adolescents on the Internet carried out by Hinduja and Patchin (2008) using material obtained from MySpace.

Copyright and Ownership

Most material accessible online will be subject to intellectual property rights (IPRs). The primary international IPR mechanism for protecting content is copyright and its associated rights. Under UK copyright law (see Copyright Designs and Patents Act (CDPA) (1988), for example, in addition to a copyright there may also be moral rights (Ch. IV, CDPA) and performance rights (Part II, CDPA) attached to a work.

As a general rule, a copyrightable work must be 'original', and 'an expression of an idea fixed in a tangible medium'. Researchers' handwritten notes, e-mails, blog posts, transcripts, web pages, and digital audio-visual recordings will thus, in most jurisdictions, automatically be copyrightable works, as they are 'expressions of ideas fixed in a tangible medium.' Many different types of work are protected by copyright, e.g., UK copyright law protects, amongst other things, literary works, artistic works, sound recordings, films broadcasts and databases. (s.3-8 CDPA). Copyright exists for a limited period - the term of copyright. Despite the harmonising role played by international agreements, different countries apply different terms of copyright protection to works. Thus, the basic term of copyright in the EU is author's life + 70 years, but in the UK the term of copyright for sound recordings is 50 years from the end of year in which they are made or published (s.12-15 CDPA).

Ownership of copyright in a work belongs, initially, to the person who created it (s.11(1) CDPA). This is subject to exceptions, which differ between countries, e.g., under UK law, copyright in works created in the course of employment does not belong to the employee, but to their employer, and thus the employer is the first owner (s.11(2) CDPA). This does not however apply to non-employee contractors, where a clear written requirement of transfer of copyright is required. A similar principle is found in U.S. law in the form of the 'work made for hire' doctrine (17 U.S.C. § 101). Ownership of copyright in a work can change hands after its initial creation, and like any property, can be bought, sold or inherited. It is important to remember that ownership of copyright in a work can be separate from physical ownership of the work.

Copying may be defined as reproducing the work in a material form, including storing the work in any medium. If someone uses a copyright work in this way without the owner's permission, or authorises someone else to do so, they will be infringing the copyright in the work (s.17 CDPA). Except in circumstances where copyright in a work has expired or the material has been expressly placed in the public domain, the default legal position is normally that it is necessary to obtain the permission of the right holder, via a licence, to make a copy of the work. Collecting data for research purposes will usually require making a copy of the relevant material. The question then is what can lawfully be done with the copy.

UK law permits the use of less than a substantial part of a copyright protected work, without the rightholder's permission (s.16 CDPA), but the UK legislation does not define 'a substantial part', and the case law on the point does not lend itself to easy interpretation. There are also express exceptions in UK copyright law, known as the 'fair dealing' provisions, which allow limited use of copyright works without the permission of the rightholder, notably for non-commercial research and private study and for criticism, review and reporting current events (s.28-31 CDPA). Use of online materials is complicated by the fact that national copyright laws vary considerably, and it may not be clear which jurisdiction's laws apply. There are provisions in U.S. law that appear similar to the UK 'fair dealing' provisions known as 'fair use' provisions (17 U.S.C. § 107), but in practice their effects are quite different, and a common mistake made by UK online researchers is to assume that acts which are permissible under U.S. law are also permissible under UK law.

Even where permission is sought to use the work, it may still be difficult to correctly identify the rightholder. Using copyright works without the rightholder's permission or other legal authorisation may open the researcher to civil action, or even criminal action, for breach of copyright. Legal action in the UK may result in injunctions against further breaches, destruction of all infringing copies, and damages for loss caused to the rightholder by the infringing copies (Charlesworth, 2009, p. 11).

If a researcher simply intends to download a copyright work from the internet for use in their research, the position is usually simple; the researcher must have an assignment (transfer of copyright ownership) from the rightholder, or a licence to use the work from the rightholder, or must otherwise be permitted by national law (e.g., via fair use or fair dealing exemptions, or insubstantial use), to use the work lawfully. Equally, if a researcher is conducting an interview via exchange of e-mail, technically the researcher will own the copyright in their questions, and the respondent will own the copyright to their answers, as both questions and answers are 'expressions of ideas fixed in a tangible medium', where the tangible media are the e-mails. The researcher will again need to seek an assignment or licence to use the respondent's work, or seek to rely upon appropriate exceptions in national law.

Copyright relating to the spoken word is complicated. For example, if an individual is talking about a subject and the discussion is not recorded in any way, it is likely that there is no copyright in those spoken words – the talk has not been 'fixed'. However, if a researcher records that speech on a tape recorder, at that point the spoken words are 'fixed' and, under UK law, a copyright crystallises. Thus, the speaker will have a copyright in

their words, and the researcher a copyright in the recording of those words. In order for a third party to use the recording, it will probably be necessary for them to seek an assignment or licence from both the speaker and the researcher who made the recording. The same will be true of an audio-visual recording of the talk, where both the speaker and the researcher who made the recording will own copyrights in the resulting recording. If the speaker is reading from a written script or paper, there will be a copyright in the text, which is already 'fixed' on paper, and a joint copyright owned by the speaker and the researcher who records the event, in the recording.

Where the researcher is an employee of a research institution, it is possible that the research institution, as their employer, will own the copyright in their notes, transcripts and recordings. For example, in the UK, where a research assistant was employed in a university-based online research project, conducting interviews via e-mail correspondence, the university would own the copyright in their portion of the e-mail correspondence. It would not therefore need to seek their permission to allow other researchers on the project to use the e-mails. However, it would be good practice to reinforce statutory provisions on copyright ownership, where they exist, with contractual provisions in employee contracts, as this will clarify the position for all parties. Non-employee contractors should always have the copyright ownership of their work set out in their contract.

There may occasionally be potential for conflicts between copyright law and other legal and ethical issues relevant to a research project. A respondent might, for example, wish to be identified as the author of their spoken words, as recorded or transcribed by a researcher. Under UK law such a request would form part of the respondent's moral rights with regard to the 'fixed' words. This may require the researcher to consider whether their research methodology has fully balanced some respondents' requirements of anonymity (which may be required under national data protection law and/or under ethical research requirements) with other respondents' requirements of identification (under copyright law).

While research respondents (and other third parties) may own copyright and/or moral rights in research data, this does not give them rights in or over research outputs, such as books, journal articles, etc. Equally, while developers of Internet research tools, such as survey software, may own intellectual property rights in those tools, this does not give them any copyright interest in research data collected using those tools, and they would not – absent any other agreement – be entitled to co-ownership in that material, or co-authorship in any publication (Welker & McCue, 2007).

Researchers seeking to collect research data online should:

- Identify which jurisdiction's copyright laws will apply; and whether the material to be collected falls within the scope of copyright protection and/or related rights;
- Identify the copyright holder, and determine the duration of the copyright. If the researcher believes the work has entered the public domain due to the expiry of copyright protection or on the basis of an explicit grant by the copyright holder, e.g., a Creative Commons public domain statement (Creative Commons, n.d.), evidence for this belief should be documented.
- Determine whether any of the uses to be made of the material during the research fall under an exception in the relevant copyright law.
- Where there are no applicable exemptions, or the exemptions do not cover all the uses to be made of the material during the research, request a licence from the rightholder to use the material for research purposes. Where a licence is granted, this should be documented.

- Where there are other rights, such as moral rights, that need to be considered, ensure that agreements are reached with rightholders to enable appropriate reuse of the data for the research.
- Ensure documentary evidence concerning the copyright status of the material collected is in a form that can be readily accessed and audited, including written statements of assignment and licence.
- in circumstances where respondents (or other third parties, e.g., contract researchers) will be sole or joint copyright holders in data generated during the research process, determine
  - whether they want an assignment of copyright (an outright transfer of the copyright from the respondent to the researcher);
  - whether they want a licence of copyright (the respondent's permission to do some of the things reserved to the copyright holder); or
  - whether any national copyright exemptions or defences would cover their proposed use.

Privacy

Many jurisdictions provide legal protections for individual privacy. These protections come in many guises. They may take the form of broad constitutional privacy protections, sector-specific laws, or laws with particular application to information about an individual - 'personally identifying 'information' (PII). Other laws may not be directly designed to protect individuals' privacy rights, but can be used to that end, such as rights provided to individuals to prevent unauthorised uses of their likeness, e.g., personality rights. Enforcement of some protections may require the individual to apply to their national courts, some may be enforceable via application to administrative bodies established by specific legislation, and others may be enforceable via mechanisms such as consumer protection laws. Collection of UCC that includes information about individuals, and which the researcher intends to use in the course of their research, will thus need to consider the types of legal rights to privacy generally, and data privacy specifically, granted to those individuals.

In the UK, the Data Protection Act 1998 (DPA 1998) provides individuals with certain rights regarding information held about them. It places obligations on those who are responsible for processing personal data (data controllers) and gives rights to those who are the subject of that data (data subjects). Processing of personal data for research purposes falls under the general provisions of the Act, but some specific research-related exemptions are provided (Charlesworth, 2008, p. 44). Data controllers (usually the researcher or the researcher's institution) are required to notify the UK Information Commissioner's office (ICO) of their intention to carry out data processing, and to conduct that processing in accordance with the Data Protection Principles contained in the Act. Failure to comply with the Act may lead to court fines for failure to notify, monetary penalties from the ICO for breaches of the Act, and legal action by data subjects, typically seeking one or more remedies including rectification or deletion of inaccurate data, the halting of unlawfully processed data, or damages for distress or losses caused by the data controller's failure to comply with the Act.

Of the legal issues discussed here, privacy, and the linked issue of liability for harm to research subjects or third parties (see below) are the two issues most often addressed through the lens of ethical guidelines and standards, particularly in terms of research involving direct interaction with human subjects. In most circumstances, therefore, researcher adherence to institutional, sectorial or representative body ethics requirements will go a long way to meeting national legal requirements; indeed (as noted in the law and ethics section above), the protections afforded by ethical oversight bodies may often outstrip the more basic protections afforded to research subjects by national privacy laws.

However, the new ways in which PII may be captured, stored, processed and archived using online research techniques mean that online researchers must still be aware of the requirements of national laws when developing practices and processes. Where ethical safeguards fail or are bypassed, researchers and their institutions may find themselves facing legal sanctions. There are numerous cautionary tales of researchers who obtained ethical clearance for their research, but failed to meet their ethical and legal responsibilities in its execution. A classic example was a UK university research project involving interviews with individuals who were abused as children, and former child abusers. During the research, the researchers ensured the privacy of the individual research subjects via various means, and only stored electronic data on specific computers held in locked offices. However, at the conclusion of the project, the research team split up, and some left the institution. None of the researchers took responsibility for ensuring the electronic data was properly anonymised and archived, or irrevocably deleted from the computers. The project computers were later deemed to be obsolete and, without institutional review of their contents, then sold or donated. This came to light when one of the computers was purchased and the new owner examined the contents of its hard drive. On discovering information about the project, which identified some of the research subjects, the purchaser alerted the local media. This was not only a clear ethical breach, but also a breach of the UK's data protection laws. It also demonstrates effectively that legal compliance has to be considered throughout the entire lifetime of a research project, that effective institutional oversight and audit has an important role to play in ensuring researcher compliance, and that reports of bad research practice can remain on the internet indefinitely (BBC, 2001).

The rapid development of new technologies can leave researchers unaware of the technical implications of the research tools they are seeking to use. Online tools may by default generate or permit the collection of significant amounts of 'background information'– data logs, IP address collection, cookies, caches, etc. This information is often 'sticky' – it can be difficult to entirely disassociate it from the 'foreground information' that the researchers are interested in. In order to use such tools responsibly, researchers need to understand the technologies involved, or to ensure they have access to informed technical support. For example, when conducting online surveys researchers may need to determine whether the survey tool they are using is suitable for the type of data being collected. Where the data includes PII, then researchers may need to consider issues such as encryption of communications between the respondent's computer and the server holding the survey, the security of the server against unauthorised access by third parties, and whether the server software or the survey tool are collecting communications data that might identify individual respondents. Researchers may also need to advise potential respondents about security issues relating to the computer the respondent is using to complete the survey, i.e., if the survey is accessed through a web browser, that the browser software may also retain data about the communication with the survey software and possibly copies of data entered into the survey. Thus, use of Internet research tools and computer systems requires researchers to do more than address the actual data they intend to collect, they should also be prepared to identify and address potential technical and administrative problems, e.g., poor research tool configuration and inappropriate levels of system security/integrity.

Researchers seeking to collect online information about living individuals ('data subjects') for use in research should prior to beginning the research:

- Identify whether the project requires collection of 'personally identifiable information' (PII) or if the research objectives can be met with anonymous data.
- Where anonymous data collection is appropriate for the research objectives take steps to:
  - Ensure the technologies to be used can reliably provide total anonymity;
  - Ensure that online research tools used, the background technology (e.g., server logs, etc.), or data subjects' actions on their computers, do not inadvertently compromise anonymity.
- Where PII collection is required to meet the research objectives:
  - Consult with appropriate institutional entities, e.g., data privacy or information rights officers, ethical review boards, or researchers with prior experience. Where the research requires large-scale collection of PII, or the type of data collected is higher-risk (e.g., data relating to ethnicity, sexuality, religion, health), consider conducting a formal privacy impact assessment (see ICO, 2008).
  - Determine what types of PII will be collected, the purpose for collecting them, and any particular legal requirements that apply to some, or all elements of that PII.
  - Determine whether the proposed collection and use of the PII for research purposes is permissible under national law, including any research-specific exemptions.
  - Ensure that formal requirements for lawful processing of PII can be met, e.g., compliance with Fair Information Processing Principles, Data Protection Principles, US-EU Safe Harbor requirements, etc.

◦ Ensure that, as far as possible, informed consent regarding use of their data has been obtained from respondents. Where informed consent cannot or will not be sought, ensure that the proposed use of PII can still meet applicable legal requirements.

◦ Consider the implications of a respondent withdrawing consent to use their PII, including how the researchers will practically deal with withdrawal of consent in terms of removal of data, etc.

◦ Determine whether the collection, use and storage of PII for research purposes requires data subjects to be notified and told about the rights they have in relation to such use, e.g., the right to request that their data not be used.

◦ Determine whether PII from the project may be lawfully passed to third parties, and whether such third parties should be identified in advance to the data subjects.

◦ Identify whether there are legal jurisdictional restrictions on transfer of PII, and that, where necessary, legal requirements for 'out of jurisdiction' transfers been met.

◦ Ascertain whether any online research tool utilised is properly configured to provide an appropriate level of security for the PII to be collected, and that reasonable steps have been taken to secure it and any underlying technology against unauthorised access. The physical security of any hardware on which PII is stored should be ensured.

◦ Take reasonable steps to ensure that anonymized research outputs, including research data anonymized after collection, cannot be used to backtrace respondents, e.g., using online search mechanisms or data triangulation.

◦ Have a documented data collection and retention process which addresses how PII collected by the researchers will be disposed of or archived in compliance with relevant laws.

• Ensure that all documentary evidence concerning the privacy, data privacy or other privacy-related measures affecting the material collected is compiled in a form that can be readily accessed and audited.

• Provide a review mechanism through which changes in the project, or in the online research tools, that might affect the project's privacy or data protection obligations, can be identified and addressed.

Liability for Content

Some content collected from online sources may expose the researcher who downloads, stores, or uses it, to either civil or criminal liability. The nature and scope of these potential liabilities for an online research project will again vary widely across jurisdictions.

Civil Liability: Defamation

A key area of potential civil liability in online research is defamation. In most jurisdictions, defamation liability is based on three criteria: publication of untrue information about an identified individual; dissemination of that information to people other than the author; and damage to the reputation of the person referred to. The person defamed will typically be seeking one or more remedies including injunctions against further publication, retractions and apologies, and financial damages to compensate them for their loss of reputation. If a researcher downloads a work containing defamatory material, or records defamatory statements made by a research subject in the course of an online interview, and then makes that material public, in the form of research data or research outputs, they may find themselves being sued for defamation along with the originator of the material or statement (Charlesworth, 2008, p. 53).

Researchers may also find themselves sued for defamation by respondents, where researchers attribute actions or views to a respondent, which the respondent does not actually hold, and which will cause damage to their reputation if others believe that they do hold them. Online research techniques may increase the risk of this form of misattribution, as some types of online interactions, e.g., email, message boards, etc., can lack the visual and other social cues that may be necessary for accurate interpretation by a researcher of a research subject's meaning in a given context.

Approaches to defamation between jurisdictions vary widely and may be counterbalanced by freedom of speech rights. However, as noted in the international section above, making research data or research publications available online may permit legal actions in jurisdictions where it is accessible.

Researchers collecting online data containing negative statements about identifiable individuals or organisations, whether by data harvesting from online sources, or via empirical research process such as interviews, should:

- Consider the reliability of the source of the negative statements; whether there is evidence to support the assertions made; and whether the statements are likely to damage the reputation of the person or organisation
- Where appropriate, seek expert advice on the defamation law applicable in their jurisdiction and any jurisdiction in which the research data, or research outputs based on the data, are intended to be made available to the public, including any relevant defences, such as innocent dissemination, legal privilege, etc.

- Determine whether solutions other than legal action may be available, as some jurisdictions, such as the UK, will permit defendants to libel actions to mitigate their liability by offering to make amends to the party defamed in advance of legal action.
- Have processes in place to deal with allegations of dissemination of defamatory statements. Damages for defamation are usually based on the extent to which the false statement has been made available. Thus, where the research data, or research outputs based on the data, are publicly available, researchers should consider whether they need to have a 'notice and takedown' process that can remove the data quickly, until an assessment of the allegations can be made.

Criminal Liability: Illegal Materials

Undertaking online research which involves accessing materials which are illegal, or may be considered to be illegal by national authorities, can be particularly risky for researchers. While the types of materials that may be illegal may vary considerably from jurisdiction to jurisdiction, pictures of child abuse and materials that facilitate or support terrorism are banned in most jurisdictions. For such material, the acts of downloading, storing and reusing may result in researchers facing arrest and criminal prosecutions being brought, even where the purpose for doing so was to carry out legitimate research.

In the UK, pictures of child abuse will fall under indecency legislation, which make it an offence to take, make, and permit to be taken, distribute, show, and possess intending to distribute or show, or publish indecent photographs or pseudo-photographs of children. The term 'indecency' is not defined in UK law, but the test is essentially whether the item in question offends current standards of propriety, or to put it another way, whether it offends contemporary community standards. Children are defined as persons under 18, or persons who appear to be under 18. Computer files, including .gif and .jpg image files, which are downloaded from FTP sites, embedded in web pages, or compiled from Usenet messages are treated as photographs. Pseudo-photographs are any image capable of being resolved into an image which appears to be a photograph and, if the image appears to show a child, then the image is treated as if that of a child. Under UK law, mere knowledgeable possession of indecent material is an offence, while the intentional downloading and/or printing out of computer data of indecent images of children from the Internet constitutes the more serious offence of 'making' of indecent photographs. There are a limited range of defences to offences under the indecency legislation (Charlesworth, 2009, p. 35).

Anti-terrorism laws are often broadly drafted and provide law enforcement and national security agencies with wide discretion to detain or prosecute individuals. In 2008, Rizwaan Sabir, a postgraduate researcher at Nottingham University in the UK downloaded a copy of an al-Qaeda training manual from a U.S. government website for use in his MA dissertation and PhD application. When he sought to print the manual, it was viewed by library staff, the police were called, and he was arrested under the Terrorism Act for suspicion of possessing extremist material. While Sabir's personal tutor and his MA supervisor advised police that his possession of the document was legitimate given his research interests, and he was later released without charge, he was held in custody for six days, and warned that he risked re-arrest if found in possession of the manual again (THES, 2008a). Legal advice in the UK following the Sabir incident was that:

... academics do have a "right" to "access" terrorist materials, whether for research or otherwise, as long as they do not "possess" them. ... Once the researcher knowingly downloads or saves the materials that he is accessing, then he is in

'possession' of terrorist materials. ... There is no 'right' to 'possess' terrorist materials and, while a genuine researcher would be able to establish a defence, the evidential burden is on the researcher to do so. (THES 2008b)

Other potential areas of content liability under UK law include extreme pornographic material (Charlesworth, 2009, p. 38) and material published in contempt of court, such as material which is prejudicial to a fair criminal trial, or fair civil proceedings (Charlesworth, 2009, p. 32).

Researchers who intend to undertake research which may involve the collection and storage of potentially illegal materials should:

- Ensure they understand the extent to which viewing, downloading and storage of such data is legal, if at all. Where there is doubt about the legality of any of these issues, then professional legal advice should be sought.
- Where viewing, downloading and storage of such material may be legal for restricted purposes, then advice should be taken on how compliance with those purposes may best be achieved. Advice might be sought from lawyers, law enforcement personnel, or institutional oversight bodies such as ethics committees.
- Document fully the research rationale for needing to collect the material, the collection methods and, where possible, the likely or actual sources of the material. There should be a documented process for the appropriate and audited disposal of the material at the end of the research.
- If working within a research institution, inform the institution of their intention to under the research, and the likely material that they will be collecting. The institution may also wish to take legal advice, or seek reassurances from law enforcement bodies that the research will not break the

law. Seeking documented clearance from their research institution will strengthen a researcher's case that they are using the material for legitimate research purposes, should their activities be questioned. In the Sabir incident, had Sabir sought institutional clearance (preferably in writing) in advance of downloading and printing the material from an appropriate institutional authority, such as a supervisor, this would likely have prevented the resulting investigation.

- Be aware that both national legal rules and ethical guidelines may require the reporting of illegal materials to the appropriate authorities

There may also be circumstances where researchers acquire, in the course of their interaction with research subjects, materials which are potentially or actually illegal, e.g., where a researcher corresponding with a research subject is sent such material by e-mail. In such circumstances, a researcher may have a legal obligation to report the material to law enforcement agencies, e.g., in the case of child abuse photographs. In the UK, retaining child abuse material provided by a research subject without reporting it to the authorities would leave the researcher open to charges of unlawful possession and/or making of indecent materials. Where researchers are collecting information from research subjects, it is increasingly common for informed consent documents to clearly state to research subjects that while their details will normally be kept private by researchers, this agreement can be overridden in cases where the law specifically requires it, or where the researcher becomes aware of the likelihood of harm to the research subject or a third party.

Liability for Harm to Research Subjects or Third Parties

Discussion of the issue of legal liability for harm to research subjects or third parties is impossible to separate from the ethical obligation to prevent, as far as possible, disproportionate harm to research subjects or third parties. Indeed, in the online context, it has been suggested that neither the legal rules nor ethical guidelines necessarily provide sufficient protection.

Legal liability for harm to research subjects or third parties, particularly in online research, tends to focus on the nature of the relationship between the researcher and the research subject. Stern, in her study of the legal and ethical responsibilities of researchers encountering what she terms 'distressing information' online, suggests that in the U.S. at least, absent a 'special relationship' of the type between a counsellor/therapist and a patient, there is no clear legal responsibility on an Internet researcher to act on material which suggests that a research subject or a third party is at risk of harm. Her reasoning is that Internet researchers are unlikely to have the necessary environmental or contextual information to determine the veracity of distressing disclosures by those studied; and communications cues available to offline researchers, such as '[t]one, volume, facial expressions, and gestures', that would permit an effective assessment of the seriousness of the disclosures, are also absent (Stern, 2003, pp. 254-255). It is debateable as to the extent to which this assessment holds true for more recent forms of online communication, including video messaging, where at least some of the cues missing from written online communications, e.g., e-mails, message boards, online forums and blogs, are more likely to be visible. However, there is currently little or no evidence to suggest that legislators or courts in any jurisdiction have reached conclusions that differ sharply from Stern's analysis.

Thus, while online research in some specific disciplines might lead a reasonable person to assume that a 'special relationship' existed, e.g., medical research, in general, liability for failure to act to prevent harm is likely to be difficult to substantiate. That having been said, there may be specific safeguard provisions in national legislation with regard to research targeting, or likely to acquire as research subjects, members of vulnerable groups, e.g., minors, or the mentally disabled. Where this is the case, researchers will need to make an assessment of whether such provisions will increase their liability for failure to act upon receipt of, or access to, 'distressing information'.

Ethical guidelines on avoidance of harm have also been criticised, not least for sometimes failing to recognise online research as being research involving human subjects; or where online research is identified as research involving human subjects, failing to take into account that harm caused may not, be restricted to individuals but may affect online communities, e.g., research on internet support groups may make individuals within those groups less inclined to use them, or use them effectively (McKee & Porter, 2009, Ch. 3).

RESEARCH PRACTICES AND PROCESSES

While the list of legal issues above may appear daunting to the new researcher, adequate preparation will ensure they rarely provide an insurmountable barrier to undertaking online research. Pre-project assessment and planning can identify the legal risks that particular online research poses, and aid the design of basic legal compliance processes proportionate to those risks, which can prevent or significantly reduce the likelihood of adverse outcomes. Indeed, probably the commonest cause of adverse legal outcomes for research projects is a simple failure by researchers to engage with the legal risks that the research topic, choice of research subjects, methodology, or choice of technology, might raise.

Each aspect of the research planning process should be considered with an eye to both the legal and ethical implications of the decisions being made. Failure to incorporate a legal risk assessment into the planning stages of a research project usually means that:

- researchers do not seek advice on potential legal issues, with which they have little or no prior experience, from appropriate sources, e.g., experienced researchers, ethics committees, university lawyers, etc.
- the implications of known issues or problems are not adequately documented and flagged for specific attention - this is particularly problematic in large multi-researcher or multi-institutional projects;
- there are no pre-defined strategies or processes for efficiently avoiding or ameliorating those legal issues/problems;
- researchers fail to identify developing legal problems; to adopt the appropriate processes for handling them; and, in multi-researcher/multi-institutional projects, to allocate responsibility for ensuing that those processes are followed.

Addressing legal risks at a late stage usually means that researchers will not have allocated sufficient project resources for additional work required to prevent or mitigate legal problems, or to access necessary legal advice or obtain insurance coverage. Such failures may be the difference between successful completion of a project and failure; between obtaining viable research data, or data which is legally compromised; or between publication and prosecution.

Preparing for Research

A legal risk assessment should identify the legal risks involved in the application of particular technologies, tools or research practices and, if carried out at an early stage, can play a role in determining which are adopted. When carrying out a risk assessment, online researchers should consider:

- *the jurisdictional boundaries of their research*, e.g., establishing whether the research has international scope, and if it does, assessing which jurisdictions' laws might apply to the research, and determining whether the laws of particular jurisdictions raise higher risks. In the case of particularly high risk jurisdictions, it may be necessary to use technical measures, e.g., blocking access to online surveys from particular countries, to limit legal exposure or to prevent possible detriments to research subjects.

- *the primary legal risks associated with their chosen research methodologies*, e.g., if the chosen method of obtaining research data is via harvesting of material held on websites, then issues such as lawful access to that data; compliance with intellectual property laws, notably copyright; and compliance with data privacy laws may be relevant. Where the research data is generated by some form of online interview, then issues such as the protection of the personal data of the research subjects, possible copyrights in interview recordings and transcripts, and liability for recording and use of recordings and transcripts may arise. Researchers planning to interact online with vulnerable groups, such as children, will need to pay particular attention to any special legal provisions for such groups, above and beyond those that apply to ordinary citizens.

- *the primary legal risks associated with the technologies and tools*, e.g., the security of technologies and tools and whether they can adequately protect data privacy. Where externally hosted tools like social networking sites (e.g., Facebook); survey tools (e.g., SurveyMonkey); and communication/video conferencing tools (e.g., Skype), are used, researchers will need to consider the appropriateness of the standard terms and conditions of the use of those tools, whether the nature of the research may require special arrangements with providers (e.g., encryption of survey answers); and whether such arrangements can relied upon.

- *how those carrying out the research will ensure compliance with particular legal obligations*, e.g., how best to accommodate the rights of data subjects under data protection law, how data will be kept secure. Designing effective legal compliance protocols can help to prevent inadvertent legal breaches, aid in ensuring research team members all understand their legal obligations, and be used as evidence of good practice in the event that the legal or ethical compliance of the project is questioned.

- *the administration of information relevant to legal compliance or legal rights*, e.g., aggregating important project-related information to permit efficient use of Internet research data. For example, a project might establish:
  - a 'copyright register' to hold details of copyright agreements, assignments and licences and other permissions relating to use and archiving of interview material, or
  - a 'retention schedule' for the research data to provide a basis on which to assess how long particular data should be held for, whether and when personal data can be anonymised, and what type of disposal mechanisms will be appropriate.

- *the administration of information-gathering tools and practices*, e.g., that processes and documentation are in place to ensure that the legal risks are understood by both researcher and research subject; that legal liability for content is appropriately allocated and explained; and that there are adequate processes in place to limit researcher and research subject exposure to liability.

- *the cost of handling legal risks*, e.g., the extent to which deploying appropriate technical and administrative mechanisms to prevent, or reduce, the legal risks identified have been adequately costed in funding proposals and, where necessary, the appropriate level of legal liability insurance acquired. It is worth noting that while universities usually have liability insurance to cover the activities of their researchers, whether particular research is adequately covered, or covered at all, will often depend upon researchers' compliance with internal ethical review and legal compliance checks.

Once the risk assessment is completed, it will be possible for the researcher to prioritise the legal risks and to determine and document how key risks are to be addressed, who is to address them, and when this is to happen. Experience suggests that the temptation for inexperienced researchers will be to concentrate solely on the technical issues involved with utilising online research technologies and tools, at the expense of matters like legal compliance, which are often viewed as mundane and boring. It is thus helpful to have a clear roadmap and timescale for addressing the legal issues raised. It also means that it is harder for work required to address legal risks to simply 'fall off the agenda' in the event of time or resource constraints (a common problem with larger research projects). The background to the risk assessment, decisions taken, and allocation of responsibilities should be contained in a risk strategy document.

Ideally, a risk assessment should be an 'end-to-end' process, that is, it should consider the life cycle of research data from its collection to its disposal at the conclusion of the research. Disposal might simply mean the deletion of data collected, but increasingly researchers are being called upon to preserve their data for future review and evaluation. Thus, it may be necessary to consider how, where, and in what form, the data is to be preserved and the likely legal issues connected with such preservation. It is increasingly common for research funders to require researchers to archive digital research materials so that they are available for future use. Funding conditions may therefore specify not just that research data is deposited, e.g., in institutional research repositories, or national research repositories, such as the UK's Economic and Social Data Service (ESDS), but that researchers provide adequate legal metadata (e.g., information identifying the copyright licences applicable to the data, or information outlining the data protection conditions applicable to its lawful processing) to permit its lawful reuse. Such requirements can also be captured in the risk strategy document.

While the initial legal risk assessment is important, it is not a panacea for all possible risks across a project's lifetime. However, if the initial risk assessment process results in a legal strategy document, this can be used as an effective basis for on-going review, as changes to project goals, methodology, online research tools, etc., during the research may all require a re-assessment of the legal risks. A danger with early legal risk assessment is that it is treated simply as a start-of-project 'box ticking' exercise, and that the outcomes then fail to translate to the actual research process. Ethics review committees can play an important role in ensuring good practice by means of research audits which take, as their starting point, the researchers' own legal risk assessments. Without a plausible mechanism of oversight and audit, the value of such assessments is likely to be reduced.

Online research is still a developing field, both in terms of the technologies available or in development, and in terms of their adoption into mainstream empirical research practice across disciplines. With this in mind, researchers should be encouraged by their institutions or representative bodies to document the legal issues they encountered during their online research activities, to determine the extent to which these were anticipated in the risk assessment, and to assess how effectively they were handled as a result. As with ethical guidelines for online research, it is important to encourage researchers to participate in discussing and developing good practice in the practical handling of legal risks in the online environment. This not only expands the legal knowledge base on which future researchers can draw, but also helps to establish and codify effective legal compliance processes. In particular, clearly established good practice legal guidelines may be influential when legislators and courts eventually come to consider how and when particular laws should be applied to online research.

Research Data Retention and Archiving

During an online research project, researchers will be continually acquiring research data. As electronic data storage becomes cheaper, there is an expectation that such research data should be archived for a minimum period of time, as a matter of course, and that archived research data should, wherever possible, be available to future researchers. In the UK, data archiving is increasingly becoming a requirement of both public and private sector research funding. Failure to comply with legal and ethical requirements during the research process may thus not only jeopardise the preservation of research data for future researchers, but also restrict researchers' ability to acquire future funding. However, if the researchers have carried out a legal risk assessment during the planning stages of the project, they should have:

- Appropriate administrative processes for ensuring that the material has been collected, stored, accessed/used and, if necessary,

disposed of, in accordance with applicable law;

- Appropriate technical measures to ensure that PII collected, stored, accessed/used and, if necessary, disposed of securely, in accordance with applicable law;

- Appropriate documentation on legal issues, and technical requirements for the guidance of the researcher(s) and others working on the project;

- Adequate metadata for the data collected to be able to comply with internal and external audit processes, or possible external legal challenges.

Completing these steps during the project will thus make the task of determining: which data should be retained and why; what form (e.g., PII or anonymized) it should be retained in; and what future uses it may be put to, a much simpler one. While there are undoubtedly legal risks associated with the collection, preservation and ultimate release to future researchers/the public of data collected for, or created in, the course of research, such risks are generally low level, and effective protection can be obtained via the type of risk assessment and risk management strategies outlined in the sections above.

No system of risk management can totally remove the threat of legal action, nor will it usually be practical/economic to attempt to achieve this. Effective risk management practices can, however, reduce the likelihood of such action and, more importantly, significantly reduce the negative effects (reputationally and financially) arising from successful legal challenges. It is important for researchers and research data repositories to consider the reasonableness of adopting, or not adopting, particular risk amelioration strategies in the context of particular types of data, and particular types of use. Provision of adequate and appropriately pitched information about legal issues to researchers depositing data, to repository staff and to those seeking to reuse research data, can build common understandings and prevent disputes.

In some jurisdictions, such as the UK, failure to adequately document legal issues pertaining to research data may lead to difficulties with Freedom of Information legislation. Under UK Freedom of Information (FoI) and Environmental Information (EIR) legislation the public have a right, subject to limited exemptions, to access information held by a UK 'public authority'. The definition of 'public authority' includes most universities, colleges, and publicly-funded research institutions. It is clear from existing decisions by the UK Information Commissioner's Office that research data is covered by the public access right. However, when making decisions about whether to release research data on receipt of a request for it under the FoI/EIR legislation, institutions will need to consider issues such as whether such a disclosure would breach data protection law (if the research data contains PII), breach copyrights or related rights (if the research data contains material in which a third party has copyright), or should be exempt because of confidentiality or commercial interests. In the absence of appropriate documentation and metadata relating to particular research data, managing compliance with the requirements of FoI/EIR legislation, whilst not compromising other legal interests, will become at best a costly and time consuming process (Charlesworth, 2009, p. 25; Shepherd, 2007; Shepherd & Ennion, 2007).

CONCLUSION

The ability to conduct research online, whether in terms of collecting and utilising existing materials (passive research) or seeking to obtain qualitative research data from research subjects (active research), can be a boon to the researcher. It permits the collection of hitherto unobtainable data, access to international material and research subjects, and the opportunity to explore new methods of researcher/research subject interactions. The ability

to publish online, or to archive research data and outputs electronically, also means that researchers can reach wider academic and public audiences, both geographically and temporally. The scope for open access to and reuse of research data and research publications, initially championed by scientific researchers, is gaining ground across academic disciplines.

These new abilities also bring researchers new requirements and responsibilities. The modern researcher needs to understand not just the changing shape of their ethical responsibilities in the online environment, but also how to achieve practical compliance, through their research methodologies/strategies, with relevant legal requirements. Those legal requirements may not just be the laws of their home country, but also the laws of the countries of their co-researchers and their research subjects. As research becomes more 'open', criticism of inadequate legal and ethical processes may come not just from traditional institutional or sectoral oversight bodies, such as ethics committees or institutional review boards, but from members of the public, the media, public interest groups and the courts. If researchers are perceived as failing to provide suitable ethical safeguards, or failing to meet legal requirements, then there will be pressure for legislators and regulators to act.

Meeting these challenges will require researchers across disciplines to review the extent to which existing processes and practices adequately address the types of ethical and legal issues which arise out of online research, data retention and publication. This will inevitably also require a re-examination of the appropriateness of the criteria upon which research oversight and audit bodies assess proposals, review on-going research and audit research outcomes. Online researchers should aim to embed legal compliance processes into their research projects, not just in the form of planning stage red light/green light risk assessments, but in terms of developing a set of structured and documented audit and compliance measures to aid and inform themselves, their research teams, relevant oversight and audit bodies, research archivists and future researchers.

REFERENCES

British Psychological Society (BPS). (2007). *Report of the Working Party on Conducting Research on the Internet: Guidelines for ethical practice in psychological research online,* Retrieved November 2, 2010, from http://www.bps.org.uk/document-download-area/document-download$.cfm?file_uuid=2B3429B3-1143-DFD0-7E5A-4BE3FDD763CC&ext=pdf

Charlesworth, A. (2003a). Information Privacy Law in the European Union: E Pluribus Unum or Ex Uno Plures. *Hastings Law Review, 54,* 931–969.

Charlesworth, A. (2003b). *Legal issues relating to the archiving of Internet resources in the UK, EU, US and Australia. Version 1.0 - 25.* London, UK: Wellcome Trust. Retrieved November 2, 2010, from http://library.wellcome.ac.uk/assets/WTL039230.pdf

Charlesworth, A. (2008). Understanding and Managing Legal Issues in Internet Research. In Fielding, N., Lee, R., & Blank, G. (Eds.), *The SAGE Handbook of Online Research Methods* (pp. 42–57). London, UK: Sage.

Charlesworth, A. (2009). *Digital Lives >> Legal & Ethical Issues Version 1.0 - 18.* London, UK: British Library. Retrieved November 2, 2010, from http://britishlibrary.typepad.co.uk/files/digital-lives-legal-ethical.pdf

Creative Commons. (n.d.). *About CC0 — "No Rights Reserved".* Retrieved November 2, 2010, from http://creativecommons.org/about/cc0

Economic and Social Research Council (ESRC). (2010). *Framework for Research Ethics.* Retrieved November 2, 2010, from http://www.esrcsociety-today.ac.uk/ESRCInfoCentre/Images/Framework for Research Ethics 2010_tcm6-35811.pdf

Enyon, R., Fry, J., & Schroeder, R. (2008). The Ethics of Internet Research. In Fielding, N., Lee, R., & Blank, G. (Eds.), *The SAGE Handbook of Online Research Methods* (pp. 23–41). London, UK: Sage.

Ess, C., & Association of Internet Researchers (AoIR). (2002). *Ethical Decision-making and Internet Research.* Retrieved November 2, 2010, from http://www.aoir.org/reports/ethics.pdf

Fielding, N., & Macintyre, M. (2006). Access Grid Nodes in Field Research. *Sociological Research Online, 11*(2). Retrieved November 2, 2010, from http://www.socresonline.org.uk/11/2/fielding.html

Fox, J., Murray, C., & Warm, A. (2003). Conducting research using web-based questionnaires: practical, methodological, and ethical considerations. *International Journal of Social Research Methodology, 6*(2), 167–180. doi:10.1080/13645570210142883

Hinduja, S., & Patchin, J. W. (2008). Personal information of adolescents on the Internet: A quantitative content analysis of MySpace. *Journal of Adolescence, 31*(1), 125–146. doi:10.1016/j.adolescence.2007.05.004

Hunter, P., & Guy, M. (2004). Metadata for Harvesting: The Open Archives Initiative, and How to Find Things on the Web. *The Electronic Library, 22*(2), 168–174. doi:10.1108/02640470410533434

Kastman, L.-A. M., & Gurak, L. J. (1999). Conducting Technical Communication Research via the Internet: Guidelines for Privacy, Permissions, and Ownership in Educational Research. *Technical Communication, 46*(4), 460–469.

McKee, H. A., & Porter, J. E. (2009). *The Ethics of Internet Research: a rhetorical, case-based process*. Witney, UK: Peter Lang.

Newman, M. (2008a, May 22). Research into Islamic terrorism led to police response. *Times Higher Education Supplement*. Retrieved November 2, 2010, from http://www.timeshighereducation.co.uk/story.asp?storycode=402125

Newman, M. (2008b, July 17). Researchers have no 'right' to study terrorist materials. *Times Higher Education Supplement*. Retrieved November 2, 2010, from http://www.timeshighereducation.co.uk/story.asp?storycode=402844

News, B. B. C. (2001, September 1). *Inquiry into sex abuse files blunder*. Retrieved from http://news.bbc.co.uk/2/hi/uk_news/1519889.stm

Shepherd, E. (2007). Freedom of Information and Records Management in the UK: What has been the Impact? *Journal of the Society of Archivists*, *28*(2), 125–138. doi:10.1080/00379810701607736

Shepherd, E., & Ennion, E. (2007). How has the implementation of the UK Freedom of Information Act 2000 affected archives and records management services? *Records Management Journal*, *17*(1), 32–51. doi:10.1108/09565690710730688

Stern, S. R. (2003). Encountering distressing information in online research: a consideration of legal and ethical responsibilities. *New Media & Society*, *5*(2), 249–266. doi:10.1177/1461444803005002006

U.S. Department of Health, Education and Welfare. (1973). *Secretary's Advisory Committee on Automated Personal Data Systems, Records, Computers, and the Rights of Citizens*. Washington, DC: Author.

Virginia Commonwealth University. (2006). *IRB Written Policies and Procedures: Use of the Internet for Recruitment and/or Research Data Collection*. Retrieved November 2, 2010, from http://www.research.vcu.edu/irb/wpp/flash/XVII-9.htm

Welker, J. A., & McCue, J. D. (2007). Authorship versus "credit" for participation in research. *Journal of the American Medical Informatics Association*, *14*(1), 16–18. doi:10.1197/jamia.M2212

ADDITIONAL READING

Adler, P. A., & Adler, P. (2002). Do university lawyers and the police define research values? In van den Hoonaard, W. C. (Ed.), *Walking the Tightrope: Ethical Issues for Qualitative Researchers* (pp. 34–42). Toronto, ON: University of Toronto Press.

Akeroyd, A. V. (1991). Personal Information and Qualitative Research Data: Some Practical and Ethical Problems arising from Data Protection Legislation. In Fielding, N. G., & Lee, R. M. (Eds.), *Using Computers in Qualitative Research* (pp. 89–106). London: Sage Publications.

Greenwood, D. J., Brydon-Miller, M., & Shafer, C. (2006). Intellectual property and action research. *Action Research*, *4*(1), 81–95. doi:10.1177/1476750306060581

Lipinski, T. A. (2006). Emerging Tort Issues in the Collection and Dissemination of Internet-Based Research Data. *Journal of Information Ethics*, *15*(2), 55–81. doi:10.3172/JIE.15.2.55

Lipinski, T. A. (2008). Emerging Legal Issues in the Collection and Dissemination of Internet-Sourced Research Data: Part I, Basic Tort Law Issues and Negligence. *International Journal of Internet Research Ethics*, *1*(1), 92–114.

Lipinski, T. A. (2009). Emerging Legal Issues in the Collection and Dissemination of Internet-Sourced Research Data: Part II, Tort Law Issues Involving Defamation. *International Journal of Internet Research Ethics*, *2*(1), 57–72.

McKee, H. A. (2008). Ethical and legal issues for writing researchers in an age of media convergence. *Computers and Composition*, *25*(1), 104–122. doi:10.1016/j.compcom.2007.09.007

Palys, T., & Lowman, J. (2000). Ethical and legal strategies for protecting confidential research information. *Canadian Journal of Law and Society*, *15*(1), 39–80.

Parry, O., & Mauthner, N. S. (2004). Whose Data are They Anyway?: Practical, Legal and Ethical Issues in Archiving Qualitative Research Data. *Sociology*, *38*(1), 139–152. doi:10.1177/0038038504039366

Sprumont, D. (1999). Legal Protection of Human Research Subjects in Europe. *European Journal of Health Law*, *6*, 25–43. doi:10.1163/15718099920522668

Van Hove, E. (1996). The Legislation on Privacy Protection and Social Research. *Computers in Human Services*, *12*(1/2), 53–68. doi:10.1300/J407v12n01_06

KEY TERMS AND DEFINITIONS

Civil Liability: Legal obligations arising from private wrongs (e.g., under UK law breaches of 'tort', defamation) or a breach of contract that is not a criminal act. Civil liability usually opens a defendant to potential responsibility for payment of damages to a private applicant, or other court-enforced penalties or orders (e.g., injunctions forbidding a defendant from engaging in an activity or course of action) in a lawsuit.

Criminal Liability: The liability that arises out of breaking a law or committing a criminal act. In criminal liability cases it is usually the state prosecuting the defendant. The penalties for criminal offences include fines and imprisonment, as well as other non-custodial punishments.

Cross-Jurisdictional: Legal jurisdiction is usually defined as the right and power to command, decide, rule, or judge. Nation states usually exert jurisdiction over the geographic territory they occupy. The Internet causes problems for traditional understandings of jurisdiction because it does not fall solely within the geographical boundaries of one nation state, but is accessible in, and has impacts upon, the majority of states – it is thus cross-jurisdictional. This leads to problems in determining which nation's laws apply to a given civil or criminal case where the action or harm at issue has its locus online.

Defamation: Publication of untrue information about an identified individual; dissemination of that information to people other than the author; and damage to the reputation of the person referred to. In the UK defamation may be by libel (written or otherwise recorded in permanent form) or by slander (verbal).

Metadata: Data that provides context or additional information about other data, e.g., information about the title, subject, author, size and copyright status of the data file of a document would constitute metadata about that document.

Moral Rights: Moral rights give the authors of literary, dramatic, musical, artistic works and film directors the rights to be identified as the author of the work or director of the film in certain circumstances, e.g., when copies are issued to the public; and to object to derogatory treatment of the work or film which amounts to a distortion or mutilation or is otherwise prejudicial to the honour or reputation of the author or director.

Performance Rights: Performers have various rights in their performances as well as in the recordings or broadcasts of their performances. Performers also have moral rights which include the rights to be identified as the performer and to object to derogatory treatment of performance.

Personally Identifiable (PII): Data about an individual that could, potentially identify that person, such as a name, fingerprints or other biometric data, email address, street address, telephone number or social security number.

User-Created Content (UCC): Also known as consumer-generated media or User-generated content. Material created by an individual or individuals, usually initially non-commercial in intent. Refers primarily to digital material placed on websites and web services, e.g., blog posts, comments on interactive websites, material such as photographs and videos uploaded to Web 2.0 services, etc.

Chapter 23
Ethical Considerations in Online Research Methods

Harsh Suri
The University of Melbourne, Australia

Fay Patel
Dalhousie University, Canada

ABSTRACT

Online research methods are gaining popularity in several disciplines as they offer numerous opportunities that were not feasible before. However, online research methods also present many challenges and complexities that give rise to ethical dilemmas for online researchers and research participants. This chapter discusses key ethical considerations in the four stages of the research process: research design, online data collection methods, data analysis methods, and online communication of research outcomes. Issues of power, voice, identity, representation, and anonymity in online research are discussed. The relationship between information and power and its implications for equity in online research is also examined. Rather than providing prescriptive recommendations, the authors use questioning as a strategic device to foster critical awareness and ethically informed decision-making among online researchers.

INTRODUCTION

Highlighting the potential social and economic impact of new media technologies globally, early advocates (Lerner, 1958; Rogers, 1962; McLuhan, 1962) recommended them as highly desirable for promoting modernity and prosperity between the 1960s and 1980s. Since the advent of the Internet

as a new media technology, online access to information has been regarded as a necessary and fast way to connect global societies (Rogers, 1995). Commonly held beliefs are that new media makes global communication more accessible, supports gender neutrality, has innovative appeal, encourages rapid response rates, provides access to new and old information sources and facilitates collaborative construction of knowledge. However, these beliefs have been challenged over time and

DOI: 10.4018/978-1-4666-0074-4.ch023

it appears that issues of access, gender neutrality, social justice, equity and intellectual property are among a wide range of contested issues across disciplinary perspectives (Mowlana, 1995; McMichael, 2005; Gurumurthy, 2004; Palomba, 2006).

Online research is relatively young with a life of about twenty years since the Internet became a primary and important source of information generation, retrieval, communication and dissemination. After being part of the ARPANET network that was solely used for military purposes in the United States in the early part of the twentieth century, the Internet was introduced first to the libraries and legal practitioners and later to the higher educational institutions. However, the pace of development of protocols for online usage of information by researchers has been relatively slow when compared with the rapid development, diversification and acceptance of the new media. This has contributed to a series of lose and ambiguous norms of engagement and protocols across different regions of the world (Rogers, 1995).

Online research methods refer to methods of designing research, collecting data, analysing data and communicating research outcomes using one or more online technologies which facilitate synchronous or asynchronous communication, presentation or co-construction of information. These technologies include emails, electronic surveys, online interviews, online discussions, web-pages, blogs, wikis and various gaming and social networking tools. *Ethics* refers to the principles, beliefs and values that espouse fairness, goodness, integrity and honesty. Research ethics and methods are intricately entwined as Markham (2007, p. 7) emphasises "that all methods decisions are in actuality ethics decisions and that all ethics decisions are in actuality methods decisions".

Ethical issues in research have remained the key focal point of validation of research for centuries and the literature is exhaustive with respect to ethical considerations in traditional face-to-face research. Ethical considerations become even more important in online research because of the elusive nature of virtual communication, the unclear boundaries of the virtual reality and the socio-cultural, political and economic factors that drive the everyday reality of research participants. It is therefore necessary to educate and inform online researchers on the pitfalls of online research and to alert them to their ethical obligations as researchers.

While the new media technologies present numerous opportunities and challenges for an online researcher, some challenges have parallels in face-to-face research and others are unique to online research. The online researcher must not only consider ethics in designing, conducting and evaluating online research methods, but also consider how research participants are assigned or denied identities, ascribed or denied their voice, and so on. Within this context, issues considered in this chapter include:

- research questions that are suitable for online research;
- influences from multiple stakeholders on the kinds of research questions to be considered;
- access to online technologies and how access affects participation levels;
- dialectical tensions between offline and online representations and identities of the researcher and the researched;
- confidentiality and anonymity in online data analysis;
- engaging the broad diversity of global communities in an effort to ensure that online research is inclusive; and
- how various stakeholders influence, and are influenced by, online presentation of research outcomes.

Most researchers are guided by their institutional review boards to ensure ethical conduct of research. For instance, Australian researchers are guided by the *National Statement on Ethical*

Conduct in Human Research developed jointly by the National Health and Medical Research Council, Australian Research Council and Australian Vice-Chancellors' Committee (NHMRC, ARC, & AVCC, 2007). We will draw upon some global themes from this document to illustrate how these themes translate specifically in an online research environment. However, as with many other publications on research ethics, this document discusses online research methods very superficially with limited discussion of Web 2.0 tools (Murthy, 2008). The most concise document on ethics in online research methods has been published by the Association of Internet Researchers (Ess & AoIR, 2002). We will draw upon this document and more recent commentaries on ethics in online research and ethics in general.

Many institutional review boards provide checklists to ensure ethical conduct of research. However, in research ethics, "there is rarely a clear cut, and context-free, set of rules or principles which can be applied without deliberation and judgement" (Pring, 2004, p. 142). We strongly believe that adherence to ethical standards cannot be promoted by adopting a punitive approach alone. Online researchers can benefit by engaging in conversations about ethics from multiple perspectives. This chapter makes no attempt to provide prescriptive recommendations to online researchers as a formulaic approach to ensure ethical standards would be counterproductive in encapsulating the complexity of interactions across cultural and national boundaries and the specific nuanced contexts that are frequently the sites of online research. According to Buchanan and Ess (2008), at most there may be agreement among diverse nations on " a range of basic values and issues, while at the same time preserving local differences in the interpretation and implementation of those values through a strategy of *ethical pluralism*" (p. 286, emphasis in original). However, they also contend that "ethical pluralism will not resolve all cultural differences and conflict in research ethics" (p. 288). We concur

with Buchanan and Ess and our chapter reiterates the conviction that it is necessary to educate and inform global communities on the risks and benefits of online research. Our discussion is geared at sensitising online researchers to a range of considerations with ethical implications in their research and to conscientise them to a point of action so that the delicate boundary between social responsibility and social justice is not overlooked. We have used questioning as a strategic device to foster critical awareness and ethically informed decision-making among online researchers.

In the next four sections, key ethical obligations of online researchers are discussed in the phases of online research design, online data collection methods, online data analysis methods and online communication of research outcomes. We will begin each of these four sections with a general discussion of key issues that all researchers, including online researchers, should be mindful of. In particular, the discussion will highlight issues that present dilemmas and challenges for online researchers. Brief references will be made to issues that arise in the blurred and critical boundaries, where relevant, as an in-depth discussion on each of these issues lies outside the scope of the chapter.

ONLINE RESEARCH DESIGN

All researchers should be mindful of emerging ethical dilemmas, many of which should be anticipated and addressed in research plans, as every piece of research is inevitably influenced by its frame of reference and embedded assumptions (Kuhn, 1970). Researchers must begin by identifying their own interests and identities and how they intersect with the research design (AERA, 2009). They must reflect upon their ontological, epistemological, axiological and political positioning with respect to the research design (Gaskell, 1988; Suri, 2008). They must not only reflect upon how they position themselves in the phenomenon being examined, but also how they are positioned by others. This is not easy as we tend to be so embedded within our own frame of reference that it is difficult to see how it influences what we see. "Many things are obscure simply because the world is too much with us. Like the fish in water, the boy in love, or the sexist among like-minded friends, we lack the perspective to see things closest to us" (Dabbs, 1982, p. 31). Nonetheless, maintaining a reflexive stance on how the emerging identities of the researcher intersect with the design and implementation of the research is crucial.

In formulating an appropriate research question, all researchers must anticipate how the interests of various stakeholders intersect with the phenomenon being studied. Potential benefits and risks for all stakeholders must be clearly identified. Key questions worth considering include: Who are the key stakeholders in this research project? Whose questions will the study examine? How can the research study influence and get influenced by the interests of various groups of stakeholders? How can potential risks be minimised especially for vulnerable groups of stakeholders?

Respect for persons and beneficence are two fundamental principles underpinning most ethical decisions. Potential benefits and risks for different stakeholders associated with the study must be clearly thought through. One could focus on assessing potential benefits and risks by drawing upon consequentialism or utilitarianism, which upholds that the "rightness or wrongness of an action should be judged in terms of whether its consequences produce more benefits than disadvantages for the greatest number of people" (Stutchbury & Fox, 2009, p. 490). Alternatively, one could adopt a deontological approach which regards "basic human rights (self-determination, privacy, informed consent, etc.) as so foundational that virtually no set of possible benefits" could justify their violation (Ess & AoIR, 2002, p. 8). While some nations, like the United States rely more on utilitarian standpoint, other nations such as the multiple groups that make up the European

Union tend to uphold the deontological standpoint (Ess & AoIR, 2002). Online researchers must carefully think through the potential risks of their research not only from the frame of reference they are subscribing to, but also from competing frames of references.

In general, researchers should opt for overt study design where the participants are made aware of any sponsoring agency and assisted in understanding the purpose of the study. Covert research may be conducted only if the research poses minimal risks to the research participants, the research contributes substantially to the community and the research purpose cannot be attained with an overt design as in some scientific disciplines (NHMRC et al., 2007). Some social scientists, for example Creswell (2009), insist that the purpose of the study must be clearly explained to the participants leaving no room for deception. If the researcher has another purpose in mind from the purpose that was shared with participants, then participants are being deceived. In addition to this the researcher has the responsibility to disclose the identity of the sponsor if the research is being sponsored. Vulnerable groups should not be further marginalized and disempowered through the research process and/or research findings (Creswell, 2009, pp. 88-89).

Online researchers frequently experience a tension between their research integrity and ethical obligations towards research participants. In general, researchers should refrain from securing a perfect research environment at the cost of compromising their participants' rights (Bruckman, 2002). For example, when researchers are faced with an obligation to obtain participant consent in a computer-mediated communication forum, they may feel that seeking explicit consent might change the flow of the conversations. Nonetheless, it is imperative that researchers do not compromise the rights of their research participants in order to secure an uninterrupted flow of conversations.

The issue of overt research, informed consent and participant confidentiality becomes more complex in an online environment. For instance, when studying online discussion forums, whose permission should the researcher, seek? Is it sufficient to seek informed consent from the moderator of the discussion forum? How can one seek informed consent if the membership of certain discussion forums is fluid and is rapidly changing? How does the researcher ensure voluntary participation and the option to opt out of the study at any stage of the project? How ethical is it for the researcher to make permanent archives of chat sessions that are typically not meant to last? Should the researcher contribute to the flow of conversation as a participant observer? Or, should the researcher lurk and observe like a "fly on the wall"? In face-to-face research, often researchers seek parental consent with minor research participants. How can the researcher establish physical age of research participants from their online identities? Online research crosses virtual borders and the signing of a consent form may not be legally binding across the different countries or may not consider the value and belief systems of different societies around the globe (Madge, 2007). Many of these questions have been highlighted by Buchanan and Ess (2008) who argue that the "heightened attention to protecting privacy, anonymity, and so on, has a strongly pragmatic dimension" (p. 285) since participants may drop off the research pool unless a strong, ongoing presence and interactive engagement is included.

Capurro and Pingel (n.d.) suggest that online communication or existence is characterised by an abstraction of personal identity, social context and global direction. The tension between face-to-face and online research is a fundamental dilemma for online researchers. On one hand, the ubiquity of the new media is enabling people to seamlessly integrate their physical identities with their virtual identities where the cyberspace is simply seen as another venue for expressing the beliefs, values and ideologies held by one. On the other hand, cyberspace is seen as an exciting space by many for constructing and co-constructing multiple and/

or fluid identities which may be distinct from ones physical identity. In this digital age, none of these identities can be privileged unquestionably as being more authentic. While some might see the physical identity as being more authentic, others may relate more closely with their online identities.

All researchers must attend to "ecological" factors such as "cultural sensitivity" and "responsive communication" (Flinders, 1992, p. 113). Online researchers must be particularly sensitive and responsive to the values, norms and language of the environment they are studying. They must adapt their online identities and activities to build mutually respectful and trusting relationships with their research participants. They must use appropriate language, be respectful of the common values and beliefs held in the group and follow the group conventions in communicating. Often skimming through the *Frequently Asked Questions* and archives of discussion forums can help researchers in understanding the subtle and nuanced norms of the group (Hall, Frederick, & Johns, 2004).

Online researchers are faced with multiple dilemmas when conducting research online, particularly because they cannot see or identify with the physical identities of their participants. At the same time, they have an access to online identities of their participants which are not necessarily congruent with their face-to-face identities. Each of these identities is an important aspect of one's being in this digital age. The relationship between online and face-to-face identities can be complex. These identities may be congruent, similar or even conflicting. Also, the relationship between these identities for the same individual may change in different situations. All of these issues must be taken into account when considering the suitability of online research design and methods.

ONLINE DATA COLLECTION METHODS

Online data collection methods are becoming popular as they allow researchers to efficiently collect information from a large number of respondents at different geographic locations. Online communications make it easy to send reminders and negotiate meeting times. Further, online data can be easily imported into statistical packages like SPSS or qualitative coding software like NVivo or ATLAS.ti to improve efficiency in data-analysis. However, unless online researchers are adequately trained and supported, online surveys can violate ethics on multiple grounds. For instance, the default option in many online survey tools requires mandatory responses which violate the option of voluntary participation.

Furthermore, tracking IP addresses, third party access, auto-fill ins, public Internet terminals, and ownership of the data contribute to a situation where research subject/participants can be easily identified - contra the fundamental promise in research ethics to protect the identity, confidentiality, and anonymity of the persons involved as subjects. A further complication here is that in traditional research settings, the researcher assumes responsibility for protecting the participants' identities, but in online research, he or she may not be solely responsible. Finally, the risks increase when certain types of [sensitive] data are being collected (Buchanan & Ess, 2009, p. 47).

Online data-collection methods are substantially affected by the digital divide. On one hand, these methods exclude a large population which does not have access to these technologies or does not feel comfortable with the new media. On the other hand, they enable participation of individuals who may have found it difficult to participate due to limited physical or social mobility or acceptance. Online reporting can also be particularly powerful in helping newer generation

of participants construct their own narratives in the form of journal entries or multimedia recordings using webcams. For example, in her study, Dillon (2010) encouraged a group of gifted adolescents to email their digital journal entries to the researcher. In face-to-face interviews, it is possible that younger participants, especially the gifted ones, may construct narratives that they believe the researcher wants to hear. They are more aware of the researcher's presence. However, the younger generation who are digital natives feel more at home in the digital space and are more likely to construct more authentic narratives in the digital space where the presence of the researcher is less invasive. It is critical to reflect on how differential levels of access and participation among different groups might skew the research findings towards the views shared by the digital haves (Murthy, 2008).

Closely related to consent is the issue of trust and confidentiality among research participants and their interpretations of trust and confidentiality as well as their right and expectation to have the outcomes of the research shared in an open forum. In an online medium, the public/private boundaries get blurred and magnified at the same time. For instance, an online discussion forum is seen by some as a platform for establishing ones credibility within that community. Hence, it becomes imperative that all contributions are adequately respected as the contributors' intellectual property. At the same time, some others regard discussion forums as platforms for sharing ones private views, feelings and beliefs and hence any references to these conversations should be adequately anonymised in published research (Ess & AoIR, 2002).

Public versus private space is increasingly complicated on the Internet because a user can transition from seemingly public spaces, to spaces that appear private, to commercial spaces without realizing that a change has taken place. Unlike more standard spaces (you notice when you leave the mall to enter your car), cyberspace flows practically seamlessly between different types of spaces and often gives the illusion of more privacy than is actually there. The environment, the intimacy of the conversations, and the medium itself contribute to a feeling of privacy and localized community rather than public space even though the spaces are open to public eye and scrutiny (Whiteman, 2007, p. 98).

At the outset of their research, online researchers must decide the extent to which the research participants' physical and online identities would be disguised. Online identities would include various online personas, which can be related to pseudonyms or avatars. Bruckman (2002) identifies the following four levels of disguise: no disguise, light disguise, moderate disguise and complete disguise. No disguise is warranted where the research participants would like public acknowledgement/recognition of their viewpoints. Light disguise would allow naming of a group and use of "verbatim quotes". Complete disguise would require special care to ensure that neither the group, nor any member of the group being studied can be identified. Here, the researcher would refrain from using verbatim quotes "if a search mechanism could link those quotes" to the online or offline identity of that person. Moderate disguise would incorporate "some features of light disguise and some of complete disguise, as appropriate to the situation" (Bruckman, 2002, p. 2).

Online researchers must respect their participants by respecting the tacit rules governing the online conversations, seeking voluntary participation through informed consent and striving for authentic representations of their participants' views. If participants wish to remain anonymous, their confidentiality must be protected in a way that cannot be intercepted by search engines. Further, the participants must be informed of the potential risks if the data can be accessed by certain agencies, under special provisions such as the USA patriot act.

Blogs are another example of a space which is perceived as public by some while private by others. The advent of Web 2.0 technologies challenges the modern notion of authorship by blurring the boundaries between individual/collaborative and personal/collective. It is sometimes assumed that everyone has the right of access to share and use information that is the intellectual property of someone else because it appears on cyberspace. However, the Internet poses a complex set of issues associated with intellectual property rights and copyright. For example, the Intellectual Property Rights (IPR) report, commissioned by the British government, found a range of different protocols of intellectual property and copyright in some of the developed and least developed countries (LDCs) where " the biases and interests of developed countries are monopolising the international copyright agenda" (Story, p. 4). Intellectual property is a growing site of conflicts and controversies as well as a new source of power and wealth due, in part, to its re-conceptualisation as a commodity of world trade and the enhanced profitability and access possibilities that digital technology has opened up (Story, p. 6).

The power of information and who has access to it, or not, should not be overlooked as access to information, or lack of it, places a person or group at an advantage or disadvantage over others. Access to the same information and the same information rights of use are important in ensuring equity. When an online research study extends across geographical and cultural boundaries, the human rights, historical representations and cultural identities of vulnerable populations must be appropriately protected. It is important to be mindful of the power attributes of the Internet and its potential to abuse the intellectual property rights and copyright of less privileged individuals and groups, especially when conducting online research. Of particular note in the IRP report are the recommendations to uphold the intellectual property rights of populations from least developed countries (LDCs) and to ensure that indigenous knowledge is respectfully acknowledged. The study found that "developed countries are regularly misappropriating, without consent, indigenous traditional knowledge from LDCs" (Story, 2002, p. 6).

It is important that online researchers consider some of the critical issues in researching sensitive topics with vulnerable populations. Online researchers must ensure that the gathering of research data is not disrespectful and intrusive to indigenous communities and their knowledge. The indigenous perspectives on the negative impact and consequences of Western research on indigenous knowledge and quality of life cannot remain underrepresented or ignored in current and future discussion on online research ethics. Indigenous perspectives must be respected and acknowledged must play a central role in research design, data collection and analysis of outcomes so that Western research models do not continue to exploit cultural values and knowledge. Contributions in the book edited by Hongladarom and Ess (2007) on cultural perspectives in information technology ethics caution us to be mindful of transgressing cultural boundaries and call to our attention the pitfalls of making assumptions about privacy, for example, and the need to respect cultural traditions. For example, Smith (1999) observes that among indigenous communities and from indigenous perspectives, the word 'research' is perceived as unfavourable. On the other hand, the values and customs of indigenous communities are sometimes regarded as barriers to successful research from Western perspectives. However, there is an indication that participatory research approaches are more favourable alternatives in indigenous research (Castellano, 2004). It is important to consider the rights of both researchers and participants. Ethical considerations in online research must embrace the principles of social justice to ensure that the rights of researchers and participants are upheld, their privileges are not withheld and that they are protected from harm.

The new media is regarded as an important venue for constructing individual and collective identities. This poses complex issues around issues of voice, identity and representation. All researchers have the ethical imperative to ensure that individual voices, identities and representations are not lost in the collective representations in ways that further marginalise vulnerable individuals (Baker, 1999). As the distinction between individual and collaborative space becomes more blurred and more magnified in the cyberspace, authentic reporting of individual identities becomes challenging for online researchers.

Stern (2003, p. 249) introduces another ethical dimension to the online researcher's portfolio, that of *encountering distressing disclosure*. She raises issues of legal responsibility and ethical and moral obligation to intervene in cases where self-disclosure to harm themselves or others is revealed in the online research. Stern argues that the online environment provides a higher risk of encountering such distressing disclosures as intent to rape, murder and commit suicide mainly because it "allows for anonymity, private authorship and public reach" (p. 250) and it also allows for "more [direct and frequent] access to the expression and communication of individuals" (p. 251). However, Stern also alerts us to the complexities and ambiguities of conducting online research that leads to such drastic outcomes. Among the complexities is the question of professional integrity among clinical researchers, their commitment to confidentiality and impartiality and to a code of professional ethics, and so on. The range of ambiguities, on the other hand, suggests that it is difficult for the online researcher to be sure that his/her interpretation of the distressing encounter, threat and risk to life is real. In a health related research project, for example, online researchers may have little access to research participants' medical records and other relevant information to verify their suspicions. It is possible that this may lead to a misinterpretation of the situation wrongly suggesting distress. Stern (2003) cites the

US case that is governed by the Belmont report that endorses the principles of respect for persons and beneficence (p. 259). In the case of America, beneficence poses a dual dilemma: should the online research protect from harm or should he/she allow the research participant to exercise free speech in line with the constitution and which value should be upheld first?

When collecting online data, research must critically reflect on a range of questions including the following: Which groups are more likely to participate in online data collection methods? How does this influence the interests of those whose perspectives may not be captured through online data collection methods? How does access to online communication technologies affect the participation level of respondents? How will the sample be identified? How representative is the sample of the entire population? How representative are the respondents of the entire population? What response rate is acceptable? Typically, response rates in online data collection methods are low. How will this be accounted for? How will the broad diversity (gender, race, ethnicity, age, disability, and so on) of participants affect their access to online participation, responses and the outcomes of the research? How will variations within different stakeholder groups be captured? Will publicly available Web 2.0 data be included in the study? How might identities of the participants revealed through the publicly available data intersect with their more private identities? When appropriate, how will the participants' ideas be acknowledged appropriately in the study? What measures will be taken to maintain the anonymity of the participants when collecting private information? How will informed consent be obtained from the participants of discussion forums? Buchanan and Ess (2008, p. 279) have discussed these "as discrete issues" while acknowledging them as intrinsically related and note that they contribute to the complexity of online research. These critical questions must be reiterated in all discussions so that online researchers can acknowledge them as fundamental issues that are deeply embedded in online research ethics rather than "as discrete issues".

ONLINE DATA ANALYSIS METHODS

All researchers must maintain a reflexive stance on how might their emerging identities influence their analysis of data. Key questions worth considering include: Why am I interested in this phenomenon? What are the ontological, epistemological, methodological, axiological and political underpinnings of my analysis? How might these assumptions influence the research outcomes? Researchers must be sensitive to the power relationships between individuals and various groups they are studying. Not only should they attend to the dominant themes emerging from their data, but also the disconfirming themes and the variations within the collective representations (AERA, 2006).

Asserting that a tension exists between face-to-face and virtual communication, Capurro and Pingel (n.d.) identify several key ethical issues. For example, a key consideration for online researchers should be the differences between the digital identities and the bodily identities and the individual and social harm resulting from the way in which the research is reported and how the outcome may impact their online or human existence in direct and indirect ways. Using the creation and use of metaphors as an example, Capurro and Pingel (n.d.) claim that since researchers may examine and manipulate online user identities in different ways, this begs the ethical question of which metaphors are emphasized at the expense of others. Another ethical consideration is about online language and it questions whether online research takes into consideration a neutral or human oriented perspective. Depending on which of these perspectives are considered then it becomes necessary for online researchers to acknowledge that the role of prior and hidden knowledge may interfere with the interpretation of the online language thereby creating further doubt about the accuracy of the analysis.

Synchronous and asynchronous sharing of online documents, cyberspace, databases and software applications opens up opportunities of collaborative research that were unconceivable before. Online technologies offer a range of opportunities for engaging various groups of people in the research process. These technologies provide numerous venues for "member-checking" (Guba & Lincoln, 1999, p. 147) or validation of research outcomes by research participants. They can be particularly useful for establishing trust and building constructive, collaborative, reciprocally beneficial relationships with key stakeholders in interpreting the research findings. Impact of the research study can be enhanced by engaging the key agents for change in formulating the key recommendations. However, the ease of data sharing also raises ethical concerns about data protection and establishing mutually agreeable boundaries with key stakeholders effectively to ensure that views of all groups, especially more vulnerable groups, such as children, indigenous groups and those with disabilities, are respected.

Key questions worth considering when using online data analysis methods include the following: What criteria will be used to select representative data? What forms of sensitivity analyses are performed? What are the different lenses which will be employed to make sense of the evidence? What steps will be taken to make sense of the evidence from the perspectives of different stakeholders? Will different stakeholders be involved in drafting recommendations stemming from the research? How did the gender difference, for example, affect online participation and in what ways were gender differences noted in participation and responses? How does the gender variable affect the outcome?

ONLINE COMMUNICATION OF RESEARCH OUTCOMES

All researchers have an obligation to "communicate their findings and the practical significance of their research in clear, straightforward, and appropriate language to relevant research populations, institutional representatives, and other stakeholders" (AERA, 2000, p. 5). Online technologies can be strategically utilised to disseminate research outcomes through multiple accessible channels, such as web-pages, YouTube, Twitter and blogs. However, online technologies have blurred the boundaries of published/unpublished, leading to multiple interpretations of the term "unpublished". For instance, putting up interim findings on publicly accessible cyberspace can sometimes interfere with copyright requirements of scholarly journals, thus limiting the options for publishing in reputed journals. Clear agreements must be established about potential venues for disseminating research outcomes at the outset of research.

Online open-access journals play an important role in providing access to scholarly information to groups which do not have access to well-resourced libraries. Several key organisations have started providing open-access to their online journals. For instance, journals on online research methods, such as *International Journal of Internet Research Ethics* and *International Journal of Internet Science*, provide open-access. However, a large proportion of top-tier journals provide restricted access. Often, academics are under pressure to publish in top-tier. This poses a difficult ethical dilemma to them: should they publish in top-tier journals which will build credibility of their work among their peers and increase the impact-factor or should they opt for open-access journals where their work is accessible to a larger population.

Online researchers can strategically utilise online technologies for disseminating their research outcomes to a wider audience in an engaging fashion. In comparison with paper-based printing, cyberspace offers multiple, less expensive, more interactive options for disseminating research outcomes. Online researchers can capitalise on this to disseminate their findings in multiple formats suitable for different groups of audience. Before commencing the research, all relevant parties, sponsoring agencies, research participants and the researcher, must agree on the dissemination strategy for research in a way that respects interests of all. The transient nature of cyberspace necessitates that a clear understanding is established as to who would be responsible for maintaining the virtual space where the findings have been published.

Key questions worth considering when using online data analysis methods include the following: What online channels will be used to communicate research outcomes? How will the research outcomes be fed back to the research participants? Who will be advantaged and who will be disadvantaged by the research outcomes? What measures are taken to appropriately communicate the caveats of the study?

The preceding discussion alerts us to a range of ethical considerations in online research which requires careful review and deep reflection from multiple perspectives. Online research remains a complex space with multiple layers of ethical considerations as Kate Oriordan (2010) reminds us: one cannot assume the space of ethics which lies between the practical need to respect ethical protocols and the pursuit of improving life conditions.

SOLUTIONS AND RECOMMENDATIONS

The chapter presents questions that online researchers must critically reflect upon to conduct their research ethically. Critical self-reflection will lead to conscientisation, which in turn, will encourage the ethical pursuit of online research. We agree with Markham's (2007, p. 10) view that "if a researcher is reflexive, he or she will see politics at work throughout the entire research enterprise".

The following solutions and recommendations are offered as broad guidelines for engaging online researchers more consciously in online research so that they will act as socially responsible global citizens who advocate social justice through the medium of their research:

1. *Critical self-reflection should become the norm in all discussions of online research and alternate research methodologies:* Historical and cultural perspectives must be interrogated as an essential part of the dialogue on online research ethics.

2. *Conscientisation and awareness of early career researchers and of learners must occur at the early stages of academic life and must be reinforced through their academic careers:* Undergraduate programs and early career researchers must embed ethical considerations in online research into their learning across disciplines.

3. *Online data gathering should be respectful of cultural norms and should value historical perspectives:* Data gathering must account for what is considered sacred to the research populations and must respond in appropriate ways so that the data gathering process does not violate human rights and does not impact negatively on the environment of the research populations.

4. *Online research analysis should include the cultural and historical perspectives of the communities who were an integral part of the research:* Interpretations of the gathered data, for example, should not be solely biased towards a Western perspective, especially when the research findings are likely to impact upon non-Western populations.

5. *Online research outcomes should be communicated through multiple channels in ways that would benefit the researched populations without bringing harm upon them:* Dissemination of research outcomes must be meaningfully and respectfully negotiated

with the communities where possible so that it can bring about beneficial changes to their quality of life.

These solutions and recommendations emphasize the imperative that is required of online researchers to ensure that the ethical pursuit of online research protects the rights, representations, identities and voices of vulnerable populations and refrains from marginalizing them further.

FUTURE RESEARCH DIRECTIONS

Future research directions in online research require more in-depth studies into the issues emerging in the foregoing discussion. Among a range of suggested topics for further research and investigation are the following:

- Respecting and recognising the overlaps and conflicts between multiple and fluid identities of research participants, such as their virtual, physical, cultural and gendered identities
- Ensuring that cultural boundaries are transgressed with sensitivity
- Acknowledging the rights to privacy of indigenous knowledge
- Creating an equitable virtual environment for all participants
- Identifying strategies in designing a socially just online research environment

CONCLUSION

The preceding discussion defies any prescriptive solutions or recommendations for ethical conduct of online research. It is premised on our belief that an ongoing critical awareness must be sought by all researchers, Once awareness and conscientisation is reached, action must be taken by researchers to ensure that they do not transgress ethical boundaries. Online research can be conducted ethically only by a genuine engagement and honest communication with the research participants. Online researchers must consider not only the groups who are able to participate in their study but must also consider those who do not have access to participate in online research. Principles of respect, trust, honesty and equity are fundamental requirements in online research if researchers want to uphold their professional and personal integrity. The foregoing discussion highlighted a number of critical aspects of online communication that online researchers must carefully think through. Researchers must carefully consider the ethical implications of their research design, implementation, analysis and dissemination from multiple perspectives in order that they subscribe to a high standard of equity. Online research will continue to present new challenges over the coming decade which requires online researchers to critically engage with a range of ethical considerations that are discussed in this chapter.

REFERENCES

American Educational Research Association (AERA). (2000). *Ethical Standards of the American Educational Research Association.* Retrieved June 22, 2010, from https://www.aera.net/AboutAERA/Default.aspx?menu_id=90&id=222

American Educational Research Association (AERA). (2006). *Standards for reporting on empirical social science research in AERA publications.* Retrieved September 1, 2006, from http://www.aera.net/uploadedFiles/Opportunities/StandardsforReportingEmpiricalSocialScience_PDF.pdf

American Educational Research Association (AERA). (2009). Standards for reporting on humanities-oriented research in AERA publications. *Educational Researcher*, *38*(6), 481–486. doi:10.3102/0013189X09341833

Baker, B. (1999). What is voice? Issues of identity and representation in the framing of reviews. *Review of Educational Research, 69*(4), 365–383.

Bruckman, A. (2002). *Ethical guidelines for research online.* Retrieved August 2, 2010, from http://www.cc.gatech.edu/≥ ~asb/ethics

Buchanan, E. A., & Ess, C. M. (2008). Internet research ethics: The field and its critical issues. In Himma, K. E., & Tavani, H. T. (Eds.), *The Handbook of Information and Computer Ethics.* Hoboken, NJ: Wiley Interscience. doi:10.1002/9780470281819.ch11

Buchanan, E. A., & Ess, C. M. (2009). Internet research ethics and the institutional review board: current practices and issues. *SIGCAS Computers and Society, 39*(3), 43–49. doi:10.1145/1713066.1713069

Capurro, R., & Pingel, C. (2002). Ethical issues of online communication research. *Ethics and Information Technology, 4*(3), 189–194. doi:10.1023/A:1021372527024

Capurro, R., & Pingel, C. (n.d.). *Internet research ethics Ethical issues of online communication research.* Retrieved July 22, 2010, from http://www.nyu.edu/projects/nissenbaum/ethics_cap_full.html

Castellano, M. B. (2004). Ethics of Aboriginal Research. *Journal of Aboriginal Health, 1*(1), 98–114.

Creswell, J. W. (2009). *Research Design Qualitative, Quantitative and Mixed method Approaches* (3rd ed.). Thousand Oaks, CA: Sage.

Dabbs, J. M. Jr. (1982). Making things visible. In Van Maanen, J., Dabbs, J. M. Jr, & Faulkner, R. R. (Eds.), *Varieties of qualitative research* (pp. 31–63). Beverly Hills, CA: Sage.

Dillon, L. (2010). Listening for voices of self: Digital journaling among gifted young adolescents. *Qualitative Research Journal, 10*(1), 13–27. doi:10.3316/QRJ1001013

Ess, C., & Association of Internet Researchers (AoIR). (2002). *Ethical decision-making and internet research: Recommendations from the AoIR ethics working committee.* Retrieved June 22, 2010, from http://www.aoir.org/reports/ethics.pdf

Flinders, D. (1992). In search of ethical guidance: Constructing a basis for dialogue. *Qualitative Studies in Education, 52*(2), 101–115. doi:10.1080/0951839920050202

Gaskell, J. (1988). Policy Research and Politics. *The Alberta Journal of Educational Research, 34*(4), 403–417.

Gurumurthy, A. (2004) *Gender and ICTs Overview Report.* Brighton, UK: Bridge Publications. Retrieved from http://www.bridge.ids.ac.uk/reports/CEP-ICTs-OR.pdf

Hall, G. J., Frederick, D., & Johns, M. D. (2004). 'NEED HELP ASAP!!!': A feminist communitarian approach to online research ethics. In Johns, M. D., Chen, S. S., & Hall, G. J. (Eds.), *Online social research: Methods, issues and ethics* (pp. 239–253). New York, NY: Peter Lang.

Hongladarom, S., & Ess, C. (Eds.). (2007). *Information Technology Ethics: Cultural Perspectives.* Hershey, PA: Information Science Reference.

Intellectual Property Law in Australia. (2010). *Introduction.* Retrieved September 10, 2010, from http://www.ipaustralia.gov.au/ip/introduction.shtml

Jonassen, D. H. (2004). *Handbook of research on educational communications and technology* (2nd ed.). Mahwah, NJ: Lawrence Erlbaum Associates.

Kuhn, T. S. (1970). *The structure of scientific revolutions* (2nd ed.). Chicago, IL: University of Chicago Press.

Lerner, D. (1958). *The passing of traditional society: Modernizing the Middle East*. Glencoe, IL: Free Press.

Madge, C. (2007). Developing a geographers' agenda for online research ethics. *Progress in Human Geography, 31*, 654–674. doi:10.1177/0309132507081496

Markham, A. (2007). Ethic as method, method as ethic: A case for reflexivity in qualitative ICT research. *Journal of Information Ethics, 15*(2), 37–54. doi:10.3172/JIE.15.2.37

McLuhan, M. (1962). *The Gutenberg Galaxy: The Making of Typographic Man*. Toronto, ON, Canada: University of Toronto Press.

McMichael, P. (2004). *Development and Social Change a global perspective* (3rd ed.). Thousand Oaks, CA: Pine Forge Press.

Mowlana, H. (1995). The communications paradox. *The Bulletin of the Atomic Scientists, 51*(4), 40–46.

Murthy, D. (2008). Digital Ethnography: An Examination of the Use of New Technologies for Social Research. *Sociology, 42*, 837–855. doi:10.1177/0038038508094565

National Health and Medical Research Council (NHMRC). Australian Research Council (ARC), & Australian Vice-Chancellors' Committee (AVCC). (2007). *National statement on ethical conduct in human research*. Retrieved June 22, 2010, from http://www.nhmrc.gov.au

Oriordan, K. (2010). *Internet research ethics: revisiting the relations between technologies, spaces, texts and people*. Retrieved February 27, 2011, from http://eresearch-ethics.org/position/internet-research-ethics-revisiting-the-relations-between-technologies-spaces-texts-and-people/

Palomba, E. (2006). *ICT technologies and intercultural issues*. Retrieved July 28, 2010, from http://www.formatex.org/micte2006/pdf/82-86.pdf

Pring, R. (2004). *Philosophy of educational research*. London, UK: Continuum.

Rhodes, S. D., Bowie, D. A., & Hergenrather, K. C. (2003). Collecting behavioural data using the World Wide Web: considerations for researchers. *Journal of Epidemiology and Community Health, 57*, 68–73. doi:10.1136/jech.57.1.68

Rogers, E. M. (1962). *Diffusion of innovations*. New York, NY: Free Press.

Rogers, E. M. (1995). *The diffusion of innovations*. New York, NY: Free Press.

Smith, L. T. (1999). *Decolonizing Methodologies: Research and Indigenous Peoples*. Dunedin, New Zealan: University of Otago Press.

Stern, S. (2003). Encountering distressing information in online research: a consideration of legal and ethical responsibilities. *New Media & Society, 5*(2), 249–266. doi:10.1177/1461444803005002006

Story, A. (2002). *Study on intellectual property rights, the Internet, and copyright*. London, UK: Commission on Intellectual Property Rights. Retrieved July 18, 2010, from http://www.iprcommission.org/papers/pdfs/study_papers/sp5_story_study.pdf

Stutchbury, K., & Fox, A. (2009). Ethics in educational research: Introducing a methodological tool for effective ethical analysis. *Cambridge Journal of Education, 39*(4), 489–504. doi:10.1080/03057640903354396

Suri, H. (2008). Ethical Considerations in Synthesising Research: Whose Representations? *Qualitative Research Journal, 8*(1), 62–73. doi:10.3316/QRJ0801062

Whiteman, E. (2007). "Just Chatting": Research Ethics and Cyberspace. *International Journal of Qualitative Methods, 6*(2), 95–105.

ADDITIONAL READING

AERA. (2000). *Ethical Standards of the American Educational Research Association.* Retrieved 2010, June 22, from AERA Web site: https://www.aera.net/AboutAERA/Default.aspx?menu_id=90&id=222

Bruckman, A. (2002). *Ethical guidelines for research online.* Retrieved 2010, August 2, from Web site: http://www.cc.gatech.edu/≥~asb/ethics

Buchanan, E. (2007).Internet Research Ethics Questions and Considerations. Encyclopedia of Information Ethics and Security 2007: 397-402

Buchanan, E. A., & Ess, C. M. (2009). Internet research ethics and the institutional review board: current practices and issues. *SIGCAS Computers and Society, 39*(3), 43–49. doi:10.1145/1713066.1713069

Ess, C., & Ao, I. R. (2002). *Ethical decision-making and internet research: Recommendations from the AoIR ethics workin committee.* Retrieved 2010, June 22, from AoIR Web site: www.aoir.org/reports/ethics.pdf

Hall, G. J., Frederick, D., & Johns, M. D. (2004). 'NEED HELP ASAP!!!': A feminist communitarian approach to online research ethics. In M. D. Johns, S. S. Chen & G. J. Hall (Eds.), *Online social research: Methods, issues and ethics* (pp. 239-253). New York: Peter Lang. Internet Research Ethics Digital Library Retrieved on 27 February 2011 from http://internetresearchethics.org/

Madge, C. (2007). Developing a geographers' agenda for online research ethics. *Progress in Human Geography, 31,* 654–674. doi:10.1177/0309132507081496

Murthy, D. (2008). Digital Ethnography: An Examination of the Use of New Technologies for Social Research. *Sociology, 42,* 837–855. doi:10.1177/0038038508094565

Stutchbury, K., & Fox, A. (2009). Ethics in educational research: Introducing a methodological tool for effective ethical analysis. *Cambridge Journal of Education, 39*(4), 489–504. doi:10.1080/03057640903354396

Suri, H. (2008). Ethical Considerations in Synthesising Research: Whose Representations? *Qualitative Research Journal, 8*(1), 62–73. doi:10.3316/QRJ0801062

Whiteman, E. (2007). "Just Chatting": Research Ethics and Cyberspace. *International Journal of Qualitative Methods, 6*(2), 95–105.

KEY TERMS AND DEFINITIONS

Ethics: Refers to the principles, beliefs and values that espouse fairness, goodness, integrity and honesty.

Intellectual Property: Refers to the original creative ideas and knowledge of an individual emanating from the mind.

Online Research Methods: Refer to methods of designing research, collecting data, analysing data and communicating research outcomes using one or more online technologies which facilitate synchronous or asynchronous communication, presentation or co-construction of information.

Compilation of References

Abrams, D., & Hogg, M. A. (1990). *Social identifications: A social psychology of intergroup relations and group processes*. New York, NY: Routledge.

Adams, J. (1999). *The social implications of hypermobility*. Paris, France: OECD.

Adey, P. (2010). *Mobility*. London, UK: Routledge.

Ali, A. K. (2005). Using the Delphi technique to search for empirical measures of local planning agency power. *Qualitative Report*, *10*(4), 718–744.

Al-Kodmany, K. (2010). Political power, governance and e-Planning. In Silva, C. N. (Ed.), *Handbook of Research on E-Planning: ICTs for Urban Development and Monitoring* (pp. 143–166). Hershey, PA: Information Science Reference. doi:10.4018/978-1-61520-929-3.ch008

Altschuld, J. W., & Thomas, P. M. (1991). Considerations in the application of a modified scree test for Delphi survey data. *Evaluation Review*, *15*(2), 179–188. doi:10.1177/0193841X9101500201

Amabile, T. M. (1985). Motivation and creativity: Effects of motivational orientation on creative writers. *Journal of Personality and Social Psychology*, *48*, 393–399. doi:10.1037/0022-3514.48.2.393

Amabile, T. M. (1996). *Creativity in context*. Boulder, CO: Westview Press.

Amabile, T. M., Hennessey, B., & Grossman, B. S. (1986). Social influences on creativity: The effects of contracted-for reward. *Journal of Personality and Social Psychology*, *50*, 14–23. doi:10.1037/0022-3514.50.1.14

American Association for Public Opinion Research (AAPOR). (2010). AAPOR report on online panels. *Public Opinion Quarterly*, *74*(4), 711–781. doi:10.1093/poq/nfq048

American Educational Research Association (AEEA) & Educational Statisticians(SIG). (2007). Research Synopsis: Statistics teachers' ideas about teaching and learning statistics at university. *Spring Newsletter*, *4*(1), 8.

American Educational Research Association (AERA). (2000). *Ethical Standards of the American Educational Research Association*. Retrieved June 22, 2010, from https://www.aera.net/AboutAERA/Default.aspx?menu_id=90&id=222

American Educational Research Association (AERA). (2006). *Standards for reporting on empirical social science research in AERA publications*. Retrieved September 1, 2006, from http://www.aera.net/uploadedFiles/Opportunities/StandardsforReportingEmpiricalSocialScience_PDF.pdf

Amnesty International. (2009). *The unseen majority: Nairobi's two million slum-dwellers*. London, UK: Author.

Anderson, A. H. (2008). Video-mediated interactions and surveys. In Conrad, F. G., & Schober, M. F. (Eds.), *Envisioning the survey interview of the future* (pp. 95–118). Hoboken, NJ: John Wiley & Sons.

Anderson, D. H., & Schneider, I. E. (1993). Using the Delphi process to identify significant recreation research-based innovations. *Journal of Park and Recreation Administration*, *11*(1), 25–36.

Anderson, J. (2004). Talking whilst walking: a geographical archaeology of knowledge. *Area*, *36*, 254–261. doi:10.1111/j.0004-0894.2004.00222.x

Anglin, G. J., Vaez, H., & Cunningham, K. L. (2004). Visual message design and learning: The role of static and dynamic illustrations. In Jonassen, D. H. (Ed.), *Handbook of Research for Educational Communications and Technology* (2nd ed., pp. 865–916). Mahwah, NJ: Lawrence Erlbaum Associates.

Anson, R. G., Fellers, J. W., Bostrom, R. P., & Chidambaram, L. (1992). Using group support systems to facilitate the research process. In *Proceedings of the 25th Hawaii International Conference on System Sciences* (Vol. 4, pp. 70-79).

Anttiroiko, A.-V. (2012). Urban Planning 2.0. *International Journal of E-Planning Research*, *1*(1), 16-30. doi:10.4018/ijepr.2012010103

Arnould, E. J., & Wallendorf, M. (1994). Market-Oriented Ethnography: Interpretation Building and Marketing Strategy Formulation. *JMR, Journal of Marketing Research*, *31*, 484–504. doi:10.2307/3151878

Astrom, J., & Granberg, M. (2007). Urban planners, wired for change? Understanding elite support for e-participation. *Journal of Information Technology & Politics*, *4*(2), 63–77. doi:10.1080/19331680802076116

Attili, G. (2007). Digital ethnographies in the planning field. *Planning Theory & Practice*, *8*(1), 90–97.

Augé, M. (1992). *Non-lieux: Introduction à une anthropologie de la surmodernité*. Paris, France: Seuil.

Axelrod, D. (1993). Using the conference model for work redesign. *Journal for Quality and Participation*, *16*(7), 58–62.

Ayling, R., & Mewse, A. J. (2009). Evaluating internet interviews with gay men. *Qualitative Health Research*, *19*(4), 566–576. doi:10.1177/1049732309332121

Baan, A., & Maznevski, M. (2008). Training for virtual collaboration: Beyond technology competencies. In Nemiro, J., Beyerlein, M. M., Bradley, L., & Beyerlein, S. (Eds.), *The handbook of high-performance virtual teams: A toolkit for collaborating across boundaries* (pp. 345–365). San Francisco, CA: Jossey-Bass.

Babbie, E. R. (2010). *The Practice of Social Research*. Independence, KY: Cengage Learning.

Bailey, D. (1992). The future search conference as a vehicle for educational change: A shared vision for Will Rogers Middle School, Sacramento, California. *The Journal of Applied Behavioral Science*, *28*(4), 520–534. doi:10.1177/0021886392284005

Baker, B. (1999). What is voice? Issues of identity and representation in the framing of reviews. *Review of Educational Research*, *69*(4), 365–383.

Baker, P. M. A., Moon, N. W., & Bakowski, A. (2007). *Access to wireless technologies for people with disabilities: Issues, opportunities, and policy options – Findings of a Policy Delphi (USDOE Grant: H133E060061 & H133E010804)*. Atlanta, GA: Georgia Institute of Technology, Rehabilitation Engineering Research Center for Wireless Technologies and Center for Advanced Communication Policy.

Baldwin, M. (1995). A future search conference: The future of information services in K-12 schools in Washington State. *Emergency Librarian*, *22*(5), 20–22.

Baltes, B. B., Dickson, M. W., Sherman, M. P., Bauer, C. C., & LaGanke, J. (2002). Computer-mediated communication and group decision making: A meta-analysis. *Organizational Behavior and Human Decision Processes*, *87*, 156–179. doi:10.1006/obhd.2001.2961

Bampton, R., & Cowton, C. (2002). The e-interview. *Forum: Qualitative Social Research*, *3*(2). Retrieved August 25, 2010, from http://www.qualitative-research.net/fqs-texte/2-02/2-02bamptoncowton-e.htm

Banister, P., Burman, E., Parker, I., Taylor, M., & Tindall, C. (1994). *Qualitative Methods in Psychology – A Research Guide*. Maidenhead, UK: Open University Press.

Banks, M. (2001). *Visual methods in social research*. London, UK: Sage.

Bannister, D., & Mair, J. M. M. (1968). *The evaluation of personal constructs*. London, UK: Academy Press.

Barker, J., & Weller, S. (2003). Is it fun?' Developing children centred research methods. *International Journal of Sociology*, *23*(1), 33–58.

Baruah, J., & Paulus, P. B. (2008). Effects of training on idea-generation in groups. *Small Group Research*, *39*, 523–541. doi:10.1177/1046496408320049

Baruch, Y. (1999). Response rate in academic studies--a comparative analysis. *Human Relations, 52*(4), 421–438. doi:10.1177/001872679905200401

Bassett, E. H., & O'Riordan, K. (2002). Ethics of Internet research: Contesting the human subjects research model. *Ethics and Information Technology, 4*, 233–247. doi:10.1023/A:1021319125207

Bat-Chava, Y. (1993). Antecedents of self-esteem in deaf people: A meta-analytic review. *Rehabilitation Psychology, 38*(4), 221–234. doi:10.1037/h0080303

Bat-Chava, Y. (1994). Group identification and self-esteem of deaf adults. *Personality and Social Psychology Bulletin, 20*(5), 494–502. doi:10.1177/0146167294205006

Bat-Chava, Y. (2000). Diversity of deaf identities. *American Annals of the Deaf, 145*(5), 420–428.

Bateson, G., & Mead, M. (1942). *Balinese Character. A Photographic Analysis*. New York, NY: New York Academy of Sciences.

Battles, H. (2010). Exploring ethical and methodological issues in Internet-based research with adolescents. *International Journal of Qualitative Methods, 9*(1), 27–39.

Battles, H. T. (2010). Exploring Ethical and Methodological Issues in Internet-Based Research with Adolescents. *International Journal of Qualitative Methods, 9*(1), 27–39.

Beal, D. J., Cohen, R. R., Burke, M. J., & McLendon, C. L. (2003). Cohesion and performance in groups: A meta-analytic clarification of construct relations. *The Journal of Applied Psychology, 88*(6), 989–1004. doi:10.1037/0021-9010.88.6.989

Bech-Larsen, T., & Nielsen, N. A. (1999). A comparison of five elicitation techniques for elicitation of attributes of low involvement. *Journal of Economic Psychology, 20*(3), 315–341. doi:10.1016/S0167-4870(99)00011-2

Bechtel, R. B. (1967). *Human movement and architecture*. Washington University.

Becker, H. S. (1974). Photography and Sociology. *Studies in the anthropology of visual communication* 1974/ 1, 3-26.

Belk, R. W., & Kozinets, R. V. (2005). Videography in marketing and consumer research. *Qualitative Market Research: An International Journal, 8*(2), 128–141. doi:10.1108/13522750510592418

Belk, R. W., & Kozinets, R. V. (2007). Camcorder society: Quality videography in consumer and marketing research. In Belk, R. W. (Ed.), *Handbook of qualitative research methods in marketing* (pp. 335–344). Cheltenham, UK: Edward Elgar.

Bell, M. W., Castronova, E., & Wagner, G. G. (2009). *Surveying the virtual world: A large scale survey in second life using the Virtual Data Collection Interface (VDCI)*. Berlin, Germany: German Institute for Economic Research (DIW Berlin)

Bell, M. W., Castronova, E., & Wagner, G. G. (in press). Virtual Assisted Self Interviewing (VASI): An expansion of survey data collection methods to virtual worlds by means of VDCI. *Journal of Virtual Worlds Research*.

Bennison, D., Warnaby, G., & Medway, D. (2007). The role of quarters in large city centres: a Mancunian case study. *International Journal of Retail & Distribution Management, 35*(8), 626–638. doi:10.1108/09590550710758612

Berger, J. (1972). *Ways of seeing*. London, UK: British Broadcasting Corporation, Penguin Press.

Berger, M. (2006). Computer assisted clinical assessment. *Child and Adolescent Mental Health, 11*(2), 64–75. doi:10.1111/j.1475-3588.2006.00394.x

Bethell, C., Fiorillo, J., Lansky, D., Hendryx, M., & Knickman, J. (2004). Online consumer surveys as a methodology for assessing the quality of the United States health care system. *Journal of Medical Internet Research, 6*(1), e2. doi:10.2196/jmir.6.1.e2

Bierlaire, M., Antonini, G., & Weber, M. (2003). *Behavioral dynamics for pedestrians*. Retrieved from http://infoscience.epfl.ch/record/86990

Bierlaire, M., & Robin, T. (2009). Pedestrian Choices. In Timmermans, H. (Ed.), *Pedestrian Behaviour: Models, Data Collection and Applications* (pp. 1–26). Bradford, UK: Emerald.

Birnbaum, M. H. (2004a). Methodological and ethical issues in conducting social psychology research via the Internet. In Sansone, C., Morf, C. C., & Panter, A. T. (Eds.), *Handbook of Methods in Social Psychology* (pp. 359–382). Thousand Oaks, CA: Sage.

Birnbaum, M. H. (2004b). Human research and data collection via the Internet. *Annual Review of Psychology, 55,* 803–832. doi:10.1146/annurev.psych.55.090902.141601

Bishop, I. (2012). On-line approaches to data delivery and visualisation in landscape planning and management. *International Journal of E-Planning Research, 1*(1), 31–41. doi: 10.4018/ijepr.2012010104

Bissell, D. (2010). Narrating Mobile Methodologies: Active and Passive Empiricisms. In Fincham, B., McGuinness, M., & Murray, L. (Eds.), *Mobile Methodologies* (pp. 53–68). Basingstoke, UK: Palgrave Macmillan.

Blanke, J. M. (2004). Copyright law in the digital age. In Brennan, L. L., & Johnson, V. E. (Eds.), *Social, Ethical and Policy Implications of Information Technology* (pp. 223–233). Hershey, PA: Information Science Publishing. doi:10.4018/978-1-59140-168-1.ch013

Blivice, S. (1974). *Pedestrian Route Choice: A Study of Walking in Munich.* Ann Arbor, MI: University of Michigan.

Bohannon, J. (2010). Game-miners grapple with massive data. *Science, 330*(6000), 30–31. doi:10.1126/science.330.6000.30-a

Bohnsack, R. (2007). *Rekonstruktive Sozialforschung, Einführung in qualitative Methoden.* Opladen: Budrich UTB.

Bohte, W., Maat, K., & Quak, W. (2008). A Method for Deriving Trip Destinations and Modes for GPS-based Travel Surveys. In Schaick, J. V., & Spek, S. V. D. (Eds.), *Urbanism on Track* (pp. 129–145). Amsterdam, The Netherlands: IOS Press.

Borgers, A., Joh, C., Kemperman, A., Kurose, S., Saarloos, D., Zhang, J., et al. (2008). *Alternative Ways of Measuring Activities and Movement Patterns of Transients in Urban Areas: International Experiences.* Paper presented at the 8th International Conference on Survey in Transport, Annecy, France.

Borgers, N., & Hox, J. (2001). Item nonresponse in questionnaire research with children. *Journal of Official Statistics, 17*(2), 321–335.

Borkan, B. (2010). The mode effect in mixed-mode surveys: Mail and Web surveys. *Social Science Computer Review, 28*(3), 371–380. doi:10.1177/0894439309350698

Borzemski, L. (2010). The Experimental Design for Data Mining to Discover Web Performance Issues in a Wide Area Network. *Cybernetics and Systems: An International Journal, 41,* 31–45. doi:10.1080/01969720903408763

Botman, S. L., & Thornberry, O. T. (1992). *Survey Design Features Correlates of Nonresponse,* pp. 309-314 in Proceedings of the Section on Survey Research Methods. Alexandria, VA: American Statistical Association.

Botschen, G., & Hemetsberger, A. (1998). Diagnosing means-end structures to determine the degree of potential marketing program standardization. *Journal of Business Research, 42*(2), 151–159. doi:10.1016/S0148-2963(97)00116-1

Botschen, G., & Thelen, E. M. (1998). Hard versus soft laddering: Implications for appropriate use. In Balderjahn, I., Mennicken, C., & Vernette, E. (Eds.), *New developments and approaches in consumer behaviour research* (pp. 321–339). Stuttgart, Germany: Schäffer-Poeschel.

Botschen, G., Thelen, E. M., & Pieters, R. (1999). Using means-end structures for benefit segmentation. *European Journal of Marketing, 33*(1-2), 38–58. doi:10.1108/EUM0000000004491

Bouchard, T. J. (1976). Field research methods: Interviewing, questionnaires, participant observation, systematic observation, unobtrusive measures. In Dunette, M. D. (Ed.), *Handbook of industrial and organizational psychology* (pp. 363–413). Chicago, IL: Rand McNally.

Bouchard, T. J., & Hare, M. (1970). Size, performance, and potential in brainstorming groups. *The Journal of Applied Psychology, 54,* 51–55. doi:10.1037/h0028621

Bourhis, A., Dubé, L., & Jacob, R. (2005). The success of virtual communities of practice: The leadership factor. *Electronic Journal of Knowledge Management, 3,* 23–34.

Bowers, C. A., Pharmer, J. A., & Salas, E. (2000). When member homogeneity is needed in work teams: A meta-analysis. *Small Group Research, 31*, 305–327. doi:10.1177/104649640003100303

Bowker, N., & Tuffin, K. (2004). Using the online medium for discursive research about people with disabilities. *Social Science Computer Review, 22*(2), 228–241. doi:10.1177/0894439303262561

Bremner, B. (2007). *Facilitating online learning adoption.* Unpublished doctoral dissertation, University of Calgary, Calgary, AB, Canada. Retrieved from http://ucalgary.summon.serialssolutions.com/search?s.q=bremner+%2B+dissertations

Briassoulis, H. (2010). Online petitions: new tools of secondary analysis? *Qualitative Research, 10*(6), 715–727. doi:10.1177/1468794110380530

Brick, J. M., Waksberg, J., & Keeter, S. (1996). Using data on interruptions in telephone service as coverage adjustments. *Survey Methodology, 22*(2), 185–197.

Bricout, J., & Baker, P. (2010). Deploying information and communication technologies to enhance participation in local governance for citizens with disabilities. *International Journal of Information Communication Technologies and Human Development, 2*(2), 34–51. doi:10.4018/jicthd.2010040103

British Psychological Society (BPS). (2007). *Report of the Working Party on Conducting Research on the Internet: Guidelines for ethical practice in psychological research online,* Retrieved November 2, 2010, from http://www.bps.org.uk/document-download-area/document-download$.cfm?file_uuid=2B3429B3-1143-DFD0-7E5A-4BE3FDD763CC&ext=pdf

British Sociology Association (BSA). (2006). *Statement of ethical practice for the British sociological association – visual sociology group,* Retrieved September 15, 2010, http://www.visualsociology.org.uk/about/ethical_statement.php

Bronner, F., & Kuijlen, T. (2007). The live or digital interviewer. A comparison between CASI, CAPI, CATI with respect to differences in response behaviour. *International Journal of Market Research, 49*(2), 167–190.

Brooks, K. W. (1979). Delphi technique: Expanding application. *North Central Association Quarterly, 54*(3), 377–385.

Brown, K., & Spinney, J. (2010). Catching a glimpse: the value of video in evoking, understanding and representing the practice of cycling. In Fincham, B., McGuinness, M., & Murray, L. (Eds.), *Mobile Methodologies* (pp. 130–151). Basingstoke, UK: Palgrave Macmillan.

Brown, N. R., & Sinclair, R. C. (1999). Estimating number of lifetime sexual partners: Men and women do it differently. *Journal of Sex Research, 36*(3), 292–297. doi:10.1080/00224499909551999

Brown, S. (1992). *Retail location: a micro-scale perspective.* Aldershot, UK: Avebury.

Brown, V. R., & Paulus, P. B. (2002). Making group brainstorming more effective: Recommendations from an associative memory perspective. *Current Directions in Psychological Science, 11*(6), 208–212. doi:10.1111/1467-8721.00202

Brown, V., Tumeo, M., Larey, T. S., & Paulus, P. B. (1998). Modeling cognitive interactions during group brainstorming. *Small Group Research, 29*, 495–526. doi:10.1177/1046496498294005

Bruckman, A. (2002). *Ethical guidelines for research online.* Retrieved August 2, 2010, from http://www.cc.gatech.edu/≥ ~asb/ethics

Bryman, A. (2008). *Social research methods* (3rd ed.). Oxford, UK: Oxford University Press.

Buchanan, E. (Ed.). (2004). *Readings in Virtual Research Ethics: Issues and controversies.* Hershey, PA: Information Science Publishing.

Buchanan, E. A., & Ess, C. M. (2009). Internet research ethics and the institutional review board: current practices and issues. *SIGCAS Computers and Society, 39*(3), 43–49. doi:10.1145/1713066.1713069

Buchwald, D., Schantz-Laursen, B., & Delmar, C. (2009). Video Diary Data Collection in Research with Children: An Alternative Method. *International Journal of Qualitative Methods, 8*(1), 12–20.

Burgess, J., & Green, J. (2009). *YouTube. Online video and participatory culture.* Cambridge, Malden, MA: Polity.

Burgess, R. G. (Ed.). (1995). *Computing and Qualitative Research*. Greenwich, CT: JAI Press.

Burke, J. G., O'Campo, P., Peak, G. L., Gielen, A. C., McDonnell, K. A., & Trochim, W. M. K. (2005). An introduction to concept mapping as a participatory public health research method. *Qualitative Health Research*, *15*(10), 1392–1410. doi:10.1177/1049732305278876

Büscher, M. Urry, J., & Witchger, K. (2010). *Mobile methods*. London, UK: Routledge.

Büscher, M. (2006). Vision in motion. *Environment & Planning A*, *38*, 281–299. doi:10.1068/a37277

Cabana, S. (1995). Motorola: Strategic planning and the search conference. *Journal for Quality and Participation*, *18*(4), 22–31.

Calabrese, F., & Ratti, C. (2006). Real time Rome. *Networks and Communication Studies*, *20*(3-4), 247–258.

Camacho, L. M., & Paulus, P. B. (1995). The role of social anxiousness in group brainstorming. *Journal of Personality and Social Psychology*, *68*, 1071–1080. doi:10.1037/0022-3514.68.6.1071

Camarada, D. (2010). Beyond citizen participation in planning: multi-agent systems for complex decision-making. In Silva, C. N. (Ed.), *Handbook of Research on E-Planning: ICTs for Urban Development and Monitoring* (pp. 404–419). Hershey, PA: Information Science Reference. doi:10.4018/978-1-61520-929-3.ch010

Cameron, A., Rosen, R. C., & Swindle, R. W. (2005). Sexual and relationship characteristics among an Internet-based sample of U.S. men with and without erectile dysfunction. *Journal of Sex & Marital Therapy*, *31*, 229–242. doi:10.1080/00926230590513447

Cantrell, M. A., & Lupinacci, P. (2007). Methodological issues in online data collection. *Journal of Advanced Nursing*, *60*(5), 544–549. doi:10.1111/j.1365-2648.2007.04448.x

Capurro, R., & Pingel, C. (n.d.). *Internet research ethics Ethical issues of online communication research*. Retrieved July 22, 2010, from http://www.nyu.edu/projects/nissenbaum/ethics_cap_full.html

Capurro, R., & Pingel, C. (2002). Ethical issues of online communication research. *Ethics and Information Technology*, *4*, 189–194. doi:10.1023/A:1021372527024

Carvin, A. (2005). *Tim Berners-Lee: Weaving a semantic web*. Retrieved from http:www.digitaldivide.net/articles/view.php?ArticleID=20

Casolara, W. M., Haynes, C. E., & McPheeters, J. (1999). Involving the community in college planning: The future search conference. *Community College Journal of Research and Practice*, *23*(2), 193–205. doi:10.1080/106689299265016

Cassell, J., & Miller, P. (2008). Is it self-administration if the computer gives you encouraging looks? In Conrad, F. G., & Schober, M. F. (Eds.), *Envisioning the survey interview of the future* (pp. 161–178). Hoboken, NJ: John Wiley & Sons. doi:10.1002/9780470183373.ch8

Castellano, M. B. (2004). Ethics of Aboriginal Research. *Journal of Aboriginal Health*, *1*(1), 98–114.

Castells, M. (1996). *The rise of the network society*. Cambridge, MA: Blackwell.

Castronova, E., & Falk, M. (2011). Virtual worlds as petri dishes for the social and behavioral sciences. In German Data Forum (Ed.), *Building on Progress – Expanding the Research Infrastructure for the Social, Economic and Behavioral Sciences* (pp. 595-606). Opladen, Germany: Budrich UniPress.

Castronova, E. (2006). On the research value of large games: Natural experiments in Norrath and Camelot. *Games and Culture*, *1*(2), 163–186. doi:10.1177/1555412006286686

Castronova, E., Bell, M. W., Cornell, R., Cummings, J. J., Falk, M., & Ross, T. (2009). Synthetic Worlds as Experimental Instruments. In Perron, B., & Wolf, M. J. P. (Eds.), *The Video Game Theory Reader 2* (pp. 272–294). New York, NY: Routledge.

Castronova, E., Cummings, J., Emigh, W., Fatten, M., Mishler, N., & Ross, T. (2009). Case Study: The economics of Arden. *Critical Studies in Media Communication*, *26*(2), 165–179. doi:10.1080/15295030902860286

Castronova, E., & Falk, M. (2009). Virtual worlds. *Games and Culture*, *4*(4), 396–407. doi:10.1177/1555412009343574

Castronova, E., & Wagner, G. G. (in press). Virtual Life Satisfaction. *Kyklos*.

Castronova, E., Williams, D., Shen, C., Ratan, R., Xiong, L., & Huang, Y. (2009). As real as real? Macroeconomic behavior in a large-scale virtual world. *New Media & Society*, *11*(5), 685–707. doi:10.1177/1461444809105346

Catania, J. A., Binson, D., Canchola, J., Pollack, L. M., Hauck, W., & Coates, T. J. (1996). Effects of interviewer gender, interviewer choice, and item wording on responses to questions concerning sexual behavior. *Public Opinion Quarterly*, *60*(3), 345–375. doi:10.1086/297758

Chan, D., & Schmitt, N. (1997). Video-based versus paper-and-pencil method of assessment in situational judgment tests: subgroup differences in test performance and face validity perceptions. *The Journal of Applied Psychology*, *82*(1), 143–159. doi:10.1037/0021-9010.82.1.143

Chang, D. (2002). Spatial Choice and Preference in Multilevel Movement Networks. *Environment and Behavior*, *34*(5), 582–615. doi:10.1177/0013916502034005002

Chang, L., & Krosnick, J. A. (2009). National surveys via RDD telephone interviewing versus the Internet. Comparing sample representativeness and response quality. *Public Opinion Quarterly*, *73*(4), 641–678. doi:10.1093/poq/nfp075

Chan, K. K., & Misra, S. (1990). Characteristics of the opinion leader: A new dimension. *Journal of Advertising*, *19*(3), 53–60.

Charlesworth, A. (2003b). *Legal issues relating to the archiving of Internet resources in the UK, EU, US and Australia. Version 1.0 - 25*. London, UK: Wellcome Trust. Retrieved November 2, 2010, from http://library.wellcome.ac.uk/assets/WTL039230.pdf

Charlesworth, A. (2009). *Digital Lives >> Legal & Ethical Issues Version 1.0 - 18*. London, UK: British Library. Retrieved November 2, 2010, from http://britishlibrary.typepad.co.uk/files/digital-lives-legal-ethical.pdf

Charlesworth, A. (2003a). Information Privacy Law in the European Union: E Pluribus Unum or Ex Uno Plures. *Hastings Law Review*, *54*, 931–969.

Charlesworth, A. (2008). Understanding and Managing Legal Issues in Internet Research. In Fielding, N., Lee, R., & Blank, G. (Eds.), *The SAGE Handbook of Online Research Methods* (pp. 42–57). London, UK: Sage.

Chen, P., & Hinton, S. M. (1999). Realtime interviewing using the World Wide Web. *Sociological Research Online*, *4*(3). doi:10.5153/sro.308

Cheung, G.-Q. (2007). *Mixed-Mode Sample Management System: An Early Glance*. Presented at International Blaise Users' Conference, Annapolis, MD.

Childs, E. (2004). *Impact of online PD on teaching practice*. Unpublished doctoral dissertation, University of Calgary, Calgary, AB, Canada.

Chou, C. (2002). Developing the e-Delphi system: A web-based forecasting tool for educational research. *British Journal of Educational Technology*, *33*(2), 233–236. doi:10.1111/1467-8535.00257

Christofides, E., Islam, T., & Desmarais, S. (2009). Gender stereotyping over instant messenger: The effects of gender and context. *Computers in Human Behavior*, *25*(4), 897–901. doi:10.1016/j.chb.2009.03.004

Chun, S. A., & Artigas, F. (2012). Sensors and Crowdsourcing for Environmental Awareness and Emergency Planning. *International Journal of E-Planning Research*, *1*(1), 56-74. doi: 10.4018/ijepr.2012010106

Church, A., Frost, M., & Sullivan, K. (2000). Transport and social exclusion in London. *Transport Policy*, *7*, 195–205. doi:10.1016/S0967-070X(00)00024-X

Claeys, C., Swinnen, A., & Abeele, P. V. (1995). Consumers' means-end chains for "think" and "feel" products. *International Journal of Research in Marketing*, *12*(3), 193–208. doi:10.1016/0167-8116(95)00021-S

Clarke, N. (2010). Writing mobility: Australia's working holiday programme. In Fincham, B., McGuinness, M., & Murray, L. (Eds.), *Mobile Methodologies* (pp. 118–129). Basingstoke, UK: Palgrave Macmillan.

Clarke, R. (1988). Information technology and dataveillance. *Communications of the ACM*, *31*(5), 512. doi:10.1145/42411.42413

Cobanoglu, C., & Cobanoglu, N. (2003). The effect of incentives in web surveys: application and ethical considerations. *International Journal of Market Research*, *45*(4), 475–488.

Cobanoglu, C., Warde, B., & Moreo, P. J. (2001). A comparison of mail, fax, and Web-based survey methods. *International Journal of Market Research*, *43*, 441–452.

Cochran, W. G. (1968). The effectiveness of adjustment by subclassification in removing bias in observational studies. *Biometrics*, *24*, 295–313. doi:10.2307/2528036

Cohen, D. J., Leviton, L. C., Isaacson, N., Tallia, A. F., & Crabtree, B. F. (2006). Online Diaries for Qualitative Evaluation. *The American Journal of Evaluation*, *27*(2), 163–184. doi:10.1177/1098214006288448

Cohen, S. G., & Gibson, C. B. (2003). In the beginning: Introduction and framework. In Gibson, C. B., & Cohen, S. G. (Eds.), *Virtual teams that work: Creating conditions for virtual team effectiveness* (pp. 1–14). San Francisco, CA: Jossey-Bass.

Collen, H., & Hoekstra, J. (2001). Values as determinants of preferences for housing attributes. *Journal of Housing and the Built Environment*, *16*(3-4), 285–306. doi:10.1023/A:1012587323814

Collier, J. Jr, & Collier, M. (1991). *Visual Anthropology: Photography as a Research Method*. Albuquerque, NM: University of New Mexico Press.

Colton, S., & Hatcher, T. (2004). *The web-based Delphi research technique as a method for content validation in HRD and adult education research*. Retrieved June 21, 2010, from http://www.mpc.edu/FacultyStaff/Sharon-Colton/Documents/Establishing%20the%20Delphi%20Technique.pdf

Comley, P. (2002). Online survey techniques: Current issues and future trends. *Interactive Marketing*, *4*(2), 156–169. doi:10.1057/palgrave.im.4340174

Connaughton, S. L., & Shuffler, M. (2007). Multinational and multicultural distributed teams: A review and future agenda. *Small Group Research*, *38*(3), 387–412. doi:10.1177/1046496407301970

Connolly, T., Jessup, L. M., & Valacich, J. S. (1990). Effects of anonymity and evaluative tone on idea generation in computer-mediated groups. *Management Science*, *36*(6), 689–703. doi:10.1287/mnsc.36.6.689

Connolly, T., Routhieaux, R. L., & Schneider, S. K. (1993). On the effectiveness of group brainstorming: Test of one underlying cognitive mechanism. *Small Group Research*, *24*(4), 490–503. doi:10.1177/1046496493244004

Converse, P. D., Wolfe, E. W., Huang, X., & Oswald, F. L. (2008). Response rates for mixed-mode surveys using mail and e-mail/Web. *The American Journal of Evaluation*, *29*(1), 99–107. doi:10.1177/1098214007313228

Cooke, N., Gorman, J. C., Pedersen, H., & Bell, B. (2007). Distributed mission environments: Effects of geographic distribution on team cognition, process, and performance. In Fiore, S. M., & Salas, E. (Eds.), *Toward a Science of Distributed Learning* (pp. 147–167). Washington, DC: American Psychological Association. doi:10.1037/11582-007

Cooper, W. H., Gallupe, R. B., Pollard, S., & Cadsby, J. (1998). Some liberating effects of anonymous electronic brainstorming. *Small Group Research*, *29*, 147–178. doi:10.1177/1046496498292001

Corbetta, P. P. (2003). *Social Research: Theory, Methods and Techniques*. Thousand Oaks, CA: Sage.

Corbett, J., & Mann, R. (2010). Tlowitsis Re-Imagined: The Use of Digital Media to Build Nation and Overcome Disconnection in a Displaced Aboriginal. *International Journal of Information Communication Technologies and Human Development*, *2*(3), 33–54. doi:10.4018/jicthd.2010070103

Cordery, J. L., & Soo, C. (2008). Overcoming impediments to virtual team effectiveness. *Human Factors and Ergonomics in Manufacturing*, *18*(5), 487–500. doi:10.1002/hfm.20119

Cornes, A., Rohan, M. J., Napier, J., & Rey, J. M. (2006). Reading the signs: Impact of signed versus written questionnaires on the prevalence of psychopathology among deaf adolescents. *The Australian and New Zealand Journal of Psychiatry*, *40*(8), 665–673.

Coskun, H., Paulus, P. B., Brown, V., & Sherwood, J. J. (2000). Cognitive stimulation and problem presentation in idea-generating groups. *Group Dynamics*, *4*(4), 307–329. doi:10.1037/1089-2699.4.4.307

Costigan, P., & Thomson, K. (1992). 'Issues in the Design of CAPI Questionnaires for Complex Surveys' in Westlake et al (eds). *Survey and Statistical Compu*ting, pp.147-156, London: North Holland.

Council of European Social Science Data Archives (CESSDA). (2010). *Research Ethics.* Retrieved March 27, 2011, from http://www.cessda.org/sharing/rights/4/index.html

Couper, M. P. (1998). *Measuring Survey Quality in a CASIC Environment*. Presented at the Survey Research Methods Section of the American Statistical Association.

Couper, M. P., Tourangeau, R., & Steiger, D. M. (2001, March 31-April 5). Social presence in web surveys. In *Proceedings of the Conference on Human Factors in Computing Systems,* Seattle, WA (pp. 412-415).

Couper, M. P. (2000). Web surveys: A review of issues and approaches. *Public Opinion Quarterly*, *64*, 464–494. doi:10.1086/318641

Couper, M. P. (2005). Technology trends in survey data collection. *Social Science Computer Review*, *23*(4), 486–501. doi:10.1177/0894439305278972

Couper, M. P. (2007). Issues of representation in eHealth research (with a focus on Web surveys). *American Journal of Preventive Medicine*, *32*(5S), S83–S89. doi:10.1016/j.amepre.2007.01.017

Couper, M. P. (2008). Technology and the survey interview/questionnaire. In Conrad, F. G., & Schober, M. F. (Eds.), *Envisioning the survey interview of the future* (pp. 58–76). Hoboken, NJ: John Wiley & Sons.

Couper, M. P., Baker, R. P., Bethlehem, J., Clark, C. Z. F., Martin, J., Nichols, W. L., & O'Reilly, J. M. (Eds.). (1998). *Computer Assisted Survey Information Collection*. New York: John Wiley.

Couper, M. P., Kapteyn, A., Schonlau, M., & Winter, J. (2007). Noncoverage and nonresponse in an Internet survey. *Social Science Research*, *36*, 131–148. doi:10.1016/j.ssresearch.2005.10.002

Couper, M. P., & Miller, P. V. (2008). Web survey methods: Introduction. *Public Opinion Quarterly*, *72*(5), 831–835. doi:10.1093/poq/nfn066

Couper, M. P., Singer, E., & Tourangeau, R. (2003). Understanding the effects of Audio-CASI on self-reports of sensitive behavior. *Public Opinion Quarterly*, *67*(3), 385–395. doi:10.1086/376948

Couper, M. P., Tourangeau, R., & Marvin, T. (2009). Taking the audio out of Audio-CASI. *Public Opinion Quarterly*, *73*(2), 281–303. doi:10.1093/poq/nfp025

Cravens, D. W., Woodruff, R. B., & Harper, J. F. (1976). *Urban public transportation goalsetting: A research approach*. Paper presented at the 54th Annual Meeting of the Transportation Research Board, Washington, DC.

Creative Commons. (n.d.). *About CC0 — "No Rights Reserved"*. Retrieved November 2, 2010, from http://creativecommons.org/about/cc0

Cresswell, T. (2006). *On the move*. New York, NY: Routledge.

Creswell, J. W. (2009). *Research Design Qualitative, Quantitative and Mixed method Approaches* (3rd ed.). Thousand Oaks, CA: Sage.

Crichton, S. (2010). Use of Digital Data. In Mills, A., Durepos, G., & Wiebe, E. (Eds.), *Encyclopedia of Case Study Research* (pp. 950–954). Thousand Oaks, CA: Sage Reference.

Crichton, S., & Childs, E. (2005). Clipping and Coding Audio Files: A Research Method to Enable Participant Voice. *International Journal of Qualitative Methods*, *4*(3). http://www.ualberta.ca/~ijqm/backissues/4_3/pdf/crichton.pdf

Crichton, S., & Kinash, S. (2003). Virtual ethnography: Interactive interviewing online as method. *Canadian Journal of Learning and Technology*, *29*(2), 101–115.

Crombie, A. (1985). The nature and types of search conferences. *International Journal of Lifelong Learning*, *4*(1), 3–33.

Cromie, J., & Ewing, M. (2009). The rejection of brand hegemony. *Journal of Business Research*, *62*(2), 218–230. doi:10.1016/j.jbusres.2008.01.029

Cummings, J. N., & Kiesler, S. (2007). Coordination costs and project outcomes in multi-university collaborations. *Research Policy*, *36*(10), 1620–1634. doi:10.1016/j.respol.2007.09.001

Cunliffe, S. (2002). Forecasting risks in the tourism industry using the Delphi technique. *Tourism*, *50*(1), 31–41.

Custer, R. L., Scarcella, J. A., & Stewart, B. R. (1999). The modified Delphi technique: A rotational modification. *Journal of Vocational and Technical Education*, *15*(2), 1–10.

Cyphert, F. R., & Gant, W. L. (1971). The Delphi technique: A case study. *Phi Delta Kappan*, *52*, 272–273.

Czajka, J. L., Hirabayashi, S. M., Little, R. J. A., & Rubin, D. B. (1992). Projecting from advance data using propensity modeling: An application to income and tax statistics. *Journal of Business & Economic Statistics*, *10*(2), 117–132. doi:10.2307/1391671

D'Agostino, R. B. Jr. (1998). Propensity score methods for bias reduction for the comparison of a treatment to a non-randomized control group. *Statistics in Medicine*, *17*, 2265–2281. doi:10.1002/(SICI)1097-0258(19981015)17:19<2265::AID-SIM918>3.0.CO;2-B

Dabbs, J. M. Jr. (1982). Making things visible. In Van Maanen, J., Dabbs, J. M. Jr, & Faulkner, R. R. (Eds.), *Varieties of qualitative research* (pp. 31–63). Beverly Hills, CA: Sage.

Daft, R. L., & Lengel, R. H. (1986). Organizational information requirements, media richness and structural design. *Management Science*, *32*(5), 554–571. doi:10.1287/mnsc.32.5.554

Dajani, J. S., Sincoff, M. Z., & Talley, W. K. (1979). Stability and agreement criteria for the termination of Delphi studies. *Technological Forecasting and Social Change*, *13*, 83–90. doi:10.1016/0040-1625(79)90007-6

Dalkey, N. C. (1972). The Delphi method: An experimental study of group opinion. In N. C. Dalkey, D. L. Rourke, R. Lewis, & D. Snyder (Eds.). *Studies in the quality of life: Delphi and decision-making* (pp. 13-54). Lexington, MA: Lexington.

Dalkey, N. C. (1969). An experimental study of group opinion. *Futures*, *1*(5), 408–426. doi:10.1016/S0016-3287(69)80025-X

Dalkey, N. C., & Helmer, O. (1963). An experimental application of the Delphi method to the use of experts. *Management Science*, *9*(3), 458–467. doi:10.1287/mnsc.9.3.458

Dant, T. (2004). Recording the 'habitus. In Pole, C. (Ed.), *Seeing is believing? Approaches to visual research* (pp. 41–60). Oxford, UK: Emerald. doi:10.1016/S1042-3192(04)07004-1

Darbyshire, P., MacDougall, C., & Schiller, W. (2005). Multiple methods in qualitative research with children: more insight or just more? *Qualitative Research*, *5*, 417–436. doi:10.1177/1468794105056921

Daston, L., & Galison, P. (2007). *Objektivität*. Frankfurt, Germany: Suhrkamp.

Davis, M. (2002). *Planet of slums*. London, UK: Verso.

De Certeau, M. (1984). *The practice of everyday life*. Berkeley, CA: University of California Press.

De Dreu, C. K. W., & Weingart, L. R. (2003). Task versus relationship conflict, team performance, and team member satisfaction: A meta-analysis. *The Journal of Applied Psychology*, *88*(4), 741–749. doi:10.1037/0021-9010.88.4.741

De Leeuw, E. (2002). The effect of computer-assisted interviewing on data quality: A review of the evidence. In J. Blasius, J. Hox, E. de Leeuw, & P. Schmidt (Eds.), *Social science methodology in the new millennium*. Opladen, Germany: Leske + Budrich.

De Leeuw, E., Hox, J., Kef, S., & Van Hattum, M. (1997). *Overcoming the problems of special interviews on sensitive topics: Computer assisted self-interviewing tailored for young children and adolescents*. Sequim, WA: Sawtooth Software Conference Proceedings.

De Leeuw, E. (2005). To mix or not to mix data collection modes in surveys. *Journal of Official Statistics*, *21*(2), 233–255.

de Leeuw, E., & de Heer, W. (2002). Trends in Household Survey Nonresponse: A Longitudinal and International Comparison. In Groves, R. M., Dillman, D. A., Eltinge, J. L., & Little, R. J. A. (Eds.), *Survey Nonresponse* (pp. 41–54). New York: Wiley.

De Leeuw, E., Hox, J., & Kef, S. (2003). Computer-assisted self-interviewing tailored for special populations and topics. *Field Methods*, *15*(3), 223–251. doi:10.1177/1525822X03254714

De Leeuw, E., Hox, J., & Snijkers, G. (1995). The effect of computer-assisted interviewing on data quality: A review. *Journal of the Market Research Society. Market Research Society*, *37*(4), 325–344.

de Loe, R. C. (1995). Exploring complex policy questions using the policy Delphi: A multi-round, interactive survey method. *Applied Geography (Sevenoaks, England)*, *15*(1), 53–68. doi:10.1016/0143-6228(95)91062-3

De Vreede, G.-J., Briggs, R. O., van Duin, R., & Enserink, B. (2000). Athletics in electronic brainstorming: Asynchronous electronic brainstorming in very large groups. In *Proceedings of the 33rd Hawaii International Conference on System Sciences.*

De Vreede, G.-J., Briggs, R. O., & Reiter-Palmon, R. (2010). Exploring asynchronous brainstorming in large groups: A field comparison of serial and parallel subgroups. *Human Factors*, *52*(2), 189–202. doi:10.1177/0018720809354748

Deeter-Schmelz, D. R., Goebel, D. J., & Kennedy, K. N. (2008). What are the characteristics of an effective sales manager? An exploratory study comparing salesperson and sales manager perspectives. *Journal of Personal Selling & Sales Management*, *28*(1), 7–20. doi:10.2753/PSS0885-3134280101

Denham, P. (2004). The impact of space and survey format on open ended responses. *Australasian Journal of Market and Social Research*, *12*(2), 11–16.

Dennis, M. (2010). *KnowledgePanel®: Processes & procedures contributing to sample representativeness & tests for self-selection bias.* Retrieved from http://www.knowledgenetworks.com/ganp/docs/KnowledgePanelR-Statistical-Methods-Note.pdf

Dennis, A. R., Aronson, J. E., Heninger, W. G., & Walker, E. (1999). Structuring time and task in electronic brainstorming. *Management Information Systems Quarterly*, *23*, 95–108. doi:10.2307/249411

Dennis, A. R., & Kinney, S. T. (1998). Testing media richness theory in the new media: The effects of cues, feedback, and task equivocality. *Information Systems Research*, *9*(3), 256–274. doi:10.1287/isre.9.3.256

Dennis, A. R., & Valacich, J. S. (1993). Computer brainstorms: More heads are better than one. *The Journal of Applied Psychology*, *78*, 531–537. doi:10.1037/0021-9010.78.4.531

Dennis, A. R., Valacich, J. S., Connolly, T., & Wynne, B. E. (1996). Process structuring in electronic brainstorming. *Information Systems Research*, *7*, 268–277. doi:10.1287/isre.7.2.268

Dennis, A. R., & Williams, M. L. (2003). Electronic brainstorming. Theory, research, and future directions. In Paulus, P. B., & Nijstad, B. A. (Eds.), *Group creativity. Innovation through collaboration* (pp. 160–178). Oxford, UK: Oxford University Press.

Dennis, A. R., & Williams, M. L. (2005). A Meta-Analysis of group side effects in electronic brainstorming: More heads are better than one. *International Journal of e-Collaboration*, *1*, 24–42. doi:10.4018/jec.2005010102

Dennis, A. R., Wixom, B. H., & Vandenberg, R. J. (2001). Understanding fit and appropriation effects in Group Support Systems via meta-analysis. *Management Information Systems Quarterly*, *25*, 167–194. doi:10.2307/3250928

Denzin, N. (1970). *The research act: a theoretical introduction to sociological methods.* New Brunswick, NJ: Transaction Publishers.

Denzin, N. K., & Lincoln, Y. S. (1994). *Handbook of qualitative methods.* London, UK: Sage.

Denzin, N. K., & Lincoln, Y. S. (2003). The Discipline and Practice of Qualitative Research. In Denzin, N. K., & Lincoln, Y. S. (Eds.), *The Landscape of Qualitative Research – Theories and Issues* (pp. 1–45). Thousand Oaks, CA: Sage.

Denzin, N. K., & Lincoln, Y. S. (2005). *The SAGE handbook of qualitative research.* Thousand Oaks, CA: Sage.

Denzin, N. K., & Lincoln, Y. S. (Eds.). (2008). *Collecting and Interpreting Qualitative Material.* Thousand Oaks, CA: Sage.

DeRosa, D. M., Smith, C. L., & Hantula, D. A. (2007). The medium matters: Mining the long-promised merit of group interaction in creative idea generation tasks in a meta-analysis of the electronic brainstorming literature. *Computers in Human Behavior, 23,* 1549–1581. doi:10.1016/j.chb.2005.07.003

Deuze, M. (2007). *Media Work.* Malden, MA: Polity Press.

Dever, J., Rafferty, A., & Valliant, R. (2008). Internet survey: can statistical adjustments eliminate coverage bias? *Survey Research Methods, 2*(2), 47–60.

Di Gangi, P. M., & Wasko, M. (2009). Steal my idea! User innovation community influence on organizational adoption of user innovations: A case study of Dell IdeaStorm. *Decision Support Systems, 48,* 303–313. doi:10.1016/j.dss.2009.04.004

Diehl, M., & Stroebe, W. (1987). Productivity loss in brainstorming groups: Toward the solution of a riddle. *Journal of Personality and Social Psychology, 53*(3), 497–509. doi:10.1037/0022-3514.53.3.497

Diehl, M., & Stroebe, W. (1991). Productivity loss in idea-generating groups: Tracking down the blocking effect. *Journal of Personality and Social Psychology, 61*(3), 392–403. doi:10.1037/0022-3514.61.3.392

Dillman, D. A. (2000). *Mail and internet surveys: The tailored design method.* New York, NY: Wiley.

Dillman, D. A., Smyth, J. D., & Christian, L. M. (2009). *Internet, mail, and mixed-mode surveys: The tailored design method* (3rd ed.). New York, NY: John Wiley & Sons.

Dillon, L. (2010). Listening for voices of self: Digital journaling among gifted young adolescents. *Qualitative Research Journal, 10*(1), 13–27. doi:10.3316/QRJ1001013

Doherty-Sneddon, G., & McAuley, S. (2000). Influence of video-mediation on adult-child interviews: Implications for the use of the live link with child witnesses. *Applied Cognitive Psychology, 14*(4), 379–392. doi:10.1002/1099-0720(200007/08)14:4<379::AID-ACP664>3.0.CO;2-T

Dohmen, T., Falk, A., Huffman, D., Sunde, U., Schupp, J., & Wagner, G. G. (in press). Individual risk attitudes: Measurement, determinants, and behavioral consequences. *Journal of the European Economic Association.*

Dornburg, C. C., Stevens, S. M., Hendrickson, S. M. L., & Davidson, G. S. (2009). Improving extreme-scale problem solving: Assessing electronic brainstorming effectiveness in an industrial setting. *Human Factors, 51*(4), 519–527. doi:10.1177/0018720809343587

Driskell, J. E., Radtke, P. H., & Salas, E. (2003). Virtual teams: Effects of technological mediation on team performance. *Group Dynamics, 7,* 297–323. doi:10.1037/1089-2699.7.4.297

Duarte, D. L., & Snyder, N. T. (2006). *Mastering virtual teams: Strategies, tools, and techniques that succeed* (3rd ed.). San Francisco, CA: Jossey-Bass.

Duffield, C. (1993). The Delphi technique: A comparison of results obtained using two expert panels. *International Journal of Nursing Studies, 30*(3), 227–237. doi:10.1016/0020-7489(93)90033-Q

Dumreicher, H., & Kolb, B. (2006). 'My house, my street', Seven fields of Spatial & Social Encounter. In D. Shehayeb, H. T. Yildiz, & P. Kellet (Eds.). *'Appropriate Home': Can we design 'appropriate' residential environments?* (pp. 97-108). Cairo, Egypt: Housing & Building National Research Centre (HBNRC).

Dumreicher, H., & Kolb, B. (2008). Place as a Social Space–Fields of Encounter Relating to the Local Sustainability Process. In *Journal of Environmental Management, Volume 87/2, Pages 201- 317*: Elsevier. doi: 10.1016/j.jenvman.2007.03.048

Dunbar, K. (1995). How scientists really reason: Scientific reasoning in real-world laboratories. In Sternberg, R. J., & Davidson, J. E. (Eds.), *The nature of insight* (pp. 365–395). Cambridge, MA: MIT Press.

Dunbar, K. (1997). How scientists think: Online creativity and conceptual change in science. In Ward, T. B., Smith, S. M., & Vaid, J. (Eds.), *Creative thought: An investigation of conceptual structures and processes* (pp. 461–493). Washington, DC: American Psychological Association. doi:10.1037/10227-017

Duncan, K. B., & Stasny, E. A. (2001). Using propensity scores to control coverage bias in telephone surveys. *Survey Methodology, 27*(2), 121–130.

Dunnette, M. D., Campbell, J., & Jaastad, K. (1963). The effect of group participation on brainstorming effectiveness for two industrial samples. *The Journal of Applied Psychology, 47*, 30–37. doi:10.1037/h0049218

Dwyer, C., & Davies, G. (2010). Qualitative methods III: animating archives, artful interventions and online environments. *Progress in Human Geography, 34*, 88–97. doi:10.1177/0309132508105005

Dykema, J., Lepkowski, J. M., & Blixt, S. (1997). The effect of interviewer and respondent behavior on data quality: Analysis of interaction coding in a validation study. In Lyberg, L., Biemer, P., Collins, M., DeLeeuw, E., Dippo, C., Schwarz, N., & Trewin, D. (Eds.), *Survey measurement and process quality* (pp. 221–248). New York, NY: Wiley.

Eagle, N., Macy, M., & Claxton, R. (2010). Network diversity and economic development. *Science, 328*(5981), 1029–1031. doi:10.1126/science.1186605

Eckhardt, E., & Anastas, J. (2007). Research methods with disabled populations. *Journal of Social Work in Disability & Rehabilitation, 6*(1-2), 233–249. doi:10.1300/J198v06n01_13

Economic and Social Research Council (ESRC). (2010). *Framework for Research Ethics*. Retrieved November 2, 2010, from http://www.esrcsocietytoday.ac.uk/ESRCInfoCentre/Images/Framework for Research Ethics 2010_tcm6-35811.pdf

Eco, U. (1991). *Einführung in die Semiotik*. Munich, Germany: UTB.

Edensor, T. (2004). Automobility and National Identity: Representation, Geography and Driving Practice. *Theory, Culture & Society, 21*(4-5), 101–120. doi:10.1177/0263276404046063

Edmondson, A. C., & Roloff, K. S. (2009). Overcoming barriers to collaboration: Psychological safety and learning in diverse teams. In Salas, E., Goodwin, G. F., & Burke, C. S. (Eds.), *Team effectiveness in complex organizations: Cross-disciplinary perspectives and approaches* (pp. 183–208). New York, NY: Routledge/Taylor & Francis.

Egger, V., Schrom-Feiertag, H., Telepak, G., & Ehrenstrasser, L. (2010). Creating a Richer Data Source for 3D Pedestrian Flow Simulations in Public Transport. In *Proceedings of the 7th International Conference on Methods and Techniques in Behavioral Research*.

Elgesem, D. (2002). What is special about the ethical issues in online research? *Ethics and Information Technology, 4*, 195–203. doi:10.1023/A:1021320510186

Elmasri, R. A., & Navathe, S. B. (2001). *Fundamentals of Database Systems*. New York: Addison-Wesley.

Elwood, S. (2006). Critical issues in participatory GIS: Deconstructions, reconstructions, and new research directions. *Transactions in GIS, 10*(5), 693–708. doi:10.1111/j.1467-9671.2006.01023.x

Emmison, M. (2004). The conceptualisation and analysis of qualitative research. In Silverman, D. (Ed.), *Qualitative research: theory, method and practice* (pp. 246–265). London, UK: Sage.

Emmison, M., & Smith, P. (2000). *Researching the visual*. London, UK: Sage.

Enyon, R., Fry, J., & Schroeder, R. (2008). The Ethics of Internet Research. In Fielding, N., Lee, R., & Blank, G. (Eds.), *The SAGE Handbook of Online Research Methods* (pp. 23–41). London, UK: Sage.

Ess, C., & Association of Internet Researchers (AoIR). (2002). *Ethical decision-making and internet research: Recommendations from the AoIR ethics working committee*. Retrieved June 22, 2010, from http://www.aoir.org/reports/ethics.pdf

Ess, C. Association of Internet Researchers Ethics Working Committee. (2002). *Ethical decision-making and Internet research: Recommendations from the AoIR Ethics Working Committee*. Chicago, IL: Association of Internet Researchers.

Esser, H. (1993). Response Set: Habit, Frame or Rational Choice? In Krebs, D., & Schmidt, P. (Eds.), *New Directions in Attitude Measurement* (pp. 293–314). Berlin, Germany: Walter de Gruyter.

Evans, J. R., & Mathur, A. (2005). The value of online surveys. *Internet Research, 15*(2), 195–219. doi:10.1108/10662240510590360

Farrell, D., & Petersen, J. C. (2010). The growth of Internet research methods and the reluctant sociologist. *Sociological Inquiry, 80*(1), 114–125. doi:10.1111/j.1475-682X.2009.00318.x

Faulx, A. L., Vela, S., Das, A., Cooper, G., Sivak, M., Isenberg, G., & Chak, A. (2005). The changing landscape of practice patterns regarding unsedated endoscopy and propofol use: A national Web survey. *Gastrointestinal Endoscopy, 62*(1), 9–15. doi:10.1016/S0016-5107(05)00518-3

Fay, M. (2008). Mobile belonging: exploring transnational feminist theory and online connectivity. In Priya Uteng, T., & Cresswell, T. (Eds.), *Gendered mobilities* (pp. 65–83). Aldershot, UK: Ashgate.

Fehr, E., Fischbacher, U., van Rosenbladt, B., Schupp, J., & Wagner, G. G. (2002). A Nation-Wide Laboratory – Examining trust and trustworthiness by integrating behavioral experiments into representative surveys. *Schmollers Jahrbuch, 122*(4), 519–542.

Fielding, N., & Macintyre, M. (2006). Access Grid Nodes in Field Research. *Sociological Research Online, 11*(2). Retrieved November 2, 2010, from http://www.socresonline.org.uk/11/2/fielding.html

Fielding, N., Lee, R. M., & Blank, G. (Eds.). (2008). *The Sage Handbook of Online Research Methods*. Los Angeles, CA: Sage.

Fincham, B. (2006). Back to the Old School: Bicycle Messengers, Employment and Ethnography. *Qualitative Research, 6*(2), 187–205. doi:10.1177/1468794106062709

Fincham, B., McGuinness, M., & Murray, L. (Eds.). (2010). *Mobile Methodologies*. Basingstoke, UK: Palgrave Macmillan.

Finholt, T. A., & Olson, G. M. (1997). From laboratories to collaboratories: A new organizational form for scientific collaboration. *Psychological Science, 8*(1), 28–36. doi:10.1111/j.1467-9280.1997.tb00540.x

Fisher, K., & Fisher, M. D. (2001). *The distance manager: A hands-on guide to managing off-site employees and virtual teams*. New York, NY: McGraw-Hill.

Fjermestad, J., & Hiltz, S. R. (1998). An assessment of group support systems experiment research: Methodology and results. *Journal of Management Information Systems, 15*, 7–149.

Flinders, D. (1992). In search of ethical guidance: Constructing a basis for dialogue. *Qualitative Studies in Education, 52*(2), 101–115. doi:10.1080/0951839920050202

Floch, J. M. (1995/2000). *Visual identities* (van Osselaer, P., & McHould, A., Trans.). London, UK: Continuum.

Flower, J. (1995). Future search: Power tool for building healthier communities. *The Healthcare Forum Journal, 38*(3), 34–42.

Flynn, L. R., Goldsmith, R. E., & Eastman, J. K. (1996). Opinion leaders and opinions seekers: Two new measurement scales. *Journal of the Academy of Marketing Science, 24*(2), 137–147. doi:10.1177/0092070396242004

Folkman Curasi, C. (2001). A critical exploration of face-to-face interviewing vs. computer-mediated interviewing. *International Journal of Market Research, 43*(4), 361–375.

Fong, J. (2008). A cross-cultural comparison of electronic word-of-mouth and country-of-origin effects. *Journal of Business Research, 61*(3), 233–242. doi:10.1016/j.jbusres.2007.06.015

Fontes, T. O., & O'Mahony, M. (2008). In-depth interviewing by instant messaging. *Social Research Update, 53*, 1-4. Retrieved from http://sru.soc.surrey.ac.uk/SRU53.pdf

Forster, E., & McCleery, A. (1999). Computer Assisted Personal Interviewing: A Method of Capturing Sensitive Information. *IASSIST Quarterly, 23*(2), 26–28.

Fox, J., Murray, C., & Warm, A. (2003). Conducting research using web-based questionnaires: practical, methodological, and ethical considerations. *International Journal of Social Research Methodology, 6*(2), 167–180. doi:10.1080/13645570210142883

Francovich, C., Reina, M., Reina, D., & Dilts, C. (2008). Trust building online: Virtual collaboration and the development of trust. In Nemiro, J., Beyerlein, M. M., Bradley, L., & Beyerlein, S. (Eds.), *The handbook of high performance virtual teams* (pp. 153–176). Hoboken, NJ: John Wiley & Sons.

Frankfort-Nachmias, C., & Nachmias, D. (2000). *Research Methods in the Social Sciences* (6th ed.). New York, NY: Worth.

Franklin, K. K., & Hart, J. K. (2007). Idea generation and exploration: Benefits and limitations of the policy Delphi research method. *Innovative Higher Education*, *31*, 237–246. doi:10.1007/s10755-006-9022-8

Franklin, K. K., & Lowry, C. (2001). Computer-mediated focus groups sessions: Naturalistic inquiry in a networked environment. *Qualitative Research*, *1*, 169–184. doi:10.1177/146879410100100204

Fraser, S., Lewis, V., Ding, S., Kellett, M., & Robinson, C. (2004). *Doing research with children and young people*. London, UK: Sage.

Freed-Taylor, M. (1994). Ethical considerations in European cross-national research. *International Social Science Journal*, *46*(4), 523–532.

Freudendal-Pedersen, M., Hartmann-Petersen, K., & Drewes Nielsen, L. (2010). Mixing methods in the search for mobile complexity. In Fincham, B., McGuinness, M., & Murray, L. (Eds.), *Mobile Methodologies* (pp. 25–42). Basingstoke, UK: Palgrave Macmillan.

Fuchs, M. (2007). Face-to-face interviews with children. Question difficulty and the impact of cognitive resources on response quality. In *Proceedings of the Survey Research Methods Section, American Statistical Association*. Retrieved from http://www.amstat.org/sections/srms/Proceedings/y2007f.html

Fuchs, M. (2009b, February 16-18). The video-enhanced web survey. Data quality and cognitive processing of questions. In *Proceedings of the Eurostat Conference on New Techniques and Technologies for Statistics*, Brussels, Belgium.

Fuchs, M., & Funke, F. (2007). Multimedia web surveys: Results from a field experiment on the use of audio and video clips in web surveys. In M. Trotman et al. (Eds.), *The Challenges of a Changing World: Proceedings of the 5th International Conference of the Association for Survey Computing* (pp. 63-80). Berkeley, CA: ASC.

Fuchs, M. (2009a). Gender-of-interviewer effects in a video-enhanced web survey. Results from a randomized field experiment. *Social Psychology*, *40*(1), 37–42. doi:10.1027/1864-9335.40.1.37

Fuchs, M., & Funke, F. (2009). Die Video-unterstützte Online-Befragung: Soziale Präsenz, soziale Erwünschtheit und Underreporting sensitiver Informationen. In Jackob, N., Schoen, H., & Zerback, T. (Eds.), *Sozialforschung im Internet: Methodologie und Praxis der Online-Befragung* (pp. 159–180). Wiesbaden, Germany: VS-Verlag.

Füller, J., Jawecki, G., & Muhlbacher, H. (2007). Innovation creation by online basketball communities. *Journal of Business Research*, *60*(1), 60–71. doi:10.1016/j.jbusres.2006.09.019

Funtowicz, S. O., & Ravetz, J. R. (1991). A new scientific methodology for global environmental issues. In Costanza, R. (Ed.), *Ecological Economics: The science and management of sustainability* (pp. 137–152). New York, NY: Columbia University Press.

Gallupe, R. B., Bastianutti, L. M., & Cooper, W. H. (1991). Unblocking brainstorms. *The Journal of Applied Psychology*, *76*(1), 137–142. doi:10.1037/0021-9010.76.1.137

Gallupe, R. B., & Cooper, W. H. (1993). Brainstorming electronically. *Sloan Management Review*, *35*, 27–36.

Gallupe, R. B., Cooper, W. H., Grise, M. L., & Bastianutti, L. M. (1994). Blocking electronic brainstorms. *The Journal of Applied Psychology*, *79*, 77–86. doi:10.1037/0021-9010.79.1.77

Gallupe, R. B., Dennis, A. R., Cooper, W. H., & Valacich, J. S. (1992). Electronic brainstorming and group size. *Academy of Management Journal*, *35*(2), 350–369. doi:10.2307/256377

Gal, S. (2002). A semiotics of the public/private distinction. *Differences: A Journal of Feminist Cultural Studies*, *13*(1), 77–95. doi:10.1215/10407391-13-1-77

Ganassali, S. (2008). The influence of the design of web survey questionnaires on the quality of responses. *Survey Research Methods*, *2*(1), 21–32.

Garren, S. T., & Chang, T. C. (2002). Improved ratio estimation in telephone surveys adjusting for noncoverage. *Survey Methodology*, *28*(1), 63–76.

Gaskell, J. (1988). Policy Research and Politics. *The Alberta Journal of Educational Research*, *34*(4), 403–417.

Gelter, I. (1987). Wortschatz und Lesefähigkeit gehörloser Schüler. *Der Sprachheilpädagoge*, *3*, 37–42.

Gengler, C. E., Klenosky, D. B., & Mulvey, M. S. (1995). Improving the graphic representation of means-end results. *International Journal of Research in Marketing, 12*(3), 245–256. doi:10.1016/0167-8116(95)00024-V

Gengler, C. E., Mulvey, M. S., & Oglethorpe, J. E. (1999). A means-end analysis of mothers' infant feeding choices. *Journal of Public Policy & Marketing, 18*(2), 172–188.

Gengler, C. E., & Reynolds, T. J. (1993). *LADDERMAP: A software tool for analyzing laddering data (Version 5.4)*. Camden, NJ: Means-End Software.

Gengler, C. E., & Reynolds, T. J. (1995). Consumer understanding and advertising strategy: Analysis and strategic translation of laddering data. *Journal of Advertising Research, 35*(4), 19–33.

Gerich, J. (2008b). Effects of social cues on response behavior. In *Proceedings of the 7th International Conference on Social Science Methodology (RC33),* Naples, Italy.

Gerich, J. (2008a). Real or virtual? Response behavior in video-enhanced self-administered computer interviews. *Field Methods, 39*(4), 985–992.

Gerich, J. (2009). Multimediale Elemente in der Computerbasierten Datenerhebung. Der Einfluss Auditiver und Visueller Elemente auf das Antwortverhalten in Befragungen. In Weichbold, M., Bacher, J., & Wolf, C. (Eds.), *Grenzen und Herausforderungen der Umfrageforschung* (pp. 107–129). Wiesbaden, Germany: Verlag für Sozialwissenschaften.

Gerich, J., & Bergmair, F. (2008). Die Anwendung Videogestützter Selbstadministrierter Computerbefragungen in der Sozialforschung mit Kindern. *Zeitschrift für Soziologie der Erziehung und Socialisation, 28*(1), 56–74.

Gerich, J., & Lehner, R. (2006). Video computer-assisted self-administered interviews for deaf respondents. *Field Methods, 18*(3), 267–283. doi:10.1177/1525822X06287535

German Data Forum. (2011). Recommendations. In German Data Forum (Ed.), *Building on Progress – Expanding the Research Infrastructure for the Social, Economic and Behavioral Sciences* (pp. 17-40). Opladen, Germany: Budrich UniPress.

Germann Molz, J. (2010). Connectivity, collaboration, search. In Büscher, M., Urry, J., & Witchger, K. (Eds.), *Mobile methods* (pp. 88–103). London, UK: Routledge.

Gibson, C. B., & Gibbs, J. L. (2006). Unpacking the concept of virtuality: The effects of geographic dispersion, electronic dependence, dynamic structure, and national diversity on team innovation. *Administrative Science Quarterly, 51*, 451–495.

Gibson, J. M. E. (1998). Using the Delphi technique to identify the content and context of nurses' continuing professional development needs. *Journal of Clinical Nursing, 7*(5), 451–459. doi:10.1046/j.1365-2702.1998.00175.x

Gies, L. (2008). How material are cyberbodies? Broadband Internet and embodied subjectivity. *Crime, Media, Culture, 4*, 311–330. doi:10.1177/1741659008096369

Giesler, M., & Pohlmann, M. (2003a). The Anthropology of File Sharing: Consuming Napster as a Gift. *Advances in Consumer Research. Association for Consumer Research (U. S.), 30*, 273–279.

Giesler, M., & Pohlmann, M. (2003b). The social form of Napster: cultivating the paradox of consumer emancipation. *Advances in Consumer Research. Association for Consumer Research (U. S.), 30*, 94–100.

Glasser, D. J., Goodman, K. W., & Einspruch, N. G. (2007). Chips, tags and scanners: Ethical challenges for radio frequency identification. *Ethics and Information Technology, 9*, 101–109. doi:10.1007/s10676-006-9124-0

Goffman, E. (1959). *The presentation of self in everyday life*. New York, NY: Doubleday Anchor Books.

Göksel, H., Judkins, D. R., & Mosher, W. D. (1991). Nonresponse adjustments for a telephone follow-up to a national in-person survey. In *Proceedings of the Survey Research Methods Section, American Statistical Association* (pp. 581-586).

Goldenberg, M. A., Klenosky, D. B., O'Leary, J. T., & Templin, T. J. (2000). A means-end investigation of Ropes course experiences. *Journal of Leisure Research, 32*(2), 208–224.

Goldsmith, R. E., & De Witt, T. S. (2003). The predictive validity of an opinion leadership scale. *Journal of Marketing Theory & Practice, 11*(1), 28–35.

Goldstein, M. F., Eckhardt, E. A., & Joyner, P. (2004). *HIV knowledge in a deaf sample: Preliminary results of a self-administered survey in American Sign Language.* Paper presented at the American Public Health Association Annual Meeting, Washington, DC.

Gong, Y., & Mackett, R. (2009). Visualizing Children's Walking Behaviour Using Portable Global Positioning (GPS) Units and Activity Monitors. In Lin, H., & Batty, M. (Eds.), *Virtual Geographic Environments* (pp. 295–310). Beijing, China: Science Press.

Gonzales, M., Hidalgo, C., & Barabasi, L. A. (2008). Understanding individual human mobility patterns. *Nature, 453,* 779–782. doi:10.1038/nature06958

Goodchild, M. F. (2007). Citizens as sensors: the world of volunteered geography. *GeoJournal, 69,* 211–221. doi:10.1007/s10708-007-9111-y

Gordon, S., & Nicholas, J. (2010, September 29-October 1). Teachers' reflections on the challenges of teaching mathematics bridging courses. In M. Sharma (Ed.), *Proceedings of the 16th UniServe Science Annual Conference - Creating ACTIVE Minds in our Science and Mathematics Students,* Sydney, NSW, Australia (pp. 35–40).

Gordon, S., Reid, A., & Petocz, P. (2007). Teachers' conceptions of teaching service statistics courses. *International Journal for the Scholarship of Teaching & Learning, 1*(1). Retrieved August 25, 2010, from http://academics.georgiasouthern.edu/ijsotl/v1n1/gordon_et_al/index.htm

Gordon, S., Reid, A., & Petocz, P. (2010). Educators' conceptions of student diversity in their classes. *Studies in Higher Education, 35*(8), 961–974. doi:10.1080/03075070903414305

Gordon, T. (2007). Energy forecasts using a "roundless" approach to running a Delphi study. *Foresight, 9*(2), 27–35. doi:10.1108/14636680710737731

Gordon, T., & Pease, A. (2006). RT Delphi: An efficient, "round-less" almost real time Delphi method. *Technological Forecasting and Social Change, 73,* 321–333. doi:10.1016/j.techfore.2005.09.005

Gore, G. (2010). Flash mob dance and the territorialisation of urban movement. *Anthropological Notebooks, 16*(3), 125–131.

Gottfredson, M. R., & Hirschi, T. (1990). *A general theory of crime.* Stanford, CA: Stanford University Press.

Graffigna, G., & Bosio, A. C. (2006). The influence of setting on findings produced in qualitative health research: A comparison between face-to-face and online discussion groups about HIV/AIDS. *International Journal of Qualitative Methods, 5*(3), 55–76.

Graiser, T. J. (2008). Online focus groups. In Fielding, N., Lee, R. M., & Blank, G. (Eds.), *The Sage Handbook of Online Research Methods* (pp. 290–306). Los Angeles, CA: Sage.

Gray, J., & Reuter, A. (1992). *Transaction Processing: Concepts and Techniques.* San Francisco: Morgan Kaufmann.

Gray, K., Chang, S., & Kennedy, G. (2010). Use of social web technologies by international and domestic undergraduate students: implications for internationalising learning and teaching in Australian universities. *Technology, Pedagogy and Education, 19*(1), 31–46. doi:10.1080/14759390903579208

Green, H., Hunter, C., & Moore, B. (1989). Assessing the environmental impact of tourism development: The use of the Delphi technique. *The International Journal of Environmental Studies, 35,* 51–62. doi:10.1080/00207238908710549

Green, H., Hunter, C., & Moore, B. (1990). Application of the Delphi technique in tourism. *Annals of Tourism Research, 17*(2), 270–279. doi:10.1016/0160-7383(90)90087-8

Green, T. D., Brown, A., & Robinson, L. (2008). *Making the most of the Web in your classroom.* Thousand Oaks, CA: Sage.

Griffiths, R. (1998). Making sameness: Place marketing and the new urban entrepreneurialism. In Oatley, N. (Ed.), *Cities, economic competition and urban policy* (pp. 41–57). London, UK: Paul Chapman.

Griffith, T. L., Mannix, E. A., & Neale, M. A. (2003). Conflict and virtual teams. In Gibson, C. B., & Cohen, S. G. (Eds.), *Virtual Teams that Work: Creating Conditions for Virtual Team Effectiveness* (pp. 335–352). San Francisco, CA: Jossey-Bass.

Griffith, T. L., Sawyer, J. E., & Neale, M. A. (2003). Virtualness and knowledge in teams: Managing the love triangle in organizations, individuals, and information technology. *Management Information Systems Quarterly*, *27*, 265–287.

Grisham, T. (2009). The Delphi technique: A method for testing complex and multifaceted topics. *International Journal of Managing Projects in Business*, *2*(1), 112–130. doi:10.1108/17538370910930545

Groves, R.M. (1987). Research on Survey Data Quality. *Public Opinion Quarterly* 51(2: 50th Anniversary Supplement): S156-S172.

Groves, R. M. (1989). *Survey Errors and Survey Costs*. New York: Wiley.

Groves, R.M. (2006). Nonresponse rates and nonresponse bias in household surveys. *Public Opinion Quarterly*, *70*(5), 646–675. doi:10.1093/poq/nfl033

Groves, R. M., & Couper, M. P. (1998). *Nonresponse in household interview surveys*. New York, NY: John Wiley.

Groves, R. M., Fowler, F. J., Couper, M. P., Lepkowski, J. M., Singer, E., & Tourangeau, R. (2004). *Survey methodology*. Hoboken, NJ: John Wiley & Sons.

Groves, R. M., & Peytcheva, E. (2008). The impact of nonresponse rates on nonresponse bias. *Public Opinion Quarterly*, *72*(2), 167–189. doi:10.1093/poq/nfn011

Gruber, T., Henneberg, S. C., Ashnai, B., Naudé, P., & Reppel, A. E. (2010). Complaint resolution management expectations in an asymmetric business-to-business context. *Journal of Business and Industrial Marketing*, *25*(5), 360–371. doi:10.1108/08858621011058124

Gruber, T., Szmigin, I., Reppel, A. E., & Voss, R. (2008). Designing and conducting online interviews to investigate interesting consumer phenomena. *Qualitative Market Research: An International Journal*, *11*(3), 256–274. doi:10.1108/13522750810879002

Gruber, T., Szmigin, I., & Voss, R. (2006). The desired qualities of customer contact employees in complaint handling encounters. *Journal of Marketing Management*, *22*(5-6), 619–642. doi:10.1362/026725706777978721

Gruber, T., Szmigin, I., & Voss, R. (2009a). Developing a deeper understanding of attributes of effective customer contact employees in personal complaint handling encounters. *Journal of Services Marketing*, *23*(6), 422–435. doi:10.1108/08876040910985889

Gruber, T., Szmigin, I., & Voss, R. (2009b). Handling customer complaints effectively - a comparison of the value maps of female and male complainants. *Managing Service Quality*, *19*(6), 6636–6656. doi:10.1108/09604520911005044

Grunert, K. G., Beckmann, S. C., & Sørensen, E. (2001). Means-end chains and laddering: An inventory of problems and an agenda for research. In Reynolds, T. J., & Olson, J. C. (Eds.), *Understanding consumer decision making - the means-end approach to marketing and advertising strategy* (pp. 69–90). Mahwah, NJ: Lawrence Erlbaum Associates.

Grunert, K. G., & Grunert, S. C. (1995). Measuring subjective meaning structures by the laddering method: Theoretical considerations and methodological problems. *International Journal of Research in Marketing*, *12*(3), 209–225. doi:10.1016/0167-8116(95)00022-T

Guiver, J. (2010). *UCLan transport institute surveys on volcano crisis for lessons learned*. Retrieved August 12, 2010, from http://www.uclan.ac.uk/schools/ssto/uclan_transport_institute_surveys_on_volcano_crisis_for_lessons_learned.php.

Gully, S. M., Devine, D. J., & Whitney, D. J. (1995). A meta-analysis of cohesion and performance: Effects of levels of analysis and task interdependence. *Small Group Research*, *26*, 497–520. doi:10.1177/1046496495264003

Gunter, B. (2000). *Media research methods*. London, UK: Sage.

Gunter, B., Nicholas, D., Huntington, P., & Williams, P. (2002). Online versus offline research: Implications for evaluating digital media. *Aslib Proceedings*, *54*(4), 229–239. doi:10.1108/00012530210443339

Guo, S., & Fraser, M. W. (2010). *Propensity score analysis: Statistical methods and applications*. Thousand Oaks, CA: Sage.

Gurumurthy, A. (2004) *Gender and ICTs Overview Report*. Brighton, UK: Bridge Publications. Retrieved from http://www.bridge.ids.ac.uk/reports/CEP-ICTs-OR.pdf

Gutman, J. (1982). A means-end chain model based on consumer categorization processes. *Journal of Marketing, 46*(2), 60–72. doi:10.2307/3203341

Gutman, J. (1997). Means-end chains as goal hierarchies. *Psychology and Marketing, 14*(6), 545–560. doi:10.1002/(SICI)1520-6793(199709)14:6<545::AID-MAR2>3.0.CO;2-7

Guy, L., & Montague, J. (2008). Analysing men's written friendship narratives. *Qualitative Research, 8*, 389–397. doi:10.1177/1468794106093635

Hahn, E. J., & Rayens, M. K. (1999). Consensus for tobacco policy among former state legislator using the policy Delphi method. *Tobacco Control, 8*, 137–140. doi:10.1136/tc.8.2.137

Haines, K., Case, S., Isles, E., Rees, I., & Hancock, A. (2004). *Extending entitlement: Making it real*. Cardiff, UK: Welsh Assembly Government.

Hall, G. J., Frederick, D., & Johns, M. D. (2004). 'NEED HELP ASAP!!!': A feminist communitarian approach to online research ethics. In Johns, M. D., Chen, S. S., & Hall, G. J. (Eds.), *Online social research: Methods, issues and ethics* (pp. 239–253). New York, NY: Peter Lang.

Hamilton, R., & Bowers, B. (2006). Internet recruitment and e-mail interviews in qualitative studies. *Qualitative Health Research, 16*, 821–835. doi:10.1177/1049732306287599

Hankinson, G. (2007). The management of destination brands: Five guiding principles based on recent developments in corporate branding theory. *Journal of Brand Management, 14*(3), 240–254. doi:10.1057/palgrave.bm.2550065

Harper, D. (1998). On the Authority of the Image: Visual Methods at the Crossroads. In N. K. Denzin & Y. S. Lincoln (Eds.), *Collecting and interpreting qualitative materials* (pp. 185-204). London, Uk: Sage

Harper, D. (1987). *Working Knowledge, Skill and Community in a Small Shop*. Chicago, IL: The University of Chicago Press.

Harper, D. (2002). Talking about Pictures: a Case for Photo Elicitation. *Visual Studies, 17*, 13–26. doi:10.1080/14725860220137345

Harris Interactive. (2008). *Election results further validate efficacy of Harris Interactive's online methodology*. New York, NY: Author.

Harter, S., & Pike, R. (1984). The pictorial scale of perceived competence and social acceptance for young children. *Child Development, 55*(6), 1969–1982. doi:10.2307/1129772

Hasson, F., Keeney, S., & McKenna, H. (2000). Research guidelines for the Delphi survey technique. *Journal of Advanced Nursing, 32*(4), 1008–1015.

Hawkins, B. (1999). *How to generate great ideas*. London, UK: Kogan Page.

Hay, I. (2005). *Qualitative Research Methods in Human Geography* (2nd ed.). New York, NY: Oxford University Press.

Healy, P. (1997). *Collaborative planning: Shaping places in fragmented societies*. Basingstoke, UK: Palgrave-Macmillan.

Heisley, D. D. (2001). Visual research: Current bias and future direction. *Advances in Consumer Research. Association for Consumer Research (U. S.), 28*(1), 45–46.

Helbing, D., Molnár, P., Farkas, I. J., & Bolay, K. (2001). Self-organizing pedestrian movement. *Environment and Planning. B, Planning & Design, 28*(3), 361–383. doi:10.1068/b2697

Helmer, O., & Rescher, N. (1959). On the epistemology of the inexact science. *Management Science, 6*, 25–53. doi:10.1287/mnsc.6.1.25

Henneberg, S. C., Gruber, T., Reppel, A. E., Ashnai, B., & Naudé, P. (2009). Complaint management expectations: An online-laddering analysis of small versus large firms. *Industrial Marketing Management, 38*(6), 584–598. doi:10.1016/j.indmarman.2009.05.008

Henrich, J., Heine, S. J., & Norenzayan, A. (2010). The weirdest people in the world? *The Behavioral and Brain Sciences, 33*(2), 1–23. doi:10.1017/S0140525X0999152X

Hertel, G., Konradt, U., & Orlikowski, B. (2004). Managing distance by interdependence: Goal setting, task interdependence, and team-based rewards in virtual teams. *European Journal of Work and Organizational Psychology*, *13*(1), 1–28. doi:10.1080/13594320344000228

Hertel, G., Konradt, U., & Voss, K. (2006). Competencies for virtual teamwork: Development and validation of a web-based selection tool for members of distributed teams. *European Journal of Work and Organizational Psychology*, *15*(4), 477–504. doi:10.1080/13594320600908187

Hewitt, M. (2002). Attitudes toward interview mode and comparability of reporting sexual behavior by personal interview and audio computer-assisted self-interviewing. Analyses of the 1995 National Survey of Family Growth. *Sociological Methods & Research*, *31*(1), 3–26. doi:10.1177/0049124102031001001

Hill, M. R. (1984). Stalking the Urban Pedestrian. *Environment and Behavior*, *16*(5), 539–550. doi:10.1177/0013916584165001

Hiltz, S. R., Johnson, K., & Turoff, M. (1986). Experiments in group decision making: Communication process and outcome in face-to-face versus computerized conferences. *Human Communication Research*, *13*, 225–252. doi:10.1111/j.1468-2958.1986.tb00104.x

Hinchcliffe, V., & Gavin, H. (2008). Internet mediated research: A critical reflection upon the practice of using instant messenger for higher educational research interviewing. *Psychology & Society*, *1*(1), 91–104.

Hinchcliffe, V., & Gavin, H. (2009). Social and virtual networks: Evaluating synchronous online interviewing using instant messenger. *Qualitative Report*, *14*(2), 318–340.

Hinds, P. J., & Mortensen, M. (2005). Understanding conflict in geographically distributed teams: The moderating effects of shared identity, shared context, and spontaneous communication. *Organization Science*, *16*(3), 290–307. doi:10.1287/orsc.1050.0122

Hinduja, S., & Patchin, J. W. (2008). Personal information of adolescents on the Internet: A quantitative content analysis of MySpace. *Journal of Adolescence*, *31*(1), 125–146. doi:10.1016/j.adolescence.2007.05.004

Hine, C. (2008). Virtual ethnography: Modes, varieties, affordances. In Fielding, N., Lee, R. M., & Blank, G. (Eds.), *The Sage Handbook of Online Research Methods* (pp. 257–268). Los Angeles, CA: Sage.

Hinkle, D. (1965). *The change of personal constructs from the viewpoint of theory of construct implications.* Unpublished doctoral dissertation, Ohio University, Athens, OH.

Hintermair, M. (2008). Self-esteem and satisfaction with life of deaf and hard-of-hearing people – A resource-oriented approach to identity work. *Journal of Deaf Studies and Deaf Education*, *13*(2), 278–300. doi:10.1093/deafed/enm054

Hoaglin, D. C., & Battaglia, M. P. (1996). A comparison of two methods of adjusting for noncoverage of nontelephone households in a telephone survey. In *Proceedings of the Survey Research Methods Section, American Statistical Association.*

Hodkinson, P., & Lincoln, S. (2008). Online journals as virtual bedrooms? Young people, identity and personal space. *Young*, *16*(1), 27–46. doi:10.1177/110330880701600103

Hoefling, T. (2008). The three-fold path of expanding emotional bandwidth in virtual teams. In Nemiro, J., Beyerlein, M. M., Bradley, L., & Beyerlein, S. (Eds.), *The handbook of high performance virtual teams* (pp. 87–104). Hoboken, NJ: John Wiley & Sons.

Holliday, R. (2000). We've been framed: visualizing methodology. *The Sociological Review*, *48*(4), 503–521. doi:10.1111/1467-954X.00230

Holt, A. (2010). Using the telephone for narrative interviewing: A research note. *Qualitative Research*, *10*(1), 113–121. doi:10.1177/1468794109348686

Holt, A. (2011). 'The terrorist in my home': teenagers' violence towards parents – constructions of parent experiences in public online message boards. *Child & Family Social Work*, *16*(4), 454–463. doi:10.1111/j.1365-2206.2011.00760.x

Holt, T. (2010). Exploring strategies for qualitative criminological and criminal justice inquiry using on-line data. *Journal of Criminal Justice Education*, *21*(4), 466–487. doi:10.1080/10511253.2010.516565

Holzwarth, P., & Niesyto, H. (2008). Representational and Discursive Self-expression of Young Migrants in the Context of Different (Media) Cultural Resources. *Forum: Qualitative Social Research, 9*(3). Retrieved September 15, 2010, from http://www.qualitative-research.net/index.php/fqs/article/view/1167

Hongladarom, S., & Ess, C. (Eds.). (2007). *Information Technology Ethics: Cultural Perspectives*. Hershey, PA: Information Science Reference.

Hookway, N. (2008). Entering the Blogosphere: Some Strategies for Using Blogs in Social Research. *Qualitative Research, 8*, 91–113. doi:10.1177/1468794107085298

Horelli, L., & Wallin, S. (2010). The future-making assessment approach as a tool for e-planning and community development—the case of Ubiquitous Helsinki. In Silva, C. N. (Ed.), *Handbook of Research on E-Planning: ICTs for Urban Development and Monitoring* (pp. 58–79). Hershey, PA: Information Science Reference. doi:10.4018/978-1-61520-929-3.ch004

Horvath, L., & Tobin, T. J. (2001). Twenty-first century teamwork: Defining competencies for virtual teams. In M. M. Beyerlein, D. A. Johnson, & S. T. Beyerlein (Eds.), *Advances in Interdisciplinary Studies of Work Teams: Vol. 8. Virtual Teams* (pp. 239-258). Bradford, UK: Emerald.

Hovgesen, H., Nielsen, T., Bro, P., & Tradisauskas. (2008). Experiences from GPS tracking of visitors in Public Parks in Denmark based on GPS technologies. In J. V. Schaick & S. V. D. Spek (Eds.), *Urbanism on Track* (pp. 65-77). Amsterdam, The Netherlands: IOS Press.

Howard, T. L. J., & Gaborit, N. (2007). Using virtual environmental technology to improve public participation in urban planning process. *Journal of Urban Planning and Development, 133*(4), 233–241. doi:10.1061/(ASCE)0733-9488(2007)133:4(233)

Hsu, C. C., & Sandford, B. A. (2007a). The Delphi technique: Making sense of consensus. *Practical Assessment, Research, & Evaluation, 12*(10). Retrieved September 1, 2007, from http://pareonline.net/getvn.asp?v=12&n=10

Hsu, C. C., & Sandford, B. A. (2007b). Minimizing non-response in the Delphi process: How to respond to non-response. *Practical Assessment, Research, & Evaluation, 12*(17). Retrieved January 15, 2008, from http://pareonline.net/getvn.asp?v=12&n=17

Hsu, C. C., & Sandford, B. A. (2010). The Delphi Technique. In Salkind, N. J. (Ed.), *Encyclopedia of Research Design*. Thousand Oaks, CA: Sage.

Hsu, S., Dehuang, N., & Woodside, A. G. (2009). Storytelling research of consumers' self-reports of urban tourism experiences in China. *Journal of Business Research, 62*(12), 1223–1254. doi:10.1016/j.jbusres.2008.11.006

Huber, G. P. (1980). Organizational science contributions to the design of decision support systems. In Fick, G., & Sprague, R. H. Jr., (Eds.), *Decision support systems: Issues and challenges*. New York, NY: Pergamon Press.

Hunter, P., & Guy, M. (2004). Metadata for Harvesting: The Open Archives Initiative, and How to Find Things on the Web. *The Electronic Library, 22*(2), 168–174. doi:10.1108/02640470410533434

Hurworth, R. (2006, September). *The use of (future) search conferences as a tool for two community development type exercises in Victoria*. Paper presented at the Australasian Evaluation Society International Conference, Darwin, NT, Australia.

Hurworth, R. (2007). The use of (future) search conferences as a qualitative improvement tool. *Qualitative Research Journal, 7*(2), 52–62. doi:10.3316/QRJ0702052

Iannacchione, V. G. (2003). Sequential weight adjustments for the location and cooperation propensity for the 1995 National Survey of Family Growth. *Journal of Official Statistics, 19*(1), 31–43.

Illingworth, N. (2001). The internet matters: Exploring the use of the internet as a research tool. *Sociological Research Online, 6*(2). Retrieved August 25, 2010, from http://www.socresonline.org.uk/6/2/illingworth.html

Intellectual Property Law in Australia. (2010). *Introduction*. Retrieved September 10, 2010, from http://www.ipaustralia.gov.au/ip/introduction.shtml

Ison, N. (2009). Having their say: e-mail interviews for research data collection with people who have verbal communication impairment. *International Journal of Social Research Methodology, 12*(2), 161–172. doi:10.1080/13645570902752365

Jacobs, J. M. (1996). *Essential assessment criteria for physical education teacher education programs: A Delphi study*. Unpublished doctoral dissertation, West Virginia University, Morgantown, WV.

James, N., & Busher, H. (2006). Credibility, authenticity and voice: dilemmas in online interviewing. *Qualitative Research, 6*(3), 403–420. doi:10.1177/1468794106065010

Jansen, B. J., Spink, A., & Saracevic, T. (2000). Real life, real users, and real needs: a study and analysis of user queries on the web. *Information Processing & Management, 36*, 207–227. doi:10.1016/S0306-4573(99)00056-4

Januszewski, A., & Molenda, M. (Eds.). (2008). *Educational technology: A definition with commentary*. Mahwah, NJ: Lawrence Erlbaum Associates.

Jessop, B., Brenner, M., & Jones, M. (2008). Theorizing sociospatial relations. *Environment and Planning. D, Society & Space, 26*, 389–401. doi:10.1068/d9107

Jett, Q. R., & George, J. M. (2003). Work interrupted: A closer look at the role of interruptions in organizational life. *Academy of Management Review, 28*(3), 494–507.

Jick, T. D. (1979). Mixing Qualitative and Quantitative Methods: Triangulation in Action. *Administrative Science Quarterly, 24*(4), 602–611. doi:10.2307/2392366

Jillson, I. A. (1975). The national drug-abuse policy Delphi: Progress report and findings to date. In Linstone, H. A., & Turoff, M. (Eds.), *The Delphi method: Techniques and applications* (pp. 124–159). Reading, MA: Addison-Wesley.

Jirón, P. (2010). Mobile borders in urban daily mobility practices in Santiago de Chile. *International Political Sociology, 4*(1), 66–79. doi:10.1111/j.1749-5687.2009.00092.x

Jobst, M., Dollner, J., & Lubanski, O. (2010). Communicating Geoinformation effectively with virtual 3D city models. In Silva, C. N. (Ed.), *Handbook of Research on E-Planning: ICTs for Urban Development and Monitoring* (pp. 120–142). Hershey, PA: Information Science Reference. doi:10.4018/978-1-61520-929-3.ch007

Johnson, J. B., Reynolds, H., & Josylin, R. (2001). *Political Science Research Methods* (4th ed.). Washington, DC: CQ Press.

Jonassen, D. H. (2004). *Handbook of research on educational communications and technology* (2nd ed.). Mahwah, NJ: Lawrence Erlbaum Associates.

Jones, H., & Twiss, B. C. (1978). *Forecasting technology for planning decision*. London, UK: Macmillan.

Jorgenson, J., & Sullivan, T. (2010). Accessing Children's Perspective through Participatory Photo Interviews. *Forum: Qualitative Social Research, 11*(1). Retrieved February 15, 2011, from http://nbn-resolving.de/urn:nbn:de:0114-fqs100189

Judd, R. C. (1972). Use of Delphi methods in higher education. *Technological Forecasting and Social Change, 4*, 173–186. doi:10.1016/0040-1625(72)90013-3

Jung, J. H., Schneider, C., & Valacich, J. S. (2010). Enhancing the motivational affordance of information systems: The effects of real-time performance feedback and goal setting in group collaboration environments. *Management Science, 56*(4), 724–742. doi:10.1287/mnsc.1090.1129

Kalaian, S. A., & Shah, H. A. (2006). *Overview of parametric and non-parametric statistical methods for analyzing*. Paper presented the 2006 Annual Meeting of the Mid-Western Educational Research Association, Columbus, OH.

Kaliski, J. (2006). Democracy takes command: The new community planning and the challenge of urban design. In Saunders, W. (Ed.), *Urban Planning Today. A Harvard Design Magazine Reader* (pp. 24–37). Minneapolis, MN: University of Minnesota Press.

Kaplan, D. H., Wheeler, J. O., & Holloway, S. R. (2009). *Urban Geography* (2nd ed.). Hoboken, NJ: John Wiley & Sons.

Karau, S. J., & Williams, K. (1993). Social loafing: A meta-analytic review and theoretical integration. *Journal of Personality and Social Psychology, 65*(4), 681–706. doi:10.1037/0022-3514.65.4.681

Kastman, L.-A. M., & Gurak, L. J. (1999). Conducting Technical Communication Research via the Internet: Guidelines for Privacy, Permissions, and Ownership in Educational Research. *Technical Communication, 46*(4), 460–469.

Katsioloudis, P. (2009). Enhancing the collection process for the Delphi technique. In *Proceedings of the 2009 ASEE Southeast Section Conference*, Marietta, GA.

Katz, L. M., Cumming, P. D., & Wallace, E. L. (2007). Computer-based donor screening: A status report. *Transfusion Medicine Reviews, 21*(1), 13–25. doi:10.1016/j.tmrv.2006.08.001

Kavaratzis, M. (2005). Place Branding: A Review of Trends and Conceptual Models. *Marketing Review, 5*(4), 329–342. doi:10.1362/146934705775186854

Kay, G. (1995). Effective meetings through electronic brainstorming. *Journal of Management Development, 14*(6), 4–25. doi:10.1108/02621719510086147

Kazmer, M. M., & Xie, B. (2008). Qualitative interviewing in internet studies: Playing with the media, playing with the method. *Information Communication and Society, 11*(2), 257–278. doi:10.1080/13691180801946333

Keeney, S., Hasson, F., & McKenna, H. P. (2001). A critical review of the Delphi technique as a research methodology for nursing. *International Journal of Nursing Studies, 38*, 195–200. doi:10.1016/S0020-7489(00)00044-4

Keeter, S., Miller, C., Kohut, A., Groves, R. M., & Presser, S. (2000). Consequences of reducing nonresponse in a large national telephone survey. *Public Opinion Quarterly, 64*, 125–148. doi:10.1086/317759

Kelbaugh, B. M. (2006). *Using electronic systems to conduct a modified Delphi study*. Paper presented at the 2006 Annual Meeting of the Mid-Western Educational Research Association, Columbus, OH.

Kelly, G. A. (1955/1991b). The psychology of personal constructs: *Vol. 1. Theory and personality*. London, UK: Routledge.

Kenten, C. (2010). Narrating Oneself: Reflections on the Use of Solicited Diaries with Diary Interviews. *Forum Qualitative Sozialforschung / Forum: Qualitative. Social Research, 11*(2). Retrieved from http://nbn-resolving.de/urn:nbn:de:0114-fqs1002160

Kenyon, S. (2006). Reshaping patterns of mobility and exclusion? The impact of virtual mobility upon accessibility, mobility and social exclusion. In Sheller, M., & Urry, J. (Eds.), *Mobile Technologies of the City* (pp. 102–120). London, UK: Routledge.

Kerlinger, F. N. (1973). *Foundations of behavioral research*. New York, NY: Holt, Rinehart, and Winston.

Kerr, N. L., Aronoff, J., & Messe, L. A. (2000). Methods of small group research. In Reis, H., & Judd, C. (Eds.), *Research methods in social psychology: A handbook*. New York, NY: Cambridge University Press.

Keul, A., & Kühberger, A. (1997). Tracking the Salzburg Tourist. *Annals of Tourism Research, 24*, 1008–1024. doi:10.1016/S0160-7383(97)00038-8

Kiesler, S., Zubrow, D., Moses, A. M., & Geller, V. (1985). Affect in computer-mediated communication: An experiment in synchronous terminal-to-terminal discussion. *Human-Computer Interaction, 1*, 77–104. doi:10.1207/s15327051hci0101_3

Kitchin, D. R., & Tate, D. N. (1999). *Conducting Research in Human Geography: Theory, Methodology and Practice* (1st ed.). London, UK: Longman.

Kivits, J. (2005). Online interviewing and the research relationship. In Hine, C. (Ed.), *Virtual Methods: Issues in social research on the internet* (pp. 35–50). Oxford, UK: Berg.

Klee, A. J. (1972). The utilization of expert opinion in decision-making. *AIChE Journal. American Institute of Chemical Engineers, 18*(6), 1107–1115. doi:10.1002/aic.690180604

Klessmann, J. (2010). Portals as a tool for public participation in urban planning. In Silva, C. N. (Ed.), *Handbook of Research on E-Planning: ICTs for Urban Development and Monitoring* (pp. 252–267). Hershey, PA: Information Science Reference. doi:10.4018/978-1-61520-929-3.ch013

Knoblauch, H., Baer, A., Laurier, E., Petschke, S., & Schnettler, B. (2008). Visual Analysis. New Developments in the Interpretative Analysis of Video and Photography. *Forum: Qualitative Social Research, 9*(3). Retrieved September 15, 2010, from http://www.qualitative-research.net/index.php/fqs/article/view/1170

Kolb, B. (2008). Involving, Sharing, Analysing—Potential of the Participatory Photo Interview. *Forum: Qualitative Social Research, 9*(3). Retrieved September 15, 2010, from http://www.qualitative-research.net/index.php/fqs/article/view/1155

Kolb, B., & Dumreicher, H. (2008). The Hammam - A living cultural heritage. *International Journal of Architectural Research, 2*(3). Retrieved September 15, 2010, from http://archnet.org/library/documents/one-document.jsp?document_id=10484

Komito, L. (2007). Community and inclusion: The impact of new communications technologies. *Irish Journal of Sociology, 16*(2), 77–96.

Kozinets, R. V. (1997). "I want to believe": A Netnography of the X-Philes' Subculture of Consumption. *Advances in Consumer Research. Association for Consumer Research (U. S.), 24*, 470–475.

Kozinets, R. V. (1998). On Netnography: Initial Reflections on Consumer Research Investigations of Cyerculture. *Advances in Consumer Research. Association for Consumer Research (U. S.), 25*, 366–371.

Kozinets, R. V. (2002). The Field behind the Screen: Using Netnography for Marketing Research in Online Communities. *JMR, Journal of Marketing Research, 39*(1), 61–72. doi:10.1509/jmkr.39.1.61.18935

Kozinets, R. V. (2007). Netnography 2.0. In Belk, R. W. (Ed.), *Handbook of Qualitative Research Methods in Marketing* (pp. 129–142). Northampton, MA: Edwards Elgar.

Kozinets, R. V. (2010). *Netnography: Doing Ethnographic Research Online*. Thousand Oaks, CA: Sage.

Kozinets, R. V., & Handelman, J. (1998). Ensouling Consumption: A Netnographic Exploration of the Meaning of Boycotting Behavior. *Advances in Consumer Research. Association for Consumer Research (U. S.), 25*(1), 475–480.

Kozinets, R. V., Hemetsberger, A., & Schau, H. J. (2008). The wisdom of consumer crowds. Collective innovation in the age of networked marketing. *Journal of Macromarketing, 28*(4), 339–354. doi:10.1177/0276146708325382

Kozlowski, S. W. J., & Ilgen, D. R. (2006). Enhancing the effectiveness of work groups and teams. *Psychological Science in the Public Interest, 7*, 77–124.

Kramer, M. (2006). *Dispossessed: life in our world's urban slums*. New York, NY: Orbis Books.

Kramer, T. J., Fleming, G. P., & Mannis, S. M. (2001). Improving face-to-face brainstorming through modeling and facilitation. *Small Group Research, 32*, 533–557. doi:10.1177/104649640103200502

Krammer, K. (2001). *Schriftsprachkompetenz gehörloser Erwachsener (Vol. 3)*. Klagenfurt, Germany: Veröffentlichungen des Forschungszentrums für Gebärdensprache und Hörgeschädigtenkommunikation der Universität Klagenfurt.

Kraut, R. E., Olson, J., Banaji, M., Bruckman, A., Cohen, J., & Couper, M. (2004). Psychological Research Online: Opportunities and Challenges. *The American Psychologist, 59*(2), 105–117. doi:10.1037/0003-066X.59.2.105

Krippendorff, K. (2004). *Content Analysis: An Introduction to Its Methodology* (2nd ed.). Thousand Oaks, CA: Sage.

Kroenke, D. M. (2001). *Database Processing: Fundamentals, Design and Implementation*. Upper Saddle River, New Jersey: Prentice Hall.

Krosnick, J. A. (1991). Response strategies for coping with the cognitive demands of attitude measures in surveys. *Applied Cognitive Psychology, 5*(3), 213–236. doi:10.1002/acp.2350050305

Kruglanski, A. W., Friedman, I., & Zeevi, G. (1971). The effects of extrinsic incentive on some qualitative aspects of task performance. *Journal of Personality, 39*, 606–617. doi:10.1111/j.1467-6494.1971.tb00066.x

Krysan, M., & Couper, M. P. (2003). Race in the live and the virtual interview: racial deference, social desirability, and activation effects in attitude surveys. *Social Psychology Quarterly, 66*(4), 364–383. doi:10.2307/1519835

Kubicek, H. (2010). The potential of e-Participation in urban planning: a European perspective. In Silva, C. N. (Ed.), *Handbook of Research on E-Planning: ICTs for Urban Development and Monitoring* (pp. 168–194). Hershey, PA: Information Science Reference. doi:10.4018/978-1-61520-929-3.ch009

Kuhn, T. S. (1970). *The structure of scientific revolutions* (2nd ed.). Chicago, IL: University of Chicago Press.

Kunimoto, N. (2004). Intimate archives: Japanese – Canadian family photograph, 1939-49. *Art History, 27*, 129–155. doi:10.1111/j.0141-6790.2004.02701005.x

Kuran, T., & McCaffery, E. J. (2004). Expanding discrimination research: Beyond ethnicity and to the Web. *Social Science Quarterly*, *85*, 713–730. doi:10.1111/j.0038-4941.2004.00241.x

Kuran, T., & McCaffery, E. J. (2008). Sex differences in the acceptability of discrimination. *Political Research Quarterly*, *61*(2), 228–238. doi:10.1177/1065912907304500

Kurose, S., Borgers, A. W. J., & Timmermans, H. J. P. (2001). Classifying pedestrian shopping behaviour according to implied heuristic choice rules. *Environment and Planning. B, Planning & Design*, *28*(3), 405–418. doi:10.1068/b2622

Kusenbach, M. (2003). The Go-Along as Ethnographic Research Tool. *Ethnography*, *4*(3), 455–485. doi:10.1177/146613810343007

Kvale, S. (1996). *InterViews: An introduction to qualitative research interviewing*. Thousand Oaks, CA: Sage.

Lamm, H., & Trommsdorff, G. (1973). Group versus individual performance on tasks requiring ideational proficiency (brainstorming). *European Journal of Social Psychology*, *3*, 361–387. doi:10.1002/ejsp.2420030402

Lange, P. G. (2008). Publicly private and privately public: Social networking on YouTube. *Journal of Computer-Mediated Communication*, *13*, 361–380. doi:10.1111/j.1083-6101.2007.00400.x

Langer, R., & Beckman, S. C. (2005). Sensitive research topics: Netnography revisited. *Qualitative Market Research*, *8*(2), 189–203. doi:10.1108/13522750510592454

Larey, T. S., & Paulus, P. B. (1995). Social comparison goal setting in brainstorming groups. *Journal of Applied Social Psychology*, *26*(18), 1579–1596. doi:10.1111/j.1559-1816.1995.tb02634.x

Large, M. (1998a). Using search conferences for building, learning, planning and implementing communities that work. *The Learning Organization*, *4*(3), 190–114.

Large, M. (1998b). Using the search conference for planning a merger participatively. *Career Development International*, *3*(2), 62–66. doi:10.1108/13620439810207554

Lashua, B., Hall, T., & Coffey, A. (2006). *Soundwalking as research method*. Paper presented at the Institute of British Geographers Annual International Conference, London, UK.

Lastowka, F., & Hunter, D. (2004). The laws of the virtual worlds. *California Law Review*, *92*(1), 1–73. doi:10.2307/3481444

Latham, A. (2003). Research Performances, and Doing Human Geography: Some Reflections on the Diary – Photograph, Diary Interview Method. *Environment and Planning*, *35*, 1993–2017. doi:10.1068/a3587

Latham, A. (2004). Researching and writing everyday accounts of the city: an introduction to the diary-photo diary-interview method. In Knowles, C., & Sweetman, P. (Eds.), *Picturing the Social Landscape: Visual methods and the sociological imagination* (pp. 117–131). London, UK: Routledge.

Laurier, E. (2010). Being there/seeing there: recording and analyzing life in the car. In Fincham, B., McGuinness, M., & Murray, L. (Eds.), *Mobile Methodologies* (pp. 103–117). Basingstoke, UK: Palgrave Macmillan.

Laurier, E., Lorimer, H., Brown, B., Juhlin, O., Nobel, A., & Perry, M. (2008). Driving and passengering: notes on the natural organization of ordinary car travel. *Mobilities*, *3*(1), 1–23. doi:10.1080/17450100701797273

Lavrakas, P. J. (Ed.). (2008). *Encyclopedia of Survey Research Methods*. Newbury Park, CA: Sage.

Leenders, R. T. A. J., Kratzer, J., & van Engelen, J. M. L. (2007). Media ensembles and new product team creativity: A tree-based exploration. In MacGregor, S. P., & Torress-Coronas Lira, T. (Eds.), *Higher Creativity for Virtual Teams: Developing Platforms for Co-Creation* (pp. 75–97). Hershey, PA: Information Science Reference. doi:10.4018/978-1-59904-129-2.ch004

Lee, S. (2006). Propensity score adjustment as a weighting scheme for volunteer panel Web surveys. *Journal of Official Statistics*, *22*(2), 329–349.

Lee, S., Brown, E. R., Grant, D., Belin, T. R., & Brick, J. M. (2009). Exploring nonresponse bias in a health survey using neighborhood characteristics. *American Journal of Public Health*, *99*, 1811–1817. doi:10.2105/AJPH.2008.154161

Lee, S., & Valliant, R. (2007). Weighting telephone samples using propensity scores. In Lepkowski, J. M., Tucker, C., & Brick, J. M. (Eds.), *Advances in telephone survey methodology* (pp. 170–186). New York, NY: Wiley. doi:10.1002/9780470173404.ch8

Lee, S., & Valliant, R. (2009). Estimation for volunteer panel Web surveys using propensity score adjustment and calibration adjustment. *Sociological Methods & Research, 37*, 319–343. doi:10.1177/0049124108329643

Lefebvre, H. (1996). *Writings on cities* (Kofman, E., & Lebas, E., Trans.). Oxford, UK: Blackwell.

Leggett Dugosh, K., Paulus, P. B., Roland, E. J., & Yang, H. C. (2001). Cognitive stimulation in brainstorming. *Journal of Personality and Social Psychology, 79*, 722–735. doi:10.1037/0022-3514.79.5.722

Lenhart, A., Fallows, D., & Horrigan, J. (2004). *Online activities and pursuits.* Retrieved from http://wwwpewtrusts.org/our_work_detail/aspx?id=50

Lepkowski, J., Kalton, G., & Kasprzyk, D. (1989). Weighting adjustments for partial nonresponse in the 1984 SIPP panel. In *Proceedings of the Survey Research Methods Section, American Statistical Association* (pp. 296-301).

Lerner, D. (1958). *The passing of traditional society: Modernizing the Middle East.* Glencoe, IL: Free Press.

Lessig, L. (2008). *Remix: Making art and commerce thrive in the hybrid economy.* New York, NY: Penguin Press.

Lessler, J. T., & O'Reilly, J. M. (1997). Mode of interview and reporting of sensitive issues: design and implementation of audio computer-assisted self-interviewing. *NIDA Research Monograph, 167*, 366–382.

Levie, W. H., & Lentz, R. (1982). Effects of Text Illustrations: A Review of Research. *Educational Communication and Technology, 30*(4), 195–232.

Levine, J. M., & Moreland, R. L. (2004). Collaboration: The social context of theory development. *Personality and Social Psychology Review, 8*(2), 164–172. doi:10.1207/s15327957pspr0802_10

Lewis, J. (2009). Redefining Qualitative Methods: Believability in the Fifth Moment. *International Journal of Qualitative Methods, 8*(2). Retrieved September 4, 2010, from http://ejournals.library.ualberta.ca/index.php/IJQM/article/view/4408/5403

Liebenberg, L. (2009). The visual image as discussion point: increasing validity in boundary crossing research. *Qualitative Research, 9*, 441–467. doi:10.1177/1468794109337877

Limb, M., & Dwyer, C. (Eds.). (2001). *Qualitative Methodologies for Geographers. Issues and debates.* London, UK: Arnold.

Lincoln, Y. S., & Guba, E. G. (1985). *Naturalistic Inquiry.* Newbury Park, CA: Sage.

Lincoln, Y., & Guba, E. (1985). *Naturalistic Enquiry.* Newbury Park, CA: Sage.

Lindeman, C. A. (1981). *Priorities within the health care system: A Delphi study.* Kansas City, MO: American Nurses' Association.

Lindqvist, P., & Nordanger, U. K. (2007). (Mis-?) using the e-Delphi method: An attempt to articulate the practical knowledge of teaching. *Journal of Research Methods and Methodological Issues, 1*(1).

Linstone, H. A., & Turoff, M. (1975). General Applications: Introduction. In Linstone, H. A., & Turoff, M. (Eds.), *The Delphi method: Techniques and applications* (pp. 75–83). Reading, MA: Addison-Wesley.

Linstone, H. A., & Turoff, M. (1975). Introduction. In Linstone, H. A., & Turoff, M. (Eds.), *The Delphi method: Techniques and applications* (pp. 3–12). Reading, MA: Addison-Wesley.

Lipton, D. S., Goldstein, M. F., Fahnbulleh, F. W., & Gertz, E. N. (1996). The Interactive Video-Questionnaire: A new technology for interviewing deaf persons. *American Annals of the Deaf, 141*(5), 370–379.

Little, R. J. A. (1993). Post-stratification: A modeler's perspective. *Journal of the American Statistical Association, 88*, 1001–1012. doi:10.2307/2290792

Little, R. J. A., & Vartivarian, S. (2005). Does weighting for nonresponse increase the variance of survey means? *Survey Methodology, 31*, 161–168.

Littleton, D. (2007). Navigating Pitfalls of Web-Based Survey Development and Administration. *Medical Reference Services Quarterly*, *26*(4), 75–83. doi:10.1300/J115v26n04_06

Lobe, B., & Vehovar, V. (2009). Towards a flexible online mixed method design with a feedback loop. *Quality & Quantity*, *43*(4), 585–597. doi:10.1007/s11135-007-9146-7

Loescher, M. (2005). Cameras at the Addy: speaking in pictures with city kids. In Grimshaw, A., & Ravetz, A. (Eds.), *Visualizing Anthropology*. Bristol, UK: Intellect. doi:10.1386/jmpr.3.2.75

Lorch, B. (2005). Auto-dependent induced shopping: exploring the relationship between power centre morphology and consumer spatial behaviour. *Canadian Journal of Urban Research*, *14*(2), 364–383.

Lorch, B. J., & Smith, M. J. (1993). Pedestrian Movement and the Downtown Enclosed Shopping Center. *Journal of the American Planning Association. American Planning Association*, *59*(1), 75–86. doi:10.1080/01944369308975846

Lorenz, L. S., & Kolb, B. (2009). Involving the Public through Participatory Visual Research Methods. In J. Tritter & K. Lutfey (Eds.), Bridging divides: patient and public involvement on both sides of the Atlantic" *Special Issue: Health Expectations*, *12*, 262-274.

Lorenz, L. S. (2010). *Brain Injury Survivors: Narratives of Rehabilitation and Healing*. Boulder, CO: Lynne Rienner.

Lucas, C. (1996). *Multicultural aspects of sociolinguistics in deaf communities*. Washington, DC: Gallaudet University Press.

Lucas, R. E. (1986). The behavioral foundations of economic theory. *The Journal of Business*, *59*(4), S401–S426.

Ludlow, J. (1975). Delphi inquires and knowledge utilization. In Linstone, H. A., & Turoff, M. (Eds.), *The Delphi method: Techniques and applications* (pp. 102–123). Reading, MA: Addison-Wesley.

Ludwig, B. G. (1994). *Internationalizing Extension: An exploration of the characteristics evident in a state university Extension system that achieves internationalization*. Unpublished doctoral dissertation, The Ohio State University, Columbus, OH.

Ludwig, B. G. (1997). Predicting the future: Have you considered using the Delphi methodology? *Journal of Extension*, *35*(5). Retrieved November 6, 2005, from http://www.joe.org/joe/1997october/tt2.html

Ludwig, D. (2001). The era of management is over. *Ecosystems (New York, N.Y.)*, *4*, 758–764. doi:10.1007/s10021-001-0044-x

Madge, C. (2007). Developing a geographers' agenda for online research ethics. *Progress in Human Geography*, *31*, 654–674. doi:10.1177/0309132507081496

Madge, C., & O'Connor, H. (2002). On-line with e-mums: exploring the Internet as a medium for research. *Area*, *34*(1), 92–102. doi:10.1111/1475-4762.00060

Madge, C., & O'Connor, H. (2005). Mothers in the making? Exploring liminality in cyber/space. *Transactions of the Institute of British Geographers*, *30*(1), 83–97. doi:10.1111/j.1475-5661.2005.00153.x

Maitland, R. (2007). Marketing National Capital Cities [Special Issue]. *Journal of Travel & Tourism Marketing*, *22*(3-4).

Malaby, T. (2006). Parlaying value: Capital in and beyond virtual worlds. *Games and Culture*, *1*(2), 141–162. doi:10.1177/1555412006286688

Mannay, D. (2010). Making the familiar strange: can visual research methods render the familiar setting more perceptible. *Qualitative Research*, *10*, 91–110. doi:10.1177/1468794109348684

Mannix, E. A., & Neale, M. A. (2005). What difference makes a difference: The promise and reality of diverse groups in organizations. *Psychological Science in the Public Interest*, *6*, 31–55. doi:10.1111/j.1529-1006.2005.00022.x

Mansour-Cole, D. (2001). Team identity formation in virtual teams. In M. M. Beyerlein, D. A. Johnson, & S. T. Beyerlein (Eds.), *Advances in Interdisciplinary Studies of Work Teams: Vol. 8. Virtual Teams* (pp. 41-58). Bradford, UK: Emerald.

Manyiwa, S., & Crawford, I. (2002). Determining linkages between consumer choices in a social context and the consumer's values: A means-end approach. *Journal of Consumer Behaviour*, *2*(1), 54–70. doi:10.1002/cb.89

Marchant, E. W. (1988). Methodological problems associated with the use of the Delphi technique: Some comments. *Fire Technology, 24*(1), 59–62. doi:10.1007/BF01039641

Marín, V. H., Delgado, L. E., & Bachmann, P. (2008). Conceptual PHES-system models of the Aysén watershed and fjord (Southern Chile): Testing a brainstorming strategy. *Journal of Environmental Management, 88*, 1109–1118. doi:10.1016/j.jenvman.2007.05.012

Markham, A. (2007). Ethic as method, method as ethic: A case for reflexivity in qualitative ICT research. *Journal of Information Ethics, 15*(2), 37–54. doi:10.3172/JIE.15.2.37

Markham, A. N. (2008). The methods, politics, and ethics of representation in online ethnography. In Denzin, N. K., & Lincoln, Y. S. (Eds.), *Collecting and Interpreting Qualitative Data* (pp. 247–284). Thousand Oaks, CA: Sage.

Marshall, C., & Rossman, G. B. (2006). *Designing qualitative research*. London, UK: Sage.

Martin, D. (2004). Reconstructing urban politics: neighbourhood activism in land-use change. *Urban Affairs Review, 39*, 589–611. doi:10.1177/1078087404263805

Mason, W., & Suri, S. (2010). Conducting behavioral research on Amazon's Mechanical Turk. *Behavioral Research Methods*.

Masser, I., & Foley, P. (1987). Delphi revisited: Expert opinion in urban analysis. *Urban Studies (Edinburgh, Scotland), 24*, 217–225. doi:10.1080/00420988720080351

Massey, D. (1994). *Space, place and gender*. Cambridge, UK: Polity Press.

Massey, D. (2005). *For space*. London, UK: Sage.

McCaffrey, D. F., Ridgeway, G., & Morral, A. R. (2004). Propensity score estimation with boosted regression for evaluating causal effects in observational studies. *Psychological Methods, 9*(4), 572–606. doi:10.1037/1082-989X.9.4.403

McCampbell, W. H., & Stewart, B. R. (1992). Career ladder programs for vocational education: Desirable characteristics. *Journal of Vocational Education Research, 17*(1), 53–68.

McCoyd, J., & Schwaber Kerson, T. (2006). Conducting intensive interviews using e-mail: a serendipitous comparative opportunity. *Qualitative Social Work, 5*(3), 389–406. doi:10.1177/1473325006067367

McCullum, C. (2002). Use of a participatory planning process as a way to build community food security. *Journal of the American Dietetic Association, 102*(7), 962–967. doi:10.1016/S0002-8223(02)90220-8

McGeary, J. (2009). A critique of using the Delphi technique for assessing evaluation capability-building needs. *Evaluation Journal of Australasia, 9*(1), 31–39.

McGuire, T. W., Kiesler, S., & Siegel, J. (1987). Group and computer-mediated discussion effects in risk decision making. *Journal of Personality and Social Psychology, 52*, 917–930. doi:10.1037/0022-3514.52.5.917

McKee, H. A., & Porter, J. E. (2009). *The Ethics of Internet Research: a rhetorical, case-based process*. Witney, UK: Peter Lang.

McLellan, E., MacQueen, K. M., & Neidig, J. L. (2003). Beyond the Qualitative Interview: Data preparation and transcription. *Field Methods, 15*, 63–84. doi:10.1177/1525822X02239573

McLuhan, M. (1962). *The Gutenberg Galaxy: The Making of Typographic Man*. Toronto, ON, Canada: University of Toronto Press.

McMichael, P. (2004). *Development and Social Change a global perspective* (3rd ed.). Thousand Oaks, CA: Pine Forge Press.

Meadow, A., Parnes, S. J., & Reese, H. (1959). Influence of brainstorming instructions and problem sequence on a creative problem solving test. *The Journal of Applied Psychology, 43*, 413–416. doi:10.1037/h0043917

Merkle, D., & Edelman, M. (2002). Nonresponse in exit polls: A comprehensive analysis. In Groves, R. M., Dillman, D. A., Eltinge, J. L., & Little, R. J. A. (Eds.), *Survey nonresponse* (pp. 243–258). New York, NY: Wiley.

Merriam, S. (1998). *Qualitative Research and Case Study Applications in Education*. San Francisco, CA: Jossey-Bass.

Michalko, M. (2001). *Cracking creativity: The secrets of creative genius*. Berkeley, CA: Tenspeed Press Edition.

Michinov, N., & Michinov, E. (2009). Advantages and pitfalls of social interactions in the digital age: Practical recommendations for improving virtual group functioning. In Heatherton, A. T., & Walcott, V. A. (Eds.), *Handbook of social Interactions in the 21st Century* (pp. 83–96). Hauppauge, NY: Nova Science Publishers.

Michinov, N., & Primois, C. (2005). Improving group productivity and creativity in on-line groups through social comparison process: New evidence for asynchronous electronic brainstorming. *Computers in Human Behavior, 21*(1), 11–28. doi:10.1016/j.chb.2004.02.004

Miller, L. E. (2006). *Determining what could/should be: The Delphi technique and its application.* Paper presented at the 2006 Annual Meeting of the Mid-Western Educational Research Association, Columbus, OH.

Milligan, C., Bingley, A., & Gatrell, A. (2005). Digging deep: Using diary techniques to explore the place of health and well-being amongst older people. *Social Science & Medicine, 61,* 1882–1892. doi:10.1016/j.socscimed.2005.04.002

Millonig, A., & Maierbrugger, G. (2010). Using semi-automated shadowing for analysing stress-induced spatiotemporal behaviour patterns of passengers in public transport infrastructures. In A. Spink, F. Grieco, O. Krips, L. Loijens, L. Noldus, & P. Zimmerman (Eds.), *Proceedings of the 7th International Conference on Methods and Techniques in Behavioural Research* (pp. 314-317).

Millonig, A., Brändle, N., Ray, M., Bauer, D., & Spek, S. V. D. (2009). Pedestrian Behaviour Monitoring: Methods and Experiences. In Gottfried, B., & Aghajan, H. (Eds.), *Behaviour Monitoring and Interpretation - BMI - Smart Environment: Ambient Intelligence and Smart Environments (Vol. 3,* pp. 11–42). Amsterdam, The Netherlands: IOS Press.

Millonig, A., & Gartner, G. (2008). *Shadowing - Tracking - Interviewing: How to Explore Human Spatio-Temporal Behaviour Patterns (Tech. Rep.).* Bremen, Germany: TZI.

Millonig, A., & Gartner, G. (2010). Show Me My Way: The Use of Human Spatio-Temporal Behaviour Patterns for Developing Ubiquitous Wayfinding Systems. In Wachowicz, M. (Ed.), *Movement-Aware Applications for Sustainable Mobility: Technologies and Approaches* (pp. 157–174). Hershey, PA: IGI Global. doi:10.4018/978-1-61520-769-5.ch010

Millonig, A., & Schechtner, K. (2007). Developing Landmark-based Pedestrian Navigation Systems. [IST]. *IEEE Transactions on Intelligent Transportation Systems, 8*(1), 43–49. doi:10.1109/TITS.2006.889439

Misanchuk, E. R., Schwier, R. A., & Boling, E. (1999). *Visual design for instructional multimedia.* Paper presented at the World Conference on Educational Multimedia, Hypermedia and Telecommunications (EDMEDIA), Chesapeake, VA.

Mitchell, V. W. (1991). The Delphi technique: An exposition and application. *Technology Analysis and Strategic Management, 3*(4), 333–358. doi:10.1080/09537329108524065

Mitroff, I., & Turoff, M. (1975). Philosophical and methodological foundations of Delphi. In Linstone, H. A., & Turoff, M. (Eds.), *The Delphi method: Techniques and applications* (pp. 17–35). Reading, MA: Addison-Wesley.

Monaco, J. (2000). *How to read a film.* Oxford, UK: Oxford University Press.

Montaquila, J., Brick, J. M., Hagedorn, M. C., Kennedy, C., & Keeter, S. (2007). Aspects of nonresponse bias in RDD telephone surveys. In Lepkowski, J. M., Tucker, C., & Brick, J. M. (Eds.), *Advances in telephone survey methodology* (pp. 561–586). New York, NY: Wiley. doi:10.1002/9780470173404.ch25

Moore, D. M., Burton, J. K., & Myers, R. J. (2004). Multiple-channel communication: The theoretical and research foundations of multimedia. In Jonassen, D. H. (Ed.), *Handbook of Research for Educational Communications and Technology* (2nd ed., pp. 979–1005). Mahwah, NJ: Lawrence Erlbaum Associates.

Moore, G., Croxford, B., Adams, M., Refaee, M., Cox, T., & Sharples, S. (2008). The photo survey research method: capturing life in the city. *Visual Studies, 23*(1), 50–62. doi:10.1080/14725860801908536

Morel, J., & Licoppe, C. (2010). Studying mobile video telephony. In Büscher, M., Urry, J., & Witchger, K. (Eds.), *Mobile methods*. London, UK: Routledge.

Morgan, D. R., Pelissero, J. P., & England, R. E. (1979). Urban planning: Using a Delphi as a decision-making aid. *Public Administration Review*, *39*(4), 380–384. doi:10.2307/976215

Morrow, V. (2008). Ethical dilemmas in research with children and young people about their social environments. *Children's Geographies*, *6*(1), 49–61. doi:10.1080/14733280701791918

Mortensen, M., & Hinds, P. (2001). Conflict and shared identity in geographically distributed teams. *The International Journal of Conflict Management*, *12*, 212–238. doi:10.1108/eb022856

Mort, G. S., & Rose, T. (2004). The effect of product type on value linkages in the means-end chain: Implications for theory and method. *Journal of Consumer Behaviour*, *3*(3), 221–234. doi:10.1002/cb.136

Mossberger, K., Tolbert, C., & McNeal, R. (Eds.). (2008). *Digital citizenship. The Internet, Society, and Participation*. Cambridge, MA: MIT Press.

Mowlana, H. (1995). The communications paradox. *The Bulletin of the Atomic Scientists*, *51*(4), 40–46.

Mullen, B., & Copper, C. (1994). The relation between group cohesiveness and performance: An integration. *Psychological Bulletin*, *115*(2), 210–227. doi:10.1037/0033-2909.115.2.210

Mullen, B., Johnson, C., & Salas, E. (1991). Productivity loss in brainstorming groups: a meta-analytic integration. *Basic and Applied Social Psychology*, *12*, 3–23. doi:10.1207/s15324834basp1201_1

Mulwanda, M., & Mutale, E. (1994). Never minds the people, shanties must go: the politics of urban land in Zambia. *Cities (London, England)*, *11*(5), 303–311. doi:10.1016/0264-2751(94)90083-3

Murray, L. (2008). Motherhood, risk and everyday mobilities. In Priya Uteng, T., & Cresswell, T. (Eds.), *Gendered mobilities* (pp. 47–63). Aldershot, UK: Ashgate.

Murray, L. (2009a). Looking at and looking back: visualization in mobile research. *Qualitative Research*, *9*(4), 469–488. doi:10.1177/1468794109337879

Murray, L. (2009b). Making the journey to school: The gendered and generational aspects of risk in constructing everyday mobility. *Health Risk & Society*, *11*(5), 471–486. doi:10.1080/13698570903183889

Murray, L. (2010). Contextualizing and mobilizing research. In Fincham, B., McGuinness, M., & Murray, L. (Eds.), *Mobile Methodologies* (pp. 13–24). Basingstoke, UK: Palgrave Macmillan.

Murry, J. P. (1992). Expectations of department chairpersons: A Delphi case study. *Journal of Staff, Program, &. Organization Development*, *10*, 13–21.

Murthy, D. (2008). Digital EthnograpShy: An Examination of the Use of New Technologies for Social Research. *Sociology*, *42*(5), 837–855. doi:10.1177/0038038508094565

Myers, M., & Newman, M. (2007). The qualitative interview in IS research: examining the craft. *Information and Organization*, *17*, 2–26. doi:10.1016/j.infoandorg.2006.11.001

Naef, M., & Schuepp, J. (2009). *Measuring Trust: Experiments and surveys in contrast and combination* (SOEPpaper No. 167). Retrieved from http://www.diw.de/de/diw_02.c.240038.de/soeppapers.html

Nagasundaram, M., & Dennis, A. R. (1993). When a group is not a group: The cognitive foundation of group idea generation. *Small Group Research*, *24*, 463–489. doi:10.1177/1046496493244003

Nass, C., Moon, Y., & Carney, P. (1999). Are respondents polite to computers? Social desirability and direct responses to computers. *Journal of Applied Social Psychology*, *29*(5), 1093–1110. doi:10.1111/j.1559-1816.1999.tb00142.x

Nass, C., Moon, Y., & Green, N. (1997). Are machines gender neutral? Gender-stereotypic responses to computers with voices. *Journal of Applied Social Psychology*, *27*(10), 864–876. doi:10.1111/j.1559-1816.1997.tb00275.x

National Health and Medical Research Council (NHM-RC). Australian Research Council (ARC), & Australian Vice-Chancellors' Committee (AVCC). (2007). *National statement on ethical conduct in human research.* Retrieved June 22, 2010, from http://www.nhmrc.gov.au

Needham, R. D., & de Loe, R. C. (1990). The policy Delphi: Purpose, structure, and application. *Canadian Geographer, 34*(2), 133–142. doi:10.1111/j.1541-0064.1990. tb01258.x

Nelson, M., & Otnes, C. (2005). Exploring cross-cultural ambivalence: a netnography of intercultural wedding message boards. *Journal of Business Research, 58*, 89–95. doi:10.1016/S0148-2963(02)00477-0

Nemiro, J. E. (2001). Assessing the climate for creativity in virtual teams. In M. M. Beyerlein, D. A. Johnson, & S. T. Beyerlein (Eds.), *Advances in Interdisciplinary Studies of Work Teams: Vol. 8. Virtual Teams* (pp. 59-84). Bradford, UK: Emerald.

Nemiro, J. E. (2002). The creative process in virtual teams. *Creativity Research Journal, 14*(1), 69–83. doi:10.1207/S15326934CRJ1401_6

Nemiro, J. E. (2008). Creativity techniques for virtual teams. In Nemiro, J., Beyerlein, M. M., Bradley, L., & Beyerlein, S. (Eds.), *The handbook of high performance virtual teams* (pp. 491–532). Hoboken, NJ: John Wiley & Sons.

Nesbary, D. (1999). *Survey Research and the World Wide Web.* Boston, MA: Allen & Bacon.

Nestor, P. G., & Schutt, R. K. (2011). *Research Methods in Psychology: Investigating Human Behavior.* Thousand Oaks, CA: Sage.

Newman, M. (2008a, May 22). Research into Islamic terrorism led to police response. *Times Higher Education Supplement.* Retrieved November 2, 2010, from http://www.timeshighereducation.co.uk/story.asp?storycode=402125

Newman, M. (2008b, July 17). Researchers have no 'right' to study terrorist materials. *Times Higher Education Supplement.* Retrieved November 2, 2010, from http://www.timeshighereducation.co.uk/story.asp?storycode=402844

Newman, W. L. (2000). *Social research Methods. Qualitative and quantitative approaches* (4th ed.). London, UK: Allyn and Bacon.

News, B. B. C. (2001, September 1). *Inquiry into sex abuse files blunder.* Retrieved from http://news.bbc.co.uk/2/hi/uk_news/1519889.stm

Neyland, D. (2006). Moving Images: The Mobility and Immobility of 'Kids Standing Still'. *The Sociological Review, 54*(2), 363–381. doi:10.1111/j.1467-954X.2006.00618.x

Nicholas, D. B., Lach, L., King, G., Scott, M., Boydell, K., & Sawatxky, B. (2010). Contrasting Internet and face-to-face focus groups for children with chronic health conditions: Outcomes and participant experiences. *International Journal of Qualitative Methods, 9*(1), 106–121.

Nicholls, W. L. II, Baker, R. P., & Martin, J. (1997). The effect of new data collection technologies on survey data quality. In Lyberg, L., Biemer, P., Collins, M., DeLeeuw, E., Dippo, C., Schwarz, N., & Trewin, D. (Eds.), *Survey measurement and process quality* (pp. 221–248). New York, NY: Wiley.

Nijstad, B. A., & Stroebe, W. (2006). How the group affects the mind: A cognitive model of idea generation in groups. *Personality and Social Psychology Review, 10*, 186–213. doi:10.1207/s15327957pspr1003_1

Nisbett, R., & Wilson, T. (1977). Telling more than We can Know: Verbal Reports on Mental Processes. *Psychological Review, 84*, 231–259. doi:10.1037/0033-295X.84.3.231

Nordin, K., & Berglund, U. (2010). Children's Maps in GIS: A Tool for Communicating Outdoor Experiences in Urban Planning. *International Journal of Information Communication Technologies and Human Development, 2*(2), 1–16. doi:10.4018/jicthd.2010040101

Norman, D. A. (2005). *Emotional design - why we love (or hate) everyday things.* New York, NY: Basic Books.

Novakowski, N., & Wellar, B. (2008). Using the Delphi technique in normative planning research: Methodological design considerations. *Environment & Planning A, 40*, 1485–1500.

Nunamaker, J. F., Dennis, A. R., Valacich, J. S., Vogel, D. R., & Georges, J. F. (1991). Electronic meeting systems to support group work. *Communications of the ACM, 34*(7), 41–61.

Nunamaker, J., Briggs, B., & Mittleman, D. (1994). Electronic meeting systems: Ten years of lessons learned. In Coleman, D., & Khanna, R. (Eds.), *Groupware: Technologies Applications* (pp. 149–193). Upper Saddle River, NJ: Prentice Hall.

Nunamaker, T. I., Applegate, L. M., & Konsyski, B. R. (1987). Facilitating group creativity: experience with a group decision support system. *Journal of Management Information Systems, 3*, 5–19.

O'Neill, S., Scott, M., & Conboy, K. (2009). What's technology got to do with it? A Delphi study on collaborative learning in distance education. In *Proceedings of 17th European Conference on Information Systems*.

O'Connor, A., Zerger, A., & Itami, B. (2005). Geotemporal tracking and analysis of tourist movement. *Mathematics and Computers in Simulation, 69*(1-2), 135–150. doi:10.1016/j.matcom.2005.02.036

O'Connor, H., & Madge, C. (2003). "Focus groups in cyberspace": using the Internet for qualitative research. *Qualitative Market Research: An International Journal, 6*(2), 133–143. doi:10.1108/13522750310470190

O'Connor, H., Madge, C., Shaw, R., & Wellens, J. (2008). Internet-based Interviewing. In Fielding, N., Lee, R. M., & Blank, G. (Eds.), *The Sage Handbook of Online Research Methods* (pp. 271–289). Los Angeles, CA: Sage.

Oevermann, U. (1993). Die objektive Hermeneutik als unverzichtbare methodologische Grundlage für die Analyse von Subjektivität. Zugleich eine Kritik der Tiefenhermeneutik. In Jung, T., & Müller-Doohm, S. (Eds.), *Wirklichkeit" im Deutungsprozess: Verstehen und Methoden in den Kultur- und Sozialwissenschaften* (pp. 106–189). Frankfurt, Germany: Suhrkamp.

Offner, A. K., Kramer, T. J., & Winter, J. P. (1996). The effects of facilitation, recording and pauses upon group brainstorming. *Small Group Research, 27*, 283–298. doi:10.1177/1046496496272005

Ohbuchi, E., Hanaizumi, H., & Hock, L. A. (2004). Barcode Readers using the Camera Device in Mobile Phones. In *Proceedings of the 2004 IEEE International Conference on Cyberworlds (CW'04)* (pp. 260-265).

Olsen, R. (2008). Computer Assisted Self-Interviewing. *Encyclopedia of Survey Research Methods*, Paul J. Lavarakas, (ed.), Sage, p. 121 – 122.

Olsen, R., & Sheets, C. (2008). Data Management. *Encyclopedia of Survey Research Methods*, Paul J. Lavarakas, (ed.), Sage, p. 177 – 180.

Olsen, R., & Sheets, C. (2008). VoIP and the Virtual Computer Assisted Telephone Interview (CATI) Facility. *Encyclopedia of Survey Research Methods*, Paul J. Lavarakas, (ed.), Sage, p. 950 – 952.

Olshfski, D., & Joseph, A. (1991). Assessing training needs of executives using the Delphi techniques. *Public Productivity & Management Review, 14*(3), 297–301. doi:10.2307/3380739

Olson, J. C., & Reynolds, T. J. (1983). Understanding consumers' cognitive structures: Implications for marketing strategy. In Percy, L., & Woodside, A. G. (Eds.), *Advertising and Consumer Psychology* (pp. 77–90). Lexington, MA: Lexington Books.

O'Muircheartaigh, C. (1997). Measurement error in surveys: A historical perspective. In Lyberg, L., Biemer, P., Collins, M., DeLeeuw, E., Dippo, C., Schwarz, N., & Trewin, D. (Eds.), *Survey measurement and process quality* (pp. 1–25). New York, NY: Wiley.

Opdenakker, R. (2006). Advantages and disadvantages of four interview techniques in qualitative research. *Forum: Qualitative Social Research, 7*(4). Retrieved August 25, 2010, from http://nbn-resolving.de/urn:nbn:de:0114-fqs0604118

O'Reilly, J. M., Hubbard, M. L., Lessler, J. T., Biemer, P. P., & Turner, C. F. (1994). Audio and video computer-assisted self-interviewing: Preliminary tests of new technologies for data collection. *Journal of Official Statistics, 10*(2), 197–214.

Oriordan, K. (2010). *Internet research ethics: revisiting the relations between technologies, spaces, texts and people.* Retrieved February 27, 2011, from http://eresearch-ethics.org/position/internet-research-ethics-revisiting-the-relations-between-technologies-spaces-texts-and-people/

Osborn, A. F. (1953). *Applied imagination.* Oxford, UK: Charles Scribner's.

Osborn, A. F. (1957). *Applied imagination; principles and procedures of creative problem-solving*. New York, NY: Scribner.

Otienoh, R. (2010). Feedback on teachers' journal entries: a blessing or a curse? *Reflective Practice: International and Multidisciplinary Perspectives, 11*(2), 143–156.

Pace, S. (2008). YouTube: An opportunity for consumer narrative analysis? *Qualitative Market Research: An International Journal, 11*(2), 213–226. doi:10.1108/13522750810864459

Pagenstecher, C. (2009). Zwangsarbeit 1939-1945. Erinnerungen und Geschichte. Ein digitales Interviewarchiv und seine Bildungsmaterialien. In D. Baranowski (Ed.), *Ich bin die Stimme der sechs Millionen. Das Videoarchiv im Ort der Information* (pp. 192-198). Berlin, Germany: Stiftung Denkmal für die ermordeten Juden Europas.

Palomba, E. (2006). *ICT technologies and intercultural issues*. Retrieved July 28, 2010, from http://www.formatex.org/micte2006/pdf/82-86.pdf

Pang, L., Morgan-Morris, V., & Howell, A. (2010). RFID in Urban Planning. In Silva, C. N. (Ed.), *Handbook of Research on E-Planning: ICTs for Urban Development and Monitoring* (pp. 388–403). Hershey, PA: Information Science Reference. doi:10.4018/978-1-61520-929-3.ch020

Panofsky, E. (2006). *Ikonographie und Ikonologie: Bildinterpretation nach dem Dreistufenmodell Erwin Panofsky*. Cologne, Germany: DuMont.

Papademas, D., & International Visual Sociology Association (IVSA). (2009). IVSA Code of Research Ethics and Guidelines. *Visual Studies, 24*(3), 250–257. doi:10.1080/14725860903309187

Parks, S. C. (1995). Challenging the future of dietetics education and credentialing—dialogue, discovery and directions: A summary of the 1994 Future Search Conference. *Journal of the American Dietetic Association, 95*(5), 598–606. doi:10.1016/S0002-8223(95)00165-4

Parnes, S. J., & Meadow, A. (1959). Effects of 'brainstorming' instructions on creative problem solving by trained and untrained subjects. *Journal of Educational Psychology, 50*, 171–176. doi:10.1037/h0047223

Parsons, J. A., Baum, S., & Johnson, T. P. (2000). *Inclusion of disabled populations in social surveys: Review and recommendations*. Chicago, IL: Survey Research Laboratory, University of Illinois at Chicago.

Patton, M. Q. (1990). *Qualitative evaluation and research methods* (2nd ed.). London, UK: Sage.

Paul, M., Hennig-Thurau, T., Gremler, D. D., Gwinner, K. P., & Wiertz, C. (2009). Toward a theory of repeat purchase drivers for consumer services. *Journal of the Academy of Marketing Science, 37*(2), 215–237. doi:10.1007/s11747-008-0118-9

Paulus, P. B. (2000). Groups, teams, and creativity: The creative potential of idea-generating groups. *Applied Psychology: An International Review, 49*(2), 237–262. doi:10.1111/1464-0597.00013

Paulus, P. B., & Brown, V. (2003). Ideational creativity in groups: Lessons from research on brainstorming. In Paulus, P. B., & Nijstad, B. (Eds.), *Group creativity: Innovation through collaboration* (pp. 110–136). New York, NY: Oxford University Press.

Paulus, P. B., & Dzindolet, M. T. (1993). Social influence processes in group brainstorming. *Journal of Personality and Social Psychology, 64*, 575–586. doi:10.1037/0022-3514.64.4.575

Paulus, P. B., & Dzindolet, M. T. (2008). Social influence, creativity, and innovation. *Social Influence, 3*, 228–247. doi:10.1080/15534510802341082

Paulus, P. B., Kohn, N., & Dzindolet, M. (2010). Teams. In Runco, M., & Pritzker, S. (Eds.), *Encyclopedia of Creativity* (2nd ed.). Amsterdam, The Netherlands: Elsevier.

Paulus, P. B., Leggett Dugosh, K. L., Dzindolet, M. T., Coskun, H., & Putman, V. L. (2002). Social and cognitive influences in group brainstorming: Predicting production gains and losses. *European Social Psychology Review, 12*, 299–325. doi:10.1080/14792772143000094

Paulus, P. B., Nakui, T., Putman, V. L., & Brown, V. R. (2006). Effects of task instructions and brief breaks on brainstorming. *Group Dynamics, 10*, 206–219. doi:10.1037/1089-2699.10.3.206

Pearce, D. G. (1988). Tourist time-budget. *Annals of Tourism Research, 15*(1), 106–121. doi:10.1016/0160-7383(88)90074-6

Peffers, K., & Gengler, C. E. (2003). How to identify new high-payoff information systems for the organization. *Communications of the ACM, 46*(1), 83–88. doi:10.1145/602421.602424

Perks, R. (2010). The Roots of Oral History: Exploring Contrasting Attitudes to Elite, Corporate, and Business Oral History in Britain and the U.S. *The Oral History Review, 37*(2), 215–224. doi:10.1093/ohr/ohq049

Peter, J. P., Olson, J. C., & Grunert, K. G. (1999). *Consumer behaviour and marketing strategy*. London, UK: McGraw-Hill.

Peters, L. M. L., & Manz, C. C. (2008). Getting virtual teams right the first time: Keys to successful collaboration in the virtual world. In Nemiro, J., Beyerlein, M. M., Bradley, L., & Beyerlein, S. (Eds.), *The handbook of high performance virtual teams* (pp. 105–130). Hoboken, NJ: John Wiley & Sons.

Petocz, P., & Reid, A. (2006). The contribution of mathematics to graduates' professional working life. In P. Jeffery (Ed.), *Australian Association for Research in Education 2005 Conference Papers*. Melbourne: AARE. Retrieved August 25, 2010, from http://www.aare.edu.au/05pap/pet05141.pdf

Pieters, R., Baumgartner, H., & Allen, D. (1995). A means-end chain approach to consumer goal structures. *International Journal of Research in Marketing, 12*(3), 227–244. doi:10.1016/0167-8116(95)00023-U

Pieters, R., Botschen, G., & Thelen, E. M. (1998). Customer desire expectations about service employees: An analysis of hierarchical reslations. *Psychology and Marketing, 15*(8), 755–773. doi:10.1002/(SICI)1520-6793(199812)15:8<755::AID-MAR3>3.0.CO;2-4

Pill, J. (1971). The Delphi method: Substance, context, a critique and an annotated bibliography. *Socio-Economic Planning Sciences, 5*, 57–71. doi:10.1016/0038-0121(71)90041-3

Pink, S. (2010). *Visualizing ethnography.* Retrieved June 20, 2010, from http://www.lboro.ac.uk/departments/ss/visualising_ethnography/

Pink, S. (2001). *Visual Ethnography*. London, UK: Sage.

Pink, S. (2007a). Walking with video. *Visual Studies, 22*, 240–252. doi:10.1080/14725860701657142

Pink, S. (2007b). *Doing Visual Ethnography: images, media and representation in research* (2nd ed.). London, UK: Sage.

Pink, S., Hubbard, P., O'Neill, M., & Radley, A. (2010). Walking across disciplines: from ethnography to arts practice. *Visual Studies, 25*(1), 1–7. doi:10.1080/14725861003606670

Pinsonneault, A., Barki, H., Gallupe, R. B., & Hoppen, N. (1999). Electronic brainstorming: the illusion of productivity. *Information Systems Research, 10*, 110–133. doi:10.1287/isre.10.2.110

Polyani, M. (2001). Towards common ground and action on repetitive strain injuries: An assessment of a future search conference. *The Journal of Applied Behavioral Science, 37*(4), 465. doi:10.1177/0021886301374005

Popkin, S., Leventhal, T., & Weismann, G. (2010). Girls in the 'hood': how safety affects the life chances of low-income girls. *Urban Affairs Review, 45*, 715–743. doi:10.1177/1078087410361572

Porter, S., & Whitcomb, M. (2005). E-mail subject lines and their effect on web survey viewing and response. *Social Science Computer Review, 23*(3), 380–387. doi:10.1177/0894439305275912

Powell, C. (2003). The Delphi technique: Myths and realities. *Journal of Advanced Nursing, 41*(4), 376–382. doi:10.1046/j.1365-2648.2003.02537.x

Powell, M. B., Wilson, C. J., & Hasty, M. K. (2002). Evaluation of the usefulness of 'Marvin'; a computerized assessment tool for investigative interviewers of children. *Computers in Human Behavior, 18*(5), 577–592. doi:10.1016/S0747-5632(02)00003-1

Pratt, T. C., & Cullen, F. T. (2000). The empirical status of Gottfredson and Hirschi's general theory of crime: A Meta-Analysis. *Criminology, 38*(3), 931–964. doi:10.1111/j.1745-9125.2000.tb00911.x

Price, C. R. (1975). Conferencing via computer: Cost effective communication for the era of forced choice. In Linstone, H. A., & Turoff, M. (Eds.), *The Delphi method: Techniques and applications* (pp. 497–516). Reading, MA: Addison-Wesley.

Priest, H. A., Stagl, K. C., Klein, C., & Salas, E. (2005). Virtual teams: Creating context for distributed teamwork. In Bowers, C., Salas, E., & Jentsch, F. (Eds.), *Creating High-Tech Teams: Practical Guidance on Work Performance and Technology* (pp. 185–212). Washington, DC: American Psychological Association. doi:10.1037/11263-009

Pring, R. (2004). *Philosophy of educational research*. London, UK: Continuum.

Prosser, J., & Burke, C. (2007). Childlike perspectives through image-based educational research. In Knowles, J. G., & Cole, A. (Eds.), *Handbook of the arts in qualitative research: perspectives, methodologies, examples and issues* (pp. 407–421). Oxford, UK: Oxford University Press.

Putman, V. L., & Paulus, P. B. (2009). Brainstorming, brainstorming rules and decision making. *The Journal of Creative Behavior, 43*, 23–39.

Quereau, T. (1995). *Creating our future together: A summary report from the future search conference series for Austin Community College* (ERIC Document Reproduction Service ED396791).

Radley, A., & Taylor, D. (2003). Remembering One's Stay in Hospital: a Study in Photography, Recovery and Forgetting. *Health, 7*(2), 129–159. doi:10.1177/1363459303007002872

Rainhorn, J.-D., Brudon-Jakobowicz, P., & Reich, M. R. (1994). Priorities for pharmaceutical policies in developing countries: Results of a Delphi survey. *Bulletin of the World Health Organization, 72*(2), 257–264.

Ramos, M., Sedivi, B. M., & Sweet, E. M. (1998). Computerized self-administered questionnaires. In Couper, M. P., Baker, R. P., Bethlehem, J., Clark, C. Z. F., Martin, J., Nicholls, W. L., & O'Reilly, J. M. (Eds.), *Computer-assisted survey information collection* (pp. 389–408). New York, NY: Wiley.

Rance, C. (2005, April 30). In Bendigo the people have spoken (p. 24). The Age.

Rangaswamy, A., & Lilien, G. L. (1997). Software tools for new product development. *JMR, Journal of Marketing Research, 34*, 177–184. doi:10.2307/3152074

Raper, J., Gartner, G., Karimi, H., & Rizos, C. (2007). A critical evaluation of location based services and their potential. *Journal of Location Based Services, 1*(1), 5–45. doi:10.1080/17489720701584069

Ravallion, M. (2001). *On the urbanization of poverty*. Washington, DC: World Bank. doi:10.1596/1813-9450-2586

Ray, M., & Schrom-Feiertag, H. (2007). Cell-based Finding and Classification of Prominent Places of Mobile Phone Users. In *Proceedings of the 4th International Symposium on Location Based Services & TeleCartography*.

Rayens, M. K., & Hahn, E. J. (2000). Building consensus using the policy Delphi method. *Policy, Politics & Nursing Practice, 1*(4), 308–315. doi:10.1177/152715440000100409

Reavey, P., & Johnson, K. (2008). Visual methodologies: using and interpreting images in qualitative psychology. In Willig, C., & Stainton-Rogers, W. (Eds.), *Handbook of Qualitative Research in Psychology*. London, UK: Sage. doi:10.4135/9781848607927.n17

Reed, B. D., Crawford, S., Couper, M. P., Cave, C., & Haefner, H. K. (2004). Pain at the vulvar vestibule—A Web survey. *Journal of Lower Genital Tract Disease, 8*, 48–57. doi:10.1097/00128360-200401000-00011

Reeves, B., & Nass, C. (1996). *The Media Equation: How People Treat Computers, Television, and New Media like Real People and Places*. Cambridge, UK: Cambridge University Press.

Reeves, G., & Jauch, L. R. (1978). Curriculum development through Delphi. *Research in Higher Education, 8*(2), 157–168. doi:10.1007/BF00992116

Reichertz, J. (1994). Selbstgefälliges zum Anziehen. In Schröer, N. (Ed.), *Interpretative Sozialforschung. Auf dem Weg zu einer hermeneutischen Wissenssoziologie* (pp. 253–280). Opladen, Germany: Westdeutscher Verlag.

Reid, A., Petocz, P., Braddock, R., Taylor, P., & McLean, K. (2006). *Professional formation: exploring students' understanding of creativity, sustainability, ethics and cross-cultural sensitivity* (Tech. Rep. GDN AP-EPRI No. 9). Seoul, Korea: Korean Education Development Institute (KEDI). Retrieved August 25, 2010, from http://eng.kedi.re.kr

Reid, A., Petocz, P., & Gordon, S. (2008). Research interviews in cyberspace. *Qualitative Research Journal, 8*(1), 47–61. doi:10.3316/QRJ0801047

Reid, A., Petocz, P., & Gordon, S. (2010). University teachers' intentions for introductory professional classes. *Journal of Workplace Learning, 22*(1-2), 67–78. doi:10.1108/13665621011012861

Reid, A., Petocz, P., Smith, G. H., Wood, L. N., & Dortins, E. (2003). Maths students' conceptions of mathematics. *New Zealand Journal of Mathematics, 32*, 163–172.

Reips, U.-D. (2001). The Web Experimental Psychology Lab: Five years of data collection on the Internet. *Behavior Research Methods, Instruments, & Computers, 33*(2), 201–211. doi:10.3758/BF03195366

Remagnino, P., Velastin, S. A., Foresti, G. L., & Trivedi, M. (2007). Novel concepts and challenges for the next generation of video surveillance systems. *Machine Vision and Applications, 18*(3-4), 135–137. doi:10.1007/s00138-006-0059-6

Reppel, A. E., Gruber, T., Szmigin, I., & Voss, R. (2007). *Conducting qualitative research online – an exploratory study into the preferred attributes of an iconic digital music player.* Paper presented at the European Advances in Consumer Research Conference, Milan, Italy.

Reppel, A. E., & Szmigin, I. (2010). Consumer-managed profiling: A contemporary interpretation of privacy in buyer-seller interactions. *Journal of Marketing Management, 26*(3-4), 321–342. doi:10.1080/02672570903566383

Reppel, A. E., Szmigin, I., & Gruber, T. (2006). The iPod phenomenon: Identifying a market leader's secret through qualitative marketing research. *Journal of Product and Brand Management, 15*(4), 239–249. doi:10.1108/10610420610679601

Reynolds, T. J., Dethloff, C., & Westberg, S. J. (2001). Advances in laddering. In Reynolds, T. J., & Olson, J. C. (Eds.), *Understanding consumer decision making - the means-end approach to marketing and advertising strategy* (pp. 91–118). Mahwah, NJ: Lawrence Erlbaum Associates.

Reynolds, T. J., Gengler, C. E., & Howard, D. J. (1995). A means-end analysis of brand persuasion through advertising. *International Journal of Research in Marketing, 12*(3), 257–266. doi:10.1016/0167-8116(95)00025-W

Reynolds, T. J., & Gutman, J. (1988). Laddering theory, method, analysis, and interpretation. *Journal of Advertising Research, 28*(1), 13–33.

Rhodes, S. D., Bowie, D. A., & Hergenrather, K. C. (2003). Collecting behavioural data using the World Wide Web: considerations for researchers. *Journal of Epidemiology and Community Health, 57*, 68–73. doi:10.1136/jech.57.1.68

Richardson, W. (2010). *Blogs, Wikis, Podcasts and Other Powerful Web Tools for Classrooms* (3rd ed.). Thousand Oaks, CA: Corwin Sage.

Richman, W. L., Weisband, S., Kiesler, S., & Drasgow, F. (1999). A meta-analytic study of social desirability distortion in computer-administered questionnaires, traditional questionnaires, and interviews. *The Journal of Applied Psychology, 84*(5), 754–775. doi:10.1037/0021-9010.84.5.754

Riediger, M. (2011). Experience Sampling. In German Data Forum (Ed.), *Building on Progress – Expanding the Research Infrastructure for the Social, Economic and Behavioral Sciences* (pp. 581-594). Opladen, Germany: Budrich UniPress.

Rodriguez, N. (2010, July 26). Exactly how much are the times a changing? *Newsweek, 56*(17).

Rogers, E. M. (1962). *Diffusion of innovations*. New York, NY: Free Press.

Rogers, E. M. (1995). *The diffusion of innovations*. New York, NY: Free Press.

Rohs, M., & Gfeller, B. (2004). Using Camera-Equipped Mobile Phones for Interacting with Real-World Objects. In *Advances in Pervasive Computing* (pp. 265–271). Zurich, Switzerland: Institute for Pervasive Computing, Department of Computer Science, ETH Zurich.

Rokeach, M. (1973). *The nature of human values*. New York, NY: Free Press.

Romer, D., Hornik, R., Stanton, B., Black, M., Li, X., Ricardo, I., & Feigelman, S. (1997). "Talking" computers: a reliable and private method to conduct interviews on sensitive topics with children. *Journal of Sex Research, 34*(1), 3–9. doi:10.1080/00224499709551859

Rose, G. (2007). *Visual methodologies: An introduction to the interpretation of visual materials*. Thousand Oaks, CA: Sage.

Rosen, B., Furst, S., & Blackburn, R. (2006). Training for virtual teams: An investigation of current practices and future needs. *Human Resource Management, 45*, 229–247. doi:10.1002/hrm.20106

Rosenbaum, P. R., & Rubin, D. B. (1983). The central role of the propensity score in observational studies for causal effects. *Biometrika, 70*(1), 41–55. doi:10.1093/biomet/70.1.41

Rosenbaum, P. R., & Rubin, D. B. (1984). Reducing bias in observational studies using subclassification on the propensity score. *Journal of the American Statistical Association, 79*(387), 516–524. doi:10.2307/2288398

Rosenberg, M. J. (1956). Cognitive structure and attitudinal affect. *Journal of Abnormal and Social Psychology, 53*(3), 367–372. doi:10.1037/h0044579

Ross, T. (2009). Constructing a virtual world as a research tool: Lessons learned from the first iteration in the development of Greenland. In *Proceedings of the International Conference on Computational Engineering (CSE 2009)*, Vancouver, BC, Canada (pp. 1163-1168).

Ross, T., & Cornell, R. D. (2010). Towards an Experimental Methodology of Virtual World Research. In *Proceedings of the 2010 Second International Conference on Games and Virtual Worlds for Serious Applications* (pp. 143-150).

Rowe, G., & Wright, G. (1999). The Delphi technique as a forecasting tool: Issues and analysis. *International Journal of Forecasting, 15*, 353–375. doi:10.1016/S0169-2070(99)00018-7

Roy, M. C., Gauvin, S., & Limayen, M. (1996). Electronic group brainstorming: The role of feedback on productivity. *Small Group Research, 27*, 215–247. doi:10.1177/1046496496272002

Sade-Beck, L. (2004). Internet ethnography: Online and offline. *International Journal of Qualitative Methods, 3*(2), 45–51.

Sandrey, M. A., & Bulger, S. M. (2008). The Delphi method: An approach for facilitating evidence based practice in athletic training. *Athletic Training Education Journal, 3*(4), 135–142.

Saris, W. E. (1991). *Computer-Assisted Interviewing*. Newbury Park: Sage.

Saunders, W. (Ed.). (2006). *Urban Planning Today: A Harvard Design Magazine Reader*. Minneapolis, MN: University of Minnesota Press.

Schechtner, K., & Schrom-Feiertag, H. (2008). Understanding and influencing spatiotemporal visitor movement in national parks based on static and dynamic sensor data. In *Proceedings of the 6th Conference on Pervasive Computing (Pervasive 2008), Workshop on Urban Atmospheres* (pp. 95-99).

Scheibe, M., Skutsch, M., & Schofer, J. (1975). Experiments in Delphi methodology. In Linstone, H. A., & Turoff, M. (Eds.), *The Delphi method: Techniques and applications* (pp. 262–287). Reading, MA: Addison-Wesley.

Schillewaert, N., & Meulemeester, P. (2005). Comparing response distributions of offline and online data collection methods. *International Journal of Market Research, 47*, 163–178.

Schirato, T., & Webb, J. (2004). *Understanding the visual*. Thousand Oaks, CA: Sage.

Schneider, J. B. (1972). The policy Delphi: A regional planning application. *Technological Forecasting and Social Change, 3*, 481–497. doi:10.1016/S0040-1625(71)80035-5

Schneider, S. J., & Edwards, B. (2000). Developing usability guidelines for Audio-CASI for respondents with limited literacy skills. *Journal of Official Statistics, 16*(3), 255–271.

Schonlau, M., van Soest, A., Kapteyn, A., & Couper, M. (2009). Selection bias in Web surveys and the use of propensity scores. *Sociological Methods & Research, 37*(3), 291–318. doi:10.1177/0049124108327128

Schroeder, J. E. (2002). *Visual consumption*. London, UK: Routledge.

Schroeder, J. E. (2007). Critical visual analysis. In Belk, R. W. (Ed.), *Handbook of qualitative research methods in marketing* (pp. 303–321). Cheltenham, UK: Edward Elgar.

Schroeder, R., & Bailenson, J. (2008). Research uses of multi-user virtual environments. In Fielding, N., Lee, R. M., & Blank, G. (Eds.), *The Sage Handbook of Online Research Methods* (pp. 327–342). Los Angeles, CA: Sage.

Schultz, R. A. (Ed.). (2006). *Contemporary issues in ethics and information technology*. London, UK: IRM Press.

Schusler, T. M. (2002). Engaging local communities in wildlife management area planning: An evaluation of the Lake Ontario Islands search conference. *Wildlife Society Bulletin, 30*(4), 1226–1237.

Schütze, F. (1976). Zur Hervorlockung und Analyse von Erzählungen thematisch relevanter Geschichten im Rahmen soziologischer Feldforschung – dargestellt an einem Projekt zur Erforschung von kommunalen Machtstrukturen. In *Arbeitsgruppe Bielefelder Soziologen: Kommunikative Sozialforschung* (pp. 159–260). Munich, Germany: Fink.

Schwartz, S. H. (1992). Universals in the content and structure of values: Theoretical advances and empirical tests in 20 countries. In Zanna, M. P. (Ed.), *Advances in experimental social psychology* (pp. 1–65). San Diego, CA: Academic Press. doi:10.1016/S0065-2601(08)60281-6

Schweitz, R. (1996). Searching for a quality environment. *Journal for Quality and Participation*, 36–40.

Scott, J. (1997). Children as respondents: Methods for improving data quality. In Lyberg, L., Biemer, P., Collins, M., DeLeeuw, E., Dippo, C., Schwarz, N., & Trewin, D. (Eds.), *Survey measurement and process quality* (pp. 331–350). New York, NY: Wiley.

Selwyn, N., & Robson, K. (1998). Using e-mail as a research tool. *Social Research Update,* 21. Retrieved August 25, 2010, from http://sru.soc.surrey.ac.uk/SRU21.html

Sengonzi, R., Demian, P., & Emmitt, S. (2009, April 1). Opportunities for e-brainstorming in pre-design processes of healthcare projects. In M. Kagioglou, J. Barlow, A. D. F Price, & C. Gray (Eds.), *Proceedings of the PhD Workshop of HaCIRIC's International Conference 2009: Improving Healthcare Infrastructures through Innovation* (pp. 32-41). Brighton, UK: HaCIRIC.

Seymour, W. S. (2001). In the flesh or online? Exploring qualitative research methodologies. *Qualitative Research, 1*(2), 147–168. doi:10.1177/146879410100100203

Shaw, D. (2003). Evaluating electronic workshops through analysing the 'brainstormed' ideas. *The Journal of the Operational Research Society, 54*(7), 692–705. doi:10.1057/palgrave.jors.2601568

Sheller, M., & Urry, J. (2006). The new mobilities paradigm. *Environment & Planning A, 38*, 207–226. doi:10.1068/a37268

Shepherd, E. (2007). Freedom of Information and Records Management in the UK: What has been the Impact? *Journal of the Society of Archivists, 28*(2), 125–138. doi:10.1080/00379810701607736

Shepherd, E., & Ennion, E. (2007). How has the implementation of the UK Freedom of Information Act 2000 affected archives and records management services? *Records Management Journal, 17*(1), 32–51. doi:10.1108/09565690710730688

Shepherd, M. M., Briggs, R. O., Reinig, B. A., Yen, J., & Nunamaker, J. F. (1996). Invoking social comparison to improve electronic brainstorming: Beyond anonymity. *Journal of Management Information Systems, 12*, 155–170.

Sheppard, S. R. J., & Cizek, P. (2009). The ethics of Google Earth: Crossing thresholds from spatial data to landscape visualisation. *Journal of Environmental Management, 90*, 2102–2117. doi:10.1016/j.jenvman.2007.09.012

Shervey, G. (2005). *Pre-service teachers and online teaching*. Unpublished master's thesis, University of Calgary, Calgary, AB, Canada.

Shields, M. C. (2003). "Giving voice" to students: using the internet for data collection. *Qualitative Research, 3*, 397–414. doi:10.1177/1468794103033007

Shirky, C. (2008). *Here comes everybody: The power of organizing without organizations*. New York, NY: Penguin.

Shoval, N. (2008). Tracking technologies and urban analysis. *Cities (London, England), 25*(1), 21–28. doi:10.1016/j.cities.2007.07.005

Shoval, N., & Isaacson, M. (2007). Tracking tourists in the digital age. *Annals of Tourism Research, 34*(1), 141–159. doi:10.1016/j.annals.2006.07.007

Shovlin, C. (2008). *Harnessing social brainstorming for business decisions.* Paper presented at the Business Intelligence Group Conference.

Sibley, M. (Ed.). (2008). Special Issue on Traditional Public Baths/Hammams in the Mediterranean *ArchNet-IJAR: International Journal of Architectural Research, (2)3*, ISSN 1994-6961. Retrieved September 15, 2010, from http://archnet.org/library/documents/one-document.jsp?document_id=10481

Siedler, T., & Sonnenberg, B. (2011). Experiments, Surveys, and the Use of Representative Samples as Reference Data. In German Data Forum (Ed.), *Building on Progress – Expanding the Research Infrastructure for the Social, Economic and Behavioral Sciences* (pp. 547-562). Opladen, Germany: Budrich UniPress.

Silva, C. N. (2007). Urban Planning and Ethics. In Rabin, J., & Berman, E. M. (Eds.), *Encyclopedia of Public Administration and Public Policy* (2nd ed.). New York, NY: CRC Press/Taylor & Francis Group. doi:10.1201/NOE1420052756.ch410

Silva, C. N. (2008a). Experimental Design. In Lavrakas, P. (Ed.), *Encyclopedia of survey research methods.* Thousand Oaks, CA: Sage.

Silva, C. N. (2008b). Research ethics in e-public administration. In Garson, G. D., & Khosrow-Pour, M. (Eds.), *Handbook of Research on Public Information Technology* (*Vol. 1*, pp. 314–322). Hershey, PA: Information Science Reference. doi:10.4018/978-1-59904-857-4.ch030

Simmel, G. (1971). The metropolis and mental life. In Simmel, G., & Wolff, K. H. (Eds.), *The Sociology of Georg Simmel* (Wolf, K. H., Trans.). New York, NY: Free Press.

Skinner, H. (2008). The emergence and development of place marketing's confused identity. *Journal of Marketing Management, 24*(9-10), 915–928. doi:10.1362/026725708X381966

Skitka, L. J., & Sargis, E. G. (2006). The Internet as psychological laboratory. *Annual Review of Psychology, 57*, 529–555. doi:10.1146/annurev.psych.57.102904.190048

Skulmoski, G. J., Hartman, F. T., & Krahn, J. (2007). The Delphi method for graduate research. *Journal of Information Technology Education, 6*, 1–21.

Slocum, N. (2005). *Participatory methods toolkit: A practitioner's manual.* Brussels, Belgium: King Baudouin Foundation and the Flemish Institute for Science and Technology Assessment.

Smith, L. T. (1999). *Decolonizing Methodologies: Research and Indigenous Peoples.* Dunedin, New Zealan: University of Otago Press.

Smith, P. J., Rao, J. N. K., Battaglia, M. P., Daniels, D., & Ezzati-Rice, T. (2001). Compensating for provider nonresponse using propensities to form adjustment cells: The National Immunization Survey. *Vital and Health Statistics, 2*(133), 1–17.

Sontag, S. (1980). *Über Fotografie.* Frankfurt, Germany: Fischer.

Sosik, J. J., Avolio, B. J., & Kahai, S. S. (1997). The impact of leadership style and anonymity on group potency and effectiveness in a GDSS environment. *The Journal of Applied Psychology, 82*, 89–103. doi:10.1037/0021-9010.82.1.89

Sosik, J. J., Kahai, S. S., & Avolio, B. J. (1998). Transformational leadership and dimensions of creativity: Motivating idea generation in computer-mediated groups. *Creativity Research Journal, 11*(2), 111–121. doi:10.1207/s15326934crj1102_3

Sparrow, N. (2006). Developing reliable online polls. *International Journal of Market Research, 48*, 659–680.

Sparrow, N., & Curtice, J. (2004). Measuring the attitudes of the general public via Internet polls: An evaluation. *International Journal of Market Research, 46*, 23–44.

Spek, S. V. D. (2008). Spatial Metro: Tracking pedestrians in historic city centres. In Schaick, J. V., & Spek, S. V. D. (Eds.), *Urbanism on Track* (pp. 79–101). Amsterdam, The Netherlands: IOS Press.

Spinello, R. (2003). The future of intellectual property. *Ethics and Information Technology, 5*, 1–16. doi:10.1023/A:1024976203396

Sproull, L., Subramani, M., Kiesler, S., Walker, J. H., & Waters, K. (1996). When the interface is a face. *Human-Computer Interaction, 11*(2), 97–124. doi:10.1207/s15327051hci1102_1

Staffans, A., Rantanen, H., & Nummi, P. (2010). Local Internet Forums. Interactive land use planning and urban development neighborhoods. In Silva, C. N. (Ed.), *Handbook of Research on E-Planning: ICTs for Urban Development and Monitoring* (pp. 80–102). Hershey, PA: Information Science Reference. doi:10.4018/978-1-61520-929-3.ch005

Stake, R. (1995). *The art of case study research*. Thousand Oaks, CA: Sage.

Steinkuehler, C., & Williams, D. (2006). Where everybody knows your (screen) name: Online games as "Third Places". *Journal of Computer-Mediated Communication*, *11*(4), 885–909. doi:10.1111/j.1083-6101.2006.00300.x

Stern, B. B., & Gould, S. J. (1988). The consumer as financial opinion leader. *Journal of Retail Banking*, *10*(2), 43–52.

Stern, J., Stackowiack, R., & Greenwald, R. (2001). *Oracle Essentials: Oracle9i, Oracle8i and Oracle 8*. Sebastopol, CA: O'Reilly.

Stern, M. J., & Dillman, D. A. (2006). Community Participaton, Social Ties, and Use of the Internet. *City & Community*, *5*(4), 409–422. doi:10.1111/j.1540-6040.2006.00191.x

Stern, S. (2003). Encountering distressing information in online research: a consideration of legal and ethical responsibilities. *New Media & Society*, *5*(2), 249–266. doi:10.1177/1461444803005002006

Stern, S. R. (2003). Encountering distressing information in online research: a consideration of legal and ethical responsibilities. *New Media & Society*, *5*(2), 249–266. doi:10.1177/1461444803005002006

Stevens, M. J., & Campion, M. A. (1994). The knowledge, skill, and ability requirements for teamwork: Implications for human resource management. *Journal of Management*, *20*, 503–530.

Stevens, M. J., & Campion, M. A. (1999). Staffing work teams: Development and validation of a selection test for teamwork settings. *Journal of Management*, *25*, 207–228. doi:10.1016/S0149-2063(99)80010-5

Stewart, K., & Williams, M. (2005). Researching online populations: The use of online focus groups for social research. *Qualitative Research*, *5*(4), 395–416. doi:10.1177/1468794105056916

Stieger, S., & Göritz, A. S. (2006). Using Instant Messaging for Internet-Based Interviews. *Cyberpsychology & Behavior*, *9*(5), 552–559. doi:10.1089/cpb.2006.9.552

Stieger, S., & Reips, U.-D. (2008). Dynamic Interviewing Program (DIP): Automatic Online Interviews via the Instant Messenger ICQ. *Cyberpsychology & Behavior*, *11*(2), 201–207. doi:10.1089/cpb.2007.0030

Stitt-Gohdes, W. L., & Crews, T. B. (2004). The Delphi technique: A research strategy for career and technical education. *Journal of Career and Technical Education*, *20*(2), 1–10.

Stone-Romero, E. F. (2002). The relative validity and usefulness of various empirical research designs. In Rogelberg, S. G. (Ed.), *Handbook of research methods in industrial and organizational psychology* (pp. 77–98). Cambridge, MA: Blackwell. doi:10.1002/9780470756669.ch4

Story, A. (2002). *Study on intellectual property rights, the Internet, and copyright*. London, UK: Commission on Intellectual Property Rights. Retrieved July 18, 2010, from http://www.iprcommission.org/papers/pdfs/study_papers/sp5_story_study.pdf

Strauss, A., & Corbin, J. (1998). *Basics of qualitative research - techniques and procedures for developing grounded theory*. Thousand Oaks, CA: Sage.

Stritter, F. T., Tresolini, C. P., & Reeb, K. G. (1994). The Delphi technique in curriculum development. *Teaching and Learning in Medicine*, *6*(2), 136–141. doi:10.1080/10401339409539662

Stroebe, W., & Diehl, M. (1994). Why groups are less effective than their members: On productivity losses in idea-generating groups. *European Review of Social Psychology*, *5*, 271–303. doi:10.1080/14792779543000084

Stroebe, W., Nijstad, B. A., & Rietzschel, E. F. (2010). Beyond productivity loss in brainstorming groups: The evolution of a question. *Advances in Experimental Social Psychology*, *43*, 157–203. doi:10.1016/S0065-2601(10)43004-X

Stubbles, R. (1992). Economic and environmental futures of the Black Hills: A Delphi study. *Great Plains Research*, *2*(1), 97–108.

Sturges, J. E., & Hanrahan, K. J. (2004). Comparing telephone and face-to-face qualitative interviewing: a research note. *Qualitative Research*, *4*(1), 107–118. doi:10.1177/1468794104041110

Stutchbury, K., & Fox, A. (2009). Ethics in educational research: Introducing a methodological tool for effective ethical analysis. *Cambridge Journal of Education*, *39*(4), 489–504. doi:10.1080/03057640903354396

Sudman, S., & Bradburn, N. M. (1974). *Response effects in surveys*. Chicago, IL: Aldine.

Suri, H. (2008). Ethical Considerations in Synthesising Research: Whose Representations? *Qualitative Research Journal*, *8*(1), 62–73. doi:10.3316/QRJ0801062

Sweet, C. (2001). Designing and conducting virtual focus groups. *Qualitative Market Research: An International Journal*, *4*(3), 130–135. doi:10.1108/13522750110393035

Syed, A. M., Hjarone, L., & Aro, A. R. (2009). The Delphi technique in developing international health policies: Experience from the SARSControl project. *The Internet Journal of Health*, *8*(2).

Szell, M., Lambiotte, R., & Thurner, S. (2010). Multi-relational organization of large-scale social networks in an online world. *Proceedings of the National Academy of Sciences of the United States of America*, *107*(31), 13636–13541. doi:10.1073/pnas.1004008107

Tajfel, H., & Turner, J. C. (1979). An integrative theory on intergroup conflict. In Austin, W., & Worchel, S. (Eds.), *The social psychology of intergroup relations* (pp. 33–48). Pacific Grove, CA: Brooks/Cole.

Taylor, D. W., Berry, P. C., & Block, C. H. (1958). Does group participation when using brainstorming facilitate or inhibit creative thinking? *Administrative Science Quarterly*, *6*, 22–47.

Taylor, H. (2000). Does Internet research work? Comparing online survey results with telephone survey. *International Journal of Market Research*, *42*, 58–63.

Taylor, H., Bremer, J., Overmeyer, C., Siegel, J. W., & Terhanian, G. (2001). The record of Internet-based opinion polls in predicting the results of 72 races in the November 2000 US elections. *International Journal of Market Research*, *43*(2), 127–135.

Taylor, R. E., & Judd, L. L. (1989). Delphi method applied to tourism. In Witt, S., & Moutinho, L. (Eds.), *Tourism marketing and management handbook*. Upper Saddle River, NJ: Prentice Hall.

Taylor, T. (2006). *Play between Worlds: Exploring Online Game Culture*. Cambridge, MA: MIT Press.

Tedlock, B. (2000). Ethnography and Ethnographic Representation. In Denzing, N., & Lincoln, Y. (Eds.), *The Handbook of Qualitative Research* (2nd ed., pp. 455–486). Thousand Oaks, CA: Sage.

Terhanian, G. (2000). *How to produce credible, trustworthy information through Internet-based survey research*. Paper presented at the Annual Meeting of the American Association for Public Opinion Research, Portland, OR.

Terhanian, G., & Bremer, J. (2000). *Confronting the selection-bias and learning effects of problems associated with Internet research*. New York, NY: Harris Interactive.

Thornton, P., Williams, A., & Shaw, W. G. (1997). Revisiting Time-Space Diaries: An Exploratory Case Study of Tourist Behavior in Cornwall, England. *Environment and Behavior A*, *29*, 1847–1867.

Tigelaar, D. E. H., Dolmans, D. H. J. M., Wolfhagen, I. H. A. P., & van Der Vleuten, C. P. M. (2004). The development and validation of a framework for teaching competencies in higher education. *Higher Education*, *48*, 253–268. doi:10.1023/B:HIGH.0000034318.74275.e4

Tourangeau, R., & Smith, T. W. (1996). Asking sensitive questions: The impact of data collection, question format, and question context. *Public Opinion Quarterly*, *60*(2), 275–304. doi:10.1086/297751

Trapl, E. S., Borawski, E. A., Storck, P. P., Lovegreen, L. D., Colabianchi, N., Cole, M. L., & Charvat, J. M. (2005). Use of audio-enhanced personal digital assistants for school-based data collection. *The Journal of Adolescent Health*, *37*(4), 296–305. doi:10.1016/j.jadohealth.2005.03.025

Tregeagle, S. (2010). Participation in child welfare services through information and communication technologies. *International Journal of Information Communication Technologies and Human Development, 2*(2), 17–33. doi:10.4018/jicthd.2010040102

Trueman, M. M., Cornelius, N., & Killingbeck-Widdup, A. J. (2007). Urban corridors and the lost city: Overcoming negative perceptions to reposition city brands. *Journal of Brand Management, 15*(1), 20–31. doi:10.1057/palgrave.bm.2550107

Truman, J., Robinson, K., Evans, A. L., Smith, D., Cunningham, L., Millward, R., & Minnis, H. (2003). The Strengths and Difficulties Questionnaire. A pilot study of a new computer version of the self-report scale. *European Child & Adolescent Psychiatry, 12*(1), 9–14. doi:10.1007/s00787-003-0303-9

Tsaur, S. H., Lin, Y. C., & Lin, J. H. (2006). Evaluating ecotourism sustainability from the integrated perspective of resource, community, and tourism. *Tourism Management, 27*, 640–653. doi:10.1016/j.tourman.2005.02.006

Tse, A. C. B. (1999). Conducting Electronic Focus Group Discussions among Chinese Respondents. *Journal of the Market Research Society. Market Research Society, 41*(4), 407–415.

Turkle, S. (1997). *Life on the Screen: Identity in the Age of the Internet*. New York, NY: Simon and Schuster.

Turner, C. F., Ku, L., Rogers, S. M., Lindberg, L. D., Pleck, J. H., & Sonenstein, F. L. (1998). Adolescent sexual behaviour, drug use, and violence: Increased reporting with computer survey technology. *Science, 280*(5365), 867–873. doi:10.1126/science.280.5365.867

Turoff, M. (1970). The design of a policy Delphi. *Technological Forecasting and Social Change, 2*, 149–171. doi:10.1016/0040-1625(70)90161-7

Turoff, M. (1975). The policy Delphi. In Linstone, H. A., & Turoff, M. (Eds.), *The Delphi method: Techniques and applications* (pp. 84–101). Reading, MA: Addison-Wesley.

Turoff, M., & Hiltz, S. R. (1995). Computer based Delphi processes. In Adler, M., & Ziglio, Z. (Eds.), *Grazing into the oracle: The Delphi method and its application to social policy and public health* (pp. 56–88). London, UK: Jessica Kingsley.

Tynan, C., McKechnie, S., & Chhuon, C. (2010). Co-creating value for luxury brands. *Journal of Business Research, 63*(11), 1156–1163. doi:10.1016/j.jbusres.2009.10.012

U.S. Department of Health, Education and Welfare. (1973). *Secretary's Advisory Committee on Automated Personal Data Systems, Records, Computers, and the Rights of Citizens*. Washington, DC: Author.

Ulschak, F. L. (1983). *Human resource development: The theory and practice of needs assessment*. Reston, VA: Reston Publishing Company.

UN-Habitat. (2002). *The state of African cities 2002*. New York, NY: Earthscan.

UN-Habitat. (2003). *The state of African cities 2003*. New York, NY: Earthscan.

UN-Habitat. (2006). *Kibera social and economic mapping: household survey report*. Nairobi, Kenya: Earthscan.

UN-Habitat. (2008). *The state of the world's cities 2008*. New York, NY: Earthscan.

UN-Habitat. (2009). *The state of the world's cities 2009*. New York, NY: Earthscan.

Urry, J. (2007). *Mobilities*. London, UK: Sage.

Valacich, J. S., Dennis, A. R., & Nunamaker, J. F. Jr. (1992). Group size and anonymity effects on computer-mediated idea generation. *Small Group Research, 23*(1), 49–73. doi:10.1177/1046496492231004

Valette-Florence, P., & Rapacchi, B. (1991). Improvements in means-end chain analysis: Using graph theory and correspondence analysis. *Journal of Advertising Research, 31*(1), 30–45.

Van Bogart, J. (1995). *Magnetic Tape Storage and Handling. A Guide for Libraries and Archives*. Retrieved August 19, 2010, from http://www.clir.org/pubs/reports/pub54/4life_expectancy.html

van Rekom, J., & Wierenga, B. (2007). On the hierarchical nature of means-end relationships in laddering data. *Journal of Business Research, 60*(4), 401–410. doi:10.1016/j.jbusres.2006.10.004

van Teijlingen, E., Pitchforth, E., Bishop, C., & Russell, E. (2006). *Delphi method and nominal group techniques in family planning and reproductive health research.* Retrieved June 7, 2010, from http://eprints.bournemouth.ac.uk/10152/1/The_Delphi_method_revised_final.pdf

Vargo, S. L., & Lusch, R. F. (2004). Evolving to a new dominant logic for marketing. *Journal of Marketing, 68,* 1–17. doi:10.1509/jmkg.68.1.1.24036

Veludo-de-Oliveira, T. M., Ikeda, A. A., & Campomar, M. C. (2006). Laddering in the practice of marketing research: barriers and solutions. *Qualitative Market Research: An International Journal, 9*(3), 297–306. doi:10.1108/13522750610671707

Venkatesh, A. (1999). Postmodern perspectives for macromarketing: An inquiry into the global information and sign economy. *Journal of Macromarketing, 19*(2), 153–169. doi:10.1177/0276146799192006

Virginia Commonwealth University. (2006). *IRB Written Policies and Procedures: Use of the Internet for Recruitment and/or Research Data Collection.* Retrieved November 2, 2010, from http://www.research.vcu.edu/irb/wpp/flash/XVII-9.htm

Voida, A., Mynatt, E. D., Erickson, T., & Kellogg, W. A. (2004). Interviewing over instant messaging. In *Proceedings of CHI '04: Extended Abstracts on Human Factors in Computing Systems,* Vienna, Austria (pp. 1344-1347). ACM Press.

Von Plato, A. (2000). Zeitzeugen und die historische Zunft. Erinnerung, kommunikative Tradierung und kollektives Gedächtnis in der qualitativen Geschichtswissenschaft – ein Problemaufriss. *BIOS. Zeitschrift für Biographieforschung und Oral History, 13,* 5–29.

Von Plato, A., Leh, A., & Thonfeld, C. (Eds.). (2010). *Hitler's Slaves. Life Stories of Forced Labourers in Nazi-Occupied Europe.* New York, NY: Berghahn Books.

Voss, R., Gruber, T., & Szmigin, I. (2007). Service quality in higher education: The role of student expectations. *Journal of Business Research, 60*(9), 949–959. doi:10.1016/j.jbusres.2007.01.020

Wadsworth, J., Johnson, A. M., Wellings, K., & Field, J. (1996). What's in a mean? - an examination of the inconsistency between men and women in reporting sexual partnerships. *Journal of the Royal Statistical Society. Series A, (Statistics in Society), 159*(1), 111–123. doi:10.2307/2983472

Walker, J. H., Sproull, L., & Subramani, R. (1994). Using a human face in an interface. In B. Adelson, S. Dumais, & J. Olson (Eds.), *Human Factors in Computing Systems: CHI'94 Conference Proceedings,* Boston, MA (pp. 85-91). ACM.

Walker, B. A., & Olson, J. C. (1991). Means-end chains: Connecting products with self. *Journal of Business Research, 22*(2), 111–118. doi:10.1016/0148-2963(91)90045-Y

Walsh, J. P., & Maloney, N. G. (2002). Computer network use, collaboration structures, and productivity. In Kiesler, S. (Ed.), *Distributed Work* (pp. 433–451). Cambridge, MA: MIT Press.

Walther, J. B. (1992). Interpersonal effects in computer-mediated interaction: A relational perspective. *Communication Research, 19,* 52–90. doi:10.1177/009365092019001003

Wang, C., & Burris, M. A. (1997). Photovoice: Concept, Methodology, and Use for Participatory Needs Assessment. *Health Education & Behavior, 24,* 369–387. doi:10.1177/109019819702400309

Wang, C., Burris, M. A., & Ping, X. Y. (1996). Chinese Village Women as Visual Anthropologists: a Participatory Approach to Reaching Policymakers. *Social Science & Medicine, 42,* 1391–1400. doi:10.1016/0277-9536(95)00287-1

Warkentin, M., Sayeed, L., & Hightower, R. (1997). Virtual teams versus face-to-face teams: An exploratory study of a web-based conference system. *Decision Sciences, 28,* 975–996. doi:10.1111/j.1540-5915.1997.tb01338.x

Warren, C., & Karner, T. (2005). The interview as social interaction and speech event. In Warren, C., & Karner, T. (Eds.), *Discovering qualitative methods: Field research, interviews, and analysis* (pp. 137–155). Los Angeles, CA: Roxbury Publishing.

Warren, S. (2005). Photograph and Voice in Critical Qualitative Management Research. *Accounting, Auditing & Accountability Journal*, *18*, 861–882. doi:10.1108/09513570510627748

Watts, L., & Lyons, G. (2010). Travel remedy kit: interventions into train lines and passenger times. In Büscher, M., Urry, J., & Witchger, K. (Eds.), *Mobile methods*. London, UK: Routledge.

Weaver, W. T. (1971). The Delphi forecasting method. *Phi Delta Kappan*, *52*(5), 267–273.

Webber, S. S., & Donahue, L. M. (2001). Impact of highly and less job-related diversity on work group cohesion and performance: A meta-analysis. *Journal of Management*, *27*, 141–162.

Webster, J., & Staples, D. S. (2006). Comparing virtual teams to traditional teams: An identification of new research possibilities. *Research in Personnel and Human Resources Management*, *25*, 181–125. doi:10.1016/S0742-7301(06)25005-9

Weisband, S., & Kiesler, S. (1996, April). Self disclosure on computer forms: Meta-analysis and implications. In *Proceedings of the Conference on Human Factors in Computing Systems*, Vancouver, BC, Canada. Retrieved from http://www.acm.org/sigchi/chi96/proceedings/papers/Weisband/sw_txt.htm

Weiss, R. S., & Boutourline, S., Jr. (1962). *A summary of fairs, pavilions, exhibits, and their audiences* (Tech. Rep.).

Welker, J. A., & McCue, J. D. (2007). Authorship versus "credit" for participation in research. *Journal of the American Medical Informatics Association*, *14*(1), 16–18. doi:10.1197/jamia.M2212

Wesner, M. S. (2008). Assessing training needs for virtual team collaboration. In Nemiro, J., Beyerlein, M. M., Bradley, L., & Beyerlein, S. (Eds.), *The handbook of high-performance virtual teams: A toolkit for collaborating across boundaries* (pp. 273–294). San Francisco, CA: Jossey-Bass.

West, M. A. (1990). The social psychology of innovation in groups. In West, M. A., & Farr, J. L. (Eds.), *Innovation and creativity at work: Psychological and organizational strategies* (pp. 309–333). Hoboken, NJ: John Wiley & Sons.

White, A., Bushin, N., Carpena-Méndez, F., & Ni Laoire, C. (2010). Using visual methodologies to explore contemporary Irish childhood. *Qualitative Research*, *10*, 143–158. doi:10.1177/1468794109356735

Whiteman, E. (2007). "Just Chatting": Research Ethics and Cyberspace. *International Journal of Qualitative Methods*, *6*(2), 95–105.

Wicklein, R. C. (1993). Identifying critical issues and problems in technology education using a modified-Delphi technique. *Journal of Technology Education*, *5*(1), 54–71.

Wiederman, M. W. (1997). The truth must be in here somewhere: examining the gender discrepancy in self-reported lifetime number of sex partners. *Journal of Sex Research*, *34*(4), 375–386. doi:10.1080/00224499709551905

Wilcox, S. (1989). *American deaf culture*. Burtonsville, MD: Linstok Press.

Wilenius, M., & Tirkkonen, J. (1997). Climate in the making: Using Delphi for Finnish climate policy. *Futures*, *29*(9), 845–862. doi:10.1016/S0016-3287(97)00061-X

Wiles, R., Prosser, J., & Bagnoli, A. Clark, A., Davies, K., Holland, S., & Renold, E. (2008). *Visual Ethics: Ethical Issues in Visual Research*. Southampton, UK: NCRM.

Williams, D. (2010a). *The promises and perils of large-scale data extraction*. Chicago, IL: MacArthur Foundation.

Williams, D. (2010b). The mapping principle, and a research framework for virtual worlds. *Communication Theory*, *20*(4), 451–470. doi:10.1111/j.1468-2885.2010.01371.x

Williams, P. (1984). Consulting the aged—A search conference approach. *Australian Journal of Adult Education*, *24*(3), 29–40.

Windle, R. (2010). *The Big Picture: What the Decline of Fixed Line Telephones will Mean to Mobile Research*, Presentation at the 2010 Mobile Research Conference. London.

Winkel, G. H., & Sasanoff, R. (1966). An approach to an objective analysis of behavior in architectural space. In Proshansky, H. M., Ittelson, W. H., & Rivlin, L. G. (Eds.), *Environmental Psychology* (pp. 619–631). New York, NY: Holt, Rinehart & Winston.

Witkin, B. R., & Altschuld, J. W. (1995). *Planning and conducting needs assessment: A practical guide.* Thousand Oaks, CA: Sage.

Woerndl, W., & Eicker, D. (2006). Creativity techniques meet the web. *International Journal of Web Based Communities, 2*(1), 100–111. doi:10.1504/IJWBC.2006.008618

Woolcock, M. (1998). Social capital and economic development: toward a theoretical synthesis and policy framework. *Theory and Society, 27*, 151–208. doi:10.1023/A:1006884930135

Wright, K. B. (2005). Researching Internet-based populations: Advantages and disadvantages of online survey research, online questionnaire authoring software packages, and Web survey services. *Journal of Computer-Mediated Communication, 10*(3).

Wuchty, S., Jones, B. F., & Uzzi, B. (2007). The increasing dominance of teams in the production of knowledge. *Science, 316*, 1036–1038. doi:10.1126/science.1136099

Wuggenig, U. (1990). Die Photobefragung als projektives Verfahren. *Angewandte Sozialforschung, 16*(1-2), 109–129.

Yeager, D. A., Krosnick, J. A., Chang, L., Javitz, H. S., Levendusky, M. S., Simpser, A., & Wang, R. (2009). *Comparing the accuracy of RDD telephone surveys and Internet surveys conducted with probability and non-probability samples.* Retrieved May 24, 2011, from http://comm.stanford.edu/faculty/krosnick/Mode%2004%20online%20supplement.pdf

Yee, N., & Bailenson, J. (2007). The Proteus Effect: The effect of transformed self-representation on behavior. *Human Communication Research, 33*(3), 271–290. doi:10.1111/j.1468-2958.2007.00299.x

Yeung, Y. (1997). Geography in an age of mega-cities. *International Social Science Journal, 49*(151), 91–104. doi:10.1111/j.1468-2451.1997.tb00008.x

Yin, R. (2008). *Case Study Research: Design and Methods* (4th ed.). Thousand Oaks, CA: Sage.

Young, S. J., & Jamieson, L. M. (2001). Delivery methodology of the Delphi: A comparison of two approaches. *Journal of Park and Recreation Administration, 19*(1), 42–58.

Yousuf, M. I. (2007). Using experts' opinions through Delphi technique. *Practical Assessment, Research, & Evaluation, 12*(4). Retrieved June 28, 2007, from http://pareonline.net/getvn.asp?v=12&n=4

Zacharias, J. (1997). The impact of layout and visual stimuli on the itineraries and perception of pedestrians in a public market. *Environment and Planning. B, Planning & Design, 24*(1), 23–35. doi:10.1068/b240023

Zacharias, J. (2000). Shopping behavior at the Alexis-Nihon Plaza in Montreal. *Journal of Shopping Center Research, 7*(2), 67–79.

Zanoli, R., & Naspetti, S. (2002). Consumer motivation in the purchase of organic food - a means-end approach. *British Food Journal, 104*(8), 643–653. doi:10.1108/00070700210425930

Zazove, P., Meador, H. E., Aikens, J. E., Nease, D. E., & Gorenflo, D. W. (2006). Assessment of depressive symptoms in deaf persons. *Journal of the American Board of Family Medicine, 19*(2), 141–147. doi:10.3122/jabfm.19.2.141

Zelnik-Manor, L., & Perona, P. (2004). Self-Tuning Spectral Clustering. In *Advances in Neural Information Processing Systems* (pp. 1601-1608).

Ziegler, R., Diehl, M., & Zijlstra, G. (2000). Idea production in nominal and virtual groups: Does computer-mediated communication improve group brainstorming? *Group Processes & Intergroup Relations, 3*(2), 141–158. doi:10.1177/1368430200032003

Zimbardo, P. (2007). *The Lucifer effect: Understanding How Good People Turn Evil.* New York, NY: Random House.

Zotero. (n.d.). *Zotero.* Retrieved May 14, 2011, from http://www.zotero.org/

About the Contributors

Carlos Nunes Silva, PhD, is Professor Auxiliar at the Institute of Geography and Spatial Planning, University of Lisbon, Portugal. He has a degree in Geography (University of Coimbra), a post-graduation in European Studies (University of Coimbra - Faculty of Law), a master degree in Human Geography: Regional and Local Planning (University of Lisbon), and a PhD in Geography: Regional and Local Planning (University of Lisbon). His research interests are mainly focused on local government policies, history and theory of urban planning, urban and metropolitan governance, urban planning ethics, research methods, e-government and e-planning. Among his recent publications is the *Handbook of Research on E-Planning: ICT for Urban Development and Monitoring* (IGI, 2010). He is the Editor-in-Chief of the *International Journal of E-Planning Research* (IJEPR).

* * *

Edward Castronova, Professor of Telecommunications, Indiana University, is a founder of scholarly online game studies and an expert on the societies of virtual worlds. Among his academic publications on these topics are two books: Synthetic Worlds (University of Chicago Press, 2005) and Exodus to the Virtual World (Palgrave, 2007). Professor Castronova teaches graduate and undergraduate courses on the design of games, the game industry, and the management of virtual societies. Outside his academic work, Professor Castronova makes regular appearances in mainstream media (60 Minutes, the New York Times, and The Economist), gives keynotes at major conferences (Austin Game Conference, Digital Games Research Association Conference, Interactive Software Federation of Europe), and consults for business (McKinsey, Vivendi, Forrester). In the longer run, Professor Castronova aims to develop online games for studying human society.

Andrew Charlesworth is Reader in IT Law in the School of Law and Department of Computer Science at the University of Bristol, where he is the Director of the cross-disciplinary Centre for IT & Law. He teaches three courses on the University of Bristol LLM Programme: IT Law, Law of E-commerce and Privacy Law. His key areas of research include data privacy, intellectual property, and e-commerce law. He has undertaken research and consultancy on legal issues arising from a range of online activities including: educational use of the web, institutional archives and repositories, web archiving, ePortfolio and PDP tools, VLEs and MLEs, institutional data sharing, Web 2.0 technologies, cloud computing and research use of personal digital collections. He has worked with, and for, a diverse range of organisations, including Hewlett Packard, Vodafone, the European Commission, the UK Information Commissioner's Office, the Wellcome Trust, and the British Library.

Susan Crichton is an associate professor at the University of British Columbia, where she teaches in the Bachelor of Education program as well as the graduate program, specializing in new media and ePublishing / digital content. Her research explores the design and development of ICT enhanced learning environments to support quality teaching and learning and the use of digital approaches for qualitative research. She studies blended learning and the use of mobile technologies for teachers and students, especially in challenging contexts. Internationally, she has worked for the Canadian International Development Agency (CIDA) and the Asian Development Bank in Western China, focusing on ICT to enhanced basic education. She has been invited to work in Bhutan, Chile, and Tanzania, principally in the area of ICT enhanced teaching and professional development. She is the founder of jiFUNzeni an organization developing ePublishing options using appropriate technologies.

Mary Dzindolet is Chair and Full Professor in the Department of Psychology and Human Ecology at Cameron University in Lawton, Oklahoma. She earned a Masters of Applied Statistics from Louisiana State University in Baton Rouge, Louisiana in 1987 and a PhD in Experimental Psychology from the University of Texas at Arlington in 1992. As a graduate student she conducted research on group creativity in the laboratory of Dr. Paul B. Paulus. She joined the faculty at Cameron University in 1993 and was selected as one of Southwest Oklahoma's Distinguished Researchers in 2001 and received the Hackler Award for Teaching Excellence in 2008. She has published over forty articles which explore group creativity or automation reliance.

Nathan Eagle is the CEO of txteagle. He also serves as an Adjunct Assistant Professor at Harvard University, a Visiting Assistant Professor at the MIT Media Laboratory and a Research Assistant Professor at Northeastern University. His research involves engineering computational tools, designed to explore how the petabytes of data generated about human movements, financial transactions, and communication patterns can be used for social good. His PhD on Reality Mining was declared one of the '10 technologies most likely to change the way we live' by the *MIT Technology Review*. Recently, he was named one of the world's top mobile phone developers by Nokia and also elected to the TR35. His academic work has been featured in *Science*, *Nature* and *PNAS*, as well as in the mainstream press.

Joachim Gerich is an Associate Professor at the Department of Sociology, unit for empirical social research at Johannes Kepler University Linz, Austria. He holds a master degree and PhD in sociology. His research interests include empirical research methods and methodology, social network research, sociology of health and disability research. Some of his recent publications are *Effects of Social Networks on the Quality of Life in an Elder and Middle-aged Deaf Community Sample* (Journal of Deaf Studies and Deaf Education, with J. Fellinger, in press); *Real Virtual? Response Behavior in Video-Enhanced Self-Administered Computer Interviews*. (Field Methods 39/4, 2008); *Visual Analôgue Scales for Mode-Independent Measurement in Self-Administered Questionnaires* (Behavior Research Methods, 39/4, 2007).

Courtney Glazer is an Associate Professor in the Department of Education at Cameron University in Lawton, Oklahoma. She earned a Masters in Arts in Learning, Design, and Technology from Stanford University in 1999 and a PhD in Instructional Technology from the University of Texas at Austin in 2003. As a graduate student she worked with online communities of practice and conducted research on distributed emotion. She joined the faculty at Cameron University in 2005 working with teacher preparation and program evaluation. She also has continued her research in emotion and online environments.

Sue Gordon is a Senior Lecturer in the Mathematics Learning Centre (and Honorary Adjunct to the Faculty of Education and Social Work) at The University of Sydney, in Australia. Sue's area of expertise is teaching and learning in higher education, particularly in the disciplines of mathematics and statistics. Her research is closely linked to her teaching and informs her teaching practice. Sue's research interests include statistics education, activity theory, and pedagogy in general. Current and previous projects (many with Peter and Anna) include seminal research on students' conceptions of mathematics and mathematics learning, researching teachers' and students' experiences of learning statistics, exploring teachers' conceptions of student diversity in their classes, investigating mathematics bridging courses and early support of students in mathematics and using statistical approaches for research in creative and qualitative disciplines.

Thorsten Gruber is a Lecturer in Marketing in the Manchester Business School, University of Manchester. Prior to that, he was engaged in postdoctoral research at the Birmingham Business School, University of Birmingham and a part-time visiting lecturer at the University of Education Ludwigsburg. He received his PhD and MBA from the University of Birmingham. His research interests include consumer complaining behavior, services marketing and the development of qualitative online research methods. His work has been published and/or is forthcoming in journals such as *Journal of the Academy of Marketing Science, Journal of Business Research, Journal of Services Marketing, Journal of Service Management, Industrial Marketing Management, Journal of Marketing Management, International Journal of Public Sector Management, Journal of Business and Industrial Marketing, Managing Service Quality, Qualitative Market Research, Journal of Product and Brand Management, Journal of Marketing for Higher Education, International Journal of Educational Management, The TQM Journal, Journal for Quality Assurance in Education*, and *Management Services Journal*.

Kathleen J. Hanrahan, PhD is a Professor at Indiana University of Pennsylvania, and is on the faculty of the Department of Criminology. She earned her doctorate at Rutgers University. Her research interests include qualitative methods, pedagogical research, and corrections with an emphasis on felony sentencing and imprisonment. Her recent projects include research on the experience of house arrest and electronic monitoring, public attitudes about imprisonment, and PC gamer's views of the impact of digital rights software on PC game piracy.

Chia-Chien Hsu received his doctorate in 2005 from The Ohio State University and is an assistant professor in the Department of Leisure and Recreation Management at Kainan University in Taiwan. He is currently working with faculty at Dayeh University on a joint research project concerning internet users' attitudes toward searching and using digital information collected by the Taiwan E-learning and Digital Archives Program. His other research interests include agri-tourism and small and medium-sized business management. Chia-Chien Hsu and Brian A. Sandford have jointly published several articles related to the topic of the Delphi technique in the Journal of *Practical Assessment, Research, & Evaluation* as well as multiple entries in the 3 volume *Encyclopedia of Research Design*, Neil J. Salkind, editor (Sage Publications, Inc.).

Rosalind Hurworth, BA (Jt Hons.) (Univ Wales, Swansea), Post Grad. Cert. Ed. (Nottingham), M.Ed. (LaTrobe), Post Grad. Dip. Sociology (Research and Survey Methods) (LaTrobe) PhD (LaTrobe), Associate Professor, is the Director of the Centre for Program Evaluation at the University of Melbourne. There she teaches qualitatively-based courses within the Master of Evaluation while also leading many national and statewide evaluations in Education and Health. Rosalind has particular expertise in running focus groups, Nominal Group Technique sessions and Search conferences, as well as in the use of photographs as data. She is also the author of *Teaching Qualitative Research* (Sense Publisher, 2008). Additionally, she has been a Past President of the Association of Qualitative Research and is the Editor of the *Evaluation Journal of Australasia (EJA)*. She has also been a recipient of the Australasian Evaluation Society's prestigious *Evaluation Training and Service Award*.

Bettina Kolb, Mag^a., Dr^{in}.phil, Sociologist experienced in visual sociology and expert for participatory visual methods like photo interview; lecturer at the Department of Sociology at the University of Vienna, member of the visual study group of the Faculty of Social Sciences. Main areas of research: visual methods of qualitative research like photo interview and photo analysis, visual methods in inter- and transdisciplinary research; cultural heritage research (the Hammam), social approach to sustainability. Projects: Social Science and photo interview in interdisciplinary and transdisciplinary projects with Oikodrom - The Vienna Institute for Urban Sustainability; in "Social studies for the hammam: representations and symbolization within a changing society" in HAMMAMED and "HAMMAM – Aspects and Multidisciplinary methods of Analysis for Mediterranean Region"; conducting photo interviews in rural Chinese villages for sustainable future scenarios in "SUCCESS – Sustainable User Concepts for China Engaging Scientific Scenarios"; consultancy for the Vienna Network for Health Promotion Schools ("WieNGS").

Guido Lang is a doctoral candidate in business with a specialization in information systems at the City University of New York. His research investigates aspects of consumer behavior in social media and electronic commerce environments. He has presented and published his work at conferences and in academic journals. In addition, he is an experienced entrepreneur in the IT services industry.

Karl Reiner Lang holds a PhD in Management Science from the University of Texas at Austin and is currently a Professor in Information Systems at Baruch College in New York City. His research interests include decision technologies, management of digital businesses, knowledge-based products and services, and issues related to the newly arising informational society. Dr. Lang's findings have been published in such diverse journals as Communications of the ACM, Journal of Management Information Systems, International Journal of Electronic Commerce, Decision Support Systems, Computational Economics, and Annals of Operations Research. He is also Associate Editor of the Decision Support Systems journal and Electronic Commerce Research and Applications.

Sunghee Lee is Research Assistant Scientist at the Survey Research Center, Institute for Social Research, University of Michigan, USA. She specializes in survey sampling and estimation techniques with an interest in inference issues with non-probability samples, including volunteer-driven Web survey samples. Her research interests also include a sampling approaches and measurement errors in data collection with racial, ethnic and linguistic minority populations from a cross-cultural perspective. Previously, she worked as Adjunct Assistant Professor at UCLA Biostatistics Department and Survey Methodologist at UCLA Center for Health Policy Research.

Almut Leh is a historian and Research Fellow at the Institute for History and Biography at the University of Hagen (Germany) and co-editor of *BIOS – Zeitschrift für Biographieforschung, Oral History und Lebensverlaufsanalysen* (Journal on Biographical Research, Oral History and Life Course Analysis). She also is a council member of the International Oral History Association and has published on German History since 1945 and the methodology of oral history. Her recent book, edited with Alexander von Plato and Christoph Thonfeld, is *Hitler's Slaves. Life Stories of Forced Labourers in Nazi-Occupied Germany*, New York – Oxford: Berghahn Books 2010.

Stanislav Mamonov is a doctoral candidate in business with a specialization in information systems at the City University of New York. His research interests include qualitative research methods and netnography.

Nicolas Michinov is currently Professor of social psychology at the University of Rennes 2 (France). He was director of a technological research team until 2008, and currently leads a social psychology research team. As a researcher in social psychology, he studies the interpersonal and intergroup processes involved in collaborative working and learning, both in face-to-face and online environments. His interests include social comparison, transactive memory, electronic brainstorming, and social identity, aiming to determine their influence on outcomes such as affect and academic performance. He is also involved in the development of new (online) research methods for the study of group processes, and in the pedagogical design of web-based learning environments.

Alexandra Millonig, born in 1972, finished her urban planning course at the Vienna University of Technology in 2005. Her Master's Thesis "Pedestrian Orientation Behaviour" received an award by the Austrian Association for Research on Road-Rail-Transport (FSV). Since 2005 she has been working as a researcher at the Dynamic Transportation Systems team of AIT Mobility where Alexandra focuses on pedestrian orientation and navigation behaviour, group-specific behaviour patterns and influencing factors as well as the user-oriented design of transport information systems. From 2007 until 2009 Alexandra was moreover working as a project assistant for the research group cartography at VUT where she is currently finishing her PhD thesis on pedestrian typologies. Both at AIT Mobility and VUT Alexandra gained extensive experience in the conceptual design, implementation and management of research projects. She was appointed FEMTech Expert of the Month June 2010 as she became visible as dedicated expert within the research domain "mobility".

Lesley Murray is a lecturer in the School of Applied Social Science, University of Brighton, UK. She previously worked as a senior strategic transport planner for the Greater London Authority and Transport for London, contributing to the Mayor of London's first transport strategy for the capital. Lesley began to develop mobile and visual methods during her work in regional government before moving into academia to carry out research on everyday mobilities and more recently on 'family'. She has recently published peer-reviewed articles on both mobile and visual methods and deliberative research and policy and has co-edited a pioneering book on mobile methodologies.

Randall Olsen is a Professor of Economics and Director of the Center for Human Resource Research (CHRR). He attended the University of Chicago, where he received his PhD in Economics. He spent a year as a post-doc at the University of Minnesota before becoming an Assistant Professor of Economics at Yale. He came to Ohio State in 1982 and started as CHRR Director in 1987. He serves as Principal Investigator on the National Longitudinal Surveys of Labor Market Experience, usually called the NLS, a study that has been ongoing since the mid 1960s. CHRR employs about 60 research professionals. He is an econometrician and labor economist who has worked extensively on the analysis and evaluation of social policy experiments, with additional research interests in theoretical econometric topics relating to microeconomic data. He has published widely in labor, econometrics and economic demography. Professor Olsen is a frequent consultant to the National Academy of Sciences Committee on National Statistics, been a reviewer on the NIH Social Science and Population Study Section a well as regular reviewer for NIH research grant applications, NIH Training Grants, program projects and Population Center grants. He has also served as a consultant on longitudinal survey programs in the UK for the Economic and Social Research Council, doing the same for the American National Election Study and for the US Department of Education.

Stefano Pace, PhD, is Assistant Professor in Marketing at Bocconi University, Department of Marketing (Milan, Italy), where he received his PhD in Business Administration & Management. He has been visiting PhD student at Wharton Business School (Sol C. Snider Research Center). His current research interests include Internet, online consumption communities, consumer behavior. His articles have been published in international journals such as 'International Marketing Review', 'European Journal of Marketing', 'European Management Journal', 'Qualitative Market Research: An International Journal', 'European Advances in Consumer Research', 'Group Decision and Negotiation'.

Fay Patel has over twenty-five years of experience as a researcher, administrator, professor and teacher in higher education in Canada, the U.S.A., New Zealand, Australia and South Africa. Her research focus includes the scholarship of teaching; curriculum mapping and review and student ratings of instruction; international development; intercultural communication; organizational culture and communication; and the diffusion of innovations and information technologies in online and face-to-face teaching and learning. Among her current co-edited and co-authored publications are *Intercultural Communication: Building a global community.* Delhi, India: Sage Publications (2011) and *Working Women: Stories of Struggle, Strife and Survival New Delhi*, India: Sage Publications (2009) and a forthcoming co-edited book with Routledge USA, *Information technology, development and social change*.

Paul B. Paulus is Distinguished Professor of Psychology in the Department of Psychology at the University of Texas at Arlington and director of the industrial/organizational program. He was formerly chair of that department and Dean of the College of Science. He has been a visiting scholar at the National Institute of Justice, the Uniformed Services University of the Health Sciences, University of Sidney, Carnegie Mellon University, the University of Pittsburgh and Bar Ilan University. He has conducted research on group creativity for 20 years, and on group and environmental processes for over 40 years. He has published eight books and over 100 papers and chapters on these and other topics. His most recent book is *Group creativity: Innovation through collaboration* (Oxford University Press) with Bernard Nijstad. His main focus recently has been on understanding the group creative process from both social and cognitive perspectives and collaborating with cognitive scientists and computer scientists to develop a detailed neural-cognitive perspective of the group creative process.

Peter Petocz is Associate Professor in the Department of Statistics at Macquarie University, Sydney. He divides his time between professional work as an applied statistician, mostly in health-related areas, and pedagogical research in statistics and mathematics education. He has authored text books and video-based learning resources for statistics learning, written widely in the field of statistics pedagogy, and held a position as editor of *Statistics Education Research Journal* for several years. Additionally, he has worked with Sue and Anna on several research projects, including investigation of teachers' approaches to teaching service statistics, their conceptions of student diversity in their classes, and the role of statistical approaches in research in creative disciplines. Joint investigations with Anna of students' views of the transition from university to professional life, and the role of dispositions such as ethics and sustainability, have recently resulted in the publication of a research monograph by Springer.

Markus Ray, born in 1981, studied electronics focusing on computer and system as well as audio and video technologies at the University of Applied Sciences Technikum Wien (MSc in 2005). In 2004 he finished his Master's thesis "Mobile GPS data collection in urban areas" at arsenal research. Since 2005 Markus has been working with the Dynamic Transportation Systems team at AIT Mobility. His main focus is the collection and analysis of mobility data on the basis of various localisation technologies such as GPS, Cell-ID, RFID or Bluetooth. Markus is responsible for the management and implementation of a number of mobility research projects.

Anna Reid is Professor of Music and Associate Dean of Learning and Teaching at the Sydney Conservatorium of Music, a faculty of the University of Sydney. She studied music performance (violoncello) and carried out research in music education, investigating students' conceptions of vocal and instrumental music. This was followed by several years in academic and research development positions in various universities. She has a wide range of qualitative research interests spanning a diversity of disciplines, including design, law and mathematics, as well as music. Her research focuses broadly on the professional formation of students through their university studies, and their conceptions of their discipline and various dispositions such as creativity, particularly in the context of performing and visual arts. Her book *From Expert Student to Novice Professional*, co-authored with Peter and two Swedish colleagues, has recently been published by Springer, and two further books are in preparation.

Alexander E. Reppel is a Senior Lecturer in Marketing at the School of Management, Royal Holloway, University of London, UK. His research interests include consumer behavior, online research methods, and the effects of marketing on society. His work has been published in journals such as the *European Journal of Marketing*, *Industrial Marketing Management* and the *Journal of Marketing Management*.

Travis Ross is a candidate in the Joint PhD Program for Cognitive Science and Telecommunications at Indiana University. His research examines the influence of social norms and social learning on player strategies, the incorporation of game theory into game design, the motivational aspects of choice in games, the role of cognitive heuristics in player choice, and the use of virtual worlds as a means to study human society. He has published in various international journals and is the founder of an online blog named *Motivate. Play.* In the past he has worked as a software developer and was a volunteer in the U.S. Peace Corps.

Brian Sandford is a tenured professor at Pittsburg State University teaching courses for the baccalaureate and Master's degrees in the Technical Teacher Education program. He serves the university on committees dealing with graduate studies, curriculum, and safety. His research interests include the professional development of part-time community college faculty in the U.S., the factors related to the retention of career and technical educators in the state of Kansas, and the use and application of the Delphi technique for data collection. Within the past 3 years his scholarly production has included: multiple entries in the recently published 3 volume Encyclopedia of Research Design, Neil J. Salkind, editor (Sage Publications, Inc.) and peer reviewed articles in the Scholar-Practitioner Quarterly, the Journal of Career and Technical Education (JCTE), and the Career and Technical Education Research Journal (CTER).

Helmut Schrom-Feiertag, born in 1973, studied telematics at Graz University of Technology focusing on information systems and computer media (MSc 2005). During his course he worked from 1993 to 2000 at the research company AVL Graz on human-machine interfaces, computer graphics for CFD and the development of multiplatform in-house software. From 2000 to 2004 Helmut worked as a graphic designer. Since 2004 he has been part of the Dynamic Transportation Systems team at AIT Mobility and is doing research on the analysis of raw mobility data, pedestrian simulation and visualisation. Helmut manages numerous research projects.

Mathew Smith, M.S. is currently pursuing his PhD at Indiana University of Pennsylvania. He is a graduate of Youngstown State University, where he studied Criminal Justice at the Undergraduate and Graduate Level. His research interests include crime and the media, and social control in online communities and Western responses to terrorism.

Judith E. Sturges, PhD is an Associate Professor at Penn State Fayette, the Eberly Campus, where she teaches courses for the Administration of Justice Department. Judith Sturges received her doctorate from Indiana University of Pennsylvania. Her current research interests include corrections with an emphasis on jails and family members of offenders, restorative justice and qualitative research methods. Her recent research as focused on the lived experience of mothers of criminal offenders, and of heroin users. She is currently exploring theories to explain the functioning of the criminal justice system.

Harsh Suri, PhD, is a Lecturer at the Centre for the Study of Higher Education, The University of Melbourne, Australia. Her research interests include issues in higher education, learning technologies, evaluation of educational change, research methods particularly qualitative research methods and methods of synthesizing research. She has developed a methodologically inclusive research synthesis (MIRS) framework for designing and evaluating research syntheses from distinct methodological orientations. Her work has been published in high status journals. Two of her early papers were recognized as outstanding presentations: Early Career Researcher Award at the Mathematics Education Research Group of Australasia (MERGA) conference in 1997 and Best Graduate Presentation at the AQR conference in 1999. She is cited in most current publications on research synthesis methods which are inclusive of qualitative research.

Isabelle Szmigin is Professor of Marketing at the University of Birmingham, UK from where she gained her PhD. She has extensive publications in the fields of consumer behavior, consumer innovativeness, services management and relationship marketing, including a book, Understanding the Consumer.

Doris Tausendfreund was born and raised in (until her teen years still West) Berlin, Germany. She did degrees in communication studies and history, going on to earn her PhD in history from the Center for Anti-Semitism Research at the Technische Universität Berlin with research on Jews living in hiding in the last years of the Third Reich and Jewish (coerced) collaboration. She has worked as a conceptual designer of web presences and is currently project manager for multimedia archives at the Freie Universität Berlin. She is author of articles on Third Reich history and the book *Erzwungener Verrat. Jüdische "Greifer" 1943–1945* (Forced Betrayal: Jewish "Catchers" 1943-1945).

Rödiger Voss is Professor of Business Administration at the HWZ University of Applied Sciences of Zurich, Center for Strategic Management. He received his PhD from the University of Education Ludwigsburg. His research interests include marketing of higher education, services marketing, and consumer behavior. His work has been published and/or is forthcoming in journals such as *Journal of Business Research, Journal of Marketing Management, Journal of Services Marketing, International Journal of Public Sector Management, International Journal of Educational Management, Qualitative Market Research, Managing Service Quality, Journal of Marketing for Higher Education, Journal for Quality Assurance in Education,* and *Management Services.*

Gert G. Wagner is Chairman of the Executive Board of DIW Berlin, Professor of Economics at the Berlin University of Technology (TUB), and Max Planck Fellow at the MPI for Human Development (Berlin). He also is chairman of the German Census Commission and German Council for Social and Economic Data, and he serves on the Advisory Board to Statistics Germany. He is a member of the Methodology and Infrastructure Committees (MIC) of ESRC/UK and an expert on the Study Commission "Growth, Wealth and Well-Being" of the German Parliament. Wagner is editor-in-chief of Schmollers Jahrbuch (Journal of Applied Social Science Studies). He published in international journals such as Industrial and Labor Relations Review, Journal of Conflict Resolution, Journal of Comparative Economics, Journal of the European Economic Association, Journal of Human Resources, Journal of Positive Psychology, Journal of Public Economics, PNAS, Psychology and Aging, Psychological Science, and Social Indicator Research.

Amy Wesolowski is a first year graduate student at Carnegie Mellon University in Engineering and Public Policy. Her research focuses on understanding population mobility and its impact on the transmission of infectious diseases. As an undergraduate at College of the Atlantic and researcher at the Santa Fe Institute, she focused on quantifying slum dynamics in Kenya using mobile phone data.

Jason Zalinger received his PhD in Communication and Rhetoric from Rensselaer Polytechnic Institute in Troy, NY. He also holds an MA in Media Ecology from NYU and a BA in English from the University of Connecticut. His dissertation—*Gmail as storyworld: How technology shapes your life narrative*—attempted to uncover the narrative architecture of Gmail and explain how changes to the interface change the shape of a user's life story. He is very interested in the emerging field of Personal Digital Archiving and believes that personal data will be the cornerstone of "Web 3.0." His work always attempts to help both academics and designers re-imagine and create systems to help users make meaning out of their personal data.

Index